HMH

into **Literature**™

Front Cover Photo Credits: (outer ring): ©momente/Shutterstock, (inner ring): ©optimarc/Shutterstock, (c) ©Carrie Garcia/ Houghton Mifflin Harcourt, (c overlay): ©Eyewire/Getty Images, (bc overlay): ©elenamiv/Shutterstock

Back Cover Photo Credits: (Units 1-6): ©Rigmanyi/Dreamstime; ©John Gomez/Shutterstock; ©Artur Debat/Moment/Getty Images; ©Garsya/Shutterstock; ©Hulton Archive/Getty Images; ©Carlos Amarillo/Shutterstock

Printed in the U.S.A.

ISBN 978-1-328-47480-3

5 6 7 8 9 10   0928   27 26 25 24 23 22 21 20

4500796916   B C D E F G

GRADE 9

Program Consultants:
Kylene Beers
Martha Hougen
Elena Izquierdo
Carol Jago
Erik Palmer
Robert E. Probst

Kylene Beers

Nationally known lecturer and author on reading and literacy; coauthor with Robert Probst of *Disrupting Thinking, Notice & Note: Strategies for Close Reading,* and *Reading Nonfiction;* former president of the National Council of Teachers of English. Dr. Beers is the author of *When Kids Can't Read: What Teachers Can Do* and coeditor of *Adolescent Literacy: Turning Promise into Practice,* as well as articles in the *Journal of Adolescent and Adult Literacy.* Former editor of *Voices from the Middle,* she is the 2001 recipient of NCTE's Richard W. Halle Award, given for outstanding contributions to middle school literacy. She recently served as Senior Reading Researcher at the Comer School Development Program at Yale University as well as Senior Reading Advisor to Secondary Schools for the Reading and Writing Project at Teachers College.

Martha Hougen

National consultant, presenter, researcher, and author. Areas of expertise include differentiating instruction for students with learning difficulties, including those with learning disabilities and dyslexia; and teacher and leader preparation improvement. Dr. Hougen has taught at the middle school through graduate levels. In addition to peer-reviewed articles, curricular documents, and presentations, Dr. Hougen has published two college textbooks: *The Fundamentals of Literacy Assessment and Instruction Pre-K–6* (2012) and *The Fundamentals of Literacy Assessment and Instruction 6–12* (2014). Dr. Hougen has supported Educator Preparation Program reforms while working at the Meadows Center for Preventing Educational Risk at The University of Texas at Austin and at the CEEDAR Center, University of Florida.

Elena Izquierdo

Nationally recognized teacher educator and advocate for English language learners. Dr. Izquierdo is a linguist by training, with a Ph.D. in Applied Linguistics and Bilingual Education from Georgetown University. She has served on various state and national boards working to close the achievement gaps for bilingual students and English language learners. Dr. Izquierdo is a member of the Hispanic Leadership Council, which supports Hispanic students and educators at both the state and federal levels. She served as Vice President on the Executive Board of the National Association of Bilingual Education and as Publications and Professional Development Chair.

Carol Jago

Teacher of English with 32 years of experience at Santa Monica High School in California; author and nationally known lecturer; former president of the National Council of Teachers of English. Ms. Jago currently serves as Associate Director of the California Reading and Literature Project at UCLA. With expertise in standards assessment and secondary education, Ms. Jago is the author of numerous books on education, including *With Rigor for All* and *Papers, Papers, Papers,* and is active with the California Association of Teachers of English, editing its scholarly journal *California English* since 1996. Ms. Jago also served on the planning committee for the 2009 NAEP Reading Framework and the 2011 NAEP Writing Framework.

Erik Palmer

Veteran teacher and education consultant based in Denver, Colorado. Author of *Well Spoken: Teaching Speaking to All Students* and *Digitally Speaking: How to Improve Student Presentations.* His areas of focus include improving oral communication, promoting technology in classroom presentations, and updating instruction through the use of digital tools. He holds a bachelor's degree from Oberlin College and a master's degree in curriculum and instruction from the University of Colorado.

Robert E. Probst

Nationally respected authority on the teaching of literature; Professor Emeritus of English Education at Georgia State University. Dr. Probst's publications include numerous articles in *English Journal* and *Voices from the Middle,* as well as professional texts including (as coeditor) *Adolescent Literacy: Turning Promise into Practice* and (as coauthor with Kylene Beers) *Disrupting Thinking, Notice & Note: Strategies for Close Reading,* and *Reading Nonfiction.* He regularly speaks at national and international conventions including those of the International Literacy Association, the National Council of Teachers of English, the Association of Supervisors and Curriculum Developers, and the National Association of Secondary School Principals. He has served NCTE in various leadership roles, including the Conference on English Leadership Board of Directors, the Commission on Reading, and column editor of the NCTE journal *Voices from the Middle.* He is also the 2004 recipient of the CEL Exemplary Leader Award.

FINDING COMMON GROUND

PAGE 1

? ESSENTIAL QUESTION:

How can we come together despite our differences?

ANALYZE & APPLY

COLLABORATE & COMPARE

INDEPENDENT READING 72

These selections can be accessed through the digital edition.

Suggested Nonfiction Connection

Key Learning Objectives

- Analyze arguments
- Analyze author's purpose and message
- Analyze tone and voice
- Analyze setting and theme
- Analyze graphic elements
- Analyze figurative language
- Analyze digital texts

 Visit the Interactive Student Edition for:

- Unit and Selection Videos
- Media Selections
- Selection Audio Recordings
- Enhanced Digital Instruction

UNIT ②
THE STRUGGLE FOR FREEDOM
PAGE 82

? **ESSENTIAL QUESTION:**

How do people find freedom in the midst of oppression?

ANALYZE & APPLY

COLLABORATE & COMPARE

Key Learning Objectives

- Analyze rhetorical devices
- Analyze text structure
- Analyze literary devices
- Analyze setting and theme
- Analyze poetic language
- Analyze setting and purpose
- Analyze multimodal texts

 Visit the Interactive Student Edition for:

- Unit and Selection Videos
- Media Selections
- Selection Audio Recordings
- Enhanced Digital Instruction

UNIT ③

THE BONDS BETWEEN US

PAGE 168

? **ESSENTIAL QUESTION:**

How do we form and maintain our connections with others?

ANALYZE & APPLY

COLLABORATE & COMPARE

© Houghton Mifflin Harcourt Publishing Company • Image Credits: (t to b) ©Courtesy, All Our Kids, Inc.; ©Victor Tondee/Shutterstock; ©Catherine Ledner/Taxi/Getty Images; ©Education Images/Universal Images Group/Getty Images ; ©Airman Michael Murphy/U.S. Department of Defense; ©Houghton Mifflin Harcourt

Key Learning Objectives

- Analyze setting and theme
- Make inferences about theme
- Analyze author's claim
- Summarize and paraphrase texts
- Evaluate details
- Analyze media messages
- Analyze plot and characterization
- Analyze diction and syntax

 Visit the Interactive Student Edition for:

- Unit and Selection Videos
- Media Selections
- Selection Audio Recordings
- Enhanced Digital Instruction

UNIT ④
SWEET SORROW
PAGE 246

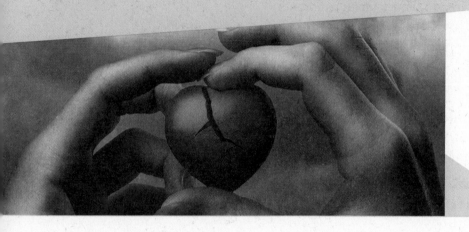

? **ESSENTIAL QUESTION:**

How can love bring both joy and pain?

ANALYZE & APPLY

COLLABORATE & COMPARE

UNIT 4

 INDEPENDENT READING 406

These selections can be accessed through the digital edition.

MYTH
Pyramus and Thisbe *from* **Metamorphoses**
by Ovid

SONNET
Sonnet 71
by Pablo Neruda

SCIENCE WRITING
from **Why Love Literally Hurts**
by Eric Jaffe

SHORT STORY
The Bass, the River, and Sheila Mant
by W.D. Wetherell

Suggested Novel Connection

NOVEL
Romiette and Julio
by Sharon Draper

© Houghton Mifflin Harcourt Publishing Company • Image Credits: (t to b) ©Mulberry Tree, 1889 (oil on canvas), Gogh, Vincent van (1853–90) / Norton Simon Collection, Pasadena, CA, USA / Bridgeman Images; ©Buena Vista Images/ Photodisc/Getty Images; ©Lightspring/Shutterstock; ©John Kuczala/Stone/Getty Images; © Getty Images RF

Key Learning Objectives

- Analyze text meaning and author's purpose
- Analyze informational text
- Generate questions
- Analyze multimodal texts
- Analyze literary devices
- Analyze parallel plots
- Analyze poetry
- Connect ideas

 Visit the Interactive Student Edition for:

- Unit and Selection Videos
- Media Selections
- Selection Audio Recordings
- Enhanced Digital Instruction

? **ESSENTIAL QUESTION:**

What does it take to survive in a crisis?

ANALYZE & APPLY

COLLABORATE & COMPARE

INDEPENDENT READING 480

These selections can be accessed through the digital edition.

ARTICLE
Adventurers Change. Danger Does Not.
by Alan Cowell

MEMOIR
from **An Ordinary Man**
by Paul Rusesabagina

POEM
Who Understands Me But Me
by Jimmy Santiago Baca

SPEECH
Truth at All Costs
by Marie Colvin

INFORMATIONAL TEXT
from **Deep Survival**
by Laurence Gonzales

Suggested Nonfiction Connection

MEMOIR
Night
by Elie Wiesel

Unit 5 Tasks

© Houghton Mifflin Harcourt Publishing Company • Image Credits: (t to b) ©Christian Kober 1/Alamy; ©PASCAL GUYOT/ AFP/Getty Images; ©Yuri Cortez/AFP/Getty Images; ©Ed Wray/AP Images; ©Sergey Nivens/Shutterstock; © Corbis RF

Key Learning Objectives
- Analyze plot
- Make inferences
- Analyze arguments and rhetorical devices
- Analyze poetic language and structure
- Analyze memoirs
- Analyze word choice

Visit the Interactive Student Edition for:
- Unit and Selection Videos
- Media Selections
- Selection Audio Recordings
- Enhanced Digital Instruction

UNIT ⑥
HEROES AND QUESTS
PAGE 492

? **ESSENTIAL QUESTION:**

What drives us to take on a challenge?

© Houghton Mifflin Harcourt Publishing Company • Image Credits: (t to b) ©Tntk/Shutterstock; ©Leemage/Universal Images Group/Getty Images; ©Jozef Klopacka/Shutterstock; ©European Space Agency; Library of Congress Prints & Photographs Division, LC-DIG-ppmsca-36895

Key Learning Objectives

• Epic heroes and epic poetry
• Analyze technical texts
• Analyze travel writing
• Evaluate graphic features
• Analyze language
• Make connections

 Visit the Interactive Student Edition for:

• Unit and Selection Videos
• Media Selections
• Selection Audio Recordings
• Enhanced Digital Instruction

SELECTIONS BY GENRE

© Houghton Mifflin Publishing Company

© Houghton Mifflin Publishing Company

HMH
Into Literature Dashboard

Easy to use and personalized for your learning.

Monitor your progress in the course.

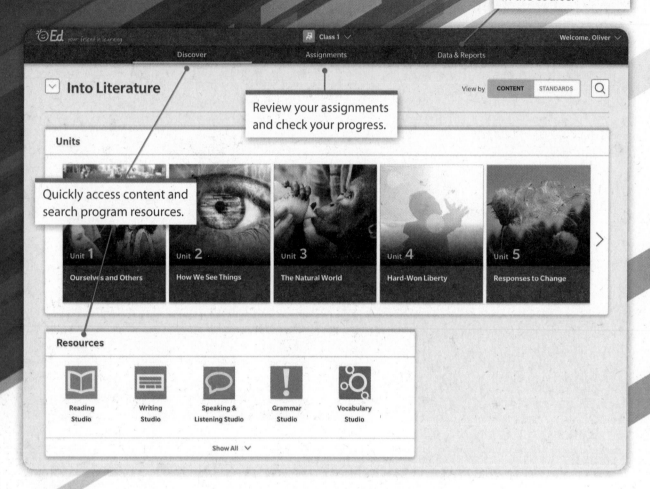

Review your assignments and check your progress.

Quickly access content and search program resources.

Into Literature

View by CONTENT STANDARDS

Units

Unit 1	Unit 2	Unit 3	Unit 4	Unit 5
Ourselves and Others	How We See Things	The Natural World	Hard-Won Liberty	Responses to Change

Resources

Reading Studio · Writing Studio · Speaking & Listening Studio · Grammar Studio · Vocabulary Studio

Show All

Online
Ed
your friend in learning

Explore Online to Experience the Power of HMH *Into Literature*

All in One Place
Readings and assignments are supported by a variety of resources to bring literature to life and give you the tools you need to succeed.

Supporting 21st-Century Skills
Whether you're working alone or collaborating with others, it takes effort to analyze the complex texts and competing ideas that bombard us in this fast-paced world. What will help you succeed? Staying engaged and organized. The digital tools in this program will help you take charge of your learning.

Ignite Your Investigation

You learn best when you're engaged. The **Stream to Start** videos at the beginning of every unit are designed to spark your interest before you read. Get curious and start reading!

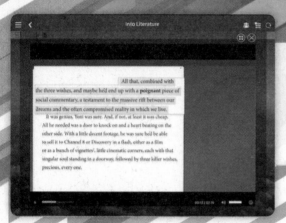

Learn How to Close Read

Close reading effectively is all about examining the details. See how it's done by watching the **Close Read Screencasts** in your eBook. Hear modeled conversations on targeted passages.

Personalized Annotations

My Notes encourages you to take notes as you read and allows you to mark the text in your own customized way. You can easily access annotations to review later as you prepare for exams.

Interactive Graphic Organizers

Graphic organizers help you process, summarize, and keep track of your learning and prepare for end-of-unit writing tasks. **Word Networks** help you learn academic vocabulary, and **Response Logs** help you explore and deepen your understanding of the **Essential Question** in each unit.

No Wi-Fi? No problem!

With HMH *Into Literature,* you always have access: download when you're online and access what you need when you're offline. Work offline and then upload when you're back online.

Communicate "Raise a Hand" to ask or answer questions without having to be in the same room as your teacher.

Collaborate Collaborate with your teacher via chat and work with a classmate to improve your writing.

HMH
Into Literature
STUDIOS

All the help you need to be successful in your literature class is one click away with the Studios. These digital-only lessons are here to tap into the skills that you already use and help you sharpen those skills for the future.

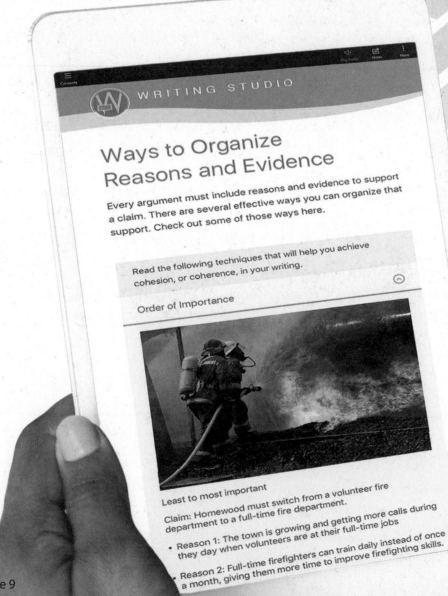

WRITING STUDIO

Ways to Organize Reasons and Evidence

Every argument must include reasons and evidence to support a claim. There are several effective ways you can organize that support. Check out some of those ways here.

Read the following techniques that will help you achieve cohesion, or coherence, in your writing.

Order of Importance

Least to most important

Claim: Homewood must switch from a volunteer fire department to a full-time fire department.

- Reason 1: The town is growing and getting more calls during they day when volunteers are at their full-time jobs

- Reason 2: Full-time firefighters can train daily instead of once a month, giving them more time to improve firefighting skills.

FM22   Grade 9

© Houghton Mifflin Harcourt Publishing Company • Image Credits: ©WAYHOME studio/Shutterstock

Easy-to-find resources, organized in five separate STUDIOS. On demand and on ED!

Look for links in each lesson to take you to the appropriate Studio.

READING STUDIO

Go beyond the book with the Reading Studio. With over 100 full-length downloadable titles to choose from, find the right story to continue your journey.

WRITING STUDIO

Being able to write clearly and effectively is a skill that will help you throughout life. The Writing Studio will help you become an expert communicator—in print or online.

SPEAKING & LISTENING STUDIO

Communication is more than just writing. The Speaking & Listening Studio will help you become an effective speaker and a focused listener.

GRAMMAR STUDIO

Go beyond traditional worksheets with the Grammar Studio. These engaging, interactive lessons will sharpen your grammar skills.

VOCABULARY STUDIO

Learn the skills you need to expand your vocabulary. The interactive lessons in the Vocabulary Studio will grow your vocabulary to improve your reading.

THE PERSPICACIOUS READER (And **yes**, you want to be one)

YOUR TEACHER AGREES!

Dr. Kylene Beers and Dr. Robert E. Probst

From Dr. Beers:

When Dr. Probst said he wanted to call this essay "The Perspicacious Reader," I had to ask him what that word meant. Did we want kids in high school to be perspicacious? Is that a good thing? Dr. Probst—who knows more words than anyone I know—said, "Of course it is good to be a perspicacious reader," and then he made me look it up. Yes, he's one of those folks who believes looking up words you don't know is good for you. So, off I went, to look it up . . .

I discovered that if you were to be a perspicacious reader, it would be a very good thing. It would mean that you were able to think deeply about what you are reading and make smart inferences. It would mean that you notice a lot as you are reading. And since we wrote a book for teachers titled **Notice and Note**, we like the idea that being a perspicacious reader means you would notice a lot as you read!

From **Both** of Us

We both think reading is one of the most important skills you will ever learn. We know that every day you read. Take a moment and think of all you read each day. Here is our combined list.

Text messages
Emails
Tweets
FB posts
Newspaper/magazine articles
How-to info for texting/using our technology
Novels we choose to read for fun
Articles for work — some we have to read and some we choose to read
Bills we get that have to be paid
Food magazines (Who do you think reads these?)
Books about teaching
Articles about technology (And who do you think reads these?)
Crossword puzzles

And then there are some things we occasionally read:

Party/wedding invitations
Birth announcements
Jokes or cartoons
Job applications
Report cards
School test results
Income tax information
Reports from doctors
Sympathy cards when someone
 has died
Information about world events

No matter what you read, we want you to read well. We want you to know what to do when you get confused because we all get confused from time to time as we read. We want you to know what to do when you come to a word you might not know (such as *perspicacious*). We want you to be able to figure out the author's theme if you are reading fiction or the author's purpose and main idea if you are reading nonfiction. We don't want you to have to wait around for someone else to tell you what the text means, which would make you dependent on that person.

We suspect, now that you're in high school, the last thing you want is to depend on others all the time. So, we want you to read smart, read critically, read closely, and always read wondering just what else there is you need to know.

But Sometimes I **Hate** to Read

We don't doubt that. You've got a lot going on in your life. Friends. Sports. Music. Jobs, maybe. Homework. Worrying about who likes whom and who is invited to what and if your grades are good and how things are going at home and who you'll sit with at lunch, stand with in the hall, go to the party with — even if you'll get invited to the party. First, it will all work out. How do we know? We've been your age. It will all work out.

What's important—along with the many other things that are important in your life right now—is to remember that you want to end up getting smarter about a lot of things each year, and the best way—yes THE BEST WAY—to do that is to make sure you become a better reader each year. So, sometimes this year your teacher may ask you to read a text that makes you say, "Really? Seriously?" We want you to dig in deep and do it because we promise there's a reason, and the reason is about making sure you, the young adult you're becoming, are prepared to deal with all the texts that get thrown your way.

Because here's what most people won't tell you: not all the texts will be honest. Right. That online ad about the used car might not mention everything you need to know. The social media post about your favorite presidential candidate just might be fake news. That Instagram photo showing everyone looking so perfect, so very happy? Chances are it was posed, shot, reshot, put through several filters, and touched up. The newspaper story about why your school district should or shouldn't build a new school might only offer one perspective. You—not a teacher, not a parent, not your best buddy—you have an obligation to yourself and to the community you live in to always ask yourself if you are reading closely enough to know when you should agree and when you shouldn't. So, we want you to always read with these three questions in mind:

If you'll do that, then we know you'll be on your way to becoming a smarter reader.

AND (Of course there is an AND) . . .

. . . we also want you to learn to read being aware of something we call

signposts.

A signpost is simply a cue an author gives you as you read that can help you figure out the theme (if reading fiction) or author's purpose (if reading nonfiction). In the same way that drivers pay attention (we hope!) to signs as they drive, we want you paying attention to signposts as you read.

© Houghton Mifflin Harcourt Publishing Company

So I'm Supposed to Read Just to Look for Signposts?

No, of course not! No one should ever set out to read an article, a chapter in a book, an online essay, a play, or a novel just to hunt for signposts. That would be like taking a drive to your favorite destination just so you can count the stop signs you see on your way there. **No!** You drive to that favorite place to see it and to enjoy the scenery along the way. But if you don't notice the stop signs or one-way signs or curve ahead signs while driving there, you might not ever get there. The signs help you make the journey safely, but noticing the signs isn't the point of the journey.

No!

The same is true of reading. You read to enjoy the journey, to learn some things along the way, and to get to the end of the text with new insights and understandings. Understanding those insights means also noticing the signposts so that you are better able to understand what the author has in mind.

The End!

IN CONCLUSION

This is a signpost showing that we are about to wrap this up!

We are always reading. We may not always be reading books, poems, articles, newspapers, webpages, or texts of any kind, but we are always reading. We read the weather, the teacher's mood, the expression on our friend's face, the demeanor of a group of strangers we encounter on the street, the unusual silence—or noise—in the hallway. We observe and listen, we try to make sense of what we have noticed, and then we act accordingly. We can't get through the day without reading.

And the essence of all of this reading—of both texts and the world around us—is simply paying attention. If we don't see the storm on the horizon, if we don't see the expression on our friend's face, if we don't see the teacher's devious grin, then we won't be able to react intelligently. Noticing is the first step.

So it is with the reading of texts. If you aren't paying attention, if you aren't noticing, then you may as well not be staring at the page at all. If you look out the window and don't notice the storm clouds forming, then you'll be drenched in the afternoon. Looking out the window without seeing what is there—noticing—does you little good.

And then you must do more. You must take note of what you have noticed. If you do notice the clouds but fail to ask yourself what they might mean, fail to recognize that they forewarn you of the approaching storm, you'll still get soaked. Noticing alone isn't enough; you have to take note of it and ask what it means.

Again, so it is with reading. If you notice what the character has said, what the author has emphasized or ignored, what the setting is like, and you don't bother asking what all that you have noticed tells you, then you may as well not have noticed it in the first place. Looking out the window and noticing the clouds—without thinking about what they mean—does you little good.

NOW WHAT?

Finally, after noticing and noting, you must do something. You must ask yourself, "So what? Now what do I need to do (or think, or feel, or say)?" If you don't reach that third step, the first two have been little more than an exercise.

Again, so it is with reading texts. If you notice what the text offers, think about it, and simply lay it aside without considering how you might change your own thinking or your own actions, then you will have missed an opportunity to grow and change. The effort of reading will have been wasted. If you notice the clouds forming, take note of that and realize that it warns you of the approaching storm, and still walk out the door without your raincoat or your umbrella, you will *still* get drenched. Reading—of the sky or of the book —should enable us to deal with life more effectively.

That's because the pages of a book allow you to explore places you've never been, meet people and characters who are far different from you, and discover through all this that reading— more than anything else— is what gives you the opportunity to reflect and in that reflection perhaps change something about yourself. Reading is a changemaker. We hope this is your year for growing and changing as a reader. We hope this is the year when, as you read, you learn to notice and note.

© Houghton Mifflin Harcourt Publishing Company

NOTICE & NOTE SIGNPOSTS

Signpost	Definition	Anchor Question(s)
FICTION		
Contrasts and Contradictions	A sharp contrast between what we would expect and what we observe the character doing; behavior that contradicts previous behavior or well-established patterns	Why would the character act (feel) this way?
Aha Moment	A character's realization of something that shifts his actions or understanding of himself, others, or the world around him	How might this change things?
Tough Questions	Questions a character raises that reveal his or her inner struggles	What does this question make me wonder about?
Words of the Wiser	The advice or insight about life that a wiser character, who is usually older, offers to the main character	What is the life lesson, and how might this affect the character?
Again and Again	Events, images, or particular words that recur over a portion of the story	Why might the author bring this up again and again?
Memory Moment	A recollection by a character that interrupts the forward progress of the story	Why might this memory be important?
NONFICTION		
Contrasts and Contradictions	A sharp contrast between what we would expect and what we observe happening. A difference between two or more elements in the text.	What is the difference, and why does it matter?
Extreme or Absolute Language	Language that leaves no doubt about a situation or an event, allows no compromise, or seems to exaggerate or overstate a case.	Why did the author use this language?
Numbers and Stats	Specific quantities or comparisons to depict the amount, size, or scale. Or, the writer is vague and imprecise about numbers when we would expect more precision.	Why did the author use these numbers or amounts?
Quoted Words	Opinions or conclusions of someone who is an expert on the subject, or someone who might be a participant in or a witness to an event. Or, the author might cite other people to provide support for a point.	Why was this person quoted or cited, and what did this add?
Word Gaps	Vocabulary that is unfamiliar to the reader—for example, a word with multiple meanings, a rare or technical word, a discipline-specific word, or one with a far-removed antecedent.	Do I know this word from someplace else? Does it seem like technical talk for this topic? Can I find clues in the sentence to help me understand the word?

READING AND WRITING ACROSS GENRES

by Carol Jago

Reading is a first-class ticket around the world. Not only can you explore other lands and cultures, but you can also travel to the past and future. That journey is sometimes a wild ride. Other books can feel like comfort food, enveloping you in an imaginative landscape full of friends and good times. Making time for reading is making time for life.

Genre

One of the first things readers do when we pick up something to read is notice its genre. You might not think of it exactly in those terms, but consider how you approach a word problem in math class compared to how you read a science fiction story. Readers go to different kinds of text for different purposes. When you need to know how to do or make something, you want a reliable, trusted source of information. When you're in the mood to spend some time in a world of fantasy, you happily suspend your normal disbelief in dragons.

In every unit of *Into Literature,* you'll find a diverse mix of genres all connected by a common theme, allowing you to explore a topic from many different angles.

GENRE:
INFORMATIONAL TEXT

COMING TO OUR SENSES
Science Essay by **Neil deGrasse Tyson**

? ESSENTIAL QUESTION:
How does our point of view shape what we think we know?

GENRE:
SHORT STORY

WHAT, OF THIS GOLDFISH, WOULD YOU WISH?
Short Story by **Etgar Keret**
translated by Nathan Englander

? ESSENTIAL QUESTION:
How do we engage with others while staying true to ourselves?

GENRE:
LITERARY NONFICTION

from TOTAL ECLIPSE
Essay by **Annie Dillard**

? ESSENTIAL QUESTION:
How do changes around us reveal who we are?

GENRE:
POETRY

ELSEWHERE
Poem by **Derek Walcott**

? ESSENTIAL QUESTION:
What do we need in order to feel free?

Writer's Craft

Learning how writers use genre to inform, to explain, to entertain, or to surprise readers will help you better understand—as well as enjoy—your reading. Imitating how professional writers employ the tools of their craft—descriptive language, repetition, sensory images, sentence structure, and a variety of other features—will give you many ideas for making your own writing more lively.

Into Literature provides you with the tools you need to understand the elements of all the critical genres and advice on how to learn from professional texts to improve your own writing in those genres.

GENRE ELEMENTS: SHORT STORY
- is a work of short fiction that centers on a single idea and can be read in one sitting
- usually includes one main conflict that involves the characters and keeps moving
- includes the basic ele of fiction—plot, chara setting, and theme
- may be based on real and historical events

GENRE ELEMENTS: INFORMATIONAL TEXT
- provides factual information
- includes evidence to support ideas
- contains text features
- includes many forms, such as news articles and essays

GENRE ELEMENTS: LITERARY NONFICTION
- shares factual information, ideas, or experiences
- develops a key insight about the topic that goes beyond the facts
- uses literary tech as figurative lang narration
- reflects a person involvement in t

GENRE ELEMENTS: POETRY
- may use figurative language, including personification
- often includes imagery that appeals to the five senses
- expresses a theme, or a "big idea" message about life

Reading with Independence

Finding a good book can sometimes be a challenge. Like every other reader, you have probably experienced "book desert" when nothing you pick up seems to have what you are looking for (not that it's easy to explain exactly what you are looking for, but whatever it is, "this" isn't it). If you find yourself in this kind of reading funk, bored by everything you pick up, give yourself permission to range more widely, exploring graphic novels, contemporary biographies, books of poetry, historical fiction. And remember that long doesn't necessarily mean boring. My favorite kind of book is one that I never want to end.

Frankenstein
Or, The Modern Prometheus
Mary Shelley

The Turn of the Screw
Henry James

Take control over your own reading with *Into Literature's* Reader's Choice selections and the HMH Digital Library. And don't forget: your teacher, librarian, and friends can offer you many more suggestions.

SHORT STORY

The Wife's Story
Ursula K. Le Guin

Is the narrator's husband, who has begun acting strangely, really one of the group, or has he become something else?

POEM

Starfish
Lorna Dee Cervantes

This poem explores the human fascination with starfish: their life cycle, beauty, and ocean habitat.

HISTORY

Crispus Attucks
Kareem Abdul-Jabbar

Learn the story of Crispus Attucks, an African American remembered as the first American to die in the Revolutionary War.

FINDING COMMON GROUND

? ***ESSENTIAL QUESTION:***

How can we come together despite our differences?

> " We may have different religions, different languages, different colored skin, but we all belong to one human race. "
>
> **Kofi Annan**

ACADEMIC VOCABULARY

Academic Vocabulary words are words you use when you discuss and write about texts. In this unit you will practice and learn five words.

☑ **enforce**   ❑ **entity**   ❑ **internal**   ❑ **presume**   ❑ **resolve**

Study the Word Network to learn more about the word **enforce**.

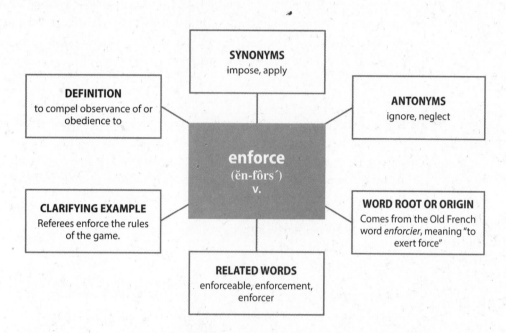

SYNONYMS
impose, apply

DEFINITION
to compel observance of or obedience to

ANTONYMS
ignore, neglect

enforce
(ĕn-fôrs´)
v.

CLARIFYING EXAMPLE
Referees enforce the rules of the game.

WORD ROOT OR ORIGIN
Comes from the Old French word *enforcier*, meaning "to exert force"

RELATED WORDS
enforceable, enforcement, enforcer

Write and Discuss Discuss the completed Word Network with a partner, making sure to talk through all of the boxes until you both understand the word, its synonyms, antonyms, and related forms. Then, fill out a Word Network for each of the four remaining words. Use a dictionary or online resource to help you complete the activity.

Go online to access the Word Networks.

RESPOND TO THE ESSENTIAL QUESTION

In this unit, you will explore how humanity can unite despite our differences and struggles. As you read, you will revisit the **Essential Question** and gather your ideas about it in the **Response Log** that appears on page R1. At the end of the unit, you will have the opportunity to write a **personal essay** about yourself, sharing an experience, opinion, or response to an event. Filling out the Response Log will help you prepare for this writing task.

You can also go online to access the Response Log.

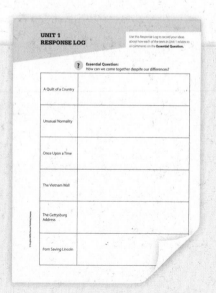

UNIT 1
RESPONSE LOG

Use this Response Log to record your ideas about how each of the texts in Unit 1 relates to or comments on the **Essential Question.**

? Essential Question:
How can we come together despite our differences?

A Quilt of a Country	
Unusual Normality	
Once Upon a Time	
The Vietnam Wall	
The Gettysburg Address	
from Saving Lincoln	

Notice & Note

READING MODEL

A QUILT OF A COUNTRY

You are about to read the argument "A Quilt of a Country." In it, you will encounter notice and note signposts that will give you clues about the essay's claims and evidence. Here are three key signposts to look for as you read this essay and other informative writing.

 For more information on these and other signposts to Notice & Note, visit the **Reading Studio**.

When you see phrases like these, pause to see if it's a **Big Questions** signpost:

- "Everyone has heard of…"
- "It goes without saying that.."
- "There was a time when…"
- "Most people know that…"

Big Questions Even in a simple conversation between two friends, there are frequent references to information that both speakers already know. Even though they may be exchanging new information, two people communicate better if they understand each other in a variety of ways. Authors count on their readers to understand certain information, such as:

- historical and current events
- shared opinions or ideas
- common words, terms, or concepts

If you're reading a text and feel lost, stop and ask yourself: **What does the author think I already know?** Read this part of "Quilt of a Country" to see one student's annotation of Big Questions.

1   That's because it was built of bits and pieces that seem discordant, like the crazy quilts that have been one of its great folk-art forms, velvet and calico and checks and brocades. Out of many, one. That is the ideal.

2   The reality is often quite different, a great national striving consisting frequently of failure. Many of the oft-told stories of the most pluralistic nation on earth are stories not of tolerance, but of bigotry. Slavery and sweatshops, the burning of crosses and the ostracism of the other. Children learn in social-studies class and in the news of the lynching of blacks, the denial of rights to women, the murders of gay men.

What does the author assume her audience understands about America?	Quindlen has an understanding of America as a melting pot, a mosaic, or a "crazy quilt."
Which historical or social events does the author assume her audience is familiar with?	The author expects that her audience knows about the historical mistreatment of African Americans and other minorities, and the struggle of women for equality.

Contrasts and Contradictions If someone tells you they are afraid of heights and then wants to try skydiving, you are likely to wonder what they really think. How can two opposites act together to form a true statement?

When an author makes two conflicting—or even contradictory--statements, it can be jarring. You might think the statements would cancel each other out. Yet authors often include **Contrasts and Contradictions** in nonfiction text to bring the reader's attention to something important. Here a student marked a Contrast and Contradiction.

> 2   It is difficult to know how to convince them that this amounts to "crown thy good with brotherhood," that <u>amid all the failures is something spectacularly successful.</u> Perhaps they understand it at this moment, when <u>enormous tragedy</u>, as it so often does, demands a time of reflection on <u>enormous blessings.</u>

When you read and encounter phrases like this, pause to see if they are **Contrasts and Contradictions** signposts:

"It may seem that ____; however …"

"For every ____, there is ____…"

"Forget what you believe in, I'm here to tell you…"

"You may think that ____ but it's really …"

Anchor Question
When you notice this signpost, stop and ask: What is the contrast or contradiction, and why does it matter?

What contrasts are expressed here?	Quindlen describes failures and successes. She also mentions "enormous tragedy" that comes with reflecting on "enormous blessings."
How do these opposites work together?	The author's point is that while contradictions exist in America, it still functions as one country.

Word Gaps Authors sometimes use terms that readers will not know. These may include specialized or technical words, or familiar words that are used in an unfamiliar or unusual way. A reader encountering unfamiliar words can ask the following questions:

- Do I know this word from some place else?
- Does this seem like technical talk for experts on this topic?
- Can I find context clues to help me understand the word?

In this example, a student underlined examples of **Word Gaps:**

> 1   America is an <u>improbable</u> idea. A <u>mongrel</u> nation built of ever-changing disparate parts . . . it is held together by a notion, the notion that all men are created equal, though everyone knows that most men consider themselves better than someone.

When you notice one of the following while reading, pause to see if it's a **Word Gaps** signpost:

Descriptive language

Multiple meanings

References to events, art, or ideas

Rare words and technical talk

Anchor Question
When you notice this signpost, stop and ask: Can I find clues in the sentence to help me understand this word?

What strategy can help you understand the words *improbable* and *mongrel*?	I can see the word "probably" and the prefix "im-" in "improbable." Context clues like "ever-changing disparate parts" help me understand the word "mongrel."

© Houghton Mifflin Harcourt Publishing Company

A QUILT OF A COUNTRY

Argument by **Anna Quindlen**

? **_ESSENTIAL QUESTION:_**

How can we come together despite our differences?

QUICK START

People say there is nothing more American than apple pie, baseball, and hot dogs. What things mean America to you? Share and explain your ideas with the class.

ANALYZE ARGUMENTS

In "A Quilt of a Country," Anna Quindlen presents an **argument** about how America works as a country. An argument presents a claim, or position, on an issue and supports it with reasons and evidence. To evaluate the strength of Quindlen's argument, you must describe these elements:

- Identify the **claim**, or Quindlen's position, on the issue.

- Look for the valid, logical **reasons** Quindlen uses to support her claim.

- Evaluate whether the **evidence** Quindlen cites for each reason is credible, or believable, and relevant to the claim. Evidence may include facts, statistics, examples, anecdotes, or quotations.

- Look for **counterarguments**, which are statements that address opposing viewpoints. Does Quindlen anticipate opposing viewpoints and provide counterarguments to disprove them?

- Look for how Quindlen offers a **concession**, or admission that an opposing viewpoint may be correct. Also, notice how she provides a **rebuttal**, or a denial that clarifies and discredits opposing viewpoints.

- Identify the audience Quindlen is addressing.

GENRE ELEMENTS: ARGUMENT

- presents a claim or position on an issue

- includes reasons or evidence that support the claim

- acknowledges and addresses counterclaims through concessions and rebuttals

EVALUATE AUTHOR'S CLAIM

To support a **claim**, authors develop and refine their ideas throughout the text. Authors develop their claims with reasons and **evidence**. Analyzing how a writer like Anna Quindlen cites evidence and develops a claim can help you make your arguments stronger.

Use a chart to help you evaluate how Anna Quindlen develops her claim in "A Quilt of a Country." First, identify her claim. Then, list specific reasons or evidence from the text. Finally, evaluate if the reason or evidence supports the claim. Would you defend her claim, or challenge it?

Read this example from a student newspaper editorial.

© Houghton Mifflin Harcourt Publishing Company

CLAIM More time should be given to students to transition between classes.	
REASONS/EVIDENCE FROM TEXT	**HOW THE REASONS/EVIDENCE SUPPORT THE CLAIM**
"Students have told me how rushed they are to gather materials from their lockers for their next classes."	The evidence is a quotation from the school counselor, an objective observer who hears from many students. Her statement is logical support for the claim because it would be easier to gather materials if students had more time.

CRITICAL VOCABULARY

discordant   **pluralistic**   **interwoven**   **diversity**

To see how many Critical Vocabulary words you already know, use them to complete the sentences.

1. During the field trip we learned about the _diversity_ of plants and animals in our area.

2. Many people describe the United States as a _pluralistic_ society.

3. The shouting kindergartners made for a _discordant_ classroom.

4. The teacher's main points were _interwoven_ with charts and graphics.

LANGUAGE CONVENTIONS

Noun Clauses A noun clause takes the place of a noun in a sentence. It is a subordinate clause that usually begins with *that, what, whatever, why, whether, how, who, whom, whoever,* or *whomever.* Like all subordinate clauses it contains a subject and a verb, but it cannot stand alone in a sentence. The noun clauses are boldfaced in these sentences:

> **What Anna Quindlen wrote** was very thoughtful.

> Throughout U.S. history, people have noted **that America is made up of many diverse cultures**.

Notice that these noun clauses could not stand alone as a sentence. They could, however, be replaced by the pronoun *it.*

ANNOTATION MODEL   **NOTICE & NOTE**

As you read, notice and note signposts, including Big Questions, Contrasts and Contradictions, and Word Gaps. Here is an example of how one reader responded to an early paragraph in "A Quilt of a Country."

This is a nation founded on a conundrum, what Mario Cuomo has characterized as "community added to individualism." These two are our defining ideals; they are also in constant conflict. Historians today bemoan the ascendancy of a kind of prideful apartheid in America, saying that the clinging to ethnicity, in background and custom, has undermined the concept of unity.

community and individualism
→ contrasts and contradictions

Author assumes I know what apartheid is.

BACKGROUND

Anna Quindlen *(b. 1953) was born in Philadelphia. She is a columnist and author who has been described as having a "common touch" because so many people relate to her writings about politics and gender-specific issues. In 1992, she became the third woman to win a Pulitzer Prize for commentary. "A Quilt of a Country" was published after the World Trade Center attacks of September 11, 2001. The piece was written at a time when many people were thinking about what it means to be an American.*

A QUILT OF A COUNTRY
Argument by Anna Quindlen

SETTING A PURPOSE

As you read, look for how the author uses an extended metaphor to convince readers of her claim, or argument. An extended metaphor is a comparison between two unlike things that is explored over and over in a variety of related ways.

1   America is an improbable idea. A mongrel[1] nation built of ever-changing disparate[2] parts, it is held together by a notion, the notion that all men are created equal, though everyone knows that most men consider themselves better than someone. "Of all the nations in the world, the United States was built in nobody's image," the historian Daniel Boorstin wrote. That's because it was built of bits and pieces that seem **discordant,** like the crazy quilts that have been one of its great folk-art forms, velvet and calico and checks and brocades. Out of many, one. That is the ideal.

2   The reality is often quite different, a great national striving consisting frequently of failure. Many of the oft-told stories of the most **pluralistic** nation on earth are stories not of tolerance,

---
[1] **mongrel:** something produced by mixing different breeds.
[2] **disparate:** distinct or not alike.

Notice & Note

You can use the side margins to notice and note signposts in the text.

discordant (dĭ-skôr´dnt) *adj.* conflicting or not being in accord

pluralistic (plŏŏr´ə-lĭs´tĭc) *adj.* consisting of many ethnic and cultural groups

**LANGUAGE
CONVENTIONS**

Annotate: Mark the two noun clauses beginning with *that* in the fifth sentence in paragraph 2.

Respond: How do these noun clauses reveal the contradictions in American society?

ANALYZE ARGUMENTS

Annotate: Mark examples of when ethnicity has divided Americans.

Summarize: What is Quindlen's claim in paragraph 3?

but of bigotry. Slavery and sweatshops, the burning of crosses and the ostracism[3] of the other. Children learn in social studies class and in the news of the lynching of blacks, the denial of rights to women, the murders of gay men. It is difficult to know how to convince them that this amounts to "crown thy good with brotherhood," that amid all the failures is something spectacularly successful. Perhaps they understand it at this moment, when enormous tragedy, as it so often does, demands a time of reflection on enormous blessings.

3   This is a nation founded on a conundrum,[4] what Mario Cuomo[5] has characterized as "community added to individualism." These two are our defining ideals; they are also in constant conflict. Historians today bemoan the ascendancy of a kind of prideful apartheid[6] in America, saying that the clinging to ethnicity, in background and custom, has undermined the concept of unity. These historians must have forgotten the past, or have gilded it. The New York of my children is no more Balkanized,[7] probably less so, than the Philadelphia of my father, in which Jewish boys would walk several blocks out of their way to avoid the Irish divide of Chester Avenue. (I was the product of a mixed marriage, across barely bridgeable lines: an Italian girl, an Irish boy. How quaint it seems now, how incendiary then.) The Brooklyn of Francie Nolan's famous tree, the Newark of which Portnoy complained, even the uninflected WASP suburbs of Cheever's characters:[8] they are ghettos, pure and simple. Do the Cambodians and the Mexicans in California coexist less easily today than did the Irish and Italians of Massachusetts a century ago? You know the answer.

4   What is the point of this splintered whole? What is the point of a nation in which Arab cabbies chauffeur Jewish passengers through the streets of New York—and in which Jewish cabbies chauffeur Arab passengers, too, and yet speak in theory of hatred, one for the other? What is the point of a nation in which one part seems to be always on the verge of fisticuffs with another, blacks and whites, gays and straights, left and right, Pole and Chinese and Puerto Rican and Slovenian? Other countries with such divisions have in fact divided into new nations with new names, but not this one, impossibly **interwoven** even in its hostilities.

interwoven
(ĭnʹtər-wōʹvən) *adj.* blended or laced together

---

[3] **ostracism:** exclusion or separation from society.
[4] **conundrum:** a riddle or a puzzle.
[5] **Mario Cuomo:** Governor of New York from 1983 until 1994.
[6] **apartheid:** a political system of racial or ethnic separation and discrimination.
[7] **Balkanized:** divided into small, uncooperative groups like countries in the Balkan Peninsula in the early 20th century.
[8] **Francie Nolan's . . . WASP suburbs of Cheever's characters:** characters in the novels *A Tree Grows in Brooklyn* and *Portnoy's Complaint;* John Cheever's characters were generally White Anglo-Saxon Protestants, or WASPs.

5   Once these disparate parts were held together by a common enemy, by the fault lines of world wars and the electrified fence of communism. With the end of the cold war[9] there was the creeping concern that without a focus for hatred and distrust, a sense of national identity would evaporate, that the left side of the hyphen—African-American, Mexican-American, Irish-American—would overwhelm the right. And slow-growing domestic traumas like economic unrest and increasing crime seemed more likely to emphasize division than community. Today the citizens of the United States have come together once more because of armed conflict and enemy attack. Terrorism has led to devastation—and unity.

6   Yet even in 1994, the overwhelming majority of those surveyed by the National Opinion Research Center agreed with this statement: "The U.S. is a unique country that stands for something special in the world." One of the things that it stands for is this vexing notion that a great nation can consist entirely of refugees from other nations, that people of different, even warring religions and cultures can live, if not side-by-side, then on either side of the country's Chester Avenues. Faced with this **diversity** there is little point in trying to isolate anything remotely resembling a national character, but there are two strains of behavior that, however tenuously, abet the concept of unity.

---

[9] **cold war:** diplomatic and economic hostility between the United States and the Soviet Union and their respective allies in the decades following World War II.

EVALUATE
AUTHOR'S CLAIM

Annotate: Mark the quotation Quindlen uses to support her claim about diversity and immigration in America.

Connect: Do you think this quotation adequately supports her claim? Why or why not?

7   There is that Calvinist undercurrent[10] in the American psyche that loves the difficult, the demanding, that sees mastering the impossible, whether it be prairie or subway, as a test of character, and so glories in the struggle of this fractured coalescing. And there is a grudging fairness among the citizens of the United States that eventually leads most to admit that, no matter what the English-only advocates try to suggest, the new immigrants are not so different from our own parents or grandparents. Leonel Castillo, former director of the Immigration and Naturalization Service and himself the grandson of Mexican immigrants, once told the writer Studs Terkel proudly, "The old neighborhood Ma-Pa stores are still around. They are not Italian or Jewish or Eastern European any more. Ma and Pa are now Korean, Vietnamese, Iraqi, Jordanian, Latin American. They live in the store. They work seven days a week. Their kids are doing well in school. They're making it. Sound familiar?"

8   Tolerance is the word used most often when this kind of coexistence succeeds, but tolerance is a vanilla-pudding word, standing for little more than the allowance of letting others live unremarked and unmolested. Pride seems excessive, given the American willingness to endlessly complain about them, them being

---

[10]**Calvinist undercurrent:** the social influence of Calvinism, a Christian religion with a strict moral code and a belief in God as absolutely sovereign.

whoever is new, different, unknown, or currently under suspicion. But patriotism is partly taking pride in this unlikely ability to throw all of us together in a country that across its length and breadth is as different as a dozen countries, and still be able to call it by one name. When photographs of the faces of all those who died in the World Trade Center destruction are assembled in one place, it will be possible to trace in the skin color, the shape of the eyes and the noses, the texture of the hair, a map of the world. These are the representatives of a mongrel nation that somehow, at times like this, has one spirit. Like many improbable ideas, when it actually works, it's a wonder.

CHECK YOUR UNDERSTANDING

Answer these questions before moving on to the **Analyze the Text** questions on the following page.

1. Which of these best describes the purpose of the selection?

   A To suggest who is responsible for the 9/11 tragedy

   B To show that America consists of different pieces that work together

   C To show how immigrants can become legal citizens

   D To prove that over time the nation's differences will disappear

2. What can the reader conclude from paragraph 2?

   F American history has always favored immigrants.

   G The American "story" has included bigotry and intolerance.

   H Democracy is an important American system.

   J The American republic has changed over time.

3. The author mentions her parents' marriage in order to —

   A show how attitudes toward immigrants have evolved over time

   B illustrate the difference between the Irish and Italian cultures

   C demonstrate how the institution of marriage has changed

   D suggest that Philadelphia was more diverse than New York

ANALYZE THE TEXT

Support your responses with evidence from the text. ▤ NOTEBOOK

1. **Summarize** What is Anna Quindlen's claim in "A Quilt of a Country"? Summarize her claim in your own words. Would you defend her claim, or challenge it?

2. **Interpret** In paragraph 1, what does Quindlen mean when she describes America as being "like the crazy quilts that have been one of its great folk-art forms"? Quindlen uses this image throughout her argument. How does this extended metaphor support her claim?

3. **Analyze** Reread Quindlen's conclusion. What specific words and phrases does she use to link the conclusion to her introduction? How do these words and phrases support her argument?

4. **Evaluate** Quindlen uses many different types of **evidence** throughout the argument to support her claim, such as examples, facts, statistics, and quotations. Identify at least three examples of evidence. Evaluate how she uses each type of evidence to support her claim.

5. **Notice & Note** Quindlen cites many instances of contrasts and contradictions to support her claim. Identify one contrast and one contradiction, and explain how each helps strengthen her argument.

RESEARCH

RESEARCH TIP
The best way to find specific information about a topic is to limit your focus. You can start with a general topic, but as you learn more about it, narrow your scope and select a topic that gives you plenty of materials to consult.

Every city or state in America has a mix of cultural groups. Research one of these groups. Record what you learn in the chart.

CULTURAL GROUP	
Percentage of overall population	
Settlement history	
Customs and traditions (for example, foods)	
Prominent members	

Extend Anna Quindlen discusses how throughout American history different cultural groups have been accepted as part of America's social fabric. What qualities of American society help immigrants to succeed?

CREATE AND DISCUSS

Compare Research with a Partner Meet with a partner to compare the results of your research into the cultural group you have chosen. Write a breakdown of the data each of you found and recorded in your charts. Then share your research.

❏ Introduce the cultural group you have chosen and where they are located.

❏ Discuss any similarities and differences between your cultural group and the one your partner chose.

❏ State a conclusion about these two cultural groups and how Quindlen's claim relates to your conclusion.

Discuss with a Small Group Have a discussion about the information partners have compiled in their research.

❏ As a group, review what each partnership has learned about their cultural groups. Make a connection with the claims and evidence Quindlen wrote about immigrants in "A Quilt of a Country."

❏ Have group members describe how their cultural group relates to Quindlen's claim. You may include personal connections or experiences as evidence. Remember to be understanding and respectful of all cultural groups.

❏ Review the conclusions that the group draws. Work together to suggest ways that cultural groups become another panel of our quilt of a country. Listen closely and respectfully to all ideas. Request assistance from peers or seek clarification as necessary.

Go to the **Speaking and Listening Studio** for help with having a group discussion.

RESPOND TO THE ESSENTIAL QUESTION

? How can we come together despite our differences?

Gather Information Review your annotations and notes on "A Quilt of a Country." Then, add relevant information to your Response Log. As you determine which information to include, think about:

UNIT 1
RESPONSE LOG

Essential Question:
How can we come together despite our differences?

A Quilt of a Country	
Unusual Normality	
Once Upon a Time	
The Vietnam Wall	
The Gettysburg Address	
from Saving Lincoln	

• ways to describe our country as a mixed group of people
• how different cultural groups come together as a nation
• how we as a nation can come together in hard times

At the end of the unit, use your notes to help you write a personal essay.

ACADEMIC VOCABULARY

As you write and discuss what you learned from the argument, be sure to use the Academic Vocabulary words. Check off each of the words that you use.

❏ **enforce**

❏ **entity**

❏ **internal**

❏ **presume**

❏ **resolve**

WORD BANK
discordant
pluralistic
interwoven
diversity

Go to the **Vocabulary Studio** for more on words with multiple meanings.

CRITICAL VOCABULARY

Practice and Apply Circle the letter of the best answer. Explain your response.

1. Which of the following would be described as **discordant**?
   a. an unskilled orchestra   **b.** birds flying in formation

2. Where would a **pluralistic** gathering most likely to be found?
   a. at a family picnic   **b.** at an international conference

3. Which of the following would be **interwoven**?
   a. a layer of frosting on a birthday cake   **b.** a musical motif heard several times throughout a movie

4. Which of the following is an example of **diversity**?
   a. an all-star team from 20 states   **b.** a set of twins

VOCABULARY STRATEGY:
Patterns of Word Changes

Words can have different meanings or be different parts of speech. Many words have several meanings listed in the dictionary. The word *equal* can mean "having the same privileges or rights." It also means "being the same or identical." Knowing different meanings can help you be an effective reader.

Words also change depending on the part of speech. The words *discordant* and *pluralistic* change spelling and meaning when the part of speech changes. Knowing how a word functions in a sentence will help you gain a complete understanding of the word's meaning.

Practice and Apply Complete the sentences with the correct word.

NOUN	VERB	ADJECTIVE
discord—lack of agreement **pluralism**—a condition of society where many groups coexist	**pluralize**—to engage in pluralism	**discordant**—conflicting **pluralistic**—consisting of many ethnic and cultural groups

1. The fact that people were shouting indicated the level of _____ during the meeting.

2. Some governmental entities claim to be _____ because people of different ethnic backgrounds work together.

3. Because the groups discussing the plan had _____ ideas, they made little progress.

LANGUAGE CONVENTIONS:
Noun Clauses

 Go to the **Grammar Studio** for more on noun clauses.

Writers use noun clauses to present complicated ideas that can replace a single word or phrase. This allows for a complete expression of ideas and a greater complexity of related concepts.

- Subject

  What Anna Quindlen wrote is still relevant today.

- Predicate Nominative

  "Pride seems excessive, given the American willingness to endlessly complain about them, them being whoever is new, different, unknown, or currently under suspicion."

- Object of a Preposition

  "This is a nation founded on a conundrum, what Mario Cuomo has characterized as 'community added to individualism.'"

- Direct Object

  Many people don't appreciate that America is made up of many diverse cultures

Practice and Apply Write your own sentences with noun phrases. You may write about the cultural group you researched earlier. When you have finished, share your sentences with a partner and compare your use of noun phrases and revise if necessary. Remember that noun phrases can start with the following words: *that, what, whatever, why, whether, how, who, whom, whoever,* or *whomever*.

UNUSUAL NORMALITY

Personal Essay by **Ishmael Beah**

? ESSENTIAL QUESTION:

How can we come together despite our differences?

QUICK START

The title of this personal essay, "Unusual Normality," is an **oxymoron**. The words *unusual* and *normal* have opposite meanings. What do you think the author meant by this title? Discuss your ideas with a small group. Can you think of any other common oxymorons, such as *open secret*?

ANALYZE PURPOSE AND MESSAGE

The **author's purpose** is the reason the writer has for writing a text. Authors may write to express thoughts or feelings, to persuade, to inform or explain, or to entertain. To determine the author's purpose in a personal essay, readers should:

- analyze the text structure. The author of this essay uses a chronological text structure to describe his experiences at one point in his life.

- analyze language, including voice and tone

- make inferences based on the author's style and message

The **message** is the central idea of the work, or what the author is trying to communicate to the audience. To determine central ideas and message in a personal essay, readers should:

- analyze the author's interpretations of events

- make inferences based on events and people the author describes

The **audience** is the people for whom the author is writing. To determine audience of a personal essay, readers should:

- analyze evidence in the text, including voice and tone

- make inferences based on details in the text and the author's message

ANALYZE VOICE AND TONE

Voice and tone are elements of an author's style.

Voice is a writer's unique use of language that allows a reader to "hear" a human personality in the writer's work. Elements of style that contribute to a writer's voice include sentence structure (or syntax), word choice (or diction), and tone.

Tone is the writer's attitude toward his or her subject. A writer communicates tone through choice of words and details.

GENRE ELEMENTS: PERSONAL ESSAY

- similar to memoirs but shorter and more focused

- explores the writer's experiences

- includes the author's feelings and reactions at the time

- written after the events in the story

LITERARY ELEMENT	EXAMPLE FROM "UNUSUAL NORMALITY"
Voice is created through sentence structure, word choice, and tone.	And I thought to myself, *What a great omen. Fresh new start to everything.*
Tone is the writer's attitude toward his or her subject, conveyed through word choice and details.	I learned a new American term for what they *did* find it. They were "weirded out" by the strange sense of humor that I had about this.

As you read, note the voice of the author and the tone of the essay, and use them as clues to the essay's purpose, message, and audience.

CRITICAL VOCABULARY

rehabilitation	counterparts	stereotype	naïve

To see how many Critical Vocabulary words you already know, write a brief answer to these questions.

1. What might **rehabilitation** for a broken leg involve?

_____

2. What might be the **counterparts** of grandmothers?

_____

3. Can a **stereotype** ever be a good thing?

_____

4. What is a **naïve** belief?

_____

LANGUAGE CONVENTIONS

Active and Passive Voice In this lesson, you will learn about the use of active and passive voice in writing. In active voice, the subject performing the action comes before the verb. The direct object *follows* the verb.

The boys played a game. The subject *boys* is the focus of the action.

In passive voice, the order is reversed.

A game was played by the boys. The focus is on the *game*.

ANNOTATION MODEL

NOTICE & NOTE

As you read, note the author's purpose and his voice and tone in the essay. You can also mark up evidence that supports your own ideas. In the model, you can see one reader's notes about "Unusual Normality."

I came to New York City in 1998. I was seventeen. ←

I entered the United States with just a passport in my hand, because somehow the baggage that I'd checked when I boarded the flight from Ivory Coast (which was tattered in ways unimaginable) didn't make it.

I stood there at the luggage rack watching all these huge bags go by, and mine didn't come. This bag held all my possessions at this point: two pairs of pants and two shirts — one long-sleeved and one short. So I just started laughing, and I didn't even bother going to the lost-baggage section to claim it.

author's purpose—express thoughts and feelings

author's voice comes from his unusual diction

this detail of author's reaction creates tone

BACKGROUND

Ishmael Beah *(b. 1980) began to write about his experiences as a way of dealing with being forced to be a child soldier in Sierra Leone in Africa. After his family was killed when he was just 12 years old, Beah was threatened with death if he didn't fight with a rebel group that was trying to overthrow the country. An American working for UNICEF brought him to the United States. Today, he is a lawyer, author, and a UN Goodwill Ambassador helping others like him.*

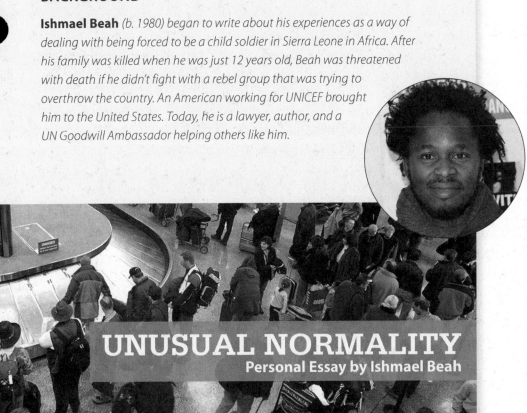

UNUSUAL NORMALITY
Personal Essay by Ishmael Beah

© Houghton Mifflin Harcourt Publishing Company • Image Credits: (t) ©Michael Loccisano/Getty Images; (c) ©DOUGLAS C. PIZAC/AP Images

SETTING A PURPOSE

As you read, pay attention to the author's reflections on the person he once was, including how he tried to fit in with people in a new place.

1 I came to New York City in 1998. I was seventeen.

2 I entered the United States with just a passport in my hand, because somehow the baggage that I'd checked when I boarded the flight from Ivory Coast (which was tattered in ways unimaginable) didn't make it.

3 I stood there at the luggage rack watching all these huge bags go by, and mine didn't come. This bag held all my possessions at this point: two pairs of pants and two shirts—one long-sleeved and one short. So I just started laughing, and I didn't even bother going to the lost-baggage section to claim it.

4 I just walked right out to meet my new adoptive mother, who was standing there with a beaming smile, waiting for me. And I explained to her what had happened, and we laughed some more.

5 We left and went into Manhattan, and that evening we went to Kmart. (After we had Chinese food and a fortune cookie that said, "You're about to have new clothes.")

6 And I thought to myself, *What a great omen. Fresh new start to everything.*

ANALYZE VOICE AND TONE

Annotate: Underline the author's thoughts, shown in italics. Circle two details in paragraphs 5–6 that caused these thoughts.

Analyze: How does the author's syntax and word choice reveal his attitude and outlook?

rehabilitation
(rē´hə-bĭl´ĭ-tā´shən) *n.* the act of being restored to good health or condition

© Houghton Mifflin Harcourt Publishing Company

MEMORY MOMENT

Notice & Note: What words indicate that the author is finished relating information about his earlier childhood? Underline these words.

Infer: Why might this information about his earlier childhood be important to the rest of the essay?

LANGUAGE CONVENTIONS

Annotate: Mark a sentence in paragraph 11 that uses passive voice.

Respond: What is the effect of this use of passive voice?

7   I was coming from a country called Sierra Leone. At age eleven, a war had started in my country. At twelve, I had become an orphan, because my mother, father, and two brothers had been killed in that war. At thirteen I was fighting as a soldier in that same war. At sixteen, after three years of war, I'd been removed from all that and had gone through **rehabilitation**, where I began learning how to deal with the memories of the war.

8   So from this experience, I had come to the United States. To have a new home, and to live with a mother who was willing to take me into her life when most people at the time were afraid of somebody like me.

9   It was a chance at living again, because all I had come to know, since I was eleven, was how to survive. I didn't know how to live. All I knew, really, up until this point in my life, was struggle. This was what I had come to expect from life, and I didn't trust in happiness or any kind of normality at all.

10   So here I was in New York, with my new mother. We needed to step into that normality.

11   But we had a lot of things to deal with, and one of the most pressing ones was that I needed to get into school. You see, the visa that I had been given was a prospective-student visa. This meant that when I arrived in the United States, I had three months to get into a school. If I didn't, I would be returned to my war-torn country, Sierra Leone.

12   Now, when I arrived, it was in the summer, so all the schools were closed. But my mother got on the phone and called every school principal she could think of in Manhattan, and tried to get them to grant me an interview.

13   When I went to some of the interviews, I was immediately denied because of the following conversation:

14   "Do you have a report card to show that you had been in school?"

15   I would say, "No, but I know I have been in school."

16   And then my mother would interject to explain the context.

17   I would sit there thinking to myself, *What do these school principals think? Do they really think that when there's a war in your village or when your town is attacked, and people are gunned down in front of you, and you're running for your life, you're thinking to yourself, "You know, I must take my report card and put it in the back of my pocket."*

18   At some of these interviews, I was able to say some of these things, thinking that it would be funny. But the school principals didn't find it funny. I learned a new American term for what they *did* find it. They were "weirded out" by the strange sense of humor that I had about this.

19   So I decided that I was going to write an entrance essay about this, and the essay was simply titled "Why I Do Not Have a Report Card."

20   With this essay, along with exams that were given to me, I was accepted to the United Nations International School and placed in the eleventh grade.

21   Thus began my two years of high school and making other teenagers confused about who I was. You see, I didn't fit into any box. I didn't have the same worries about what shoes or clothes I wore. And so my teenage **counterparts** always wanted to find out why I was like that. Why I didn't worry about my essays or exams or things.

22   And of course I couldn't tell them, because I felt that they were not ready to hear the truth. What was I going to say?

23   During a break from class, "Hey, you know, I was a child soldier at thirteen. Let's go back to class now."

24   So I was silent, mostly. I didn't say much. I would just smile. And this made them more curious.

25   They would say to me, "You're such a weird kid."

26   And I would respond by saying, "No, no, no. I'm not weird. *Weird* has a negative connotation. I prefer the word *unusual*. It has a certain sophistication and gravitas¹ to it that suits my character."

27   And of course when I was finished saying this, they would look at me and say, "Why don't you speak like a normal person?"

28   The reason I spoke like this was because of my British-African English that I'd learned, which was the only formal English that I knew. So whenever I spoke, people felt ill at ease, particularly my fellow teenagers. They thought, *What is wrong with this fellow?*

29   Some of them, though, didn't find it as strange. They thought maybe my English was like this because I was from some royal African family.

30   So throughout my high-school years, I tried to make my English less formal, so that my friends would not feel disturbed by it. (However, I did not dispute the fact that I was from some royal African family or that I was a prince. Because, you see, sometimes some **stereotypes** have their benefits, and I certainly took advantage of that.)

31   But I needed to be silent about my background, because I also felt like I was being watched. When I got into the school, some of the other parents were not very happy that somebody with my background was in school with their children. And I realized that the way I conducted myself would determine whether they would ever let another child who had been through war into such a school.

counterparts
(koun´tər-pärts´) *n.* people or things that have the same characteristics and function as another

ANALYZE VOICE AND TONE
Annotate: Mark the author's word choices and syntax that create the tone of paragraphs 21–27.

Draw Conclusions: What attitude does the author have toward his teenaged counterparts?

stereotype
(stĕr´ē-ə-tīp´) *n.* one that is thought of as conforming to a set type or image

---

¹ **gravitas** (grăv´ĭ-täs): seriousness, being solemn and respected.

© Houghton Mifflin Harcourt Publishing Company • Image Credits: ©monkeybusinessimages/iStock/Getty Images Plus/Getty Images

ANALYZE VOICE AND TONE

Annotate: In paragraphs 39–42, mark the words Beah uses to show the differences between himself and the "tough kids" of New York.

Compare: How does the violence of the "tough kids" differ from the violence the author has known?

32   But even with all of these attitudes, and with my silence, I started making friends. To them it was sufficient that I was just some kid who lived in the East Village, who was from an African country.

33   And these kids were tough (they told me). Because they lived in a tough city, New York. And therefore *they* were tough.

34   They had been to the Bronx. They had been to Bed-Stuy. They had taken the train there. They had gotten into fights and won.

35   So they would say things to me like, "If you want to survive the streets of New York City, we need to teach you a few things."

36   And I'd be like, "Okay, sure. I'm open to learning."

37   And they would tell me things about how to be tough and stuff, and I would say, "Well, thank you very much. I truly appreciate this advice that you're giving me."

38   They were like, "No worries, our African brother. Anytime, anytime."

39   Truth was, I'd been to some of these places that they spoke about, these neighborhoods, and I knew that the people who lived there didn't glorify violence the way they did. They didn't have time to pretend, because they lived in it, just like I had.

40   I noticed that these kids had a sort of *idea* of violence that they'd never really *lived*. They glorified it in a way, because they'd never actually experienced it at all.

41   When I walked with them, I observed that I paid more attention to the people who walked past us—how the person walked, which way they were coming from. I didn't take the same route twice, because I didn't want to develop a predictable path. These were all habits that were formed from my experiences, but I noticed that my

new friends didn't do that at all. So I knew they were just saying these things to seem tough to me.

42   Now, I did enjoy listening to my new friends that I had made. I enjoyed listening to them tremendously, because I wished, when I listened to them, that the only violence I knew was the violence that I imagined.

43   And listening to them allowed me to experience childhood in a way that I hadn't known was possible. It let me be a normal kid.

44   So I listened to them, and we hung out all the time, and through that I participated in what was left of my childhood.

45   I got to be a child again with them; the only worries that we had were when we went rollerblading without any protective gear. We took our brakes off, and sometimes we would avoid hitting an old lady by falling into a trash can on the street, and we laughed about it.

46   These things meant a lot to me.

47   After about a year of being friends with these boys, one of them decided to invite a group of us, about ten of us, to upstate New York. His family had property up there, and he said we were going there for the weekend to play a game called paintball.

48   I said, "Well, what is that?"

49   And he said, "Oh, man, you've never played paintball? You're gonna love it. It's a great game. The fellows and I, we always play it. And don't worry, we'll teach it to you, and we'll protect you.

50   "You use these balls of paint, and you shoot people," and he explained the basics of the game to me.

51   I said, "Okay, that sounds interesting."

52   And I thought, *If these guys who only pretend about violence can play it, it must not be that difficult a game.*

53   But of course I didn't say this. I just thought these things. So I went with them upstate to a humongous property that had trees and creeks that ran into a bigger river—this beautiful open place.

54   But as soon as we arrived, I began to memorize the terrain immediately, and this was from habit. I knew how many paces it took to get to the house, how many paces it took to the first tree, to the first bush, to the shed. I learned the spaces between the trees.

55   Overnight, while everybody was sleeping, I tried to replay some of these things in my head—to memorize the terrain.

56   And this was all out of habit, because where I came from, in my previous life, this kind of skill set could determine whether you lived or died.

57   In the morning, at breakfast, they were pumped up.

58   Everyone was saying, "Yeah, the game is gonna be awesome today."

59   And so after we finished breakfast, I was introduced to the game of paintball. They showed me the weapon, how you can shoot it. And I allowed them to teach me to shoot things.

AGAIN AND AGAIN

Notice & Note: Mark a thought about his friends that the author revisits, this time in a paintball game.

Predict: Based on this thought, make a prediction about what will happen during the paintball game.

© Houghton Mifflin Harcourt Publishing Company

ANALYZE PURPOSE
AND MESSAGE

Annotate: Mark words and
phrases in paragraph 67–71
that reveal Beah's actions
during paintball.

Interpret: Why does Beah
fight the way he does during
the paintball game? How does
this help reveal the author's
message?

60   They were very macho about it.

61   They said to me, "This is how you shoot, you aim like this."

62   I said, "Okay." I tried it a few times. I deliberately missed.

63   Then they showed me the camouflage and the combat gear and
everything.

64   And then everybody was ready to go, and they were amped up,
and all like, "Yeah, we're gonna go out! We're gonna DO THIS!!"

65   They decided we were going to play one-on-one. And then, after,
we would play team games.

66   So they started painting their faces, getting into this idea of war
that they knew.

67   I declined putting the face paint on, and I wanted to give them a
hint about my past, but then I thought, *You know what? I'm going to
have fun with this.*

68   So we went off into the bush, and when one of them shouted,
"Yeah, let the war begin! I'm going to bring pain to all of you! I'm
going to show you how it's done!" I thought to myself, *First rule of
warfare, you never belittle your opponent.*

69   But I didn't say this. I went into the bushes. I already knew where
to go, because I had memorized the layout of the place.

70   And so I would hide. I would wait for them. I would climb a
tree here. I would hide under certain shrubs. And they would come
rolling around, jumping, doing all kinds of things, things they'd
probably seen in movies about how people act in war.

71   I would just wait for them. And after they were done exhausting
themselves, I would come up behind them, and I would shoot the
paintball at them.

72   This went on all day. And when we came back that night, during
dinner, they talked about it.

73   You know: *How come you're so good? You're sure you've never
played paintball before?*

74   I said, "No, I have never played paintball before. I'm just a quick
learner, and you guys explained the game to me, and you are really
great teachers. This is why I'm able to play so well."

75   But they said, "That can't be all."

76   Some of the kids' parents were there, and the kids said to them,
"'This guy, he comes up on you. You can't even hear him coming at
all."

77   And I said, "Well, you know, I grew up in a village. And I used to
be a hunter when I was a boy, so I know how to blend into the forest,
like a chameleon[2]. I know how to adapt to my environment."

---

[2] **chameleon** (kə-mēl´yən) *n.* a tropical lizard that can change color

78   And they looked at me and said, "You're a very strange fellow, man. But you're *badass* at paintball."

79   I said, "Well, thank you. Thank you very, very much."

80   So this went on. We never got to play the group game. We played as individuals all throughout the weekend, because they wanted to beat me, and so they started to team up with each other. I would see them doing this, and then I would come up with a kind of watered-down version of another guerrilla tactic,[3] just to play with them.

81   For example, sometimes I would walk backwards and then stand where my footsteps "began" and hide. They would follow my footprints, and then I would come up behind them.

82   Anyway, at some point I decided that I was going to sit out the game, just so that they could enjoy it. And I saw a sense of relief on all of their faces.

---

[3] **guerrilla tactic** (gə-rĭl´ə tăk´tĭk): warfare techniques practiced by small bands of native fighters harassing and surprising larger armies.

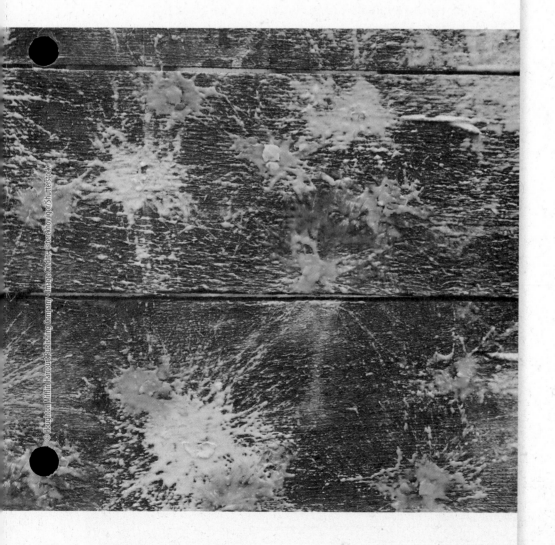

© Houghton Mifflin Harcourt Publishing Company • Image Credits: ©Stretch Photography/Blend Images/Getty Images

ANALYZE VOICE AND TONE

Annotate: Mark the words in paragraphs 88–90 that show the author's attitude towards his classmates and the paintball game.

Interpret: Describe the author's attitude toward his classmates and the paintball game in your own words.

83   They were like, *Oh, well, FINALLY!*

84   When I returned, I told my mother about this game. And my mother, being a mother, was immediately worried.

85   She said, "Oh, did that bring up something for you?"

86   And I said, "No, it didn't, absolutely."

87   Because I know the difference between pretend war and real war.

88   But it was interesting for me to observe how my friends perceived what war is.

89   The next day at school, these friends of mine talked about the awesome weekend of paintball we'd had. But they never said how I'd won all the games. And I said nothing at all.

90   They never invited me back to play paintball with them. And I didn't ask to be invited back.

91   I so wanted to talk to them about the war while we were playing the game. I wanted to explain certain things, but I felt that if they knew about my background, they would no longer allow me to be a child. They would see me as an adult, and I was worried that they would fear me.

92   My silence allowed me to experience things, to participate in my childhood, to do things I hadn't been able to do as a child.

93   It was only years later that they learned why I had won the game.

94   But I wish I had been able to tell them early on, because I wanted them to understand how lucky they were to have a mother, a father, grandparents, siblings.[4] People who annoyed them by caring about them so much and calling them all the time to make sure they were okay.

95   I wanted to tell them that they were so lucky to have this **naïve** innocence about the world. I wanted them to understand that it was extremely lucky for them to only play *pretend* war and never have to do the real thing. And that their **naïve** innocence about the world was something for which I no longer had the capacity.

---

[4] **siblings** (sĭb´lĭngs): *n.* brothers or sisters, individuals sharing one or more parents

ANALYZE PURPOSE AND MESSAGE

Annotate: Mark the sentences in paragraphs 92–95 that reveal the author's message.

Interpret: What is the author's message, and what does it reveal about the author's purpose for writing and who he sees as his audience?

naïve
(nī-ēv´) *adj.* lacking worldly experience or understanding

CHECK YOUR UNDERSTANDING

Answer these questions before moving on to the **Analyze the Text** questions on the following page.

1 Which of these best describes the purpose of the selection?

   A To explain how the author became a great paintball player

   B To show how people who think they are tough are really weak

   C To explain how the past made the author appreciate his new life

   D To describe how it was impossible for the author to escape his past

2 At the conclusion of the essay —

   F the author's friends invite him to play paintball again

   G the author tells his friends about his past

   H the author finally gets into a good school

   J the author explains what he wanted to tell his friends

3 Which of the following is not true about the author, Ishmael Beah?

   A The author fought as a soldier in a war when he was a child.

   B The author did not know how to play paintball before this story.

   C The author is from a royal African family.

   D The author took school very seriously.

ANALYZE THE TEXT

Support your responses with evidence from the text. NOTEBOOK

1. **Interpret** Ishmael Beah's use of language—his word choice and syntax—establishes an individual voice and tone. Describe the essay's voice and tone, citing examples from the selection.

2. **Cite Evidence** What are some of the ways that the author differs from his classmates? Cite evidence from the text in your answer.

3. **Analyze** Review the last sentence of paragraph 31. Use details in this sentence to help you infer a reason or purpose Beah might have had for writing this essay.

4. **Synthesize** How does the text structure—a personal essay—enable the author to deliver his message effectively? Explain your answer using examples from the text.

5. **Notice & Note** Think about the Memory Moments you noticed during this story. What skills and habits did the author learn as a child soldier that helped him both in New York and in the paintball game?

RESEARCH

RESEARCH TIP
At the end of an article, an author will often list the references he or she used to write the piece. Explore these links, which can reveal details that might lead to greater understanding of the topic.

Conflicts in the African nations of Sierra Leone, Sudan, and the Democratic Republic of the Congo brought the world's attention to children forced to serve as soldiers. Use these countries as well as terms such as "Lost Boys of Sudan" as keywords to find relevant sources about specific groups of child soldiers and the related conflicts. Verify that your sources are valid and your information is accurate. Record what you learn in the chart.

ARTICLE TITLE AND SOURCE	DETAILS OF CONFLICT

Connect In the last paragraph of "Unusual Normality," the author discusses losing his naïve innocence. Continue your research about these child soldiers to learn about other children who have lost their childhood to war. Find out about the role of U.S. resettlement efforts, including details about individuals who escaped life as one of these child soldiers.

CREATE AND PRESENT

Write a Summarizing Report Write a three-to-four paragraph report in which you summarize your findings about child soldiers.

- ❏ Write about the facts and details you have learned about the topic, synthesizing information from a variety of sources. Compare sources to each other to reveal biases.

- ❏ As you write about U.S. resettlement efforts for refugees, include any specific stories or accounts of specific child soldiers.

- ❏ Maintain meaning and logical order as you write your report.

Debate with a Small Group Have a debate about what should be done about the problem of children forced to become soldiers.

- ❏ In your group, review the topic and the research individuals have done. Isolate the issues and areas of the topic that are controversial. Decide what your group position will be on the question.

- ❏ As you participate in the debate, use appropriate register (degree of formality), vocabulary, and tone to help convey your points. Listen actively to others' positions, respond appropriately, and adjust your responses when new evidence causes you to change your views.

- ❏ Review the ideas discussed in the debate, and summarize conclusions. Use evidence from your research sources to support your conclusions.

 Go to the **Writing Studio** for more on writing an informative report.

Go to the **Speaking and Listening Studio** for help with holding a debate.

RESPOND TO THE ESSENTIAL QUESTION

 How can we come together despite our differences?

Gather Information Review your annotations and notes on "Unusual Normality." Then, add relevant information to your Response Log. As you determine which information to include, think about:

- how Beah's attitudes toward school reflect his background
- why and how Beah tries to fit in to his new environment and make friends
- what factors help Beah appreciate his new life

At the end of the unit, use your notes to help you write a personal essay.

ACADEMIC VOCABULARY

As you write and discuss what you learned from the essay, be sure to use the Academic Vocabulary words. Check off each of the words that you use.

- ❏ **enforce**
- ❏ **entity**
- ❏ **internal**
- ❏ **presume**
- ❏ **resolve**

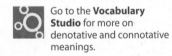
WORD BANK

rehabilitation

counterparts

stereotype

naïve

CRITICAL VOCABULARY

Practice and Apply Circle the letter of the best answer to each question. Then, explain your response.

1. Which of the following would be part of **rehabilitation**?
   a. constructing something from new parts
   b. nursing an injured animal

2. Which of the following are **counterparts**?
   a. the governors of two neighboring states
   b. the sky and the clouds floating through it

3. Which of the following is a **stereotype**?
   a. tall people play basketball
   b. I like music

4. Which of the following is a **naïve** action?
   a. putting your money in a savings account
   b. trusting a stranger with all your money

VOCABULARY STRATEGY:
Denotative and Connotative Meanings

Some words have both a **denotative** and **connotative meaning**. A denotative meaning is the meaning of the word that you would find in a dictionary. A word's connotative meaning includes the feelings and ideas that people may connect with a word. For example, someone may be described as *slender* or *skinny*. The denotative meanings of the words are similar. But *skinny* implies that someone is too thin. It has a negative connotation, while *slender* has a positive connotation.

Go to the **Vocabulary Studio** for more on denotative and connotative meanings.

Practice and Apply Read these sentences. Then, state the denotative and connotative meanings of the boldfaced words.

1. The man wore **tattered** clothes to the mall. She had **torn** the sleeve on her favorite shirt.

   _____

2. She **laughed** at the joke. He **cackled** when she finished telling the story.

   _____

3. She had a **weird** way of talking. His songs were **quirky**.

   _____

LANGUAGE CONVENTIONS: ACTIVE AND PASSIVE VOICE

Writers may use either active or passive voice in their writing. Active voice is easier to read and understand, flows more smoothly, and uses fewer words. Ishmael Beah uses active voice in the sentence below, with the subject *mother* first, and then the verb *called*, followed by the direct object *principal*.

But my <u>mother</u> got on the phone and <u>called</u> every school <u>principal</u>...

However, passive voice is appropriate when writers want to bring attention to the one receiving the action (the principal in the sentence above) instead of the one doing the action (the mother). The sentence could have been written as:

Every school principal was called by my mother on the phone.

Writers can choose to use passive voice for emphasis.

In "Unusual Normality," notice how Ishmael Beah uses both active and passive voice for different effects:

- Active: focus on the subject *I* not the direct object *term*.

  <u>I learned</u> a new American <u>term</u> for what they *did* find it.

- Passive: focus on the *visa,* not on who gave it to him.

  You see, the <u>visa</u> that I had been given was a prospective-student visa.

Practice and Apply Write your own sentences with active and passive voice. Your sentences can be about your own experiences in school or those of someone you know. When you have finished, share your sentences with a partner and compare your use of active and passive voice.

Go to the **Grammar Studio** for more on active and passive voice.

ONCE UPON A TIME

Short Story by **Nadine Gordimer**

ESSENTIAL QUESTION:

How can we come together despite our differences?

QUICK START

What is something you fear? What is something that others in your family fear? Think about and discuss ways these fears shape and affect your lives.

ANALYZE SETTING AND THEME

The **setting** of a story is the time and place of the action of the story. Setting often shapes a story's events or plot, including the story's conflict.

The main message of a story is the **theme**, which can be enhanced or advanced by the setting. As you analyze "Once Upon a Time," make inferences, or logical guesses, about the theme by considering the details and symbols Gordimer includes. Pay particular attention to the characters' actions and motivations, as well as the setting—including the historical background—to help you infer the theme. Looking for the Signposts and asking questions about them as you read can also help you find the theme of a story.

GENRE ELEMENTS: SHORT STORY

- includes the basic elements of fiction—setting, characters, plot, conflict, and theme
- centers on one particular moment or event in life
- can be read in one sitting

LITERARY ELEMENT	EXAMPLES
A story's **setting** can shape the events of a story.	**In a house, in a suburb, in a city, there were a man and his wife….**
Look for clues to a story's **theme** throughout the story, such as changes in details of the setting.	So from every window and door in the house… they now saw the trees and sky through bars….

ANALYZE PLOT: SUBPLOTS

A **subplot** is an additional storyline that runs parallel to the main story. Sometimes subplots are used as framing devices at the beginning or end of a story.

Subplots may involve characters who are less important or another story that is happening outside the main, focused story. Subplots are usually linked to the main plot of the story in some way.

In "Once Upon a Time," the subplot involves the author's struggle to write a children's story. One night she is awakened by a noise and begins to imagine dangers in her home.

CRITICAL VOCABULARY

| distend | intention | audacious | intrusion | serrated |

To see how many Critical Vocabulary words you already know, use them to complete the sentences.

1. The motorcyclist's stunt was terrifying and _____.

2. The thief's _____ in the middle of the night scared the whole family.

3. The businesswomen said it was her _____ to buy the company for cash.

4. The bacterial infection caused the baby's stomach to _____.

5. The knife was sharp because it was _____.

LANGUAGE CONVENTIONS

Prepositional Phrases are phrases consisting of a preposition and an object of the preposition, usually a noun or a pronoun. Prepositional phrases provide more information about the noun or verb in a sentence. Think about the information prepositional phrases add to the following sentences from the selection.

. . . she implored her employers to have burglar bars attached <u>to the doors and windows of the house</u> . . .

So <u>from every window and door in the house where they were living happily ever after</u> they now saw the trees and sky through bars . . .

ANNOTATION MODEL   NOTICE & NOTE

As you read, note the author's use of setting and subplots to advance the theme of the story. You can also mark up evidence that supports your own ideas. In the model, you can see one reader's notes about "Once Upon a Time."

<u>I couldn't find a position in which my mind would let go of my body—release me to sleep again.</u> So I began to tell myself a story; a bedtime story.

In a house, in a suburb, in a city, <u>there were a man and his wife who loved each other very much and were living happily ever after.</u>

This might be the end of a subplot, and the start of the main plot.

This is a very simple setting; I think it's going to get more complicated.

BACKGROUND

Nadine Gordimer *(1923–2014) was born in South Africa. Her family was privileged and white in a country that practiced apartheid—an official policy of segregation of nonwhite South Africans. Gordimer became politically opposed to the policy. Her early works, such as* The Soft Voice of the Serpent *and* The Lying Days, *explore themes of exile and the effects of apartheid on life in South Africa. Before apartheid ended in 1994, some of Gordimer's writings were banned by the South African government. Gordimer was awarded many literary prizes, including the Nobel Prize for Literature in 1991.*

ONCE UPON A TIME

Short Story by Nadine Gordimer

SETTING A PURPOSE

As you read, pay attention to the way that the author builds a portrait of the suburb as a setting that should be safe but becomes something else.

1   Someone has written to ask me to contribute to an anthology of stories for children. I reply that I don't write children's stories; and he writes back that at a recent congress/book fair/seminar a certain novelist said every writer ought to write at least one story for children. I think of sending a postcard saying I don't accept that I "ought" to write anything.

2   And then last night I woke up—or rather was wakened without knowing what had roused me.

3   A voice in the echo chamber of the subconscious?

4   A sound.

5   A creaking of the kind made by the weight carried by one foot after another along a wooden floor. I listened. I felt the apertures of my ears **distend** with concentration. Again: the creaking. I was waiting for it; waiting to hear if it indicated that feet were moving from room to room, coming up the passage—to my door. I have no burglar bars, no gun under the pillow, but

Notice & Note

You can use the side margins to notice and note signposts in the text.

LANGUAGE CONVENTIONS
Annotate: Mark the two prepositional phrases in paragraph 3.

Respond: What information do these prepositional phrases provide?

distend
(dĭ-stĕnd´) *v.*
to bulge or expand.

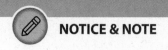
ANALYZE SUBPLOTS

Annotate: Mark words and phrases in paragraphs 6 and 7 that tell how the author feels at this point in the story.

Analyze: What mood do these words create?

I have the same fears as people who do take these precautions, and my windowpanes are thin as rime,[1] could shatter like a wineglass. A woman was murdered (how do they put it) in broad daylight in a house two blocks away, last year, and the fierce dogs who guarded an old widower and his collection of antique clocks were strangled before he was knifed by a casual laborer he had dismissed without pay.

6   I was staring at the door, making it out in my mind rather than seeing it, in the dark. I lay quite still—a victim already—but the arrhythmia[2] of my heart was fleeing, knocking this way and that against its body-cage. How finely tuned the senses are, just out of rest, sleep! I could never listen intently as that in the distractions of the day; I was reading every faintest sound, identifying and classifying its possible threat.

7   But I learned that I was to be neither threatened nor spared. There was no human weight pressing on the boards, the creaking was a buckling, an epicenter[3] of stress. I was in it. The house that surrounds me while I sleep is built on undermined ground; far beneath my bed, the floor, the house's foundations, the stopes[4] and passages of gold mines have hollowed the rock, and when some face trembles, detaches, and falls, three thousand feet below, the whole house shifts slightly, bringing uneasy strain to the balance and counterbalance of brick, cement, wood, and glass that hold it as a structure around me. The misbeats of my heart tailed off like the last muffled flourishes on one of the wooden xylophones made by the Chopi and Tsonga[5] migrant miners who might have been down there, under me in the earth at that moment. The stope where the fall was could have been disused, dripping water from its ruptured veins; or men might now be interred there in the most profound of tombs.

8   I couldn't find a position in which my mind would let go of my body—release me to sleep again. So I began to tell myself a story; a bedtime story.

AHA MOMENT

Notice & Note: Mark sentences that tell what caused the sudden change in the author's decision not to write a story for children.

Infer: Why did the author change her mind?

9   In a house, in a suburb, in a city, there were a man and his wife who loved each other very much and were living happily ever after. They had a little boy, and they loved him very much. They had a cat and a dog that the little boy loved very much. They had a car and a caravan trailer for holidays, and a swimming pool which was fenced so that the little boy and his playmates would not fall in and drown. They had a housemaid who was absolutely trustworthy and an

---

[1] **rime** (rīm): a coating of frost
[2] **arrhythmia** (ə-rĭth′mē-ə): an irregular heartbeat
[3] **epicenter:** the focal point
[4] **stopes:** step-like holes or trenches made by miners
[5] **Chopi and Tsonga** (chō′pē and tsôn′ga): ethnic groups that live in Mozambique

itinerant[6] gardener who was highly recommended by the neighbors. For when they began to live happily ever after, they were warned by that wise old witch, the husband's mother, not to take on anyone off the street. They were inscribed in a medical benefit society, their pet dog was licensed, they were insured against fire, flood damage, and theft, and subscribed to the local Neighborhood Watch, which supplied them with a plaque for their gates lettered YOU HAVE BEEN WARNED over the silhouette of a would-be intruder. He was masked; it could not be said if he was black or white, and therefore proved the property owner was no racist.

10   It was not possible to insure the house, the swimming pool, or the car against riot damage. There were riots, but these were outside the city, where people of another color were quartered. These people were not allowed into the suburb except as reliable housemaids and gardeners, so there was nothing to fear, the husband told the wife. Yet she was afraid that some day such people might come up the street and tear off the plaque YOU HAVE BEEN WARNED and open the gates and stream in. . . . Nonsense, my dear, said the husband, there are police and soldiers and tear gas and guns to keep them away. But to please her—for he loved her very much and buses were being burned, cars stoned, and schoolchildren shot by the police in those quarters out of sight and hearing of the suburb—he had electronically controlled gates fitted. Anyone who pulled off the sign YOU HAVE BEEN WARNED and tried to open the gates would have to announce his **intentions** by pressing a button and speaking into a receiver relayed to the house. The little boy was fascinated by the device and used it as a walkie-talkie in cops and robbers play with his small friends.

11   The riots were suppressed, but there were many burglaries in the suburb and somebody's trusted housemaid was tied up and shut in a cupboard by thieves while she was in charge of her employers' house. The trusted housemaid of the man and wife and little boy was so upset by this misfortune befalling a friend left, as she herself often was, with responsibility for the possessions of the man and his wife and the little boy, that she implored her employers to have burglar bars attached to the doors and windows of the house, and an alarm system installed. The wife said, she is right, let us take heed of her advice. So from every window and door in the house where they were living happily ever after they now saw the trees and sky through bars, and when the little boy's pet cat tried to climb in by the fanlight[7] to keep him company in his little bed at night, as it customarily had done, it set off the alarm keening[8] through the house.

© Houghton Mifflin Harcourt Publishing Company

---

[6] **itinerant:** frequently traveling to different places
[7] **fanlight:** an arched window, usually over a door
[8] **keening:** wailing or crying

ANALYZE SETTING AND THEME

Annotate: What fear does the wife have? How does her husband reassure her that they are safe? Mark sentences in paragraph 10 that show the fear and the husband's reassurances.

Predict: What do you think will happen next?

intention
(ĭn-tĕn´shən) *n.*
purpose or plan.

audacious
(ô-dā´shəs) *adj.* bold, rebellious.

ANALYZE SETTING AND THEME

Annotate: Mark the phrases and sentences in paragraph 13 that suggest the wife's desire to help is in conflict with the family's fear.

Analyze: How might this conflict relate to the author's theme, or message?

12   The alarm was often answered—it seemed—by other burglar alarms, in other houses, that had been triggered by pet cats or nibbling mice. The alarms called to one another across the gardens in shrills and bleats and wails that everyone soon became accustomed to, so that the din roused the inhabitants of the suburb no more than the croak of frogs and musical grating of cicadas'[9] legs. Under cover of the electronic harpies'[10] discourse intruders sawed the iron bars and broke into homes, taking away hi-fi equipment, television sets, cassette players, cameras and radios, jewelry and clothing, and sometimes were hungry enough to devour everything in the refrigerator or paused **audaciously** to drink the whiskey in the cabinets or patio bars. Insurance companies paid no compensation for single malt, a loss made keener by the property owner's knowledge that the thieves wouldn't even have been able to appreciate what it was they were drinking.

13   Then the time came when many of the people who were not trusted housemaids and gardeners hung about the suburb because they were unemployed. Some importuned for a job: weeding or painting a roof; anything, *baas*,[11] madam. But the man and his wife remembered the warning about taking on anyone off the street. Some drank liquor and fouled the street with discarded bottles. Some begged, waiting for the man or his wife to drive the car out of the electronically operated gates. They sat about with their feet in the gutters, under the jacaranda trees that made a green tunnel of the street—for it was a beautiful suburb, spoiled only by their presence— and sometimes they fell asleep lying right before the gates in the midday sun. The wife could never see anyone go hungry. She sent the trusted housemaid out with bread and tea, but the trusted housemaid said these were loafers and *tsotsis*,[12] who would come and tie her up and shut her in a cupboard. The husband said, she's right. Take heed of her advice. You only encourage them with your bread and tea. They are looking for their chance. . . . And he brought the little boy's tricycle from the garden into the house every night, because if the house was surely secure, once locked and with the alarm set, someone might still be able to climb over the wall or the electronically closed gates into the garden.

14   You are right, said the wife, then the wall should be higher. And the wise old witch, the husband's mother, paid for the extra bricks as her Christmas present to her son and his wife—the little boy got a Space Man outfit and a book of fairy tales.

---

[9] **cicadas** (sĭ-kā´ dəs): large, loud insects
[10] **harpies:** mythological creatures who were part woman and part bird
[11] **baas** (bäs): a white person in a position of authority in relation to nonwhites
[12] **tsotsis** (tsō´tsēs): dishonest, untrustworthy people

© Houghton Mifflin Harcourt Publishing Company

© Houghton Mifflin Harcourt Publishing Company • Image Credits: ©Jason Edwards/National Geographic Magazines/ Getty Images

15   But every week there were more reports of **intrusion**: in broad daylight and the dead of night, in the early hours of the morning, and even in the lovely summer twilight—a certain family was at dinner while the bedrooms were being ransacked upstairs. The man and his wife, talking of the latest armed robbery in the suburb, were distracted by the sight of the little boy's pet cat effortlessly arriving over the seven-foot wall, descending first with a rapid bracing of extended forepaws down on the sheer vertical surface, and then a graceful launch, landing with a swishing tail within the property. The whitewashed wall was marked with the cat's comings and goings; and on the street side of the wall there were larger red-earth smudges that could have been made by the kind of broken running shoes, seen on the feet of unemployed loiterers, that had no innocent destination.

16   When the man and wife and little boy took the pet dog for its walk round the neighborhood streets they no longer paused to admire this show of roses or that perfect lawn; these were hidden

intrusion
(ĭn-trōō´shən) *n.* act of trespass or invasion.

CONTRASTS AND CONTRADICTIONS

Notice & Note: Mark contrasts and contradictions between the "perfect" suburb and the walls and other protections that the neighbors have built.

Summarize: How has the suburb changed, and why?

behind an array of different varieties of security fences, walls, and devices. The man, wife, little boy, and dog passed a remarkable choice: there was the low-cost option of pieces of broken glass embedded in cement along the top of walls, there were iron grilles ending in lance points, there were attempts at reconciling the aesthetics of prison architecture with the Spanish Villa style (spikes painted pink) and with the plastic urns of neoclassical facades (twelve-inch pikes finned like zigzags of lightning and painted pure white). Some walls had a small board affixed, giving the name and telephone number of the firm responsible for the installation of the devices. While the little boy and the pet dog raced ahead, the husband and wife found themselves comparing the possible effectiveness of each style against its appearance; and after several weeks when they paused before this barricade or that without needing to speak, both came out with the conclusion that only one was worth considering. It was the ugliest but the most honest in its suggestion of the pure concentration-camp style, no frills, all evident efficacy. Placed the length of walls, it consisted of a continuous coil of stiff and shining metal **serrated** into jagged blades, so that there would be no way of climbing over it and no way through its tunnel without getting entangled in its fangs. There would be no way out, only a struggle getting bloodier and bloodier, a deeper and sharper hooking and tearing of flesh. The wife shuddered to look at it. You're right, said the husband, anyone would think twice. . . . And they took heed of the advice on a small board fixed to the wall: Consult DRAGON'S TEETH The People For Total Security.

serrated
(sĕr´ā´tĭd) *adj.* having a jagged, saw-toothed edge.

17 Next day, a gang of workmen came and stretched the razor-bladed coils all round the walls of the house where the husband and wife and little boy and pet dog and cat were living happily ever after. The sunlight flashed and slashed off the serrations, the cornice of razor thorns encircled the home, shining. The husband said, Never mind. It will weather. The wife said, You're wrong. They guarantee it's rustproof. And she waited until the little boy had run off to play before she said, I hope the cat will take heed. . . . The husband said, Don't worry, my dear, cats always look before they leap. And it was true that from that day on, the cat slept in the little boy's bed and kept to the garden, never risking a try at breaching security.

ANALYZE SETTING AND THEME

Annotate: Mark the words that reveal the shocking ending of the story.

Connect: Think about the characters' actions and motivations that led to this ending. What can you infer about the theme, or message, of this story?

18 One evening, the mother read the little boy to sleep with a fairy story from the book the wise old witch had given him at Christmas. Next day, he pretended to be the prince who braves the terrible thicket of thorns to enter the palace and kiss the Sleeping Beauty back to life: he dragged a ladder to the wall, the shining coiled tunnel was just wide enough for his little body to creep in, and with the first fixing of its razor teeth in his knees and hands and head he screamed and struggled deeper into its tangle. The trusted housemaid and the itinerant gardener, whose "day" it was, came running, the first to see

and to scream with him, and the itinerant gardener tore his hands trying to get at the little boy. Then the man and his wife burst wildly into the garden and for some reason (the cat, probably), the alarm set up wailing against the screams while the bleeding mass of the little boy was hacked out of the security coil with saws, wire cutters, choppers, and they carried it—the man, the wife, the hysterical trusted housemaid, and the weeping gardener—into the house.

CHECK YOUR UNDERSTANDING

Answer these questions before moving on to the **Analyze the Text** section on the following page.

1 The author included the opening paragraph about not writing children's stories to —

   A argue why children's stories are not important

   B compare herself to other authors

   C show how she came to write a fairy tale

   D explain why her story is not like other children's stories

2 Which of the following is a central theme in the story?

   F Private security measures are important for people's safety.

   G Sometimes people must suppress the majority population.

   H People shouldn't allow fear to dictate their actions and isolate them.

   J Police and law enforcement can control robberies and intrusions.

3 The author's purpose for writing the selection was most likely to —

   A warn about outsiders trying to invade your home

   B explore different home security systems

   C tell about a curse that was placed on a neighborhood

   D show the dangers of fear and paranoia

ANALYZE THE TEXT

Support your responses with evidence from the text. NOTEBOOK

1. **Connect** Nadine Gordimer wrote many stories about the injustices of apartheid. She was also active in bringing change to the political entities of South Africa. Even though her books were banned in South Africa for a time, she resolved to stay instead of living in exile. What do you learn about Gordimer's political point of view by reading this story? Explain your ideas using evidence from the story.

2. **Infer** Authors often leave things unstated in a story, leaving the reader with questions about the outcome. What can you infer about what Gordimer leaves unstated at the end of her story? How does it relate to her statements about the family living "happily ever after"?

3. **Infer** What is the theme of this story? Explain how Gordimer develops this theme through the story's setting.

4. **Identify Patterns** How is the structure of this story similar to a fairy tale? How does the story's subplot contribute to the structure? Cite details from the text to support your answer.

5. **Notice & Note** What actions do the husband, wife, and their neighbors do again and again because of their fear of outsiders? How does this reveal the story's theme?

RESEARCH

RESEARCH TIP

Search general terms like *fairy tale, tall tale,* and *bedtime story,* as well as the titles of these types that you encounter. Remember that each source will suggest other search terms that may or may not prove to be useful.

Fairy tales are one of the oldest forms of writing and originally came from oral stories passed down through cultures. Research and read a few well-known fairy tales, and write a summary for each fairy tale. Record what you learn in the chart, citing your sources. Then share your findings with a partner and discuss the structure and characteristics of each fairy tale.

FAIRY TALE AND SOURCE	SUMMARY

Connect In paragraph 7, Gordimer references a number of different home security systems. With a small group, discuss whether anyone knows about these protections or has seen them being used. Have them discuss what happens to the effectiveness of an alarm that falsely goes off too many times.

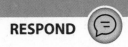

CREATE AND PRESENT

Write a Fairy Tale With a partner create a modern fairy tale based on a community or school event that has happened already or you have observed.

- ❏ Introduce the setting and the characters.
- ❏ Include magical or made-up elements like talking animals or creative settings.
- ❏ Have the tale demonstrate some truth about life or a central message.

Present to the Class You and your partner should decide how you would like to present your fairy tale.

- ❏ You can rehearse it and then act it out.
- ❏ You can record it and then show the video.
- ❏ You can present the story and read it aloud or share illustrations.

If you encounter challenges in your process, change the presentation to fit your needs.

Go to the **Writing Studio** for more on writing narratives.

Go to the **Speaking and Listening Studio** for help with presenting a play or acting in a film.

RESPOND TO THE ESSENTIAL QUESTION

 How can we come together despite our differences?

Gather Information Review your annotations and notes on "Once Upon a Time." Then, add relevant information to your Response Log. As you determine which information to include, think about:

- how the family becomes increasingly isolated
- what happens to a society when fear takes over people's lives
- what the cat might symbolize as the people in the story shut themselves off from others

At the end of the unit, use your notes to help you write a personal essay.

ACADEMIC VOCABULARY

As you write and discuss what you learned from the short story, be sure to use the Academic Vocabulary words. Check off each of the words that you use.

- ❏ **enforce**
- ❏ **entity**
- ❏ **internal**
- ❏ **presume**
- ❏ **resolve**

WORD BANK
distend
intention
audacious
intrusion
serrated

CRITICAL VOCABULARY

Practice and Apply Choose which of the two situations best fits the word's meaning.

1. distend

   a. After the Thanksgiving meal our stomachs were uncomfortably full.

   b. Platters of food completely covered the holiday table.

2. intention

   a. The soccer player showed his determination to shoot for the goal.

   b. The soccer player's purpose was to play better in the next game.

3. audacious

   a. The daring boy brought gum to the computer lab.

   b. A teacher caught the mischievous boy.

4. intrusion

   a. The newspaper talked about the girl's wrongful entrance into the clubhouse.

   b. The girl's interruption of the conversation made the club members unhappy.

5. serrated

   a. The edge of the paper was cut into a decorative pattern.

   b. The toothed edge of the paper looked like a set of teeth.

VOCABULARY STRATEGY:
Words from Latin

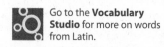

Go to the **Vocabulary Studio** for more on words from Latin.

Etymologies show the origin and historical development of a word. For example, the Critical Vocabulary word *distend* comes from the Latin word *distendere*, which means "to stretch." Exploring the etymology of words can help you clarify their precise meanings and expand your vocabulary.

WORD AND DEFINITION	ETYMOLOGY
surround "to enclose on all sides"	from the Latin *super-* + *unda* "to flow over in waves"

Practice and Apply

Follow these steps for each Critical Vocabulary word, using a chart like the one above:

- Find the etymology of each word in a dictionary. If you need help, in the front or the back of your dictionary there will be a section that explains how the etymology is noted and what the abbreviations mean.
- Compare the Latin definition of each word with the English definition. Are they the same? How does the English definition relate to the Latin meaning?

LANGUAGE CONVENTIONS:
Prepositional Phrases

Authors use different types of phrases to add variety and interest to their writing. **Prepositional phrases** are phrases that consist of a preposition and an object of the preposition, such as a noun or a pronoun. Here are some common prepositions and phrases that can be created with them.

PREPOSITION	OBJECT OF PREPOSITION	PREPOSITIONAL PHRASE
from	the street	from the street
before	the rain	before the rain
during	the game	during the game
until	her test	until her test
outside	the gate	outside the gate

Read the following sentence from the story.

> **In a house, in a suburb, in a city, there were a man and his wife who loved each other very much and were living happily ever after.**

Nadine Gordimer might have written the sentence this way:

> **In a suburban house, there were a man and his wife who loved each other very much and were living happily ever after.**

While the second sentence conveys the same meaning, it doesn't hold the same interest as the original sentence. In the original sentence, the author uses the prepositional phrases to create a unique sentence structure that adds variety and emphasis. The prepositional phrases used one after another, *in a house, in a suburb, in a city,* help the author change gears from a story about something that happened to her to a story about another family. The phrases mimic the way a storyteller might use a steady beat or rhythm to start a story.

Notice also that Gordimer used commas to set off each prepositional phrase to emphasize each prepositional phrase.

Examine another sentence from "Once Upon a Time":

> **One evening, the mother read the little boy to sleep <u>with a fairy story from the book</u> the wise old witch had given him <u>at Christmas.</u>**

Although Gordimer could have written several shorter sentences, this sentence with a series of prepositional phrases conveys the sense of a fairy tale. The prepositional phrases add details to the sentence.

Notice that here the prepositional phrases are not set off with commas.

Practice and Apply Rewrite the beginning of your modern fairy tale. Use prepositional phrases to add detail and enhance the storytelling rhythm. Use proper punctuation to set off prepositional phrases.

Go to the **Grammar Studio** for more on prepositional phrases.

THE VIETNAM WALL

Poem by **Alberto Ríos**

ESSENTIAL QUESTION:

How can we come together despite our differences?

QUICK START

How much do you know about the Vietnam Veterans Memorial? List three things you think are true and three questions you have. Share your assumptions and questions with your group.

ANALYZE GRAPHIC ELEMENTS

Think of a few of the **graphic elements** you've seen in the texts you've read. Your list might include photos, headings, captions, sidebar features, charts, and words emphasized in boldfaced or italic type. Each graphic element is there for a specific purpose; it adds to your experience as a reader and contributes to what you know about the text.

Poets create graphic effects through the way they organize type on the page. The author of "The Vietnam Wall" made intentional decisions about graphic elements including line length, punctuation, capitalization, word position, and the overall shape of the poem on the page.

FROM "THE VIETNAM WALL"	GRAPHIC ELEMENTS
I **Have seen it** **And I like it: The magic,** **The way like cutting onions** **It brings water out of nowhere.**	• The word "I" by itself on line 1 focuses the reader's attention on the speaker. • Ending line 2 in the middle of a thought builds tension. • The colon in line 3 tells the reader that more information is coming about what the author likes and why.

In this poem, most lines are short, averaging about five words each. The narrator speaks in short, choppy phrases. This effect builds suspense and suggests that the narrator's experience of the wall is an emotional experience. As a whole, the poem visually resembles the physical structure of the wall.

GENRE ELEMENTS: POETRY

- includes imagery that appeals to the senses
- includes sound devices such as rhyme, alliteration, assonance, consonance, and repetition
- creates a mood
- expresses a theme, or message about life

© Houghton Mifflin Harcourt Publishing Company

ANALYZE FIGURATIVE LANGUAGE

A writer using literal language states the facts. **Figurative language** makes a point by comparing two things that are dissimilar. Examples of figurative language include similes, metaphors, and personification.

Similes and metaphors are the basic elements of figurative language. A **simile** uses *like* or *as* to compare two unlike things. A **metaphor** directly compares two things by saying that one thing *is* another. Figurative language creates mental pictures that help the reader visualize what the poet is describing.

WRITING STYLE	EXAMPLE
Literal Language	At seven feet, seven inches tall, basketball player Manute Bol was taller than his opponents.
Figurative Language	**Simile:** Manute Bol loomed over opponents like a grown man in a crowd of toddlers.
	Metaphor: To Bol, the opposing guards were the grass beneath his tremendous feet.

Authors use **personification** to give human qualities to an object, animal, or idea. Personification can emphasize an idea or create an emotional effect.

PERSONIFICATION IN "THE VIETNAM WALL"	EFFECT
Invisible from one side, a scar Into the skin of the ground From the other, a black winding Appendix line.	The author compares the memorial to a scar from an appendix operation. This **personification** helps readers understand that the Vietnam War left a "scar" on the American conscience.

As you read "The Vietnam Wall," watch for examples of graphic elements and figurative language. Notice what the author conveys through the use of these elements, and the effect they have on you.

ANNOTATION MODEL

NOTICE & NOTE

As you read, makes notes about the graphic elements and figurative language that are striking to you. Write your observations as well as your questions in the margins of your text. This model shows one reader's notes about lines 17–21 of "The Vietnam Wall."

One name. And then more
Names, long lines, lines of names until
They are the shape of the U.N. building
Taller than I am: I have walked
Into a grave.

"lines," "names" → repeated words for emphasis

metaphor compares seeing the wall to walking into a grave

BACKGROUND

The Vietnam Veterans Memorial was dedicated in 1982 to commemorate the 2.7 million military men and women who served in the Vietnam conflict. There are approximately 58,272 names inscribed in the wall in chronological order from the first death, injury, or missing-in-action date to the last. The polished black granite V-shaped wall was designed by Maya Lin.

Alberto Ríos *(b. 1952) grew up in the U.S.-Mexican border town of Nogales, Arizona. He has published numerous award-winning books of poetry, three books of short stories, and a memoir. In 2013, Ríos was named the first Poet Laureate of Arizona. He lives in Tempe and teaches at Arizona State University.*

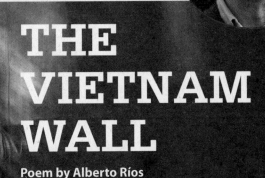

THE VIETNAM WALL

Poem by Alberto Ríos

SETTING A PURPOSE

As you read, consider how the poem expresses the reaction of visitors to the Vietnam Veterans Memorial. Write down the questions and observations you generate as you read.

I
Have seen it
And I like it: The magic,
The way like cutting onions
5 It brings water out of nowhere.
Invisible from one side, a scar
Into the skin of the ground
From the other, a black winding
Appendix line.
10   A dig.
    An archaeologist can explain.
The walk is slow at first
Easy, a little black marble wall
Of a dollhouse,

© Houghton Mifflin Harcourt Publishing Company • Image Credits: (t) ©David Levenson/Getty Image; (c) ©Nicholas Kamm/AFP/G...

Notice & Note

You can use the side margins to notice and note signposts in the text.

ANALYZE GRAPHIC ELEMENTS
Annotate: Circle the one word in line 1.

Connect: Why do you think this is the only word in the first line?

15 A smoothness, a shine
The boys in the street want to give.
One name. And then more
Names, long lines, lines of names until
They are the shape of the U.N. building[1]
20 Taller than I am: I have walked
Into a grave.
And everything I expect has been taken away, like that, quick:
      The names are not alphabetized.
      They are in the order of dying.
25   An alphabet of—somewhere—screaming.
I start to walk out. I almost leave
But stop to look up names of friends,
My own name. There is somebody
Severiano Ríos.
30 Little kids do not make the same noise
Here, junior high school boys don't run
Or hold each other in headlocks.
No rules, something just persists
Like pinching on St. Patrick's Day
35 Every year for no green.
      No one knows why.
Flowers are forced
Into the cracks
Between sections
40 Men have cried
At this wall.
I have
Seen them.

---

[1] **U. N. Building:** headquarters of the United Nations in New York City.

© Houghton Mifflin Harcourt Publishing Company

CHECK YOUR UNDERSTANDING

Answer these questions before moving on to the **Analyze the Text** section on the following page.

1 Which of the following is an example of figurative language used to describe the memorial?

 A *The boys in the street want to give*

 B *Names, long lines, lines of names*

 C *My own name. There is somebody / Severiano Ríos.*

 D *A scar into the skin of the ground*

2 The speaker compares the wall to —

 F a dollhouse

 G St. Patrick's Day

 H his relative

 J onions

3 At one point, the speaker starts to leave the memorial. Why does he decide to stay?

 A To see why people are screaming

 B To look for names he recognizes

 C To leave flowers

 D To visit the U.N. Building

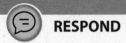

ANALYZE THE TEXT

Support your responses with evidence from the text. ▤ NOTEBOOK

1. **Interpret** Reread lines 20–25. What image is conveyed by the metaphor? How does that image express the speaker's emotions?

2. **Evaluate** Over the course of the poem, the author describes several responses to the wall. What are they? Cite text evidence for each.

3. **Analyze** The Vietnam Veterans Memorial forms a V-shape. How does the physical shape of the poem reflect the shape of the wall?

4. **Draw Conclusions** What is the central idea of the poem? How does the poet use his subject—the Vietnam Veterans Memorial—to convey that central idea?

5. **Identify Patterns** What words or images appear in this poem again and again? What is the effect of this repetition?

RESEARCH

RESEARCH TIP
Be sure to use only reputable sources for your information, including sites you know and trust, those your teachers recommend, and those with *.edu, .org,* or *.gov* addresses.

Search for photos of the Vietnam Veterans Memorial. Look for images that depict different views of the wall and include people's reactions to it. Sketch two images that had an impact on you, and tell why.

SKETCH OF IMAGE	YOUR THOUGHTS

CREATE AND PRESENT

Create an Imagery Board With a partner or a small group, create an imagery board in which you find photos that relate to "The Vietnam Wall," to the memorial itself, or to images mentioned in the poem.

❏ Search online or draw pictures of at least 3–5 images from the poem.

❏ Match those images with specific lines from the poem.

❏ Take notes about the meanings of the images and how they enhance your understanding of both the Vietnam Veterans Memorial and the poem. Think about what each image conveys and how it appeals to different senses or emotions.

Present Your Work Share your imagery board with another group, or you may have a gallery walk with different image boards in the class.

❏ Describe each image and tell why you chose those images.

❏ Read the lines of the poem and interpret them for your classmates.

❏ Explain why you chose each of these images.

❏ Speak slowly and clearly and look at your audience as you share your ideas. Use language that is appropriate for your audience.

❏ Listen carefully as others present, and ask thoughtful questions. Point out differences in images and interpretations between groups.

Go to the **Speaking and Listening Studio** for help with having a group discussion.

RESPOND TO THE ESSENTIAL QUESTION

? How can we come together despite our differences?

Gather Information Review your annotations and notes on "The Vietnam Wall" and add relevant details to your response log. As you determine which information to include, think about how memorials honoring the dead can bring people together.

At the end of the unit, you will use your notes to write a personal essay.

ACADEMIC VOCABULARY

As you write and discuss what you learned from the poem, be sure to use the Academic Vocabulary words. Check off each of the words that you use.

❏ **enforce**

❏ **entity**

❏ **internal**

❏ **presume**

❏ **resolve**

SPEECH

THE GETTYSBURG ADDRESS

by **Abraham Lincoln**

pages 57–59

COMPARE ACROSS GENRES

Notice how the same speech appears as written text and then as part of a movie production. How do the different formats affect your understanding of the writer's message? After you review both selections, you will collaborate with a small group on a final project.

ESSENTIAL QUESTION:

How can we come together despite our differences?

FILM CLIP

from SAVING LINCOLN

page 67

The Gettysburg Address

QUICK START

During difficult times, good leaders address people with words that inspire and encourage them. What should a leader say when things are going wrong? With a group, discuss what a strong leader has said to you when you have been discouraged.

ANALYZE PURPOSE AND AUDIENCE

A person may write a speech for one or more reasons. These reasons are called the **author's purpose**. An author's purpose might be to inform or explain, to persuade, to express thoughts or feelings, or to entertain. Writers also craft their speeches for a particular **audience,** or group of people.

SPEAKER'S PURPOSE	INTENDED EFFECT ON AUDIENCE
Inform or explain	The audience gains new information from the speech.
Persuade	The audience is persuaded to adopt the speaker's position on an argument.
Express thoughts and feelings	The audience gets a better sense of who the speaker is and what he or she cares about.
Entertain	The audience is amused or experiences enjoyment.

As you read "The Gettysburg Address," note how Lincoln addresses his audience and how he achieves his purpose.

ANALYZE RHETORICAL DEVICES

To help advance a purpose, an author will often use **rhetorical devices**, or specific words and language structures that make a message memorable. Rhetorical devices to look for in "The Gettysburg Address" include:

- **Repetition:** the use of the same word or words more than once. Repetition is used to emphasize key ideas.
- **Parallelism:** a form of repetition in which a grammatical pattern is repeated. Parallelism is used to create rhythm and evoke emotions.
- **Understatement:** a technique of creating emphasis by saying less than is literally true. Understatement can be used for humorous effect, to create satire, or to achieve a restrained tone.

As you read "The Gettysburg Address," notice the repeated words and parallel clauses and phrases, such as *we are engaged, we are met, we have come.* Also look for statements that may downplay, or lessen, the seriousness of the situation. Think about how Lincoln uses repetition, parallelism, and understatement to advance his purpose.

GENRE ELEMENTS: SPEECH

- directly addresses and connects with audiences
- uses rhetorical devices to achieve specific purposes
- contains a clear message, stated near the beginning
- ends memorably

CRITICAL VOCABULARY

To preview the Critical Vocabulary words, match the words to their definitions.

1. In a flash of inspiration, Michel was suddenly able to _____ a brilliant plan to earn money.	a. conceive
2. When the mouse saw a cat about to pounce, the mouse feared she would _____.	b. detract
3. After earning a poor grade on a math quiz, Asha would _____ to study harder for the next quiz.	c. resolve
4. One faulty firework did not _____ from an amazing fireworks show.	d. perish

LANGUAGE CONVENTIONS

One grammatical feature that makes Abraham Lincoln's rhetoric so effective is his use of **parallel structure**, or the repetition of grammatical forms within a sentence. The repetition can occur at the word, phrase, or clause level. Lincoln uses parallel structure as a rhetorical device to express and connect ideas that are related or equal in importance, and to create rhythm and evoke emotions. Here is an example of parallel words from "The Gettysburg Address":

The brave men, <u>living</u> and <u>dead</u>, who struggled here have consecrated it, far above our poor power to <u>add</u> or <u>detract</u>.

As you read "The Gettysburg Address," watch for repetition of words, phrases, and clauses.

ANNOTATION MODEL

NOTICE & NOTE

Here is how you might annotate to identify the parallel structures Lincoln uses.

Four score and seven years ago our fathers brought forth on this continent, a new nation, <u>conceived in liberty, and dedicated to the proposition that all men are created equal.</u>

Now we are engaged in a great civil war, testing whether that nation, or any nation <u>so conceived and so dedicated</u>, can long endure.

Lincoln sets a serious tone and purpose by talking about how America was founded based on the ideas of freedom and equality.

parallel structure → "so conceived," "so dedicated"

BACKGROUND

*President **Abraham Lincoln** (1809–1865) is considered an American hero for preserving the Union and emancipating the slaves. He was a skillful politician, leader, and orator. One of his most famous speeches was delivered at the dedication of the National Cemetery at Gettysburg, Pennsylvania, in 1863, site of one of the most deadly battles of the Civil War. The victory for the Union forces marked a turning point in the Civil War, but losses on both sides at Gettysburg were staggering: 28,000 Confederate soldiers and 23,000 Union soldiers were killed or wounded. Lincoln was assassinated by John Wilkes Booth in 1865. Lincoln's dedication to the ideals of freedom and equality continue to inspire people around the world.*

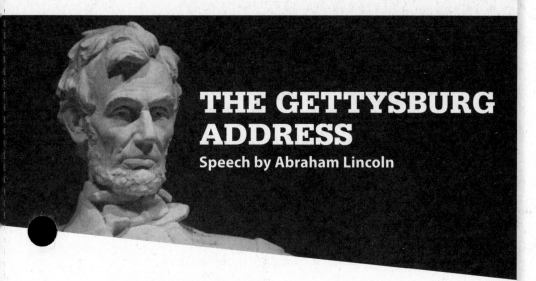

THE GETTYSBURG ADDRESS

Speech by Abraham Lincoln

PREPARE TO COMPARE

As you read, pay attention to how Lincoln's speech emphasizes the importance of ending the Civil War and reuniting the country. This information will help you compare this speech with the video that follows it. If you come across words or passages you do not understand, ask for help from your classmates or your teacher.

1   Four score and seven[1] years ago our fathers brought forth on this continent a new nation, **conceived** in liberty and dedicated to the proposition that all men are created equal.

2   Now we are engaged in a great civil war, testing whether that nation, or any nation so conceived and so dedicated, can long endure. We are met on a great battlefield of that war. We have come to dedicate a portion of that field, as a final resting place for those who here gave their lives that that nation might live. It is altogether fitting and proper that we should do this.

---

[1] **four score and seven:** eighty-seven.

© Houghton Mifflin Harcourt Publishing Company • Image Credits: ©ksb/Shutterstock

Notice & Note

You can use the side margins to notice and note signposts in the text.

---

conceive
(kən-sēv´) *v.* to form or develop in the mind; devise

ANALYZE PURPOSE AND AUDIENCE

Annotate: Underline a sentence that tells why the audience has gathered.

Respond: How does Lincoln's tone reflect the audience and occasion?

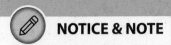

NOTICE & NOTE

3   But in a larger sense, we cannot dedicate—we cannot consecrate[2]—we cannot hallow[3]—this ground. The brave men, living and dead who struggled here have consecrated it, far above our poor power to add or **detract**. The world will little note, nor long remember what we say here, but it can never forget what they did here. It is for us, the living, rather to be dedicated here to the unfinished work which they who fought here have thus far so nobly advanced. It is rather for us to be here dedicated to the great task remaining before us—that from these honored dead we take increased devotion to that cause for which they gave the last full measure of devotion—that we here highly **resolve** that these dead shall not have died in vain—that this nation, under God, shall have a new birth of freedom—and that government of the people, by the people, for the people shall not **perish** from the earth.

---

[2] **consecrate:** to dedicate as sacred.
[3] **hallow:** define as holy.

IN THIS TEMPLE
AS IN THE HEARTS OF THE PEOPLE
FOR WHOM HE SAVED THE UNION
THE MEMORY OF ABRAHAM LINCOLN
IS ENSHRINED FOREVER

CHECK YOUR UNDERSTANDING

Answer these questions before moving on to the **Analyze the Text** questions on the following page.

1 In the Gettysburg Address, Lincoln's main idea is that —

   A the soldiers died because of injustice

   B these men would not die in vain

   C the Civil War was over after the Battle of Gettysburg

   D America deserved independence and freedom

2 What historic event does Lincoln mention at the beginning of the speech?

   F The Emancipation Proclamation

   G The arrival of European colonists

   H The founding of the United States

   J The end of the Civil War

3 What does Lincoln want the audience to do?

   A Continue supporting the war effort

   B Reject the idea of war

   C End the Civil War

   D Enlist in the army

ANALYZE THE TEXT

Support your responses with evidence from the text. NOTEBOOK

1. **Analyze** Why did Lincoln write and deliver "The Gettysburg Address"? What were his two main purposes? Explain using evidence from the speech.

2. **Interpret** The word *dedicate* is repeated several times in the speech. What does *dedicate* mean? What idea does Lincoln emphasize with the repetition of this word?

3. **Identify Patterns** Identify two examples of parallel structure in the speech. How does Lincoln use parallel structure to persuade the audience to accept his message?

4. **Draw Conclusions** Seminal U.S. documents often refer to themes and ideals that are important to the audience they address. What is the **theme**, or underlying message, of "The Gettysburg Address"? Is this theme still important today? Explain the American ideals that the speech upholds.

5. **Notice & Note** Lincoln refers to a "great civil war" and notes that Gettysburg is "a great battlefield of that war." Why do you think Lincoln wanted his audience to believe Gettysburg was important and significant?

RESEARCH

RESEARCH TIP
Choose your sources carefully as you research this topic. Look for valid, reliable sources that cite historical documents. Message boards or presentations by other students may not be reliable sources.

At the time of Lincoln's speech, only the people physically gathered with him at Gettysburg would have heard it. Everyone else would have been aware of it only through word of mouth or through newspaper reports. Find out more about the people who were present to hear Lincoln speak. What were they doing at Gettysburg? What were their reactions? How did the media report on the speech?

RESEARCH QUESTIONS	DETAILS	URL/SOURCE
Who was the audience for the speech?		
What was the audience's reaction to the speech?		
How did the media cover the speech?		

Connect Share what you learn in a panel discussion or brief presentation. Be sure to identify the source for each piece of information you use to support your ideas.

CREATE AND PRESENT

Deliver an Oral Presentation "The Gettysburg Address" is one of the most famous speeches in U.S. history. Prepare an oral presentation in which you critique the speech for its effectiveness.

- ❑ Reread the speech silently to yourself, making notes about Lincoln's main points and the important ideas he emphasizes.

- ❑ Take notes about the rhetorical devices that Lincoln includes, such as repetition, parallelism, and understatement. Write down examples, describing the effect of each device.

- ❑ Make a list of points that you want to make about the speech.

Discuss with a Small Group To refine your presentation, discuss your ideas with a small group.

- ❑ Summarize the points you want to make. Choose a main idea and support it with specific examples from the speech.

- ❑ After revising your points and creating your presentation, practice your presentation with a partner or small group. Give each other feedback about eye contact, speaking rate, volume, and body language.

- ❑ Use the feedback from your partner or small group to deliver the presentation to your class. Acknowledge that different people may want to emphasize different words or phrases in the speech or may have different reactions to parts of the speech.

 Go to the **Speaking and Listening Studio** for help with oral presentations.

RESPOND TO THE ESSENTIAL QUESTION

? How can we come together despite our differences?

Gather Information Review your annotations and notes on "The Gettysburg Address." Highlight those that help answer the Essential Question. Then, add relevant details to your Response Log.

ACADEMIC VOCABULARY

As you write and discuss what you learned from the speech, be sure to use the Academic Vocabulary words. Check off each of the words that you use.

- ❑ **enforce**
- ❑ **entity**
- ❑ **internal**
- ❑ **presume**
- ❑ **resolve**

© Houghton Mifflin Harcourt Publishing Company

The Gettysburg Address 61

WORD BANK

conceive   resolve

detract   perish

 Go to the **Vocabulary Studio** for more on multiple-meaning words.

CRITICAL VOCABULARY

Practice and Apply Choose which Critical Vocabulary word is most closely associated with the underlined word or phrase in each sentence.

1. Additional details in a speech sometimes <u>take away from</u> the whole message.

2. A special election can be used to <u>decide</u> a tie in the vote for the student body president.

3. It takes a creative person <u>to form an idea</u> in his or her mind about an important issue and then convey that message to an audience.

4. Sometimes organizations such as clubs <u>come to an end</u> when the members are no longer interested.

VOCABULARY STRATEGY:
Multiple-Meaning Words

Words that have more than one definition are considered **multiple-meaning words**. To determine a word's appropriate meaning within a text, you need to look for context clues in the words, sentences, and paragraphs that surround it. Look at the word *fitting* in this sentence from the Gettysburg Address:

It is altogether <u>fitting</u> and proper that we should do this.

The word *fitting* can mean "the act of trying on clothes" or "a small part for a machine." However, the word *proper* is a context clue that tells you that the correct meaning of *fitting* in this sentence is "appropriate."

Practice and Apply Find these multiple-meaning words in the speech: *engaged* (paragraph 2), *testing* (paragraph 2), *poor* (paragraph 3), *measure* (paragraph 3). Working with a partner, use context clues to determine each word's meaning as it is used in the speech.

1. Determine how the word functions in the sentence. Is it a noun, an adjective, a verb, or an adverb?

2. If the sentence does not provide enough information, read the paragraph in which the word appears and consider the larger context of the speech.

3. Write down your definition.

LANGUAGE CONVENTIONS
Parallel Structure

As you read "The Gettysburg Address," look for examples of **parallel structure** in Lincoln's words, phrases, and clauses. Then evaluate how this rhetorical device creates a poetic and rhythmic effect that helps make the words and ideas in this speech powerful and memorable.

Type of Structure	Example from the Gettysburg Address
parallel words	living and dead

Type of Structure	Example from the Gettysburg Address
parallel phrases	of the people, by the people, for the people

Type of Structure	Example from the Gettysburg Address
parallel clauses	we cannot dedicate—we cannot consecrate—we cannot hallow

Practice and Apply With a partner, look back at "The Gettysburg Address" and identify additional examples of parallel structure. Then imagine you were at Gettysburg on the day President Lincoln delivered his speech. Write a brief letter to Lincoln explaining how you were affected by his remarks. Use parallel structure at least twice in your letter. Exchange letters with a partner and discuss how effectively you each used parallel structure to communicate your message to Lincoln.

FILM CLIP

from SAVING LINCOLN

page 67

COMPARE ACROSS GENRES

Now that you've read "The Gettysburg Address," watch an excerpt from the film *Saving Lincoln*. The clip shows the actor who plays Abraham Lincoln delivering the speech. Think about how your reaction to viewing and listening to the speech is different from your experience of reading it. After you are finished, you will collaborate with a small group on a final project that involves an analysis of both formats.

? ESSENTIAL QUESTION:

How can we come together despite our differences?

SPEECH

THE GETTYSBURG ADDRESS

by **Abraham Lincoln**

pages 57–59

from **Saving Lincoln**

QUICK START

Nowadays, it seems like we have a video record of almost everything that happens. But actors on stage or on film can still retell events so that we see them in a new way. Think about a recent event in the news. How could actors portray that event to reveal the meaning of it? Discuss with a partner.

ANALYZE DIGITAL TEXTS

A film about the life of a famous person is often called a biopic (biography picture). Script writers and directors must do a great deal of research before filming a biopic. They have to find information about not just the famous person, but also the time period in which he or she lived. This information shapes decisions about settings and costumes.

In the biopic *Saving Lincoln,* director Salvador Litvak used a green screen stage, on which actors are filmed in front of a blank green screen. The director, editors, and special effects artists can then add details to the background to make it look like the actors are in any number of settings.

Litvak also used a technique of adding historical photographs as backdrops to the filmed action. As you watch the film, look to the background behind the actors. The images you see are real photographs laid behind the actors.

GENRE ELEMENTS: FILM

- created for a specific purpose or reason
- combines visual and sound techniques
- may use film techniques such as camera shots, lighting, music, and other special effects

ANALYZE SPECIAL EFFECTS

In film and other digital texts, a **special effect** is an illusion created so that the audience "sees" something that is not happening naturally. Fight scenes, car crashes, mythical monsters—all of these details in a movie are put together by special effects artists.

Special effects in films are usually categorized into practical effects and computer-generated effects.

- A **practical effect** is any effect created without the help of a computer. For example, producers might sprinkle water while filming to make it look like it is raining or make up an actor to look like a zombie.

- Today, film crews have almost limitless capacities for creating **computer-generated imagery**, or CGI. By using computers, they can place actors in outer space, create fires and explosions, animate magical creatures, and even create computer-generated characters.

As you watch the clip from *Saving Lincoln,* notice how the director has made the scene resemble something from the past. Look at the costumes, props, and the set. List details in a chart like this and write whether you think the effects are physical or computer-generated.

FILM TECHNIQUE	PRACTICAL EFFECT OR CGI?	EFFECT ON AUDIENCE

BACKGROUND

Saving Lincoln *is a biopic, released in 2013, that is partly about Abraham Lincoln. Saving Lincoln is told from the point of view of Ward Hill Lamon, who was Lincoln's law partner in Illinois and a longtime friend. When Lincoln became president, Lamon acted as his main bodyguard, preventing several assassination attempts. Saving Lincoln ends up telling part of Lamon's life story as well. In this way, it is a biopic of both men. Film director Salvador Litvak researched Lincoln and Lamon's friendship by reading through letters and diaries from both of them. In this excerpt from the film, a voiceover describes what Lamon thinks is Lincoln's purpose for delivering the speech. Then we watch and hear the address delivered by the actor playing Lincoln.*

PREPARE TO COMPARE

As you watch the film, pay attention to how the actor playing Lincoln presents the speech. Note how he emphasizes certain words or phrases and uses body language to get his points across. **NOTEBOOK**

To view the video, log in online and select **"from SAVING LINCOLN"** from the unit menu.

As needed, pause the video to make notes about how the director and actors involved in the film created an interpretation of Lincoln's speech. Replay or rewind so that you can clarify anything you do not understand.

ANALYZE MEDIA

Support your responses with evidence from the text. 📔 NOTEBOOK

1. **Summarize** How does the narrator, Ward Hill Lamon, provide context for the presentation of the speech?

2. **Analyze** How would you describe Lincoln's audience, as shown in the film? What is their response to the speech?

3. **Infer** Based on the title of the film and the background information you read, what do you think is the focus of *Saving Lincoln*?

4. **Evaluate** How does the director make use of special effects and costumes to create geographic and historical effects?

5. **Draw Conclusions** Why do you think the director included the scene where Lamon reads newspaper reactions to the speech? Consider what biographical information this adds to the movie.

RESEARCH

RESEARCH TIP
Most search engines have options that allow you to view results in the form of images and videos. Further filter options let you view certain kinds of videos; for example, you can choose to view videos of certain lengths.

As one of the most famous speeches in the English language, "The Gettysburg Address" has been recorded and filmed by many actors and narrators. Find other interpretations—video or audio—of the speech online. Take notes on how each version gives you a different insight, or enables you to understand the speech's message in a new way.

URL OF VIDEO OR AUDIO CLIP	NOTES ABOUT PRESENTATION OF SPEECH

Connect At the time of Lincoln's speech, recording equipment had not been invented. Actors and readers today have to imagine what he sounded and looked like as he spoke to his audience. Think about the meaning of Lincoln's speech. How do you think he looked and sounded while speaking? Which interpretation most closely matches your vision?

CREATE AND PRESENT

Review the Film Write a review of how the director of *Saving Lincoln* portrayed the Gettysburg Address.

❑ First, describe the setting and context of the film clip.

❑ Then, write your impressions of the actors, costumes, and special effects.

❑ Finally, state your opinion about how the director added to moviegoers' understanding of the historical event.

Hold a Panel Discussion Using your opinions from your review, as well as your notes about the other interpretations of Lincoln's speech, hold a panel discussion about the effectiveness of different interpretations of the speech.

❑ Before the discussion, make a list of points you would like to make about both *Saving Lincoln* and other recordings you have found. Cue up other recordings in case you need to play them for the rest of the panel.

❑ Establish rules for speaking. Will speakers go in order? When will the rest of the group be able to respond to a viewer's points?

❑ Hold the discussion with your panel. State your opinions about the different pieces of media and back them up with evidence. Listen and respond to your group members' opinions.

 Go to the **Writing Studio** for help with writing informative texts.

 Go to the **Speaking and Listening Studio** for help with holding a panel discussion.

RESPOND TO THE ESSENTIAL QUESTION

 How can we come together despite our differences?

Gather Information Review your annotations and notes on the excerpt from *Saving Lincoln*. Think about Lincoln's message and how the audience is shown reacting to it. Then, add relevant details to your Response Log.

At the end of the unit, you will use your notes to write a personal essay.

ACADEMIC VOCABULARY

As you write and discuss what you learned about the film presentation of "The Gettysburg Address," be sure to use the Academic Vocabulary words. Check off each of the words that you use.

❑ **enforce**

❑ **entity**

❑ **internal**

❑ **presume**

❑ **resolve**

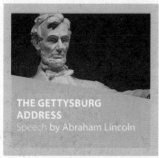

THE GETTYSBURG ADDRESS
Speech by Abraham Lincoln

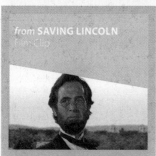

from **SAVING LINCOLN**
Film Clip

Collaborate & Compare

COMPARE ACROSS GENRES

When you compare two or more presentations of the same material in different formats, you **synthesize** the information: You make connections and combine ideas, which deepens your understanding. It's easier to do this when the texts you're comparing are the same genre—for example, two poems. But sometimes you can get a more thorough understanding of the topic by experiencing the material in different ways—say, by reading a print version of it and watching actors perform it.

In a small group, complete the Venn Diagram with similarities and differences in how the written speech and the film affect your understanding of the material. One example is completed for you.

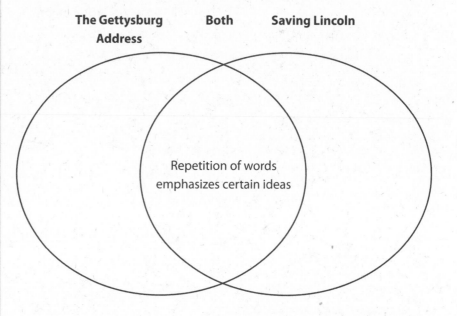

The Gettysburg Address **Both** **Saving Lincoln**

Repetition of words emphasizes certain ideas

ANALYZE THE TEXTS

Discuss these questions in your group.

1. **Contrast** What do the introductory voiceover and the brief scene after Lincoln delivers his speech tell you about its purpose and the immediate response to it?

2. **Evaluate** An audience member in the film reacts to the speech by saying that it was unusually short. Evaluate why Lincoln might have kept the speech so short.

3. **Connect** What did you visualize when you were reading the text of the speech? Compare that to how the director staged the speech.

4. **Analyze** How does the actor playing Lincoln use voice and body language to communicate the message of the speech?

DISCUSS AND PRESENT

You have developed an understanding of "The Gettysburg Address" through multiple avenues, including the printed text, several readings of the speech, and the film clip. Now, your group can discuss your overall understanding of the purpose and message of "The Gettysburg Address." Follow these steps:

1. **Synthesize Ideas** Review the different interpretations of the speech that you have studied—the transcript of the speech and the excerpt from the film as well as any performances or recordings you found online. How was the speech presented? How did each interpretation add to your understanding of the speech's purpose, meaning, and impact, as well as its audience?

Record your thoughts on the speech. You can use this framework to synthesize what you learn:

Information gained from written speech:	Information gained from film of speech:
Information gained from online source:	Information gained from class discussion:

My understanding of the speech's purpose:
My understanding of the speech's meaning:
My understanding of the speech's impact:
My understanding of the speech's audience:

2. **Listen and Share Ideas** In your group, state your understanding of the speech's purpose, meaning, and impact, as well as its actual audience. Use details from the sources to support your interpretation of the speech. Ask questions about words or phrases you don't understand.

3. **Come to a Consensus** Based on the discussion, can the group construct a statement about the speech, telling its purpose, meaning, and impact? Together, write a summary statement about "The Gettysburg Address" and its effect on the audience.

INDEPENDENT READING

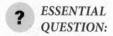
How can we come together despite our differences?

Reader's Choice

Setting a Purpose Select one or more of these options from your eBook to continue your exploration of the Essential Question.

- Read the descriptions to see which text grabs your interest.
- Think about which genres you enjoy reading.

Notice & Note

In this unit, you practiced asking **Big Questions** and noticing and noting two signposts: **Contrasts and Contradictions** and **Word Gaps**. As you read independently, these signposts and others will aid your understanding. Below are the anchor questions to ask when you read literature and nonfiction.

Reading Literature: Stories, Poems, and Plays		
Signpost	**Anchor Question**	**Lesson**
Contrasts and Contradictions	Why did the character act that way?	p. 419
Aha Moment	How might this change things?	p. 171
Tough Questions	What does this make me wonder about?	p. 494
Words of the Wiser	What's the lesson for the character?	p. 171
Again and Again	Why might the author keep bringing this up?	p. 170
Memory Moment	Why is this memory important?	p. 418

Reading Nonfiction: Essays, Articles, and Arguments		
Signpost	**Anchor Question(s)**	**Lesson**
Big Questions	What surprised me? What did the author think I already know? What challenged, changed, or confirmed what I already knew?	p. 248 p. 2 p. 84
Contrasts and Contradictions	What is the difference, and why does it matter?	p. 3
Extreme or Absolute Language	Why did the author use this language?	p. 85
Numbers and Stats	Why did the author use these numbers or amounts?	p. 249
Quoted Words	Why was this person quoted or cited, and what did this add?	p. 85
Word Gaps	Do I know this word from someplace else? Does it seem like technical talk for this topic? Do clues in the sentence help me understand the word?	p. 3

You can preview these texts in Unit 1 of your eBook.

Then, check off the text or texts that you select to read on your own.

POEM

Facing It
Yusef Komunyakaa

The narrator struggles with memories of fallen comrades as he contemplates the Vietnam Veterans memorial.

BLOG

Making the Future Better, Together
Eboo Patel

Could George Washington's views about unity and diversity be relevant today?

SPEECH

Oklahoma Bombing Memorial Address
Bill Clinton

President Bill Clinton takes a stand against the fear, hatred, and violence that can divide a nation.

SHORT STORY

Night Calls
Lisa Fugard

A girl uses her gift of mimicking bird calls to create a bond with her emotionally distant father.

POEM

Theme for English B
Langston Hughes

The poet who says he often does not "want to be a part of you" nevertheless acknowledges that we learn from each other.

Collaborate and Share   Work with a partner to discuss what you learned from at least one of your independent readings.

- Give a brief synopsis or summary of the text.

- Describe any signposts that you noticed in the text and explain what they revealed to you.

- Describe what you most enjoyed or found most challenging about the text. Give specific examples.

- Decide if you would recommend the text to others. Why or why not?

Go to the **Reading Studio** for more resources on **Notice & Note.**

Write a Personal Essay

As you read this unit, you focused on how people from different backgrounds and with different experiences can come together as human beings. For this writing task, you will write a personal essay related to this topic. A personal essay is a short work of nonfiction in which the writer expresses an opinion or provides insight based on personal experiences. For an example of a well-written personal essay you can use as a mentor text, review the essay "Unusual Normality."

As you write your essay, you will want to look at the notes you made in your Response Log, which you filled out after reading the texts in this unit.

Writing Prompt

Read the information in the box below.

This is the topic or context for your essay.

> Our differences can help us explore and understand more of the world and what it means to be human.

Think carefully about the following question.

This is the Essential Question for the unit. How would you answer this question, based on the texts in this unit and your personal experience?

> How can we come together despite our differences?

Think about events in your own experience that relate to this topic.

Write a personal essay about how differences between people can be opportunities rather than obstacles.

Be sure to—

Review these points as you write and again when you finish. Make any needed changes.

- ❏ write an introduction that catches the reader's attention and presents the topic of the essay
- ❏ write about an event from your own life or something you've noticed in the world around you
- ❏ use transitions to connect related ideas
- ❏ use appropriate register (level of formality), vocabulary, tone, and voice.
- ❏ end by sharing your insights about the value of diversity in a school, a community, or a country

① Plan

Before you begin to write your personal essay, you need to have an idea of what you want to explore in your writing. In this case, you will write about an event or experience that helped you to understand something about the value of diversity. Your essay will be more interesting if you describe the challenges you faced in your experience, as the author did in "Unusual Normality."

You also need to think about what you hope to achieve in your essay and who you are writing it for—your purpose and your audience. One way to choose what to write about is to brainstorm. Use the chart below to help you. When you have finished filling out the chart, circle the event you would like to write about for this essay.

Personal Essay Brainstorming Chart	
Experience or Event	**What I Thought and Felt About It**

Background Reading Review the notes you have taken in your Response Log after reading the texts in this unit. These texts provide background reading that will help you think about what you want to say in your essay.

Go to **Writing as a Process: Planning and Drafting** for help planning your essay.

Notice & Note
From Reading to Writing

As you plan your personal essay, apply what you've learned about signposts to your own writing. Remember that writers use common features, called signposts, to help convey their message to readers.

Think about how you can incorporate an **Aha Moment** into your essay.

Go to the **Reading Studio** for more resources on Notice & Note.

Use the notes from your Response Log as you plan your essay.

Organize Your Ideas After you have chosen an event to write about, you need to organize your ideas. First, write a statement of the topic you're going to explore. That will lead to the narrative part of the essay: telling about the event from your life that affected how you thought and felt about differences among people. In your conclusion, you will explain the insight you gained from the experience you just described. Use the chart below to help you organize your ideas. Then, use it to make an outline. If you find that you do not have enough to write about, you may need to go back to your brainstorming chart and choose a different event.

Personal Essay: Being True to Yourself
Topic Statement

Event from Your Life
How it started:
What happened:
How it ended:

Conclusion

You might prefer to draft your essay online.

❷ Develop a Draft

Once you have completed your planning activities, you will be ready to begin drafting your personal essay. Refer to your Graphic Organizer and the outline you have created, as well as any notes you took as you studied the texts in the unit. These will provide a kind of map for you to follow as you write. Using a word processor or online writing application makes it easier to make changes or move sentences around later when you are ready to revise your first draft.

© Houghton Mifflin Harcourt Publishing Company

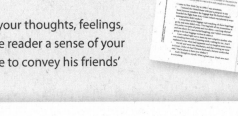

Use the Mentor Text

Author's Craft

As you draft your essay, be sure to communicate your thoughts, feelings, and responses to events. You also want to give the reader a sense of your personality. Note how Ishmael Beah uses dialogue to convey his friends' thoughts and feelings as well as his own.

> They would say to me, "You're such a weird kid."
> And I would respond by saying, "No, no, no. I'm not weird. *Weird* has a negative connotation. I prefer the word *unusual*. It has a certain sophistication and gravitas to it that suits my character."

The author uses dialogue to reveal his personality and view of the world.

Apply What You've Learned Use the techniques of narration, including dialogue, to convey thoughts and feelings.

Genre Characteristics

Your personal essay should describe your feelings at the time of the event or experience, as well as thoughts and insights that came later. Notice how Beah reflects on his decision not to tell his friends about his past in "Unusual Normality."

> But I wish I had been able to tell them early on, because I wanted them to understand how lucky they were to have a mother, a father, grandparents, siblings.

The author reflects on how he feels about choices he made in the past.

Apply What You've Learned As you describe your life experience, comment on its meaning for you in order to help the reader understand the reactions you had at the time and after it happened.

③ Revise

Go to **Writing as a Process: Revising and Editing** for help revising your essay.

On Your Own After you write your draft, you will use the process of revision to improve your essay. The Revision Guide will help you focus on specific elements to make your writing stronger.

REVISION GUIDE		
Ask Yourself	**Tips**	**Revision Techniques**
1. Does my introduction present my topic in a way that makes people want to read my essay?	**Highlight** the introduction.	**Reword** your topic in a way that stimulates your readers' curiosity.
2. Have I told an event from my life in a clear, coherent way?	**Underline** time clues.	**Add** words and phrases that make the time order clear.
3. Have I used the active voice whenever possible?	**Note** any use of the passive voice.	**Change** passive voice to active voice if the active voice would be more effective.
4. Have I made the event feel real to the reader?	**Underline** dialogue and details that show where and with whom the experience happened.	**Add** dialogue and descriptive, sensory details about the place and the people.
5. Is the first-person point of view used consistently?	**Note** anywhere the point of view changes.	**Change** third-person pronouns to first-person pronouns as necessary.
6. Does my essay reveal why the experience was significant?	**Underline** comments you have made about the event.	**Add** statements that explain the event's importance and meaning to you.

ACADEMIC VOCABULARY

As you conduct your **peer review,** try to use these words. Ask questions if you do not understand any of the vocabulary words.

❏ enforce

❏ entity

❏ internal

❏ presume

❏ resolve

With a Partner After you have worked through the Revision Guide on your own, exchange papers with a partner. Evaluate each other's drafts in a peer review. Help your partner accomplish his or her purpose in writing. Ask questions about anything you did not understand. Explain how you think your partner's draft could be revised and what your specific suggestions for revision are.

When giving feedback to your partner, include praise for what he or she has done well.

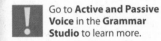

❹ Edit

Once you have addressed the organization, development, and flow of ideas in your essay, you can look to improve the finer points of your draft. Edit for the proper use of standard English conventions and make sure to correct any misspellings or grammatical errors.

Language Conventions

- **Active and Passive Voice** Most of the time, writers use active voice.
- **Active voice** indicates that the subject of the sentence is performing the action of the sentence. (*I baked the bread.*)
- **Passive voice** indicates that the subject of the sentence is being acted upon. (*The bread was baked.*)

> ! Go to **Active and Passive Voice** in the **Grammar Studio** to learn more.

The chart contains examples of active and passive voice verbs from "Unusual Normality."

VERB VOICE	EXAMPLE
Active	So here I was in New York, with my new mother. We needed to step into that normality.
Passive	At age eleven, a war had started in my country.

❺ Publish

Finalize your essay and choose a way to share it with your audience. Consider these options:

- Present your essay as a speech to the class.
- Post your essay as a blog on a classroom or school website.

Use the scoring guide to evaluate your essay.

WRITING TASK SCORING GUIDE: PERSONAL ESSAY

	Organization/Progression	Development of Ideas	Use of Language and Conventions
4	• The organization is effective and appropriate to the purpose. • All ideas are focused on the topic specified in the prompt. • Transitions clearly show the relationship among ideas.	• The introduction catches the reader's attention, clearly states the topic. • The essay contains an appropriate, clearly narrated life experience. • The writer includes details and uses devices such as dialogue to make the event or experience vivid. • The conclusion effectively communicates the meaning and significance of the event.	• Language and word choice is purposeful and precise. • Verb tenses are correct and consistent. • Active voice is used whenever possible. • Spelling, capitalization, and punctuation are correct. • Grammar, usage, and mechanics are correct.
3	• The organization is, for the most part, effective and appropriate to the purpose. • Most ideas are focused on the topic specified in the prompt. • A few more transitions are needed to show the relationship among ideas.	• The introduction is semi-engaging. The topic is stated. • The essay contains a fairly appropriate and clearly narrated life experience. • The writer includes some details. • The conclusion explains the meaning of the event.	• Language is for the most part specific and clear. • Verb tenses are mostly correct and consistent. • Active voice is used most of the time. • Some spelling, capitalization, and punctuation mistakes are present. • Some grammar and usage errors occur.
2	• The organization is evident but is not always appropriate to the purpose. • Only some ideas are focused on the topic specified in the prompt. • More transitions are needed to show the relationship among ideas.	• The introduction is not engaging. The topic is stated, but not clearly. • The essay contains vaguely narrated life experience. • The writer includes insufficient details. • The conclusion tries to explain and connect the meaning of the event, but does not do it well.	• Language is somewhat vague. • There are occasional errors in verb tense. • Active voice is used more than passive voice. • Spelling, capitalization, and punctuation errors occur but do not make reading difficult. • Grammar and usage are often incorrect, but the writer's ideas are still clear.
1	• The organization is not appropriate to the purpose. • Ideas are not focused on the topic specified in the prompt. • No transitions are used, making the essay difficult to understand.	• The introduction is missing or confusing. • There are not details about the event or experience. • The writer does not convey the meaning of the experience. • The conclusion is missing.	• Language is inappropriate for the text. • Verb tenses are confused. • Active voice is rarely used. • Many spelling, capitalization, and punctuation errors are present. • Grammatical and usage errors confuse the writer's ideas.

Reflect on the Unit

In this writing task, you wrote about your own experience after reading about the experiences of others in the readings in this unit. Now is a good time to reflect on what you have learned.

Reflect on the Essential Question

- How can we come together despite our differences? How has your answer to this question changed since you first considered it when you started this unit?

- What are some examples from the texts you've read that show how our differences can be opportunities rather than obstacles?

Reflect on Your Reading

- Which selections were the most interesting or surprising to you?

- From which selection did you learn the most about the value of diversity?

Reflect on the Writing Task

- What difficulties did you encounter while working on your personal essay? How might you avoid them next time?

- What part of the essay was the easiest and hardest to write? Why?

- What improvements did you make to your essay as you were revising?

SELECTIONS
- "Quilt of a Country"
- "Unusual Normality"
- "Once Upon a Time"
- "The Vietnam Wall"
- "The Gettysburg Address"
- from *Saving Lincoln*

THE STRUGGLE FOR FREEDOM

? **ESSENTIAL QUESTION:**

How do people find freedom in the midst of oppression?

> " If there is no struggle, there is no progress. "
>
> Frederick Douglass

ACADEMIC VOCABULARY

Academic Vocabulary words are words you use when you discuss and write about texts. In this unit you will practice and learn five words.

☑ decline   ❑ enable   ❑ impose   ❑ integrate   ❑ reveal

Study the Word Network to learn more about the word **decline**.

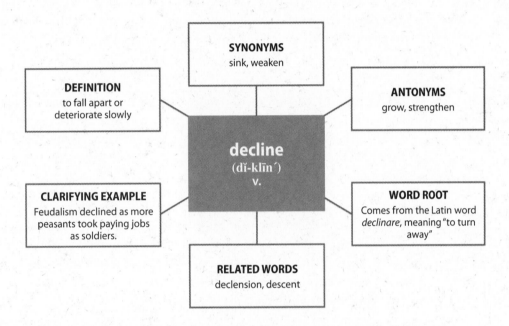

SYNONYMS
sink, weaken

ANTONYMS
grow, strengthen

DEFINITION
to fall apart or deteriorate slowly

decline
(dĭ-klīn´)
v.

WORD ROOT
Comes from the Latin word *declinare*, meaning "to turn away"

CLARIFYING EXAMPLE
Feudalism declined as more peasants took paying jobs as soldiers.

RELATED WORDS
declension, descent

Write and Discuss Discuss the completed Word Network with a partner, making sure to talk through all of the boxes until you both understand the word, its synonyms, antonyms, and related forms. Then, fill out a Word Network for each of the four remaining words. Use a dictionary or online resource to help you complete the activity.

 Go online to access the Word Networks.

RESPOND TO THE ESSENTIAL QUESTION

In this unit, you will explore the universal desire for freedom. As you read, you will revisit the **Essential Question** and gather your ideas about it in the **Response Log** that appears on page R2. At the end of the unit, you will have the opportunity to write a **research report** about the difficulties people have as they struggle for freedom. Filling out the Response Log will help you prepare for this writing task.

 You can also go online to access the Response Log.

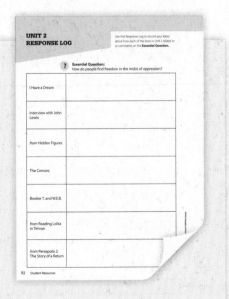

© Houghton Mifflin Harcourt Publishing Company

I HAVE A DREAM

You are about to read the speech "I Have a Dream." In it, you will notice and note questions and signposts that will give you clues about the topic of the speech and the intentions of the author. Here are three key signposts to look for as you read this speech and other works of nonfiction.

For more information on these and other questions and signposts in Notice & Note, visit the **Reading Studio.**

When you read a speech like this one, pause to **challenge, change, or confirm** what you know:

"At first I thought . . . , but . . ."

"I had to rethink . . ."

"My understanding changed when . . ."

"I was right/wrong about . . ."

Big Questions Whenever we read something, we start with what we already know. You probably have heard the words "I Have a Dream" and know that Martin Luther King Jr. said those words. As you read the speech this time, think about what those words truly mean. Ask yourself: **What challenged, changed, or confirmed what I knew?**

Imagine you have dropped a few items from a high point, including a feather, a paper clip, a magnet, a piece of paper, a balloon, and a pen. Which items hit the floor first? You know some facts about gravity and air resistance, but not everything will happen the way you expect. The rate at which some items fall may confirm what you already knew, while others may change or challenge your assumptions. The same thing happens when you read.

Read this part of "I Have a Dream" to see a student's annotation of a Big Question.

> So we've come here today to dramatize a shameful condition. In a sense we've come to our nation's capital to cash a check. When the architects of our republic wrote the magnificent words of the Constitution and the Declaration of Independence, they were signing a promissory note to which every American was to fall heir. This note was the promise that all men, yes, black men as well as white men, would be guaranteed the unalienable rights of life, liberty, and the pursuit of happiness.
>
> It is obvious today that America has defaulted on this promissory note insofar as her citizens of color are concerned.

What statements confirm, change, or challenge what you already know?	1. The Declaration of Independence says all men, regardless of the color of their skin, have the right to "life, liberty, and the pursuit of happiness."
	2. Dr. King says that America has "defaulted" on this promise for people of color.

Extreme or Absolute Language Imagine you are passionate about a subject and determined to persuade people that you are right. You might use absolute words such as "always" and "never" to emphasize your point. You might use powerful or exaggerated images to sway your audience's opinion.

This kind of strong language in a speech can influence the reader's thinking. **Extreme or Absolute Language** often reveals what is most important to a speaker. Pay attention to the speaker's language in order to identify and understand his or her point of view. Here's an example of a student underlining Extreme or Absolute Language:

> Now is the time to make real the promises of democracy; now is the time to rise from <u>the dark and desolate valley of segregation to the sunlit path of racial justice</u>; now is the time to lift our nation from the quicksands of racial injustice to the solid rock of brotherhood . . .

When you see **Extreme or Absolute Language** as you read, pause to note:

"This language shows . . . about the author."

"The author used this language because . . ."

"The language emphasizes the author's point by . . ."

Anchor Question
When you notice this signpost, ask: Why did the author use this language?

What statement sounds absolute or extreme to you?	"the dark and desolate valley of segregation to the sunlit path of racial justice"
Why did the author use this language?	He wants to help his audience picture the brutality and injustice of segregation.

Quoted Words Sometimes you need proof to persuade readers of your opinion or claim. You might cite the words of someone important to prove your point, or share the perspective of someone who was there. Quoting their words can strengthen your argument. Authors and speakers often use **Quoted Words** to reinforce important ideas. Quoted Words might include:

- the conclusions of someone who is an expert on the subject
- someone who witnessed an event

When you come across quoted words, ask yourself why this expert was quoted and what he or she helps you understand about the topic. In this example, a student underlined instances of Quoted Words:

> I say to you today, my friends, even though we face the difficulties of today and tomorrow, I still have a dream. … I have a dream that one day this nation will rise up and live out the true meaning of its creed, <u>"We hold these truths to be self-evident; that all men are created equal."</u>

When you see **Quoted Words** as you read, pause to note:

"This quote comes from . . ."

"This quote means . . ."

"The author uses these words to . . ."

"This quote reinforces the author's message by . . ."

Anchor Question
When you notice this signpost, ask: Why was this person quoted or cited, and what did this add?

What words are quoted?	"We hold these truths to be self-evident; that all men are created equal."
Why did Martin Luther King Jr. quote or cite this sentence?	It is from the Declaration of Independence. Dr. King says that this is the "creed" of our nation. It is an ideal that our country believes in firmly.

I HAVE A DREAM

Speech by **Martin Luther King Jr.**

? **ESSENTIAL QUESTION:**

How do people find freedom in the midst of oppression?

QUICK START

Have you ever been treated differently for any reason? How did it make you feel? Write a paragraph describing what happened and how you reacted.

ANALYZE ARGUMENTS

One way to analyze Martin Luther King Jr.'s speech is to look at it as an argument. To analyze an argument, you think about how each part works.

PART OF AN ARGUMENT	EXAMPLE FROM SPEECH
The central idea of an argument is the **claim**.	. . . the Negro still is not free; one hundred years later, the life of the Negro is still sadly crippled by the manacles of segregation and the chains of discrimination . . .
The author must support the claim with **evidence** and examples.	We can never be satisfied as long as the Negro is the victim of the unspeakable horrors of police brutality . . . we cannot be satisfied as long as the Negro's basic mobility is from a smaller ghetto to a larger one . . .
To persuade an audience of a claim, the author may **appeal** to the audience by connecting with their personal lives.	Some of you have come fresh from narrow jail cells. Some of you have come from areas where your quest for freedom left you battered by the storms of persecution and staggered by the winds of police brutality.
In the **conclusion**, the author sums up the claim with a strong statement about what the audience should believe.	I have a dream that my four little children will one day live in a nation where they will not be judged by the color of their skin, but by the content of their character.

ANALYZE RHETORICAL DEVICES

Rhetorical devices are techniques writers use to enhance their arguments and communicate more effectively. Rhetorical devices can evoke an emotional response in an audience and make the message memorable.

RHETORICAL DEVICES	EXAMPLE FROM SPEECH
Repetition repeats the same word(s) for emphasis.	Again and again we must rise to the majestic heights of meeting physical force with soul force.
Parallelism uses similar grammatical constructions to express related or equally important ideas. It often creates a rhythm.	Let freedom ring from Stone Mountain of Georgia; let freedom ring from Lookout Mountain of Tennessee; let freedom ring from every hill and molehill of Mississippi. "From every mountainside, let freedom ring."
An **extended metaphor** makes a lengthy comparison between two unlike things to emphasize an important idea.	Instead of honoring this sacred obligation, America has given the Negro people a bad check, a check which has come back marked "insufficient funds."

GENRE ELEMENTS: SPEECH

- directly addresses and connects with audiences
- uses rhetorical devices to achieve specific purposes
- contains a clear message, stated near the beginning
- ends memorably

© Houghton Mifflin Harcourt Publishing Company

CRITICAL VOCABULARY

default	desolate	degenerate	inextricably	redemptive

To see how many Critical Vocabulary words you already know, use them to complete the sentences.

1. That story will always be _____ linked with childhood experiences.

2. If you _____ on a loan, your personal credit rating will be affected.

3. The moors are wide and _____, far from the noisy streets of London.

4. Calm music is _____, freeing my soul from worry.

5. Our talk will _____ into a fight if we don't find common ground.

LANGUAGE CONVENTIONS

Repetition and Parallelism Two devices King uses that make his rhetoric effective are repetition and parallelism—expressing related ideas using similar grammatical constructions. Using these devices, King creates a strong rhythm in his speech and links his ideas in listeners' minds.

Repetition

But one hundred years later, the Negro still is not free . . . one hundred years later, the Negro lives on a lonely island of poverty in the midst of a vast ocean of material prosperity; one hundred years later, the Negro is still languishing in the corners of American society and finds himself in exile in his own land.

Parallelism

. . . we will be able to work together, to pray together, to struggle together, to go to jail together, to stand up for freedom together . . .

ANNOTATION MODEL

NOTICE & NOTE

As you read, notice and note signposts, including **Big Questions, Extreme or Absolute Language,** and **Quoted Words.** In the model, you can see one reader's notes about "I Have a Dream."

I am happy to join with you today in what will go down in history as the greatest demonstration for freedom in the history of our nation.

Dr. King uses extreme language to emphasize the historical importance of the event.

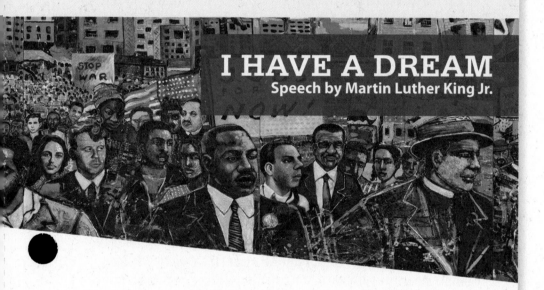

BACKGROUND

On August 28, 1963, thousands of Americans marched on Washington, D.C., to urge Congress to pass a civil rights bill. Martin Luther King Jr. delivered his "I Have a Dream" speech on the steps of the Lincoln Memorial before more than 250,000 people. This momentous event was called the March on Washington.
Martin Luther King Jr. *(1929–1968) came from a family of preachers. As pastor of a Baptist Church in Alabama, King honed his rhetorical skills. Preaching a philosophy of nonviolence, his leadership helped bring about the passage of the Civil Rights Act of 1964. Awarded the Nobel Peace Prize, King continued his work for justice and equality until he was assassinated in 1968.*

I HAVE A DREAM
Speech by Martin Luther King Jr.

SETTING A PURPOSE

As you read, monitor your comprehension by rereading and reviewing your background knowledge. Think about how this speech confirms, changes, or challenges what you know.

1   I am happy to join with you today in what will go down in history as the greatest demonstration for freedom in the history of our nation.

2   Five score[1] years ago, a great American, in whose symbolic shadow we stand today, signed the Emancipation Proclamation.[2] This momentous decree came as a great beacon light of hope to millions of Negro slaves who had been seared in the flames of withering injustice. It came as a joyous daybreak to end the long night of their captivity.

---

[1] **five score:** 100; *score* means "twenty." (This phrasing recalls the beginning of Abraham Lincoln's Gettysburg Address: "Four score and seven years ago . . .")

[2] **Emancipation Proclamation:** a document signed by President Lincoln in 1863, during the Civil War, declaring that all slaves in states still at war with the Union were free.

Notice & Note

You can use the side margins to notice and note signposts in the text.

ANALYZE ARGUMENTS

Annotate: Underline King's claim. Mark details and evidence in paragraphs 3–5 that support his claim.

Analyze: What does King believe should happen?

default
(dǐ-fôlt´) *v.* to fail to keep a promise to repay a loan.

desolate
(děs´ə-lǐt) *adj.* unhappy; lonely.

EXTREME OR ABSOLUTE LANGUAGE

Notice & Note: Mark examples of extreme or absolute language in paragraph 7.

Infer: What does King mean by "the whirlwinds of revolt"?

3   But one hundred years later, the Negro still is not free; one hundred years later, the life of the Negro is still sadly crippled by the manacles of segregation and the chains of discrimination; one hundred years later, the Negro lives on a lonely island of poverty in the midst of a vast ocean of material prosperity; one hundred years later, the Negro is still languishing in the corners of American society and finds himself in exile in his own land.

4   So we've come here today to dramatize a shameful condition. In a sense we've come to our nation's capital to cash a check. When the architects of our republic wrote the magnificent words of the Constitution and the Declaration of Independence, they were signing a promissory note[3] to which every American was to fall heir. This note was the promise that all men, yes, black men as well as white men, would be guaranteed the unalienable rights of life, liberty, and the pursuit of happiness.

5   It is obvious today that America has **defaulted** on this promissory note insofar as her citizens of color are concerned. Instead of honoring this sacred obligation, America has given the Negro people a bad check, a check which has come back marked "insufficient funds." But we refuse to believe that the bank of justice is bankrupt. We refuse to believe that there are insufficient funds in the great vaults of opportunity of this nation. And so we've come to cash this check, a check that will give us upon demand the riches of freedom and the security of justice.

6   We have also come to this hallowed spot to remind America of the fierce urgency of now. This is no time to engage in the luxury of cooling off or to take the tranquilizing drug of gradualism. Now is the time to make real the promises of democracy; now is the time to rise from the dark and **desolate** valley of segregation to the sunlit path of racial justice; now is the time to lift our nation from the quicksands of racial injustice to the solid rock of brotherhood; now is the time to make justice a reality for all of God's children. It would be fatal for the nation to overlook the urgency of the moment. This sweltering summer of the Negro's legitimate discontent will not pass until there is an invigorating autumn of freedom and equality.

7   Nineteen sixty-three is not an end, but a beginning. And those who hope that the Negro needed to blow off steam and will now be content will have a rude awakening if the nation returns to business as usual. There will be neither rest nor tranquility in America until the Negro is granted his citizenship rights. The whirlwinds of revolt will continue to shake the foundations of our nation until the bright day of justice emerges.

---

[3] **promissory note:** a written promise to repay a loan.

© Houghton Mifflin Harcourt Publishing Company

8   But there is something that I must say to my people, who stand on the worn threshold which leads into the palace of justice. In the process of gaining our rightful place, we must not be guilty of wrongful deeds. Let us not seek to satisfy our thirst for freedom by drinking from the cup of bitterness and hatred. We must forever conduct our struggle on the high plain of dignity and discipline. We must not allow our creative protests to **degenerate** into physical violence. Again and again we must rise to the majestic heights of meeting physical force with soul force. The marvelous new militancy, which has engulfed the Negro community, must not lead us to a distrust of all white people. For many of our white brothers, as evidenced by their presence here today, have come to realize that their destiny is tied up with our destiny. And they have come to realize that their freedom is **inextricably** bound to our freedom. We cannot walk alone. And as we walk, we must make the pledge that we shall always march ahead. We cannot turn back.

degenerate
(dĭ-jĕn´ər-āt) *v.*
to decline morally.

inextricably
(ĭn-ĕk´strĭ-kə-blē) *adv.*
in a way impossible to untangle.

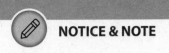
LANGUAGE
CONVENTIONS

Annotate: Underline the repetition and parallelism that King uses in paragraph 9.

Respond: Why is this use of repetition effective?

redemptive
(rĭ-dĕmp´tĭv) *adj.*
causing freedom or salvation

ANALYZE RHETORICAL
DEVICES

Annotate: Mark the phrase that is repeated throughout paragraphs 11–15.

Connect: How does the meaning of this phrase change and evolve?

9   There are those who are asking the devotees of civil rights, "When will you be satisfied?" We can never be satisfied as long as the Negro is the victim of the unspeakable horrors of police brutality; we can never be satisfied as long as our bodies, heavy with the fatigue of travel, cannot gain lodging in the motels of the highways and the hotels of the cities; we cannot be satisfied as long as the Negro's basic mobility is from a smaller ghetto to a larger one; we can never be satisfied as long as our children are stripped of their selfhood and robbed of their dignity by signs stating For Whites Only; we cannot be satisfied as long as the Negro in Mississippi cannot vote and a Negro in New York believes he has nothing for which to vote. No! No, we are not satisfied, and we will not be satisfied until "justice rolls down like waters and righteousness like a mighty stream."

10   I am not unmindful that some of you have come here out of great trials and tribulations. Some of you have come fresh from narrow jail cells. Some of you have come from areas where your quest for freedom left you battered by the storms of persecution and staggered by the winds of police brutality. You have been the veterans of creative suffering. Continue to work with the faith that unearned suffering is **redemptive**. Go back to Mississippi. Go back to Alabama. Go back to South Carolina. Go back to Georgia. Go back to Louisiana. Go back to the slums and ghettos of our Northern cities, knowing that somehow this situation can and will be changed. Let us not wallow in the valley of despair.

11   I say to you today, my friends, even though we face the difficulties of today and tomorrow, I still have a dream. It is a dream deeply rooted in the American dream. I have a dream that one day this nation will rise up and live out the true meaning of its creed, "We hold these truths to be self-evident; that all men are created equal." I have a dream that one day on the red hills of Georgia, sons of former slaves and the sons of former slave owners will be able to sit down together at the table of brotherhood. I have a dream that one day even the state of Mississippi, a state sweltering with the heat of injustice, sweltering with the heat of oppression, will be transformed into an oasis of freedom and justice. I have a dream that my four little children will one day live in a nation where they will not be judged by the color of their skin, but by the content of their character.

12   I have a dream today!

13   I have a dream that one day down in Alabama—with its vicious racists, with its Governor having his lips dripping with the words of interposition and nullification[4]— one day right there in Alabama,

---

[4] **Governor . . . nullification:** Rejecting a federal order to desegregate the University of Alabama, Governor George Wallace claimed that the principle of nullification (a state's alleged right to refuse a federal law) allowed him to resist federal "interposition," or interference, in state affairs.

little black boys and black girls will be able to join hands with little white boys and white girls as sisters and brothers.

14   I have a dream today!

15   I have a dream that one day every valley shall be exalted, and every hill and mountain shall be made low. The rough places will be plain and the crooked places will be made straight, "and the glory of the Lord shall be revealed, and all flesh shall see it together."

QUOTED WORDS

Notice & Note: Mark the quotation Dr. King uses in paragraph 15.

Analyze: What is he quoting from? Why is this effective?

ANALYZE RHETORICAL DEVICES

Annotate Mark the extended metaphor King uses in paragraphs 16–17, including details that develop it.

Interpret: Explain Dr. King's vision in your own words.

16   This is our hope. This is the faith that I go back to the South with. With this faith we will be able to hew out of the mountain of despair a stone of hope. With this faith we will be able to transform the jangling discords of our nation into a beautiful symphony of brotherhood. With this faith we will be able to work together, to pray together, to struggle together, to go to jail together, to stand up for freedom together, knowing that we will be free one day. And this will be the day. This will be the day when all of God's children will be able to sing with new meaning, "My country 'tis of thee, sweet land of liberty, of thee I sing. Land where my fathers died, land of the pilgrims' pride, from every mountainside, let freedom ring." And if America is to be a great nation, this must become true.

17   So let freedom ring from the prodigious hilltops of New Hampshire; let freedom ring from the mighty mountains of New York; let freedom ring from the heightening Alleghenies of Pennsylvania; let freedom ring from the snowcapped Rockies of Colorado; let freedom ring from the curvaceous slopes of California. But not only that. Let freedom ring from Stone Mountain of Georgia; let freedom ring from Lookout Mountain of Tennessee; let freedom ring from every hill and molehill of Mississippi. "From every mountainside, let freedom ring."

18   And when this happens, and when we allow freedom to ring, when we let it ring from every village and every hamlet, from every state and every city, we will be able to speed up that day when all of God's children—black men and white men, Jews and Gentiles, Protestants and Catholics—will be able to join hands and sing in the words of the old Negro spiritual, "Free at last. Free at last. Thank God Almighty, we are free at last."

CHECK YOUR UNDERSTANDING

Answer these questions before moving on to the **Analyze the Text** section on the following page.

1 Martin Luther King Jr.'s main purpose in "I Have a Dream" is to —

  A celebrate the end of slavery and oppression of African Americans

  B urge all people to peacefully work together for racial equality

  C give a lecture about the Emancipation Proclamation

  D describe his dreams and interpret them for his audience

2 In paragraph 5, King uses the extended metaphor of a check to —

  F persuade demonstrators that they should avoid banks

  G give an example of poverty in his community

  H explain that America must keep its promise of freedom for all people

  J ask the government to provide more financial assistance

3 How does King appeal to the emotions of his audience?

  A He tells a story from the Christian Bible.

  B He uses repetition and parallelism to create rhythm.

  C He uses complicated, unfamiliar vocabulary.

  D He interprets the Declaration of Independence.

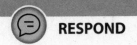

ANALYZE THE TEXT

Support your responses with evidence from the text. 📓 NOTEBOOK

1. **Summarize** The central point of an argument is the **claim**. What is King's claim in this speech? What evidence does he cite to support his claim?

2. **Interpret** Review paragraph 8. Who is King's audience in this paragraph? How does King want his audience to work toward racial justice? Explain your answer and cite evidence from the text.

3. **Analyze** Find examples of parallelism in paragraph 6. What effect does the parallel structure create? What point is King emphasizing?

4. **Evaluate** Why do you think King's "I Have a Dream" speech is remembered as one of the most significant speeches in American history? Explain what makes the speech memorable and how it contributes to the ideal of an American society.

5. **Notice & Note** Explain how King uses extreme or absolute language to persuade his audience. Give at least two examples. Do you think he uses this technique effectively? Explain.

RESEARCH TIP
The best search terms are very specific. Along with King's name, include the name of his speech and the form you want, such as text, image, or video, in order to find exactly what you are looking for.

RESEARCH

It's one thing to read a speech, but it's even better to listen to it or to be an audience member. Find a version of Martin Luther King Jr.'s speech in audio or video form. On the chart, explain what you noticed in the audio or video version, and how that is different from what you noticed in the text.

FORM OF SPEECH	WHAT I NOTICED	IMPACT ON ME
Text		
Audio/Video		

Connect In paragraph 9, Dr. King says that people ask civil rights activists, "When will you be satisfied?" Reread the paragraph and write a response about how his main idea in that part of the speech applies today. Share your response with a small group.

CREATE AND DISCUSS

Write a Response Listen to a recording or watch a video of Martin Luther King Jr.'s "I Have a Dream" speech. Write a short response to describe how listening to the speech enhances your understanding of the topic.

- ❑ Listen to the recording or watch "I Have a Dream" at least twice. Follow along using the written speech.

- ❑ Annotate the written speech as you listen or watch. As you follow along, take notes on how hearing the speech changes your understanding of it. Is your emotional response different when you hear Dr. King read the speech?

- ❑ Summarize your overall response to the speech, including how your understanding of the speech changed as you listened to King speak.

Discuss with a Small Group Have a panel discussion to share personal thoughts and feelings about the speech.

- ❑ Review the text and decide which parts of the speech had a different impact as you listened to the recording.

- ❑ Have members prepare personal thoughts and feelings in response to the recording. Appoint a discussion leader to facilitate sharing.

- ❑ Have each group member share and discuss the impact of the recording on their understanding of the speech and how it affected them personally to hear King deliver the speech. All students should listen closely and respectfully before asking questions or making comments.

- ❑ Students can help one other define or describe terms or ideas when words in the text are unfamiliar.

Go to the **Speaking and Listening Studio** for help with having a group discussion.

RESPOND TO THE ESSENTIAL QUESTION

 How do people find freedom in the midst of oppression?

Gather Information Review your annotations and notes on "I Have a Dream." Then, add relevant information to your Response Log. As you determine which information to include, think about:

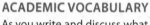

- how Dr. King urged his audience to fight oppression
- how racial inequality can lead to injustice
- why it is important to understand that freedom takes many forms

At the end of the unit, use your notes to help you write a research report.

ACADEMIC VOCABULARY

As you write and discuss what you learned from the speech, be sure to use the Academic Vocabulary words. Check off each of the words that you use.

- ❑ **decline**
- ❑ **enable**
- ❑ **impose**
- ❑ **integrate**
- ❑ **reveal**

© Houghton Mifflin Harcourt Publishing Company

WORD BANK
default
desolate
degenerate
inextricably
redemptive

CRITICAL VOCABULARY

Practice and Apply Answer the following questions in complete sentences, incorporating the Critical Vocabulary words and their meanings.

1. Look back at paragraph 5. Why does King say that America has **defaulted** on its promise?

_____

2. Look back at paragraph 6. In what ways is segregation **desolate**?

_____

3. Look back at paragraph 8. How is physical violence a good example of how protests might **degenerate**?

_____

4. Look back at paragraph 8. How is the freedom of all people **inextricably** bound together?

_____

5. Look back at paragraph 10. How and why does King use the word **redemptive** to link the concepts of freedom and religious faith?

_____

VOCABULARY STRATEGY:
Antonyms

Go to the **Vocabulary Studio** for more on antonyms.

Antonyms are words with opposite meanings. Recognizing antonyms can help you understand new vocabulary words. For example, the word *cheerful* is an antonym for the Critical Vocabulary word *desolate*. Use an online or print thesaurus to find antonyms.

Practice and Apply Use a thesaurus to find an antonym for each of the remaining Critical Vocabulary words. Then, write sentences using each antonym.

1. **default**

_____

2. **degenerate**

_____

3. **inextricably**

_____

4. **redemptive**

_____

LANGUAGE CONVENTIONS:
Repetition and Parallelism

Martin Luther King Jr. uses the techniques of repetition and parallelism to express his ideas. These patterns emphasize his important ideas and make his speech flow rhythmically. Through these techniques, he links ideas together and builds upon them.

Repetition refers to repeated words or phrases. Sometimes phrases are repeated throughout a sentence. Other times they are repeated throughout a paragraph, or between paragraphs. This is a way to link ideas together.

> **We can never be satisfied as long as the Negro is the victim of the unspeakable horrors of police brutality; we can never be satisfied as long as our bodies, heavy with the fatigue of travel, cannot gain lodging in the motels of the highways and the hotels of the cities . . .**

Here, Dr. King gives many reasons why "we can never be satisfied." He links his reasons together by repeating the same phrase again and again.

Parallelism refers to a similar sentence or phrase structure that is repeated within a sentence or paragraph. Speakers often use parallelism to highlight similarities or differences.

> **I have a dream that one day every valley shall be exalted, and every hill and mountain shall be made low. The rough places will be plain and the crooked places will be made straight . . .**

Here, Dr. King uses parallelism to highlight the contrasts, or differences in his imagery. Similar sentence structure is used in both phrases.

Practice and Apply Look back at the response you wrote to listening or watching the speech for Create and Discuss. Find two or three places where you can revise your wording to use the techniques of repetition or parallelism. Write your revised response below.

PODCAST

from INTERVIEW WITH JOHN LEWIS

NPR Podcast

? **ESSENTIAL QUESTION:**

How do people find freedom in the midst of oppression?

QUICK START

Have you ever had to overcome fear or other obstacles to stand up for yourself? Discuss your reaction with the class.

ANALYZE A PODCAST

GENRE ELEMENTS: PODCAST INTERVIEW

- centered around a conversation between a host or interviewer and one or more guests
- exists in a digital format, usually as a series of downloadable files available by subscription
- generally intended to entertain and/or inform

The purpose of a digital media product or text is usually to inform, entertain, persuade, or express the feelings or thoughts of those who created it. **Podcasts** are digital audio files available on the Internet. They can be downloaded to devices, and listeners can subscribe to series of podcasts.

Creators of podcasts use spoken word, or narration, and other sound elements. Podcasts are especially suited for sharing personal experiences often in the form of audio interviews.

Sound elements are what you hear in a podcast.

PODCASTS	Digital audio files that can be downloaded from the Internet
SOUND ELEMENTS	Music or other sounds created by singing, playing instruments, or using computer-generated tones; creates a mood
VOICE NARRATION	The words as well as the expression and quality of voice

ANALYZE AUTHOR'S PURPOSE

The **author's purpose** is the author's reason for writing. People who participate in interviews also have a purpose. In a podcast interview, the interviewer's purpose is to elicit useful information from the interviewee. The interviewee's purpose may be to inform, entertain, express thoughts and feelings, or persuade the audience. John Lewis may have had a specific purpose in agreeing to the interview with NPR. His knowledge of critical events in American history merits analysis and preservation, and his interview with Terry Gross helps to ensure that.

BACKGROUND

John Lewis *(b. 1940) is one of the "Big Six" civil rights activists of the 1960s Civil Rights Movement, as well as a U.S. Representative in Congress. Lewis was born in Alabama in 1940, during a time when segregation was in full force. As a teen, he was inspired by Dr. Martin Luther King Jr. and Rosa Parks. He began college in 1957, and participated in civil rights marches, helping to plan the March on Washington in 1963. In 1965, he led the march from Selma, Alabama, with Hosea Williams and was beaten so badly by state troopers that his skull was fractured. His actions helped persuade President Johnson to enact the 1965 Voting Rights Act. The Act was intended to overcome legal barriers at the state and local levels that prevented African Americans from exercising their right to vote. Lewis's life in politics has been dedicated to voting rights, fighting poverty, and supporting public education. He has created a graphic novel series to teach young people about the marches for civil rights.*

SETTING A PURPOSE

Before listening, make a prediction about what John Lewis will discuss in the podcast, which was recorded in 2009. Afterward, check to see if your prediction was correct.

To listen to the podcast, log in online and select **"from INTERVIEW WITH JOHN LEWIS"** from the unit menu.

As needed, pause the recording to make notes about your predictions or what you might want to talk about later. Replay or rewind so that you can clarify anything you do not understand.

ANALYZE PODCASTS

Support your responses with evidence from the podcast. ▤ NOTEBOOK

1. **Cause/Effect** The interviewer asks John Lewis about what caused him to go against his mother's wishes and get involved in civil rights marches. What does he say inspired him to organize and march with other activists?

2. **Analyze** What is the interviewer's purpose as she begins to ask questions of John Lewis? Describe the approach she takes to get Lewis to share his story.

3. **Draw Conclusions** What factors motivated John Lewis to fight for voting rights? Explain why Lewis felt that the risks were worth taking to change the society he lived in.

4. **Interpret** What does John Lewis mean when he says he focused on "bringing down those signs"? How does his story about listening to Dr. King talk about activism in Montgomery help you understand what his main goals were?

5. **Cite Evidence** What do you think was Lewis's purpose in agreeing to be interviewed? Cite evidence from the interview to support your answer.

RESEARCH

RESEARCH TIP
Be sure to check the websites you use to ensure that they are reliable and credible sources of information. Sites of well-known news organizations are a good place to start, and sites with the suffix .org tend to be more reliable than commercial sites.

John Lewis is a longtime member of Congress with a long list of civil rights achievements. Research Lewis's many accomplishments and their impact on others. Record what you learn in the chart.

ACCOMPLISHMENTS	EFFECTS

Connect In the interview, John Lewis says that he felt that Dr. King was speaking directly to him, saying that he, too, could "make a contribution." With a small group, discuss how John Lewis's contributions have had an impact on your own community's rights and freedoms.

CREATE AND PRESENT

Create a Multimedia Presentation Using photos and images from your research on John Lewis, create a multimedia presentation about one aspect of Lewis's career. Present it to the class or post it online.

❏ Select photos and images that help to explain one aspect of John Lewis's career, such as an event in which he played a key role or one of his major accomplishments.

❏ Then, use presentation software to create a multimedia presentation about this aspect of Lewis's career. Prepare notes to guide you in speaking about the parts of the presentation. Choose language that suits your topic and purpose. Then, practice your presentation, noting when you should pause or change the volume of your voice for effect.

❏ Give your final presentation to the class in person and/or online.

Discuss with a Small Group Have a discussion about how information in "Interview with John Lewis" can help to inspire people to resist oppressive laws and fight for freedom.

❏ As a group, review the interview and decide which information is relevant to the discussion topic. Use the podcast player functions to replay important aspects of the interview and help you locate relevant information for the discussion.

❏ Have group members prepare ideas and details that relate to the topic.

❏ Review the ideas together and suggest which ones can help people fight when rights are denied. Listen closely and respectfully to all ideas.

Go to the **Speaking and Listening Studio** for more on creating a multimedia presentation.

Go to the **Speaking and Listening Studio** for more on participating in a collaborative discussion.

RESPOND TO THE ESSENTIAL QUESTION

? How do people find freedom in the midst of oppression?

Gather Information Review your notes on "Interview with John Lewis." Then, add relevant information to your Response Log. As you determine which information to include, think about:

• the ways in which marginalized groups of people are oppressed

• what happens to people when they are denied their rights

• how oppressed people can fight for equal standing in their society

At the end of the unit, use your notes to help you write a research report.

UNIT 2
RESPONSE LOG

Essential Question:
How do people find freedom in the midst of oppression?

I Have a Dream	
Interview with John Lewis	
from Hidden Figures	
The Censors	
Booker T. and W.E.B.	
from Reading Lolita in Tehran	
from Persepolis 2: The Story of a Return	

R2 Student Resources

ACADEMIC VOCABULARY

As you write and discuss what you learned from the podcast, be sure to use the Academic Vocabulary words. Check off each of the words that you use.

❏ **decline**

❏ **enable**

❏ **impose**

❏ **integrate**

❏ **reveal**

from
HIDDEN
FIGURES

History Writing by **Margot Lee Shetterly**

© Houghton Mifflin Harcourt Publishing Company • Image Credits: ©NASA Langley Research Center

? ***ESSENTIAL QUESTION:***

How do people find freedom in the midst of oppression?

QUICK START

What do you know about opportunities that were once closed to African Americans, women, or other minorities? Name some jobs a woman or an African American might not have been able to apply for in the past.

ANALYZE TEXT STRUCTURE

Authors use a variety of **text structures.** These include thesis or main idea and details; cause and effect; problem and solution; and chronology, or time order. Most historical texts are a combination of chronology, main idea, and cause and effect. Sometimes these organizational designs are intertwined.

As you read, keep track of the important events, the order in which they happen, any causal relationships, and key ideas.

GENRE ELEMENTS:
HISTORY WRITING
• uses chronological order
• is a form of informational text
• includes evidence to support ideas
• contains text features to help the reader absorb and retain information

TEXT STRUCTURES	EXAMPLE FROM *HIDDEN FIGURES*
Narration of an Event	By 1943, the American aircraft industry was the largest, most productive, and most sophisticated in the world, making three times more planes than the Germans, who were fighting on the other side of the war.
Cause and Effect	But in the spring of 1943, with World War II in full swing and many men off serving in the military . . . employers were beginning to hire women to do jobs that had once belonged *only* to men.
Thesis/Important Ideas	The NACA's mission was . . . to help the United States develop the most powerful and efficient airplanes in the world. . . . World leaders felt that the country that ruled the skies would win the war.

MAKE PREDICTIONS

To read historical text effectively, it is important to **make predictions** as you read. A prediction is an informed guess about what the author is about to say.

- Before you read, use text features such as the title, headings, and background information to make initial predictions about the text.

- As you read, use text structure as well as genre characteristics to correct your initial predictions and to predict what you will read about next.

- After you read, confirm your predictions. They may not always be correct. If the author surprises you, your predictions will help you evaluate and remember the unexpected information.

Use a chart like this one to help you make and evaluate your predictions:

WHAT I KNOW	MY PREDICTION	WAS IT CORRECT?

CRITICAL VOCABULARY

| simulate | assess | maneuver | analytical |

To see how many Critical Vocabulary words you already know, use them to complete the sentences.

1. I always _____ a new situation to determine its opportunities and dangers.

2. Someone with a(n) _____ mind is usually a good problem solver.

3. It can be difficult to _____ in a tight space.

4. Computers can now _____ the experience of flying an airplane.

LANGUAGE CONVENTIONS

Pronoun-Antecedent Agreement In this lesson, you will learn about the agreement of a pronoun with its antecedent. A singular pronoun replaces or refers to a singular noun, and a plural pronoun replaces a plural noun.

This executive order opened up new and exciting opportunities for African Americans, allowing them to work side by side with white people during the war.

In this sentence from the selection, the plural pronoun *them* refers back to the plural noun *African Americans*. Both words are plural, so they are in agreement.

ANNOTATION MODEL

NOTICE & NOTE

As you read, note the author's use of text structures, or organizational designs, in the article. Mark text that shows how the author used structure to organize the text. In the model, you can see one reader's notes about *Hidden Figures*.

A few years earlier, an ad like this would have been unthinkable—most employers never would have considered a woman for a job that had always been performed by a man. But in the spring of 1943, with [World War II in full swing] and [many men off serving in the military], the country needed all the help it could get. Employers were beginning to hire women to do jobs that had once belonged *only* to men.

time clues—helps set chronology

key idea about women and work

These details explain why the situation changed.

BACKGROUND

Before World War II, most women did not work outside their homes. When the United States entered the war, the lack of working men created opportunities for women, including the women written about in Hidden Figures.
Margot Lee Shetterly *(b. 1969) grew up in Hampton, Virginia, near the Langley Research Center. As she began to learn about the history of African American women mathematicians at Langley, she researched and wrote about them in a bestselling book, which has since been made into the popular movie* Hidden Figures.

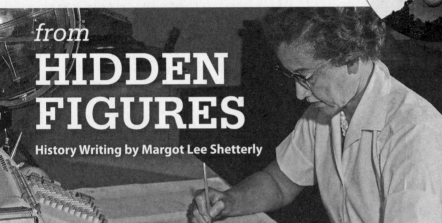

from
HIDDEN FIGURES

History Writing by Margot Lee Shetterly

SETTING A PURPOSE

As you read, pay attention to the details that explain why the work African American women did at Langley was important to them and why it was important to the country.

1   The newspaper ad caught the attention of many women. It read: "Reduce your household duties! Women who are not afraid to roll up their sleeves and do jobs previously filled by men should call the Langley Memorial Aeronautical Laboratory."

2   A few years earlier, an ad like this would have been unthinkable—most employers never would have considered a woman for a job that had always been performed by a man. But in the spring of 1943, with World War II in full swing and many men off serving in the military, the country needed all the help it could get. Employers were beginning to hire women to do jobs that had once belonged *only* to men.

Notice & Note

You can use the side margins to notice and note signposts in the text.

MAKE PREDICTIONS
Annotate: Mark at least two details in paragraphs 1 and 2 that help you predict what this article is about.

Predict: What do you think you will learn by reading this article?

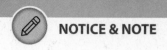
3   This particular ad was placed by the National Advisory Committee for Aeronautics (NACA), a government agency dedicated to studying the science of flying. The NACA shared a campus with the US Army Air Corps in Hampton, Virginia, a city in the southeastern part of the state, next to the Chesapeake Bay.

4   The NACA's mission was important and unique: to help the United States develop the most powerful and efficient airplanes in the world. Airplanes moved military troops, tracked enemies, and launched bombs. World leaders felt that the country that ruled the skies would win the war. President Franklin D. Roosevelt believed in the importance of air power, so two years earlier, in 1941, he had challenged the nation to increase its production of airplanes to fifty thousand units a year. At that time, the industry had manufactured only three thousand planes a year.

5   The NACA and private industry were up for the challenge. By 1943, the American aircraft industry was the largest, most productive, and most sophisticated in the world, making three times more planes than the Germans, who were fighting on the other side of the war.

"Victory through Air Power!"

6   Before manufacturers built the airplanes, the designs were developed, tested, and refined at the Langley Memorial Aeronautical Laboratory, which was where the NACA had first begun its operations, in 1917. The engineers created wind tunnels to **simulate**, or imitate, different conditions a plane could encounter when flying. This helped the engineers to test airplane parts as well as whole aircraft, examining them for any problems, like air disturbance and uneven wing geometry.

7   After that testing, pilots flew the planes, trying to **assess** how the machines handled in the air. Did the aircraft roll unexpectedly? Did it stall? Was it hard to guide or **maneuver**? Making small changes to the design added up to a difference in performance. Even tiny improvements in speed and efficiency multiplied over millions of pilot miles added to a difference that could tip the balance of the war.

8   People working at Langley knew that they were doing their part to win the war. "Victory through air power!" said Henry Reid, the engineer-in-charge of the Langley Laboratory. And the workers took their mission to heart.

WANTED: Female Mathematicians

9   Each of the engineers at the Langley Memorial Aeronautical Laboratory required the support of a number of other workers: craftsmen to build the airplane models, mechanics to maintain the test tunnels, and "number crunchers" to process the data that was collected during the tests. For the engineers, a plane was basically a complex physics experiment. Physics is the science of matter, energy, and motion. Physics meant math, and math meant mathematicians. At the Langley Laboratory, mathematicians meant women.

© Houghton Mifflin Harcourt Publishing Company

10   Female mathematicians had been on the job at Langley since 1935. And it didn't take long for the women to show that they were just as good or even better at computing than many of the male engineers. But few of the women were granted the title "mathematician," which would have put them on equal footing with some male employees. Instead, they were classified as "subprofessionals," a title that meant they could be paid less.

11   At Langley, the female mathematicians were called "computers." They did the computations to turn the results of the raw data gathered by the engineers into a more useful form. Today we think of computers as machines, but in the 1940s, a computer was just someone whose job it was to do computations, a flesh-and-blood woman who was very good with numbers.

12   In 1943, it was difficult for the Langley Laboratory to find as many qualified women as they needed. A recruiter from the National Advisory Committee for Aeronautics visited colleges in search of young women with **analytical** or mathematical skills.

The Human Computers

13   When the managers couldn't satisfy the demand with only white employees, the government decided to hire African Americans. A civil rights leader named A. Philip Randolph encouraged President Roosevelt to sign an executive order—a law that ordered the

© Houghton Mifflin Harcourt Publishing Company • Image Credits: (L) ©NASA • (M) ©NASA Langley Research Center • (R) ©NASA

Dorothy Vaughan

Katherine Johnson

Mary Jackson

LANGUAGE CONVENTIONS

Annotate: Underline the pronoun in the second sentence of paragraph 11. Then find the antecedent of the pronoun and circle it.

Respond: Why does the author use pronouns instead of repeating the same nouns?

analytical
(ăn´ə-lĭt´ ĭ kəl) *adj.* able to analyze, or understand something by breaking it down into parts.

ANALYZE STRUCTURE

Annotate: In paragraph 13, sentence 1, underline the cause and circle the effect.

Infer: What does this cause-and-effect relationship explain about the decision to hire African American women as mathematicians at Langley?

© Houghton Mifflin Harcourt Publishing Company

desegregation of the federal government and defense industry and created the Fair Employment Practices Committee. This executive order opened up new and exciting opportunities for African Americans, allowing them to work side-by-side with white people during the war.

CITE EVIDENCE

Annotate: Mark the African American colleges listed in paragraph 14.

Connect: How did employers figure out which applicants were African Americans? Cite evidence to support your response.

14   The federal government also helped create special training classes at black colleges, where people could learn the skills they would need to be successful in the war jobs. Black newspapers like the *Norfolk Journal and Guide* published articles telling their readers to apply for these new job openings. And there were many applicants! The applications were not supposed to consider race—a recent law had done away with the requirement that the application must include a photo—but it wasn't hard for employers to figure out which job candidates were black. African Americans did not have access to white colleges and universities, so black applicants came from black colleges, such as West Virginia State University, Howard University, Hampton Institute, and Arkansas Agricultural, Mechanical & Normal College. Many of the African-American candidates had years of teaching experience as well as math and science degrees.

15   Once hired, the black mathematicians were assigned to a separate work space in the Warehouse Building on the west side of the Langley campus. The East Area Computers were all white; the West Area Computers were all black, except for the supervisor and her assistant, who were white women.

CONTRASTS AND CONTRADICTIONS

Notice & Note: Mark parts of the text in paragraphs 15–17 that show a contrast or contradiction between how much the African American female mathematicians were needed and how they were treated.

Analyze: What was the difference and why does it matter?

16   There had always been African-American employees at Langley, but they had worked as janitors, cafeteria workers, mechanic's assistants, and groundskeepers. Hiring black mathematicians—that was something new. For the most part, the engineers welcomed extra hands, even if those hands were black. The Langley Laboratory was operating around the clock to test airplanes to be flown by American soldiers in the war: everyone had a job to do.

17   Hampton, Virginia, where the Langley campus was located, was very much a southern town. State law and Virginia custom meant that African Americans did not ride the same buses or eat in the same cafeterias or use the same bathrooms as whites. The Langley staff had to prepare for the arrival of the African-American mathematicians. One of the tasks: creating metal bathroom signs that read "Colored Girls."

18 For the black women, the experience of working at a laboratory offered the chance to do interesting work that would help support the war effort. Walking into an unfamiliar environment wasn't easy for the women of the new West Area Computing Office, but each of them was eager for the opportunity to help their country and prove that they, too, could be excellent mathematicians.

CHECK YOUR UNDERSTANDING

Answer these questions before moving on to the **Analyze the Text** section on the following page.

1 The purpose of the National Advisory Committee for Aeronautics (NACA) during World War II was to —

A train mathematicians

B provide jobs for women

C mass produce airplanes to be used in war

D help the airline industry develop good airplanes

2 Female mathematicians had worked at Langley since —

F it began its operations in 1917

G 1935, a few years before the start of World War II

H the beginning of World War II

J just after World War II

3 Which idea is most important in the selection?

A The U.S. needed good aircraft in World War II.

B The first female mathematicians at Langley were white.

C President Franklin Roosevelt believed in air power.

D African American women were successful mathematicians at Langley.

ANALYZE THE TEXT

Support your responses with evidence from the text. 📓 NOTEBOOK

1. **Predict** Review the predictions you made before and as you read. How did text features and the characteristics of history writing help you make correct predictions? Which predictions did you have to correct as you read?

2. **Cause/Effect** During the 1940s, women were able to get jobs for the first time in many industries. What event caused that to happen?

3. **Summarize** Review paragraphs 6–7. What tests and improvements performed at Langley helped the U.S. airplane industry? Give at least two examples.

4. **Infer** From the information given in paragraph 10, what inferences can you draw about attitudes towards woman at Langley? From the information given in paragraphs 15 and 16, what inferences can you draw about attitudes towards African Americans at Langley?

5. **Notice & Note** In paragraph 2, the author uses this extreme language: "...A few years earlier, an ad like this would have been unthinkable...." How does the word "unthinkable" convey people's attitude toward women in the work place at the time?

RESEARCH

RESEARCH TIP
Frame your research in the form of a question. This will help you to make sure you include all the different keywords that you need to get a specific result.

African American women served in several important roles during World War II. Research the participation of African American women in the groups listed in the chart below. Record what you learn on the right side of the chart.

GROUP	CONTRIBUTION
Nurses	
6888th Central Postal Battalion	
Factory Workers	

Extend Find a poster or photograph of the World War II icon "Rosie the Riveter," which shows a white woman. Then find a photograph of a black "Rosie the Riveter." What do these posters show about the attitude of women entering the workplace during World War II? How does this help you understand *Hidden Figures*? Share your thoughts with a small group.

CREATE AND DISCUSS

Write a Blog Post Write a three- to four-paragraph blog about the African American female mathematicians at Langley.

- ❑ Introduce the topic and express your main idea about the "human computers."
- ❑ Then, tell about the situation at Langley before and during the war.
- ❑ In your final paragraph, state your conclusion about the "Hidden Figures."

Discuss with a Small Group Have a discussion about how information in *Hidden Figures* can help someone understand the history of segregation in the United States.

- ❑ As a group, review the text and decide which information is relevant to the discussion topic. Use the headings to help you locate the information.
- ❑ Have group members prepare ideas and details that relate to the topic.
- ❑ Review the ideas together and generate questions about topics you might want to learn more about. Listen closely and respectfully to all ideas.

 Go to the **Writing Studio** for more on writing an informative essay.

Go to the **Speaking and Listening Studio** for help with participating in a collaborative discussion.

RESPOND TO THE ESSENTIAL QUESTION

? How do people find freedom in the midst of oppression?

Gather Information Review your annotations and notes on *Hidden Figures*. Then, add relevant information to your Response Log. As you determine which information to include, think about:

- the forms of discrimination the female mathematicians at Langley faced
- how they overcame discrimination
- how these mathematicians helped in the fight against oppression

At the end of the unit, use your notes to help you write a research report.

UNIT 2
RESPONSE LOG

Essential Question
How do people find freedom in the midst of oppression?

I Have a Dream	
Interview with John Lewis	
from Hidden Figures	
The Censors	
Booker T. and W.E.B.	
from Reading Lolita in Tehran	
from Persepolis 2: The Story of a Return	

R2 Student Resources

ACADEMIC VOCABULARY

As you write and discuss what you learned from the history, be sure to use the Academic Vocabulary words. Check off each of the words that you use.

- ❑ **decline**
- ❑ **enable**
- ❑ **impose**
- ❑ **integrate**
- ❑ **reveal**

WORD BANK
simulate
assess
maneuver
analytical

Go to the **Vocabulary Studio** for more on reference sources.

CRITICAL VOCABULARY

Practice and Apply Work with a partner to write the dialogue for a brief scene that depicts the meaning of but does not mention each Critical Vocabulary word. Then swap your scene with another pair. Pairs will then analyze each other's scenes and identify the word that is being conveyed in each one. Here are some ideas:

• a character is **simulating** something

• a character **assessing** a situation or another character

• a character is **maneuvering** through a difficult space

• a situation requires **analytical** thinking

VOCABULARY STRATEGY:
Reference Sources

When you read an informational text, looking up words or terms in print and digital **reference sources** such as dictionaries, glossaries or thesauruses can help you better understand the text. These resources help you clarify and validate your understanding of the precise and appropriate meaning of technical or discipline-based vocabulary.

Reference sources can be used along with context clues. You may encounter an unfamiliar word for which you are able to discover a meaning from the context in which the word appears. Here is a sentence from the selection:

> The engineers created wind tunnels to <u>simulate</u>, or imitate, different conditions a plane could encounter when flying.

The word "imitate" and the context of "wind tunnels" and "different conditions" help you get the meaning of the word *simulate*. When you look the word up in a reference source to confirm the meaning, you may see a specific technical definition of the word. This will help clarify your understanding of the word's use in the text.

> **simulate** *v.* (sĭm´yə-lāt´) to produce the features of an event or process in a way that seems real but is not, usually for training or testing purposes.

Practice and Apply The words below are also used in *Hidden Figures*. Look them up in a dictionary, glossary, or thesaurus, using context clues from the text to help you choose the appropriate definition for the word. In the text margin, write the definition that fits the sentence.

1. refined (paragraph 6)

2. engineers (paragraph 6)

3. performance (paragraph 7)

4. process (paragraph 9)

LANGUAGE CONVENTIONS:
Pronoun-Antecedent Agreement

Pronouns take the place of nouns so that speakers and writers can avoid sounding repetitious. Pronouns can also make sentences clearer, but only if they agree with the nouns they replace—their antecedents.

A singular noun replaces a singular pronoun, and a plural noun replaces a plural pronoun. There are usually words, phrases, or even clauses between the antecedent and the pronoun, and those can sometimes be confusing. But you can simply look for the noun that the pronoun replaces and match the number of that noun.

Here are some examples of pronoun-antecedent agreement from *Hidden Figures*:

Go to the **Grammar Studio** for more on pronoun-antecedent agreement.

- These pronouns are separated from their antecedents by phrases and are in a new clause.

  > **<u>People</u> working at Langley knew that <u>they</u> were doing <u>their</u> part to win the war.**

- The pronoun is in a new clause.

  > **<u>President Franklin D. Roosevelt</u> believed in the importance of air power, so two years earlier, in 1941, <u>he</u> had challenged the nation to increase its production of airplanes to fifty thousand units a year.**

- The pronoun is in a new sentence.

  > **Did the <u>aircraft</u> roll unexpectedly? Did <u>it</u> stall?**

Practice and Apply Write a paragraph about the female mathematicians described in *Hidden Figures*. Use at least three pronouns in your paragraph. Make sure that they agree with their antecedents.

THE CENSORS

Short Story by **Luisa Valenzuela**

translated by David Unger

© Houghton Mifflin Harcourt Publishing Company • Image Credits: ©Lena Lir/Shutterstock

? ESSENTIAL QUESTION:

How do people find freedom in the midst of oppression?

QUICK START

The short story you are about to read is about government censorship. Can you think of a situation in which it might be acceptable for a government to censor information? Discuss your thoughts with the class.

ANALYZE LITERARY DEVICES

Literary devices are techniques used by authors to communicate their experiences and ideas. Here are definitions of three literary devices used in "The Censors."

DEVICE	DEFINITION
Foreshadowing	**Foreshadowing** is a writer's use of clues to hint at events that will occur later in the story. It creates suspense, making readers eager to find out what will happen next.
Irony	**Irony** takes place when something happens that is the opposite of what readers would expect. **Verbal irony** is when what is said is the opposite of what is meant. **Situational irony** is when a character or reader expects one thing to happen but something else happens.
Idiom	An **Idiom** is a commonly-used expression that means something other than the literal meaning of its words.

GENRE ELEMENTS: SHORT STORY

- includes the basic elements of fiction—setting, characters, plot, conflict, and theme
- centers on one particular moment or event in the main character's life
- can be read in one sitting

ANALYZE SETTING AND THEME

The **setting**—the time and place in which a story occurs—can play an important role in developing the **theme,** or central message, of a story. Valenzuela wrote this story in Argentina in an atmosphere of censorship, suppression, and violence. She drew on the mood of fear and oppression to create the setting of this story and inform its theme.

As you read "The Censors," notice examples of how the story's cultural and social setting shape the theme.

CRITICAL VOCABULARY

To see how many Critical Vocabulary words you already know, use them to complete the sentences.

irreproachable   staidness   negligence   subversive

1. Rebel troops committed _____ acts against the government.

2. My father's love of routine makes many people accuse him of _____.

3. The auto company's _____ led to the faulty part on the car.

4. The mayor was considered very respectable and _____ in her character.

LANGUAGE CONVENTIONS

Colons and Semicolons In this lesson, you will learn about the effective use of colons and semicolons. Both types of punctuation indicate pauses in a sentence. Colons introduce related information. Semicolons show a connection between two separate ideas that are related in some way. Here is a sentence from the story:

. . . Juan didn't join in; after thinking it over, he reported him to his superiors . . . .

The semicolon emphasizes the contrast between the two ideas: not only did Juan not join in, but also he took the action of reporting the man to his superiors.

As you read, look for the author's use of colons and semicolons and how they contribute to the message.

ANNOTATION MODEL   **NOTICE & NOTE**

As you read, mark passages that might foreshadow later events in the story. You can also note your thoughts and questions. This model shows one reader's notes from a passage in "The Censors."

Juan knows there won't be a problem with the letter's contents, that it's irreproachable, harmless. But what about the rest? He knows that they examine, sniff, feel, and read between the lines of each and every letter, and check its tiniest comma and most accidental stain. He knows that all letters pass from hand to hand and go through all sort of tests in the huge censorship offices and that, in the end, very few continue on their way. Usually it takes months, even years, if there aren't any snags; all this time the freedom, maybe even the life, of both sender and receiver is in jeopardy.

Who is doing this and why?

Why are there censorship offices?

What is putting their life in jeopardy? This sounds ominous.

BACKGROUND

Luisa Valenzuela (b. 1938) was born in Argentina and published her first story at the age of seventeen. After graduating from the University of Buenos Aires, she moved to Paris and traveled abroad for several years. She returned home in 1974 to find political turmoil and oppression. A fascist dictatorship, a system of government in which a leader suppresses opposition through violent means, now ruled Argentina. Despite threats of censorship and physical harm, she began using her writing to document the horrors of life under a dictator.

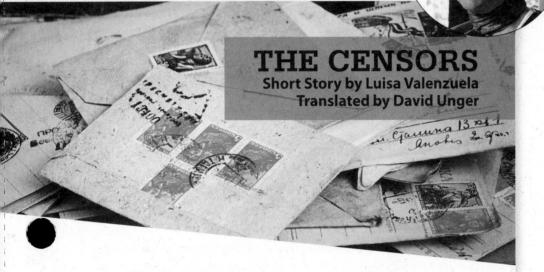

THE CENSORS
Short Story by Luisa Valenzuela
Translated by David Unger

SETTING A PURPOSE

As you read, pay attention to the clues that reveal how Juan's feelings about his work change.

1   Poor Juan! One day they caught him with his guard down before he could even realize that what he had taken as a stroke of luck was really one of fate's dirty tricks. These things happen the minute you're careless and you let down your guard, as one often does. Juancito let happiness—a feeling you can't trust—get the better of him when he received from a confidential source Mariana's new address in Paris and he knew that she hadn't forgotten him. Without thinking twice, he sat down at his table and wrote her a letter. *The* letter that keeps his mind off his job during the day and won't let him sleep at night (what had he scrawled, what had he put on that sheet of paper he sent to Mariana?).

Notice & Note

You can use the side margins to notice and note signposts in the text.

ANALYZE LITERARY DEVICES

Annotate: Mark the idioms used by the author in paragraph 1.

Interpret: Explain the meaning of each idiom. What tone, or attitude toward the character and the audience, do the idioms create?

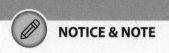

irreproachable

(ĭr´ĭ-prō´chə-bəl) *adj.* without fault or blame; perfect.

ANALYZE SETTING AND THEME

Annotate: Mark descriptions of setting in paragraph 2.

Synthesize: What is life like for people where Juan lives? How might this setting shape the author's theme, or message about life?

staidness

(stād´nĭs) *n.* the quality of being steady, calm, and serious.

negligence

(nĕg´lĭ-jəns) *n.* carelessness or failure to take normal precautions.

2   Juan knows there won't be a problem with the letter's contents, that it's **irreproachable**, harmless. But what about the rest? He knows that they examine, sniff, feel, and read between the lines of each and every letter, and check its tiniest comma and most accidental stain. He knows that all letters pass from hand to hand and go through all sorts of tests in the huge censorship offices and that, in the end, very few continue on their way. Usually it takes months, even years, if there aren't any snags; all this time the freedom, maybe even the life, of both sender and receiver is in jeopardy. And that's why Juan's so down in the dumps: thinking that something might happen to Mariana because of his letters. Of all people, Mariana, who must finally feel safe there where she always dreamed she'd live. But he knows that the *Censor's Secret Command* operates all over the world and cashes in on the discount in air rates; there's nothing to stop them from going as far as that hidden Paris neighborhood, kidnapping Mariana, and returning to their cozy homes, certain of having fulfilled their noble mission.

3   Well, you've got to beat them to the punch, do what everyone tries to do: sabotage the machinery, throw sand in its gears, get to the bottom of the problem so as to stop it.

4   This was Juan's sound plan when he, like many others, applied for a censor's job—not because he had a calling or needed a job: no, he applied simply to intercept his own letter, a consoling but unoriginal idea. He was hired immediately, for each day more and more censors are needed and no one would bother to check on his references.

5   Ulterior motives couldn't be overlooked by the *Censorship Division*, but they needn't be too strict with those who applied. They knew how hard it would be for those poor guys to find the letter they wanted and even if they did, what's a letter or two when the new censor would snap up so many others? That's how Juan managed to join the *Post Office's Censorship Division*, with a certain goal in mind.

6   The building had a festive air on the outside which contrasted with its inner **staidness**. Little by little, Juan was absorbed by his job and he felt at peace since he was doing everything he could to get his letter for Mariana. He didn't even worry when, in his first month, he was sent to *Section K* where envelopes are very carefully screened for explosives.

7   It's true that on the third day, a fellow worker had his right hand blown off by a letter, but the division chief claimed it was sheer **negligence** on the victim's part. Juan and the other employees were allowed to go back to their work, albeit feeling less secure. After work, one of them tried to organize a strike to demand higher wages for unhealthy work, but Juan didn't join in; after thinking it over, he reported him to his superiors and thus got promoted.

8   You don't form a habit by doing something once, he told himself as he left his boss's office. And when he was transferred to *Section J,* where letters are carefully checked for poison dust, he felt he had climbed a rung in the ladder.

9   By working hard, he quickly reached *Section E* where the job was more interesting, for he could now read and analyze the letters' contents. Here he could even hope to get hold of his letter which, judging by the time that had elapsed, had gone through the other sections and was probably floating around in this one.

ANALYZE LITERARY DEVICES

Annotate: Mark instances of foreshadowing in paragraphs 6–8.

Analyze: Describe how the foreshadowing contributes to the story's tone.

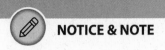

10   Soon his work became so absorbing that his noble mission blurred in his mind. Day after day he crossed out whole paragraphs in red ink, pitilessly chucking many letters into the censored basket. These were horrible days when he was shocked by the subtle and conniving ways employed by people to pass on **subversive** messages; his instincts were so sharp that he found behind a simple 'the weather's unsettled' or 'prices continue to soar' the wavering hand of someone secretly scheming to overthrow the Government.

11   His zeal brought him swift promotion. We don't know if this made him happy. Very few letters reached him in *Section B*—only a handful passed the other hurdles—so he read them over and over again, passed them under a magnifying glass, searched for microprint with an electronic microscope, and tuned his sense of smell so that he was beat by the time he made it home. He'd barely manage to warm up his soup, eat some fruit, and fall into bed, satisfied with having done his duty. Only his darling mother worried, but she couldn't get him back on the right road. She'd say, though it wasn't always true: Lola called, she's at the bar with the girls, they miss you, they're waiting for you. Or else she'd leave a bottle of red wine on the table. But Juan wouldn't overdo it: any distraction could make him lose his edge and the perfect censor had to be alert, keen, attentive, and sharp to nab cheats. He had a truly patriotic task, both self-denying and uplifting.

12   His basket for censored letters became the best fed as well as the most cunning basket in the whole *Censorship Division*. He was about to congratulate himself for having finally discovered his true mission, when his letter to Mariana reached his hands. Naturally, he censored it without regret. And just as naturally, he couldn't stop them from executing him the following morning, another victim of his devotion to his work.

ANALYZE LITERARY DEVICES

Annotate: Mark an instance of situational irony that occurs twice in this paragraph.

Evaluate: What might this ironic statement foreshadow about Juan?

CHECK YOUR UNDERSTANDING

Answer these questions before moving on to the **Analyze the Text** section on the following page.

1 Why does Juan apply for the censorship job?

A His mother asked him to.

B He wants to intercept his letter.

C He thinks he would be good at it.

D He needs to make money.

2 Which of the following sentences explains how Juan feels when he is promoted to Section J?

F "He felt he had climbed a rung in the ladder."

G He felt he had "finally discovered his true mission."

H He felt "down in the dumps."

J "He felt at peace."

3 At the conclusion of the story, Juan —

A is promoted to head censor

B escapes to Paris

C has Mariana executed

D is executed

ANALYZE THE TEXT

Support your responses with evidence from the text.　NOTEBOOK

1. **Infer** Revisit the final paragraph of the text. In your own words, what is the story's message, or **theme**? How is it influenced by the setting?

2. **Analyze** In his career as a censor, Juan moves from Section K to Section B. Describe the pacing or progression of his advancement. Besides the section letters, what devices and word choices does the author use to speed up or slow down the pace of the story?

3. **Cite Evidence** How does the author **foreshadow**, or hint at, the changes that will occur in Juan's personality and his life? Provide examples of foreshadowing along with the changes they foretell.

4. **Compare** Compare Juan's work goal or motivation near the beginning of the story with his goal or motivation near the end. How does the author communicate the way this change occurs?

5. **Evaluate** Why does Juan censor his own letter "without regret"? How is his final action as a censor an example of irony, or a seeming contradiction? How does this ending illustrate Valenzuela's point of view about the political situation in Argentina?

RESEARCH

RESEARCH TIP
Remember to write ideas in your own words. When a direct quote is used, be sure to properly cite the source.

During times of war, the U.S. government censored the postal system as well as other methods of communication. In a small group, brainstorm questions you have about censorship in U.S. history.

Record your questions in a chart like the one below. Then choose a topic for further research, and record your findings in the chart.

Summarize your research findings in a short informational report, including your citations. Share your findings with your group.

DEVELOP A QUESTION	MY QUESTIONS AND RESEARCH TOPICS
Brainstorm questions about this topic, including what you would like to know about how and why censorship occurred.	
GATHER RESEARCH	**RESEARCH FINDINGS AND CITATIONS**
Research and take notes on one or more of the questions you developed. Make sure to properly cite sources.	

Connect How does the censorship described by Valenzuela in "The Censors" compare to ways in which the U.S. government censored communication in times of war?

CREATE AND DISCUSS

Write a Letter In the character of Juan, write the one-page letter you imagine he wrote to Mariana at the beginning of the story.

- ❏ Write the letter to Mariana as Juan.
- ❏ Underline passages of the letter that a censor might conceal.
- ❏ Annotate the letter to explain why those passages would be censored.

Discuss with Your Class Share your letter with the class first without the annotations and then with the annotations.

- ❏ Read the letter to the class. Discuss what phrases or sentences they might censor and why.
- ❏ Share a copy of the letter with annotations. Discuss your annotations and your reasoning for censoring those sections.
- ❏ Review the phrases that you or your classmates would choose to censor. Discuss what they might have in common and what made you more likely to choose them.

Go to the **Speaking and Listening Studio** for more on participating in a collaborative discussion.

RESPOND TO THE ESSENTIAL QUESTION

 How do people find freedom in the midst of oppression?

Gather Information Review your annotations and notes on "The Censor." Then, add relevant information to your Response Log. As you determine which information to include, think about:

- the impact that oppression has on individuals
- how choices are limited under oppression
- how freedom can grow or survive during times of oppression

At the end of the unit, use your notes to help you write a research report.

UNIT 2 RESPONSE LOG

Essential Question: How do people find freedom in the midst of oppression?

I Have a Dream	
Interview with John Lewis	
from Hidden Figures	
The Censors	
Booker T. and W.E.B.	
from Reading Lolita in Tehran	
from Persepolis 2: The Story of a Return	

R2   Student Resources

ACADEMIC VOCABULARY

As you write and discuss what you learned from the short story, be sure to use the Academic Vocabulary words. Check off the words that you use.

- ❏ **decline**
- ❏ **enable**
- ❏ **impose**
- ❏ **integrate**
- ❏ **reveal**

WORD BANK
irreproachable
staidness
negligence
subversive

CRITICAL VOCABULARY

Practice and Apply Circle the letter of the best answer to each question. Then, discuss your responses with a partner.

1. Which of the following shows **irreproachable** behavior?
   a. someone who returns money that was dropped on the street
   b. someone who tends to be private and shy at parties

2. Which of the following is a description of **staidness**?
   a. a person who speaks with a formal tone
   b. a person who speaks with great emotion

3. Which of the following demonstrates **negligence**?
   a. spilled water is left on the floor, causing someone to slip
   b. a small child gets angry and throws her toy

4. Which of the following is a **subversive** act?
   a. voting for a new mayor
   b. disrupting a peaceful protest

VOCABULARY STRATEGY:
Suffixes That Form Nouns

Go to the **Vocabulary Studio** for more on suffixes.

The Critical Vocabulary words *staidness* and *negligence* are formed by adding a noun **suffix** to an adjective, or describing word. Something that is *staid* shows *staidness*; someone who is *negligent* reveals his *negligence*. Noticing word patterns will help you more quickly develop an accurate definition for any unfamiliar words you encounter in your reading. Here are some common noun suffixes you will see in English words.

SUFFIXES	MEANINGS	EXAMPLES
-ance, -ence	act or condition of	radiance, excellence
-cy	state or condition of	sufficiency, redundancy
-dom	state, rank, or condition	officialdom, martyrdom
-hood	state or condition of	likelihood, childhood

Practice and Apply For each row of the chart, identify an additional example that uses the suffix shown. With each word you choose, follow these steps:

1. Identify the base—that is, the main word part without the suffix. Note the part of speech (adjective, verb, noun) and meaning of each base word.

2. Write a definition for each word you chose that incorporates the base word meaning and the suffix meaning.

3. Finally, use each word you chose in a sentence.

LANGUAGE CONVENTIONS:
Colons and Semicolons

An author's use of punctuation not only can help readers understand the message but also can help create meaning and tone. In "The Censors," Luisa Valenzuela uses colons and semicolons to great effect.

Read the following sentence from the story.

And that's why Juan's so down in the dumps: thinking that something might happen to Mariana because of his letters.

The author could instead have written the sentence this way:

Juan's down in the dumps from thinking that something might happen to Mariana because of his letters.

By setting up the sentence as she does, the author involves readers in making meaning. The two-part sentence provides readers with a question (What's bothering Juan?) followed by its answer (thinking that he's endangered Mariana). Readers naturally pause at the colon to prepare for what comes after it. Here are some other common uses of colons.

USES OF COLONS	
Purpose	Example
illustrate or provide an example of what was just stated	Argentina has seen much political turmoil: since World War II, the nation has endured numerous military coups and dictatorships.
introduce a quotation	Valenzuela is no stranger to censorship: "I wrote…thinking that I should write in illegible handwriting so that no one could read over my shoulder."
introduce a list	Valenzuela has lived in many places: Paris, New York, Barcelona, and Buenos Aires.

Valenzuela also uses semicolons effectively. For example, here is another sentence from "The Censors":

Usually it takes months, even years, if there aren't any snags; all this time the freedom, maybe even the life, of both sender and receiver is in jeopardy.

Valenzuela could have chosen to create two separate sentences; her use of the semicolon shows that the second idea results from the first.

Practice and Apply Look back at the letter you created in this selection's Create and Discuss. Revise the letter to add at least one colon and one semicolon. Then discuss with a partner how each punctuation mark you added clarified meaning or tone.

Go to the **Grammar Studio** for more on colons and semicolons.

BOOKER T. AND W.E.B.

Poem by **Dudley Randall**

? *ESSENTIAL QUESTION:*

How do people find freedom in the midst of oppression?

QUICK START

The poem you are about to read depicts an imaginary conversation between Booker T. Washington (1856–1915) and W.E.B. Du Bois (1868–1963), two men who had very different ideas about what African Americans should do to improve their lives in the late 19th and early 20th centuries. How much do you already know about these men? What questions do you have about them? Record what you know and want to know in the chart. After you read the poem, you'll do research to find out more about both of them.

BOOKER T. WASHINGTON	W.E.B. DU BOIS

ANALYZE POETIC ELEMENTS

Most poets try to create word pictures in their poems that help readers see, hear, feel, smell, and even taste the experiences they present. Such word pictures are called **imagery**. The imagery in a poem can help to describe things and to convey the feeling of the poem. When you read poems, pay attention to the how the poet's use of imagery affects you as a reader.

Underline the imagery that appeals to your sense of hearing in this excerpt from Edgar Allen Poe's poem "The Raven."

> Once upon a midnight dreary, while I pondered, weak and weary,
> Over many a quaint and curious volume of forgotten lore—
> While I nodded, nearly napping, suddenly there came a tapping,
> As of some one gently rapping, rapping at my chamber door.
> "'Tis some visitor," I muttered, "tapping at my chamber door—
> Only this and nothing more."

GENRE ELEMENTS: POETRY

- includes imagery that appeals to the senses
- includes sound devices such as rhyme, alliteration, assonance, consonance, and repetition
- creates a mood
- expresses a theme, or message about life

© Houghton Mifflin Harcourt Publishing Company

ANALYZE POETIC LANGUAGE

"Booker T. and W.E.B." is an imaginary debate between two early leaders of the African American community. The leaders' conflicting perspectives are revealed through dialogue, as they attempt to change each other's mind. To this end, they employ several techniques to argue their points.

Diction includes the poet's choice of words as well as syntax—the way of arranging words in sentences. Diction may be formal or informal. Readers should pay close attention to a poet's word choice and syntax, and notice the mood and tone they create.

An **idiom** is an expression whose meaning differs from the actual meaning of the words. "Bought the farm" is an idiom that means someone has died.

Understatement is the technique of deliberately making a subject seem less important that it really is. Using understatement, a topic or idea is described with less force than expected. Understatement can allow an interaction to remain polite, despite the intensity of the disagreement.

As you read, use the chart to record examples of diction, idiom, and understatement. Think about how these techniques affect the tone, or attitude, of each speaker. Note connotations of each speaker's word choices.

DEVICES	EXAMPLES AND EFFECTS
diction	
idiom	
understatement	

ANNOTATION

NOTICE & NOTE

As you read, note each speaker's diction and use of idiom and understatement. This model shows a reader's notes about the first stanza of "Booker T. and W.E.B."

"It seems to me," said Booker T.,

"It shows a mighty lot of cheek

To study chemistry and Greek

When Mister Charlie needs a hand

To hoe the cotton on his land,

And when Miss Ann looks for a cook,

Why stick your nose inside a book?"

The speaker sounds as if he is being modest by saying "It seems to me." This might be an example of understatement.

He uses idioms like "mighty lot of cheek" to make W.E.B.'s ideas seem wrong-headed.

Why "Mister" Charlie, "Miss" Ann?

BACKGROUND

Dudley Randall *(1914–2000) grew up in Detroit, Michigan. In 1981, he was named poet laureate of Detroit. In this poem, Randall depicts the title characters' clash over the path to equality for African Americans. Booker T. Washington believed that African Americans should work hard and save money to earn the equality they deserved. W.E.B. Du Bois advocated agitation and protest to demand equal treatment. Their dispute split the black community into a "conservative" side that supported Washington and a "radical" side that supported Du Bois.*

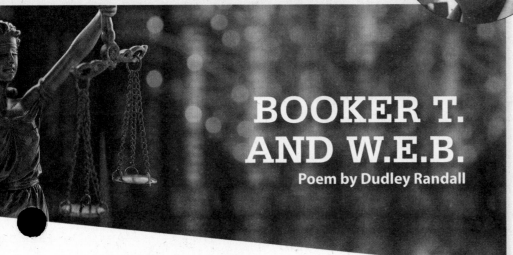

BOOKER T. AND W.E.B.
Poem by Dudley Randall

SETTING A PURPOSE

As you read, pay attention to the way the speakers talk to each other and argue their points.

(*Booker T. Washington and W.E.B. Du Bois*)
"It seems to me," said Booker T.,
"It shows a mighty lot of cheek[1]
To study chemistry and Greek
When Mister Charlie needs a hand
5　To hoe the cotton on his land,
And when Miss Ann looks for a cook,
Why stick your nose inside a book?"

"I don't agree," said W.E.B.,
"If I should have the drive to seek
10　Knowledge of chemistry or Greek,
I'll do it. Charles and Miss can look
Another place for hand or cook.

---

[1] **cheek:** rude or impertinent boldness; disrespect.

© Houghton Mifflin Harcourt Publishing Company • Image Credits: (t) ©Detroit Free Press/ZUMA Press Inc/Alamy; (c) ©utah778/iStock/Getty Images Plus/Getty Images

Notice & Note

You can use the side margins to notice and note signposts in the text.

ANALYZE POETIC LANGUAGE

Annotate: In line 11, mark the way W.E.B. refers to the people Booker T. calls "Mister Charlie" and "Miss Ann" in the first stanza.

Interpret: Why do the two men refer to these people in different ways? What does this reveal about the men and the way they see themselves in relation to Charles and Ann?

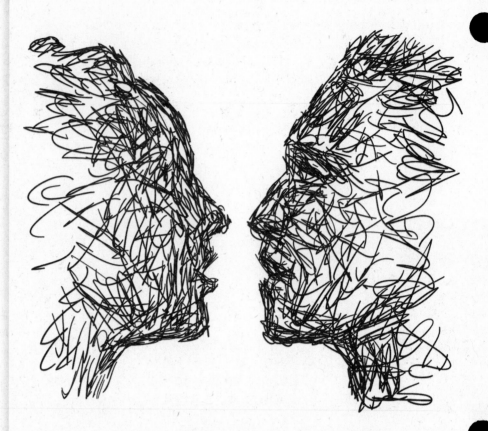

Some men rejoice in skill of hand,
And some in cultivating land,
15 But there are others who maintain
The right to cultivate the brain."

"It seems to me," said Booker T.,
"That all you folks have missed the boat
Who shout about the right to vote,
20 And spend vain days and sleepless nights
In uproar over civil rights.
Just keep your mouths shut, do not grouse,
But work, and save, and buy a house."

ANALYZE POETIC ELEMENTS

Annotate: Mark examples of imagery in lines 24-32.

Interpret: What sense or senses does the imagery appeal to? What ideas does it emphasize?

"I don't agree," said W.E.B.,
25 "For what can property avail
If dignity and justice fail?
Unless you help to make the laws,
They'll steal your house with trumped-up clause.
A rope's as tight, a fire as hot,
30 No matter how much cash you've got.
Speak soft, and try your little plan,

But as for me, I'll be a man."

"It seems to me," said Booker T.—

"I don't agree,"
35 Said W.E.B.

CHECK YOUR UNDERSTANDING

Answer these questions before moving on to the **Analyze the Text** section on the following page.

1 In the lines *Charles and Miss can look / Another place for hand or cook*, the word *hand* means —

   A applause

   B driver

   C laborer

   D ability

2 At the end of line 22, the word *grouse* means —

   F look for clues; investigate

   G ground-dwelling bird

   H complain; grumble

   J ability or talent

3 Which is the most accurate paraphrase of W.E.B. Du Bois's meaning in lines 31–32?

   A You try it your way. I'm going to keep fighting.

   B You are too soft-spoken to win an argument with me.

   C Your quiet approach is a good one. I will take your advice.

   D Your plan is too impractical to be successful.

© Houghton Mifflin Harcourt Publishing Company

ANALYZE THE TEXT

Support your responses with evidence from the text. 📓 NOTEBOOK

1. **Analyze** Reread and paraphrase line 2, focusing on the word *cheek*. What does Booker T.'s choice of that word suggest to you about his opinion of W.E.B.?

2. **Infer** Reread lines 1–7. Who are "Mister Charlie" and "Miss Anne"? How does Booker T. think they should be treated? Does his attitude surprise you? Why or why not?

3. **Infer** Reread lines 8–11. What are some synonyms you could use in place of the word *drive* in line 9? What does W.E.B.'s choice of that word suggest to you about his opinion of Booker T.?

4. **Synthesize** Review the third and fourth stanzas. How do Booker T. and W.E.B.'s views of the fight for civil rights differ? Use evidence from the poem in your answer.

5. **Interpret** What is the effect of the use of rhyme and the repetition of the phrases "It seems to me" and "I don't agree"? What attitude does each phrase convey? How does this highlight the differences between the men? Use evidence from the poem in your answer.

RESEARCH

RESEARCH TIP
When you conduct online research, be sure to evaluate the credibility of websites. Web addresses ending in .gov, .edu, or .org are the work of large groups. Because these sites are frequently reviewed, they are often more reliable and credible than other sites.

Find out more about the views of Booker T. Washington and W.E.B. Du Bois regarding the issues mentioned in the poem. Work with a partner to research their lives, influences, and points of view on those issues. Use what you learn to summarize their views in this chart.

ISSUE	BOOKER T. WASHINGTON	W.E.B. DU BOIS
What the focus of education should be		
What people should strive to achieve		
How best to gain civil rights and political power		

Extend Look for other poems by Dudley Randall and compare their subject matter to "Booker T. and W.E.B." What similarities do you notice? How are the poems different?

CREATE AND DEBATE

Assess the Viewpoints Expand on the chart you used in the research activity to define the pros and cons of each man's position on the issues listed.

- ❏ In your opinion, what are the strengths and weaknesses of each man's position on the issues of education, life goals, and civil rights/political power?
- ❏ How do you think each man would feel about the same issues if he were alive today?
- ❏ Conduct additional research as necessary.

Conduct a Debate Work with your classmates to conduct a team debate on the ideas of Booker T. Washington and W.E.B. Du Bois. Use the ideas and information you gathered and conduct additional research to prepare your arguments. Then hold your debate in front of your class.

- ❏ Speak in a loud, clear voice so everyone can hear and understand you. Use a formal tone and appropriate vocabulary.
- ❏ Stand up straight and make eye contact with your opponents and your audience. Use facial expressions and natural gestures to add emphasis to your words.
- ❏ Use evidence from your research to support your arguments. Adjust your views in light of persuasive evidence from your classmates.
- ❏ Listen actively while others are speaking, and don't interrupt.
- ❏ Evaluate your preparation for and participation in the debate.

Go to the **Speaking and Listening Studio** for more on giving a presentation.

RESPOND TO THE ESSENTIAL QUESTION

 How do people find freedom in the midst of oppression?

Gather Information Review your annotations and notes on "Booker T. and W.E.B." Then add relevant information to your Response Log. As you determine which information to include, think about:

- What are some different paths to gaining freedom and equality?
- What are the effects of oppression?
- Must we change within ourselves before we can change society?

At the end of the unit, use your notes to help you write a research report.

UNIT 2 RESPONSE LOG

Use this Response Log to record your ideas about how each of the texts in Unit 2 relate to or comments on the **Essential Question.**

? Essential Question: How do people find freedom in the midst of oppression?

I Have a Dream	
Interview with John Lewis	
From Hidden Figures	
The Censors	
Booker T. and W.E.B.	
from Reading Lolita in Tehran	
from Persepolis 2: The Story of a Return	

R2 Student Resource

ACADEMIC VOCABULARY

As you write and discuss what you learned from the poem, be sure to use the Academic Vocabulary words. Check off each of the words that you use.

- ❏ **decline**
- ❏ **enable**
- ❏ **impose**
- ❏ **integrate**
- ❏ **reveal**

© Houghton Mifflin Publishing Company

MEMOIR

from

READING LOLITA IN TEHRAN

by **Azar Nafisi**

pages 139–141

COMPARE ACROSS GENRES

As you read, notice the presentations of the two texts, as well as how these two different genres help the authors share their personal stories. Then, look for ways that the ideas in the two texts relate to each other. After you read both selections, you will collaborate with a small group on a final project.

? **ESSENTIAL QUESTION:**

How do people find freedom in the midst of oppression?

GRAPHIC MEMOIR

from

PERSEPOLIS 2: THE STORY OF A RETURN

by **Marjane Satrapi**

translated by Anjali Singh

pages 149–151

from **Reading Lolita in Tehran**

QUICK START

Throughout history and across cultures, women have experienced different treatment and faced different social expectations than men. With a group, discuss ways that males and females are treated differently in your culture.

ANALYZE RHETORICAL DEVICES

Azar Nafisi uses rhetorical questions to engage the audience and to make a point. **Rhetorical questions** are questions that do not require or expect an answer. Depending on the context, they are often posed for dramatic effect. For example:

RHETORICAL QUESTION FROM SELECTION	MEANING
How can I create this other world outside the room?	Nafisi uses the rhetorical question as an opener to explain why she creates an imaginary scene involving Sanaz.
Does she compare her own situation with her mother's when she was the same age?	The question engages readers and invites them to consider any background knowledge they have about Iran's history.
Is she aware, Sanaz, of her own power?	Nafisi uses the rhetorical question to provide dramatic effect and to give meaning to the questions that follow.

ANALYZE SETTING AND PURPOSE

The setting and purpose of a text reveal important information. As you analyze the effect of setting and purpose on *Reading Lolita in Tehran*, consider:

- **Setting:** The **setting** is where a text occurs. Iran requires women to live according to a specific set of laws that govern their dress and behavior.
- **Purpose:** The **purpose** reflects why an author wrote a text—what she hopes to communicate. In *Reading Lolita in Tehran*, Nafisi discusses how she taught a small group of women in her home in Tehran after she stopped teaching at an Iranian university.
- **Author's point of view:** The **author's point of view** is how an author thinks or feels about a subject. Azar Nafisi wrote her book after she left Iran to live abroad. Her perspective as a woman and scholar who had once lived under an oppressive regime influences how she approaches the topic and constructs the text.

Setting, purpose, and point of view all help shape the **main idea**, or message the author wants to convey. As you read the excerpt from *Reading Lolita in Tehran*, note how the writer uses the setting and point of view to accomplish her purpose and convey her feelings about her experiences.

**GENRE ELEMENTS:
MEMOIR**

- records actual events based on the writer's observations
- dependent on the author's point of view
- looks back at specific event or series of events
- shares the author's feelings and what she has learned

CRITICAL VOCABULARY

segregate	allocate	irrelevant	convert

To preview the Critical Vocabulary words, replace each boldfaced word with a different word or words that have the same meaning.

1. Be sure to (**segregate**) _____ the different types of recycling into different waste containers.

2. The school decided to (**allocate**) _____ some money to buy a new playground swing set.

3. She revised her paragraph to remove any (**irrelevant**) _____ details.

4. We are free to keep our religious beliefs and not (**convert**) _____ to another way of thinking.

LANGUAGE CONVENTIONS: VERB TENSE

In her memoir, Nafisi alternates between past and present tense, using each in a consistent way.

When she uses present tense, as in, "Let's imagine one of the girls, say Sanaz, leaving my house . . ." she focuses the reader's attention on the thoughts and feelings of that one student. When Nafisi uses past tense, as in, "They were never free of the regime's definition of them as Muslim women," she is reflecting more generally on the events and atmosphere of Iran.

As you read the excerpt from *Reading Lolita in Tehran*, watch for ways the author uses present and past tense verbs.

ANNOTATION MODEL

NOTICE & NOTE

Here are one student's annotations about setting and purpose.

from **Reading Lolita in Tehran**

How can I create this other world outside the room? I have no choice but to appeal once again to your imagination. Let's imagine one of the girls, say Sanaz, leaving my house and let us follow her from there to her final destination. She says her good-byes and puts on her black robe and scarf over her orange shirt and jeans, coiling her scarf around her neck to cover her huge gold earrings.

> The first sentence shows that the author's purpose for writing is to describe what life is like for Iranian women outside her study group.

> The phrase "black robe and scarf" tells me that the text is set somewhere where women must completely cover themselves when outside.

BACKGROUND

The Iranian Revolution in the late 1970s resulted in the overthrow of the pro-western Shah of Iran. Iranians established a theocracy, or religious government, based on the rule of Islam. The new government passed laws that segregate men and women and that force women to adhere to an Islamic dress code. Iranian women are required to wear veils that cover their hair and neck and coats that cover their arms and legs.

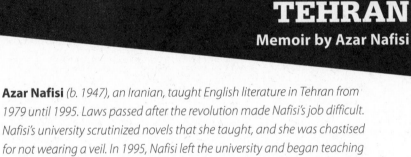

from

READING LOLITA IN TEHRAN

Memoir by Azar Nafisi

Azar Nafisi (b. 1947), an Iranian, taught English literature in Tehran from 1979 until 1995. Laws passed after the revolution made Nafisi's job difficult. Nafisi's university scrutinized novels that she taught, and she was chastised for not wearing a veil. In 1995, Nafisi left the university and began teaching a small group of women in her home, where they were free to discuss books, like Lolita, that were considered unacceptable by Iranian authorities. In 1997, she left Iran for the United States, where she now teaches.

PREPARE TO COMPARE

As you read, make note of the kind of information included in a narrative memoir. You will compare this genre to Persepolis 2, which is in the form of a graphic novel. If you encounter words or ideas you don't understand, ask your classmates or teacher for assistance.

1 How can I create this other world outside the room? I have no choice but to appeal once again to your imagination. Let's imagine one of the girls, say Sanaz, leaving my house and let us follow her from there to her final destination. She says her goodbyes and puts on her black robe and scarf over her orange shirt and jeans, coiling her scarf around her neck to cover her huge gold earrings. She directs wayward strands of hair under the scarf, puts her notes into her large bag, straps it on over her

Notice & Note

You can use the side margins to notice and note signposts in the text.

LANGUAGE CONVENTIONS
Annotate: Underline examples of present tense verbs.

Respond: How do the present tense verbs help you understand the current living conditions of the women?

ANALYZE SETTING AND PURPOSE

Annotate: Mark text evidence that discusses the setting.

Respond: What is the setting for this memoir? What do you think the author's purpose is for writing it?

EXTREME OR ABSOLUTE LANGUAGE

Notice & Note: Mark text that quotes messages conveyed by the culture in which the women live.

Interpret: Why might the author have included these quoted messages?

segregate

(sĕg´rĭ-gāt´) *v.* to cause people to be separated based on gender, race, or other factors.

allocate

(ăl´ə-kāt´) *v.* to assign or designate for.

shoulder and walks out into the hall. She pauses a moment on top of the stairs to put on thin lacy black gloves to hide her nail polish.

2   We follow Sanaz down the stairs, out the door and into the street. You might notice that her gait[1] and her gestures have changed. It is in her best interest not to be seen, not be heard or noticed. She doesn't walk upright, but bends her head towards the ground and doesn't look at passersby. She walks quickly and with a sense of determination. The streets of Tehran and other Iranian cities are patrolled by militia, who ride in white Toyota patrols, four gun-carrying men and women, sometimes followed by a minibus. They are called the Blood of God. They patrol the streets to make sure that women like Sanaz wear their veils properly, do not wear makeup, do not walk in public with men who are not their fathers, brothers or husbands. She will pass slogans on the walls, quotations from Khomeini[2] and a group called the Party of God: MEN WHO WEAR TIES ARE U.S. LACKEYS.[3] VEILING IS A WOMAN'S PROTECTION. Beside the slogan is a charcoal drawing of a woman: her face is featureless and framed by a dark chador.[4] MY SISTER, GUARD YOUR VEIL. MY BROTHER, GUARD YOUR EYES.

3   If she gets on a bus, the seating is **segregated**. She must enter through the rear door and sit in the back seats, **allocated** to women. Yet in taxis, which accept as many as five passengers, men and women are squeezed together like sardines, as the saying goes, and the same goes with minibuses, where so many of my students complain of being harassed by bearded and God-fearing men.

4   You might well ask, What is Sanaz thinking as she walks the streets of Tehran? How much does this experience affect her? Most probably, she tries to distance her mind as much as possible from her surroundings. Perhaps she is thinking of her brother, or of her distant boyfriend and the time when she will meet him in Turkey. Does she compare her own situation with her mother's when she was the same age? Is she angry that women of her mother's generation could walk the streets freely, enjoy the company of the opposite sex, join the police force, become pilots, live under laws that were among the most progressive in the world regarding women? Does she feel humiliated by the new laws, by the fact that after the revolution, the age of marriage was lowered from eighteen to nine, that stoning became once more the punishment for adultery and prostitution?

5   In the course of nearly two decades, the streets have been turned into a war zone, where young women who disobey the rules are hurled into patrol cars, taken to jail, flogged, fined, forced to wash the toilets and humiliated, and as soon as they leave, they go back

---

[1] **gait:** manner of walking.

[2] **Khomeini** (kō-mā´ nē): Ruhollah Khomeini (1902–1989), religious and political leader of Iran after the 1979 revolution.

[3] **U.S. lackeys:** people who serve United States policies. The Iranian government is hostile to the U.S. because it supported the former Shah of Iran.

[4] **chador** (chə´-dər): a long scarf that covers a Muslim woman's hair, neck, and shoulders.

and do the same thing. Is she aware, Sanaz, of her own power? Does she realize how dangerous she can be when her every stray gesture is a disturbance to public safety? Does she think how vulnerable the Revolutionary Guards are who for over eighteen years have patrolled the streets of Tehran and have had to endure young women like herself, and those of other generations, walking, talking, showing a strand of hair just to remind them that they have not **converted**?

6   We have reached Sanaz's house, where we will leave her on her doorstep, perhaps to confront her brother on the other side and to think in her heart of her boyfriend.

7   These girls, my girls, had both a real history and a fabricated one. Although they came from very different backgrounds, the regime that ruled them had tried to make their personal identities and histories **irrelevant**. They were never free of the regime's definition of them as Muslim women.

NOTICE & NOTE

ANALYZE RHETORICAL DEVICES

Annotate: Mark the rhetorical questions in paragraph 5.

Respond: What is the effect of these questions?

convert

(kən-vûrt´) v. to change one's system of beliefs.

irrelevant

(ĭr-rĕl´ə-vənt) adj. insignificant, unimportant.

CHECK YOUR UNDERSTANDING

Answer these questions before moving on to the **Analyze the Text** section on the following page.

1 This passage is mostly about —

   A the author's opinion of universities in Iran

   B the author's experience with her daughters

   C the author's opinion of the government of Iran

   D the author's experience with a female literature group

2 How does the genre of this selection allow the author to share her point of view?

   F In this informational text, the author notes specific facts about Iran.

   G In this memoir, the author shares her observations of situations she experienced in Iran.

   H In this informational text, the author provides her opinion about Iran.

   J In this memoir, the author tells a story based on historical events.

3 In the first paragraph, the description of Sanaz tells you that she —

   A openly disobeys laws governing how women in Iran must dress

   B has more freedom in how she dresses than other women in Iran

   C is interested in fashion even though she has to cover herself

   D is more concerned with what people think of her than she is with following the laws governing women

© Houghton Mifflin Harcourt Publishing Company

ANALYZE THE TEXT

Support your responses with evidence from the text. NOTEBOOK

1. **Infer** This excerpt opens with a clue to the author's purpose. What is it? How does she use details of setting to achieve her purpose? Cite text evidence in your response.

2. **Analyze** Why might Iranian authorities have imposed such stringent laws on women?

3. **Conclude** What can you determine about how Sanaz and the other women in the literature group cope with the laws about their behavior and appearance?

4. **Notice & Note** Nafisi repeatedly uses rhetorical questions. How are they effective in conveying her point of view? Explain with evidence from the text.

RESEARCH

RESEARCH TIP
Be sure to check the websites you use to ensure that they are reliable and credible sources of information. Sites of well-known news organizations are a good place to start, and sites with the suffix *.org* tend to be more reliable than commercial sites.

Find out more about how the Iranian government and society has or has not changed since 2003, when Nafisi's memoir was written. Research modern Iranian politics, society, and culture based on information from two or three reliable websites. Keep track of your sources in a chart like the one shown. Remember to use quotation marks around text taken word-for-word from your sources.

TITLE	URL/ SOURCE	PARAPHRASED OR QUOTED INFORMATION

Connect What generalizations can you make about how Iranian government and society have changed since 2003? Discuss in a small group.

CREATE AND PRESENT

Create a Podcast With a partner, use what you've learned from this memoir and your research to create a podcast about Iran today.

❏ Start with an attention-getting anecdote.

❏ Present specific information about Iranian government and society. Support these statements with evidence you cited from your research.

❏ End with a summary of the information.

Present to a Small Group Take turns playing your podcast for your group and listening to others' podcasts.

Write a summary of what you have learned about modern-day Iranian society. Then reflect on what you have learned in order to answer these questions:

❏ In what ways do Iranian women today respond to the restrictions put on them?

❏ How do you think you would respond if the United States experienced societal change as dramatic as Iran's?

Go to the **Speaking and Listening Studio** for help using media in a presentation.

RESPOND TO THE ESSENTIAL QUESTION

? How do people find freedom in the midst of oppression?

Gather Information Review your annotations and notes on *Reading Lolita in Tehran* and highlight those that help answer the Essential Question. Then, add relevant details to your Response Log.

ACADEMIC VOCABULARY

As you write and discuss what you learned from the memoir *Reading Lolita in Tehran*, be sure to use the Academic Vocabulary words. Check off each of the words that you use.

❏ **decline**

❏ **enable**

❏ **impose**

❏ **integrate**

❏ **reveal**

WORD BANK

segregate

allocate

irrelevant

convert

Go to the **Vocabulary Studio** for more on denotative and connotative meanings.

CRITICAL VOCABULARY

Practice and Apply   Use your understanding of the Critical Vocabulary words to answer the following questions.

1. Are your friends' opinions ever **irrelevant**? Explain.

2. If your job were to **allocate** money to the clubs or sports teams at school, how would you do it?

3. Why might you **segregate** children according to age?

4. Is someone who believes fiercely in something likely to **convert**? Explain.

VOCABULARY STRATEGY:
Denotative and Connotative Meanings

A word's denotation is its strict dictionary definition. But many words have slight nuances or differences in meaning. These nuances, or connotations, have associated meanings and emotions. Nafisi explains that in Iran, the buses are segregated. The Critical Vocabulary word segregate has a similar denotation to the word separate. They both mean "to set apart." But the word segregate has an altogether different connotation. To segregate suggests separating people or things forcefully, often in an unfair way.

Practice and Apply: For each Critical Vocabulary word below, write the word's denotation. Then write the connotation of the word as it appears in the story.

VOCABULARY WORD	DENOTATION	CONNOTATION
allocate		
irrelevant		
convert		

LANGUAGE CONVENTIONS:
Verb Tense

In her memoir, Nafisi alternates between past and present tense, using each tense in a consistent way. When she uses **present tense**, Nafisi refers the reader to the actions taking place in the women's literature group, as if they are currently taking place. When the author uses **past tense**, she reflects on her time with the women, as well as on the events and atmosphere of Iran.

She <u>doesn't</u> walk upright, but <u>bends</u> her head towards the ground and <u>doesn't</u> look at passersby.	By using present tense as if the actions are currently taking place, the author creates a more vivid, immediate picture of her students.

These girls, my girls, <u>had</u> both a real history and a fabricated one.	By using past tense, the author reflects on the women in the literature group.

Practice and Apply Locate two additional sentences that use present tense verbs and two additional sentences that use past tense verbs. Write the sentences and describe how the author uses the verb tenses to make her point.

PRESENT TENSE	EFFECT OF THE VERB TENSE
1.	
2.	

PAST TENSE	EFFECT OF THE VERB TENSE
1.	
2.	

© Houghton Mifflin Harcourt Publishing Company

GRAPHIC MEMOIR

from
PERSEPOLIS 2 : THE STORY OF A RETURN

by **Marjane Satrapi**
translated by Anjali Singh
pages 149–151

COMPARE ACROSS GENRES

Now that you've read the excerpt from *Reading Lolita in Tehran*, read the excerpt from *Persepolis 2* and explore how this graphic memoir connects to some of the same ideas. As you read, think about how the graphic novel genre helps the author of *Persepolis 2* tell her personal story. After you are finished, you will collaborate with a small group on a final project that involves an analysis of both texts.

? **ESSENTIAL QUESTION:**

How do people find freedom in the midst of oppression?

MEMOIR

from
READING LOLITA IN TEHRAN

by **Azar Nafisi**
pages 139–141

from **Persepolis 2: The Story of a Return**

QUICK START

Throughout history, people have found ways to advocate for change. Whether it is students hoping to see change in their schools or citizens protesting against their governments, people possess the capability to effect change. With a group, discuss ways that people have protested against injustice throughout history.

ANALYZE MULTIMODAL TEXTS

Authors choose a format that tells their personal story in a compelling way. Different formats emphasize details that help to tell the story. The challenge for readers or viewers is to determine which details are emphasized and how those details convey the author's message.

A **graphic novel** tells a story or conveys information in a series of frames that show action, along with narrative text and the characters' words. In graphic novels, both words and images work together to convey the work's meaning and to advance the author's point of view, or how he or she feels about a subject. Where a comic book tells a continuing story over a series of issues that are published over time, perhaps once a month or four issues over the course of a year, a graphic novel tells a stand-alone story that is usually bound as a single book. Graphic novels also tend to be longer than comic books.

Graphic novels can be fiction, such as historical fiction, realistic fiction, and science fiction; nonfiction, such as history or informational text; fantasy; and many other types.

© Houghton Mifflin Harcourt Publishing Company

**GENRE ELEMENTS:
GRAPHIC NOVEL**

- uses sequential art to tell a story in different panels
- content can be fiction or nonfiction
- text appears in captions and in dialogue and thought balloons

MAIN TYPES OF GRAPHIC NOVELS	
Manga	Manga is read from top to bottom and right to left, a traditional Japanese reading pattern
Personal Narratives	Autobiographical stories that tell about the author's experiences and observations
Nonfiction	Similar to a personal narrative, but the author tells a personal story to call attention to a social issue or cause

As you read this excerpt from *Persepolis 2,* notice how Marjane Satrapi tells her story through words and stark black and white images. In this excerpt, the author's perspective as a young woman out of place in a rigid and uncompromising society is reflected in the way the main character's face is drawn. It is also shown in panels revealing her thoughts and interactions with others.

EVALUATE PRINT AND GRAPHIC FEATURES

In graphic novels, authors integrate print and graphic features to achieve their purpose for writing. **Print features** help readers pay attention to important words. **Graphic features** help readers visualize or make pictures in their minds. Words or images alone do not fully communicate the author's message in a graphic novel.

PRINT FEATURES	GRAPHIC FEATURES
large print	illustrations
bold print	graphs
italics	maps
underlining	photographs
font size	charts/tables
font type	sketches
colored print	drawings
quotation marks	cartoons
punctuation	pictures

Careful readers must study details in the drawings, as well as read the captions, speech bubbles, and thought balloons, to understand the author's point of view.

Graphic novel authors may represent text in different ways.

- **Speech bubbles** show words that the characters are speaking directly.
- **Thought balloons** convey what is going on in characters' minds.
- **Captions** contain the narrative, allowing the author to speak directly to the reader.

As you read the excerpt from *Persepolis 2*, note how words and images work together to convey the author's message.

BACKGROUND

Since the Iranian Revolution of the late 1970s, "morality police" ensure that people comply with the laws in Iran. People who do not comply may be taken to the morality police headquarters to be questioned, beaten, or jailed.

Marjane Satrapi *(b. 1969) was born in Iran. After the revolution, her parents sent her to school in Europe. Later, she studied illustration. Persepolis 1 tells the story of Satrapi's childhood in Iran, and Persepolis 2 tells the story of her adolescence in Europe and Iran and of her struggle to fit in. Persepolis, a movie based on both books, has won many awards. Satrapi lives in Paris.*

from PERSEPOLIS 2:
THE STORY OF A RETURN
Graphic Novel by Marjane Satrapi
translated by Anjali Singh

PREPARE TO COMPARE

As you read, pay attention to how the author uses graphic novel elements to tell her personal story. Look for ways that Satrapi's story is similar to and different from that of Azar Nafisi. Write down any questions you generate as you read.

Notice & Note

You can use the side margins to notice and note signposts in the text.

ANALYZE MULTIMODAL TEXTS

Annotate: Make a checkmark on a panel in which emotion is shown.

Respond: How does the image pair with the words to convey the author's emotion about her experiences?

CONTRASTS & CONTRADICTIONS

Notice & Note: Mark with a star a panel that contradicts your view of how you would expect the world to be.

Interpret: Why might the author have presented you with this information?

EVALUATE PRINT AND GRAPHIC FEATURES

Annotate: Circle a speech bubble and underline a caption.

Respond: How do the speech bubble and the caption convey different types of information?

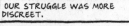

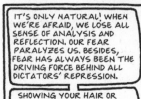

CHECK YOUR UNDERSTANDING

Answer these questions before moving on to the **Analyze the Text** section on the following page.

1 This passage is mostly about —

   A how women tried to escape from Iran

   B how women tried to educate themselves in Iran

   C how women rebelled against oppression in Iran

   D how women sought to overthrow the government of Iran

2 How does the presentation of the text allow the author to share her point of view?

   F The realistic fiction text tells how life has changed for the author.

   G The informational text provides the reader with facts about life in Iran.

   H The graphic novel format allows the reader to learn about Iran's cultural history.

   J The graphic novel format allows the reader to visually see and read about the author's experiences.

3 How does the caption in the second panel add to the reader's understanding of the text?

   A The factual information in the caption explains why the revolution occurred.

   B The factual information in the caption provides historical background for the text.

   C The opinions in the caption help explain the author's point of view.

   D The opinions in the caption help explain why people demonstrated against the government.

ANALYZE THE TEXT

Support your responses with evidence from the text. ⬜ NOTEBOOK

1. **Infer** How does the main character in the text feel about any power she may possess? Does she feel powerful or powerless? Why?

2. **Analyze** Look at the second and third panels in the text. How does the author use both words and graphics to make a point about how the people's struggle has changed?

3. **Infer** The narrator says that she spent an entire day at the committee because of a pair of red socks. What might red socks have **symbolized**, or represented, to the committee?

4. **Interpret** The narrator's facial expression remains the same in each of the panels. How would you describe it? How does this visual consistency help reveal the author's point of view?

5. **Notice & Note** Reread the last part of the speech bubble in the final panel. What contrast or contradiction points to the author's larger message?

RESEARCH

RESEARCH TIP
It's always easier to begin a research project by creating a research plan. First, identify exactly what you want to learn. Then, think about sources that would be helpful to use.

Graphic novels can convey information about real or fictional events. They can also communicate information about characters' dress, attitude, and emotions. Look at several graphic novels, paying attention to what kinds of information are conveyed by the images alone. For example, images could convey details about the setting, what characters look like, their emotions, plot events, and even theme. Take notes on what kinds of information are included and how they are conveyed.

GRAPHIC NOVEL	INFORMATION AND HOW IT IS CONVEYED

Extend Describe how the graphic novel structure can provide different information about a subject than is possible with a narrative format.

CREATE AND DISCUSS

Write an Argumentative Essay Write a three- to four-paragraph essay in which you address the genre of graphic novels.

❏ Introduce your essay by describing the format of graphic novels.

❏ Then, explain similarities and differences between graphic novels and other narrative formats. Think about how graphic novels are similar to and different from prose texts and plays.

❏ In your final paragraph, state whether you think graphic novels should be considered as important a genre as print-only texts.

Share and Discuss Opinions With a small group, discuss graphic novels as a genre. How do you feel about reading graphic novels? Do you feel that they are an effective way of communicating information? Why or why not?

❏ Review the characteristics of a graphic novel. Discuss how graphic novels differ from comic books.

❏ Then, discuss graphic novels you have read. Note how the graphic novel may or may not have enhanced the author's ability to communicate her story.

❏ Finally, end by recommending a graphic novel and/or noting a graphic novel that you would like to read.

 Go to the **Writing Studio** for more on writing arguments.

Go to the **Speaking and Listening Studio** for help with having a group discussion.

RESPOND TO THE ESSENTIAL QUESTION

 ? How do people find freedom in the midst of oppression?

Gather Information Review your annotations and notes on *Persepolis 2*. Examine how the main character creates freedom for herself in the midst of oppression. Think about the character's actions, motivations, and traits as you respond. Then, add relevant details to your Response Log.

At the end of the unit, use your notes to write a research report.

ACADEMIC VOCABULARY

As you write and discuss what you learned about *Persepolis 2*, be sure to use the Academic Vocabulary words. Check off each of the words that you use.

❏ **decline**

❏ **enable**

❏ **impose**

❏ **integrate**

❏ **reveal**

MEMOIR
from **READING LOLITA IN TEHRAN**
by Azar Nafisi

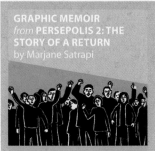

GRAPHIC MEMOIR
from **PERSEPOLIS 2: THE STORY OF A RETURN**
by Marjane Satrapi

Collaborate and Compare

COMPARE ACROSS GENRES

Both *Reading Lolita in Tehran* and *Persepolis* 2 discuss life in Iran following the Iranian Revolution of the 1970s. Even though the texts address a similar topic, they do so using different genres. Both print and graphic novel formats allow the author to communicate her story to the reader, but only one uses illustrations integrated with text.

In a small group, discuss the common elements in the two selections. Take notes in the chart below about the authors' purpose, message, and use of language. On your own, write a few sentences describing your personal reactions to reading about the same general topic in two genres. Which genre did you prefer? Why?

ELEMENTS	READING LOLITA IN TEHRAN	PERSEPOLIS 2
AUTHOR'S PURPOSE		
AUTHOR'S MESSAGE		
USE OF LANGUAGE		

Notes about my reactions to the two selections:

_____

_____

ANALYZE THE TEXTS

Discuss these questions in your group.

1. **Connect** How is the way the authors communicate with readers similar and different in the texts?

2. **Compare** What information is presented in both texts?

3. **Analyze** What is the effect of using language only, as opposed to combining language and images? Are any aspects of the story gained by using images and/or lost by using fewer words in a graphic novel?

4. **Synthesize** What have you learned from these sources together about the status of women in Iran since the Iranian Revolution?

COLLABORATE AND PRESENT

Now your group can continue exploring the ideas in these texts by collaborating to create a graphic novel version of the excerpt from *Reading Lolita in Tehran*. Follow these steps:

1. **Brainstorm** Imagine that Nafisi had written her memoir in the form of a graphic novel. Brainstorm how to recast the selection into a graphic novel. Think about how to create panels to convey the story.

2. **Create Storyboards** Create sequential storyboards to tell Nafisi's story.
   ❏ **Illustrate** the panels with hand-drawn images or with computer-generated images.

   ❏ **Decide** how to use speech bubbles and captions to convey the specific activities of the women's literature group and captions to describe the setting in Iran.

   ❏ **Use** details from the memoir that you think advance the story.

3. **Discuss What You Have Learned** After partners or groups present their graphic novels to the class, discuss how effectively they convey Nafisi's message. Communicate and accept suggestions for improvement in a constructive manner. Think about how your graphic novel conveys the contrasts between what occurs in the women's literature group and what occurs in Iranian society as a whole.

4. **Reflect on Your Work** Evaluate your role in creating the graphic novel and in the group discussion. Jot down notes about your preparation for and participation in this activity. What were your main contributions?

PROJECT TIP
Plan your graphic novel as a group. Then divide the work equally among members of the group.

INDEPENDENT READING

? **ESSENTIAL QUESTION:**

How do people find freedom in the midst of oppression?

Reader's Choice

Setting a Purpose Select one or more of these options from your eBook to continue your exploration of the Essential Question.

- Read the descriptions to see which text grabs your interest.
- Think about which genres you enjoy reading.

Notice & Note

In this unit, you practiced asking **Big Questions** and noticing and noting two signposts: **Extreme or Absolute Language** and **Quoted Words.** As you read independently, these signposts and others will aid your understanding. Below are the anchor questions to ask when you read literature and nonfiction.

Reading Literature: Stories, Poems, and Plays		
Signpost	**Anchor Question**	**Lesson**
Contrasts and Contradictions	Why did the character act that way?	p. 419
Aha Moment	How might this change things?	p. 171
Tough Questions	What does this make me wonder about?	p. 494
Words of the Wiser	What's the lesson for the character?	p. 171
Again and Again	Why might the author keep bringing this up?	p. 170
Memory Moment	Why is this memory important?	p. 418

Reading Nonfiction: Essays, Articles, and Arguments		
Signpost	**Anchor Question(s)**	**Lesson**
Big Questions	What surprised me? What did the author think I already knew? What challenged, changed, or confirmed what I already knew?	p. 248 p. 2 p. 84
Contrasts and Contradictions	What is the difference, and why does it matter?	p. 3
Extreme or Absolute Language	Why did the author use this language?	p. 85
Numbers and Stats	Why did the author use these numbers or amounts?	p. 249
Quoted Words	Why was this person quoted or cited, and what did this add?	p. 85
Word Gaps	Do I know this word from someplace else? Does it seem like technical talk for this topic? Do clues in the sentence help me understand the word?	p. 3

You can preview these texts in Unit 2 of your eBook.

Then, check off the text or texts that you select to read on your own.

POEM

We Wear the Mask
Paul Laurence Dunbar

The poem's speaker conceals great pain under "the mask" that "lies."

SHORT STORY

The Prisoner Who Wore Glasses
Bessie Head

A political prisoner combines cleverness and courage to get the best of a brutal overseer.

HISTORY WRITING

Reforming the World
from **America's Women**
Gail Collins

Middle class women become radicalized as they fight for equality and the right to vote.

AUTOBIOGRAPHY

from **Long Walk to Freedom**
Nelson Mandela

Nelson Mandela shows fearlessness and humility as he devotes his life to ending apartheid in South Africa.

SPEECH

Eulogy for Martin Luther King Jr.
Robert F. Kennedy

Robert Kennedy, as presidential candidate, delivers news that shocks the nation.

Collaborate and Share   Get with a partner to discuss what you learned from at least one of your independent readings.

- Give a brief synopsis or summary of the text.

- Describe any signposts that you noticed in the text and explain what they revealed to you.

- Describe what you most enjoyed or found most challenging about the text. Give specific examples.

- Decide if you would recommend the text to others. Why or why not?

Go to the **Reading Studio** for more resources on **Notice & Note**.

Write a Research Report

Go to the **Writing Studio** for help writing your report.

This unit focuses on how people find freedom in a society that oppresses them. For this writing task, you will write a research report. For a research report, you gather information from a number of different, valid sources about a specific topic and write about what you have discovered. For an example of a well-written research report you can use as a mentor text, review the selection *Hidden Figures*.

As you write your report, you will want to look at the notes you made in your Response Log after reading the texts in this unit. Include words and terms you learned from your research.

Writing Prompt

Read the information in the box below.

This is the general topic or context for your report.

> Throughout history, people in many societies have fought for the freedom and equality they were denied.

Think carefully about the following question.

This is the Essential Question for the unit. How would you answer this question, based on the texts in this unit?

> How do people find freedom in the midst of oppression?

Think about how you will find a specific topic for your report.

Write a research report about one event, or a person or group of people, connected to the struggle for freedom.

Be sure to—

Review these points as you write and again when you finish. Make any needed changes.

❑ research your topic using only valid sources and keep careful notes about your sources

❑ narrow your topic so that it is specific to one event, person, or group of people

❑ write an introduction that catches the reader's attention and clearly states your topic

❑ organize your information in a logical way

❑ connect related ideas effectively

❑ avoid plagiarism by paraphrasing or quoting sources

❑ write a final paragraph that summarizes your information or draws a conclusion

❑ cite your sources correctly at the end of the report

① Plan

Before you begin to write your research report, you need to research the topic of how people have fought for the freedom and equality they were denied. Be sure to use only valid, accurate sources for your research. Check sources for omissions, which may show bias. Also look for faulty reasoning, such as loaded language. While you are researching, narrow the topic to focus on one specific event, person, or group in the struggle for freedom, such as the first African American female doctor and challenges she faced, or Cesar Chavez and the struggle for migrant workers. Develop questions that you would like to answer through your research and write them down. Keep track of the sources you are using so that you can credit them appropriately in your report. When you have enough information, write a thesis statement to express your main idea. You also need to think about the purpose of your report and the audience you are writing it for. Use the chart below to help you organize your research.

Research Report Planning Chart	
Specific Research Topic	
Thesis Statement:	**Source 1:**
	Information:
Source 2:	**Source 3:**
Information:	**Information:**

Go to **Conducting Research: Starting Your Research** for help planning your report.

Notice & Note
From Reading to Writing

As you plan your research report, apply what you've learned about signposts to your own writing. Remember that writers use common features, called signposts, to help convey their message to readers.

Think about how you can incorporate **Quoted Words** into your report.

 Go to the **Reading Studio** for more resources on Notice & Note.

Use the notes from your Response Log as you plan your report.

Background Reading Review the notes you have taken in your Response Log after reading the texts in this unit. These texts provide key ideas that will help you think about what you want to say in your report.

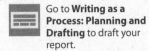

Go to **Writing as a Process: Planning and Drafting** to draft your report.

Organize Your Ideas After you have researched your topic, you need to organize your ideas. In your introduction, you will state your thesis. You will also introduce the event, person, or people you have chosen. The body of your report can be a narrative, told in chronological order. Or it can be several important ideas, supported by details. In your conclusion, you summarize your research. You might include a statement about the overall importance of your topic; or questions that remain unanswered.

Research Report
Introduction
Body Point 1:   Point 2:   Point 3:
Conclusion
Sources

Go online to find examples of documentation that use the MLA or APA style. Choose one style and use it consistently for your sources.

❷ Develop a Draft

Once you have completed your planning activities, you will be ready to begin drafting your research report. Refer to your Graphic Organizer and the outline you have created, as well as any notes you took as you studied the selections in the unit. These will provide a kind of map for you to follow as you write. Use a word processing program or online writing app to make it easier to make changes or move sentences around. Finally, be sure to list your sources at the end of the report using a standard method of documentation such as that of the Modern Language Association (MLA) or the American Psychological Association (APA).

Use the Mentor Text

▶ Author's Craft

A clearly stated thesis makes everything that follows clearer and easier to understand. Look at the way the author states the thesis in *Hidden Figures*.

> . . . in the spring of 1943, with World War II in full swing and many men off serving in the military, the country needed all the help it could get. Employers were beginning to hire women to do jobs that had once belonged only to men.

The author uses dates and other facts to state her thesis clearly and convincingly.

Apply What You've Learned State the thesis of your research report clearly. If you have trouble doing that, you may not have narrowed your topic sufficiently.

▶ Genre Characteristics

One of the most important qualities of a good research report is clearly stated ideas, with precise use of language. Note the way the author explains why Langley needed so many people to do mathematical computations.

> Each of the engineers at the Langley Memorial Aeronautical Laboratory required the support of a number of other workers: craftsmen to build the airplane models, mechanics to maintain the test tunnels, and "number crunchers" to process the data that was collected during the tests.

The author states her idea clearly and completely.

Apply What You've Learned Use precise language to state your ideas as your write your research report. If your language seems vague, try adding more specific details to make it more precise.

3 Revise

Go to **Writing as a Process: Revising and Editing** for help revising your report.

On Your Own Once you have written your draft, you will use the process of revision to turn that draft into an effective piece of writing. The Revision Chart will help you focus on specific elements to make your writing stronger.

REVISION GUIDE		
Ask Yourself	**Tips**	**Revision Techniques**
1. Does my introduction grab the readers' attention?	**Highlight** the introduction.	**Add** an interesting fact, example, or quotation that illustrates the topic.
2. Does my introduction clearly state the thesis?	**Underline** the thesis statement.	**Reword** the thesis statement to make it clearer. If necessary, narrow the topic.
3. Are my main ideas organized in a clear and logical way?	**Highlight** each main idea. **Underline** transitions.	**Reorder** ideas so that each one flows easily to the next. **Add** appropriate transitions to connect ideas and clarify the organization.
4. Do I support each main idea with relevant details?	**Underline** each supporting fact, definition, example, or quotation.	**Add** facts, details, examples, or quotations to support ideas.
5. Do my pronouns consistently agree with their antecedents?	**Underline** any place where pronoun agreement is not clear.	**Change** pronouns to agree with their antecedents.
6. Have I used the correct format to cite information for my sources?	**Highlight** each source of information that you have used.	**Add** any information that you have omitted and correct format errors.

ACADEMIC VOCABULARY

As you conduct your peer review, try to use these words.

- ❑ decline
- ❑ enable
- ❑ impose
- ❑ integrate
- ❑ reveal

With a Partner After you have worked through the Revision Guide on your own, exchange papers with a partner. Evaluate each other's drafts in a **peer review.** Try to see how your partner could better accomplish his or her purpose in writing. Explain how you think your partner's draft should be revised and what your specific suggestions are.

When receiving feedback from your partner, listen carefully and take notes so that you can remember the revision suggestions.

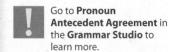

④ Edit

Once you have addressed the organization, development, and flow of ideas in your report, you can look to improve the finer points of your draft. Edit for the proper use of standard English conventions and make sure to correct any misspellings or grammatical errors.

> **!** Go to **Pronoun Antecedent Agreement** in the **Grammar Studio** to learn more.

Language Conventions

Pronoun-Antecedent Agreement An antecedent is the noun to which a pronoun refers. A pronoun must "agree with," or match, its antecedent.

- A **singular pronoun** must replace a singular noun.
- A **plural pronoun** must replace a plural noun.

The chart contains examples of pronoun-antecedent agreement from *Hidden Figures*.

PRONOUN TYPE	EXAMPLE
Singular pronoun	<u>President Franklin D. Roosevelt</u> believed in the importance of air power, so two years earlier, in 1941, <u>he</u> had challenged the <u>nation</u> to increase <u>its</u> production of airplanes to fifty thousand units a year.
Plural pronoun	<u>People</u> working at Langley knew that <u>they</u> were doing <u>their</u> part to win the war.

⑤ Publish

Finalize your report and choose a way to share it with your audience. Consider these options:

- Present your report as a speech to the class.
- Produce your report as a podcast to be posted on a classroom or school website.

Use the scoring guide to evaluate your report.

WRITING TASK SCORING GUIDE: RESEARCH REPORT

	Organization/Progression	Development of Ideas	Use of Language and Conventions
4	• The organization is effective and appropriate to the purpose. • All ideas are focused on the topic specified in the prompt. • Transitions clearly show the relationship among ideas.	• The introduction catches the reader's attention, clearly states the topic. • The report contains a clear and insightful thesis statement. • The topic is well developed with clear main ideas supported by specific and well-chosen facts, details, examples, etc. • The report is based on multiple, valid research sources.	• Language and word choice is purposeful and precise. • Pronouns agree with their antecedents. • Spelling, capitalization, and punctuation are correct. • Grammar, usage, and mechanics are correct. • Research sources are cited correctly using a standard format.
3	• The organization is, for the most part, effective and appropriate to the purpose. • Most ideas are focused on the topic specified in the prompt. • A few more transitions are needed to show the relationship among ideas.	• The introduction could be more engaging. The topic is stated. • The report contains a clear thesis statement. • The development of ideas is clear because the writer uses specific and appropriate facts, details, examples, and quotations. • The report is based on at least two valid research sources.	• Language is for the most part specific and clear. • Pronoun-antecedent agreement is usually clear. • There are some spelling, capitalization, and punctuation mistakes. • Some grammar and usage errors occur. • Research sources are cited with some formatting errors.
2	• The organization is evident but is not always appropriate to the purpose. • Only some ideas are focused on the topic specified in the prompt. • More transitions are needed to show the relationship among ideas.	• The introduction is not engaging. The topic is not clear. • The thesis statement does not express a clear point. • The development of ideas is minimal. The writer uses facts, details, examples, etc. that are inappropriate or ineffectively presented. • The report is based on at least one valid research source.	• Language is somewhat vague and unclear. • There are occasional errors in pronoun-antecedent agreement. • Spelling, capitalization, and punctuation, as well as grammar and usage, are often incorrect but do not make reading difficult. • Research sources are cited using incorrect format.
1	• The organization is not appropriate to the purpose. • Ideas are not focused on the topic specified in the prompt. • No transitions are used, making the report difficult to understand.	• The introduction is missing or confusing. • The thesis statement is missing. • The development of ideas is weak. Supporting facts, details, examples, or quotations are unreliable, vague, or missing. • The report is not based on research sources, or the research sources cited are not valid.	• Language is inappropriate for the text. • Pronouns do not agree with their antecedents. • Many spelling, capitalization, and punctuation errors are present. • Grammatical and usage errors confuse the writer's ideas. • No research sources are cited.

Create a Podcast

You will now adapt your research report as a podcast that your classmates can listen and respond to. You also will listen to their podcasts, ask questions to better understand their ideas, and help them improve their work.

Go to **Using Media in a Presentation** in the **Speaking and Listening Studio** for help planning and crafting your presentation.

① Adapt Your Report as a Podcast

Review your research report, and use the chart below to guide you as you adapt your report and follow instructions for creating a script and effects for your podcast. Ensure that the vocabulary, language, and tone of your podcast are appropriate for your audience. Also, make sure to link your ideas clearly using connecting words to transition smoothly from one idea to the next.

Podcast Planning Chart		
Title and Introduction	How will you revise your title and introduction to capture the listener's attention? Is there a catchier way to state your thesis? Consider putting your thesis in the form of a question that you can then answer.	
Audience	Who is your audience? What information will your audience already know? What information can you exclude? What should you add?	
Effective Language and Organization	Which parts of your report should be simplified? What can you change to strike a more informal voice and tone? Make sure you use standard language conventions so your ideas are clear to listeners.	
Sound	Think about whether you want to begin your podcast with music or sound effects. What kind of music is appropriate to the topic? Are there sound effects you can use that will help you create a mood?	

As you work to improve your podcast and those of your classmates, follow these rules of constructive criticism:

❏ **Accept the other person's purpose and try to help them achieve it.**

❏ **Begin your comments with the strong points of the work.**

❏ **Remember that the best criticism is both kind and truthful.**

② Practice with a Partner or Group

When your script is ready and you've decided on whether to have music and/or sound effects, practice before you record.

Practice Effective Verbal Techniques

❏ **Enunciation** Replace words that you stumble over, and rearrange sentences so that your delivery is smooth.

❏ **Voice Modulation and Register** Change the tone and pitch of your voice (louder, softer, higher, lower) to show enthusiasm and emphasis.

❏ **Speaking Rate** Speak slowly enough that listeners understand you. Pause briefly now and then to let them consider important points.

❏ **Microphone Skills** Practice to see how far your mouth should be from the microphone to record clearly without making distracting noises.

Create Your Podcast

❏ **Recording Location** If your school doesn't have a music practice room or a studio, find a room with as little outside sound as possible.

❏ **Editing** If your school has audio editing software, or if you can download an open source app, use that to clean up the start and finish of your podcast after you have recorded it.

❏ **Music** Find appropriate music free for your podcast from archive.org or the Library of Congress music collection. You can also use music from your own collection as long as you use it only for this school assignment.

❏ **Sound Effects** You can download free sound effects from many different sites online.

Provide and Consider Advice for Improvement

As an audience, listen closely to the podcast. Evaluate its impact, purpose, point of view, and any rhetorical devices used. Take notes about ways that podcasters can improve their presentations and more effectively present their ideas. Paraphrase and summarize each presenter's key ideas and main points to confirm your understanding and ask questions to clarify any confusing ideas.

As a podcaster, pay attention to feedback and consider ways to improve your podcast to make it more effective. Remember to ask for suggestions about your music and sound effects, if you chose to use them.

③ Post Your Podcast

Use the advice you received during practice to make final changes to your podcast. Then, make it available to your classmates.

Reflect on the Unit

As you were planning your research report, you reviewed your thoughts about the reading you have done in this unit. Now is a good time to reflect on what you have learned.

Reflect on the Essential Question

- How do people find freedom in the midst of oppression? How has your answer to this question changed since you first considered it when you started this unit?

- What are some examples from the texts you've read that show how people find freedom?

Reflect on Your Reading

- Which selections were the most interesting or surprising to you?

- From which selection did you learn the most about finding freedom in the midst of oppression?

Reflect on the Writing Task

- What difficulties did you encounter while working on your research report? How might you avoid them next time?

- What part of the report was the easiest and hardest to write? Why?

- What improvements did you make to your report as you were revising?

- What changes did you need to make to your report to make it work as a podcast?

UNIT 2 SELECTIONS
- "I Have a Dream"
- "Interview with John Lewis"
- from *Hidden Figures*
- "The Censors"
- "Booker T. and W.E.B."
- from *Reading Lolita in Tehran*
- from *Persepolis 2: The Story of a Return*

THE BONDS BETWEEN US

? *ESSENTIAL QUESTION:*

How do we form and maintain our connections with others?

> **The welfare of each of us is dependent fundamentally upon the welfare of all of us.**
>
> Theodore Roosevelt

ACADEMIC VOCABULARY

Academic Vocabulary words are words you use when you discuss and write about texts. In this unit, you will practice and learn five words.

☑ **capacity** ☐ **confer** ☐ **emerge** ☐ **generate** ☐ **trace**

Study the Word Network to learn more about the word **capacity**.

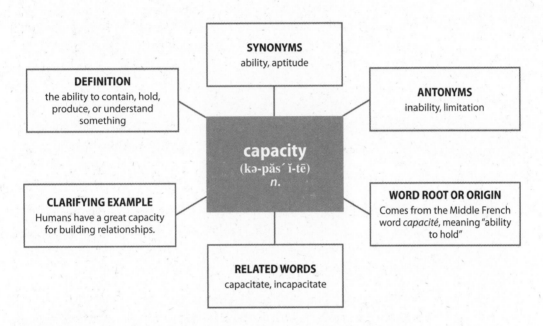

SYNONYMS
ability, aptitude

DEFINITION
the ability to contain, hold, produce, or understand something

ANTONYMS
inability, limitation

capacity
(kə-păs´ ĭ-tē)
n.

CLARIFYING EXAMPLE
Humans have a great capacity for building relationships.

WORD ROOT OR ORIGIN
Comes from the Middle French word *capacité*, meaning "ability to hold"

RELATED WORDS
capacitate, incapacitate

Write and Discuss Discuss the completed Word Network with a partner, making sure to talk through all of the boxes until you both understand the word, its synonyms, antonyms, and related forms. Then, fill out a Word Network for each of the remaining four words. Use a dictionary or online resource to help you complete the activity.

 Go online to access the Word Networks.

RESPOND TO THE ESSENTIAL QUESTION

In this unit, you will read various genres that explore what links us to family, friends, pets, and community. As you read, you will revisit the **Essential Question** and gather your ideas about it in the **Response Log** that appears on page R3. At the end of the unit, you will have the opportunity to write a **short story** about interpersonal connections. Filling out the Response Log will help you prepare for this writing task.

 You can also go online to access the Response Log.

UNIT 3 RESPONSE LOG

Use this Response Log to record your ideas about how each of the texts in Unit 3 relates to or comments on the **Essential Question.**

? Essential Question:
How do we form and maintain our connections with others?

The Grasshopper and the Bell Cricket	
Monkey See, Monkey Do, Monkey Connect	
With Friends Like These . . .	
AmeriCorps NCCC: Be the Greater Good	
Loser	
At Dusk	

Notice & Note

For more information on these and other signposts to Notice & Note, visit the **Reading Studio**.

THE GRASSHOPPER AND THE BELL CRICKET

You are about to read the short story "The Grasshopper and the Bell Cricket." In it, you will notice and note signposts that provide clues about the story's setting and themes. Here are three key signposts to look for as you read this short story and other works of fiction.

When you see a word or phrase repeated several times in a text, pause to see if it is an **Again and Again**.

Again and Again Have you ever been reading a story when you begin to notice that a word, an event, or an image keeps popping up over and over? This isn't an accident or an oversight by the author. Pay attention—the author is trying to tell you something.

When a word, image or event in a story comes up **Again and Again**, you know it's important, but you might not immediately know *why* it's important. The repetition might give you clues about characters or setting, foreshadow an important event, or help you to understand the story's themes.

The paragraphs below illustrate a student's annotation within "The Grasshopper and the Bell Cricket" and a response to a Notice & Note signpost.

Anchor Question
When you notice this signpost, ask: *Why might the author keep bringing this up?*

> "Does anyone want a grasshopper?" A boy . . . suddenly straightened up and shouted . . . .
> "Does anyone want a grasshopper? A grasshopper!"
> "I do! I do!" Four or five more children came running up . . . . The boy called out a third time.
> "Doesn't anyone want a grasshopper?"
> Two or three more children came over.
> "Yes. I want it."
> It was a girl . . . The boy . . . thrust out his fist that held the insect at the girl.

What words are repeated?	"anyone want a grasshopper?"
What is the significance of the repetition?	The boy repeats his offer until the girl, the one he really wants to give the grasshopper to, says she'd like to have it.

Aha Moment Here's a familiar story: a detective snoops around and asks questions in order to solve a murder mystery. Using intuition and keen intelligence, the detective combs through the clues until they all fall into place and suddenly--aha! —mystery solved!

A character experiencing an **Aha Moment** may:

- reach a broader understanding about something or someone
- discover a way to resolve a conflict or problem
- soon begin to think or act differently

Read this part of "The Grasshopper and the Bell Cricket" to see a student's annotation of an Aha Moment:

> 21   By the light of his . . . lantern . . . [the boy] glanced at the girl's face.
>
> 22   Oh, I thought . . . How silly of me not to have understood his actions until now!

When you see phrases like these, pause to see whether it's an **Aha Moment**:

"All of a sudden…"

"for the first time…"

"and just like that…"

"I realized…"

Anchor Question
When you notice this signpost, ask: *How might this change things?*

What words tell you that something has changed?	Oh, I thought...How silly of me not to have understood his actions until now.
What might this realization tell you about the characters?	The boy likes the girl.

Words of the Wiser In this situation, a wiser character—who is often older—offers insight or advice about life to the main character. This insight comes from having life experiences that the main character has yet to have. The advice often suggests a theme. Here's an example of a student finding and marking an instance of **Words of the Wiser**:

> 25   Even if you have the wit to look by yourself in a bush away from the other children, there are not many bell crickets in the world. Probably you will find a girl like a grasshopper whom you think is a bell cricket.

When you see a phrase like this, pause to see if it is a **Words of the Wiser**:

"I have learned over the years . . ."

"I now realize . . ."

Anchor Question
When you notice this signpost, ask: *What's the lesson for the character?*

What kind of advice is the wiser character giving Fujio?	The wiser character is advising Fujio that there are only a few people in the world who will be special to him.
What's the life lesson?	The lesson is to seek people who capture your heart.

© Houghton Mifflin Harcourt Publishing Company

THE GRASSHOPPER AND THE BELL CRICKET

Short Story by **Yasunari Kawabata**

translated by Lane Dunlop and J. Martin Holman

© Houghton Mifflin Harcourt Publishing Company • Image Credits: ©allnow/Shutterstock

? **ESSENTIAL QUESTION:**

How do we form and maintain our connections with others?

QUICK START

Nature is all around you. Every day, you experience nature in many ways—by feeling the sun on your face or the wind in your hair, or by smelling the ocean air. Take a moment to list the elements of nature you encounter each day and how they affect you. Then turn to a partner and share your thoughts.

ANALYZE SETTING AND THEME

The time and place of a short story's action is the setting. **Setting** can also include the social and cultural environment in which the action of the story takes place. "The Grasshopper and the Bell Cricket" was written in the early twentieth century by a Japanese author. Knowing some characteristics of Japanese culture will help you better understand the role of setting in the story and how the setting influences the theme.

- Traditionally nature is quite important in Japanese culture. The roots of this reverence for nature come from the Shinto religion, which honors all aspects of the natural world: water, rocks, trees, sun, birds, and insects.

- Instead of hoping to tame nature, Japanese culture aims to live in harmony with it. Japanese culture shows both respect and gratitude for nature.

- In Japan, as in other cultures, crickets are symbols of good luck. The bell cricket is an insect appreciated for its song, not its beauty.

As you read the story, pay attention to the details of setting and the atmosphere they create. Think about how this contributes to the mood of the story and helps reveal the story's **theme** or themes.

MAKE INFERENCES ABOUT THEME

The **theme** of a story, or its central idea, may express an attitude or an underlying message about life or human nature. Themes are seldom stated directly. Instead, you must make **inferences**, or logical guesses, about them using evidence in the text and your own common sense. To determine theme, think about the experiences story characters go through, and note key statements that say something about life or people in general. Then ask yourself, "What conclusions can I draw about theme using these details?"

The chart below shows three key subjects in "The Grasshopper and the Bell Cricket." As you read the story, record plot details related to these subjects. Then make inferences from these details and use your own knowledge to write three themes for the story.

KEY SUBJECTS	STORY EVIDENCE	THEMES
love		
nature		
finding someone special to you		

GENRE ELEMENTS: SHORT STORY

- includes the four basic elements of fiction—setting, characters, plot, and theme
- usually develops one major conflict
- can be read in one sitting

CRITICAL VOCABULARY

lozenge	loiter	emanate	sheepish	discernible

To see how many Critical Vocabulary words you already know, use them to complete the sentences.

1. Jason's _____ expression showed that he had broken the vase.

2. The gravestone was so old that the writing on it was barely _____.

3. The principal told us not to _____ in the halls between classes.

4. Every morning, delicious smells _____ from the corner bakery.

5. Louisa's new sweater has a large, red _____ shape on it.

LANGUAGE CONVENTIONS

Verb Phrases In this lesson, you will learn that a sentence may have a single-word verb or a verb phrase. A **verb phrase** consists of a main verb and one or more helping verbs. Helping verbs can also be used to indicate ability or permission. Common helping verbs include all tenses of *to be, to have, to do.*

In a verb phrase, the helping verbs add meaning to the main verb.

- They can indicate the time of the main verb: I **will read** *Snow Country*.

- They can indicate obligation: You **should read** it too.

- They can indicate possibility: I **might read** *The Master of Go* instead.

ANNOTATION MODEL

NOTICE & NOTE

As you read, take notes about signposts you notice, including **Again and Again, Aha Moment**, and **Words of the Wiser**. Here is an example of how one reader responded to the opening of "The Grasshopper and the Bell Cricket."

Behind the white board fence of the school playground, from a dusky clump of bushes under the black cherry trees, <u>an insect's voice</u> could be heard. . . . One of the neighborhood children had heard an insect sing on this slope one night.

Insect → sound again and again

The narrator must love nature or bugs. Maybe the insect will be important in the story somehow.

BACKGROUND

Yasunari Kawabata *(1899–1972) was born in Osaka, Japan, and became an orphan when he was quite young. This experience may have led to the themes of loneliness and death in much of his writing. He published his first story, "The Izu Dancer," in 1926, and he became a major author in Japan after his novel* Snow Country *was published in 1948. In 1968, he was awarded the Nobel Prize in Literature "for his narrative mastery, which with great sensibility expresses the essences of the Japanese mind."*

THE GRASSHOPPER AND THE BELL CRICKET

Short Story by Yasunari Kawabata
translated by Lane Dunlop and J. Martin Holman

SETTING A PURPOSE

As you read, consider the way the narrator talks about nature and describes his surroundings.

1 Walking along the tile-roofed wall of the university, I turned aside and approached the upper school. Behind the white board fence of the school playground, from a dusky clump of bushes under the black cherry trees, an insect's voice could be heard. Walking more slowly and listening to that voice, and feeling reluctant to part with it, I turned right so as not to leave the playground behind. When I turned to the left, the fence gave way to an embankment[1] planted with orange trees. At the corner, I exclaimed with surprise. My eyes gleaming at what they saw up ahead, I hurried forward with short steps.

2 At the base of the embankment was a bobbing cluster of beautiful varicolored lanterns, such as one might see at a festival in a remote country village. Without going any farther, I knew that it was a group of children on an insect chase among the bushes of the embankment. There were about twenty lanterns.

---

[1] **embankment:** a man-made elevated area of land used to prevent flooding or to raise a roadway.

Notice & Note

You can use the side margins to notice and note signposts in the text.

ANALYZE SETTING

Annotate: In paragraphs 1–2, mark the interactions between characters and nature.

Infer: What aspects of Japanese culture do these details illustrate?

MAKE INFERENCES ABOUT THEME

Annotate: Paragraph 3 takes place in the narrator's imagination. Mark text that expresses the narrator's admiration for the children.

Connect: Why do you think the author goes into such detail in an imaginary scene? What conclusions can you draw about theme using these details?

AGAIN AND AGAIN

Notice & Note: In paragraph 3, the narrator says that each day the children make new lanterns. Mark the explanation the narrator provides.

Connect: Why do you think the children do this?

lozenge
(lŏz´ĭnj) *n.* a diamond-shaped object.

loiter
(loi´tər) *v.* to stand or wait idly.

emanate
(ĕm´ə-nāt) *v.* to emit or radiate from.

Not only were there crimson, pink, indigo, green, purple, and yellow lanterns, but one lantern glowed with five colors at once. There were even some little red store-bought lanterns. But most of the lanterns were beautiful square ones that the children had made themselves with love and care. The bobbing lanterns, the coming together of children on this lonely slope—surely it was a scene from a fairy tale?

3   One of the neighborhood children had heard an insect sing on this slope one night. Buying a red lantern, he had come back the next night to find the insect. The night after that, there was another child. This new child could not buy a lantern. Cutting out the back and front of a small carton and papering it, he placed a candle on the bottom and fastened a string to the top. The number of children grew to five, and then to seven. They learned how to color the paper that they stretched over the windows of the cutout cartons, and to draw pictures on it. Then these wise child-artists, cutting out round, three-cornered, and **lozenge** leaf shapes in the cartons, coloring each little window a different color, with circles and diamonds, red and green, made a single and whole decorative pattern. The child with the red lantern discarded it as a tasteless object that could be bought at a store. The child who had made his own lantern threw it away because the design was too simple. The pattern of light that one had in hand the night before was unsatisfying the morning after. Each day, with cardboard, paper, brush, scissors, penknife, and glue, the children made new lanterns out of their hearts and minds. Look at my lantern! Be the most unusually beautiful! And each night, they had gone out on their insect hunts. These were the twenty children and their beautiful lanterns that I now saw before me.

4   Wide-eyed, I **loitered** near them. Not only did the square lanterns have old-fashioned patterns and flower shapes, but the names of the children who had made them were cut in squared letters of the syllabary.[2] Different from the painted-over red lanterns, others (made of thick cutout cardboard) had their designs drawn onto the paper windows, so that the candle's light seemed to **emanate** from the form and color of the design itself. The lanterns brought out the shadows of the bushes like dark light. The children crouched eagerly on the slope wherever they heard an insect's voice.

5   "Does anyone want a grasshopper?" A boy, who had been peering into a bush about thirty feet away from the other children, suddenly straightened up and shouted.

6   "Yes! Give it to me!" Six or seven children came running up. Crowding behind the boy who had found the grasshopper, they

---

[2] **syllabary** (sĭl´ə-bĕr-ē): A set of written characters for a language, with each character representing a syllable.

peered into the bush. Brushing away their outstretched hands and spreading out his arms, the boy stood as if guarding the bush where the insect was. Waving the lantern in his right hand, he called again to the other children.

7 "Does anyone want a grasshopper? A grasshopper!"

8 "I do! I do!" Four or five more children came running up. It seemed you could not catch a more precious insect than a grasshopper. The boy called out a third time.

9 "Doesn't anyone want a grasshopper?"

10 Two or three more children came over.

11 "Yes. I want it."

12 It was a girl, who just now had come up behind the boy who'd discovered the insect. Lightly turning his body, the boy gracefully bent forward. Shifting the lantern to his left hand, he reached his right hand into the bush.

13 "It's a grasshopper."

14 "Yes. I'd like to have it."

15 The boy quickly stood up. As if to say "Here!" he thrust out his fist that held the insect at the girl. She, slipping her left wrist under the string of her lantern, enclosed the boy's fist with both hands. The boy quietly opened his fist. The insect was transferred to between the girl's thumb and index finger.

16 "Oh! It's not a grasshopper. It's a bell cricket." The girl's eyes shone as she looked at the small brown insect.

17 "It's a bell cricket! It's a bell cricket!" The children echoed in an envious chorus.

18 "It's a bell cricket. It's a bell cricket."

19 Glancing with her bright intelligent eyes at the boy who had given her the cricket, the girl opened the little insect cage hanging at her side and released the cricket in it.

20 "It's a bell cricket."

21 "Oh, it's a bell cricket," the boy who'd captured it muttered. Holding up the insect cage close to his eyes, he looked inside it. By the light of his beautiful many-colored lantern, also held up at eye level, he glanced at the girl's face.

22 Oh, I thought. I felt slightly jealous of the boy, and **sheepish**. How silly of me not to have understood his actions until now! Then I caught my breath in surprise. Look! It was something on the girl's breast that neither the boy who had given her the cricket, nor she who had accepted it, nor the children who were looking at them noticed.

AHA MOMENT

Notice & Note: In paragraphs 7–16, mark how the boy's behavior toward the girl is different from the way he acts toward the other children.

Compare: What can you infer about his feelings toward her?

LANGUAGE CONVENTIONS

Annotate: Mark the verb phrase that uses a form of the helping verb *have* in paragraph 21.

Connect: What is the effect of this verb phrase? What subtle shift in time does the verb phrase help express?

sheepish
(shē´pǐsh) *adj.* showing embarrassment.

discernible
(dĭ-sûr´nə-bəl) *adj.*
recognizable or noticeable.

ANALYZE SETTING AND THEME

Annotate: In paragraphs 23 and 24, mark the places where the narrator talks about the red and green colors coming from the lanterns.

Analyze: What insight does the narrator have about the red and green colors coming from Fujio and Kiyoko's lanterns? Why is the time of day an important element of the setting?

23   In the faint greenish light that fell on the girl's breast, wasn't the name "Fujio" clearly **discernible**? The boy's lantern, which he held up alongside the girl's insect cage, inscribed his name, cut out in the green papered aperture, onto her white cotton kimono. The girl's lantern, which dangled loosely from her wrist, did not project its pattern so clearly, but still one could make out, in a trembling patch of red on the boy's waist, the name "Kiyoko." This chance interplay of red and green—if it was chance or play—neither Fujio nor Kiyoko knew about.

24   Even if they remembered forever that Fujio had given her the cricket and that Kiyoko had accepted it, not even in dreams would Fujio ever know that his name had been written in green on Kiyoko's breast or that Kiyoko's name had been inscribed in red on his waist, nor would Kiyoko ever know that Fujio's name had been inscribed in green on her breast or that her own name had been written in red on Fujio's waist.

25   Fujio! Even when you have become a young man, laugh with pleasure at a girl's delight when, told that it's a grasshopper, she is given a bell cricket; laugh with affection at a girl's chagrin when, told that it's a bell cricket, she is given a grasshopper.

26   Even if you have the wit to look by yourself in a bush away from the other children, there are not many bell crickets in the world. Probably you will find a girl like a grasshopper whom you think is a bell cricket.

27   And finally, to your clouded, wounded heart, even a true bell cricket will seem like a grasshopper. Should that day come, when it seems to you that the world is only full of grasshoppers, I will think it a pity that you have no way to remember tonight's play of light, when your name was written in green by your beautiful lantern on a girl's breast.

WORDS OF THE WISER

Notice & Note: In paragraphs 25–27, underline the references to grasshoppers and circle references to bell crickets.

Draw Conclusions: What is the narrator advising Fujio about?

CHECK YOUR UNDERSTANDING

Answer these questions before moving on to the **Analyze the Text** questions on the following page.

1 Which of the following is true?

   A The narrator is annoyed with the children.

   B A grasshopper is rare, and a bell cricket is common.

   C Fujio sees his name reflected onto Kiyoko's kimono.

   D The children are looking in some bushes for insects.

2 Where is Fujio when he finds the grasshopper?

   F He is climbing the embankment.

   G He is at a distance from the other children.

   H He is sitting next to the narrator.

   J He and Kiyoko are standing together.

3 What does the narrator see on the clothing of Fujio and Kiyoko?

   A A bell cricket

   B A grasshopper

   C The reflection of each others' names

   D Multicolored circle and diamond shapes

ANALYZE THE TEXT

Support your responses with evidence from the text. 📓 NOTEBOOK

1. **Cite Evidence** In what ways is setting important in this story? How does the setting connect to themes about love, nature, or being an individual?

2. **Interpret** The narrator spends a great deal of time observing and commenting on the children's lanterns in paragraphs 2–4. What does he appreciate about the lanterns? What could the lanterns symbolize? Cite evidence from the text to support your ideas.

3. **Analyze** In paragraphs 16–21, what opinions does the narrator express about people? Why is it important to understand the role of bell crickets in Japanese culture in order to understand the narrator's point of view? Explain using details from the story.

4. **Infer** Determine the **theme**, or underlying message, that the narrator expresses in paragraph 26 when he thinks, "Even if you have the wit to look by yourself in a bush away from the other children, there are not many bell crickets in the world. Probably you will find a girl like a grasshopper whom you think is a bell cricket."

5. **Notice & Note** The narrator experiences back-to-back Aha Moments beginning in paragraph 22. How does the story change after these Aha Moments? Cite text evidence to support your response.

RESEARCH

Japan is famous for its arts and crafts, including paper lanterns and origami. Conduct research to identify and explore the history of three Japanese art forms. Record what you learn in the chart and jot down other questions that come to you as you work.

ART FORM	INFORMATION ABOUT ART FORM AND ITS SIGNIFICANCE

Extend Think about the children's lanterns in the story and their qualities that impress the narrator. What do these details and the art forms you researched help you understand about Japanese culture?

CREATE AND DISCUSS

Write an Informal Letter Write an informal letter to Fujio or Kiyoko in which you describe the results of your research on Japanese art forms and ask the questions that occurred to you during your research.

❏ Begin your letter with a greeting, usually "Dear …" and end your letter with a friendly closing such as "Sincerely," "Yours Truly," or "Regards."

❏ Include an introductory paragraph to explain your purpose for writing. Then write 1–3 paragraphs in the body of your letter. Go into detail about the ideas you mentioned in the introduction.

❏ Finally, write a concluding paragraph in which you restate your purpose for writing and add any final thoughts you may have.

Discuss with a Small Group Have a discussion on the information compiled about Japanese art forms and the questions generated during research.

❏ As a group, review what members learned about Japanese art forms. Discuss what these art forms might reveal about Japanese culture and connect these ideas with information in the story.

❏ Next, have group members share questions that came up during their research. Create a list of questions and any answers.

❏ Finally, review the conclusions about Japanese culture. Discuss ways it has influenced artistic and popular activities in the United States today. Remember to listen closely and respectfully to all ideas.

> Go to the **Speaking and Listening Studio** for help with having a group discussion.

RESPOND TO THE ESSENTIAL QUESTION

 How do we form and maintain our connections with others?

Gather Information Review your annotations and notes on "The Grasshopper and the Bell Cricket." Then add relevant information to your Response Log. As you determine which information to include, think about:

- the message in this story about connections between people
- the ways in which you form and maintain connection with friends
- how relationships with your closest friends are different from your connections with other friends and acquaintances

At the end of the unit, use your notes to help you write a short story.

ACADEMIC VOCABULARY

As you write and discuss what you learned from the short story, be sure to use the Academic Vocabulary words. Check off each of the words that you use.

❏ **capacity**
❏ **confer**
❏ **emerge**
❏ **generate**
❏ **trace**

WORD BANK

lozenge   sheepish
loiter   discernable
emanate

CRITICAL VOCABULARY

Practice and Apply Answer the questions to show your understanding of the Critical Vocabulary words. Use a dictionary or thesaurus as needed.

1. Which would you be more likely to do if you are feeling **sheepish**: blush and grin or scowl and shout? Why?

2. If a room **emanates** light, can you see the light or not? Why?

3. Which would be more **discernible**, something written in crayon or in invisible ink? Why?

4. If I **loiter**, do I run away, or do I hang around? Why?

5. Which item has a **lozenge** shape: a kite or an egg? Why?

Go to the **Vocabulary Studio** for more on context clues.

VOCABULARY STRATEGY:
Context Clues

When you read, you can use **context clues** to understand unfamiliar words. **Context** is how a word relates to the overall meaning of a sentence, paragraph, or piece of writing.

Here are some types of context clues you may find in texts:

SYNONYMS OR DEFINITION	CONTRAST	EXAMPLES
The text may provide a definition or a synonym.	The text may give an antonym, or contrasting information.	The text may list examples of the word.

Look at this example from the story:

> Then these wise child-artists, cutting out round, three-cornered, and <u>lozenge</u> leaf shapes in the cartons . . .

You read that *lozenge* is part of a list of shapes, an example of a shape. You also know from contrasting information that a *lozenge* is not round or three-cornered.

Practice and Apply Locate these words in the story: *discarded* (paragraph 3), *crouched* (paragraph 4), and *inscribed* (paragraph 23). Then use context clues to write definitions for each word. Check your definitions in a dictionary.

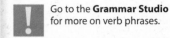

LANGUAGE CONVENTIONS:
Verb Phrases

Go to the **Grammar Studio** for more on verb phrases.

Verb phrases are a combination of one or more helping verbs and a main verb. In "The Grasshopper and the Bell Cricket," Yasunari Kawabata uses many verb phrases to express shifts in time.

By using the verb phrase *might see*, the author sets up a comparison— between the lanterns on the embankment and lanterns at a festival.

> **At the base of the embankment was a bobbing cluster of beautiful varicolored lanterns, such as one <u>might see</u> at a festival in a remote country village.**

Here, the author uses the verb phrase *had made* to show that the children made the lanterns in the past—prior to the narrator seeing them.

> **But most of the lanterns were beautiful square ones which the children <u>had made</u> themselves with love and care.**

Other words can interrupt the parts of a verb phrase. Here, *does* and *want* create the verb phrase, which is interrupted by the subject, a structure common with questions.

> **<u>Does</u> anyone <u>want</u> a grasshopper?**

The table shows some common helping verbs. You can use these verbs in their different forms in verb phrases.

COMMON HELPING VERBS IN VERB PHRASES		
be	can	am
do	have	may
might	shall	should
will	would	could

Practice and Apply With a partner, review the letters you created in response to the selection's Create and Discuss assignment. Note the use of verb phrases in your letters. Help each other revise verb phrases to make your writing more effective in showing shifts in time, or work together to create sentences that contain verb phrases. Remember to consider the tense of the verbs as you are revising.

MONKEY SEE, MONKEY DO, MONKEY CONNECT

Science Writing by **Frans de Waal**

? ***ESSENTIAL QUESTION:***

How do we form and maintain our connections with others?

QUICK START

Have you ever been with a group when one of you got the giggles, and soon no one could stop laughing? Share your experience with a partner or the class.

MONITOR COMPREHENSION

When you **monitor** comprehension, you check your own understanding as you read. You can do this by using strategies, including the ones below. You might have to modify the strategy you use to suit your own needs:

STRATEGY	WHAT IT MEANS
Use background knowledge	Consider what you already know as you read and how this helps you understand the text.
Reread	Read a paragraph, page, or section again to see what you missed or to clarify an idea.
Annotate	Mark important facts, key passages, or vocabulary you want to remember.
Ask questions	Look for answers to questions such as *what, why*, and *how* as you read the text.

GENRE ELEMENTS: SCIENCE WRITING

- introduces a key idea, sometimes a surprising one
- uses analogies or examples to illustrate concepts
- may use scientific terminology or refer to established theories
- generally sticks to facts, not opinions

ANALYZE AUTHOR'S CLAIM

A **claim** is the author's position on a topic or issue. The science article "Monkey See, Monkey Do, Monkey Connect" is an informational text that states a specific claim about the behavior of human beings. Although Frans de Waal is an expert on the topic, it is not enough for him to simply state his claim and expect readers to accept what he is saying. He must **support** his claim throughout the essay with reasons, or declarations made to justify an action, decision, or belief; and with **evidence**, such as facts, details, and examples. He should end with a convincing **conclusion**.

As a reader, it is your job to consider an author's claim and determine if the claim is valid.

First, identify the author's credibility, or if the author is a believable source.
- *Is the author an expert on the topic?*
- *What qualifications does the author have to speak about the topic?*

Next, note the reasons and evidence the author provides.
- *Do the reasons make sense? Are they logical?*
- *Is the evidence relevant?*

Finally, decide if you agree with the author's claim based on the reasons and evidence. You can either defend the author's claim or challenge it if the reasons and evidence do not lead you to the same conclusion. Either way, you will use text evidence to support your position.

CRITICAL VOCABULARY

empathy   synchronization   contagion   cognition   implication

To see how many Critical Vocabulary words you already know, use them to complete the sentences.

1. When Catherine came to class with the flu, the _____ quickly spread.

2. I was impressed by the _____ of the swimmers' movements.

3. Humans can think through more difficult problems because they have a higher capacity for _____ than other primates.

4. _____ is the ability to understand what another person is feeling.

5. What is the _____ of the new dress code on outfits for picture day?

LANGUAGE CONVENTIONS

Colons A colon can introduce a list, explanation, or quotation; emphasize an idea; or connect ideas. Use a colon only after an independent clause.

correct	For french toast, you need five ingredients: eggs, bread, butter, cinnamon, and maple syrup.
incorrect	For french toast you need: eggs, bread, butter, cinnamon, and maple syrup.

As you read the article, note the author's use of colons and their function.

ANNOTATION MODEL

NOTICE & NOTE

As you read, note the author's claims and the reasons and evidence he gives to support them. Mark information that supports your own ideas; and record questions you have. In the model, you can see one reader's notes about "Monkey See, Monkey Do, Monkey Connect."

What intrigues me most about laughter is how it spreads. <u>It's almost impossible not to laugh when everybody else is.</u> There have been laughing epidemics, in which no one could stop and <u>some even died</u> in a prolonged fit. There are laughing churches and laugh therapies based on the <u>healing power of laughter.</u> The must-have toy of 1996—Tickle Me Elmo—laughed hysterically after being squeezed three times in a row. All of this because <u>we love to laugh and can't resist joining laughing around us.</u>

Is this going to be part of the author's claim?·

People have died from laughing?

Is this a reason? Or evidence?

BACKGROUND

Frans B.M. de Waal *(b. 1948) was born in the Netherlands. Trained in biology, de Waal analyzes the behaviors and social interactions of primates, an order of mammals that includes monkeys, chimpanzees, gorillas, lemurs, and homo sapiens, or humans. He is the director of The Living Links Center at the Yerkes National Primate Research Center in Lawrenceville, Georgia, and the author of numerous books including Chimpanzee Politics.*

MONKEY SEE, MONKEY DO, MONKEY CONNECT

Science Writing by Frans de Waal

SETTING A PURPOSE

As you read, monitor your comprehension by annotating, using background knowledge, rereading, and asking questions as appropriate.

1 What intrigues me most about laughter is how it spreads. It's almost impossible not to laugh when everybody else is. There have been laughing epidemics, in which no one could stop and some even died in a prolonged fit. There are laughing churches and laugh therapies based on the healing power of laughter. The must-have toy of 1996—Tickle Me Elmo—laughed hysterically after being squeezed three times in a row. All of this because we love to laugh and can't resist joining laughing around us. This is why comedy shows on television have laugh tracks and why theater audiences are sometimes sprinkled with "laugh plants": people paid to produce raucous laughing at any joke that comes along.

Notice & Note

You can use the side margins to notice and note signposts in the text.

MONITOR COMPREHENSION

Annotate: Mark context clues in paragraph 1 that suggest the meaning of the word *raucous*.

Infer: How would you define *raucous* as it is used in the last sentence of paragraph 1?

WORD GAPS

Notice & Note: In paragraph 2, what clues from the sentence help you understand the word *suppress*?

Infer: Do you think this is a technical term, or could it be used in everyday conversation?

2   The infectiousness of laughter even works across species. Below my office window at the Yerkes Primate Center, I often hear my chimps laugh during rough-and-tumble games, and I cannot suppress a chuckle myself. It's such a happy sound. Tickling and wrestling are the typical laugh triggers for apes, and probably the original ones for humans. The fact that tickling oneself is notoriously ineffective attests to its social significance. And when young apes put on their play face, their friends join in with the same expression as rapidly and easily as humans do with laughter.

3   Shared laughter is just one example of our primate sensitivity to others. Instead of being Robinson Crusoes sitting on separate islands,[1] we're all interconnected, both bodily and emotionally. This may be an odd thing to say in the West, with its tradition of individual freedom and liberty, but *Homo sapiens*[2] is remarkably easily swayed in one emotional direction or another by its fellows.

---

[1] **Robinson Crusoes . . . islands:** Crusoe, the title character of Daniel Defoe's 1719 novel, was stranded alone on a tropical island.

[2] *Homo sapiens* (hō´mō sā´pē-ənz): the species of primates that includes humans.

4   This is precisely where **empathy** and sympathy start—not in the higher regions of imagination, or the ability to consciously reconstruct how we would feel if we were in someone else's situation. It began much more simply, with the **synchronization** of bodies: running when others run, laughing when others laugh, crying when others cry, or yawning when others yawn. Most of us have reached the incredibly advanced stage at which we yawn even at the mere mention of yawning—as you may be doing right now!—but this is only after lots of face-to-face experience.

5   Yawn **contagion**, too, works across species. Virtually all animals show the peculiar "paroxystic respiratory cycle characterized by a standard cascade of movements over a five- to ten-second period," which is the way the yawn has been defined. I once attended a lecture on involuntary pandiculation (the medical term for stretching and yawning) with slides of horses, lions, and monkeys—and soon the entire audience was pandiculating. Since it so easily triggers a chain reaction, the yawn reflex opens a window onto mood transmission,

LANGUAGE CONVENTIONS

Annotate: Mark the sentence in paragraph 4 in which a colon introduces a list of examples.

Analyze: What does the list that follows the colon give examples of?

empathy
(ĕm´pə-thē) *n.* the ability to understand and identify with another's feelings.

synchronization
(sĭng-krə-nĭ-zā´shən) *n.* coordinated, simultaneous action.

contagion
(kən-tā´jən) *n.* the spreading from one to another.

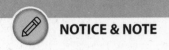
MONITOR COMPREHENSION

Annotate: Mark clues in paragraph 4–6 that hint at the meaning of *yawn contagion*.

Analyze: What is *yawn contagion?*

ANALYZE AUTHOR'S CLAIM

Annotate: Paragraphs 8 and 9 each provide an example supporting the author's claim that primates, including humans, share primate sensitivity. Mark lines that summarize each example.

Summarize: Paraphrase each example, then define *primate sensitivity*.

an essential part of empathy. This makes it all the more intriguing that chimpanzees yawn when they see others do so.

6   Yawn contagion reflects the power of unconscious synchrony, which is as deeply ingrained in us as in many other animals. Synchrony may be expressed in the copying of small body movements, such as a yawn, but also occurs on a larger scale, involving travel or movement. It is not hard to see its survival value. You're in a flock of birds and one bird suddenly takes off. You have no time to figure out what's going on: You take off at the same instant. Otherwise, you may be lunch.

7   Or your entire group becomes sleepy and settles down, so you too become sleepy. Mood contagion serves to coordinate activities, which is crucial for any traveling species (as most primates are). If my companions are feeding, I'd better do the same, because once they move off, my chance to forage will be gone. The individual who doesn't stay in tune with what everyone else is doing will lose out like the traveler who doesn't go to the restroom when the bus has stopped.

8   The herd instinct produces weird phenomena. At one zoo, an entire baboon troop gathered on top of their rock, all staring in exactly the same direction. For an entire week they forgot to eat, mate, and groom. They just kept staring at something in the distance that no one could identify. Local newspapers were carrying pictures of the monkey rock, speculating that perhaps the animals had been frightened by a UFO. But even though this explanation had the unique advantage of combining an account of primate behavior with proof of UFOs, the truth is that no one knew the cause except that the baboons clearly were all of the same mind.

9   Finding himself in front of the cameras next to his pal President George W. Bush, former British prime minister Tony Blair—known to walk normally at home—would suddenly metamorphose into a distinctly un-English cowboy. He'd swagger with arms hanging loose and chest puffed out. Bush, of course, strutted like this all the time and once explained how, back home in Texas, this is known as "walking." Identification is the hook that draws us in and makes us adopt the situation, emotions, and behavior of those we're close to. They become role models: We empathize with them and emulate[3] them. Thus children often walk like the same-sex parent or mimic their tone of voice when they pick up the phone.

10   How does one chimp imitate another? Does he identify with the other and absorb its body movements? Or could it be that he doesn't need the other and instead focuses on the problem faced by the other? This can be tested by having a chimpanzee show another how to open a puzzle box with goodies inside. Maybe all that the

---

[3] **emulate:** to imitate or behave like.

© Houghton Mifflin Harcourt Publishing Company

watching ape needs to understand is how the thing works. He may notice that the door slides to the side or that something needs to be lifted up. The first kind of imitation involves reenactment of observed manipulations; the second merely requires technical know-how.

11   Thanks to ingenious studies in which chimps were presented with a so-called ghost box, we know which of these two explanations is correct. A ghost box derives its name from the fact that it magically opens and closes by itself so that no actor is needed. If technical know-how were all that mattered, such a box should suffice. But in fact, letting chimps watch a ghost box until they're bored to death—with its various parts moving and producing rewards hundreds of times—doesn't teach them anything.

12   To learn from others, apes need to see actual fellow apes: Imitation requires identification with a body of flesh and blood. We're beginning to realize how much human and animal cognition runs via the body. Instead of our brain being like a little computer that orders the body around, the body-brain relation is a two-way street. The body produces internal sensations and communicates with other bodies, out of which we construct social connections and an appreciation of the surrounding reality. Bodies insert themselves into everything we perceive or think. Did you know, for example, that physical condition colors perception? The same hill is assessed as steeper, just from looking at it, by a tired person than by a well-rested one. An outdoor target is judged as farther away than it really is by a person burdened with a heavy backpack than by one without it.

13   Or ask a pianist to pick out his own performance from among others he's listening to. Even if this is a new piece that the pianist has performed only once, in silence (on an electronic piano and without headphones on), he will be able to recognize his own play. While listening, he probably recreates in his head the sort of bodily sensations that accompany an actual performance. He feels the closest match listening to himself, thus recognizing himself through his body as much as through his ears.

14   The field of "embodied" **cognition** is still very much in its infancy but has profound **implications** for how we look at human relations. We involuntarily enter the bodies of those around us so that their movements and emotions echo within us as if they're our own. This is what allows us, or other primates, to re-create what we have seen others do. Body mapping is mostly hidden and unconscious, but sometimes it "slips out," such as when parents make chewing mouth movements while spoon-feeding their baby. They can't help but act the way they feel their baby ought to. Similarly, parents watching a singing performance of their child often get completely into it, mouthing every word. I myself still remember as a boy standing on the sidelines of soccer games and involuntarily making kicking or jumping moves each time someone I was cheering for got the ball.

ANALYZE AUTHOR'S CLAIM

Annotate: In paragraph 12, the author asserts the claim that "[our bodies and the bodies of others of our species] insert themselves into everything we perceive or think." He then gives three examples of ways we use our bodies to perceive the world. Mark those examples in paragraphs 12 and 13.

Analyze: Restate each example in your own words.

cognition
(kŏg-nĭsh´ən) *n.* the process or pattern of gaining knowledge.

implication
(ĭm-plĭ-kā´shən) *n.* consequence or effect.

15 The same can be seen in animals, as illustrated in an old black-and-white photograph from Wolfgang Köhler's classic tool-use studies on chimpanzees. One ape, Grande, stands on boxes that she has stacked up to reach bananas hung from the ceiling, while Sultan watches intently. Even though Sultan sits at a distance, he raises his arm in precise synchrony with Grande's grasping movement. Another example comes from a chimpanzee filmed while using a heavy rock as a hammer to crack nuts. The actor is being observed by a younger ape, who swings his own (empty) hand down in sync every time the first one strikes the nut. Body mapping provides a great shortcut to imitation.

16 When I see synchrony and mimicry—whether it concerns yawning, laughing, dancing, or aping—I see social connection and bonding. I see an old herd instinct that has been taken up a notch. It goes beyond the tendency of a mass of individuals galloping in the same direction, crossing the river at the same time. The new level requires that one pay better attention to what others do and absorb how they do it. For example, I knew an old monkey matriarch with a curious drinking style. Instead of the typical slurping with her lips from the surface, she'd dip her entire underarm in the water, then lick the hair on her arm. Her children started doing the same, and then her grandchildren. The entire family was easy to recognize.

17 There is also the case of a male chimpanzee who had injured his fingers in a fight and hobbled around leaning on a bent wrist instead of his knuckles. Soon all of the young chimpanzees in the colony were walking the same way in single file behind the unlucky male. Like chameleons changing their color to match the environment, primates automatically copy their surroundings.

18 When I was a boy, my friends in the south of the Netherlands always ridiculed me when I came home from vacations in the north, where I played with boys from Amsterdam. They told me that I

MONITOR COMPREHENSION

Annotate: Locate and mark the word *mimicry* in paragraph 16. Reread to identify several terms in the surrounding text that provide context clues for the meaning of *mimicry*.

Draw Conclusions: Summarize the meanings of the words you identified and determine which of them is closest in meaning to *mimicry*.

talked funny. Unconsciously, I'd return speaking a poor imitation of the harsh northern accent.

19   The way our bodies—including voice, mood, posture, and so on—are influenced by surrounding bodies is one of the mysteries of human existence, but one that provides the glue that holds entire societies together. It's also one of the most underestimated phenomena, especially in disciplines that view humans as rational decision makers. Instead of each individual independently weighing the pros and cons of his or her own actions, we occupy nodes within a tight network that connects all of us in both body and mind.

CHECK YOUR UNDERSTANDING

Answer these questions before moving on to the **Analyze the Text** section on the following page.

1 In the paragraph 2 sentence, *The fact that tickling oneself is notoriously ineffective attests to its social significance*, <u>notoriously</u> means —

   A unfavorably

   B humorously

   C famously

   D seriously

2 In paragraph 18, the author includes an anecdote, or brief story about himself. Its purpose is to —

   F connect with readers who have had a similar experience

   G support the author's claim about language and accents

   H provide an example of unconscious synchrony

   J show the herd mentality regarding human bullying

3 Which idea is supported by information throughout the selection?

   A Humans unconsciously imitate the actions and behaviors of other humans.

   B Laughter has a healing psychological effect on all primates, including humans.

   C Humans learn best by imitating other humans.

   D Sympathy and empathy are critical to the formation of meaningful human relationships.

ANALYZE THE TEXT

Support your responses with evidence from the text. 📓 NOTEBOOK

1. **Analyze** An author carefully chooses words and phrases to establish **tone**, or a particular attitude toward his or her subject. Some authors use formal language to convey a serious tone, while others use a more conversational style. What tone does de Waal establish in the opening paragraphs of his essay? What words and phrases create this tone?

2. **Cite Evidence** What is the primary claim that emerges in this essay? Provide evidence from the text to support your idea.

3. **Infer** What is the "herd instinct"? According to de Waal, what is the positive side of people watching and imitating one another? What might be a potential downside of this part of human nature?

4. **Draw Conclusions** What, according to de Waal, is the "glue that holds entire societies together"? What do you think are his strongest pieces of evidence in support of that claim?

5. **Notice & Note** Reread the final paragraph of the selection. How might the author's conclusions create an Aha Moment, causing the reader to see human behavior in a new light?

RESEARCH

Brainstorm at least three questions you have after reading the selection "Monkey See, Monkey Do, Monkey Connect." Are you curious about Dr. de Waal and his credentials? Do you want to learn more about an aspect of his or other scientists' research? The Yerkes Primate Center? Or something else? List your questions, put a star by the question that interests you most, then research its answer. Write down additional questions that occur to you during your research.

RESEARCH TIP
When you conduct online research, be sure to evaluate the credibility of websites. Web addresses that end in .gov, .edu, or .org are the work of large groups. Because these sites are frequently reviewed, they are often more reliable than other sites. Use them and other sites you trust, including those your teachers recommend.

INITIAL BRAINSTORM QUESTIONS	ADDITIONAL QUESTIONS

CREATE AND DEBATE

Take a Position The author of "Monkey See, Monkey Do, Monkey Connect" presents one view of the ways in which humans relate to one another. Do you agree with his view, or do you believe that people are, or should be, "Robinson Crusoes sitting on separate islands"?

- ❏ Review your notes and annotations, consider your own research, and reflect on what you already know.

- ❏ Write a position statement in which you state your claim clearly, using appropriate academic and content vocabulary.

- ❏ Create a list of reasons and evidence that support your claim using the article, your own research, and other logical reasons.

Participate in a Debate Choose sides for or against a stated claim and use reasons and evidence to support your position.

- ❏ As a class, choose a position statement to argue for or against.

- ❏ In teams, prepare an opening statement, a list of supporting reasons and evidence, and a concluding statement.

- ❏ Listen actively as the other team present arguments. Allow them to respond to each of your team's arguments with counter-arguments.

Go to the **Speaking and Listening Studio** for help having a group discussion.

RESPOND TO THE ESSENTIAL QUESTION

 How do we form and maintain our connections with others?

Gather Information Review your annotations and notes on "Monkey See, Monkey Do, Monkey Connect." Then add relevant information to your Response Log. As you determine which information to include, think about:

- what we can learn from the infectiousness of laughter and the fact that it's impossible to tickle oneself

- the author's observations on how imitating others of one's species can affect an individual's survival

- benefits an individual gains from the formation of lasting connections

At the end of the unit, use your notes to help you write a short story.

ACADEMIC VOCABULARY

As you write and discuss what you learned from the scientific article, be sure to use the Academic Vocabulary words. Check off each of the words that you use.

- ❏ **capacity**
- ❏ **confer**
- ❏ **emerge**
- ❏ **generate**
- ❏ **trace**

© Houghton Mifflin Harcourt Publishing Company

WORD BANK
empathy
synchronization
contagion
cognition
implication

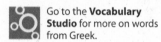
Go to the **Vocabulary Studio** for more on words from Greek.

CRITICAL VOCABULARY

Practice and Apply Explain which Critical Vocabulary word listed above is most closely associated with the familiar word shown below.

1. Which vocabulary word is associated with *thinking*?

2. Which vocabulary word is associated with *suggestion*?

3. Which vocabulary word is associated with *feeling*?

4. Which vocabulary word is associated with *disease*?

5. Which vocabulary word is associated with *coordination*?

VOCABULARY STRATEGY:
Words from Greek

Many English words contain Greek roots. The Critical Vocabulary word *synchronization* contains the prefix *syn-*, meaning "with or together," combined with the Greek root *chrono*, which means "time." *Chrono* is the basis of many other words in our everyday vocabulary.

THE GREEK ROOT *CHRONO*	
chronic	anachronistic
chronicle	synchronicity

Use your understanding of the root *chrono* and context clues in the sentences below to understand meaning of the words in the chart. Under each sentence, write down the meaning of the italicized word.

1. My sister has a *chronic* cough that has kept her awake for weeks.

_____

2. The book will *chronicle* the history of our community.

_____

3. A computer is *anachronistic* on the set of a play about colonial life.

_____

4. It was *synchronicity* that we bumped into each other without planning to meet.

_____

Practice and Apply The Critical Vocabulary word *empathy* contains the Greek root, *pathos*. Work with a partner to define *pathos* and create a chart of words that contain the root. Write sentences with the words you identify.

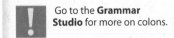

LANGUAGE CONVENTIONS:
Colons

Go to the **Grammar Studio** for more on colons.

Authors use colons to add clarity to their writing. They also use colons for emphasis in order to draw attention to key ideas. In an essay, colons commonly introduce a list, quotation, or independent clause.

USE OF A COLON	EXAMPLE
In this sentence from the selection, notice how de Waal uses a colon to lead to a key idea, a definition of the term "laugh plants."	This is why comedy shows on television have laugh tracks and why theater audiences are sometimes sprinkled with "laugh plants": people paid to produce raucous laughing at any joke that comes along.
In this passage from the selection, the colon has a different purpose. It introduces a list.	It began much more simply, with the synchronization of bodies: running when others run, laughing when others laugh, crying when others cry, or yawning when others yawn.
Now read the same sentence without the colon. Consider how the sentence loses clarity without the colon to introduce the list.	It began much more simply, with the synchronization of bodies running when others run, laughing when others laugh, crying when others cry, or yawning when others yawn.
You can also use a colon to introduce a long quotation or a related independent clause. This sentence from the selection is an example.	They become role models: We empathize with them and emulate them.

When an independent clause follows a colon, should that clause begin with a capital letter? Experts disagree. If your assignment is to follow a certain style (APA, MLA, Chicago Manual of Style, and so on) be sure to look up the rule in that style manual. In general, it's up to the individual but it is important to be consistent.

Practice and Apply Write two paragraphs summarizing key points in the article, "Monkey See, Monkey Do, Monkey Connect." Use colons in at least three places. At least one colon should introduce a list and one should introduce a quotation or independent clause.

WITH FRIENDS LIKE THESE . . .

Informational Text by **Dorothy Rowe**

? ESSENTIAL QUESTION:

How do we form and maintain our connections with others?

QUICK START

Why do certain people become your friends and not others? How do you stay friends? With a partner, discuss the factors that make you likely to become friends with someone and factors that determine whether the person becomes your long-term friend.

SUMMARIZE AND PARAPHRASE TEXTS

Two skills that will help you understand a text—and communicate your understanding to others—are **summarizing** and **paraphrasing**.

When you **summarize** a text, you briefly retell the main ideas in your own words, while maintaining meaning and logical order. The **central idea** is the main point that the author wants you to understand. To keep your summary **objective**, include only the author's ideas.

When you **paraphrase** a text, you restate its ideas in your own words. Paraphrasing helps you clarify the author's meaning because you must understand it before you can rephrase it. An effective paraphrase maintains both the author's meaning and the logical order in which the ideas are presented. As you read, makes notes about the key idea in each paragraph. This will help you grasp the central idea of the selection. When you come across a long or confusing sentence, take time to paraphrase it.

EVALUATE DETAILS

To determine key ideas in a text, you need to **evaluate details**. Authors of informational texts support their ideas with several types of details. These can include key words and terms, facts and examples, statistics, quotations or ideas from experts, and real-world anecdotes.

As you read each paragraph or section of an informational text, ask yourself what types of details the author includes. After you read, determine the key idea of the paragraph based on the details by asking yourself questions:

- How do these details relate to each other?

- What key idea do these details support?

- How reliable are the details? How clear and accurate are they?

- How well do the details support the main idea of the text?

Use a chart like this to organize the most important details and the key ideas:

PARAGRAPH NUMBER	MOST IMPORTANT DETAILS	KEY IDEA

**GENRE ELEMENTS:
INFORMATIONAL TEXT**

- provides factual information

- includes evidence to support ideas

- may contains text features to organize ideas

- includes many forms, such as news articles and essays

CRITICAL VOCABULARY

validate	assess	derive

To see how many Critical Vocabulary words you already know, use them to complete the sentences.

1. We always _____ the options on the menu before we try a new restaurant.

2. The popularity of those websites will always _____ from their focus on celebrities.

3. The mayor hopes that re-election will _____ her leadership.

LANGUAGE CONVENTIONS

Adjective and Adverb Phrases A **prepositional phrase** is a phrase that consists of a preposition, its object, and any modifiers of the object. Authors use prepositional phrases to add information and enhance a sentence. In this lesson, you will learn about two types of prepositional phrases: **adjective phrases** and **adverb phrases.** Here is an example from the selection of each:

We are constantly assessing how safe our sense <u>of being a person</u> is.

Friends are central <u>to this all-important sense of validation</u>.

The underlined phrase in the first sentence is an adjective phrase modifying the noun *sense*. The underlined phrase in the second sentence is an adverb phrase modifying the adjective *central*. As you read "With Friends Like These . . .," note the author's use of adjective and adverb phrases.

ANNOTATION MODEL

NOTICE & NOTE

As you read, mark the details the author uses to support her ideas. Note what types of details they are, and evaluate their effectiveness. When you finish the selection, summarize the main idea. Here is an example of how one reader responded to "With Friends Like These . . .":

We value friends, but the path of friendship, like love, rarely runs smooth.①We may feel jealous of a friend's achievements when we want to feel happy for her.②We might find it hard to give friends objective advice, unrelated to the person we want them to be.③We can be reluctant to allow each other to change, sometimes falling out in a way that is painful for all involved. And yet friendships are vitally important, central to our enjoyment of life.

1, 2, and 3: examples of friendship not running smoothly; effective because anyone with friends can relate

Key idea: friendships important but challenging

BACKGROUND

Dorothy Rowe *(b. 1930) is an Australian-born psychologist who has lived in England since 1968. During her career, she has studied the ways in which people make meaning and the biological basis of mental disorders. Rowe is the author of 16 books. In 2010, London's* Daily Telegraph *included Rowe on its list of the 100 most powerful women in Britain in business, academia, and politics.*

WITH FRIENDS LIKE THESE . . .

Informational Text by Dorothy Rowe

SETTING A PURPOSE

As you read, pay attention to whether the author appears to be drawing on scientific studies or personal experience to support her ideas.

1   We value friends, but the path of friendship, like love, rarely runs smooth. We may feel jealous of a friend's achievements when we want to feel happy for her. We might find it hard to give friends objective advice, unrelated to the person we want them to be. We can be reluctant to allow each other to change, sometimes falling out in a way that is painful for all involved. And yet, friendships are vitally important; central to our enjoyment of life.

2   More fundamentally, friendships are essential to our sense of who we are. Neuroscientists have shown that our brain does not reveal to us the world as it is, but rather as possible interpretations of what is going on around us, drawn from our past experience. Since no two people ever have exactly the same experience, no two people ever see anything in exactly the same way.

Notice & Note

You can use the side margins to notice and note signposts in the text.

SUMMARIZE AND PARAPHRASE TEXTS

Annotate: Mark a sentence that you find long or confusing in paragraphs 1–3.

Interpret: Paraphrase the sentence. How does the sentence you chose relate to the ideas in the first three paragraphs? Explain your answer.

3   Most of our brain's constructions are unconscious. Early in our life our stream of conscious and unconscious constructions create, like a real stream, a kind of whirlpool that quickly becomes our most precious possession, that is, our sense of being a person, what we call "I", "me", "myself." Like a whirlpool, our sense of being a person cannot exist separately from the stream that created it.

4   Because we cannot see reality directly, all our ideas are guesses about what is going on. Thus our sense of being a person is made up of these guesses. All the time we are creating ideas about who we are, what is happening now, what has happened in our world, and what our future will be. When these ideas are shown by events to be reasonably accurate, that is, our ideas are **validated**, we feel secure in ourselves, but when they are proved wrong, we feel that we are falling apart.

5   Friends are central to this all-important sense of validation. When a friend confirms to us that the world is as we see it, we feel safer, reassured. On the other hand, when we say, "I'm shattered," or "I'm losing my grip," we might not be using clichés to describe a bad day but talking about something quite terrifying that we are experiencing: our sense of who we are is being challenged. So terrifying is this experience that we develop many different tactics aimed at warding off invalidation and defending ourselves against being annihilated as a person.

Emotional support

6 We are constantly **assessing** how safe our sense of being a person is. Our assessments are those interpretations we call emotions. All our emotions relate to the degree of safety or danger our sense of being a person is experiencing. So important are these interpretations to our survival that we do not need to put them into words, although of course we can. Our positive emotions are interpretations to do with safety, while the multitude of negative emotions define the particular kind of danger and its degree. Joy is: "Everything is the way I want it to be"; jealousy is: "How dare that person have something that is rightly mine."

7   We can be invalidated by events such as the bankruptcy of the firm that employs us, but most frequently we are invalidated by other people.

8   A friend told me how her husband had used her password and pin to drain her bank account and fund his secret gambling habit. Losing her savings was a terrible blow, but far worse was her loss of trust in the person she saw as her best friend.

9   When she described herself as falling apart, I assured her that what was falling apart were some of her ideas. All she had to do was

© Houghton Mifflin Harcourt Publishing Company

validate
(văl´ĭ-dāt) *v.* to establish the value, truth, or legitimacy of

CONTRASTS AND CONTRADICTIONS

Notice & Note: What phrase indicates the author is introducing contrasting details in paragraph 5? Mark it in the text.

Interpret: How does the contrast in this paragraph illustrate the importance of validation?

assess
(ə-sĕs´) *v.* to evaluate

LANGUAGE CONVENTIONS
ANNOTATE: Mark two adjective or adverb phrases in paragraphs 7–9.

ANALYZE: For each adjective or adverb phrase, describe how it adds information to the sentence.

EVALUATE DETAILS

Annotate: In paragraph 10, circle one example of how a friendship can be risky. Underline one example of how a friendship can be helpful.

Evaluate: How can the contrasting examples you marked be expressed as a key idea?

to endure a period of uncertainty until she could construct ideas that better reflected her situation.

10   Friendship can be rewarding but, like all relationships, it can also be risky. Other people can let us down, insult or humiliate us, leading us to feel diminished and in danger. Yet we need other people to tell us when we have got our guesses right, and, when we get things wrong, to help us make more accurate assessments. Live completely on your own and your guesses will get further and further away from reality.

11   The degree of risk we perceive from our friends relates directly to the degree of self-confidence we feel. When confident of ourselves, we feel that we can deal with being invalidated; when lacking self-confidence, we often see danger where no danger need exist. Take jealousy, for example. Feeling self-confident, we can rejoice in our friend's success at a new job; feeling inferior, we see danger and try to defend ourselves with: "It's not fair." We can fail to see that our friendship should be more important to us than our injured pride.

12   Our levels of confidence also relate to how ready we are to accept change, and how able we are to allow our friends to change. To feel secure in ourselves, we need to be able to predict events reasonably accurately. We think we know our friends well, and so can predict what they will do. We create a mental image of our friends, and we want to keep them within the bounds of that image. Our need to do this can override our ability to see our friends in the way they see themselves. We do not want them to change because then we would have to change our image of them. Change creates uncertainty, and uncertainty can be frightening.

© Houghton Mifflin Harcourt Publishing Company • Image Credits: ©Artville/Getty Images

Falling out

13 However, an inability to allow change can lead to the end of a friendship. Falling out with a friend shows us that our image of them, from which we **derive** our predictions about that friend, is wrong; and if that is the case, our sense of being a person is threatened.

14   If we lose a friend, we have to change how we see ourselves and our life. Each of us lives in our own individual world of meaning. We need to find friends whose individual world is somewhat similar to our own so that we are able to communicate with one another.

15   The people who can validate us best are those we can see as equals, and with whom there can be mutual affection, trust, loyalty and acceptance. Such people give us the kind of validation that builds a lasting self-confidence despite the difficulties we encounter.

16   These are our true friends.

derive
(dĭ-rīv´) *v.* to obtain or extract from

SUMMARIZE AND PARAPHRASE TEXTS
Annotate: Mark two details in paragraphs 13–16 that indicate the selection's central idea.

Summarize: In two to four sentences, write an objective summary of the selection.

CHECK YOUR UNDERSTANDING

Answer these questions before moving on to the **Analyze the Text** section on the following page.

1 Many of the author's supporting details come from —

A sociology and television shows

B neuroscience and day-to-day life

C her own friendships in high school

D a documentary film about relationships

2 The author probably included the information in paragraph 6 to —

F explain why emotions are important to our survival

G demonstrate that joy is the key to friendship

H show that joy and jealousy cannot be put into words

J describe how emotions are connected to our sense of being a person

3 How does the author support the idea that the degree of perceived risk and the degree of self-confidence are related?

A By including an example about jealousy over a friend's new job

B By defining the qualities that lead to self-confidence

C By including examples of normal risks taken in healthy friendships

D By comparing two of her friends with varying degrees of self-confidence

ANALYZE THE TEXT

Support your responses with evidence from the text. NOTEBOOK

1. **Infer** Reread the first paragraph. What **tone**, or attitude, is created by the author's use of the first-person pronouns *we* and *our*? Why do you think she chose to introduce her topic to readers in this way?

2. **Evaluate** In paragraphs 2–4, the author develops her ideas with details from the fields of neuroscience and psychology. How does she connect this information to the key idea that "friendships are essential to our sense of who we are"?

3. **Analyze** In paragraph 12, the author discusses people's capacity to accept change. Why does she introduce these ideas immediately before the section "Falling out"?

4. **Cite Evidence** In paragraph 15, the author makes this claim: "The people who can validate us best are those we can see as equals, and with whom there can be mutual affection, trust, loyalty and acceptance." What evidence does the author provide to support this claim? Is she justified in making it?

5. **Notice & Note** What information challenged, changed, or confirmed what you already knew about friendship? Paraphrase key ideas and details from the text in your answer.

RESEARCH

RESEARCH TIP
When researching an unfamiliar or complex topic, look for sources geared toward a general audience. Technical sources assume that the audience is knowledgeable about the terms and concepts of the academic field. Newspaper articles and books meant for the general reader will be easier to understand.

In paragraph 2 of "With Friends Like These . . ." Dorothy Rowe introduces concepts about friendship based on research by neuroscientists. Find another article about friendship and neuroscience. After you read the article, **freewrite**, or write your thoughts continuously without stopping, for 2 minutes. Record your thoughts about friendship in the chart below.

ARTICLE TITLE AND TOPIC	FREEWRITE

Connect Share your response to the article with a partner. Talk about ways in which the ideas in your article relate to the ideas in "With Friends Like These . . ." Did anything in the second article cause you to change your views about friendship? Note details that caused you to adjust your perspective.

© Houghton Mifflin Harcourt Publishing Company

CREATE AND PRESENT

Write a Personal Essay Using your notes, charts, and marked-up selection, write a personal essay about how the key ideas in "With Friends Like These . . ." and in your self-selected article relate to your own friendships.

- ❏ Introduce the topic and tell readers how you relate to the key ideas overall. Cite evidence from both your own experiences and the texts.

- ❏ Refer to the characteristics of true friends listed in paragraph 15. Use synonyms if Rowe's wording is too technical.

- ❏ In your final paragraph, discuss how your approach toward friendship might change based on what you learned.

Present a Scene With a partner, present a two- to three-minute scene in which two teenagers meet and discover the ideal friend.

- ❏ Share your essay with your partner. Based on your essays and notes, brainstorm a list of the qualities of an ideal friend.

- ❏ Write a script for your scene. Think about how to communicate your ideas through words, actions, and body language. Include a prop.

- ❏ Rehearse your scene. Practice speaking clearly and loudly, facing your audience, and pausing for dramatic effect. Use a synonym if you cannot remember an exact word from your script.

 Go to the **Writing Studio** for more on writing a narrative.

Go to the **Speaking and Listening Studio** for help with giving a presentation.

RESPOND TO THE ESSENTIAL QUESTION

 ? How do we form and maintain our connections with others?

Gather Information Review your "With Friends Like These . . ." notes and annotations. Then, add relevant information to your Response Log. As you determine which information to include, think about:

- how friendships help create and validate our sense of self
- the role of self-confidence in perceiving risk and accepting change
- the conditions and characteristics that promote long, successful friendships

At the end of the unit, use your notes to help you write a short story.

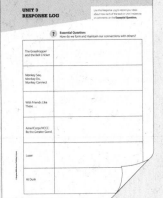

ACADEMIC VOCABULARY

As you write and discuss what you learned from the informational text, be sure to use the Academic Vocabulary words. Check off each of the words that you use.

- ❏ **capacity**
- ❏ **confer**
- ❏ **emerge**
- ❏ **generate**
- ❏ **trace**

CRITICAL VOCABULARY

WORD BANK
validate
assess
derive

Practice and Apply Working with a partner, develop a brief scene that depicts the meaning of each Critical Vocabulary word but does not include the word. Swap your scenes with another pair. Pairs will then analyze each other's scenes and identify the Critical Vocabulary word that is being conveyed in each one. Start by briefly describing each idea below.

1. An experience makes a character feel **validated**. Idea for scene:

   _____

2. A character **assesses** a situation or another character. Idea for scene:

   _____

3. A character **derives** an idea from something he or she observes. Idea for scene:

   _____

Go to the **Vocabulary Studio** for more on print and digital sources.

VOCABULARY STRATEGY:
Print and Digital Resources

Many informational texts include words and phrases that are specific to a particular discipline. Dorothy Rowe draws on psychology and neurology to support the ideas in "With Friends Like These . . . ." To clarify and validate your understanding of technical words, you can look them up in **print and digital resources** such as glossaries, encyclopedias, technical dictionaries, and print dictionaries. If you find more than one definition for a word, context clues can help you choose the appropriate definition.

Practice and Apply The words below appear in "With Friends Like These . . . ." Look up each word in a print or digital dictionary, glossary, or thesaurus. Then, use the word in an original sentence that demonstrates your understanding of the word as it is used in the text.

1. constructions

   _____

2. unconscious

   _____

3. perceive

   _____

LANGUAGE CONVENTIONS:
Adjective and Adverb Phrases

A **prepositional phrase** is a phrase that consists of a preposition, its object, and any modifiers of the object. Prepositional phrases that modify nouns or pronouns are called **adjective phrases**. Prepositional phrases that modify verbs, adjectives, or adverbs are called **adverb phrases**.

"With Friends Like These . . ." opens with these sentences:

> **We value friends, but the path of friendship, like love, rarely runs smooth. We may feel jealous of a friend's achievements when we want to feel happy for her.**

The prepositional phrase *of friendship* functions as an adjective modifying *path*. The phrases *of a friend's achievements* and *for her* act as adverbs modifying *jealous* and *happy*. Notice how removing the adverb phrases makes the second sentence much less specific:

> **We may feel jealous when we want to feel happy.**

This chart shows sentences from the selection that use prepositional phrases as either adjectives or adverbs. Read each sentence carefully and note the relationship between the phrase and the word it modifies. There may be other words between the phrase and the word it modifies.

ADJECTIVE PHRASE	ADVERB PHRASE
Each of us lives in our own individual world of meaning. (modifies the noun *world*)	**More fundamentally, friendships are essential to our sense of who we are.** (modifies the adjective *essential*)

Practice and Apply Write a summary of the author's ideas about how friendships validate our sense of who we are. Then, revise your paragraph to include at least one of each kind of phrase shown in the chart—a prepositional phrase that functions as an adjective and a prepositional phrase that functions as an adverb.

Go to the **Grammar Studio** for more on adjective and adverb phrases.

PUBLIC SERVICE ANNOUNCEMENT

AMERICORPS NCCC: BE THE GREATER GOOD

by The Corporation for National and Community Service

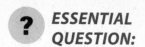

? ESSENTIAL QUESTION:

How do we form and maintain our connections with others?

QUICK START

Think about times when you have helped other people or your community. How do you feel when you are contributing to other people's health and happiness? List three words describing those feelings.

ANALYZE MEDIA MESSAGES

GENRE ELEMENTS: PUBLIC SERVICE ANNOUNCEMENT

- appeals to audience emotions through visuals and music
- sends a clear, compelling message
- calls the audience to action
- takes the form of a video or a radio broadcast

A **public service announcement** (PSA) is a type of advertisement. Like other advertisements, a PSA is structured to achieve a purpose. A television commercial, for example, is usually created to encourage people to buy something. A PSA's purpose is to inform the audience as well as encourage viewers to take action. For example, a PSA might ask people to donate goods and services to victims of a natural disaster. Although PSAs are meant to persuade and to influence viewers, the information that they convey is fact-based and unbiased.

PSAs are **multimodal texts**. They communicate a message through multiple media techniques, or modes, including written text, audio tracks, video, and special effects. When you analyze a multimodal text you should consider individual media modes as well as the combined effect of those modes. Most PSAs include these elements:

CLEAR AND CONCISE MESSAGE	message or central idea is clear even without the audio
LOGICAL PRESENTATION	visuals, text, and music are arranged logically to convey the central idea
EMOTIONAL HOOK	visuals and music evoke, or bring forth, particular emotions to engage the audience
CRITICAL INFORMATION	important information is included, such as the name of the organization or statistics
CALL TO ACTION	viewers understand what the announcement wants them to do

BACKGROUND

A public service announcement (PSA) is a message usually produced for television or radio about a topic or issue of interest to the public. Media and news organizations distribute PSAs at no charge. This particular announcement is for a program that is part of the Corporation for National and Community Service, a federal agency that provides support to volunteer organizations and to individual volunteers around the country. The program, which is called AmeriCorps NCCC (National Civilian Community Corps), develops leaders and strengthens communities through team-based community service.

SETTING A PURPOSE

As you view the video, pay attention to how the visuals, music, and text contribute to the PSA's message. NOTEBOOK .

To view the video, log in online and select **"AMERICORPS NCCC: BE THE GREATER GOOD"** from the unit menu.

As needed, pause the video to make notes about how the visuals, music, and text work together to communicate each idea. Replay or rewind so that you can clarify anything you do not understand.

ANALYZE MEDIA

Support your answers with evidence from the video. ☷ NOTEBOOK

1. **Summarize** In your own words, describe jobs that a volunteer for AmeriCorps NCCC might perform.

2. **Infer** How does AmeriCorps NCCC want the audience to feel about volunteering as part of a team? What audio and visuals in the PSA help communicate this? Cite specific words, scenes or images in your response.

3. **Integrate** Describe the music, lighting, camera angle and perspective used in the video. In what way do they support the purpose of the video?

4. **Synthesize** Explain the title and last line "Be the Greater Good." How does this phrase relate to the voiceover statements that begin "You're a . . ."?

5. **Critique** Think about the purpose of the PSA. Consider the hook, the call to action, and the techniques used to present information. Do you think "Be the Greater Good" is an effective PSA? Why or why not?

RESEARCH

In a small group, research two additional PSAs on topics people in your group care about. Compare and contrast the use of media elements, and determine the main message that each PSA sends.

TITLE OF PSA	PSA 1	PSA 2
Voiceover: Language style and techniques		
Visual techniques		
Sound/music techniques		
Special effects		
Message		

RESEARCH TIP
When researching PSAs, watch out for advertisements that do not fit the genre. Navigate away from any video that appears biased, not based on facts, or focused on a commercial product. Review any accompanying notes that identify the creator, publication date, and purpose of the PSA. Find the website or the organization that sponsors the PSA; it is most likely reputable if its URL ends in *.org, .edu,* or *.gov.*

Extend Compare the two PSAs you researched. Which PSA communicates its main message more effectively? How?

CREATE AND PRESENT

Create a Public Service Announcement In a small group, create a PSA script or storyboard in which you send a message and deliver a call to action.

❏ Brainstorm a list of issues people in your group care about, then come to a consensus on a topic.

❏ Determine a compelling way to hook your audience. Think about how to best use audio, video, and voiceover text to achieve your purpose.

❏ Find factual information to include in your PSA. Credit your sources.

❏ Write the script and/or storyboard for your PSA to organize the multiple streams of information you want to present.

Present a Public Service Announcement Turn your plan into a finished product, which your group will present to the class.

❏ Choose the format for your presentation: audio (for a radio broadcast), video, or poster presentation.

❏ Make a list of equipment you will need, and consult with your teacher and media center about obtaining it.

❏ Assign specific roles and responsibilities to each group member so that all elements of your PSA are covered.

❏ When delivering your presentation, keep in mind the message and call to action that you want the audience to hear. Use speaking rate, volume, and pauses to emphasize your message.

Go to the **Writing Studio** for more on producing and publishing with technology.

Go to the **Speaking and Listening Studio** for more on using media in a presentation.

RESPOND TO THE ESSENTIAL QUESTION

? How do we form and maintain our connections with others?

Gather Information Review your notes on "AmeriCorps NCCC: Be the Greater Good." Then, add relevant information to your Response Log. As you determine which information to include, think about:

- How helping people enhances your connection to them
- The benefits to working as part of a group to help others

At the end of the unit, use your notes to help you write a short story.

UNIT 3 RESPONSE LOG	
Essential Question: How do we form and maintain our connections with others?	
The Grasshopper and the Bell Cricket	
Monkey See, Monkey Do, Monkey Connect	
With Friends Like These . . .	
AmeriCorps NCCC: Be the Greater Good	
Loser	
At Dusk	

ACADEMIC VOCABULARY

As you write and discuss what you learned from the public service announcement, be sure to use the Academic Vocabulary words. Check off each of the words that you use.

❏ **capacity**

❏ **confer**

❏ **emerge**

❏ **generate**

❏ **trace**

COMPARE THEMES

As you read, notice how authors working in two different genres address similar themes. What messages do these texts relate about the world in general? How do the authors express those messages? After you review both selections, you will collaborate with a small group on a final project.

? **ESSENTIAL QUESTION:**

How do we form and maintain our connections with others?

Loser

QUICK START

Think about something you have lost that meant a lot to you. How did you try to find it? Would you have given up something else of value in order to get it back? Write for a few minutes about the thing you lost and what it meant to you.

ANALYZE PLOT

Authors usually write fictional stories in chronological, or **linear**, order. This means the author reveals plot events in the order that the characters experience them. Sometimes, however, an author will create a **non-linear plot**. They may use these literary devices:

- **Flashbacks:** the placement of earlier events into the present action, often by having a character recall something that happened in the past.

- **Foreshadowing:** a technique that warns readers of future events.

- **Subplots:** a device in which less important events happen at about the same time as the main plot, but in a separate place and to different characters.

As you read "Loser," notice the sequence of plot events and the author's use of flashbacks. How do the flashbacks help push the plot forward and help you better understand the story's characters and messages?

ANALYZE CHARACTERIZATION

The way a writer creates and develops characters' personalities is known as **characterization.** Authors develop complex yet believable characters by describing what they do, say, and think, as well as how they interact with other characters. These details about the characters often shape the story's themes. Use a chart like the one below to record text details that reveal the personality of this story's main character. Then, make an inference or ask a question about each detail.

TEXT EVIDENCE	EXAMPLES	INFERENCES AND QUESTIONS
Character's words and actions		
Character's thoughts and observations		
What others say to and about the character		

As you read "Loser," note how the author uses the main character's traits and experiences to relate messages about life.

© Houghton Mifflin Harcourt Publishing Company

CRITICAL VOCABULARY

knack   skeptic   scam   insistent

To see how many Critical Vocabulary words you already know, use them to complete the sentences below.

1. I am a(n) _____ and don't believe in ghosts or UFOs.

2. If an offer seems too good to be true, it could be a(n) _____ .

3. I didn't want another piece of pie, but my aunt was _____.

4. Take the broken phone to Olivia, who has a(n) _____ for fixing them.

LANGUAGE CONVENTIONS
Active and Passive Voice

In a sentence in the **active voice**, the subject performs the action. In the sentence below from the selection, the subject (the neighbors) did the action (discovered):

> **The neighbors discovered his talent accidentally. . .**

In the **passive voice**, the subject (his talent) is being acted upon:

> **His talent was discovered by the neighbors accidentally.**

Writers usually use the active voice because it is clear and direct. They may use the passive voice to emphasize the object or the action, rather than who or what did it.

As you read "Loser," look for examples of sentences written in the active voice and in the passive voice.

ANNOTATION MODEL

NOTICE & NOTE

Here is how one student annotated plot developments in "Loser."

Once there was an orphan who had a knack for finding lost things. Both his <u>parents had been killed when he was eight years old</u>—they were swimming in the ocean when it turned wild with waves, and each had tried to save the other from drowning. The boy woke up from a nap, on the sand, alone. After the tragedy, the community adopted and raised him, and a few years after the deaths of his parents, he began to have a sense of objects even when they weren't visible. This ability continued growing in power through his teens and (by his twenties) he was able to actually sniff out lost sunglasses, keys, contact lenses and sweaters.

The author starts the story with a flashback to tell about the day the boy became an orphan.

The story is set years later, when he is in his twenties.

BACKGROUND

Aimee Bender *(b.1969) is an American writer whose short stories have been published in many magazines and journals, as well as read aloud on radio broadcasts and podcasts. Her five books, all collections of short stories, have won several awards. Bender often writes about realistic-seeming characters set in our real world, but with slightly magical or fantastical elements. The following story, "Loser," appeared in her book* The Girl in the Flammable Skirt, *which was first published in 1988. Bender lives with her family in Los Angeles, where she teaches creative writing at the University of Southern California.*

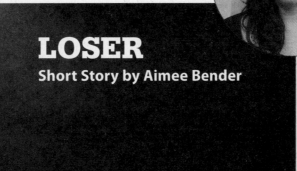

LOSER
Short Story by Aimee Bender

PREPARE TO COMPARE

As you read, think about how the characters' experiences connect to your own or to those of other characters you have read about. Ask yourself what the events tell you about the characters in this story.

1 Once there was an orphan who had a **knack** for finding lost things. Both his parents had been killed when he was eight years old—they were swimming in the ocean when it turned wild with waves, and each had tried to save the other from drowning. The boy woke up from a nap, on the sand, alone. After the tragedy, the community adopted and raised him, and a few years after the deaths of his parents, he began to have a sense of objects even when they weren't visible. This ability continued growing in power through his teens and by his twenties, he was able to actually sniff out lost sunglasses, keys, contact lenses and sweaters.

2 The neighbors discovered his talent accidentally—he was over at Jenny Sugar's house one evening, picking her up for a date, when Jenny's mother misplaced her hairbrush, and was walking around, complaining about this. The young man's nose twitched and he turned slightly toward the kitchen and pointed to the drawer where the spoons and knives were kept. His date burst into laughter. Now that would be quite a silly place to put

© Houghton Mifflin Harcourt Publishing Company • Image Credits: (t) ©Agence Opale/Alamy; (c) ©woolzian/iStock/Getty Images Plus/Getty Images

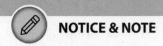

ANALYZE PLOT

Annotate: How do other people find out about the young man's gift? Mark the words that tell the reader.

Predict: How do you think people will treat the young man now that they know this?

skeptic
(skĕp´tĭk) *n.* someone who doubts something.

scam
(skăm) *n.* a plan to cheat others, often out of money.

insistent
(ĭn-sĭs´tənt) *adj.* demanding that something happen or refusing to accept that it will not happen.

ANALYZE PLOT

Annotate: Mark words the author uses to establish time in this part of the story.

Analyze: How does the author shift from past events to the current or main events of the story?

the brush, she said, among all that silverware! and she opened the drawer to make her point, to wave with a knife or brush her hair with a spoon, but when she did, boom, there was the hairbrush, matted with gray curls, sitting astride the fork pile.

3   Jenny's mother kissed the young man on the cheek but Jenny herself looked at him suspiciously all night long.

4   You planned all that, didn't you, she said, over dinner. You were trying to impress my mother. Well you didn't impress me, she said.

5   He tried to explain himself but she would hear none of it and when he drove his car up to her house, she fled before he could even finish saying he'd had a nice time, which was a lie anyway. He went home to his tiny room and thought about the word lonely and how it sounded and looked so lonely, with those two l's in it, each standing tall by itself.

6   As news spread around the neighborhood about the young man's skills, people reacted two ways: there were the deeply appreciative and the **skeptics**. The appreciative ones called up the young man regularly. He'd stop by on his way to school, find their keys, and they'd give him a homemade muffin. The skeptics called him over too, and watched him like a hawk; he'd still find their lost items but they'd insist it was an elaborate **scam** and he was doing it all to get attention. Maybe, declared one woman, waving her index finger in the air, Maybe, she said, he steals the thing so we think it's lost, moves the item, and then comes over to save it! How do we know it was really lost in the first place? What is going on?

7   The young man didn't know himself. All he knew was the feeling of a tug, light but **insistent**, like a child at his sleeve, and that tug would turn him in the right direction and show him where to look. Each object had its own way of inhabiting space, and therefore messaging its location. The young man could sense, could smell, an object's presence—he did not need to see it to feel where it put its gravity down. As would be expected, items that turned out to be miles away took much harder concentration than the ones that were two feet to the left.

8   When Mrs. Allen's little boy didn't come home one afternoon, that was the most difficult of all. Leonard Allen was eight years old and usually arrived home from school at 3:05. He had allergies and needed a pill before he went back out to play. That day, by 3:45, a lone Mrs. Allen was wreck. Her boy rarely got lost—only once had that happened in the supermarket but he'd been found quite easily under the produce tables, crying; this walk home from school was a straight line and Leonard was not a wandering kind.

9   Mrs. Allen was just a regular neighbor except for one extraordinary fact—through an inheritance, she was the owner of a gargantuan[1] emerald she called the Green Star. It sat, glass-cased, in her kitchen, where everyone could see it because she insisted that

---
[1] **gargantuan** (gär-găn´chōō-ən): huge.

it be seen. Sometimes, as a party trick, she'd even cut steak with its beveled[2] edge.

10   On this day, she removed the case off the Green Star and stuck her palms on it. Where is my boy? she cried. The Green Star was cold and flat. She ran, weeping, to her neighbor, who calmly walked her back home; together, they gave the house a thorough search, and then the neighbor, a believer, recommended calling the young man. Although Mrs. Allen was a skeptic, she thought anything was a worthwhile idea, and when the line picked up, she said, in a trembling voice:

11   You must find my boy.

12   The young man had been just about to go play basketball with his friends. He'd located the basketball in the bathtub.

13   You lost him? said the young man.

14   Mrs. Allen began to explain and then her phone clicked.

15   One moment please, she said, and the young man held on.

16   When her voice returned, it was shaking with rage.

17   He's been kidnapped! she said. And they want the Green Star!

18   The young man realized then it was Mrs. Allen he was talking to, and nodded. Oh, he said, I see. Everyone in town was familiar with Mrs. Allen's Green Star. I'll be right over, he said.

19   The woman's voice was too run with tears to respond.

20   In his basketball shorts and shirt, the young man jogged over to Mrs. Allen's house. He was amazed at how the Green Star was all exactly the same shade of green. He had a desire to lick it.

21   By then, Mrs. Allen was in hysterics.

22   They didn't tell me what to do, she sobbed. Where do I bring my emerald? How do I get my boy back?

23   The young man tried to feel the scent of the boy. He asked for a photograph and stared at it—a brown-haired kid at his kindergarten graduation—but the young man had only found objects before, and lost objects at that. He'd never found anything, or anybody, stolen. He wasn't a policeman.

24   Mrs. Allen called the police and one officer showed up at the door.

25   Oh it's the finding guy, the officer said. The young man dipped his head modestly. He turned to his right; to his left; north; south. He got a glimmer of a feeling toward the north and walked out the back door, through the backyard. Night approached and the sky seemed to grow and deepen in the darkness.

---

[2] **beveled (bĕv´əld):** cut at sloping angles.

ANALYZE CHARACTERIZATION

Annotate: Mark details that show what other characters think of the young man.

Analyze: What can you infer about the young man from what the neighbors say?

ANALYZE CHARACTERIZATION

Annotate: Mark information that the author tells you about the young man's actions.

Analyze: What do the young man's actions tell you about his character?

ANALYZE PLOT

Annotate: Mark verbs that signal a flashback.

Analyze: How does the author use these flashbacks to connect to the young man's talent?

26   What's his name again? he called back to Mrs. Allen.

27   Leonard, she said. He heard the policeman pull out a pad and begin to ask basic questions.

28   He couldn't quite feel him. He felt the air and he felt the tug inside of the Green Star, an object displaced from its original home in Asia. He felt the tug of the tree in the front yard which had been uprooted from Virginia to be replanted here, and he felt the tug of his own watch which was from his uncle; in an attempt to be fatherly, his uncle had insisted he take it but they both knew the gesture was false.

29   Maybe the boy was too far away by now.

30   He heard the policeman ask: What is he wearing?

31   Mrs. Allen described a blue shirt, and the young man focused in on the blue shirt; he turned off his distractions and the blue shirt, like a connecting radio station, came calling from the northwest. The young man went walking and walking and about fourteen houses down he felt the blue shirt shrieking at him and he walked right into the backyard, through the back door, and sure enough, there were four people watching TV including the tear-stained boy with a runny nose eating a candy bar. The young man scooped up the boy while the others watched, so surprised they did nothing, and one even muttered: Sorry, man.

ANALYZE CHARACTERIZATION

Annotate: Mark details that tell you about the young man's character.

Explain: How does the author use the young man's actions and thoughts here to tell you about his character?

32   For fourteen houses back, the young man held Leonard in his arms like a bride. Leonard stopped sneezing and looked up at the stars and the young man smelled Leonard's hair, rich with the memory of peanut butter. He hoped Leonard would ask him a question, any question, but Leonard was quiet. The young man answered in his head: Son, he said, and the word rolled around, a marble on a marble floor. Son, he wanted to say.

33   When he reached Mrs. Allen's door, which was wide open, he walked in with quiet Leonard and Mrs. Allen promptly burst into tears and the policeman slunk out the door.

34   She thanked the young man a thousand times, even offered him the Green Star, but he refused it. Leonard turned on the TV and curled up on the sofa. The young man walked over and asked him

about the program he was watching but Leonard stuck a thumb in his mouth and didn't respond.

35   Feel better, he said softly. Tucking the basketball beneath his arm, the young man walked home, shoulders low.

36   In his tiny room, he undressed and lay in bed. Had it been a naked child with nothing on, no shoes, no necklace, no hairbow, no watch, he could not have found it. He lay in bed that night with the trees from other places rustling and he could feel their confusion. No snow here. Not a lot of rain. Where am I? What is wrong with this dirt?

37   Crossing his hands in front of himself, he held on to his shoulders. Concentrate hard, he thought. Where are you? Everything felt blank and quiet. He couldn't feel a tug. He squeezed his eyes shut and let the question bubble up: Where did you go? Come find me. I'm over here. Come find me.

38   If he listened hard enough, he thought he could hear the waves hitting.

AGAIN AND AGAIN

Notice & Note: Mark identical or similar words and phrases that repeat in the last two paragraphs.

Analyze: What do the words and phrases tell you about the young man's thoughts?

CHECK YOUR UNDERSTANDING

Answer these questions before moving on to the **Analyze the Text** section on the following page.

1 What happened to the young man's parents?

A They drowned.

B They abandoned him.

C They were kidnapped.

D They were in a car accident.

2 The neighbors discover the boy's talent when he finds —

F Leonard

G his parents

H a hairbrush

J the Green Star

3 What helps the young man find Leonard?

A The Green Star

B The boy's shirt

C The waves

D The trees

ANALYZE THE TEXT

Support your responses with evidence from the text. 📓 NOTEBOOK

1. **Analyze** **Personification** is the assigning of human traits to non-human objects. How does the author use personification for effect in this story?

2. **Compare** In fiction, a **foil** is a character whose personality and attitude contrast sharply with those of another character. How does the character of Leonard act as a foil for the young man?

3. **Evaluate** The word *loser* can be a cruel insult. It can also refer to someone who loses a competition. Why do you think the author used "Loser" as the story's title? Do you think it fits the story? Why or why not?

4. **Critique** Do you think the author has created a complex character in the young man? Is he a believable character, even with his unusual gift?

5. **Notice & Note** Reread the last paragraph. How does this Memory Moment—the young man's flashback—help you understand how the story explores the theme of loss?

RESEARCH

RESEARCH TIP
Use search terms such as *common themes* or *literature themes* to find lists of themes commonly used by authors. If a theme sounds like it might relate to "Loser," search for the specific theme to learn more about it.

Most works of fiction, including "Loser," explore multiple themes. Some themes are commonly found throughout literature and other works of fiction, such as plays and movies. Look online for lists of common fictional themes. Which themes do you think fit the story in "Loser"? List three themes that you think the author addresses. Cite evidence from the text that supports your choices.

THEME	HOW "LOSER" REFLECTS THIS THEME

Connect Add a column to your chart. List books, movies, and shows you know that address the themes you discovered.

CREATE AND PRESENT

Freewrite Use the chart of themes you researched and evidence from the text that connects to those themes. You will write a statement about how the story explores the different themes. To get started, freewrite to develop your ideas.

❏ For each theme, write your understanding of what the theme says about human nature and life. Then write why you think this theme connects to "Loser."

❏ List examples from the text that support the presence of the theme.

❏ Use your freewriting to draft a three-paragraph statement about the theme in "Loser."

Discuss with a Small Group To refine your ideas, discuss them with a small group.

❏ Tell your group the three themes you believe are explored in "Loser." Explain your thinking by citing the evidence from the short story.

❏ Listen carefully and respond appropriately to your group members. Jot down the three themes each person lists and then listen as they explain why they chose each one.

❏ Ask questions about your group members' points to clarify what you don't understand. You may all have chosen different themes—after all, there are countless themes found in literature!

Go to the **Writing Studio** for more on drafting a statement.

Go to the **Speaking and Listening Studio** for help with participating in collaborative discussions.

RESPOND TO THE ESSENTIAL QUESTION

 How do we form and maintain our connections with others?

Gather Information Review your annotations and notes on "Loser" and highlight those that help answer the Essential Question. Then, add relevant details to your Response Log.

ACADEMIC VOCABULARY
As you write and discuss what you learned from the short story, be sure to use the Academic Vocabulary words. Check off each of the words that you use.

❏ **capacity**

❏ **confer**

❏ **emerge**

❏ **generate**

❏ **trace**

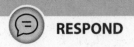

CRITICAL VOCABULARY

Practice and Apply Answer these questions to demonstrate your understanding of each Critical Vocabulary word.

WORD BANK

knack   scam

skeptic   insistent

1. What is something that you have a **knack** for doing?

_____

2. When have you been a **skeptic** about something other people believe in?

_____

3. How can you tell whether an email offer is a **scam**?

_____

4. What are you **insistent** on doing during this school year?

_____

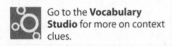

Go to the **Vocabulary Studio** for more on context clues.

VOCABULARY STRATEGY:
Context Clues

The **context** of a word can give you important clues about the word's meaning, including both its denotation and connotation. Sometimes writers provide specific clues such as those shown in the chart.

SPECIFIC CONTEXT CLUES		
Type of Clue	**Key Words/Phrases**	**Example**
Definition or restatement of the meaning of the word	or, which is, that is, in other words, also known as, also called	His first conjecture, **or guess**, was correct.
example following an unfamiliar word	such as, like, as if, for example, especially, including	She loved macabre stories, **such as those by Stephen King.**
comparison with a more familiar word or concept	as, like, also, similar to, in the same way, likewise	Despite his physical suffering, his mind was as **lucid** as any **rational** person's.
contrast with a familiar word or experience	unlike, but, however, although, on the other hand, on the contrary	Unlike her **clumsy** partner, she was an **agile** dancer.
cause-and-effect relationship in which one term is familiar	because, since, when, consequently, as a result, therefore	Because that perfume has a **sharp** scent, I chose a more **subtle** fragrance.

Practice and Apply Working with a partner, use context clues to define these words from "Loser": *matted* (paragraph 2), *hysterics* (paragraph 21) and *gesture* (paragraph 28). For each word, determine its part of speech in the sentence, write your understanding of the meaning of the word based on the context clues, then verify the meaning of the word in a dictionary.

LANGUAGE CONVENTIONS:
Active and Passive Voice

Go to the **Grammar Studio** for more help with active and passive voice.

The **voice** of a verb tells whether its subject performs or receives the action expressed by the verb. When the subject performs the action, the verb is in the **active voice**. When the subject is the receiver of the action, the verb is in the **passive voice**.

You might think writers should always use active voice, as it makes the action clear. However, sometimes writers want to emphasize the receiver of the action. *I was hit by the car* is written in the passive voice to emphasize how the accident affected the subject, *I*. Writing *The car hit me* changes the emphasis to the car.

In other cases, writers cannot or do not want to specify the subject. For example, *Kate was elected president* is written in the passive voice. Rewriting the sentence in the active voice requires knowing who voted (for example, *The class elected Kate president; The students elected Kate president; The group elected Kate president*). The writer might not know who voted; or might want to keep the subject vague in order to focus on a more important point.

Look at the examples of sentences from "The Loser" written in the active and passive voice.

ACTIVE VOICE	PASSIVE VOICE
After the tragedy, the community adopted and raised him. . .	Both of his parents had been killed when he was eight years old. . .
Jenny's mother kissed the young man on the cheek but Jenny herself looked at him suspiciously all night long.	. . .he'd been found quite easily under the produce tables. . .

Practice and Apply Write a one-paragraph summary of the story "Loser," using only active voice. Then look through your paragraph. Which sentences could you rewrite in the passive voice? Rewrite your paragraph and evaluate which sentence structures make the paragraph easier to understand.

SUMMARY

_____

_____

_____

_____

POEM

AT DUSK

by **Natasha Trethewey**

pages 229–231

COMPARE THEMES

Read "At Dusk" to explore how this poem addresses some of the same themes as the short story "Loser." As you read, ask yourself what ideas the author expresses about life or human nature and if those ideas overlap with the ideas in "Loser." After you are finished, you will collaborate with a small group on a final project that involves an analysis of both texts.

? **ESSENTIAL QUESTION:**

How do we form and maintain our connections with others?

SHORT STORY

LOSER

by **Aimee Bender**

pages 217–221

At Dusk

QUICK START

Dusk is the time of day just after the sun has set, when the light on earth and in the sky grows dimmer. People have long associated that time of day with certain emotions. What feelings and memories do you have about dusk? What words would you use to describe this time of day? Discuss with a partner.

ANALYZE DICTION AND SYNTAX

Poets choose words and phrases to convey a specific **tone**—that is, an attitude toward a subject; a **mood**—the feeling or atmosphere; and a **voice**—use of language that creates a personality we can "hear."

Diction is an author's choice of words. **Syntax** is the arrangement of those words into phrases and sentences. The diction and syntax the author uses throughout "At Dusk" contribute to the poem's tone, mood, and voice.

The examples below show how these elements of the author's style contribute to the poem's theme, or message.

LINES FROM POEM	EFFECT ON TONE, MOOD, OR VOICE
the cat lifts her ears, turns first / toward the voice, then back / to the constellation of fireflies flickering / near her head. It's as if she can't decide/ whether to leap over the low hedge, /...or stay where she is.	Here, the poet has chosen to describe the cat's motions in detail—she "lifts her ears, turns first toward the voice..."—which creates a tone of fascination regarding the cat.
street lamps just starting to hum / the backdrop of evening	The poet uses the sensory details of the street lamps "starting to hum" to signal the darkening of the scene as evening falls. This creates a dark, quiet mood.
She's given up calling for now, left me / to imagine her inside the house waiting, / perhaps in a chair in front of the TV, / or walking around, doing small tasks;	The poet has the speaker wonder about what her neighbor is doing inside her house, and she lists several possibilities. This establishes the speaker's curious, imaginative voice.

As you read "At Dusk," make note of the author's diction and syntax choices. Use a chart like the one above to guide your interpretation of the effects of Trethewey's diction and syntax on tone, mood, and voice.

GENRE ELEMENTS: POETRY

- uses figurative language, including personification
- includes imagery that appeals to the senses and expresses emotions
- expresses a theme, or a message about life

CREATE MENTAL IMAGES

Poets use **imagery,** or descriptive words and phrases that recreate sensory experiences for the reader. These descriptions help you make **mental images** of what the poet wants you to visualize. Think of the pictures the words and phrases paint, and ask yourself how you would experience those scenes using your senses.

Review the excerpts from the poem in the chart on the previous page. As you read them the first time, you might have quickly pictured the scene. Now reread them in the chart below, and think more specifically: What did you visualize?

street lamps just starting to hum / the backdrop of evening

the cat lifts her ears, turns first / toward the voice, then back / to the constellation of fireflies flickering / near her head. It's as if she can't decide / whether to leap over the low hedge, / . . . or stay where she is

She's given up calling for now, left me / to imagine her inside the house waiting, / perhaps in a chair in front of the TV

As you read "At Dusk," make mental images of the scene to help you understand the poet's message.

ANNOTATION MODEL

NOTICE & NOTE

Here are annotations about mental images one student created based on the poem.

At first I think she is calling a child,
my neighbor, leaning through her doorway
at dusk, street lamps just starting to hum
the backdrop of evening. Then I hear
the high-pitched wheedling we send out
to animals who know only sound, not
the meanings of our words—*here here*—
nor how they sometimes fall short.

I have a mental image of a neighborhood street that is pretty quiet—you can hear the street lamps humming—and a neighbor leaning out the door, calling as the speaker watches. The neighbor is whistling or making high-pitched sounds: the noises we make when we call for our pets.

BACKGROUND

Natasha Trethewey (b. 1966) was named United States Poet Laureate in 2012. Her role, she says, is "to be the biggest promoter of poetry; someone who's really got to do the work of bringing poetry to the widest audience possible." A native of Gulfport, Mississippi, Trethewey has published several collections of poetry and is a professor of English at Northwestern University in Evanston, Illinois. She has won many honors, including the Pulitzer Prize for poetry in 2007 for her book Native Guard.

AT DUSK

Poem by Natasha Trethewey

PREPARE TO COMPARE

As you read, think about how the author uses language not just to convey a scene, but also to make a statement about life. What mood does the scene create for the reader? How do the tone, mood, and voice contribute to the poem's theme?

At first I think she is calling a child,
my neighbor, leaning through her doorway
at dusk, street lamps just starting to hum
the backdrop of evening. Then I hear
5 the high-pitched wheedling we send out
to animals who know only sound, not
the meanings of our words—*here here*—
nor how they sometimes fall short.
In another yard, beyond my neighbor's
10 sight, the cat lifts her ears, turns first
toward the voice, then back
to the constellation of fireflies flickering
near her head. It's as if she can't decide
whether to leap over the low hedge,
15 the neat row of flowers, and bound
onto the porch, into the steady circle

Notice & Note

You can use the side margins to notice and note signposts in the text.

AGAIN AND AGAIN

Notice & Note: Mark an example of repeated words.

Interpret: What is the effect of this repetition?

of light, or stay where she is: luminous
possibility—all that would keep her
away from home—flitting before her.
20 I listen as my neighbor's voice trails off.
She's given up calling for now, left me
to imagine her inside the house waiting,
perhaps in a chair in front of the TV,
or walking around, doing small tasks;
25 left me to wonder that I too might lift
my voice, sure of someone out there,
send it over the lines stitching here
to there, certain the sounds I make
are enough to call someone home.

CHECK YOUR UNDERSTANDING

Answer these questions before moving on to the **Analyze the Text** section on the following page.

1 Why is the neighbor calling out her door?

    A To greet the speaker

    B To ask for her children

    C To call her cat home

    D To ask for help

2 What does the speaker see in another neighbor's yard?

    F A light

    G A child

    H A cat

    J A TV

3 The poem ends with the speaker thinking about —

    A what the neighbor wants

    B what the cat will do

    C calling someone home

    D how to help the neighbor

ANALYZE THE TEXT

Support your responses with evidence from the text. 📓 NOTEBOOK

1. **Interpret** The speaker talks about the cat not hearing meanings of our words "nor how they sometimes fall short" (line 8). What might this mean?

2. **Infer** What might keep the cat from returning home? What might the image of a "constellation of fireflies flickering" represent?

3. **Analyze** What is the tone of this poem? What words and phrases convey the tone?

4. **Draw Conclusions** Explain the significance of the title "At Dusk."

5. **Notice & Note** What realization does the speaker come to at the end of the poem, and how might this Aha Moment affect the speaker's actions in the future?

RESEARCH

The different times of the day, and the feelings that they evoke in people, are common subjects for poets. Go online and find another poem set at dusk, as well as poems set at dawn and at night. Compare the poems. How does the mood in each poem differ? Record words and phrases that contribute to the poems' moods and messages.

RESEARCH TIP

Some poems might have the words *dawn, dusk,* or *night* in the title, but don't limit your search to those. You can also search, for example, "poems set at sunrise" or "poems about evening."

TIME OF DAY	POEM	DESCRIPTIVE WORDS AND PHRASES
Dawn		
Dusk		
Night		

Extend Choose a poem about a time of day that is meaningful for you, and that you would like to read to the class. Have your teacher approve it, and then share it with a partner. Describe the mood of the poem to your partner.

CREATE AND PRESENT

Present an Oral Reading Using either "At Dusk", or a poem you discovered during your research, plan a poetry reading for your group. The focus of the poetry reading will be appropriate **prosody**, or expressive reading.

Go to the **Speaking and Listening Studio** for help with presenting a recitation.

❏ Read the poem to yourself, making note of line breaks and punctuation. Determine how the poet means for the words to flow.

❏ Think about the tone, mood, and voice of the poem. This will determine how you use the elements of prosody—timing, phrasing, emphasis, and intonation—to interpret the poem for your listeners.

❏ Practice reading the poem aloud with a partner.

Discuss with a Small Group Hold a poetry reading with your group.

❏ Read your poem to your classmates. Use gestures and body language as needed, but focus on how your voice conveys the meaning and feeling of the poem.

❏ Listen carefully as the members of your group read their poems. Make mental images based on each poem's descriptive details. Take notes on the critique form given to you by your teacher. Answer any questions your classmates have about the poem's diction or meaning.

❏ After everyone has read, exchange information from your critique form with group members. Discuss how you gain a sense of the poets' voice, mood, and tone from hearing the poems read aloud.

RESPOND TO THE ESSENTIAL QUESTION

? How do we form and maintain our connections with others?

Gather Information Review your annotations and notes on "At Dusk" and highlight those that help answer the Essential Question. Then, add relevant details to your Response Log.

ACADEMIC VOCABULARY

As you write and discuss what you learned from the poem, be sure to use the Academic Vocabulary words. Check off each of the words that you use.

❏ **capacity**

❏ **confer**

❏ **emerge**

❏ **generate**

❏ **trace**

LOSER
Short Story by Aimee Bender

AT DUSK
Poem by Natasha Trethewey

Collaborate & Compare

COMPARE THEMES

Now that you have read "Loser" and "At Dusk," you can compare how the authors developed themes in their work. You may have noticed some overlap in themes between the two texts, but the authors used different techniques and were working in different **genres**, or literary categories, to express those ideas.

Both authors rely on characterization, setting, plot, and use of language to communicate their themes. Review the texts with a partner. Use a chart like the one below to record your ideas about how the authors have used these elements to develop their themes. Cite specific text evidence where you can. You will **synthesize**, or combine, the information from your chart to draft a theme statement about both works.

	"LOSER"	"AT DUSK"
Characterization		
Setting		
Plot		
Use of Language		

ANALYZE THE TEXTS

Discuss these questions in your group.

1. **Compare** What themes did you discover in both "Loser" and "At Dusk"? How do the authors' attitudes toward those themes differ?

2. **Evaluate** Both authors use **symbols**—people, places, objects, or activities—that stand for something beyond themselves. Choose a symbol from each text and evaluate how the author uses it to add meaning to the text.

3. **Connect** How did creating mental images help you understand both texts? Cite examples from each text.

4. **Connect** The young man in "Loser" and the speaker in "At Dusk" share some qualities. Do you relate to either or both of their feelings or experiences? Explain.

COLLABORATE AND PRESENT

In your group, create a theme statement about "Loser" and "At Dusk." Your group will write a statement describing how the themes you found apply to both texts. You will also describe how the authors develop these themes using characterization, setting, plot, and language.

1. **Synthesize Ideas** Discuss the charts you used to compare the texts and other notes you took while reading. Where are the overlaps in theme between the texts? Collaborate to draft a statement with a description of themes the works share. Include an explanation of how each author developed those themes, citing text evidence and drawing on your own experiences and background knowledge.

2. **Present** Each group will present its statement to the class. As there are countless themes in literature, you may have focused on different ones. Listen to other groups' ideas and think about how the evidence in the texts supports different themes.

3. **Discuss and Reflect** A **theme** is an important idea about life or human nature. It is likely that the themes you have analyzed in both texts relate to your life or the lives of people around you. As a group, discuss how the themes in the texts enrich your understanding of the world around you.

© Houghton Mifflin Harcourt Publishing Company

INDEPENDENT READING

? *ESSENTIAL QUESTION:*

How do we form and maintain our connections with others?

Reader's Choice

Setting a Purpose   Select one or more of these options from your eBook to continue your exploration of the Essential Question.

- Read the descriptions to see which text grabs your interest.
- Think about which genres you enjoy reading.

Notice & Note

In this unit, you practiced noticing and noting these signposts: **Words of the Wiser, Aha Moment,** and **Again and Again.** As you read independently, these signposts and others will aid your understanding. Below are the anchor questions to ask when you read literature and nonfiction.

Reading Literature: Stories, Poems, and Plays		
Signpost	**Anchor Question**	**Lesson**
Contrasts and Contradictions	Why did the character act that way?	p. 419
Aha Moment	How might this change things?	p. 171
Tough Questions	What does this make me wonder about?	p. 494
Words of the Wiser	What's the lesson for the character?	p. 171
Again and Again	Why might the author keep bringing this up?	p. 170
Memory Moment	Why is this memory important?	p. 418

Reading Nonfiction: Essays, Articles, and Arguments		
Signpost	**Anchor Question(s)**	**Lesson**
Big Questions	What surprised me? What did the author think I already knew? What challenged, changed, or confirmed what I already knew?	p. 248 p. 2 p. 84
Contrasts and Contradictions	What is the difference, and why does it matter?	p. 3
Extreme or Absolute Language	Why did the author use this language?	p. 85
Numbers and Stats	Why did the author use these numbers or amounts?	p. 249
Quoted Words	Why was this person quoted or cited, and what did this add?	p. 85
Word Gaps	Do I know this word from someplace else? Does it seem like technical talk for this topic? Do clues in the sentence help me understand the word?	p. 3

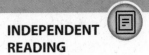
You can preview these texts in Unit 3 of your eBook.

Then, check off the text or texts that you select to read on your own.

The Power of a Dinner Table
David Brooks

Close bonds form when a couple opens their home and hearts to local teens.

POEM

The Debt
Tim Seibles

The poet explores how history can teach us to treat one another with more humanity.

INFORMATIONAL TEXT

from War
Sebastian Junger

Under what circumstances would you give your life for someone else?

SHORT STORY

A Worn Path
Eudora Welty

In this story set in the deep South, a woman overcomes harsh obstacles to take care of someone she loves.

POEM

My Ceremony for Taking
Lara Mann

A poet finds a way to heal herself after her family splits apart.

Collaborate and Share   Work with a partner to discuss what you learned from at least one of your independent readings.

- Give a brief synopsis or summary of the text.
- Describe any signposts that you noticed in the text and explain what they revealed to you.
- Describe what you most enjoyed or found most challenging about the text. Give specific examples.
- Decide whether you would recommend the text to others. Why or why not?

Go to the **Reading Studio** for more resources on **Notice & Note.**

Go to **Writing Narratives** in the **Writing Studio** for help writing a short story.

Write a Short Story

This unit focuses on the connections each of us has with family, friends, pets, and community. For this writing task, you will write a short story that shows how we connect with others. Think about how the selections you have read use narrative techniques to explore interpersonal connections. For an example of a well-written short story you can use as a mentor text, review the story "Loser."

As you write your story, you will want to look at the notes you made in your Response Log after reading the texts in this unit.

Writing Prompt

Read the information in the box below.

This is the topic or context for your story.

> We connect with others through what we see, hear, say, and do.

Think carefully about the following question.

This is the Essential Question for the unit. How would you answer this question, based on the text in this unit?

Be sure to follow the instructions that explain exactly what you are supposed to write.

> How do we form and maintain our connections with others?

Write a short story about an event that reveals something about how we connect with each other.

Review these points as you write and again when you finish. Make any needed changes.

Be sure to—

❑ begin by introducing a setting, a narrator, and a main character

❑ have an engaging plot with a central conflict

❑ provide a clear progression of events, using transitions to connect paragraphs and ideas

❑ use a variety of narrative techniques to develop characters, plot, theme, and suspense or surprise

❑ include sensory language and descriptive details

❑ end with a logical and satisfying resolution to the conflict

1 Plan

Every short story begins with an idea. It may come from something you've seen, heard, or experienced. If you keep a journal, look it over for ideas. Look through a photo book or images online for inspiration. Think about things that connect people to one another, such as interests, beliefs, goals, ethnicity, neighborhood, or family. Building on one of these connections, write down ideas for characters, setting, plot, conflict, and theme. Use the chart below to help you plan your story.

Short Story Planning Chart
Type of Connection (interests, goals, family, etc.)

Characters	Setting

Conflict	Plot

Theme

Background Reading Review the notes you have taken in your Response Log after reading the texts in this unit. These texts provide background reading that will help you think about what you want to say in your short story.

Go to **Writing Narratives: Narrative Context** for help planning your short story.

Notice & Note
From Reading to Writing

As you plan your short story, apply what you've learned about signposts to your own writing. Remember that writers use common features, called signposts, to help convey their message to readers. Think about how you can incorporate an **Aha Moment** into your short story.

Go to the **Reading Studio** for more resources on **Notice & Note**.

Use the notes from your Response Log as you plan your short story.

UNIT 3
RESPONSE LOG

? Essential Question:
How do we form and maintain our connections with others?

The Grasshopper and the Bell Cricket	
Monkey See, Monkey Do, Monkey Connect	
With Friends Like These ...	
AmeriCorps NCCC: Be the Greater Good!	
Loser	
At Dusk	

© Houghton Mifflin Harcourt Publishing Company

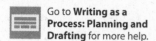
Go to **Writing as a Process: Planning and Drafting** for more help.

Organize Your Ideas Draw upon the techniques you identified in the texts as you organize your own ideas in an outline or graphic organizer. Consider these points:

- How can the beginning of your story engage readers?
- What is the story's plot? What is the central conflict?
- What is the progression of events? How do the events lead to a climax—a turning point or moment of greatest intensity?
- How is the conflict resolved? How does the story end?
- Which point of view will you use in your story?
- Create an outline or use this plot line to plan your story.

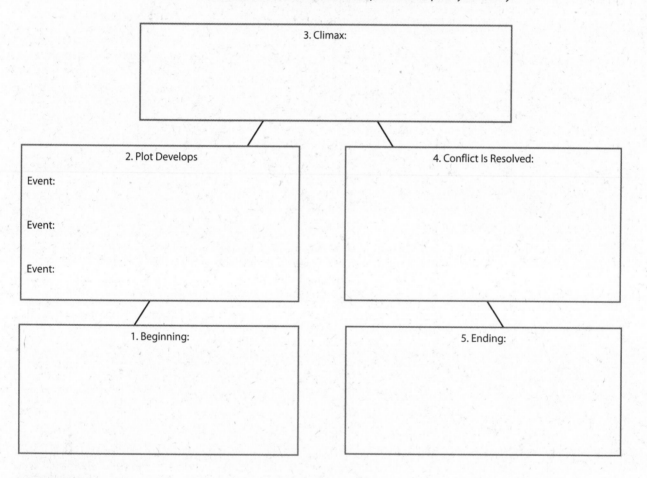

You might prefer to draft your short story online.

② Develop a Draft

Once you have completed your planning activities, you will be ready to begin drafting your short story. Refer to your graphic organizer and/or the outline you have created, as well as any notes you took as you studied the texts in the unit. These will provide a kind of map for you to follow as you write. Use a word processor or online writing application to make it easier for you to make changes and move sentences around later when you are ready to revise your first draft.

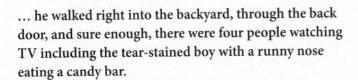

Use the Mentor Text

Author's Craft

Sensory and descriptive details can be very effective in drawing the reader into a story, even when the details seem to be small and unimportant. Note the way the author uses details in "Loser."

> … he walked right into the backyard, through the back door, and sure enough, there were four people watching TV including the tear-stained boy with a runny nose eating a candy bar.

The author makes the scene seem very real by giving vivid details about the boy's appearance.

Apply What You've Learned When describing your characters and setting, be creative in your use of sensory and descriptive details.

Genre Characteristics

"Loser" uses a consistent point of view. The entire story is told by a third-person narrator with a clear voice. The narrator is outside the story and can talk about the feelings and thoughts of all the characters. At the same time, the narrator focuses primarily on the unnamed young man at the center of the story.

> He went home to his tiny room and thought about the word lonely and how it sounded and looked so lonely, with those two l's in it, each standing tall by itself.

The narrator is telling exactly what is in the heart and mind of the young man.

Apply What You've Learned You can choose a third-person point of view like the one in "Loser," using pronouns like "he" and "she," or you can choose a first-person point of view, using the pronoun "I." First-person point of view is limited to the thoughts and feelings of one character but has a more personal feeling. Whichever one you choose, use it throughout your story.

3 Revise

Go to **Writing as Process: Revising and Editing** for help revising your short story.

On Your Own In your first draft, you put your ideas together and see how they work. Then, you can do important and creative work while revising, including bringing color to your story by introducing effective descriptions. Use sensory details, including well-chosen adjectives and vivid verbs. Also, make sure you use effective transitions between paragraphs. For example, you might mention something at the end of one paragraph and then refer back to it in the first sentence of the next paragraph. The Revision Guide will help you focus on specific elements to make your writing stronger.

REVISION GUIDE

Ask Yourself	Tips	Revision Techniques
1. Does the narrative begin in an engaging way and introduce characters, setting, conflict, and point of view?	**Underline** the opening and **mark** clues about the characters, setting, conflict, or point of view.	**Revise** your introduction to begin with action or dialogue, and **add** details about the characters, setting, or conflict.
2. Do narrative techniques and precise language bring the story to life?	**Underline** dialogue, sensory details, and vivid verbs.	**Add** dialogue, sensory details, and vivid verbs where they are lacking.
3. Does the plot build steadily, without getting slow or sluggish?	**Mark** important plot points.	**Make cuts** if the story goes on too long without advancing the plot.
4. Are suspense or surprise used effectively?	**Mark** passages that build tension or reveal a surprise.	**Add** details that build tension. **Add** a surprising event.
5. Is the narrative told from a consistent point of view?	**Note** any places where the point of view changes.	**Change** pronouns to make the point of view consistent.
6. Are there clear transitions between paragraphs?	**Note** any confusion moving from one paragraph to another.	**Revise** paragraph transitions to make them clearer.
7. Does the conclusion resolve the conflict in a logical way?	**Underline** the part where the conflict is or should be resolved	**Add** dialogue or narration that logically resolves the conflict.

ACADEMIC VOCABULARY

As you conduct your **peer review**, try to use these words.

❏ capacity

❏ confer

❏ emerge

❏ generate

❏ trace

With a Partner After you have worked through the Revision Guide on your own, exchange papers with a partner. Evaluate each other's drafts in a **peer review**. Begin by giving your partner praise for what he or she has done well. Then try to see how your partner could better accomplish his or her purpose in writing. Explain how you think your partner's draft should be revised and what your specific suggestions for revision are.

When receiving feedback from your partner, listen attentively and ask questions to make sure you fully understand the revision suggestions.

4 Edit

So that your readers can fully appreciate your story, edit for proper use of standard English conventions and make sure to correct any misspellings or grammatical errors.

Language Conventions

Spell Plural Nouns Most plural nouns are made by adding either -*s* or -*es*.

- To form the plural of **most nouns**, including those ending in *o*, add -*s*.
- To form the plural of **a few nouns that end in *o***, such as *hero, tomato, potato,* and *echo,* and all nouns that end in *s, sh, ch, x, or z,* add -*es*.
- When a singular noun ends in ***y* with a consonant** before it, change the *y* to *i* and add -*es*.
- When a singular noun ends in ***y* with a vowel** (*a, e, i, o, u*) before it, just add -*s*.

The chart has examples of nouns from "Loser" and the correct plural spellings.

> Go to **Spelling Rules** in the **Grammar Studio** to learn more.

NOUNS	PLURALS
orphan, parent, neighbor, sweater, object, nose, kitchen, sleeve, location, case, marble	orphans, parents, neighbors, sweaters, objects, noses, kitchens, sleeves, locations, cases, marbles
hairbrush, search, watch	hairbrushes, searches, watches
tragedy, community, ability, twenty, allergy, party, candy	tragedies, communities, abilities, twenties, allergies, parties, candies
year, key, boy, guy	years, keys, boys, guys

5 Publish

Finalize your story and choose a way to share it with your audience. Consider these options:

- Present your story to the class by reading it aloud. Be sure to use different voices for different characters.
- Self-publish your story by printing it in a readable font and adding a cover with an illustration you draw yourself or download. Make the finished product available to other students.

Use the scoring guide to evaluate your short story.

WRITING TASK SCORING GUIDE: SHORT STORY

	Organization /Progression	Development of Ideas	Use of Language and Conventions
4	• The organization is effective and appropriate to the purpose. • Events serve the plot and/or the character development. • The conflict of the story is presented, developed, and resolved. • The story is told from a consistent point of view.	• The beginning of the story catches the reader's attention and begins to introduce the conflict. • The theme emerges from the plot events and character development. • The conclusion resolves the conflict and supports the theme.	• Language and word choice is precise and descriptive. • Complex sentences are used well. • Spelling, capitalization, and punctuation are correct. • Grammar, usage, and mechanics are correct.
3	• The organization is, for the most part, effective and appropriate to the purpose. • Most events serve the plot and/or the character development. • The conflict of the story is presented, developed, and resolved fairly well. • The story is told from a mostly consistent point of view.	• The beginning of the story catches the reader's attention fairly well and begins to introduce the conflict. • For the most part, the theme emerges from the plot events and character development. • The conclusion resolves the conflict and supports the theme well enough for the story to be enjoyable.	• Language is for the most part specific and descriptive. • Complex sentences are used. • There are some spelling, capitalization, and punctuation mistakes. • Some grammar and usage errors occur.
2	• The organization is evident but is not always appropriate to the purpose. • Only some events serve the plot and/or the character development. • The conflict of the story needs to be better presented, developed, and resolved. • The story is told from an inconsistent point of view.	• The beginning of the story does not catch the reader's attention well and the introduction of the conflict is vague. • The theme does not emerge from the plot events and character development in a clear way, but it does exist. • The conclusion does not resolve the conflict and support the theme well.	• Language is somewhat vague and lacking in detail. • Spelling, capitalization, and punctuation, as well as grammar and usage, are often incorrect but do not make reading too difficult.
1	• The organization is not appropriate to the purpose. • Events do not serve the plot and/or the character development. • The conflict of the story is not presented, developed, and resolved. • The story does not show evidence of a point of view.	• The beginning of the story does not catch the reader's attention and conflict is missing. • The theme does not emerge from the plot events and character development. • The conclusion does not resolve the conflict and support the theme.	• Language is inappropriate for the text. • Many spelling, capitalization, and punctuation errors are present. • Grammatical and usage errors confuse the writer's ideas.

Reflect on the Unit

You've encountered a lot of ideas about connection in this unit, and you've written a story that brings together some of those ideas with ideas of your own. Now is a good time to reflect on what you have learned.

Reflect on the Essential Question

- How do we form and maintain our connections with others? How has your answer to this question changed since you first considered it when you started this unit?

- What are some examples from the texts you've read that show how we form and maintain our connections with others?

Reflect on Your Reading

- Which selections were the most interesting to you? Which ones were the most moving?

- From which selection did you learn the most about making connections in a complex society?

Reflect on the Writing Task

- What difficulties did you encounter while working on your short story? How might you handle them differently next time?

- What part of the short story was the easiest and which part was the hardest to write? Why?

- What improvements did you make to your story as you were revising?

© Houghton Mifflin Harcourt Publishing Company

UNIT 3 SELECTIONS
- "The Grasshopper and the Bell Cricket"
- "Monkey See, Monkey Do, Monkey Connect"
- "With Friends Like These . . ."
- "AmeriCorps NCCC: Be the Greater Good"
- "Loser"
- "At Dusk"

SWEET SORROW

©Houghton Mifflin Harcourt Publishing Company • Image Credits: (t) ©Garsya/Shutterstock; (b) ©PinkCat/Shutterstock

? **ESSENTIAL QUESTION:**

How can love bring both joy and pain?

" **Love is the great intangible.** "

Diane Ackerman

ACADEMIC VOCABULARY

Academic Vocabulary words are words you use when you discuss and write about texts. In this unit, you will practice and learn five words.

☑ **attribute**   ❑ **commit**   ❑ **expose**   ❑ **initiate**   ❑ **underlie**

Study the Word Network to learn more about the word **attribute**.

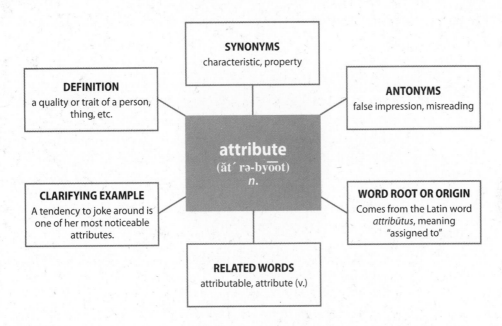

SYNONYMS
characteristic, property

DEFINITION
a quality or trait of a person, thing, etc.

ANTONYMS
false impression, misreading

attribute
(ăt´ rə-byōōt)
n.

CLARIFYING EXAMPLE
A tendency to joke around is one of her most noticeable attributes.

WORD ROOT OR ORIGIN
Comes from the Latin word *attribūtus*, meaning "assigned to"

RELATED WORDS
attributable, attribute (v.)

Write and Discuss Discuss the completed Word Network with a partner, making sure to talk through all of the boxes until you both understand the word, its synonyms, antonyms, and related forms. Then, fill out a Word Network for each of the remaining four words. Use a dictionary or online resource to help you complete the activity.

Go online to access the Word Networks.

RESPOND TO THE ESSENTIAL QUESTION

In this unit, you will explore the nature of love and the conflicts surrounding it. As you read, you will revisit the **Essential Question** and gather your ideas about it in the **Response Log** that appears on page R4. At the end of the unit, you will have the opportunity to write a **literary analysis**. Filling out the Response Log will help you prepare for this writing task.

You can also go online to access the Response Log.

**UNIT 4
RESPONSE LOG**

Use this Response Log to record your ideas about how each of the texts in Unit 4 relates to or comments on the **Essential Question**.

? **Essential Question:**
How can love bring both joy and pain?

The Price of Freedom	
Love's Vocabulary	
My Shakespeare	
The Tragedy of Romeo and Juliet	
Having It Both Ways	
Superheart	

R4   Student Resources

THE PRICE OF FREEDOM

For more information on these and other signposts to Notice & Note, visit the **Reading Studio**.

You are about to read the personal essay "The Price of Freedom." In it, you will notice and note signposts that will give you clues about the essay's claims and evidence. Here are three key signposts to look for as you read this essay.

Big Questions When listening to a narrative, you expect the unexpected. The point of telling a story is to entertain or inform the listener, and a key element of storytelling is surprise. Just when the audience thinks it knows what is going to happen, there's a twist that makes the story memorable. As you read this essay, think about the **Big Question:** What surprised me?

When authors introduce a surprising element, they are drawing the reader's attention to the story, as well as making a point about why this story is special. Authors offer the unexpected in a variety of ways:

- a story begins one way, the expected route, and then shifts suddenly
- a surprise lets the author take readers places they might not want to go
- a shift reveals hidden sides of a character and explores their abilities
- a plot twist teases the reader to guess the ending

The paragraphs below illustrate a student's annotation of "The Price of Freedom" and responses to the Big Question.

> During the evening he drew out of his pocket a small velvet box. <u>And inside there was a gold chain with a Star of David and a dove of peace hanging on it.</u>
> He said simply, "I'd like you to have this."
> "Thank you so much," I stammered. "I'm terribly touched, but I couldn't possibly accept it."
> He looked so sad. So disappointed.
> He said, "Please do, oh, please do. All my family in France has perished in a German concentration camp. I've nobody left in the world. And I'd like to think somebody remembers me. Somebody perhaps even thinks of me when I'm over there."

What surprised you in this passage? Why?	I was surprised that someone would offer a stranger such a precious gift. The author was surprised, too!
Why do you think the author included this incident in her essay?	Maybe she wanted to show an agent who had lost all his family, yet wanted to be remembered by someone.

Numbers and Stats A writer's use of specific numbers and statistics provides concrete detail in an essay. Numbers and statistics work along with words to give a clear picture of the facts for the reader.

If a writer states that there were "a lot of spies" in the war, it is up to the reader to imagine what "a lot of" means. But, if a specific number is used such as, "2,786 spies died," then readers can clearly visualize how many lives were lost. The same is true of statistics. A writer referring to an increase in missions leaves the reader wondering how much of an increase. If the writer specifies a 70% increase, readers can judge for themselves if the increase is significant. Here a student marked two examples of **Numbers and Stats**:

> . . . He needed nerves of steel, because once infiltrated, <u>his life expectancy was six weeks</u> . . . After all, <u>he was an old man—he was almost thirty-five</u>.

When you read and encounter phrases like these, see if it's a **Numbers and Stats** signpost:

"But on reaching the ripe old age of eighteen. …

"… in and out of four languages."

"… their long, tough, six-month training."

Anchor Question: When you notice this signpost, stop and ask: Why did the author use these numbers?

How does the author use a number to shock the reader with the possibility of death?	The author says a spy could die within six weeks of entering enemy territory.
How does the author use a nonspecific word and then a statistic to play off each other?	She says he was old. When she adds that he is thirty-five, I realized the agent was a young man, and she was even younger.

Word Gaps Authors will often mention terms that some readers will not know. Sometimes these include specialized or technical concepts, or familiar words used in an unusual way. A reader encountering a **Word Gap** can:

- Consider the context in which the word is used. What is it likely to mean?
- Ask if this seems like technical talk for experts on the subject.
- Define specialized words with a search engine, dictionary or thesaurus.

In this example, a student underlined two Word Gaps.

> He smiled and raised his hand to his red <u>parachutist beret</u>. A final salute.
> He was infiltrated that night.
> I never saw him again.
> The mission was successful, but he didn't return. And I was left with a little <u>cameo</u> of a perfect love.

When you notice one of the following while reading, pause to see if it's a **Word Gaps** signpost:

- Descriptive language
- Multiple meanings
- References to events, art, or ideas
- Rare words and technical talk

Anchor Question: When you notice this signpost, stop and ask: Do clues in the sentence help me understand the word?

What context clues explain the meaning of "parachutist beret"?	He raises his hand in a salute so his hand would go to his head touching a cap a parachutist would wear.
How does the word "cameo" sum up the type of relationship the author had?	A cameo is a small portrait, like a little picture, or an image, like their brief encounter.

© Houghton Mifflin Harcourt Publishing Company

THE PRICE OF FREEDOM

Personal Essay by **Noreen Riols**

? *ESSENTIAL QUESTION:*

How can love bring both joy and pain?

QUICK START

Secret agents are often portrayed as glamorous, daring characters in movies and books. Why do you think an agent's job might be dangerous and deadly? Write a few sentences about what you think happens to secret agents if they get caught.

ANALYZE TEXT MEANINGS

Most texts have both explicit, or openly stated, meanings; and implicit, or implied, meanings. Your job as a reader is to figure out these explicit and implicit meanings, using references from the text for support.

Follow these steps to determine a text's meanings.

1. Read the complete text without taking any notes.

2. Reread the text, focusing on the main ideas and the most important details. This time take notes, listing key words, main ideas with their supporting details, and quotations that make strong points.

3. Make an **inference**, or logical assumption, about key ideas in the text. Inferences are based on details in the text plus your own knowledge and experience.

4. Draw a **conclusion** about Riols's main message by reviewing key details in the text and the inferences you made. Ask yourself: What do most of the ideas and details have in common? What does Riols want her readers to know?

CREATE MENTAL IMAGES

Mental Images are pictures or scenes you create in your mind as you read. You become part of the creative process and "see" what you are reading. Mental images help you become more involved in what you are reading and as a result, pay closer attention to the details of the text. This helps to deepen your understanding and enjoyment of the text.

Write down mental images the author's words create in your mind in a chart similar to this one.

MENTAL IMAGES	EXAMPLE FROM THE SELECTION
A shocking, surprising vision	He was leaping like a demented kangaroo in and out of four languages.
A portrait of human emotion	For me it was a revelation to see their different reactions. Some returned with their nerves absolutely shattered, in shreds. Their hands were shaking uncontrollably as they lit cigarette after cigarette.
A snapshot of an intense moment	As I walked through the door, I turned. He was standing on the pavement, watching me. He smiled and raised his hand to his red parachutist beret. A final salute.

© Houghton Mifflin Harcourt Publishing Company

GENRE ELEMENTS: PERSONAL ESSAY

- similar to memoirs but shorter and more focused
- explores the writer's experiences
- includes the writer's feelings and reactions at the time

CRITICAL VOCABULARY

seductive	demented	hordes	sabotage
infiltration	decoy	adulate	annihilate

To see how many Critical Vocabulary words you already know, write brief answers to these questions.

1. What does it mean to **annihilate** something with **sabotage**? _____

2. How would a **seductive decoy** operate? _____

3. How would **demented hordes** fight in battle? _____

4. How would pretending to **adulate** help **infiltration**? _____

LANGUAGE CONVENTIONS

Sentence Variety In this lesson, you will learn about using sentence variety for different effects. Writers often vary their writing by alternating short and long sentences. This creates a rhythm that keeps the reader interested. Notice how the long sentence below contains several facts in one clear statement.

Before they were returned to London at the end of their month in Beaulieu—and it was in London, in their country section, that their fate would be decided—each one had an interview with our commandant, Colonel Woolrych.

Sometimes writers will purposely create sentence fragments to emphasize an idea or image. In the second sentence below, the author stresses the man's unhappiness by using a different adjective in a fragment.

He looked so sad. <u>So disappointed.</u>

ANNOTATION MODEL

NOTICE & NOTE

As you read, note the author's use of details that help you create mental images. Here is one reader's response to the first paragraphs of "The Price of Freedom."

> But when I went to sign on, I was taken aside and <u>closeted in a kind of windowless broom cupboard</u> with a →   high-ranking army officer, who began asking me an awful lot of questions which had nothing to do with the navy.
>   He was <u>leaping like a demented kangaroo in and out of four languages.</u> And he seemed very surprised that I could keep up.

I can picture this—a tiny, dark office.

I can imagine how strange and funny the officer must have seemed.

My inference is that the officer is testing the author for skills as an agent.

BACKGROUND

Noreen Riols (b. 1926) was born in Malta in Italy to English parents. She now lives in a seventeenth-century house in a little town near Versailles in France. Among her many books is The Secret Ministry of Ag. & Fish, published in 2014 in several countries. Riols is a recipient of the Chevalier de la Legion d'Honneur, France's highest award. This essay is based on her service with The Special Operations Executive, a volunteer fighting force created by Winston Churchill to go behind German lines in Europe and blow up trains, bridges, and factories. He ordered them to "set Europe ablaze!"

THE PRICE OF FREEDOM

Personal Essay by Noreen Riols

SETTING A PURPOSE

As you read, pay attention to the author's descriptions of the emotional suffering of agents she worked with. Compare it to the suffering the author herself experienced.

1 During World War II, I was a pupil at the French Lycée[1] in London. But on reaching the ripe old age of eighteen, I was obliged to abandon my studies and either join the armed forces or work in a munitions factory[2].

2 Well, that option did not thrill me. So I decided to become a member of the Women's Royal Naval Service. Because I liked the hat. I thought it was most **seductive**.

3 But when I went to sign on, I was taken aside and closeted in a kind of windowless broom cupboard with a high-ranking army officer, who began asking me an awful lot of questions which had nothing to do with the navy.

---

[1] **French Lycée** (lī´-say´): secondary school in France.
[2] **munitions** (myōō-nĭsh´əns) **factory**: a place where weapons and ammunition are manufactured.

© Houghton Mifflin Harcourt Publishing Company • Image Credits: (t) ©Ben Gold/Camera Press/Redux Pictures; (c) ©elwynn/Shutterstock

seductive
(sĭ-dŭk´tĭv) *adj.* tempting, alluring.

ANALYZE TEXT MEANINGS
Annotate: Mark the sentences in paragraphs 3–4 that describe the army officer's odd behavior.

Infer: What can you infer about his bizarre behavior? (Hint: he speaks several languages during their meeting.)

demented
(dĭ-měn´tĭd) *adj.* suffering from dementia, crazy, foolish.

horde
(hôrd) *n.* a large group or crowd, a swarm.

sabotage
(săb´ə-täzh) *n.* deliberate destruction of property; an act of damage to stop something.

infiltration
(ĭn-fĭl-trā´shən) *n.* the act or process of passing in secret through enemy lines.

NUMBERS AND STATS

Notice & Note: Mark a statistic that reveals how dangerous an agent's job is.

Interpret: How does this statistic account for the agent's fears?

ANALYZE TEXT MEANING

Annotate: Mark text that describes why the radio operator's job was the most dangerous.

Draw Conclusions: Why would a radio operator be easy for the Gestapo to find?

4   He was leaping like a **demented** kangaroo in and out of four languages. And he seemed very surprised that I could keep up.

5   He sent me to a large building in central London. Oh, I knew it well. But like the **hordes** of people who passed by every day, never had I imagined or even suspected that this was the headquarters of Churchill's secret army. And that behind those walls, members of every occupied country were organizing acts of **sabotage**, and the **infiltration** of secret agents into enemy territory at night, by parachute, fishing boat, felucca[3], and submarine.

6   Without realizing what had happened, I had been recruited into the hidden world of secret agents on special missions. (But I never got my seductive hat.)

7   I was assigned to "F" for France section. It was an exhausting but exciting, thrilling, exhilarating life, full of action and emotion. We lived some very intense moments.

8   I got to know an awful lot of agents. And I shared many confidences with those who were about to leave. They told me of their concerns for their families—many of them were married with young children—and of their own apprehension of torture and of death.

9   They knew they only had a 50 percent chance of coming back. And they were afraid.

10   Brave men are always afraid. Courage isn't the absence of fear. It's the willingness—the guts, if you like—to face the fear.

11   They faced their fears. And they left.

12   I remember one. He was a Jew. A radio operator. And he was going in on a second mission. Well, for a Jew to go in at all was extremely dangerous. But many did—we had quite a few Jewish agents. But a radio operator? A second mission?

13   A radio operator was the most stressful, hazardous, dangerous mission of all. He lived on his nerves. He could never relax. He was always on the run, always with the Gestapo[4] just a couple of steps behind him. He needed nerves of steel, because once infiltrated, his life expectancy was six weeks.

14   I was with this agent on the night before he left. Oh, there was no romantic association; I was just keeping him company. After all, he was an old man—he was almost thirty–five.

15   During the evening he drew out of his pocket a small velvet box. And inside there was a gold chain with a Star of David and a dove of peace hanging on it.

16   He said simply, "I'd like you to have this."

17   "Thank you so much," I stammered. "I'm terribly touched, but I couldn't possibly accept it."

18   He looked so sad. So disappointed.

---

[3] **felucca** (fə-lŭk´ə): a swift and narrow sailing vessel.
[4] **Gestapo** (gə-shtä´pō): German internal security police known for terrorist methods.

19   He said, "Please do, oh, please do. All my family in France has perished in a German concentration camp. I've nobody left in the world. And I'd like to think that somebody remembers me. Somebody perhaps even thinks of me when I'm over there."

20   So I took his little box, promising to look after it and give it back to him when he returned.

21   But he didn't return.

22   Those who did return were taken immediately for a debriefing[5], and I often accompanied the two debriefing officers.

23   For me it was a revelation to see their different reactions. Some returned with their nerves absolutely shattered, in shreds. Their hands were shaking uncontrollably as they lit cigarette after cigarette.

24   Others were as cool as cucumbers. And I realized then that we all have a breaking point. And we can never know until we're faced with the situation what that breaking point actually is. Perhaps that is why departing agents were strongly urged if arrested by the Gestapo to take the cyanide[6] pill, which was always hidden somewhere around their person, before they left. It would kill them within two minutes.

25   I grew up attending those debriefing sessions.

26   Many of those agents weren't very much older than I. Hearing their incredible stories, witnessing their courage, their total dedication, I changed almost overnight from a teenager to a woman.

27   One snowy Saturday evening in early February, I was told that I was to leave and go down to Beaulieu. Now, Beaulieu was the last of the many secret training schools. These training schools were dotted all over England. And the future agents attended each one in turn during their long, tough, six–month training. Beaulieu, or Group B

LANGUAGE CONVENTIONS
Annotate: Mark the long sentence in paragraph 24.

Respond: What details does the sentence convey? Why might the author have chosen to communicate this information in one long sentence rather than two or three shorter ones?

---

[5] **debriefing** (dē-brē´fĭng): the act or process of interviewing after an assignment to obtain information.

[6] **cyanide** (sī´ə-nīd): a powerful chemical poison.

© Houghton Mifflin Harcourt Publishing Company • Image Credits: ©Gary Eason/Alamy

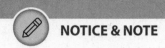

CREATE MENTAL IMAGES

Annotate: Mark the details about place in paragraph 29.

Synthesize: What mental images do they create for you?

decoy
(dē´koi) *n.* a means to trick or attract.

as it was called, was in Hampshire, deep in the New Forest. Only six women worked there during the war, and I am the last survivor.

28   We were used as decoys. We worked in the neighboring seaside towns of Bournemouth and Southampton. My pitch was usually Bournemouth.

29   It was there that we taught future agents how to follow someone—find out where they were going, who they were seeing— without being detected. How to detect if someone were following *them* and throw them off. How to pass messages without any sign of recognition or even moving our lips. This took place on the beach, in the park, on benches in the town, in telephone booths, and in the tearooms above the Gaumont Cinema.

30   The last exercise was reserved for those future agents whom the instructors thought might talk. Now, the instructors were with them all the time. They watched their every movement. They analyzed it all. And if they thought that they might talk, they would have a carefully prearranged setup meeting between a **decoy** and a future agent in one of the two grand hotels in Bournemouth.

31   (Of course, if I had taken part in the earlier exercises, I couldn't take part in that one, because they would know me, and then one of the other women took over.)

32   The meeting would take place in the bar or the lounge, followed by an intimate dinner tête-à-tête. It was our job to get them to talk— to betray themselves, in fact.

33   The Brits didn't talk much. Foreigners sometimes did, especially young ones. Oh, I understood. They were lonely. They were far from their homes and their families. They didn't even know if they would *have* a home, or even a country, to go back to once the war was over. And it was flattering to have a young girl hanging on their every word. Before they were returned to London at the end of their month in Beaulieu—and it was in London, in their country section, that

NOTICE & NOTE

their fate would be decided—each one had an interview with our commandant, Colonel Woolrych. (We called him Woolly Bags behind his back.) He had all the reports from the different training schools, and he made his final report that went back to London and carried a lot of weight.

34   Now, if they had talked, during the interview a door would open and I, or another decoy, would walk in.

35   Woolly Bags would say, "Do you know this woman?" And they would realize they'd been tricked . . . .

36   On the eve of my nineteenth birthday, I fell madly, hopelessly in love with an agent. He was one of our best agents. A crack. He'd just returned from a very successful second mission, and he was **adulated.** He was a legend in the section. I'd heard all about him, but I never thought I'd meet him.

37   Then, suddenly one evening, he was there. Our eyes locked across a crowded room. And it was as if a magnet drew us irresistibly towards each other.

38   I couldn't believe that he could love me. He was handsome. He was twelve years older than I. He was a hero.

39   He must have met many beautiful, sophisticated, elegant, gorgeous women. (Oh, he had—he told me. But he said he'd been looking for me.) Our idyll lasted three months, until he left on his next mission.

40   I was terrified. It was a very dangerous mission. They said only he could carry it off. I was so afraid. But he reassured me. He said he was a survivor. And he promised me that this would be his last mission, and when he came back, he'd never leave me again. We'd grow old together.

41   The day he left, we had lunch, just the two of us, in a little intimate restaurant. We both knew that it would be many months perhaps before we'd be together again.

adulate
(ăj´ə-lāt) *v.* to praise or admire excessively.

WORD GAPS

Notice & Note: Mark any words in paragraph 39 whose meaning you are not sure about.

Analyze: How can you use context to determine meaning?

© Houghton Mifflin Harcourt Publishing Company • Image Credits: ©Bert Hardy/Hulton Archive/Getty Images

The Price of Freedom   257

Noreen Riols in France, 2014

42   We kept emotion out of our conversation. I think we were both afraid of breaking down. I know if we hadn't, I would have broken down, and I'd have begged him not to go.

43   I imagine you've all been in love. Can you picture what it's like to be terribly in love, and know that all you have is a few hours, this moment in time?

44   He took me back to the office, and we said good–bye at the bus stop. I don't think we even said "good–bye."

45   As I walked through the door, I turned. He was standing on the pavement, watching me. He smiled and raised his hand to his red parachutist beret. A final salute.

46   He was infiltrated that night.

47   I never saw him again.

48   The mission was successful, but he didn't return. And I was left with a little cameo of a perfect love. Perfect, perhaps, because it had been so brief.

49   When the news that I'd dreaded came through, they tried to comfort me. They told me I should be proud. He was incredibly courageous—a wonderful man, who realized that there was a force of

LANGUAGE CONVENTIONS

Annotate: Mark the longest sentence in paragraph 49.

Respond: How does this sentence link the man with the larger issues the author is writing about?

evil in the world that had to be **annihilated**, but that freedom has a price tag. He paid that price with his life.

annihilate
(ə-nī´ə-lāt): *v.* to destroy completely.

50   But I didn't want a dead hero. I didn't want a medal in a velvet box. I wanted Bill.

51   All those agents in the secret army were volunteers. They didn't have to go. But they went. Almost half of them never returned. Like Bill, they gave their youth, their joie de vivre, their hopes and dreams for the future.

52   They gave their all, for us.

53   They gave their todays, so that we might have our tomorrow.

CHECK YOUR UNDERSTANDING

Answer these questions before moving on to the **Analyze the Text** section on the following page.

1 The primary purpose of the selection is —

A to explain the sorts of things special agents did in Europe during WW II

B to have readers understand the sacrifices special agents made during WW II

C to encourage other citizens to make the ultimate sacrifice

D to tell a little-known tale of mystery and wartime intrigue

2 As the essay begins —

F the author tells about her difficulties caused by falling in love with the wrong guy

G the author explains the importance of patriotism when stopping evil

H the author demonstrates how agents had to be carefully screened

J the author describes how she came to work with secret agents

3 Which sentence invites the reader to make a personal connection with the author's story?

A *Courage isn't the absence of fear.*

B *I grew up attending those debriefing sessions.*

C *I imagine you've all been in love.*

D *They gave their todays so that we might have our tomorrows.*

ANALYZE THE TEXT

Support your responses with evidence from the text. ▤ NOTEBOOK

1. **Connect** Describe two mental images you created as you read. What details in the text did you use to create the pictures in your mind?

2. **Infer** Make an inference about why special agents might have been encouraged to use their cyanide pill if captured. Identify where the text provides explicit information, and the implicit meaning that led to your inference.

3. **Interpret** What skills were special agents taught in secret training school? Why might they have been useful?

4. **Evaluate** Do you think the author was right to accept the necklace from the Jewish radio operator? Why or why not?

5. **Notice & Note** Which statistics persuaded you of the dangers secret agents faced?

RESEARCH

Several intelligence agencies formed in the United States and Great Britain during and after World War II. For example, in 1942 the Office of Strategic Services (OSS) was established in the United States. Research the jobs people did at these agencies. Record what you learn in the chart.

WORLD WAR II AGENCIES	JOBS EMPLOYEES PERFORMED

Extend In 1954, the Soviet Union formed its own security agency, the KGB. With a partner, research how KGB agents operated against intelligence agents from other countries during the Cold War.

RESEARCH TIP
Be careful when choosing sources for your research. Make sure the websites you use are reliable and relevant to your search.

© Houghton Mifflin Harcourt Publishing Company

CREATE AND DISCUSS

Write a Professional Letter Imagine you live in the country where one of the agencies you researched has its headquarters. Write a one-page letter to the agency asking questions about their organization or expressing interest in working with them.

❏ Express your willingness to help your country and make sacrifices.

❏ Ask for more detailed information about the jobs available and what skills would be required.

❏ Use the words and terms you have learned while reading the essay and researching these agencies.

Discuss with a Small Group Share your letters with your fellow budding secret agents.

❏ Determine the effectiveness of the letters.

❏ Think like a working spy who is looking to recruit new agents, just like the army officer who interviewed the author of the essay.

❏ Discuss which agency you would like to work for and why.

Go to the **Writing Studio** for more on writing using formal style.

Go to the **Speaking and Listening Studio** for more on participating in collaborative discussions.

RESPOND TO THE ESSENTIAL QUESTION

 How can love bring both joy and pain?

Gather Information Review your annotations and notes on "The Price of Freedom." Then, add relevant information to your Response Log. As you determine which information to include, think about how wartime might intensify both the joy and pain of love.

At the end of the unit, use your notes to help you write a literary analysis.

ACADEMIC VOCABULARY

As you write and discuss what you learned from the essay, be sure to use the Academic Vocabulary words. Check off each of the words that you use.

❏ **attribute**

❏ **commit**

❏ **expose**

❏ **initiate**

❏ **underlie**

WORD BANK
seductive
demented
hordes
sabotage
infiltration
decoy
adulate
annihilate

CRITICAL VOCABULARY

Practice and Apply Circle the letter of the best answer to each question. Then, explain your response.

1. Which of the following could be used when describing bees?
   a. decoy   **b.** horde

2. Which of the following would be used when talking about heroes?
   a. adulate   **b.** annihilate

3. Which of the following could be described as **seductive**?
   a. danger   **a.** sadness

4. Which of the following would be used when seeking secret information about an enemy country?
   a. infiltration   **b.** sabotage

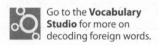 Go to the **Vocabulary Studio** for more on decoding foreign words.

VOCABULARY STRATEGY:
Foreign Words

The author of "The Price of Freedom" lived and worked in France so it's not surprising that she used many French words. **Foreign words and phrases** often appear in writing that has as its subject matter the cultures of different nations. Some foreign words and terms are commonly used in English, even though they retain their foreign spelling. You can find definitions in a dictionary. But often you can determine meaning through context.

Practice and Apply Underline the foreign word or phrase in each sentence. Then, use context clues to determine meaning. In your own words, write a sentence with the foreign term.

1. Alone, away from all others, the two lovebirds had a tête-à-tête with their heads held close to each other to listen to every word.

   _____

2. Before the war, she was filled with genuine joie de vivre that kept her celebrating her existence, but after the war, the world was a sad place.

   _____

3. The artist's studio had many beautiful paintings; but the pièce de résistance was the large, stunning self-portrait.

   _____

4. No one could explain her mysterious je ne sais quoi which left her admirers wondering, "I can't exactly say what is so appealing about her."

   _____

LANGUAGE CONVENTIONS:
Sentence Variety

Writers often use a variety of sentence lengths to create different effects in their work. Noreen Riols, author of "The Price of Freedom," sometimes combines complete sentences into one longer sentence. Notice the three underlined subjects and predicates in the sentence below.

> **I know** if we hadn't, **I would have broken** down, and **I'd have begged** him not to go.

Riols varies her style by using long sentences, short sentences, and even fragments—short, incomplete sentences. Fragments are complete thoughts but often lack subjects or predicates. Authors use fragments to create a more informal, conversational style. They also use fragments to call attention to a detail or idea.

> **But many did—we had quite a few Jewish agents. But a radio operator? A second mission?**

In the passage above, the author wants to emphasize the agent's willingness to risk his life in a second, hazardous mission.

In addition, Riols uses fragments to reveal her inner thoughts. The casual tone she uses to share her thoughts makes readers feel she is talking directly to them. Here is an example, using slang to reinforce the informal tone.

> **He was one of our best agents. A crack. He'd just returned from a very successful mission, and he was adulated.**

Practice and Apply Write a short passage about a topic that interests you. Try combining your own sentences into longer sentences. Also, practice writing fragments. When you have finished, share your writing with a partner and discuss how you incorporated variety into your writing by varying sentence length and structure.

Go to the **Grammar Studio** for more on sentence variety.

LOVE'S VOCABULARY

Essay by **Diane Ackerman**

? *ESSENTIAL QUESTION:*

How can love bring both joy and pain?

QUICK START

The author of "Love's Vocabulary" calls love a concept that no one can define. Brainstorm with classmates words that define or describe love.

ANALYZE INFORMATIONAL TEXT

Informational text is nonfiction writing that delivers facts and details about a specific topic. The author's purpose usually is to inform, but the writing often also entertains or persuades. The characteristics and structural elements of expository informational text include:

- thesis or main idea, which is a statement of the author's purpose as well as the text's main idea

- supporting evidence, such as examples that explain or clarify the thesis

- text features, such as headings and subheadings, that organize ideas

- visual aids, such as pictures, graphs, charts, and timelines

- a conclusion that summarizes the thesis

Informational text also uses types of **organizational design** to frame the information the writer presents. Organizational patterns include:

- comparison and contrast

- problem and solution

- cause and effect

"Love's Vocabulary" is organized as an extended discussion of the meaning of a single word.

GENRE ELEMENTS: ESSAY

- explores and explains a single topic

- may include the writer's own thoughts or experiences

- provides factual information supported with evidence

- uses a specific organizational structure

GENERATE QUESTIONS

Asking questions is an important part of active reading. In order to understand main ideas and supporting details, readers should generate questions about what they are reading. As a reader, you should ask questions:

- to help eliminate confusion about a text

- to focus on parts of the text

- to seek answers by finding specific evidence

- to guide you to inferences about meaning and author's purpose

- to explore a topic and gain greater understanding

Use a chart similar to the one here to keep track of your questions while reading. You can also record your questions in your Response Log.

TEXT PASSAGE	REASON TO QUESTION	QUESTION	ANSWER

CRITICAL VOCABULARY

intangible	guise	increment	supple	gradation

To see how many Critical Vocabulary words you already know, use them to complete the sentences.

1. Gymnasts perform intense workouts so their bodies stay _____.

2. Thieves use the _____ of respectability to steal from victims.

3. If you look at the squirrel's fur you will see a _____ in the color.

4. The director's contributions to the play were _____ but important.

5. We were paid our salary in a daily_____ of ninety dollars each.

LANGUAGE CONVENTIONS

Participial Phrases Writers use many techniques to keep their writing vivid and interesting. Sometimes, they do this through sentence structure—for example, by using participial phrases.

Participial phrases use verbs as adjectives. Like adjectives, they modify nouns or pronouns. Notice that the participial phrase in this sentence describes what the young lovers are doing.

Laughing wildly, the young lovers ignored everyone else in the room.

The lovers are ignoring and laughing. But *laughing* is combined with the adverb *wildly* to become a phrase that describes them as more than just *young*. The participial phrase could be placed in other positions in the sentence and make sense. However, it is usually placed in front of, or close to the noun it describes.

ANNOTATION MODEL

NOTICE & NOTE

As you read, note how this essay reflects characteristics of informational text. Write questions in the margins. Here is one reader's notes on "Love's Vocabulary."

Love's Vocabulary ←

Love is the great intangible. In our nightmares, we can create beasts out of pure emotion. Hate stalks the streets with dripping fangs, fear flies down narrow alleyways on leather wings, and jealousy spins sticky webs across the sky. In daydreams, we can maneuver with poise, foiling an opponent, scoring high on fields of glory while crowds cheer, cutting fast to the heart of an adventure. But what dream state is love? Frantic and serene, vigilant and calm, wrung-out and fortified, explosive and sedate—love commands a vast army of moods.

— The title and first sentence tell me the author's topic and her thesis.

She develops her thesis using examples and supporting details.

BACKGROUND

Diane Ackerman (b. 1948), *author of* A Natural History of the Senses, An Alchemy of Mind, *and* The Zookeeper's Wife, *which was made into a film in 2017, weaves her love of science and natural history into her poetry, fiction, and nonfiction. Her memoir,* One Hundred Names for Love, *chronicles her husband's struggle to reclaim language after a stroke. In describing that time, Ackerman said, "I've always transcended best by pretending that I'm Margaret Mead viewing a scene for the first time or an alien from another planet regarding the spectacle of life on Earth and discovering how spectacular, unexpected, and beautiful it is."*

LOVE'S VOCABULARY

Essay by Diane Ackerman

SETTING A PURPOSE

As you read, imagine that the author is sitting beside you and you can ask her whenever you don't understand something. Write down your questions.

1   Love is the great **intangible**. In our nightmares, we can create beasts out of pure emotion. Hate stalks the streets with dripping fangs, fear flies down narrow alleyways on leather wings, and jealousy spins sticky webs across the sky. In daydreams, we can maneuver with poise, foiling an opponent, scoring high on fields of glory while crowds cheer, cutting fast to the heart of an adventure. But what dream state is love? Frantic and serene, vigilant and calm, wrung-out and fortified, explosive and sedate—love commands a vast army of moods. Hoping for victory, limping from the latest skirmish, lovers enter the arena once again. Sitting still, we are as daring as gladiators.

2   When I set a glass prism on a windowsill and allow the sun to flood through it, a spectrum of colors dances on the floor. What we call "white" is a rainbow of colored rays packed into a small space. The prism sets them free. Love is the white light

Notice & Note

You can use the side margins to notice and note signposts in the text.

intangible
(ĭn-tăn´jə-bəl) *n.* something that is difficult to grasp or explain.

LANGUAGE CONVENTIONS
Annotate: Mark the author's use of three participial phrases in paragraph 1.

Analyze: What is the effect of these phrases?

guise
(gīz) *n.* form or outward appearance; outfit.

of emotion. It includes many feelings which, out of laziness and confusion, we crowd into one simple word. Art is the prism that sets them free, then follows the gyrations[1] of one or a few. When art separates this thick tangle of feelings, love bares its bones. But it cannot be measured or mapped. Everyone admits that love is wonderful and necessary, yet no one can agree on what it is. I once heard a sportscaster say of a basketball player, "He does all the intangibles. Just watch him do his dance." As lofty as the idea of love can be, no image is too profane to help explain it. Years ago, I fell in love with someone who was both a sport and a pastime. At the end, he made fade-away jump shots in my life. But, for a while, love did all the intangibles. It lets us do our finest dance.

3   *Love.* What a small word we use for an idea so immense and powerful it has altered the flow of history, calmed monsters, kindled works of art, cheered the forlorn, turned tough guys to mush, consoled the enslaved, driven strong women mad, glorified the humble, fueled national scandals, bankrupted robber barons, and made mincemeat of kings. How can love's spaciousness be conveyed in the narrow confines of one syllable? If we search for the source of the word, we find a history vague and confusing, stretching back to the Sanskrit *lubhyati* ("he desires"). I'm sure the etymology rambles back much farther than that, to a one-syllable word heavy as a heartbeat. Love is an ancient delirium, a desire older than civilization, with taproots[2] stretching deep into dark and mysterious days.

4   We use the word *love* in such a sloppy way that it can mean almost nothing or absolutely everything. It is the first conjugation[3] students of Latin learn. It is a universally understood motive for crime. "Ah, he was in love," we sigh, "well, that explains it." In fact, in some European and South American countries, even murder is forgivable if it was "a crime of passion." Love, like truth, is the unassailable defense. Whoever first said "love makes the world go round" (it was an anonymous Frenchman) probably was not thinking about celestial mechanics, but the way love seeps into the machinery of life to keep generation after generation in motion. We think of love as a positive force that somehow ennobles the one feeling it. When a friend confesses that he's in love, we congratulate him.

5   In folk stories, unsuspecting lads and lasses ingest love potions and quickly lose their hearts. As with all intoxicants, love comes in many **guises** and strengths. It has a mixed bouquet, and may include some piquant ingredients.[4] One's taste in love will have a lot to do with one's culture, upbringing, generation, religion, era, gender, and

---

[1] **gyrations** (jī-rā´shəns): spiral or circular movements.
[2] **taproots** (tăp´rōōts): the main roots of a tree or plant from which other roots grow.
[3] **conjugation** (kŏn-jə-gā´shən): in grammar, the various forms of a verb.
[4] **piquant** (pē´kənt) **ingredients:** components that make something pleasantly spicy.

© Houghton Mifflin Harcourt Publishing Company

so on. Ironically, although we sometimes think of it as the ultimate Oneness, love isn't monotone or uniform. Like a batik[5] created from many emotional colors, it is a fabric whose pattern and brightness may vary. What is my goddaughter to think when she hears her mother say: "I love Ben & Jerry's Cherry Garcia ice cream"; "I really loved my high school boyfriend"; "Don't you just love this sweater?"; "I'd love to go to the lake for a week this summer"; "Mommy loves you." Since all we have is one word, we talk about love in **increments** or unwieldy ratios. "How much do you love me?" a child asks. Because the parent can't answer *I* (verb that means unconditional parental love) *you*, she may fling her arms wide, as if welcoming the sun and sky, stretching her body to its limit, spreading her fingers to encompass all of Creation, and say: "This much!" Or: "Think of the biggest thing you can imagine. Now double it. I love you a hundred times that much!"

6   When Elizabeth Barrett Browning wrote her famous sonnet "How do I love thee?" she didn't "count the ways" because she had an arithmetical turn of mind, but because English poets have always had to search hard for personal signals of their love. As a society, we are embarrassed by love. We treat it as if it were an obscenity. We reluctantly admit to it. Even saying the word makes us stumble and blush. Why should we be ashamed of an emotion so beautiful and natural? In teaching writing students, I've sometimes given them the assignment of writing a love poem. "Be precise, be individual, and be descriptive. But don't use any clichés," I caution them, "or any curse words." Part of the reason for this assignment is that it helps them understand how inhibited we are about love. Love is the most important thing in our lives, a passion for which we would fight or die, and yet we're reluctant to linger over its name. Without a **supple** vocabulary, we can't even talk or think about it directly. On the other hand, we have many sharp verbs for the ways in which human beings can hurt one another, dozens of verbs for the subtle **gradations** of hate. But there are pitifully few synonyms for love. Our vocabulary of love and lovemaking is so paltry that a poet has to choose among clichés, profanities, or euphemisms. Fortunately, this has led to some richly imagined works of art. It has inspired poets to create their own private vocabularies. Mrs. Browning sent her husband a poetic abacus[6] of love, which in a roundabout way expressed the sum of her feelings. Other lovers have tried to calibrate their love in equally ingenious ways. In "The Flea," John Donne watches a flea suck blood from his arm and his beloved's, and rejoices that their blood marries in the flea's stomach.

7   Yes, lovers are most often reduced to comparatives and quantities. "Do you love me more than her?" we ask. "Will you love me less if I

---

[5] **batik** (bə-tēk´): colorful design created by applying different dyes and wax to fabric.
[6] **abacus** (ăb´ə-kəs): a device for performing calculations by manipulating beads strung on wires in a rectangular frame.

© Houghton Mifflin Harcourt Publishing Company

NOTICE & NOTE

ANALYZE INFORMATIONAL TEXT
Annotate Mark the examples cited in paragraph 5.

Connect How do these sentences serve as supporting details for the author's thesis that love is "intangible," not easily defined?

increment
(ĭn´krə-mənt) *n.* an addition or increase by a standard measure of growth.

CONTRASTS AND CONTRADICTIONS

Annotate: Mark the sentences in paragraph 6 in which the author introduces the negative ideas people have about love.

Compare: Is the author contradicting herself? Explain.

supple
(sŭp´əl) *adj.* flexible or easily adaptable.

gradation
(grā-dā´shən) *n.* a slight, successive change in color, degree or tone.

GENERATE QUESTIONS

Annotate: Mark the sentences in paragraph 8 where the author introduces a woman from ancient Egypt into the essay.

Evaluate: What questions could readers ask about why the author uses this example in a discussion of love?

WORD GAPS

Annotate: Mark two words in paragraph 8 that many readers might not know.

Interpret: Why do you think the author uses unusual words like these?

don't do what you say?" We are afraid to face love head on. We think of it as a sort of traffic accident of the heart. It is an emotion that scares us more than cruelty, more than violence, more than hatred. We allow ourselves to be foiled by the vagueness of the word. After all, love requires the utmost vulnerability. We equip someone with freshly sharpened knives; strip naked; then invite him to stand close. What could be scarier?

8   If you took a woman from ancient Egypt and put her in an automobile factory in Detroit, she would be understandably disoriented. Everything would be new, especially her ability to stroke the wall and make light flood the room, touch the wall elsewhere and fill the room with summer's warm breezes or winter's blast. She'd be astonished by telephones, computers, fashions, language, and customs. But if she saw a man and woman stealing a kiss in a quiet corner, she would smile. People everywhere and everywhen understand the phenomenon of love, just as they understand the appeal of music, finding it deeply meaningful even if they cannot explain exactly what that meaning is, or why they respond viscerally to one composer and not another. Our Egyptian woman, who prefers the birdlike twittering of a sistrum,[7] and a twentieth-century man, who prefers the clashing jaws of heavy metal, share a passion for music that both would understand. So it is with love. Values, customs, and protocols may vary from ancient days to the present, but not the majesty of love. People are unique in the way they walk, dress, and gesture, yet we're able to look at two people—one wearing a business suit, the other a sarong[8]—and recognize that both of them are clothed. Love also has many fashions, some bizarre and (to our taste) shocking, others more familiar, but all are part of a phantasmagoria[9] we know. In the Serengeti[10] of the heart, time and nation are irrelevant. On that plain, all fires are the same fire.

9   Remember the feeling of an elevator falling in your chest when you said good-bye to a loved one? Parting is more than sweet sorrow, it pulls you apart when you are glued together. It feels like hunger pains, and we use the same word, *pang*. Perhaps this is why Cupid is depicted with a quiver of arrows, because at times love feels like being pierced in the chest. It is a wholesome violence. Common as child birth, love seems rare nonetheless, always catches one by surprise, and cannot be taught. Each child rediscovers it, each couple redefines it, each parent reinvents it. People search for love as if it were a city lost beneath the desert dunes, where pleasure is the law, the streets are lined with brocade cushions, and the sun never sets.

---

[7] **sistrum** (sĭs′trəm): an ancient percussion instrument that sounds like a metal rattle.

[8] **sarong** (sə-rông′): a traditional Southeast Asian woman's garment made from a long piece of fabric that is wrapped around the body.

[9] **phantasmagoria** (făn-tăz-mə-gôr′ē-ə): a dreamlike sequence of surreal images or events.

[10] **Serengeti** (sĕr-ən-gĕt′ē): a vast plain in Tanzania known for its migratory animals.

10   If it's so obvious and popular, then what is love? I began researching this book because I had many questions, not because I knew at the outset what answers I might find. Like most people, I believed what I had been told: that the idea of love was invented by the Greeks, and romantic love began in the Middle Ages. I know now how misguided such hearsay is. We can find romantic love in the earliest writings of our kind. Much of the vocabulary of love, and the imagery lovers use, has not changed for thousands of years. Why do the same images come to mind when people describe their romantic feelings? Custom, culture, and tastes vary, but not love itself, not the essence of the emotion.

NOTICE & NOTE

ANALYZE INFORMATIONAL TEXT

Annotate: Mark the sentence in paragraph 10 that acts as a conclusion to the essay.

Draw Conclusions: How does this sentence expand upon the author's thesis?

CHECK YOUR UNDERSTANDING

Answer these questions before moving on to the **Analyze the Text** section on the following page.

1   The author refers to Cupid in order to —

   A cite a reason why love is part of cultural mythology

   B suggest his arrows symbolize the pain of loved ones parting

   C quote an expert in the field of romance and passion

   D prove that love is timeless and is a part of every culture

2   Which sentence best conveys the difficulty of defining the word *love*?

   F *How can love's spaciousness be conveyed in the narrow confines of one syllable?*

   G *Love is an ancient delirium, a desire older than civilization, with taproots stretching deep into dark and mysterious days.*

   H *We think of love as a positive force that somehow ennobles the one feeling it.*

   J *As a society, we are embarrassed by love.*

3   Which of the following describes the essay's organizational design?

   A The author traces the history of love as recorded in art through societies.

   B The author discusses the problems love causes and solutions humans find.

   C The author explores many ways humans define the word *love*.

   D The author seeks the causes of love and its effects.

ANALYZE THE TEXT

Support your responses with evidence from the text.   NOTEBOOK

1. **Infer** Ackerman begins by stating that "Love is the great intangible." What does she mean by this statement? What details and examples in the first two paragraphs help to support this thesis?

2. **Evaluate** In paragraph 3, what human qualities does Ackerman attribute to love? Describe the tone she creates by this use of personification.

3. **Analyze** In paragraph 3, what does the author say is the source of the word *love*? Why is this important information for the structure and purpose of the essay?

4. **Interpret** In paragraph 8, Ackerman writes, "Values, customs, and protocols may vary from ancient days to the present, but not the majesty of love." What does she mean by this statement? What example does she use to develop this idea?

5. **Notice & Note** Why does Ackerman include Quoted Words—references to Elizabeth Barrett Browning's poem "How Do I Love Thee?" and John Donne's poem "The Flea"? Why would you expect to see citations like this in an informational text?

RESEARCH

Diane Ackerman' essay explores many of the ways Americans define or demonstrate their love for each other. In other countries, love is expressed in different ways according to differing customs. Research how people from other countries and regions—for example, Latin America, France, and Japan—express their love and what is allowed or not allowed for those in love.

COUNTRY	DEFINITIONS AND CULTURAL EXPRESSIONS OF LOVE

Connect In the United States, people use a variety of words and phrases to say "I love you." Use a thesaurus to explore all the ways we say we love each other. Discuss the different connotations of these words and phrases.

CREATE AND PRESENT

Discuss the Author's Statement Discuss in small groups Diane Ackerman's statement that as a society we are "embarrassed" and "inhibited" by love.

Go to the **Speaking and Listening Studio** for help with small-group discussions.

❏ Discuss the points the author makes in paragraph 6 to support her statement. Which points are valid? Which would you challenge?

❏ Do her descriptions match what you have observed in movies, books, or the behavior of people around you?

❏ Take notes about your views and those of others.

Present in a Panel Discussion Have representatives of each group assemble a formal panel discussion to present the results of each group. If possible, put together two panels with differing opinions. All speakers should use appropriate register (degree of formality), vocabulary, tone, and voice when they discuss.

Go to the **Speaking and Listening Studio** for help with having a panel discussion.

❏ Have a representative summarize their group's critique of the author's statement, citing text evidence.

❏ Members should discuss their views and opinions about the statement, citing the text as well as their own observations.

❏ Each member should write a summary of the panel discussion that synthesizes how we discuss love as a society.

RESPOND TO THE ESSENTIAL QUESTION

? How can love bring both joy and pain?

Gather Information Review your annotations and notes on "Love's Vocabulary." Then, add relevant information to your Response Log. As you determine which information to include, think about:

- how Ackerman demonstrates the difficulties of defining love
- some of the joys she discusses in connection with love
- how she characterizes the pains of love

At the end of the unit, use your notes to help you write a literary analysis.

ACADEMIC VOCABULARY

As you write and discuss what you learned from the essay, be sure to use the Academic Vocabulary words. Check off each of the words that you use.

❏ **attribute**

❏ **commit**

❏ **expose**

❏ **initiate**

❏ **underlie**

CRITICAL VOCABULARY

WORD BANK
intangible
guise
increment
supple
gradation

Practice and Apply Circle the letter of the best answer to each question. Then, explain your response.

1. Which of the following would be described as **intangible**?
   a. school supplies donated to a class

   b. encouragement given to students

2. Which of the following is a **guise**?
   a. a costume worn to a party

   b. a fresh coat of paint on a house

3. Which of the following is an example of an **increment**?
   a. exit ramps on a freeway

   b. a degree of body temperature on a thermometer

4. Which of the following is usually **supple**?
   a. a new branch on a sapling

   b. a loaf of frozen bread

5. Which of the following is an example of a **gradation**?
   a. an argument breaking out over an insult

   b. a subtle shift of tone in a conversation

VOCABULARY STRATEGY:
Synonyms

Go to the **Vocabulary Studio** for more on synonyms.

When you encounter an unfamiliar word in an essay, you can often determine its meaning by substituting a **synonym**—a word with a similar meaning—for the unfamiliar word. For example, in the first line of the essay, Ackerman uses the Critical Vocabulary word *intangible*. The context clue "dream state" later in the paragraph indicates something unsubstantial. The synonym *unsubstantial* makes sense in the sentence.

Practice and Apply Work with a partner to locate these words in the essay: *immense* (paragraph 3), *ennobles* (paragraph 4), *monotone* (paragraph 5), *inhibited* (paragraph 6). Follow these steps:

1. Look for a context clue in the sentence or paragraph where the unfamiliar word occurs.

2. Use context clues to determine meaning and think of a synonym that fits.

3. Substitute your synonym for the unfamiliar word to see if it makes sense.

4. Consult a dictionary or a thesaurus to confirm the meaning.

LANGUAGE CONVENTIONS:
Participial Phrases

A **participle** is a verb form that functions as an adjective. Like adjectives, participles modify nouns and pronouns. Most participles are present-participle forms, ending in *-ing*, or past-participle forms, ending in *-ed* or *-en*. A **participial phrase** is a group of words that consists of either the present or past participle form of a verb and its modifiers. For example, the participial phrase in this sentence from "Love's Vocabulary" consists of a present participle (sitting) and an adverb (still):

> **Sitting still, we are as daring as gladiators.**

The phrase *sitting still* modifies the pronoun *we*. The author could have conveyed the same information this way:

> **We are sitting still. We are as daring as gladiators.**

However, the rhythm of these two sentences is choppy and uninteresting. Reread Ackerman's sentence and notice how her use of a participial phrase to combine the ideas adds variety and interest to her writing.

Several participial phrases may be used in one sentence to show different actions. Ackerman creates a sense of drama and builds interest by using participial phrases in combination to show several actions:

> **Hoping for victory, limping from the latest skirmish, lovers enter the arena once again.**

Here, two participial phrases, separated by commas, modify the noun *lovers*. Ackerman could have written simply, "Lovers enter the arena once again." However, she includes participial phrases to tell us more about the lovers. She adds meaning by describing the lovers' states of mind and by presenting a dramatic visual image.

Participial phrases may be placed at the beginning, the middle, or the end of a sentence. When using participial phrases in your own writing, it is important to place them carefully and to use punctuation correctly for clarity.

Practice and Apply Look back at the summary of the discussion about love and embarrassment you wrote for this selection's Create and Present activity. Revise it to add at least three participial phrases. Then discuss with your group how the participial phrases improve the meaning or tone of the summary.

Go to the **Grammar Studio** for more on participial phrases.

VIDEO AND POEM

MY SHAKESPEARE

Video and poem by
Kate Tempest

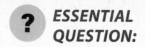

? ESSENTIAL QUESTION:

How can love bring both joy and pain?

QUICK START

Kate Tempest's poem and video explore William Shakespeare's legacy in everyday life. Think about other literature, art, or music from long ago that remains relevant to modern life. List a few authors, artists, or works from the past and briefly note how they are still important today.

GENRE ELEMENTS: VIDEO

- created for a specific purpose or reason
- combines visual and sound techniques
- may use film techniques such as camera shots, lighting, music, and other special effects

ANALYZE MULTIMODAL TEXTS

Multimodal texts present information and ideas in more than one mode, or method, such as through images, words, and sound effects. One type of multimodal text, often called performance art, consists of a video of a writer performing a written work. Elements, which include the writer's tone of voice, movements and gestures, are chosen to convey the writer's purpose and message or theme.

Sound Elements are what you hear in a video:

MUSIC	sounds created with singing, instruments, or computer-generated tones; sets the mood
SOUND EFFECTS	added sounds that contribute to mood or emphasize a point
SPEAKER'S TECHNIQUES	tempo, rhythm, and tone of voice

Visual Elements are what you see in a video:

FRAMING	people and objects within the "frame" of a screen or image, including background images
SPECIAL EFFECTS	includes manipulated video images and fast- or slow-motion sequences
CAMERA SHOTS	a single, continuous view taken by a camera
SPEAKER'S TECHNIQUES	facial expressions, movements, and gestures

BACKGROUND

Kate Tempest *(b. 1985) is a London-born poet, playwright, and rapper. She began performing at age 16 and has performed all over the world, winning acclaim and awards at music festivals and poetry slams. Her first collection of poetry,* Everything Speaks in its Own Way, *was published in 2012 and includes a CD and a DVD along with the text. The Royal Shakespeare Company commissioned Kate to write and perform "My Shakespeare" for the World Shakespeare Festival in 2012. Thousands of artists from around the world participated in this festival. Her latest work,* Let Them Eat Chaos, *was nominated for the 2017 Mercury Prize for Album of the Year in the United Kingdom and Ireland.*

SETTING A PURPOSE

As you watch and read, pause to note any questions that you have. Then share your questions with a small group or with your teacher to clarify your understanding.

To view the video, log in online and select **"MY SHAKESPEARE"** from the unit menu.

As needed, pause the video to make notes about Kate Tempest's performance of her poem "My Shakespeare," including how her performance techniques, sound effects, and camera shots engage the audience and add meaning to the poem. Replay or rewind to review anything you do not understand.

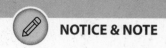
My Shakespeare

Performance by Kate Tempest

He's in every lover who ever stood alone beneath a window,
In every jealous whispered word,
in every ghost that will not rest.
He's in every father with a favorite,
5 Every eye that stops to linger
On what someone else has got, and feels the tightening in their
    chest.

He's in every young man growing boastful,
Every worn out elder, drunk all day;
muttering false prophecies and squandering their lot.
10 He's there—in every mix-up that spirals far out of control—and
    never seems to end,
even when its beginnings are forgot.

He's in every girl who ever used her wits. Who ever did her best.
In every vain admirer,
Every passionate, ambitious social climber,
15 And in every misheard word that ever led to tempers fraying,
Every pawn that moves exactly as the player wants it to,
And still remains convinced that it's not playing.

He's in every star crossed lover, in every thought that ever set your
teeth on edge, in every breathless hero, stepping closer to the ledge,
20 his is the method in our madness, as pure as the driven snow—his is
the hair standing on end, he saw that all that glittered was not gold.
He knew we hadn't slept a wink, and that our hearts were upon our
sleeves, and that the beast with two backs had us all upon our knees
as we fought fire with fire, he knew that too much of a good thing,
25 can leave you up in arms, the pen is mightier than the sword, still
his words seem to sing our names as they strike, and his is the milk
of human kindness, warm enough to break the ice—his, the green
eyed monster, in a pickle, still, discretion is the better part of valor,
his letters with their arms around each others shoulders, swagger
30 towards the ends of their sentences, pleased with what they've done,
his words are the setting for our stories—he has become a poet who
poetics have embedded themselves deep within the fabric of our
language, he's in our mouths, his words have tangled round our own
and given rise to expressions so effective in expressing how we feel,
35 we can't imagine how we'd feel without them.

© Houghton Mifflin Harcourt Publishing Company

ANALYZE MULTIMODAL TEXTS

Annotate: Mark where the words in the written poem differ from the ones delivered in the video.

Infer: Why do you think the poet changed the words of the poem? How do the changes alter the meaning?

See—he's less the tights and garters—more the sons demanding
    answers from the absence of their fathers.
The hot darkness of your last embrace.
He's in the laughter of the night before, the tightened jaw of the
    morning after,
He's in us. Part and parcel of our Royals and our rascals.
40 He's more than something taught in classrooms, in language that's
    hard to understand,
he's more than a feeling of inadequacy when we sit for our exams,
He's in every wise woman, every pitiful villain,
Every great king, every sore loser, every fake tear.
His legacy exists in the life that lives in everything he's written,
45 And me, I see him everywhere, he's my Shakespeare.

NOTICE & NOTE

ANALYZE MULTIMODAL TEXTS

Annotate: In the last two lines, underline words the poet emphasizes in her video delivery. Circle places where the poet pauses.

Connect: What does the poet's delivery of these lines add to the meaning of the poem? What is your personal reaction to these lines?

CHECK YOUR UNDERSTANDING

Answer these questions before moving on to the **Analyze the Text** section on the following page.

1 The speaker in the poem feels that Shakespeare's legacy belongs to her because —

   A she understands the language he uses

   B she has read many of his plays and can quote them

   C she is following in his footsteps as a poet

   D she recognizes his influence in the world around her

2 What is the phrase "tights and garters" used to represent?

   F How people used to dress

   G Something irrelevant to modern life

   H Costumes designed for a theater production

   J Clothing that is uncomfortable to wear

3 What is an important idea in the poem?

   A Shakespeare's words have become part of everyday life.

   B Shakespeare's works should be taught in every classroom.

   C Shakespeare's understanding of the world was advanced for his time.

   D Shakespeare's plays covered a wide range of topics and situations.

ANALYZE POEM AND VIDEO

Support your responses with evidence from the video and text. ▤ NOTEBOOK

1. **Infer** What does the repetition of the words "in every" throughout the poem signal to readers? What message does Tempest convey through these words?

2. **Cite Evidence** Explain the statement that Shakespeare is "in our mouths, his words have tangled round our own . . ." What evidence does the author provide to support this idea?

3. **Analyze** In the last stanza, Tempest acknowledges the negative ideas that today's young people might have about Shakespeare. How do the text and the video work together to refute these ideas?

4. **Synthesize** Explain how the poet uses visual elements, sound elements, and speaking techniques to develop the meaning of her poem through the video.

5. **Evaluate** What do the poem's final words, "my Shakespeare" mean? What evidence from the poem supports this meaning?

RESEARCH

RESEARCH TIP
When researching something from the past, look for accounts and information from that time. For example, search for newspaper articles about the event or reviews written about a performance.

Kate Tempest wrote the poem "My Shakespeare" for the World Shakespeare Festival in 2012. In a small group, research the 2012 World Shakespeare Festival and the productions it inspired. From the chart below, assign each group member a topic to research. Record your findings in the chart, and share them with the group.

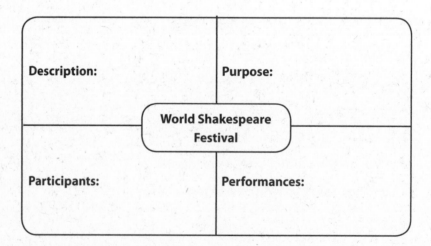

Extend Find another video of a performance from the World Shakespeare Festival. Think about what you see and hear in the video and how the images are arranged. With a partner, discuss how the video adds meaning to the text being performed.

CREATE AND PRESENT

Write a Poem Write a three-to four-stanza poem about a work, artist, or author that has influenced you. Review your notes on the Quick Start activity before you begin.

- ❏ Think about the ideas you want to explore in your poem. For example, you might want to write about how the work, artist, or author has changed your view of yourself or of the world. Write a list of your ideas.

- ❏ Arrange your ideas in a logical or artistic order.

- ❏ Draft your poem using literary devices such as repetition to emphasize ideas. Use rhythm and a rhyme scheme that will best convey your thoughts and feelings.

- ❏ Revise and edit your poem as needed.

Produce a Video With a partner, create a video performance of your poem.

- ❏ Decide what your audience will see and hear in the video, including the speaking techniques, camera shots, music, and background images.

- ❏ Practice reading the poem aloud, emphasizing different words or phrases until it sounds the way you want it to.

- ❏ Record your video. You may want to use video editing software to arrange images and add audio and visual elements.

- ❏ Present your video to the class. Combine the videos into a class film about how artists affect our lives.

> Go to the **Speaking and Listening Studio** for more on giving a presentation.

RESPOND TO THE ESSENTIAL QUESTION

? How can love bring both joy and pain?

Gather Information Review your annotations and notes on "My Shakespeare." Then, add relevant information to your Response Log. As you determine which information to include, think about:

- why Shakespeare is still relevant today
- the role of love in the situations described in the poem
- how experiences of joy and pain are captured in the poem

At the end of the unit, use your notes to help you write a literary analysis.

ACADEMIC VOCABULARY
As you write and discuss what you learned from the poem, be sure to use the Academic Vocabulary words. Check off each of the words that you use.

- ❏ **attribute**
- ❏ **commit**
- ❏ **expose**
- ❏ **initiate**
- ❏ **underlie**

My Shakespeare 281

SHAKESPEAREAN DRAMA

Shakespeare's 38 plays may be more popular today than they were in Elizabethan times. While Shakespeare's comedies and histories remain crowd-pleasing classics, his tragedies are perhaps his most powerful works. One of the most famous, *The Tragedy of Romeo and Juliet*, relates the tale of two love-struck teens caught in the tensions between their feuding families.

CHARACTERISTICS OF SHAKESPEAREAN TRAGEDY

A **tragedy** is a drama that results in a catastrophe for the main characters. Shakespearean tragedies offer more than just despair; they provide comic moments that counter the underlying tension of the plot. Before you read, familiarize yourself with some character types and dramatic conventions of Shakespearean tragedy.

Characters	Dramatic Conventions
Tragic Hero • the protagonist, or central character • usually fails or dies because of a character flaw or a cruel twist of fate	**Soliloquy** • a speech given by a character alone • exposes a character's thoughts and feelings to the audience
Antagonist • the adversary or hostile force opposing the protagonist • can be a character, a group of characters, or a nonhuman entity	**Aside** • a character's remark that others on stage do not hear • reveals the character's private thoughts
Foil • a character whose personality and attitude contrast sharply with those of another character • emphasizes another character's attributes and traits	**Dramatic Irony** • when the audience knows more than the characters; helps build suspense
	Comic Relief • a humorous scene or speech meant to relieve tension; the contrast can heighten the seriousness of the action

THE LANGUAGE OF SHAKESPEARE

Blank Verse Shakespeare wrote his plays primarily in blank verse: unrhymed lines of **iambic pentameter**, a meter that contains five unstressed syllables (˘), each followed by a stressed syllable (´). Read the following line aloud, emphasizing each stressed syllable:

Here's múch tŏ dó wĭth háte bŭt móre wĭth lóve.

© Houghton Mifflin Harcourt Publishing Company • Image Credits: ©AKaiser/Shutterstock

While this pattern forms the general rule, variations in the rhythm prevent the play from sounding monotonous. As you read, pay close attention to places where characters speak in rhyming poetry instead of unrhymed verse.

Allusion An allusion is a reference to a literary or historical person or event that the audience is expected to know. Shakespeare's audience was familiar with Greek and Roman mythology and the Bible, so his plays include many references to these works. For example, Mercutio refers to the mythological god of love when he says, "Borrow Cupid's wings and soar with them . . ." (Act I, Scene 4).

ELIZABETHAN THEATER

A Wide Audience Though acting companies toured throughout England, London was the center of the Elizabethan stage. One reason that London's theaters did so well was that they attracted an avid audience of rich and poor alike. In fact, Elizabethan theaters were among the few forms of entertainment available to working class people, and one of the only places where people of all classes could mix.

The Globe In 1599, Shakespeare and other shareholders of The Lord Chamberlain's Men built the Globe Theater, a three-story wooden structure with an open courtyard at its center where the actors performed on an elevated platform. The theater held 3,000 people, with most of them standing near the courtyard stage in an area known as the pit. The pit audience paid the lowest admission fee—usually just one penny. Theater-goers willing and able to pay more sat in the covered inner balconies that surrounded the courtyard.

Staging Elizabethan theater relied heavily on the audience's imagination. Most theaters had no curtains, no lighting, and very little scenery. Instead, props, sound effects, and certain lines of dialogue defined the setting of a scene. While the staging was simple, the scenes were hardly dull. Flashing swords, brightly colored banners, and elegant costumes contributed to the spectacle. The costumes also helped audience members imagine that women appeared in the female roles, which were actually performed by young men. In Shakespeare's time, women could not belong to theater companies in England— Elizabethan society considered it highly improper for a woman to appear on stage.

THE TRAGEDY OF ROMEO AND JULIET

Drama by **William Shakespeare**

? **ESSENTIAL QUESTION:**

How can love bring both joy and pain?

QUICK START

Sketch a scene or image that you associate with the story of Romeo and Juliet.

ANALYZE LITERARY DEVICES

Shakespeare uses a variety of literary devices in *The Tragedy of Romeo and Juliet* to create complex and believable characters, establish mood and setting, and develop suspense. As you read the play, start a word wall of any terms or phrases you find interesting or challenging. Add to this word wall as you continue to read.

Characters In creating his characters, Shakespeare often uses a **foil**, a character who contrasts with one of his major characters. Mercutio is one of the most famous foils in literature, his ironic wit contrasting with Romeo's romanticism and his fierce family pride contrasting with Romeo's desire for peace between the Montagues and the Capulets.

Setting Since Shakespearean theaters did not have stage sets with false trees and painted walls, the playwright had to create a sense of where the characters were by using **descriptive dialogue**. It's difficult to make that dialogue sound natural, but Shakespeare does it in this line from Act I, Scene 5: "More light, you knaves! and turn the tables up, / And quench the fire, the room is grown too hot."

Mood Shakespeare is brilliant at varying moods and building tension. Then he breaks that tension with such devices as **comic relief**, in which he uses word play. For example, Shakespeare's **puns** make use of a word's multiple meanings, or they play on its sound. One of Shakespeare's most powerful literary devices for mood building is the **soliloquy**, in which a character who is alone—or thinks he or she is alone—speaks his or her innermost thoughts and feelings. The overlapping soliloquies in the balcony scene of *The Tragedy of Romeo and Juliet* (Act II, Scene 2), which gradually become a dialogue, create a mood of romance and longing. Other literary devices Shakespeare uses include **oxymorons**, expressions containing an apparent contradiction ("parting is such sweet sorrow"); and **similes** ("My bounty is as boundless as the sea, / My love as deep; the more I give to thee, / The more I have, for both are infinite.").

Suspense Shakespeare builds suspense even when the audience is so familiar with a story that it knows how the play ends. One device he uses is **dramatic irony**, in which the audience knows what one or more of the people on stage does not know. For example, Juliet pours out her heart in the balcony scene, not knowing that Romeo is listening. Another important device for building suspense is **foreshadowing**. At several points in the play characters refer, often unknowingly, to what will happen in the future.

**GENRE ELEMENTS:
DRAMA**

- written to be performed by actors in front of an audience
- tells a story through characters' words and actions
- includes stage directions with important details that explain what's happening
- may be divided into acts, which are in turn divided into scenes
- may show that the time or place of the action has changed by starting a new act or scene

ANALYZE PARALLEL PLOTS

Romeo and Juliet is not a simple love story with a **linear**, or straightforward, plot. It is a complex drama featuring **parallel plots**, separate story lines that happen at the same time and are linked by common characters and themes. The chart can help you identify the parallel plots in the play.

PLOT	PURPOSE
The love story of Romeo and Juliet	How does this main plot intertwine with the other parallel plots?
The feud between the Capulets and the Montagues	How does this plot contribute to the drama of the play?
Romeo's unrequited love for Rosaline	What does this show us about Romeo?
Juliet's marriage proposal from Paris	What do we learn about Juliet and her relationship with her family?

LANGUAGE CONVENTIONS

Parallel structure is the repetition of certain words, phrases, or grammatical structures. It adds emphasis or improves the rhythm of a piece of writing. Here is a line from the play with parallel structure underlined.

"O, shut the door! And when thou hast done so, / Come weep with me— past hope, past cure, past help!"

ANNOTATION MODEL

NOTICE & NOTE

As you read, note clues about the setting, plot, and characters of *The Tragedy of Romeo and Juliet*. This model shows one reader's notes about the Prologue.

Two households, both alike in dignity,
In fair Verona, where we lay our scene,
From <u>ancient grudge</u> break to new mutiny,
Where civil blood makes civil hands unclean.
From forth the fatal loins of these two foes,
A pair of star-crossed lovers take their life,
Whose misadventured piteous overthrows
Doth with <u>their death</u> bury their parents' strife.

These two families must have been fighting for a long time.

This foreshadows the way the play ends.

BACKGROUND

William Shakespeare *(1564–1616) has long been considered the greatest writer in the English language—and perhaps the greatest playwright of all time. Four hundred years after their premier performances, his plays remain more popular than ever, and they have been produced more often and in more countries than those of any other author. Despite Shakespeare's renown, we have relatively few details about his life and career as an actor, poet, and playwright.*

THE TRAGEDY OF ROMEO AND JULIET

Drama by
William Shakespeare

Shakespeare came from Stratford-upon-Avon, a small village about 90 miles northwest of London, and was probably born in 1564. Though no records exist, we assume that he attended the local grammar school. In 1582, he married Anne Hathaway, the daughter of a farmer. The couple's first child arrived in 1583, and twins, a boy and a girl, followed two years later.

We know nothing about the next seven years of Shakespeare's life, but he likely left his family behind and joined a traveling theater troupe. His trail resurfaces in London, where he had become a successful poet and playwright. He wrote for and acted with The Lord Chamberlain's Men, a popular theater troupe. By 1597, the year that The Tragedy of Romeo and Juliet was published, he had become a shareholder of the theater company. As his popularity grew, Shakespeare also became part owner of London's Globe Theater. In 1603, King James I became a patron of the Globe Theater, and the theater troupe became known as The King's Men.

In 1609, Shakespeare published his sonnets, a series of poems that received wide popular acclaim. Shakespeare then began to take advantage of his wealth and fame, spending more time in Stratford-upon-Avon and retiring there permanently around 1612. He would write no more plays after that year. No records confirm the cause or date of his death; a monument marking his gravesite indicates that he died on April 23, 1616. Although we have little data documenting his life, more pages have been written about Shakespeare than about any author in the history of Western civilization.

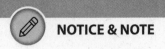
Notice & Note

You can use the side margins to notice and note signposts in the text.

SETTING A PURPOSE

Look for clues that reveal the personalities of Romeo and Juliet. Write down any questions you generate during reading.

THE TIME: The 14th century

THE PLACE: Verona (və-rō′nə) and Mantua (măn′chōō-ə) in northern Italy

CAST

The Montagues

Lord Montague (mŏn′tə-gyōō)
Lady Montague
Romeo, son of Montague
Benvolio (bĕn-vō′lē-ō), nephew of Montague and friend of Romeo
Balthasar (băl′thə-sär), servant to Romeo
Abram, servant to Montague

The Capulets

Lord Capulet (kăp′yōō-lĕt)
Lady Capulet
Juliet, daughter of Capulet
Tybalt (tĭb′əlt), nephew of Lady Capulet
Nurse to Juliet
Peter, servant to Juliet's nurse
Sampson, servant to Capulet
Gregory, servant to Capulet
An Old Man of the Capulet family

Others

Prince Escalus (ĕs′kə-ləs), ruler of Verona
Mercutio (mĕr-kyōō′shē-ō), kinsman of the prince and friend of Romeo
Friar Laurence, a Franciscan priest
Friar John, another Franciscan priest
Count Paris, a young nobleman, kinsman of the prince
Apothecary (ə-pŏth′ĭ-kĕr-ē)
Page to Paris
Chief Watchman
Three Musicians
An Officer
Chorus
Citizens of Verona, **Gentlemen** and **Gentlewomen** of both houses, **Maskers, Torchbearers, Pages, Guards, Watchmen, Servants,** and **Attendants**

Prologue

[*Enter* Chorus.]

Chorus. Two households, both alike in dignity,
In fair Verona, where we lay our scene,
From ancient grudge break to new mutiny,
Where civil blood makes civil hands unclean.
5 From forth the fatal loins of these two foes,
A pair of star-crossed lovers take their life,
Whose misadventured piteous overthrows
Doth with their death bury their parents' strife.
The fearful passage of their death-marked love,
10 And the continuance of their parents' rage,
Which, but their children's end, naught could remove,
Is now the two hours' traffic of our stage,
The which if you with patient ears attend,
What here shall miss, our toil shall strive to mend.

[*Exit.*]

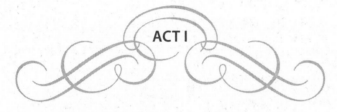

ACT I

Scene 1 *A public square in Verona.*

[*Enter* Sampson *and* Gregory, *servants of the house of Capulet, armed with swords and bucklers* (*shields*).]

Sampson. Gregory, on my word, we'll not carry coals.

Gregory. No, for then we should be colliers.

Sampson. I mean, an we be in choler, we'll draw.

Gregory. Ay, while you live, draw your neck out of collar.

5 **Sampson.** I strike quickly, being moved.

Gregory. But thou art not quickly moved to strike.

Sampson. A dog of that house of Montague moves me.

Gregory. To move is to stir, and to be valiant is to stand.
Therefore, if thou art moved, thou runnest away.

10 **Sampson.** A dog of that house shall move me to stand. I will
take the wall of any man or maid of Montague's.

Gregory. That shows thee a weak slave, for the weakest goes to
the wall.

3–4 ancient . . . unclean: A new outbreak of fighting (**mutiny**) between families has caused the citizens of Verona to have one another's blood on their hands.

6 star-crossed: doomed. The position of the stars when the lovers were born was not favorable. In Shakespeare's day, people took astrology very seriously.

7 misadventured: unlucky.

11 but: except for; **naught:** nothing.

14 what . . . mend: The play will fill in the details not mentioned in the prologue.

1–2 we'll not carry coals: we won't stand to be insulted; **colliers:** those involved in the dirty work of hauling coal, who were often the butt of jokes.
3–4 in choler: angry; **collar:** a hangman's noose.

11 take the wall: walk. People of higher rank had the privilege of walking closer to the wall, to avoid any water or garbage in the street.

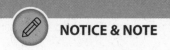
14–24 Sampson's tough talk includes boasts about his ability to overpower women.

Sampson. 'Tis true; and therefore women, being the weaker
15   vessels, are ever thrust to the wall. Therefore push I will Montague's men from the wall and thrust his maids to the wall.

Gregory. The quarrel is between our masters and us their men.

Sampson. 'Tis all one. I will show myself a tyrant. When I have fought with the men, I will be cruel with the maids: I will cut
20   off their heads.

Gregory. The heads of the maids?

Sampson. Ay, the heads of the maids, or their maidenheads. Take it in what sense thou wilt.

Gregory. They must take it in sense that feel it.

25   **Sampson.** Me they shall feel while I am able to stand; and 'tis known I am a pretty piece of flesh.

28 poor-John: a salted fish, considered fit only for poor people to eat.

Gregory. 'Tis well thou art not fish; if thou hadst, thou hadst been poor-John. Draw thy tool! Here comes two of the house of Montagues.

[*Enter* Abram *and* Balthasar, *servants to the Montagues.*]

30   **Sampson.** My naked weapon is out. Quarrel! I will back thee.

Gregory. How? turn thy back and run?

Sampson. Fear me not.

Gregory. No, marry. I fear thee!

33 marry: a short form of "by the Virgin Mary" and so a mild exclamation.

Sampson. Let us take the law of our sides; let them begin.

35   **Gregory.** I will frown as I pass by, and let them take it as they list.

34–44 Gregory and Sampson decide to pick a fight by insulting the Montague servants with a rude gesture (**bite my thumb**).

Sampson. Nay, as they dare. I will bite my thumb at them; which is disgrace to them, if they bear it.

Abram. Do you bite your thumb at us, sir?

Sampson. I do bite my thumb, sir.

40   **Abram.** Do you bite your thumb at us, sir?

Sampson [*aside* to Gregory]. Is the law of our side if I say ay?

Gregory [*aside* to Sampson]. No.

Sampson. No, sir, I do not bite my thumb at you, sir; but I bite my thumb, sir.

45   **Gregory.** Do you quarrel, sir?

Abram. Quarrel, sir? No, sir.

Sampson. But if you do, sir, I am for you. I serve as good a man as you.

ANALYZE PARALLEL PLOTS
Annotate: The storyline of the feud between the Capulets and Montagues runs parallel to the storyline of Romeo and Juliet. Mark the line(s) where the argument between the servants of the two households begins.

Predict: How might this parallel plot affect the main plot of the "star-crossed lovers"?

Abram. No better.

50 **Sampson.** Well, sir.

[*Enter* Benvolio, *nephew of Montague and first cousin of Romeo.*]

Gregory [*aside* to Sampson]. Say "better." Here comes one of my master's kinsmen.

Sampson. Yes, better, sir.

Abram. You lie.

55 **Sampson.** Draw, if you be men. Gregory, remember thy swashing blow.

[*They fight.*]

Benvolio. Part, fools!   [*beats down their swords*]
Put up your swords. You know not what you do.

[*Enter* Tybalt, *hot-headed nephew of Lady Capulet and first cousin of Juliet.*]

Tybalt. What, art thou drawn among these heartless hinds?
60 Turn thee, Benvolio! look upon thy death.

Benvolio. I do but keep the peace. Put up thy sword,
Or manage it to part these men with me.

Tybalt. What, drawn, and talk of peace? I hate the word
As I hate hell, all Montagues, and thee.
65 Have at thee, coward!

[*They fight.*]

[*Enter several of both houses, who join the fray; then enter* Citizens *and* Peace Officers, *with clubs.*]

Officer. Clubs, bills, and partisans! Strike! beat them down!

Citizens. Down with the Capulets! Down with the Montagues!

[*Enter old* Capulet *and* Lady Capulet.]

Capulet. What noise is this? Give me my long sword, ho!

Lady Capulet. A crutch, a crutch! Why call you for a sword?

70 **Capulet.** My sword, I say! Old Montague is come
And flourishes his blade in spite of me.

[*Enter old* Montague *and* Lady Montague.]

Montague. Thou villain Capulet!—Hold me not, let me go.

Lady Montague. Thou shalt not stir one foot to seek a foe.

[*Enter* Prince Escalus, *with attendants. At first no one hears him.*]

59 heartless hinds: cowardly servants.

63 drawn: with your sword out.

65 have at thee: Defend yourself.

66 bills, and partisans: spears.

69 A crutch . . . sword: You need a crutch more than a sword.

© Houghton Mifflin Harcourt Publishing Company

74–81 The prince is furious about the street fighting caused by the feud. He orders the men to drop their weapons and pay attention.

77 pernicious: destructive.

82–90 Three... peace: The prince holds Capulet and Montague responsible for three recent street fights, each probably started by an offhand remark or insult (**airy word**). He warns that they will be put to death if any more fights occur.

Exeunt: the plural form of *exit*, indicating that more than one person is leaving the stage.

97 Who ... abroach: Who reopened this old argument?

99 adversary: enemy.
100 ere: before.

107 on part and part: some on one side, some on the other.

110 fray: fight.

113 drave: drove.

115 rooteth: grows.

Prince. Rebellious subjects, enemies to peace,
75 Profaners of this neighbor-stained steel—
Will they not hear? What, ho! you men, you beasts,
That quench the fire of your pernicious rage
With purple fountains issuing from your veins!
On pain of torture, from those bloody hands
80 Throw your mistempered weapons to the ground
And hear the sentence of your moved prince.
Three civil brawls, bred of an airy word
By thee, old Capulet, and Montague,
Have thrice disturbed the quiet of our streets
85 And made Verona's ancient citizens
Cast by their grave beseeming ornaments
To wield old partisans, in hands as old,
Cankered with peace, to part your cankered hate.
If ever you disturb our streets again,
90 Your lives shall pay the forfeit of the peace.
For this time all the rest depart away.
You, Capulet, shall go along with me;
And, Montague, come you this afternoon,
To know our farther pleasure in this case,
95 To old Freetown, our common judgment place.
Once more, on pain of death, all men depart.

[*Exeunt all but* Montague, Lady Montague, *and* Benvolio.]

Montague. Who set this ancient quarrel new abroach?
Speak, nephew, were you by when it began?

Benvolio. Here were the servants of your adversary
100 And yours, close fighting ere I did approach.
I drew to part them. In the instant came
The fiery Tybalt, with his sword prepared;
Which, as he breathed defiance to my ears,
He swung about his head and cut the winds,
105 Who, nothing hurt withal, hissed him in scorn.
While we were interchanging thrusts and blows,
Came more and more, and fought on part and part,
Till the Prince came, who parted either part.

Lady Montague. O, where is Romeo? Saw you him today?
110 Right glad I am he was not at this fray.

Benvolio. Madam, an hour before the worshiped sun
Peered forth the golden window of the East,
A troubled mind drave me to walk abroad,
Where, underneath the grove of sycamore
115 That westward rooteth from the city's side,

So early walking did I see your son.
Towards him I made, but he was ware of me
And stole into the covert of the wood.
I—measuring his affections by my own,
120 Which then most sought where most might not be found,
Being one too many by my weary self—
Pursued my humor, not pursuing his,
And gladly shunned who gladly fled from me.

Montague. Many a morning hath he there been seen,
125 With tears augmenting the fresh morning's dew,
Adding to clouds more clouds with his deep sighs;
But all so soon as the all-cheering sun
Should in the farthest East begin to draw
The shady curtains from Aurora's bed,
130 Away from light steals home my heavy son
And private in his chamber pens himself,
Shuts up his windows, locks fair daylight out,
And makes himself an artificial night.
Black and portentous must this humor prove
135 Unless good counsel may the cause remove.

Benvolio. My noble uncle, do you know the cause?

Montague. I neither know it nor can learn of him.

Benvolio. Have you importuned him by any means?

Montague. Both by myself and many other friends;
140 But he, his own affections' counselor,
Is to himself—I will not say how true—
But to himself so secret and so close,
So far from sounding and discovery,
As is the bud bit with an envious worm
145 Ere he can spread his sweet leaves to the air
Or dedicate his beauty to the sun.
Could we but learn from whence his sorrows grow,
We would as willingly give cure as know.

[*Enter* Romeo *lost in thought.*]

Benvolio. See, where he comes. So please you step aside,
150 I'll know his grievance, or be much denied.

Montague. I would thou wert so happy by thy stay
To hear true shrift. Come, madam, let's away.

[*Exeunt* Montague *and* Lady.]

Benvolio. Good morrow, cousin.

Romeo.   Is the day so young?

Benvolio. But new struck nine.

117–123 made: moved; **covert:** covering. Romeo saw Benvolio coming and hid in the woods. Benvolio himself was seeking solitude and did not go after him.

124–135 Romeo has been seen wandering through the woods at night, crying. At dawn he returns home and locks himself in his room. Montague feels that his son needs guidance.
129 Aurora's bed: Aurora was the goddess of the dawn.

134 portentous: indicating evil to come; threatening.

138 importuned: asked in an urgent way.

140 his own affections' counselor: Romeo keeps to himself.

143–148 so far from . . . know: Finding out what Romeo is thinking is almost impossible. Montague compares his son to a young bud destroyed by the bite of a worm before it has a chance to open its leaves. Montague wants to find out what is bothering Romeo so he can help him.

152 shrift: confession.

153 cousin: any relative or close friend. The informal version is *coz*.

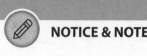

162–165 love: references to Cupid, the god of love, typically pictured as a blind boy with wings and a bow and arrow. Anyone hit by one of his arrows falls in love instantly.

Romeo.   Ay me! sad hours seem long.
155 Was that my father that went hence so fast?

Benvolio. It was. What sadness lengthens Romeo's hours?

Romeo. Not having that which having makes them short.

Benvolio. In love?

Romeo. Out—

160 **Benvolio.** Of love?

Romeo. Out of her favor where I am in love.

Benvolio. Alas that love, so gentle in his view,
Should be so tyrannous and rough in proof!

Romeo. Alas that love, whose view is muffled still,
165 Should without eyes see pathways to his will!
Where shall we dine?—O me! What fray was here?—
Yet tell me not, for I have heard it all.

Here's much to do with hate, but more with love.
Why then, O brawling love! O loving hate!
170 O anything, of nothing first create!
O heavy lightness! serious vanity!
Misshapen chaos of well-seeming forms!
Feather of lead, bright smoke, cold fire, sick health!
Still-waking sleep, that is not what it is!
175 This love feel I, that feel no love in this.
Dost thou not laugh?

Benvolio.   No, coz, I rather weep.

Romeo. Good heart, at what?

Benvolio.   At thy good heart's oppression.

Romeo. Why, such is love's transgression.
Griefs of mine own lie heavy in my breast,
180 Which thou wilt propagate, to have it prest
With more of thine. This love that thou hast shown
Doth add more grief to too much of mine own.
Love is a smoke raised with the fume of sighs;
Being purged, a fire sparkling in lovers' eyes;
185 Being vexed, a sea nourished with lovers' tears.
What is it else? A madness most discreet,
A choking gall, and a preserving sweet.
Farewell, my coz.

Benvolio.   Soft! I will go along.
An if you leave me so, you do me wrong.

190 **Romeo.** Tut! I have lost myself; I am not here:
This is not Romeo, he's some other where.

Benvolio. Tell me in sadness, who is that you love?

Romeo. What, shall I groan and tell thee?

Benvolio.   Groan? Why, no;
But sadly tell me who.

195 **Romeo.** Bid a sick man in sadness make his will.
Ah, word ill urged to one that is so ill!
In sadness, cousin, I do love a woman.

Benvolio. I aimed so near when I supposed you loved.

Romeo. A right good markman! And she's fair I love.

200 **Benvolio.** A right fair mark, fair coz, is soonest hit.

Romeo. Well, in that hit you miss. She'll not be hit
With Cupid's arrow. She hath Dian's wit,
And, in strong proof of chastity well armed,
From Love's weak childish bow she lives unharmed.

© Houghton Mifflin Harcourt Publishing Company

ANALYZE LITERARY DEVICES
Annotate: Romeo, confused and upset about love, describes his feelings using oxymorons, or contradictory expressions. Mark some of these expressions.

Analyze: How do these oxymorons help show the complexity of what Romeo is feeling?

176–182 Benvolio expresses his sympathy for Romeo. Romeo replies that this is one more problem caused by love. He now feels worse than before because he must carry the weight of Benvolio's sympathy along with his own grief.

184 purged: cleansed (of the smoke).
185 vexed: troubled.
187 gall: something causing bitterness or hate.

188 soft: Wait a minute.

192 sadness: seriousness.

201–204 She'll … unharmed: The girl isn't interested in falling in love. She is like Diana, the goddess of chastity.

**205–207 She will not
... gold:** She is not swayed by
Romeo's love or his wealth.

205 She will not stay the siege of loving terms,
    Nor bide the encounter of assailing eyes,
    Nor ope her lap to saint-seducing gold.
    O, she is rich in beauty; only poor
    That, when she dies, with beauty dies her store.

210 **Benvolio.** Then she hath sworn that she will still live chaste?

**212–213 for beauty
... posterity:** She wastes
her beauty, which will not
be passed on to future
generations.

Romeo. She hath, and in that sparing makes huge waste;
For beauty, starved with her severity,
Cuts beauty off from all posterity.
She is too fair, too wise, wisely too fair

215 To merit bliss by making me despair.
    She hath forsworn to love, and in that vow
    Do I live dead that live to tell it now.

**215–216 to merit ...
despair:** The girl will reach
heaven (**bliss**) by being so
virtuous, which causes Romeo
to feel despair; **forsworn to:**
sworn not to.

Benvolio. Be ruled by me: forget to think of her.

Romeo. O, teach me how I should forget to think!

220 **Benvolio.** By giving liberty unto thine eyes:
    Examine other beauties.

221–222 'Tis ... more: That
would only make me appreciate
my own love's beauty more.

Romeo.   'Tis the way
To call hers (exquisite) in question more.
These happy masks that kiss fair ladies' brows,
Being black, puts us in mind they hide the fair.

223 Masks were worn by
Elizabethan women to protect
their faces from the sun.

225 He that is strucken blind cannot forget
    The precious treasure of his eyesight lost.
    Show me a mistress that is passing fair,
    What doth her beauty serve but as a note
    Where I may read who passed that passing fair?

**227–229 Show me ...
fair:** A woman who is
exceedingly (passing) beautiful
will only remind me of my love,
who is even prettier.

230 Farewell. Thou canst not teach me to forget.

Benvolio. I'll pay that doctrine, or else die in debt.

231 I'll pay ... debt: I'll
convince you you're wrong, or
die trying.

[*Exeunt.*]

Scene 2 *A street near the Capulet house.*

[*Enter* Capulet *with* Paris, *a kinsman of the Prince, and* Servant.]

1 bound: obligated.

Capulet. But Montague is bound as well as I,
In penalty alike; and 'tis not hard, I think,
For men so old as we to keep the peace.

4 reckoning: reputation.

Paris. Of honorable reckoning are you both,
5 And pity 'tis you lived at odds so long.
  But now, my lord, what say you to my suit?

6 what say ... suit: Paris is
asking for Capulet's response to
his proposal to marry Juliet.

Capulet. But saying o'er what I have said before:
My child is yet a stranger in the world,
She hath not seen the change of fourteen years;

10 Let two more summers wither in their pride
Ere we may think her ripe to be a bride.

   Paris. Younger than she are happy mothers made.

   Capulet. And too soon marred are those so early made.
   The earth hath swallowed all my hopes but she;
15 She is the hopeful lady of my earth.
   But woo her, gentle Paris, get her heart;
   My will to her consent is but a part.
   An she agree, within her scope of choice
   Lies my consent and fair according voice.
20 This night I hold an old accustomed feast,
   Whereto I have invited many a guest,
   Such as I love, and you among the store,
   One more, most welcome, makes my number more.
   At my poor house look to behold this night
25 Earth-treading stars that make dark heaven light.
   Such comfort as do lusty young men feel
   When well-appareled April on the heel
   Of limping Winter treads, even such delight
   Among fresh female buds shall you this night
30 Inherit at my house. Hear all, all see,
   And like her most whose merit most shall be;
   Which, on more view of many, mine, being one,
   May stand in number, though in reck'ning none.
   Come, go with me.   [*to* Servant, *giving him a paper*]
                        Go, sirrah, trudge about
35 Through fair Verona; find those persons out
   Whose names are written there, and to them say,
   My house and welcome on their pleasure stay.

   [*Exeunt* Capulet *and* Paris.]

   Servant. Find them out whose names are written here! It is
   written that the shoemaker should meddle with his yard and the
40 tailor with his last, the fisher with his pencil and the painter
   with his nets; but I am sent to find those persons whose names
   are here writ, and can never find what names the writing person
   hath here writ. I must to the learned. In good time!

   [*Enter* Benvolio *and* Romeo.]

   Benvolio. Tut, man, one fire burns out another's burning;
45 One pain is lessened by another's anguish;
   Turn giddy, and be holp by backward turning;
   One desperate grief cures with another's languish.
   Take thou some new infection to thy eye,
   And the rank poison of the old will die.

10 Let two more summers . . . pride: let two more years pass.

14 The earth . . . she: All my children are dead except Juliet.

16 woo her: try to win her heart.

18–19 An . . . voice: I will give my approval to the one she chooses.

20 old accustomed feast: a traditional or annual party.

29–33 among . . . none: Tonight at the party you will see the loveliest girls in Verona, including Juliet. When you see all of them together, your opinion of Juliet may change.

34 sirrah: a term used to address a servant.

38–43 The servant cannot read. He confuses the craftsmen and their tools, tapping a typical source of humor for Elizabethan comic characters.

44–49 Tut, man . . . die: Benvolio says Romeo should find a new love—that a "new infection" will cure the old one.

55 God-den: good evening. Romeo interrupts his lament to talk to the servant.

56 God gi' go-den: God give you a good evening.

69 Rosaline: This is the woman that Romeo is in love with. Mercutio, a friend of both Romeo and the Capulets, is also invited to the party.

72 whither: where.

81 crush a cup of wine: slang for "drink some wine."

50 **Romeo.** Your plantain leaf is excellent for that.

Benvolio. For what, I pray thee?

Romeo. For your broken shin.

Benvolio. Why, Romeo, art thou mad?

Romeo. Not mad, but bound more than a madman is;
Shut up in prison, kept without my food,
55 Whipped and tormented and—God-den, good fellow.

Servant. God gi' go-den. I pray, sir, can you read?

Romeo. Ay, mine own fortune in my misery.

Servant. Perhaps you have learned it without book. But I pray, can you read anything you see?

60 **Romeo.** Ay, if I know the letters and the language.

Servant. Ye say honestly. Rest you merry!

[Romeo's *joking goes over the clown's head. He concludes that* Romeo *cannot read and prepares to seek someone who can.*]

Romeo. Stay, fellow; I can read.   [*He reads.*]
"Signior Martino and his wife and daughters;
County Anselmo and his beauteous sisters;
65 The lady widow of Vitruvio;
Signior Placentio and his lovely nieces;
Mercutio and his brother Valentine;
Mine uncle Capulet, his wife, and daughters;
My fair niece Rosaline and Livia;
70 Signior Valentio and his cousin Tybalt;
Lucio and the lively Helena."
[*gives back the paper*]
A fair assembly. Whither should they come?

Servant. Up.

Romeo. Whither?

75 **Servant.** To supper, to our house.

Romeo. Whose house?

Servant. My master's.

Romeo. Indeed I should have asked you that before.

Servant. Now I'll tell you without asking. My master is the great
80 rich Capulet; and if you be not of the house of Montagues, I
pray come and crush a cup of wine. Rest you merry!

[*Exit.*]

Benvolio. At this same ancient feast of Capulet's
Sups the fair Rosaline whom thou so lovest,
With all the admired beauties of Verona.

85 Go thither, and with unattainted eye
Compare her face with some that I shall show,
And I will make thee think thy swan a crow.

Romeo. When the devout religion of mine eye
Maintains such falsehood, then turn tears to fires;
90 And these, who, often drowned, could never die,
Transparent heretics, be burnt for liars!
One fairer than my love? The all-seeing sun
Ne'er saw her match since first the world begun.

Benvolio. Tut! you saw her fair, none else being by,
95 Herself poised with herself in either eye;
But in that crystal scales let there be weighed
Your lady's love against some other maid
That I will show you shining at this feast,
And she shall scant show well that now shows best.

100 **Romeo.** I'll go along, no such sight to be shown,
But to rejoice in splendor of mine own.

[*Exeunt.*]

Scene 3 *Capulet's house.*

[*Enter* Lady Capulet *and* Nurse.]

Lady Capulet. Nurse, where's my daughter? Call her forth to me.

Nurse. Now, by my maidenhead at twelve year old,
I bade her come. What, lamb! what, ladybird!
God forbid! Where's this girl? What, Juliet!

[*Enter* Juliet.]

5 **Juliet.** How now? Who calls?

Nurse. Your mother.

Juliet. Madam, I am here. What is your will?

Lady Capulet. This is the matter—Nurse, give leave awhile,
We must talk in secret. Nurse, come back again;
10 I have remembered me, thou's hear our counsel.
Thou knowest my daughter's of a pretty age.

Nurse. Faith, I can tell her age unto an hour.

Lady Capulet. She's not fourteen.

Nurse.   I'll lay fourteen of my teeth—
And yet, to my teen be it spoken, I have but four—
15 She's not fourteen. How long is it now
To Lammastide?

Lady Capulet. A fortnight and odd days.

85 unattainted: unbiased; unprejudiced.

88–91 When . . . liars: If the love I have for Rosaline, which is like a religion, changes because of such a lie (that others may be more beautiful), let my tears be turned to fire and my eyes be burned.

94–99 Tut . . . best: You've seen Rosaline alone; now compare her with some other women.

100–101 Romeo agrees to go to the party, but only to see Rosaline.

8–11 give leave . . . counsel: Lady Capulet seems nervous, not sure whether she wants the nurse to stay or leave; **of a pretty age:** of an attractive age, ready for marriage.

14 teen: sorrow.

16 Lammastide: August 1, a religious feast day. It is two weeks (**a fortnight**) away.

17–49 The nurse babbles about Juliet's childhood. Her own daughter, Susan, was the same age as Juliet, and died in infancy, leaving the nurse available to become a wet nurse (that is, breastfeed) to Juliet. An earthquake happened on the day she stopped breastfeeding Juliet (**she was weaned**).

27 laid wormwood to my dug: applied a plant with a bitter taste to her breast to discourage the child from breastfeeding.

33 tetchy: cranky.

34–35 Shake . . . trudge: When the dove house shook, I knew enough to leave.

37 by the rood: by the cross of Christ (a mild oath).

39 broke her brow: cut her forehead.

42–49 "Yea," . . . "Ay": The nurse's husband made a crude joke, asking the baby whether she'd fall the other way (on her back) when she was older. Although Juliet didn't understand the question, she stopped crying (**stinted**) and answered "Yes." The nurse finds the story so funny that she can't stop retelling it.

Nurse. Even or odd, of all days in the year,
Come Lammas Eve at night shall she be fourteen.
Susan and she (God rest all Christian souls!)
20 Were of an age. Well, Susan is with God;
She was too good for me. But, as I said,
On Lammas Eve at night shall she be fourteen;
That shall she, marry; I remember it well.
'Tis since the earthquake now eleven years;
25 And she was weaned (I never shall forget it),
Of all the days of the year, upon that day.
For I had then laid wormwood to my dug,
Sitting in the sun under the dovehouse wall.
My lord and you were then at Mantua—
30 Nay, I do bear a brain—But, as I said,
When it did taste the wormwood on the nipple
Of my dug and felt it bitter, pretty fool,
To see it tetchy and fall out with the dug!
Shake, quoth the dovehouse! 'Twas no need, I trow,
35 To bid me trudge.
And since that time it is eleven years,
For then she could stand alone; nay, by the rood,
She could have run and waddled all about;
For even the day before, she broke her brow;
40 And then my husband (God be with his soul!
'A was a merry man) took up the child.
"Yea," quoth he, "dost thou fall upon thy face?
Thou wilt fall backward when thou has more wit,
Wilt thou not, Jule?" And, by my holidam,
45 The pretty wretch left crying, and said "Ay."
To see now how a jest shall come about!
I warrant, an I should live a thousand years,
I never should forget it. "Wilt thou not, Jule?" quoth he,
And, pretty fool, it stinted, and said "Ay."

50 **Lady Capulet.** Enough of this. I pray thee hold thy peace.

Nurse. Yes, madam. Yet I cannot choose but laugh
To think it should leave crying and say "Ay."
And yet, I warrant, it had upon its brow
A bump as big as a young cock'rel's stone;
55 A perilous knock; and it cried bitterly.
"Yea," quoth my husband, "fallst upon thy face?
Thou wilt fall backward when thou comest to age,
Wilt thou not, Jule?" It stinted, and said "Ay."

Juliet. And stint thou too, I pray thee, nurse, say I.

Nurse. Peace, I have done. God mark thee to his grace!
Thou wast the prettiest babe that e'er I nursed.
An I might live to see thee married once,
I have my wish.

Lady Capulet. Marry, that "marry" is the very theme
65 I came to talk of. Tell me, daughter Juliet,
How stands your disposition to be married?

Juliet. It is an honor that I dream not of.

Nurse. An honor? Were not I thine only nurse,
I would say thou hadst sucked wisdom from thy teat.

70 **Lady Capulet.** Well, think of marriage now. Younger than you,
Here in Verona, ladies of esteem,
Are made already mothers. By my count,
I was your mother much upon these years
That you are now a maid. Thus then in brief:
75 The valiant Paris seeks you for his love.

Nurse. A man, young lady! lady, such a man
As all the world—why he's a man of wax.

Lady Capulet. Verona's summer hath not such a flower.

Nurse. Nay, he's a flower, in faith—a very flower.

80 **Lady Capulet.** What say you? Can you love the gentleman?
This night you shall behold him at our feast.
Read o'er the volume of young Paris' face,

64 Marry . . . "marry": two different usages of the same word—the first meaning "by the Virgin Mary" and the second meaning "to wed."

73–74 I was . . . maid: I was your mother at about your age, yet you are still unmarried.

77 a man of wax: a man so perfect he could be a wax statue, of the type sculptors once used as models for their works.

82–89 Read . . . cover: Lady Capulet uses an extended metaphor that compares Paris to a book that Juliet should read.

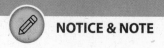
84 every several lineament: each separate feature (of Paris's face).

87 margent . . . eyes: She compares Paris's eyes to the margin of a page, where notes are written to explain the content.

88–91 This . . . hide: This beautiful book (Paris) needs only a cover (wife) to become even better. He may be hiding even more wonderful qualities inside.

96 Women get bigger (pregnant) when they marry.

98–100 I'll look . . . fly: I'll look at him with the intention of liking him, if simply looking can make me like him; **endart:** look deeply, as if penetrating with a dart.

103–104 extremity: great confusion; **straight:** immediately.

105 the County stays: Count Paris is waiting for you.

And find delight writ there with beauty's pen;
Examine every several lineament,
85 And see how one another lends content;
And what obscured in this fair volume lies
Find written in the margent of his eyes.
This precious book of love, this unbound lover,
To beautify him only lacks a cover.
90 The fish lives in the sea, and 'tis much pride
For fair without the fair within to hide.
That book in many's eyes doth share the glory,
That in gold clasps locks in the golden story;
So shall you share all that he doth possess,
95 By having him making yourself no less.

Nurse. No less? Nay, bigger! Women grow by men.

Lady Capulet. Speak briefly, can you like of Paris' love?

Juliet. I'll look to like, if looking liking move;
But no more deep will I endart mine eye
100 Than your consent gives strength to make it fly.

[*Enter a* Servingman.]

Servingman. Madam, the guests are come, supper served up, you called, my young lady asked for, the nurse cursed in the pantry, and everything in extremity. I must hence to wait. I beseech you follow straight.

105 **Lady Capulet.** We follow thee. [*Exit* Servingman.] Juliet, the County stays.

Nurse. Go, girl, seek happy nights to happy days.

[*Exeunt.*]

Scene 4 *A street near the Capulet house.*

[*Enter* Romeo, Mercutio, Benvolio, *with five or six other* Maskers; Torchbearers.]

Romeo. What, shall this speech be spoke for our excuse?
Or shall we on without apology?

Benvolio. The date is out of such prolixity.
We'll have no Cupid hoodwinked with a scarf,
5 Bearing a Tartar's painted bow of lath,
Scaring the ladies like a crowkeeper;
Nor no without-book prologue, faintly spoke
After the prompter, for our entrance;
But let them measure us by what they will,
10 We'll measure them a measure, and be gone.

1–10 What, shall this . . . be gone: Romeo asks whether they should send a messenger announcing their arrival at the party. Benvolio says that they'll dance one dance (**measure them a measure**) and then leave.

Romeo. Give me a torch. I am not for this ambling;
Being but heavy, I will bear the light.

Mercutio. Nay, gentle Romeo, we must have you dance.

Romeo. Not I, believe me. You have dancing shoes
15 With nimble soles; I have a soul of lead
So stakes me to the ground I cannot move.

Mercutio. You are a lover. Borrow Cupid's wings
And soar with them above a common bound.

Romeo. I am too sore enpierced with his shaft
20 To soar with his light feathers, and so bound
I cannot bound a pitch above dull woe.
Under love's heavy burden do I sink.

Mercutio. And, to sink in it, should you burden love—
Too great oppression for a tender thing.

25 **Romeo.** Is love a tender thing? It is too rough,
Too rude, too boist'rous, and it pricks like thorn.

Mercutio. If love be rough with you, be rough with love.
Prick love for pricking, and you beat love down.
Give me a case to put my visage in.
30 A visor for a visor! What care I
What curious eye doth quote deformities?
Here are the beetle brows shall blush for me.

Benvolio. Come, knock and enter, and no sooner in
But every man betake him to his legs.

35 **Romeo.** A torch for me! Let wantons light of heart
Tickle the senseless rushes with their heels;
For I am proverbed with a grandsire phrase,
I'll be a candle-holder and look on;
The game was ne'er so fair, and I am done.

40 **Mercutio.** Tut, dun's the mouse, the constable's own word!
If thou art Dun, we'll draw thee from the mire
Of, save your reverence, love, wherein thou stickst
Up to the ears. Come, we burn daylight, ho!

Romeo. Nay, that's not so.

Mercutio.   I mean, sir, in delay
45 We waste our lights in vain, like lamps by day.
Take our good meaning, for our judgment sits
Five times in that ere once in our five wits.

Romeo. And we mean well in going to this masque;
But 'tis no wit to go.

12 heavy: sad. Romeo makes a joke based on the meanings of *heavy* and *light*.

14–32 Romeo continues to talk about his sadness, while Mercutio jokingly makes fun of him to try to cheer him up.

29–32 Give . . . for me: Give me a mask for an ugly face. I don't care if people notice my appearance. Here, look at my bushy eyebrows.

34 betake . . . legs: dance.

35–38 Let . . . look on: Let playful people tickle the grass (**rushes**) on the floor with their dancing. I'll follow the old saying (**grandsire phrase**) and just be a spectator.

40–43 Tut . . . daylight: Mercutio jokes, using various meanings of the word dun, which sounds like Romeo's last word, done. He concludes by saying they should not waste time (**burn daylight**).

53–95 Mercutio talks of Mab, queen of the fairies, a folktale character well-known to Shakespeare's audience. His language includes vivid descriptions, puns, and satires of people; and ultimately he gets caught up in his own wild imaginings.

55 agate stone: jewel for a ring.

57 atomies: tiny creatures.

59 spinners' legs: spiders' legs.

61 traces: harness.

Mercutio.   Why, may one ask?

50 **Romeo.** I dreamt a dream tonight.

Mercutio.   And so did I.

Romeo. Well, what was yours?

Mercutio.   That dreamers often lie.

Romeo. In bed asleep, while they do dream things true.

Mercutio. O, then I see Queen Mab hath been with you.
She is the fairies' midwife, and she comes
55 In shape no bigger than an agate stone
On the forefinger of an alderman,
Drawn with a team of little atomies
Athwart men's noses as they lie asleep;
Her wagon spokes made of long spinners' legs,
60 The cover, of the wings of grasshoppers;
Her traces, of the smallest spider's web;

Her collars, of the moonshine's wat'ry beams;
Her whip, of cricket's bone; the lash, of film;
Her wagoner, a small grey-coated gnat,
65 Not half so big as a round little worm
Pricked from the lazy finger of a maid;
Her chariot is an empty hazelnut,
Made by the joiner squirrel or old grub,
Time out o' mind the fairies' coachmakers.
70 And in this state she gallops night by night
Through lovers' brains, and then they dream of love;
O'er courtiers' knees, that dream on curtsies straight;
O'er lawyers' fingers, who straight dream on fees;
O'er ladies' lips, who straight on kisses dream,
75 Which oft the angry Mab with blisters plagues,
Because their breaths with sweetmeats tainted are.
Sometime she gallops o'er a courtier's nose,
And then dreams he of smelling out a suit,
And sometime comes she with a tithe-pig's tail
80 Tickling a parson's nose as 'a lies asleep,
Then dreams he of another benefice.
Sometime she driveth o'er a soldier's neck,
And then dreams he of cutting foreign throats,
Of breaches, ambuscadoes, Spanish blades,
85 Of healths five fathom deep; and then anon
Drums in his ear, at which he starts and wakes,
And being thus frighted, swears a prayer or two
And sleeps again. This is that very Mab
That plaits the manes of horses in the night
90 And bakes the elflocks in foul sluttish hairs,
Which once untangled much misfortune bodes.
This is the hag, when maids lie on their backs,
That presses them and learns them first to bear,
Making them women of good carriage.
95 This is she—

Romeo.   Peace, peace, Mercutio, peace!
Thou talkst of nothing.

Mercutio.   True, I talk of dreams;
Which are the children of an idle brain,
Begot of nothing but vain fantasy;
Which is as thin of substance as the air,
100 And more inconstant than the wind, who woos
Even now the frozen bosom of the North
And, being angered, puffs away from thence,
Turning his face to the dew-dropping South.

68 joiner: carpenter.

77–78 Sometimes she . . . suit: Sometimes Mab makes a member of the king's court dream of receiving special favors.

81 benefice: a well-paying position for a clergyman.

84 ambuscadoes: ambushes; **Spanish blades:** high-quality Spanish swords.

89 plaits: braids.

96–103 True . . . South: Mercutio is trying to keep Romeo from taking his dreams too seriously.

© Houghton Mifflin Harcourt Publishing Company

106–111 Romeo, still depressed, fears that some terrible event caused by the stars will begin at the party. Remember the phrase "star-crossed lovers" from the prologue.

Benvolio. This wind you talk of blows us from ourselves.
105 Supper is done, and we shall come too late.

Romeo. I fear, too early; for my mind misgives
Some consequence, yet hanging in the stars,
Shall bitterly begin his fearful date
With this night's revels and expire the term
110 Of a despised life, closed in my breast,
By some vile forfeit of untimely death.
But he that hath the steerage of my course
Direct my sail! On, lusty gentlemen!

Benvolio. Strike, drum.

[*Exeunt.*]

Scene 5 *A hall in Capulet's house; the scene of the party.*

[Servingmen *come forth with napkins.*]

First Servingman. Where's Potpan, that he helps not to take way? He shift a trencher! he scrape a trencher!

Second Servingman. When good manners shall lie all in one or two men's hands, and they unwashed too, 'tis a foul thing.

5 **First Servingman.** Away with the joint-stools, remove the court-cupboard, look to the plate. Good thou, save me a piece of marchpane and, as thou lovest me, let the porter let in Susan Grindstone and Nell. Anthony, and Potpan!

Second Servingman. Ay, boy, ready.

10 **First Servingman.** You are looked for and called for, asked for and sought for, in the great chamber.

Third Servingman. We cannot be here and there too. Cheerly, boys! Be brisk awhile, and the longer liver take all.

[*Exeunt.*]

[Maskers *appear with* Capulet, Lady Capulet, Juliet, *all the* Guests, *and* Servants.]

Capulet. Welcome, gentlemen! Ladies that have their toes
15 Unplagued with corns will have a bout with you.
Ah ha, my mistresses! which of you all
Will now deny to dance? She that makes dainty,
She I'll swear hath corns. Am I come near ye now?
Welcome, gentlemen! I have seen the day
20 That I have worn a visor and could tell
A whispering tale in a fair lady's ear,
Such as would please. 'Tis gone, 'tis gone, 'tis gone!

1–13 These opening lines are a comic conversation among three servants as they work.

2 trencher: wooden plate.

6–7 plate: silverware and silver plates; **marchpane:** marzipan, a sweet made from almond paste.

14–27 Capulet welcomes his guests and invites them all to dance. He alternates talking with his guests and telling the servants what to do.

17–18 She that . . . corns: Any woman too shy to dance will be assumed to have corns, ugly and painful growths on the toes.

20 visor: mask.

© Houghton Mifflin Harcourt Publishing Company

You are welcome, gentlemen! Come, musicians, play.
A hall, a hall! give room! and foot it, girls.

[*Music plays and they dance.*]

25 More light, you knaves! and turn the tables up,
And quench the fire, the room is grown too hot.
Ah, sirrah, this unlooked-for sport comes well.
Nay, sit, nay, sit, good cousin Capulet,
For you and I are past our dancing days.
30 How long is't now since last yourself and I
Were in a mask?

Second Capulet. By'r Lady, thirty years.

Capulet. What, man? 'Tis not so much, 'tis not so much!
'Tis since the nuptial of Lucentio,
Come Pentecost as quickly as it will,
35 Some five-and-twenty years, and then we masked.

Second Capulet. 'Tis more, 'tis more! His son is elder, sir;
His son is thirty.

Capulet.   Will you tell me that?
His son was but a ward two years ago.

Romeo [*to a* Servingman]. What lady's that, which doth enrich
    the hand
40 Of yonder knight?

Servant. I know not, sir.

Romeo. O, she doth teach the torches to burn bright!
It seems she hangs upon the cheek of night
Like a rich jewel in an Ethiop's ear—
45 Beauty too rich for use, for earth too dear!
So shows a snowy dove trooping with crows
As yonder lady o'er her fellows shows.
The measure done, I'll watch her place of stand
And, touching hers, make blessed my rude hand.
50 Did my heart love till now? Forswear it, sight!
For I ne'er saw true beauty till this night.

Tybalt. This, by his voice, should be a Montague.
Fetch me my rapier, boy. What, dares the slave
Come hither, covered with an antic face
55 To fleer and scorn at our solemnity?
Now, by the stock and honor of my kin,
To strike him dead I hold it not a sin.

Capulet. Why, how now, kinsman? Wherefore storm you so?

Tybalt. Uncle, this is a Montague, our foe;

NOTICE & NOTE

28–38 Capulet and his relative watch the dancing as they talk of days gone by.

33 nuptial: marriage.

44–45 Ethiop's ear: the ear of an Ethiopian (African); for earth too dear: too precious for this world.

52–57 Tybalt recognizes Romeo's voice and tells his servant to get his sword (rapier). He thinks Romeo has come to make fun of (fleer) their party.

© Houghton Mifflin Harcourt Publishing Company

60 A villain, that is hither come in spite
   To scorn at our solemnity this night.

Capulet. Young Romeo is it?

Tybalt.   'Tis he, that villain Romeo.

Capulet. Content thee, gentle coz, let him alone.
   'A bears him like a portly gentleman,
65 And, to say truth, Verona brags of him
   To be a virtuous and well-governed youth.
   I would not for the wealth of all this town
   Here in my house do him disparagement.
   Therefore be patient, take no note of him.
70 It is my will; the which if thou respect,
   Show a fair presence and put off these frowns,
   An ill-beseeming semblance for a feast.

Tybalt. It fits when such a villain is a guest.
   I'll not endure him.

64 portly: dignified.

68 do him disparagement: speak critically or insultingly to him.

72 semblance: outward appearance.

© Houghton Mifflin Harcourt Publishing Company • Image Credits: (tc) ©AKaiser/Shutterstock; (c) Paramount Pictures/Courtesy The Everett Collection

Capulet.   He shall be endured.
75 What, goodman boy? I say he shall. Go to!
Am I the master here, or you? Go to!
You'll not endure him? God shall mend my soul!
You'll make a mutiny among my guests!
You will set cock-a-hoop! You'll be the man.

80 **Tybalt.** Why, uncle, 'tis a shame.

Capulet.   Go to, go to!
You are a saucy boy. Is't so, indeed?
This trick may chance to scathe you. I know what.
You must contrary me! Marry, 'tis time.—
Well said, my hearts!—You are a princox—go!
85 Be quiet, or—More light, more light!—For shame!
I'll make you quiet; what!—Cheerly, my hearts!

Tybalt. Patience perforce with willful choler meeting
Makes my flesh tremble in their different greeting.
I will withdraw; but this intrusion shall,
90 Now seeming sweet, convert to bitter gall.

[*Exit.*]

Romeo. If I profane with my unworthiest hand
This holy shrine, the gentle fine is this:
My lips, two blushing pilgrims, ready stand
To smooth that rough touch with a tender kiss.

95 **Juliet.** Good pilgrim, you do wrong your hand too much,
Which mannerly devotion shows in this;
For saints have hands that pilgrims' hands do touch,
And palm to palm is holy palmers' kiss.

Romeo. Have not saints lips, and holy palmers too?

100 **Juliet.** Ay, pilgrim, lips that they must use in prayer.

Romeo. O, then, dear saint, let lips do what hands do!
They pray; grant thou, lest faith turn to despair.

Juliet. Saints do not move, though grant for prayers' sake.

Romeo. Then move not while my prayer's effect I take.
105 Thus from my lips, by thine my sin is purged.

[*kisses her*]

Juliet. Then have my lips the sin that they have took.

Romeo. Sin from my lips? O trespass sweetly urged!
Give me my sin again.

[*kisses her*]

---

75 goodman boy: a term used to address an inferior; **Go to:** Stop, that's enough!

79 set cock-a-hoop: cause everything to be upset.

82–83 scathe: harm; **I know … contrary me:** I know what I'm doing! Don't you dare challenge my authority.

84–86 Capulet intersperses his angry speech to Tybalt with comments to his guests and servants.

87–90 Patience . . . gall: Tybalt says he will restrain himself, but his suppressed anger (**choler**) makes his body shake.

91–108 Romeo and Juliet are in the middle of the dance floor, with eyes only for each other. They touch the palms of their hands. Their conversation revolves around Romeo's comparison of his lips to pilgrims who have traveled to a holy shrine. Juliet goes along with the comparison.

105 purged: washed away.

© Houghton Mifflin Harcourt Publishing Company

108 kiss by the book: Juliet could mean "You kiss like someone who has practiced." Or she could be teasing Romeo, meaning "You kiss coldly, as though you had learned how by reading a book."

109 At the nurse's message, Juliet walks to her mother.

115 shall have the chinks: shall become rich.

116 my life . . . debt: my life belongs to my enemy.

120 towards: coming up.

ANALYZE LITERARY DEVICES

Annotate: Foreshadowing is the use of hints or clues to suggest events that will happen later in the story. Mark the line(s) where Juliet's words foreshadow what will come later in the play.

Analyze: What do these lines suggest about Juliet's fate?

137–138 Too early . . . too late: I fell in love with him before I learned who he is; **prodigious:** abnormal; unlucky.

Juliet.   You kiss by the book.

Nurse. Madam, your mother craves a word with you.

110 **Romeo.** What is her mother?

Nurse.   Marry, bachelor,
Her mother is the lady of the house.
And a good lady, and a wise and virtuous.
I nursed her daughter that you talked withal.
I tell you, he that can lay hold of her
115 Shall have the chinks.

Romeo.   Is she a Capulet?
O dear account! my life is my foe's debt.

Benvolio. Away, be gone, the sport is at the best.

Romeo. Ay, so I fear; the more is my unrest.

Capulet. Nay, gentlemen, prepare not to be gone;
120 We have a trifling foolish banquet towards.

[*They whisper in his ear.*]

Is it e'en so? Why then, I thank you all.
I thank you, honest gentlemen. Good night.
More torches here! [*Exeunt* Maskers.] Come on then, let's to bed.
Ah, sirrah, by my fay, it waxes late;
125 I'll to my rest.

[*Exeunt all but* Juliet *and* Nurse.]

Juliet. Come hither, nurse. What is yond gentleman?

Nurse. The son and heir of old Tiberio.

Juliet. What's he that now is going out of door?

Nurse. Marry, that, I think, be young Petruchio.

130 **Juliet.** What's he that follows there, that would not dance?

Nurse. I know not.

Juliet. Go ask his name.—If he be married,
My grave is like to be my wedding bed.

Nurse. His name is Romeo, and a Montague,
135 The only son of your great enemy.

Juliet. My only love, sprung from my only hate!
Too early seen unknown, and known too late!
Prodigious birth of love it is to me
That I must love a loathed enemy.

© Houghton Mifflin Harcourt Publishing Company

140 **Nurse.** What's this? what's this?

Juliet. A rhyme I learnt even now
Of one I danced withal.

[*One calls within, "Juliet."*]

Nurse. Anon, anon!
Come, let's away; the strangers all are gone.

[*Exeunt.*]

CHECK YOUR UNDERSTANDING

Answer these questions before moving on to the selection activities.

1 What role does Benvolio play in the fights that occur in Scene 1?

   A He starts the fights.

   B He runs away from the fights.

   C He tries to break up the fights.

   D He encourages others to fight.

2 Romeo's parents are concerned about him because —

   F they think his friend Mercutio is a bad influence on him

   G they're afraid he'll be arrested for fighting in the streets

   H they don't want him to be on friendly terms with the Capulets

   J they know something is bothering him but don't know what it is

3 Where do Romeo and Juliet first meet?

   A In a tavern

   B In a public square

   C At a costume party

   D At the Montagues' house

ANALYZE THE TEXT

Support your responses with evidence from the text. ⊟ NOTEBOOK

1. **Interpret** An important **theme**, or message, in *Romeo and Juliet* is the struggle against fate, or forces that determine how a person's life will turn out. Explain how Act I's Prologue establishes the fate of the main characters and introduces the struggles they will face. Why do you think Shakespeare tells the audience the fate of the main characters before the play begins?

2. **Predict** Review the foreshadowing in Scene 5, line 133, where Juliet says: "My grave is like to be my wedding bed." Paraphrase this line, then predict what event it foreshadows.

3. **Analyze** A **foil** is a character who highlights, through sharp contrast, the qualities of another character. Identify two sets of characters in Act I who are foils for each other. What do you learn about the characters by seeing them contrasted to one another?

4. **Identify** *Romeo and Juliet* is a play that deals with serious and tragic events, yet Shakespeare weaves in jokes and comical situations throughout Act I. One example is the conversation among the servants at the beginning of Scene 5. Identify other examples of **comic relief** in the first act.

5. **Notice & Note** In Act 1, Scene 5, there is an Aha Moment when Romeo realizes that Juliet is a Capulet (lines 116–117). How might this change the direction of the plot?

CREATE AND PRESENT

Speaking Activity: Discussion In *Romeo and Juliet*, characters are motivated by passion and strong emotions.

❑ Notice that throughout Act I, Shakespeare contrasts themes of love and hate through characters' words and actions.

❑ Work with a partner to identify passages that express love or hate. Often these emotions are expressed using the dramatic conventions of asides and soliloquies.

❑ Read the passages aloud with your partner. Read with feeling to express the emotions that underlie the words. Ask questions about any words or language you do not understand.

❑ Discuss what dramatic effect Shakespeare creates by pairing these two emotions in the first act of the play. Listen closely and respectfully to your partner's ideas.

❑ Write a summary that outlines the main points of your discussion.

Go to the **Speaking and Listening Studio** for more on participating in collaborative discussions.

SETTING A PURPOSE

Look for words and phrases that reveal the developing relationship between Romeo and Juliet and the intensity of their feelings for each other. Write down any questions you generate during reading.

Prologue

[*Enter* Chorus.]

Chorus. Now old desire doth in his deathbed lie,
And young affection gapes to be his heir.
That fair for which love groaned for and would die,
With tender Juliet matched, is now not fair.
5 Now Romeo is beloved, and loves again,
Alike bewitched by the charm of looks;
But to his foe supposed he must complain,
And she steal love's sweet bait from fearful hooks.
Being held a foe, he may not have access
10 To breathe such vows as lovers use to swear,
And she as much in love, her means much less
To meet her new beloved anywhere;
But passion lends them power, time means, to meet,
Temp'ring extremities with extreme sweet.

[*Exit.*]

1–4 Now . . . fair: Romeo's love for Rosaline (**old desire**) is now dead. His new love for Juliet (**young affection**) replaces the old.

7 but . . . complain: Juliet, a Capulet, is Romeo's supposed enemy, yet she is the one to whom he must plead (**complain**) his love.

14 Temp'ring . . . sweet: moderating great difficulties with extreme delights.

ACT II

Scene 1 *A lane by the wall of Capulet's orchard.*

[*Enter* Romeo *alone.*]

Romeo. Can I go forward when my heart is here?
Turn back, dull earth, and find thy center out.

[*climbs the wall and leaps down within it*]

[*Enter* Benvolio *with* Mercutio.]

Benvolio. Romeo! my cousin Romeo! Romeo!

Mercutio.   He is wise,
And, on my life, hath stol'n him home to bed.

5 **Benvolio.** He ran this way, and leapt this orchard wall.
Call, good Mercutio.

Mercutio.   Nay, I'll conjure too.

1–2 Can . . . out: How can I leave when Juliet is still here? My body (**dull earth**) has to find its heart (**center**).

6 conjure: use magic to call him.

8–21 Appear . . . us: Mercutio jokes about Romeo's lovesickness.

ANALYZE LITERARY DEVICES

Annotate: Character foils have contrasting traits. Read the exchange between Mercutio and Benvolio in lines 16–42 and mark Benvolio's responses.

Analyze: How does Benvolio act as a foil to Mercutio in this scene?

23–29 'Twould . . . raise up him: It would anger him if I called a stranger to join his beloved (**mistress**), but I'm only calling Romeo to join her.

31 To be . . . night: to keep company with the night, which is as gloomy as Romeo is.

34 medlar: a fruit that looks like a small brown apple.

39 truckle bed: trundle bed, a small bed that fits beneath a bigger one.

Romeo! humors! madman! passion! lover!
Appear thou in the likeness of a sigh;
Speak but one rhyme, and I am satisfied!
10 Cry but "Ay me!" pronounce but "love" and "dove";
Speak to my gossip Venus one fair word,
One nickname for her purblind son and heir,
Young Adam Cupid, he that shot so trim
When King Cophetua loved the beggar maid!
15 He heareth not, he stirreth not, he moveth not;
The ape is dead, and I must conjure him.
I conjure thee by Rosaline's bright eyes,
By her high forehead and her scarlet lip,
By her fine foot, straight leg, and quivering thigh,
20 And the demesnes that there adjacent lie,
That in thy likeness thou appear to us!

Benvolio. An if he hear thee, thou wilt anger him.

Mercutio. This cannot anger him. 'Twould anger him
To raise a spirit in his mistress' circle
25 Of some strange nature, letting it there stand
Till she had laid it and conjured it down.
That were some spite; my invocation
Is fair and honest and in his mistress' name
I conjure only but to raise up him.

30 **Benvolio.** Come, he hath hid himself among these trees
To be consorted with the humorous night.
Blind is his love, and best befits the dark.

Mercutio. If love be blind, love cannot hit the mark.
Now will he sit under a medlar tree
35 And wish his mistress were that kind of fruit
As maids call medlars when they laugh alone.
Oh, Romeo, that she were, O, that she were
An open et cetera, thou a pop'rin pear!
Romeo, good night. I'll to my truckle bed;
40 This field-bed is too cold for me to sleep.
Come, shall we go?

Benvolio.   Go then, for 'tis in vain
To seek him here that means not to be found.

[*Exeunt.*]

© Houghton Mifflin Harcourt Publishing Company

Scene 2 *Capulet's orchard.*

[*Enter* Romeo.]

Romeo. He jests at scars that never felt a wound.

[*Enter* Juliet *above at a window.*]

But soft! What light through yonder window breaks?
It is the East, and Juliet is the sun!
Arise, fair sun, and kill the envious moon,
5 Who is already sick and pale with grief
That thou her maid art far more fair than she.
Be not her maid, since she is envious;
Her vestal livery is but sick and green,
And none but fools do wear it; cast it off.
10 It is my lady; O, it is my love!
O that she knew she were!
She speaks, yet she says nothing. What of that?
Her eye discourses; I will answer it.
I am too bold; 'tis not to me she speaks.
15 Two of the fairest stars in all the heaven,
Having some business, do entreat her eyes
To twinkle in their spheres till they return.
What if her eyes were there, they in her head?
The brightness of her cheek would shame those stars
20 As daylight doth a lamp; her eyes in heaven
Would through the airy region stream so bright
That birds would sing and think it were not night.
See how she leans her cheek upon her hand!
O that I were a glove upon that hand,
25 That I might touch that cheek!

Juliet.   Ay me!

Romeo.   She speaks.
O, speak again, bright angel! for thou art
As glorious to this night, being o'er my head,
As is a winged messenger of heaven
Unto the white-upturned wond'ring eyes
30 Of mortals that fall back to gaze on him
When he bestrides the lazy-pacing clouds
And sails upon the bosom of the air.

Juliet. O Romeo, Romeo! wherefore art thou Romeo?
Deny thy father and refuse thy name!
35 Or, if thou wilt not, be but sworn my love,
And I'll no longer be a Capulet.

1 He jests . . . wound: Romeo has overheard Mercutio and comments that Mercutio makes fun of love because he has never been wounded by it.

13–14 Her eye . . . speaks: Romeo shifts back and forth between wanting to speak to Juliet and being afraid.
15–22 Two of . . . not night: Romeo compares Juliet's eyes to stars in the sky.

25 Juliet begins to speak, not knowing that Romeo is nearby.

26–32 thou art . . . of the air: He compares Juliet to an angel (**winged messenger of heaven**) who stands on (**bestrides**) the clouds.

33 wherefore: why. Juliet asks why Romeo is who he is—someone from her enemy's family.

Romeo [*aside*]. Shall I hear more, or shall I speak at this?

Juliet. 'Tis but thy name that is my enemy.
Thou art thyself, though not a Montague.
40 What's Montague? It is nor hand, nor foot,
Nor arm, nor face, nor any other part
Belonging to a man. O, be some other name!
What's in a name? That which we call a rose
By any other name would smell as sweet.
45 So Romeo would, were he not Romeo called,
Retain that dear perfection which he owes
Without that title. Romeo, doff thy name;
And for that name, which is no part of thee,
Take all myself.

Romeo.   I take thee at thy word.
50 Call me but love, and I'll be new baptized;
Henceforth I never will be Romeo.

Juliet. What man art thou that, thus bescreened in night,
So stumblest on my counsel?

Romeo.   By a name
I know not how to tell thee who I am.
55 My name, dear saint, is hateful to myself,
Because it is an enemy to thee.
Had I it written, I would tear the word.

Juliet. My ears have yet not drunk a hundred words
Of that tongue's utterance, yet I know the sound.
60 Art thou not Romeo, and a Montague?

Romeo. Neither, fair saint, if either thee dislike.

Juliet. How camest thou hither, tell me, and wherefore?
The orchard walls are high and hard to climb,
And the place death, considering who thou art,
65 If any of my kinsmen find thee here.

Romeo. With love's light wings did I o'erperch these walls;
For stony limits cannot hold love out,
And what love can do, that dares love attempt.
Therefore thy kinsmen are no let to me.

70 **Juliet.** If they do see thee, they will murder thee.

Romeo. Alack, there lies more peril in thine eye
Than twenty of their swords! Look thou but sweet,
And I am proof against their enmity.

43–47 Juliet tries to convince herself that a name is just a meaningless word that has nothing to do with the person. She asks Romeo to get rid of (**doff**) his name.

52–53 Juliet is startled that someone hiding (**bescreened**) nearby hears her private thoughts (**counsel**).

ANALYZE PARALLEL PLOTS
Annotate: Mark the words in lines 62–67 that refer to the feud between the Capulets and Montagues.

Analyze: How does the parallel plot of the feud affect the romance between Romeo and Juliet?

66–69 With . . . me: Love helped me climb (**o'erperch**) the walls. Neither walls nor your relatives are a hindrance (**let**) to me.

72–73 Look . . . enmity: Smile on me, and I will be defended against my enemies' hatred (**enmity**).

Juliet. I would not for the world they saw thee here.

75 **Romeo.** I have night's cloak to hide me from their sight;
And but thou love me, let them find me here.
My life were better ended by their hate
Than death prorogued, wanting of thy love.

Juliet. By whose direction foundst thou out this place?

80 **Romeo.** By love, that first did prompt me to enquire.
He lent me counsel, and I lent him eyes.
I am no pilot, yet, wert thou as far
As that vast shore washed with the farthest sea,
I would adventure for such merchandise.

78 than death . . . love: than my
death postponed (**prorogued**)
if you don't love me.

85 **Juliet.** Thou knowest the mask of night is on my face;
Else would a maiden blush bepaint my cheek
For that which thou hast heard me speak tonight.
Fain would I dwell on form—fain, fain deny
What I have spoke; but farewell compliment!
90 Dost thou love me? I know thou wilt say "Ay";
And I will take thy word. Yet, if thou swearst,
Thou mayst prove false. At lovers' perjuries,
They say Jove laughs. O gentle Romeo,
If thou dost love, pronounce it faithfully.
95 Or if thou thinkst I am too quickly won,
I'll frown, and be perverse, and say thee nay,
So thou wilt woo; but else, not for the world.
In truth, fair Montague, I am too fond,
And therefore thou mayst think my 'havior light;
100 But trust me, gentleman, I'll prove more true
Than those that have more cunning to be strange.
I should have been more strange, I must confess,
But that thou overheardst, ere I was ware,
My true love's passion. Therefore pardon me,
105 And not impute this yielding to light love,
Which the dark night hath so discovered.

Romeo. Lady, by yonder blessed moon I swear,
That tips with silver all these fruit-tree tops—

Juliet. O, swear not by the moon, the inconstant moon,
110 That monthly changes in her circled orb,
Lest that thy love prove likewise variable.

Romeo. What shall I swear by?

Juliet.   Do not swear at all;
Or if thou wilt, swear by thy gracious self,
Which is the god of my idolatry,
115 And I'll believe thee.

Romeo.   If my heart's dear love—

Juliet. Well, do not swear. Although I joy in thee,
I have no joy of this contract tonight.
It is too rash, too unadvised, too sudden;
Too like the lightning, which doth cease to be
120 Ere one can say "It lightens." Sweet, good night!
This bud of love, by summer's ripening breath,
May prove a beauteous flow'r when next we meet.

Good night, good night! As sweet repose and rest
Come to thy heart as that within my breast!

125 **Romeo.** O, wilt thou leave me so unsatisfied?

Juliet. What satisfaction canst thou have tonight?

Romeo. The exchange of thy love's faithful vow for mine.

Juliet. I gave thee mine before thou didst request it;
And yet I would it were to give again.

130 **Romeo.** Wouldst thou withdraw it? For what purpose, love?

Juliet. But to be frank and give it thee again.
And yet I wish but for the thing I have.
My bounty is as boundless as the sea,
My love as deep; the more I give to thee,
135 The more I have, for both are infinite.
I hear some noise within. Dear love, adieu!

[Nurse *calls within*.]

Anon, good nurse! Sweet Montague, be true.
Stay but a little, I will come again.

[*Exit*.]

Romeo. O blessed, blessed night! I am afeard,
140 Being in night, all this is but a dream,
Too flattering-sweet to be substantial.

[*Re-enter* Juliet, *above*.]

Juliet. Three words, dear Romeo, and good night indeed.
If that thy bent of love be honorable,
Thy purpose marriage, send me word tomorrow,
145 By one that I'll procure to come to thee,
Where and what time thou wilt perform the rite;
And all my fortunes at thy foot I'll lay
And follow thee my lord throughout the world.

Nurse [*within*]. Madam!

150 **Juliet.** I come, anon.—But if thou meanst not well,
I do beseech thee—

Nurse [*within*].   Madam!

Juliet.   By-and-by I come.—
To cease thy suit and leave me to my grief.
Tomorrow will I send.

Romeo.   So thrive my soul—

Juliet. A thousand times good night! [*Exit*.]

ANALYZE LITERARY DEVICES

Annotate: Mark the lines that contain foreshadowing.

Analyze: How do these lines foreshadow what may come later?

150–151 But if . . . thee: Juliet is still worried that Romeo is not serious.

155 **Romeo.** A thousand times the worse, to want thy light!
Love goes toward love as schoolboys from their books;
But love from love, towards school with heavy looks.

[*Enter* Juliet *again, above.*]

Juliet. Hist! Romeo, hist! O for a falc'ner's voice
To lure this tassel-gentle back again!
160 Bondage is hoarse and may not speak aloud;
Else would I tear the cave where Echo lies,
And make her airy tongue more hoarse than mine
With repetition of my Romeo's name.
Romeo!

165 **Romeo.** It is my soul that calls upon my name.
How silver-sweet sound lovers' tongues by night,
Like softest music to attending ears!

Juliet. Romeo!

Romeo.   My sweet?

Juliet.   What o'clock tomorrow
Shall I send to thee?

Romeo.   By the hour of nine.

170 **Juliet.** I will not fail. 'Tis twenty years till then.
I have forgot why I did call thee back.

Romeo. Let me stand here till thou remember it.

Juliet. I shall forget, to have thee still stand there,
Rememb'ring how I love thy company.

175 **Romeo.** And I'll still stay, to have thee still forget,
Forgetting any other home but this.

Juliet. 'Tis almost morning. I would have thee gone—
And yet no farther than a wanton's bird,
That lets it hop a little from her hand,
180 Like a poor prisoner in his twisted gyves,
And with a silk thread plucks it back again,
So loving-jealous of his liberty.

Romeo. I would I were thy bird.

Juliet.   Sweet, so would I.
Yet I should kill thee with much cherishing.
185 Good night, good night! Parting is such sweet sorrow,
That I shall say good night till it be morrow.

[*Exit.*]

Romeo. Sleep dwell upon thine eyes, peace in thy breast!
Would I were sleep and peace, so sweet to rest!
Hence will I to my ghostly father's cell,

190 His help to crave and my dear hap to tell.

[*Exit.*]

Scene 3 *Friar Laurence's cell in the monastery.*

[*Enter* Friar Laurence *alone, with a basket.*]

Friar Laurence. The grey-eyed morn smiles on the frowning
    night,
Chequ'ring the Eastern clouds with streaks of light;
And flecked darkness like a drunkard reels
From forth day's path and Titan's fiery wheels.
5 Now, ere the sun advance his burning eye
The day to cheer and night's dank dew to dry,
I must upfill this osier cage of ours
With baleful weeds and precious-juiced flowers.
The earth that's nature's mother is her tomb,
10 What is her burying grave, that is her womb;
And from her womb children of divers kind
We sucking on her natural bosom find;
Many for many virtues excellent,
None but for some, and yet all different.
15 O, mickle is the powerful grace that lies
In plants, herbs, stones, and their true qualities;
For naught so vile that on the earth doth live
But to the earth some special good doth give;
Nor aught so good but, strained from that fair use,
20 Revolts from true birth, stumbling on abuse.
Virtue itself turns vice, being misapplied,
And vice sometimes by action dignified.
Within the infant rind of this small flower
Poison hath residence, and medicine power;
25 For this, being smelt, with that part cheers each part;
Being tasted, slays all senses with the heart.
Two such opposed kings encamp them still
In man as well as herbs—grace and rude will;
And where the worser is predominant,
30 Full soon the canker death eats up that plant.

[*Enter* Romeo.]

Romeo. Good morrow, father.

Friar Laurence.   Benedicite!
What early tongue so sweet saluteth me?
Young son, it argues a distempered head
So soon to bid good morrow to thy bed.
35 Care keeps his watch in every old man's eye,
And where care lodges sleep will never lie;

190 dear hap: good fortune.

4 Titan is the god whose chariot pulls the sun into the sky each morning.

7 osier cage: willow basket.

9–12 The earth . . . find: The same earth that acts as a tomb is also the womb, or birthplace, of various useful plants that people can harvest.

15–18 mickle: great. The friar says that nothing from the earth is so evil that it doesn't do some good.

28 grace and rude will: good and evil. Both exist in people as well as in plants.

31 Benedicite (bĕ-nĕ-dī´sĭ-tē´): God bless you.

33–42 it argues . . . tonight: Only a disturbed (**distempered**) mind could make you get up so early. Old people may have trouble sleeping, but it is not normal for someone as young as you. Or were you up all night?

© Houghton Mifflin Harcourt Publishing Company • Image Credits: (c) ©Mary Evans/BHE Productions/Ronald Grant/Everett Collection, Inc.; (d) ©vectorkat/Shutterstock

But where unbruised youth with unstuffed brain
Doth couch his limbs, there golden sleep doth reign.
Therefore thy earliness doth me assure
40 Thou art uproused with some distemp'rature;
Or if not so, then here I hit it right—
Our Romeo hath not been in bed tonight.

Romeo. That last is true, the sweeter rest was mine.

Friar Laurence. God pardon sin! Wast thou with Rosaline?

45 **Romeo.** With Rosaline, my ghostly father? No.
    I have forgot that name, and that name's woe.

Friar Laurence. That's my good son! But where hast thou been
    then?

Romeo. I'll tell thee ere thou ask it me again.
    I have been feasting with mine enemy,
50 Where on a sudden one hath wounded me
    That's by me wounded. Both our remedies
    Within thy help and holy physic lies.
    I bear no hatred, blessed man, for, lo,
    My intercession likewise steads my foe.

55 **Friar Laurence.** Be plain, good son, and homely in thy drift.
    Riddling confession finds but riddling shrift.

Romeo. Then plainly know my heart's dear love is set
    On the fair daughter of rich Capulet;
    As mine on hers, so hers is set on mine,
60 And all combined, save what thou must combine
    By holy marriage. When, and where, and how
    We met, we wooed, and made exchange of vow,
    I'll tell thee as we pass; but this I pray,
    That thou consent to marry us today.

65 **Friar Laurence.** Holy Saint Francis! What a change is here!
    Is Rosaline, that thou didst love so dear,
    So soon forsaken? Young men's love then lies
    Not truly in their hearts, but in their eyes.
    Jesu Maria! What a deal of brine
70 Hath washed thy sallow cheeks for Rosaline!
    How much salt water thrown away in waste,
    To season love, that of it doth not taste!
    The sun not yet thy sighs from heaven clears,
    Thy old groans ring yet in mine ancient ears.
75 Lo, here upon thy cheek the stain doth sit
    Of an old tear that is not washed off yet.
    If e'er thou wast thyself, and these woes thine,
    Thou and these woes were all for Rosaline.
    And art thou changed? Pronounce this sentence then:
80 Women may fall when there's no strength in men.

Romeo. Thou chidst me oft for loving Rosaline.

Friar Laurence. For doting, not for loving, pupil mine.

Romeo. And badest me bury love.

Friar Laurence.   Not in a grave
    To lay one in, another ought to have.

49–56 Romeo tries to explain the situation, asking for help both for himself and his "foe" (Juliet). The friar does not understand Romeo's convoluted language and asks him to speak clearly so that he can help.

69 brine: salt water— that is, the tears that Romeo has been shedding for Rosaline.

80 Women . . . men: If men are so weak, women may be forgiven for sinning.

81–82 chidst: scolded. The friar replies that he scolded Romeo for being lovesick, not for loving.

85–88 She whom . . . spell: Romeo says that the woman he loves feels the same way about him. That wasn't true of Rosaline. The friar replies that Rosaline knew that he didn't know what real love is.

91–92 For this . . . prove: this marriage may work out so well; **rancor:** bitter hate.

WORDS OF THE WISER

Notice & Note: Mark Friar Laurence's advice to Romeo in the last line of Scene 3.

Respond: What is Friar Laurence trying to make Romeo understand?

3 man: servant.

6–12 Tybalt . . . dared: Tybalt, still angry with Romeo, has sent a letter challenging Romeo to a duel. Benvolio says that Romeo will accept Tybalt's challenge and fight him.

15 blind bow-boy's butt-shaft: Cupid's dull practice arrow. Mercutio suggests that Romeo fell in love with very little work on Cupid's part.

18–24 More than . . . hay: Prince of Cats refers to a cat in a fable, named Tybalt. Mercutio makes fun of Tybalt's new style of dueling, comparing it to singing (**pricksong**). *Passado, punto reverso*, and *hay* were terms used in the new dueling style.

---

85 **Romeo.** I pray thee chide not. She whom I love now
Doth grace for grace and love for love allow.
The other did not so.

Friar Laurence.   O, she knew well
Thy love did read by rote, that could not spell.
But come, young waverer, come go with me.
90 In one respect I'll thy assistant be;
For this alliance may so happy prove
To turn your households' rancor to pure love.

Romeo. O, let us hence! I stand on sudden haste.

Friar Laurence. Wisely, and slow. They stumble that run fast.

[*Exeunt.*]

Scene 4 *A street.*

[*Enter* Benvolio *and* Mercutio.]

Mercutio. Where the devil should this Romeo be?
Came he not home tonight?

Benvolio. Not to his father's. I spoke with his man.

Mercutio. Why, that same pale hard-hearted wench, that
Rosaline,
5 Torments him so that he will sure run mad.

Benvolio. Tybalt, the kinsman to old Capulet,
Hath sent a letter to his father's house.

Mercutio. A challenge, on my life.

Benvolio. Romeo will answer it.

10 **Mercutio.** Any man that can write may answer a letter.

Benvolio. Nay, he will answer the letter's master, how he dares,
being dared.

Mercutio. Alas, poor Romeo, he is already dead! stabbed with a
white wench's black eye; shot through the ear with a love song;
15 the very pin of his heart cleft with the blind bow-boy's butt-shaft;
and is he a man to encounter Tybalt?

Benvolio. Why, what is Tybalt?

Mercutio. More than Prince of Cats, I can tell you. O, he's the
courageous captain of compliments. He fights as you sing
20 pricksong—keeps time, distance, and proportion; rests me his
minim rest, one, two, and the third in your bosom! the very
butcher of a silk button, a duelist, a duelist! a gentleman of the
very first house, of the first and second cause. Ah, the immortal
passado! the *punto reverso!* the *hay!*

25 **Benvolio.** The what?

Mercutio. The pox of such antic, lisping, affecting fantasticoes—these new tuners of accent! "By Jesu, a very good blade! a very tall man! a very good whore!" Why, is not this a lamentable thing, grandsire, that we should be thus afflicted with these strange flies,
30 these fashion-mongers, these perdona-mi's, who stand so much on the new form that they cannot sit at ease on the old bench? O, their bones, their bones!

[*Enter* Romeo, *no longer moody.*]

Benvolio. Here comes Romeo! here comes Romeo!

Mercutio. Without his roe, like a dried herring. O, flesh, flesh,
35 how art thou fishified! Now is he for the numbers that Petrarch flowed in. Laura, to his lady, was but a kitchen wench (marry, she had a better love to berhyme her), Dido a dowdy, Cleopatra a gypsy, Helen and Hero hildings and harlots, Thisbe a grey eye or so, but not to the purpose. Signior Romeo, bon jour! There's
40 a French salutation to your French slop. You gave us the counterfeit fairly last night.

Romeo. Good morrow to you both. What counterfeit did I give you?

Mercutio. The slip, sir, the slip. Can you not conceive?

45 **Romeo.** Pardon, good Mercutio. My business was great, and in such a case as mine a man may strain courtesy.

Mercutio. That's as much as to say, such a case as yours constrains a man to bow in the hams.

Romeo. Meaning, to curtsy.

50 **Mercutio.** Thou hast most kindly hit it.

Romeo. A most courteous exposition.

Mercutio. Nay, I am the very pink of courtesy.

Romeo. Pink for flower.

Mercutio. Right.

55 **Romeo.** Why, then is my pump well-flowered.

Mercutio. Well said! Follow me this jest now till thou hast worn out thy pump, that, when the single sole of it is worn, the jest may remain, after the wearing, solely singular.

Romeo. Oh, single-soled jest, solely singular for the singleness!

60 **Mercutio.** Come between us, good Benvolio! My wits faint.

Romeo. Switch and spurs, switch and spurs! or I'll cry a match.

Mercutio. Nay, if our wits run the wild-goose chase, I am done; for thou hast more of the wild goose in one of thy wits than, I

26–32 The pox . . . their bones: Mercutio continues to make fun of people who embrace new styles and new manners of speaking.

ANALYZE LITERARY DEVICES

Annotate: Mercutio refers to Petrarch, a poet, and uses literary and classical allusions to make fun of Romeo's lovesickness. Mark the allusions in Mercutio's speech.

Analyze: What is Mercutio's point in using these comparisons to mock Romeo's love?

39–44 bon jour: "Good day" in French; **There's . . . last night:** Here's a greeting to match your fancy French trousers (**slop**). You did a good job of getting away from us last night. (A piece of counterfeit money was called a **slip**.)

55 pump: shoe; **well-flowered:** Shoes with flowerlike designs.

61 Switch . . . match: Keep going, or I'll claim victory.

64–65 Was . . . goose: Have I proved that you are a foolish person?

73 cheveril: kidskin, which is flexible. Mercutio means that a little wit stretches a long way.

LANGUAGE CONVENTIONS

Annotate: Underline the parallel construction in lines 77–80.

Analyze: What is the effect of this parallel construction?

80–81 great natural: an idiot, like a jester or clown who carries a fool's stick (**bauble**).

---

am sure, I have in my whole five. Was I with you there for the
65 goose?

Romeo. Thou wast never with me for anything when thou wast not there for the goose.

Mercutio. I will bite thee by the ear for that jest.

Romeo. Nay, good goose, bite not!

70 **Mercutio.** Thy wit is a very bitter sweeting; it is a most sharp sauce.

Romeo. And is it not, then, well served in to a sweet goose?

Mercutio. O, here's a wit of cheveril, that stretches from an inch narrow to an ell broad!

75 **Romeo.** I stretch it out for that word "broad," which, added to the goose, proves thee far and wide a broad goose.

Mercutio. Why, is not this better now than groaning for love? Now art thou sociable, now art thou Romeo; now art thou what thou art, by art as well as by nature. For this driveling love is like
80 a great natural that runs lolling up and down to hide his bauble in a hole.

Benvolio. Stop there, stop there!

Mercutio. Thou desirest me to stop in my tale against the hair.

Benvolio. Thou wouldst else have made thy tale large.

Mercutio. O, thou art deceived! I would have made it short; for I
was come to the whole depth of my tale, and meant indeed to
occupy the argument no longer.

[*Enter* Nurse *and* Peter, *her servant. He is carrying a large fan.*]

Romeo. Here's goodly gear!

Mercutio. A sail, a sail!

90 **Benvolio.** Two, two! a shirt and a smock.

Nurse. Peter!

Peter. Anon.

Nurse. My fan, Peter.

Mercutio. Good Peter, to hide her face; for her fan's the fairer of
95 the two.

Nurse. God ye good morrow, gentlemen.

Mercutio. God ye good-den, fair gentlewoman.

Nurse. Is it good-den?

Mercutio. 'Tis no less, I tell ye, for the bawdy hand of the dial is
100 now upon the prick of noon.

Nurse. Out upon you! What a man are you!

Romeo. One, gentlewoman, that God hath made himself to mar.

Nurse. By my troth, it is well said. "For himself to mar," quoth'a?
Gentlemen, can any of you tell me where I may find the young
105 Romeo?

Romeo. I can tell you; but young Romeo will be older when you
have found him than he was when you sought him. I am the
youngest of that name, for fault of a worse.

Nurse. You say well.

110 **Mercutio.** Yea, is the worst well? Very well took, i' faith! wisely,
wisely.

Nurse. If you be he, sir, I desire some confidence with you.

Benvolio. She will endite him to some supper.

Mercutio. A bawd, a bawd, a bawd! So ho!

115 **Romeo.** What hast thou found?

Mercutio. No hare, sir; unless a hare, sir, in a lenten pie, that is
something stale and hoar ere it be spent.

[*sings*]

> "An old hare hoar,
> And an old hare hoar,

NOTICE & NOTE

88–89 goodly gear: something fine to joke about; **a sail:** Mercutio likens the nurse in all her petticoats to a huge ship coming toward them.

93 Fans were usually carried only by fine ladies. The nurse is trying to pretend that she is more than a servant.

112–113 confidence: The nurse means *conference*; she uses big words without understanding their meaning; **endite:** Benvolio makes fun of the nurse by using this word rather than *invite*.

114–124 Mercutio calls the nurse a **bawd,** or woman who runs a house of prostitution. His song uses the insulting puns **hare,** a rabbit or prostitute, and **hoar,** old.

© Houghton Mifflin Harcourt Publishing Company

120 Is very good meat in Lent.
But a hare that is hoar,
Is too much for a score
When it hoars ere it be spent."

Romeo, will you come to your father's? We'll to dinner thither.

125 **Romeo.** I will follow you.

Mercutio. Farewell, ancient lady. Farewell, [*sings*] lady, lady, lady.

[*Exeunt* Mercutio *and* Benvolio.]

Nurse. Marry, farewell! I pray you, sir, what saucy merchant was this that was so full of his ropery?

Romeo. A gentleman, nurse, that loves to hear himself talk and
130 will speak more in a minute than he will stand to in a month.

Nurse. An 'a speak anything against me, I'll take him down, an 'a
were lustier than he is, and twenty such Jacks; and if I cannot,
I'll find those that shall. Scurvy knave! I am none of his flirt-gills;
I am none of his skainsmates. [*turning to* Peter] And thou must
135 stand by too, and suffer every knave to use me at his pleasure?

Peter. I saw no man use you at his pleasure. If I had, my weapon
should quickly have been out, I warrant you. I dare draw as soon
as another man, if I see occasion in a good quarrel, and the law
on my side.

140 **Nurse.** Now, afore God, I am so vexed that every part about me
quivers. Scurvy knave! Pray you, sir, a word; and as I told you,
my young lady bade me enquire you out. What she bid me say,
I will keep to myself; but first let me tell ye, if ye should lead her
into a fool's paradise, as they say, it were a very gross kind of
145 behavior, as they say; for the gentlewoman is young; and
therefore, if you should deal double with her, truly it were an ill
thing to be offered to any gentlewoman, and very weak dealing.

Romeo. Nurse, commend me to thy lady and mistress. I protest
unto thee—

150 **Nurse.** Good heart, and i' faith I will tell her as much. Lord,
Lord! she will be a joyful woman.

Romeo. What wilt thou tell her, nurse? Thou dost not mark me.

Nurse. I will tell her, sir, that you do protest, which, as I take it,
is a gentlemanlike offer.

155 **Romeo.** Bid her devise
Some means to come to shrift this afternoon;
And there she shall at Friar Laurence' cell
Be shrived and married. Here is for thy pains.

Nurse. No, truly, sir; not a penny.

160 **Romeo.** Go to! I say you shall.

Nurse. This afternoon, sir? Well, she shall be there.

Romeo. And stay, good nurse, behind the abbey wall.
Within this hour my man shall be with thee
And bring thee cords made like a tackled stair,
165 Which to the high topgallant of my joy
Must be my convoy in the secret night.
Farewell. Be trusty, and I'll quit thy pains.
Farewell. Commend me to thy mistress.

Nurse. Now God in heaven bless thee! Hark you, sir.

170 **Romeo.** What sayst thou, my dear nurse?

Nurse. Is your man secret? Did you ne'er hear say,
Two may keep counsel, putting one away?

Romeo. I warrant thee my man's as true as steel.

Nurse. Well, sir, my mistress is the sweetest lady. Lord, Lord!
175 when 'twas a little prating thing—O, there is a nobleman in
town, one Paris, that would fain lay knife aboard; but she, good
soul, had as lief see a toad, a very toad, as see him. I anger her
sometimes, and tell her that Paris is the properer man; but I'll
warrant you, when I say so, she looks as pale as any clout in the
180 versal world. Doth not rosemary and Romeo begin both with a
letter?

Romeo. Ay, nurse, what of that? Both with an R.

Nurse. Ah, mocker! that's the dog's name. R is for the—No; I
know it begins with some other letter; and she hath the prettiest
185 sententious of it, of you and rosemary, that it would do you good
to hear it.

Romeo. Commend me to thy lady.

Nurse. Ay, a thousand times. [*Exit* Romeo.] Peter!

Peter. Anon.

190 **Nurse.** Peter, take my fan, and go before, and apace.

[*Exeunt.*]

Scene 5 *Capulet's orchard.*

[*Enter* Juliet.]

Juliet. The clock struck nine when I did send the nurse;
In half an hour she promised to return.
Perchance she cannot meet him. That's not so.
O, she is lame! Love's heralds should be thoughts,
5 Which ten times faster glide than the sun's beams

164–165 tackled stair: rope ladder; **topgallant:** highest point.

167 quit thy pains: reward you.

174–177 The nurse begins to babble about Paris' proposal but says that Juliet would rather look at a toad than at Paris.

179–186 clout: old cloth; **the versal world:** the entire world; **Doth not . . . hear it:** The nurse tries to recall a clever saying that Juliet made up about Romeo and rosemary, the herb, but cannot remember it. She is sure that the two words couldn't begin with *R* because this letter sounds like a snarling dog; **sententious:** The nurse means *sentences*.

190 apace: quickly.

4–6 Love's . . . hills: Love's messengers should be thoughts, which travel ten times faster than sunbeams.

© Houghton Mifflin Harcourt Publishing Company

© Houghton Mifflin Harcourt Publishing Company

7 nimble-pinioned . . . Love: Swift-winged doves pull the chariot of Venus, goddess of love.

Driving back shadows over lowering hills.
Therefore do nimble-pinioned doves draw Love,
And therefore hath the wind-swift Cupid wings.
Now is the sun upon the highmost hill
10 Of this day's journey, and from nine till twelve
Is three long hours; yet she is not come.
Had she affections and warm youthful blood,
She would be as swift in motion as a ball;
My words would bandy her to my sweet love,

14 bandy: toss.

15 And his to me.
But old folks, many feign as they were dead—
Unwieldy, slow, heavy, and pale as lead.
[*Enter* Nurse *and* Peter.] O God, she comes! O honey nurse,
    what news?
Hast thou met with him? Send thy man away.

16 feign as: act as if.

20 **Nurse.** Peter, stay at the gate.

[*Exit* Peter.]

21–22 The nurse teases Juliet by putting on a sad face as if the news were bad.

Juliet. Now, good sweet nurse—O Lord, why lookst thou sad?
Though news be sad, yet tell them merrily;
If good, thou shamest the music of sweet news
By playing it to me with so sour a face.

25–26 give me . . . I had: Leave me alone for a while. I ache all over because of the running back and forth I've been doing.

25 **Nurse.** I am aweary, give me leave awhile.
Fie, how my bones ache! What a jaunce have I had!

Juliet. I would thou hadst my bones, and I thy news.
Nay, come, I pray thee speak. Good, good nurse, speak.

Nurse. Jesu, what haste! Can you not stay awhile?
30 Do you not see that I am out of breath?

Juliet. How art thou out of breath when thou hast breath
To say to me that thou art out of breath?
The excuse that thou dost make in this delay
Is longer than the tale thou dost excuse.
35 Is thy news good or bad? Answer to that.
Say either, and I'll stay the circumstance.
Let me be satisfied, is't good or bad?

36 I'll . . . circumstance: I'll wait for the details.

38 simple: foolish.

Nurse. Well, you have made a simple choice; you know not how
to choose a man. Romeo? No, not he. Though his face be better
40 than any man's, yet his leg excels all men's; and for a hand and a
foot, and a body, though they be not to be talked on, yet they are
past compare. He is not the flower of courtesy, but, I'll warrant
him, as gentle as a lamb. Go thy ways, wench; serve God. What,
have you dined at home?

45 **Juliet.** No, no. But all this did I know before.
What say he of our marriage? What of that?

Nurse. Lord, how my head aches! What a head have I!
It beats as it would fall in twenty pieces.
My back o' t'other side—ah, my back, my back!
50 Beshrew your heart for sending me about
To catch my death with jauncing up and down!

Juliet. I' faith, I am sorry that thou art not well.
Sweet, sweet, sweet nurse, tell me, what says my love?

Nurse. Your love says, like an honest gentleman, and a courteous,
55 and a kind, and a handsome, and, I warrant, a virtuous—Where
is your mother?

Juliet. Where is my mother? Why, she is within.
Where should she be? How oddly thou repliest!
"Your love says, like an honest gentleman,
'Where is your mother?'"

Nurse.   O God's Lady dear!
60 Are you so hot? Marry come up, I trow.
Is this the poultice for my aching bones?
Hence forward do your messages yourself.

Juliet. Here's such a coil! Come, what says Romeo?

Nurse. Have you got leave to go to shrift today?

65 **Juliet.** I have.

Nurse. Then hie you hence to Friar Laurence' cell;
There stays a husband to make you a wife.
Now comes the wanton blood up in your cheeks:
They'll be in scarlet straight at any news.
70 Hie you to church; I must another way,
To fetch a ladder, by the which your love
Must climb a bird's nest soon when it is dark.
I am the drudge, and toil in your delight;
But you shall bear the burden soon at night.
75 Go; I'll to dinner; hie you to the cell.

Juliet. Hie to high fortune! Honest nurse, farewell.

[*Exeunt.*]

Scene 6 *Friar Laurence's cell.*

[*Enter* Friar Laurence *and* Romeo.]

Friar Laurence. So smile the heavens upon this holy act
That after-hours with sorrow chide us not!

Romeo. Amen, amen! But come what sorrow can,
It cannot countervail the exchange of joy

50–51 Beshrew . . . down:
Curse you for making me endanger my health by running around.

60–61 Marry . . . bones:
Control yourself! Is this the treatment I get for my pain?

63 coil: fuss.

70–72 The nurse will get the ladder that Romeo will use to climb to Juliet's room after they are married.

1–2 So smile . . . us not: May heaven so bless this act that we won't regret it in the future (**after-hours**).

4 countervail: outweigh.

© Houghton Mifflin Harcourt Publishing Company • Image Credits: (t) ©Paramount/Photofest; (bg) ©vectorkat/Shutterstock

9–15 These . . . slow: The friar compares Romeo's passion to gunpowder and the fire that ignites it—both are destroyed—then to honey, whose sweetness can destroy the appetite. He reminds Romeo to practice moderation in love.

5 That one short minute gives me in her sight.
   Do thou but close our hands with holy words,
   Then love-devouring death do what he dare—
   It is enough I may but call her mine.

Friar Laurence. These violent delights have violent ends
10 And in their triumph die, like fire and powder,
   Which, as they kiss, consume. The sweetest honey
   Is loathsome in his own deliciousness
   And in the taste confounds the appetite.
   Therefore love moderately: long love doth so;
15 Too swift arrives as tardy as too slow.

[*Enter* Juliet.]

   Here comes the lady. O, so light a foot
   Will ne'er wear out the everlasting flint.
   A lover may bestride the gossamer
   That idles in the wanton summer air,
20 And yet not fall; so light is vanity.

Juliet. Good even to my ghostly confessor.

Friar Laurence. Romeo shall thank thee, daughter, for us both.

Juliet. As much to him, else is his thanks too much.

23 As much to him: I give the same greeting to Romeo that he offers to me.

24–29 if the measure . . . encounter: If you are as happy as I am and have more skill to proclaim it, then sweeten the air by singing of our happiness to the world.

Romeo. Ah, Juliet, if the measure of thy joy
25 Be heaped like mine, and that thy skill be more

To blazon it, then sweeten with thy breath
This neighbor air, and let rich music's tongue
Unfold the imagined happiness that both
Receive in either by this dear encounter.

30 **Juliet.** Conceit, more rich in matter than in words,
Brags of his substance, not of ornament.
They are but beggars that can count their worth;
But my true love is grown to such excess
I cannot sum up sum of half my wealth.

35 **Friar Laurence.** Come, come with me, and we will make short work;
For, by your leaves, you shall not stay alone
Till Holy Church incorporate two in one.

[*Exeunt.*]

30–31 Conceit . . . ornament:
True understanding (**conceit**)
needs no words.

CHECK YOUR UNDERSTANDING

Answer these questions before moving on to the **Analyze the Text** questions
on the following page.

1 Why is Friar Laurence pleased that Romeo has fallen in love with Juliet?

   A He never liked Rosaline and is glad Romeo found someone new
   to love.

   B He thinks it means the feud between the Montagues and Capulets
   will end.

   C He's sure that Romeo has made a careful and thoughtful decision.

   D He hopes that by marrying Juliet, Romeo will finally grow up.

2 Which of the following is a central theme in Act 2?

   F Love can transcend society's boundaries.

   G Older people are always wiser than younger people.

   H Any serious situation can be lightened by a few jokes.

   J Venturing outside one's social group can be dangerous.

3 As the act ends, Romeo and Juliet —

   A change their minds about marriage

   B make up after a lovers' quarrel

   C discuss their fears about the future

   D are about to be married

ANALYZE THE TEXT

Support your responses with evidence from the text. ☰ NOTEBOOK

1. **Analyze** In Act II, Scene 2, Juliet says, "What's in a name? That which we call a rose / By any other name would smell as sweet" (lines 43–44). What does she mean? How does this comparison relate to one of the conflicts in her life?

2. **Cite Evidence** In Scene 3, why is Friar Laurence suspicious of Romeo's declaration of love for Juliet? What is his motivation for agreeing to marry Romeo and Juliet, despite his reservations?

3. **Draw Conclusions** Identify at least one soliloquy and one aside in Act II. Explain what each example reveals about the character who speaks it.

4. **Compare** Compare Romeo's behavior before he meets Juliet with his behavior after they declare their love for each other. What do you learn about Romeo's character from the change in his behavior?

5. **Notice & Note** In literature, a **motif** is a repeated image, idea, or theme. Explain the light/dark or day/night motif in Romeo's speech at the beginning of Act II, Scene 2. What does he mean when he refers to Juliet as "the sun"? Where else in Act II does this Again and Again motif appear?

CREATE AND PRESENT

Debate Both Friar Laurence and Mercutio have personal attributes that put them at odds with Romeo's passion. Analyze their differences and hold a debate in which each character presents his point of view.

- ❏ Working with two other students, discuss the characteristics of Friar Laurence, Mercutio, and Romeo. What differences do these three demonstrate in Act II?

- ❏ With each person in your group taking the point of view of one of these characters, debate Romeo's plan to marry Juliet.

- ❏ Work together to write a summary of your debate.

Go to the **Speaking and Listening Studio** for more on participating in collaborative discusssions.

SETTING A PURPOSE

Notice how events begin to shift in a more ominous or dangerous direction in this act. Write down any questions you generate during reading.

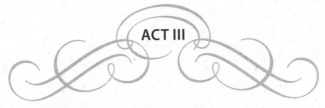

ACT III

Scene 1 *A public place.*

[*Enter* Mercutio, Benvolio, Page, *and* Servants.]

Benvolio. I pray thee, good Mercutio, let's retire.
The day is hot, the Capulets abroad,
And if we meet, we shall not scape a brawl,
For now, these hot days, is the mad blood stirring.

5 **Mercutio.** Thou art like one of those fellows that, when he enters
the confines of a tavern, claps me his sword upon the table and
says "God send me no need of thee!" and by the operation of the
second cup draws him on the drawer, when indeed there is no
need.

10 **Benvolio.** Am I like such a fellow?

Mercutio. Come, come, thou art as hot a Jack in thy mood as
any in Italy; and as soon moved to be moody, and as soon
moody to be moved.

Benvolio. And what to?

15 **Mercutio.** Nay an there were two such, we should have none
shortly, for one would kill the other. Thou! why, thou wilt
quarrel with a man that hath a hair more or a hair less in his
beard than thou hast. Thou wilt quarrel with a man for cracking
nuts, having no other reason but because thou hast hazel eyes.
20 What eye but such an eye would spy out such a quarrel? Thy
head is as full of quarrels as an egg is full of meat; and yet thy
head hath been beaten as addle as an egg for quarreling. Thou
hast quarreled with a man for coughing in the street, because he
hath wakened thy dog that hath lain asleep in the sun. Didst
25 thou not fall out with a tailor for wearing his new doublet before
Easter? with another for tying his new shoes with old riband?
And yet thou wilt tutor me from quarreling!

Benvolio. An I were so apt to quarrel as thou art, any man should
buy the fee simple of my life for an hour and a quarter.

30 **Mercutio.** The fee simple? O simple!

[*Enter* Tybalt *and others.*]

3–4 we shall . . . stirring: We shall not avoid a fight, since the heat makes people ill-tempered.

7–8 by the . . . drawer: feeling the effects of a second drink, is ready to fight (**draw on**) the waiter who's pouring the drinks (**drawer**).

12–13 as soon moved . . . to be moved: as likely to get angry and start a fight.

ANALYZE LITERARY DEVICES

Annotate: Mark one or more lines in which Mercutio teases his friend by insisting that Benvolio is quick to pick a fight.

Respond: How is Mercutio's teasing an example of irony?

25 doublet: jacket.
26 riband: ribbon or laces.

28–29 An I . . . quarter: If I picked fights as quickly as you do, anybody could own me for the smallest amount of money.

Benvolio. By my head, here come the Capulets.

Mercutio. By my heel, I care not.

Tybalt. Follow me close, for I will speak to them. Gentlemen, good den. A word with one of you.

35 **Mercutio.** And but one word with one of us? Couple it with something; make it a word and a blow.

Tybalt. You shall find me apt enough to that, sir, an you will give me occasion.

Mercutio. Could you not take some occasion without giving?

40 **Tybalt.** Mercutio, thou consortest with Romeo.

Mercutio. Consort? What, dost thou make us minstrels? An thou make minstrels of us, look to hear nothing but discords. Here's my fiddlestick; here's that shall make you dance. Zounds, consort!

45 **Benvolio.** We talk here in the public haunt of men.
Either withdraw unto some private place
And reason coldly of your grievances,
Or else depart. Here all eyes gaze on us.

Mercutio. Men's eyes were made to look, and let them gaze.
50 I will not budge for no man's pleasure, I.

40–44 consortest: are friends with; Mercutio pretends to misunderstand him, assuming that Tybalt is insulting him by calling Romeo and him a **consort**, a group of traveling musicians. He then refers to his sword as his **fiddlestick**, the bow for a fiddle.

[*Enter* Romeo.]

Tybalt. Well, peace be with you, sir. Here comes my man.

Mercutio. But I'll be hanged, sir, if he wear your livery.
Marry, go before to field, he'll be your follower!
Your worship in that sense may call him man.

55 **Tybalt.** Romeo, the love I bear thee can afford
No better term than this: thou art a villain.

Romeo. Tybalt, the reason that I have to love thee
Doth much excuse the appertaining rage
To such a greeting. Villain am I none.
60 Therefore farewell. I see thou knowst me not.

Tybalt. Boy, this shall not excuse the injuries
That thou hast done me; therefore turn and draw.

Romeo. I do protest I never injured thee,
But love thee better than thou canst devise
65 Till thou shalt know the reason of my love;
And so, good Capulet, which name I tender
As dearly as mine own, be satisfied.

Mercutio. O calm, dishonorable, vile submission!
Alla stoccata carries it away.

51–54 Mercutio again pretends to misunderstand Tybalt. By **my man**, Tybalt means "the man I'm looking for." Mercutio takes it to mean "my servant." (**Livery** is a servant's uniform.)

57–59 I forgive your anger because I have reason to love you.

61 Boy: an insulting term of address.

66 tender: cherish.

68–70 Mercutio assumes that Romeo is afraid to fight. *Alla stoccata* is a move used in sword fighting.

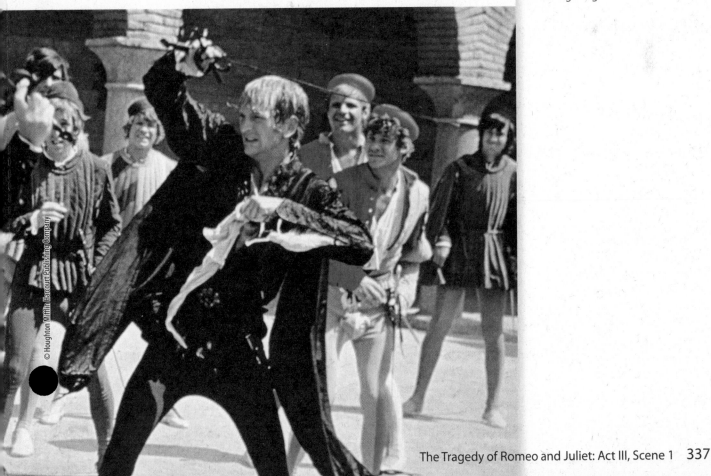

72–74 nothing but . . . eight: I intend to take one of your nine lives (as a cat supposedly has) and give a beating to the other eight.

79 *passado*: a sword fighting maneuver.

80–84 Romeo wants Benvolio to help him stop the fight. They are able to hold back Mercutio.

83 bandying: fighting.

85 A plague . . . sped: I curse both the Montagues and the Capulets. I am destroyed.

ANALYZE LITERARY DEVICES

Annotate: Mark the section in lines 90–96 where Mercutio uses rhythm to express his feelings.

Analyze: Why does Mercutio speak to Romeo in such a rhythmic way at this moment?

[*draws*]

70 Tybalt, you ratcatcher, will you walk?

Tybalt. What wouldst thou have with me?

Mercutio. Good King of Cats, nothing but one of your nine lives. That I mean to make bold withal, and, as you shall use me hereafter, dry-beat the rest of the eight. Will you pluck your
75 sword out of his pilcher by the ears? Make haste, lest mine be about your ears ere it be out.

Tybalt. I am for you.

[*draws*]

Romeo. Gentle Mercutio, put thy rapier up.

Mercutio. Come, sir, your *passado!*

[*They fight.*]

80 **Romeo.** Draw, Benvolio; beat down their weapons.
Gentlemen, for shame! forbear this outrage!
Tybalt, Mercutio, the Prince expressly hath
Forbid this bandying in Verona streets.
Hold, Tybalt! Good Mercutio!

[Tybalt, *under* Romeo's *arm, thrusts* Mercutio *in, and flies with his* Men.]

Mercutio.   I am hurt.
85 A plague o' both your houses! I am sped.
Is he gone and hath nothing?

Benvolio.   What, art thou hurt?

Mercutio. Ay, ay, a scratch, a scratch. Marry, 'tis enough.
Where is my page? Go, villain, fetch a surgeon.

[*Exit* Page.]

Romeo. Courage, man. The hurt cannot be much.

90 **Mercutio.** No, 'tis not so deep as a well, nor so wide as a church door; but 'tis enough, 'twill serve. Ask for me tomorrow, and you shall find me a grave man. I am peppered, I warrant, for this world. A plague o' both your houses! Zounds, a dog, a rat, a mouse, a cat, to scratch a man to death! A braggart, a rogue, a
95 villain, that fights by the book of arithmetic! Why the devil came you between us? I was hurt under your arm.

Romeo. I thought all for the best.

Mercutio. Help me into some house, Benvolio,
Or I shall faint. A plague o' both your houses!

© Houghton Mifflin Harcourt Publishing Company

100 They have made worms' meat of me. I have it,
And soundly too. Your houses!

[*Exit, supported by* Benvolio.]

Romeo. This gentleman, the Prince's near ally,
My very friend, hath got this mortal hurt
In my behalf—my reputation stained
105 With Tybalt's slander—Tybalt, that an hour
Hath been my kinsman, O sweet Juliet,
Thy beauty hath made me effeminate
And in my temper softened valor's steel!

[*Reenter* Benvolio.]

Benvolio. O Romeo, Romeo, brave Mercutio's dead!
110 That gallant spirit hath aspired the clouds,
Which too untimely here did scorn the earth.

Romeo. This day's black fate on more days doth depend;
This but begins the woe others must end.

[*Reenter* Tybalt.]

Benvolio. Here comes the furious Tybalt back again.

115 **Romeo.** Alive in triumph, and Mercutio slain?
Away to heaven respective lenity,
And fire-eyed fury be my conduct now!
Now, Tybalt, take the "villain" back again
That late thou gavest me, for Mercutio's soul
120 Is but a little way above our heads,
Staying for thine to keep him company.
Either thou or I, or both, must go with him.

Tybalt. Thou, wretched boy, that didst consort him here,
Shalt with him hence.

Romeo.   This shall determine that.

[*They fight.* Tybalt *falls.*]

125 **Benvolio.** Romeo, away, be gone!
The citizens are up, and Tybalt slain.
Stand not amazed. The Prince will doom thee death
If thou art taken. Hence, be gone, away!

Romeo. O, I am fortune's fool!

Benvolio.   Why dost thou stay?

[*Exit* Romeo.]

[*Enter* Citizens.]

102–108 This gentleman . . . valor's steel: My friend has died protecting my reputation against a man who has been my relative for only an hour. My love for Juliet has made me less manly and brave.

110 aspired: soared to.

112–113 This day's . . . must end: This awful day will be followed by more of the same.

116 respective lenity: considerate mildness.

CONTRASTS AND CONTRADICTIONS

Notice & Note: Mark the section in lines 115–122 where Romeo says something out of character.

Analyze: What causes the sudden change in Romeo's character?

124 The sword fight probably goes on for several minutes, till Romeo runs his sword through Tybalt.

129 I am fortune's fool: Fate has made a fool of me.

130 Citizen. Which way ran he that killed Mercutio?
Tybalt, that murderer, which way ran he?

Benvolio. There lies that Tybalt.

Citizen.   Up, sir, go with me.
I charge thee in the Prince's name obey.

[*Enter* Prince *with his* Attendants, Montague, Capulet, *their* Wives,
and others.]

Prince. Where are the vile beginners of this fray?

135–136 Benvolio says he can tell (**discover**) what happened.

135 Benvolio. O noble Prince, I can discover all
The unlucky manage of this fatal brawl.
There lies the man, slain by young Romeo,
That slew thy kinsman, brave Mercutio.

Lady Capulet. Tybalt, my cousin! O my brother's child!
140 O Prince! O cousin! O husband! O, the blood is spilled
Of my dear kinsman! Prince, as thou art true,
For blood of ours shed blood of Montague.
O cousin, cousin!

**141–142 as thou . . .
Montague:** If your word is good, you will sentence Romeo to death for killing a Capulet.

Prince. Benvolio, who began this bloody fray?

146–147 Romeo, that . . . was: Romeo talked calmly (**fair**) and told Tybalt to think how trivial (**nice**) the argument was.

145 Benvolio. Tybalt, here slain, whom Romeo's hand did slay.
Romeo, that spoke him fair, bid him bethink
How nice the quarrel was, and urged withal
Your high displeasure. All this—uttered
With gentle breath, calm look, knees humbly bowed—

150–151 could . . . peace: could not quiet the anger of Tybalt, who would not listen to pleas for peace.

150 Could not take truce with the unruly spleen
Of Tybalt deaf to peace, but that he tilts
With piercing steel at bold Mercutio's breast;
Who, all as hot, turns deadly point to point,
And, with a martial scorn, with one hand beats
155 Cold death aside and with the other sends
It back to Tybalt, whose dexterity

156–157 whose dexterity retorts it: whose skill returns it.

Retorts it. Romeo he cries aloud,
"Hold, friends! friends, part!" and swifter than his tongue,
His agile arm beats down their fatal points,

159–160 his agile . . . rushes: He rushed between them and pushed down their swords.

160 And 'twixt them rushes; underneath whose arm
An envious thrust from Tybalt hit the life
Of stout Mercutio, and then Tybalt fled,
But by-and-by comes back to Romeo,
Who had but newly entertained revenge,

164 entertained: thought of.

165 And to't they go like lightning; for, ere I
Could draw to part them, was stout Tybalt slain;
And, as he fell, did Romeo turn and fly.
This is the truth, or let Benvolio die.

© Houghton Mifflin Harcourt Publishing Company

Lady Capulet. He is a kinsman to the Montague;
170 Affection makes him false, he speaks not true.
Some twenty of them fought in this black strife,
And all those twenty could but kill one life.
I beg for justice, which thou, Prince, must give.
Romeo slew Tybalt; Romeo must not live.

175 **Prince.** Romeo slew him; he slew Mercutio.
Who now the price of his dear blood doth owe?

Montague. Not Romeo, Prince; he was Mercutio's friend;
His fault concludes but what the law should end,
The life of Tybalt.

Prince.   And for that offense
180 Immediately we do exile him hence.
I have an interest in your hate's proceeding,
My blood for your rude brawls doth lie a-bleeding;
But I'll amerce you with so strong a fine
That you shall all repent the loss of mine.
185 I will be deaf to pleading and excuses;
Nor tears nor prayers shall purchase out abuses.
Therefore use none. Let Romeo hence in haste,
Else, when he is found, that hour is his last.
Bear hence this body, and attend our will.
190 Mercy but murders, pardoning those that kill.

[*Exeunt.*]

Scene 2 *Capulet's orchard.*

[*Enter* Juliet *alone.*]

Juliet. Gallop apace, you fiery-footed steeds,
Toward Phoebus' lodging! Such a wagoner
As Phaëton would whip you to the West,
And bring in cloudy night immediately.
5 Spread thy close curtain, love-performing night,
That runaways' eyes may wink, and Romeo
Leap to these arms, untalked of and unseen.
Lovers can see to do their amorous rites
By their own beauties; or, if love be blind,
10 It best agrees with night. Come, civil night,
Thou sober-suited matron, all in black,
And learn me how to lose a winning match,
Played for a pair of stainless maidenhoods.
Hood my unmanned blood bating in my cheeks

178–179 Romeo is guilty only of avenging Mercutio's death, which the law would have done anyway.

179–190 The prince banishes Romeo from Verona. He angrily points out that one of his own relatives is dead because of the feud and declares that Romeo will be put to death unless he flees immediately.

2–3 Phoebus: Apollo, the god of the sun; **Phaëton:** a mortal who lost control of the sun's chariot when he drove it too fast.

14–16 Hood . . . modesty: Juliet asks that the darkness hide her blushing cheeks on her wedding night.

LANGUAGE CONVENTIONS

Annotate: Mark the places in Juliet's speech (lines 1–35) where Shakespeare uses parallel structure—repetition of certain words, phrases, or grammatical structures for emphasis or other effects.

Analyze: How does parallel construction enhance what Juliet is saying in this section?

26–27 I have . . . possessed it: Juliet protests that she has gone through the wedding ceremony (**bought the mansion**) but is still waiting to enjoy the rewards of marriage.

34 the cords: the rope ladder.

37–42 well-a-day: an expression used when someone has bad news. The nurse wails and moans without clearly explaining what has happened, leading Juliet to assume that Romeo is dead.

45–50 Juliet's "I" means "aye," or "yes." A **cockatrice** is a mythological beast whose glance kills its victims.

51 my weal or woe: my happiness or sorrow.

53–56 God . . . mark: an expression meant to scare off evil powers, similar to "Knock on wood"; **corse:** corpse; **swounded:** fainted.

15 With thy black mantle; till strange love, grown bold,
Think true love acted simple modesty.
Come, night; come, Romeo, come; thou day in night;
For thou wilt lie upon the wings of night
Whiter than new snow on a raven's back.
20 Come, gentle night; come, loving, black-browed night;
Give me my Romeo; and, when he shall die,
Take him and cut him out in little stars,
And he will make the face of heaven so fine
That all the world will be in love with night
25 And pay no worship to the garish sun.
O, I have bought the mansion of a love,
But not possessed it; and though I am sold,
Not yet enjoyed. So tedious is this day
As is the night before some festival
30 To an impatient child that hath new robes
And may not wear them. Oh, here comes my nurse,

[*Enter* Nurse, *wringing her hands, with the ladder of cords in her lap.*]

And she brings news; and every tongue that speaks
But Romeo's name speaks heavenly eloquence.
Now, nurse, what news? What hast thou there? the cords
35 That Romeo bid thee fetch?

Nurse.   Ay, ay, the cords.

Juliet. Ay me! what news? Why dost thou wring thy hands?

Nurse. Ah, well-a-day! he's dead, he's dead, he's dead!
We are undone, lady, we are undone!
Alack the day! he's gone, he's killed, he's dead!

40 **Juliet.** Can heaven be so envious?

Nurse.   Romeo can,
Though heaven cannot. O Romeo, Romeo!
Who ever would have thought it? Romeo!

Juliet. What devil art thou that dost torment me thus?
This torture should be roared in dismal hell.
45 Hath Romeo slain himself? Say thou but "I,"
And that bare vowel "I" shall poison more
Than the death-darting eye of a cockatrice.
I am not I, if there be such an "I,"
Or those eyes shut, that make thee answer "I."
50 If he be slain, say "I," or if not, "no."
Brief sounds determine of my weal or woe.

Nurse. I saw the wound, I saw it with mine eyes,
(God save the mark!) here on his manly breast.
A piteous corse, a bloody piteous corse;

© Houghton Mifflin Harcourt Publishing Company

55 Pale, pale as ashes, all bedaubed in blood,
    All in gore blood. I swounded at the sight.

Juliet. O, break, my heart! poor bankrout, break at once!
To prison, eyes; ne'er look on liberty!
Vile earth, to earth resign; end motion here,
60 And thou and Romeo press one heavy bier!

Nurse. O Tybalt, Tybalt, the best friend I had!
O courteous Tybalt! honest gentleman!
That ever I should live to see thee dead!

Juliet. What storm is this that blows so contrary?
65 Is Romeo slaughtered, and is Tybalt dead?
My dear-loved cousin, and my dearer lord?
Then, dreadful trumpet, sound the general doom!
For who is living, if those two are gone?

Nurse. Tybalt is gone, and Romeo banished;
70 Romeo that killed him, he is banished.

Juliet. O God! Did Romeo's hand shed Tybalt's blood?

Nurse. It did! it did! alas the day, it did!

Juliet. O serpent heart, hid with a flow'ring face!
Did ever dragon keep so fair a cave?
75 Beautiful tyrant! fiend angelical!
Dove-feathered raven! wolvish-ravening lamb!
Despised substance of divinest show!
Just opposite to what thou justly seemst,
A damned saint, an honorable villain!
80 O nature, what hadst thou to do in hell
When thou didst bower the spirit of a fiend
In mortal paradise of such sweet flesh?
Was ever book containing such vile matter
So fairly bound? O, that deceit should dwell
85 In such a gorgeous palace!

Nurse.   There's no trust,
No faith, no honesty in men; all perjured,
All forsworn, all naught, all dissemblers.
Ah, where's my man? Give me some aqua vitae.
These griefs, these woes, these sorrows make me old.
90 Shame come to Romeo!

Juliet.   Blistered be thy tongue
For such a wish! He was not born to shame.
Upon his brow shame is ashamed to sit;
For 'tis a throne where honor may be crowned
Sole monarch of the universal earth.

57–60 Juliet say her heart is broken and bankrupt (**bankrout**). She wants to be buried with Romeo, sharing his burial platform (**bier**).

ANALYZE LITERARY DEVICES
Annotate: Mark examples of oxymorons in lines 73–85.

Respond: How do these oxymorons help make Juliet a complex yet believable character?

81 bower . . . fiend: give a home to the spirit of a demon.

86–87 all perjured . . . dissemblers: All are liars and pretenders.
88 aqua vitae: brandy.

95 O, what a beast was I to chide at him!

Nurse. Will you speak well of him that killed your cousin?

Juliet. Shall I speak ill of him that is my husband?
Ah, poor my lord, what tongue shall smooth thy name
When I, thy three-hours' wife, have mangled it?
100 But wherefore, villain, didst thou kill my cousin?
That villain cousin would have killed my husband.
Back, foolish tears, back to your native spring!
Your tributary drops belong to woe,
Which you, mistaking, offer up to joy.
105 My husband lives, that Tybalt would have slain;
And Tybalt's dead, that would have slain my husband.
All this is comfort; wherefore weep I then?
Some word there was, worser than Tybalt's death,
That murdered me. I would forget it fain;
110 But O, it presses to my memory
Like damned guilty deeds to sinners' minds!
"Tybalt is dead, and Romeo—banished."
That "banished," that one word "banished,"
Hath slain ten thousand Tybalts. Tybalt's death
115 Was woe enough, if it had ended there;
Or, if sour woe delights in fellowship
And needly will be ranked with other griefs,
Why followed not, when she said "Tybalt's dead,"
Thy father, or thy mother, nay, or both,
120 Which modern lamentation might have moved?
But with a rearward following Tybalt's death,
"Romeo is banished"—to speak that word
Is father, mother, Tybalt, Romeo, Juliet,
All slain, all dead. "Romeo is banished"—
125 There is no end, no limit, measure, bound,
In that word's death; no words can that woe sound.
Where is my father and my mother, nurse?

Nurse. Weeping and wailing over Tybalt's corse.
Will you go to them? I will bring you thither.

130 **Juliet.** Wash they his wounds with tears? Mine shall be spent,
When theirs are dry, for Romeo's banishment.
Take up those cords. Poor ropes, you are beguiled,
Both you and I, for Romeo is exiled.
He made you for a highway to my bed;
135 But I, a maid, die maiden-widowed.
Come, cords; come, nurse. I'll to my wedding bed;
And death, not Romeo, take my maidenhead!

Nurse. Hie to your chamber. I'll find Romeo

102–106 Juliet is uncertain whether her tears should be of joy or of sorrow.

114–127 If the news of Tybalt's death had been followed by the news of her parents' deaths, Juliet would have felt grief. To follow the story of Tybalt's death with the news of Romeo's banishment creates a sorrow so deep it cannot be expressed in words.

132 beguiled: cheated.

135–137 I . . . maidenhead: I will die a widow without ever really having been a wife. Death, not Romeo, will be my husband.

To comfort you. I wot well where he is.
140 Hark ye, your Romeo will be here at night.
I'll to him; he is hid at Laurence' cell.

Juliet. O, find him! give this ring to my true knight
And bid him come to take his last farewell.

[*Exeunt.*]

Scene 3 *Friar Laurence's cell.*

[*Enter* Friar Laurence.]

Friar Laurence. Romeo, come forth; come forth, thou fearful man.
Affliction is enamored of thy parts,
And thou art wedded to calamity.

[*Enter* Romeo.]

Romeo. Father, what news? What is the Prince's doom?
5 What sorrow craves acquaintance at my hand
That I yet know not?

Friar Laurence.   Too familiar
Is my dear son with such sour company.
I bring thee tidings of the Prince's doom.

Romeo. What less than doomsday is the Prince's doom?

10 **Friar Laurence.** A gentler judgment vanished from his lips—
Not body's death, but body's banishment.

Romeo. Ha, banishment? Be merciful, say "death";
For exile hath more terror in his look,
Much more than death. Do not say "banishment."

15 **Friar Laurence.** Hence from Verona art thou banished.
Be patient, for the world is broad and wide.

Romeo. There is no world without Verona walls,
But purgatory, torture, hell itself.
Hence banished is banish'd from the world,
20 And world's exile is death. Then "banishment,"
Is death misterm'd. Calling death "banishment,"
Thou cuttst my head off with a golden axe
And smilest upon the stroke that murders me.

Friar Laurence. O deadly sin! O rude unthankfulness!
25 Thy fault our law calls death; but the kind Prince,
Taking thy part, hath rushed aside the law,
And turned that black word death to banishment.
This is dear mercy, and thou seest it not.

Romeo. 'Tis torture, and not mercy. Heaven is here,
30 Where Juliet lives; and every cat and dog

---

139 **wot:** know.

2 **Affliction . . . parts:** Trouble loves you.

4 **doom:** sentence.

9 **doomsday:** death.

10 **vanished:** came.

17–23 **There is . . . murders me:** Being exiled outside Verona's walls is as bad as being dead. And yet you smile at my misfortune.

▶ WORDS OF THE WISER

Notice & Note: Mark the line(s) where Friar Laurence gives insight into Romeo's predicament.

Infer: What lesson is Friar Laurence trying to teach Romeo?

33–35 More validity . . . than Romeo: Even flies that live off the dead (**carrion**) will be able to get closer to Juliet than Romeo will.

And little mouse, every unworthy thing,
Live here in heaven and may look on her;
But Romeo may not. More validity,
More honorable state, more courtship lives
35 In carrion flies than Romeo. They may seize
On the white wonder of dear Juliet's hand
And steal immortal blessing from her lips,
Who, even in pure and vestal modesty,

Still blush, as thinking their own kisses sin;
40 But Romeo may not—he is banished.
This may flies do, when I from this must fly;
They are free men, but I am banished.
And sayst thou yet that exile is not death?
Hadst thou no poison mixed, no sharp-ground knife,
45 No sudden mean of death, though ne'er so mean,
But "banished" to kill me—"banished"?
O friar, the damned use that word in hell;
Howling attends it! How hast thou the heart,
Being a divine, a ghostly confessor,
50 A sin-absolver, and my friend professed,
To mangle me with that word "banished"?

Friar Laurence. Thou fond mad man, hear me a little speak.

Romeo. O, thou wilt speak again of banishment.

Friar Laurence. I'll give thee armor to keep off that word;
55 Adversity's sweet milk, philosophy,
To comfort thee, though thou art banished.

Romeo. Yet "banished"? Hang up philosophy!
Unless philosophy can make a Juliet,
Displant a town, reverse a prince's doom,
60 It helps not, it prevails not. Talk no more.

Friar Laurence. O, then I see that madmen have no ears.

Romeo. How should they, when that wise men have no eyes?

Friar Laurence. Let me dispute with thee of thy estate.

Romeo. Thou canst not speak of that thou dost not feel.
65 Wert thou as young as I, Juliet thy love,
An hour but married, Tybalt murdered,
Doting like me, and like me banished,
Then mightst thou speak, then mightst thou tear thy hair,
And fall upon the ground, as I do now,
70 Taking the measure of an unmade grave.

[Nurse *knocks within.*]

Friar Laurence. Arise; one knocks. Good Romeo, hide thyself.

Romeo. Not I; unless the breath of heartsick groans
Mist-like infold me from the search of eyes.

[*knock*]

Friar Laurence. Hark, how they knock! Who's there? Romeo, arise;
75 Thou wilt be taken.—Stay awhile!—Stand up;

[*knock*]

44–46 Hadst . . . to kill me: Couldn't you have killed me with poison or a knife instead of with that awful word *banished*?

52 fond: foolish.

54–56 The friar offers philosophical comfort and counseling (**adversity's sweet milk**) as a way to overcome hardship.

63 dispute: discuss; **estate:** situation.

72–73 Romeo will hide only if his sighs create a mist and shield him from sight.

© Houghton Mifflin Harcourt Publishing Company

Run to my study.—By-and-by!—God's will,
What simpleness is this.—I come, I come!

[*knock*]

Who knocks so hard? Whence come you? What's your will?

Nurse [*within*]. Let me come in, and you shall know my errand.
80 I come from Lady Juliet.

Friar Laurence.   Welcome then.

[*Enter* Nurse.]

Nurse. O holy friar, O, tell me, holy friar,
Where is my lady's lord, where's Romeo?

Friar Laurence. There on the ground, with his own tears made
     drunk.

Nurse. O, he is even in my mistress' case,
85 Just in her case! O woeful sympathy!
Piteous predicament! Even so lies she,
Blubb'ring and weeping, weeping and blubbering.
Stand up, stand up! Stand, an you be a man.
For Juliet's sake, for her sake, rise and stand!
90 Why should you fall into so deep an O?

Romeo [*rises*]. Nurse—

Nurse. Ah sir! ah sir! Well, death's the end of all.

Romeo. Spakest thou of Juliet? How is it with her?
Doth not she think me an old murderer,
95 Now I have stained the childhood of our joy
With blood removed but little from her own?
Where is she? and how doth she? and what says
My concealed lady to our canceled love?

Nurse. O, she says nothing, sir, but weeps and weeps;
100 And now falls on her bed, and then starts up,
And Tybalt calls; and then on Romeo cries,
And then down falls again.

Romeo.   As if that name,
Shot from the deadly level of a gun,
Did murder her; as that name's cursed hand
105 Murdered her kinsman. O tell me, friar, tell me,
In what vile part of this anatomy
Doth my name lodge? Tell me, that I may sack
The hateful mansion.

[*draws his dagger*]

Friar Laurence.   Hold thy desperate hand.
Art thou a man? Thy form cries out thou art;
110 Thy tears are womanish, thy wild acts denote

84–85 he is even ... her case: He is acting the same way that Juliet is.

90 into so deep an O: into such deep grief.

96 blood ... from her own: the blood of a close relative of hers.

98 concealed lady: secret bride.

102 that name: the name Romeo.

106–108 in what vile part ... mansion: Romeo asks where in his body (**anatomy**) his name can be found so that he can cut the name out.
108–125 Hold thy ... bedeck thy shape, thy love, thy wit: You're not acting like a man. Would you send your soul to hell by committing suicide (**doing damned hate upon thyself**)? Why do you curse your birth, heaven, and earth? You are refusing to make good use of your advantages, just as a miser refuses to spend his money.

The unreasonable fury of a beast.
Unseemly woman in a seeming man!
Or ill-beseeming beast in seeming both!
Thou hast amazed me. By my holy order,
115 I thought thy disposition better tempered.
Hast thou slain Tybalt? Wilt thou slay thyself?
And slay thy lady too that lives in thee,
By doing damned hate upon thyself?
Why railst thou on thy birth, the heaven, and earth?
120 Since birth and heaven and earth, all three do meet
In thee at once; which thou at once wouldst lose.
Fie, fie, thou shamest thy shape, thy love, thy wit,
Which, like a usurer, aboundst in all,
And usest none in that true use indeed
125 Which should bedeck thy shape, thy love, thy wit.
Thy noble shape is but a form of wax,
Digressing from the valor of a man;
Thy dear love sworn but hollow perjury,
Killing that love which thou hast vowed to cherish;
130 Thy wit, that ornament to shape and love,
Misshapen in the conduct of them both,
Like powder in a skilless soldier's flask,
Is set afire by thine own ignorance,
And thou dismembered with thine own defense.
135 What, rouse thee, man! Thy Juliet is alive,
For whose dear sake thou wast but lately dead.
There art thou happy. Tybalt would kill thee,
But thou slewest Tybalt. There art thou happy.
The law, that threatened death, becomes thy friend
140 And turns it to exile. There art thou happy.
A pack of blessings light upon thy back;
Happiness courts thee in her best array;
But, like a misbehaved and sullen wench,
Thou poutst upon thy fortune and thy love.
145 Take heed, take heed, for such die miserable.
Go get thee to thy love, as was decreed,
Ascend her chamber, hence and comfort her.
But look thou stay not till the watch be set,
For then thou canst not pass to Mantua,
150 Where thou shalt live till we can find a time
To blaze your marriage, reconcile your friends,
Beg pardon of the Prince, and call thee back
With twenty hundred thousand times more joy
Than thou wentst forth in lamentation.
155 Go before, nurse. Commend me to thy lady,
And bid her hasten all the house to bed,
Which heavy sorrow makes them apt unto.

LANGUAGE CONVENTIONS
Annotate: Mark the places in Friar Laurence's speech (lines 108–144) where Shakespeare uses parallel construction.

Analyze: What is the effect of parallel construction in this speech?

126–134 The friar explains how by acting as he is, Romeo is misusing his shape (his outer form or body), his love, and his wit (his mind or intellect).

148–149 look . . . Mantua: Leave before the guards take their places at the city gates; otherwise you will not be able to escape.

151 blaze . . . friends: announce your marriage and get the families (**friends**) to stop feuding.

Romeo is coming.

Nurse. O Lord, I could have stayed here all the night
160 To hear good counsel. O, what learning is!
My lord, I'll tell my lady you will come.

Romeo. Do so, and bid my sweet prepare to chide.

[Nurse *offers to go and turns again.*]

Nurse. Here is a ring she bid me give you, sir.
Hie you, make haste, for it grows very late.

[*Exit.*]

165 **Romeo.** How well my comfort is revived by this!

Friar Laurence. Go hence; good night; and here stands all your
    state:
Either be gone before the watch be set,
Or by the break of day disguised from hence.
Sojourn in Mantua. I'll find out your man,
170 And he shall signify from time to time
Every good hap to you that chances here.
Give me thy hand. 'Tis late. Farewell; good night.

Romeo. But that a joy past joy calls out on me,
It were a grief so brief to part with thee.
175 Farewell.

[*Exeunt.*]

Scene 4 *Capulet's house.*

[*Enter* Capulet, Lady Capulet, *and* Paris.]

Capulet. Things have fall'n out, sir, so unluckily
That we have had no time to move our daughter.
Look you, she loved her kinsman Tybalt dearly,
And so did I. Well, we were born to die.
5 'Tis very late; she'll not come down tonight.
I promise you, but for your company,
I would have been abed an hour ago.

Paris. These times of woe afford no time to woo.
Madam, good night. Commend me to your daughter.

10 **Lady Capulet.** I will, and know her mind early tomorrow;
Tonight she's mewed up to her heaviness.

[Paris *offers to go and* Capulet *calls him again.*]

Capulet. Sir Paris, I will make a desperate tender
Of my child's love. I think she will be ruled
In all respects by me; nay more, I doubt it not.

---

162 bid . . . chide: Tell Juliet to get ready to scold me for the way I've behaved.

166–171 and here . . . here: Either leave before the night watchmen go on duty, or get out at dawn in a disguise. Stay awhile in Mantua. I'll find your servant and send messages to you about what good things are happening here.

1–2 Things have . . . our daughter: Such terrible things have happened that we haven't had time to persuade (**move**) Juliet to think about your marriage proposal.

8 Sad times are not good times for talking of marriage.

11 Tonight she is locked up with her sorrow.

12 desperate tender: bold offer.

15 Wife, go you to her ere you go to bed;
   Acquaint her here of my son Paris' love
   And bid her (mark you me?) on Wednesday next—
   But, soft! what day is this?

   Paris.   Monday, my lord.

   Capulet. Monday! ha, ha! Well, Wednesday is too soon.
20 A Thursday let it be—a Thursday, tell her,
   She shall be married to this noble earl.
   Will you be ready? Do you like this haste?
   We'll keep no great ado—a friend or two;
   For hark you, Tybalt being slain so late,
25 It may be thought we held him carelessly,

ANALYZE PARALLEL PLOTS
Annotate: In this scene, Shakespeare continues the parallel plot of Paris's marriage proposal to Juliet. Mark the spot in lines 12–21 where Lord Capulet says that he will convince Juliet to marry Paris.

Predict: How will this parallel plot affect the main plot of Romeo and Juliet's romance?

23 no great ado: no big festivity.

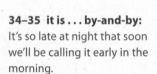

Being our kinsman, if we revel much.
Therefore we'll have some half a dozen friends,
And there an end. But what say you to Thursday?

Paris. My lord, I would that Thursday were tomorrow.

30 **Capulet.** Well, get you gone. A Thursday be it then.
Go you to Juliet ere you go to bed;
Prepare her, wife, against this wedding day.
Farewell, my lord.—Light to my chamber, ho!
Afore me, it is so very very late

35 That we may call it early by-and-by.
Good night.

[*Exeunt.*]

34–35 it is . . . by-and-by:
It's so late at night that soon
we'll be calling it early in the
morning.

Scene 5 *Capulet's orchard.*

[*Enter* Romeo *and* Juliet *above, at the window.*]

Juliet. Wilt thou be gone? It is not yet near day.
It was the nightingale, and not the lark,
That pierced the fearful hollow of thine ear.
Nightly she sings on yond pomegranate tree.

5 Believe me, love, it was the nightingale.

2 It was . . . lark: The
nightingale sings at night; the
lark sings in the morning.

Romeo. It was the lark, the herald of the morn;
No nightingale. Look, love, what envious streaks
Do lace the severing clouds in yonder East.
Night's candles are burnt out, and jocund day

10 Stands tiptoe on the misty mountain tops.
I must be gone and live, or stay and die.

9 Night's candles: stars.

Juliet. Yond light is not daylight; I know it, I.
It is some meteor that the sun exhales
To be to thee this night a torchbearer

15 And light thee on thy way to Mantua.
Therefore stay yet; thou needst not to be gone.

12–25 Juliet continues to
pretend it is night to keep
Romeo from leaving. Romeo
says he'll stay if Juliet wishes it,
even if it means death.

Romeo. Let me be ta'en, let me be put to death.
I am content, so thou wilt have it so.
I'll say yon grey is not the morning's eye,

20 'Tis but the pale reflex of Cynthia's brow;
Nor that is not the lark whose notes do beat
The vaulty heaven so high above our heads.
I have more care to stay than will to go.
Come, death, and welcome! Juliet wills it so.

25 How is't, my soul? Let's talk; it is not day.

20 Cynthia's brow: Cynthia
is another name for Diana, the
Roman goddess of the moon.
She was often pictured with a
crescent moon on her forehead.

Juliet. It is, it is! Hie hence, be gone, away!
It is the lark that sings so out of tune,
Straining harsh discords and unpleasing sharps.

26 Romeo's mention of death
frightens Juliet, and she urges
him to leave quickly.

Some say the lark makes sweet division;
30 This doth not so, for she divideth us.
Some say the lark and loathed toad changed eyes;
O, now I would they had changed voices too,
Since arm from arm that voice doth us affray,
Hunting thee hence with hunt's-up to the day!
35 O, now be gone! More light and light it grows.

Romeo. More light and light—more dark and dark our woes!

[*Enter* Nurse, *hastily.*]

Nurse. Madam!

Juliet. Nurse?

Nurse. Your lady mother is coming to your chamber.
40 The day is broke; be wary, look about.

[*Exit.*]

29 division: melody.

31–34 I wish the lark had the voice of the hated (**loathed**) toad, since its voice is frightening us apart and acting as a morning song for hunters (**hunt's-up**).

The Tragedy of Romeo and Juliet: Act III, Scene 5   353

Juliet. Then, window, let day in, and let life out.

Romeo. Farewell, farewell! One kiss, and I'll descend.

[*He starts down the ladder.*]

Juliet. Art thou gone so, my lord, my love, my friend?
I must hear from thee every day in the hour,
45 For in a minute there are many days.
O, by this count I shall be much in years
Ere I again behold my Romeo!

Romeo. Farewell!
I will omit no opportunity
50 That may convey my greetings, love, to thee.

Juliet. O, thinkst thou we shall ever meet again?

Romeo. I doubt it not; and all these woes shall serve
For sweet discourses in our time to come.

Juliet. O God, I have an ill-divining soul!
55 Methinks I see thee, now thou art below,
As one dead in the bottom of a tomb.
Either my eyesight fails, or thou lookst pale.

Romeo. And trust me, love, in my eye so do you.
Dry sorrow drinks our blood. Adieu! adieu!

[*Exit.*]

60 **Juliet.** O Fortune, Fortune! all men call thee fickle.
If thou art fickle, what dost thou with him
That is renowned for faith? Be fickle, Fortune,
For then I hope thou wilt not keep him long
But send him back.

Lady Capulet. [*within*]. Ho, daughter! are you up?

65 **Juliet.** Who is't that calls? It is my lady mother.
Is she not down so late, or up so early?
What unaccustomed cause procures her hither?

[*Enter* Lady Capulet.]

Lady Capulet. Why, how now, Juliet?

Juliet.   Madam, I am not well.

Lady Capulet. Evermore weeping for your cousin's death?
70 What, wilt thou wash him from his grave with tears?
An if thou couldst, thou couldst not make him live.
Therefore have done. Some grief shows much of love;
But much of grief shows still some want of wit.

Juliet. Yet let me weep for such a feeling loss.

75 **Lady Capulet.** So shall you feel the loss, but not the friend

---

46 much in years: very old.

54–56 I have . . . tomb: Juliet sees an evil vision of the future.

59 Dry . . . blood: People believed that sorrow drained the blood from the heart, causing a sad person to look pale.

60–62 fickle: changeable in loyalty or affection. Juliet asks fickle Fortune why it has anything to do with Romeo, who is the opposite of fickle.

67 What . . . hither: What unusual reason brings her here?

72–73 have . . . wit: Stop crying (**have done**). A little grief is evidence of love, while too much grief shows a lack of good sense (**want of wit**).

Which you weep for.

Juliet.   Feeling so the loss,
I cannot choose but ever weep the friend.

Lady Capulet. Well, girl, thou weepst not so much for his death
As that the villain lives which slaughtered him.

80 **Juliet.** What villain, madam?

Lady Capulet.   That same villain Romeo.

Juliet [*aside*]. Villain and he be many miles asunder.—
God pardon him! I do, with all my heart;
And yet no man like he doth grieve my heart.

Lady Capulet. That is because the traitor murderer lives.

85 **Juliet.** Ay, madam, from the reach of these my hands.
Would none but I might venge my cousin's death!

Lady Capulet. We will have vengeance for it, fear thou not.
Then weep no more. I'll send to one in Mantua,
Where that same banished runagate doth live,
90 Shall give him such an unaccustomed dram
That he shall soon keep Tybalt company;
And then I hope thou wilt be satisfied.

Juliet. Indeed I never shall be satisfied
With Romeo till I behold him—dead—
95 Is my poor heart so for a kinsman vexed.
Madam, if you could find out but a man
To bear a poison, I would temper it;
That Romeo should, upon receipt thereof,
Soon sleep in quiet. O, how my heart abhors
100 To hear him named and cannot come to him,
To wreak the love I bore my cousin Tybalt
Upon his body that hath slaughtered him!

Lady Capulet. Find thou the means, and I'll find such a man.
But now I'll tell thee joyful tidings, girl.

105 **Juliet.** And joy comes well in such a needy time.
What are they, I beseech your ladyship?

Lady Capulet. Well, well, thou hast a careful father, child;
One who, to put thee from thy heaviness,
Hath sorted out a sudden day of joy
110 That thou expects not nor I looked not for.

Juliet. Madam, in happy time! What day is that?

Lady Capulet. Marry, my child, early next Thursday morn
The gallant, young, and noble gentleman,
The County Paris, at Saint Peter's Church,

81–102 In these lines Juliet's words have double meanings. To avoid lying to her mother, she chooses her words carefully. They can mean what her mother wants to hear—or what Juliet really has on her mind.

89 runagate: runaway.
90 unaccustomed dram: poison.

93–102 dead: This could refer either to Romeo or to Juliet's heart. Juliet says that if her mother could find someone to carry a poison to Romeo, she would mix (**temper**) it herself.

115 Shall happily make thee there a joyful bride.

Juliet. Now by Saint Peter's Church, and Peter too,
He shall not make me there a joyful bride!
I wonder at this haste, that I must wed
Ere he that should be husband comes to woo.
120 I pray you tell my lord and father, madam,
I will not marry yet; and when I do, I swear
It shall be Romeo, whom you know I hate,
Rather than Paris. These are news indeed!

Lady Capulet. Here comes your father. Tell him so yourself,
125 And see how he will take it at your hands.

[*Enter* Capulet *and* Nurse.]

Capulet. When the sun sets the air doth drizzle dew,
But for the sunset of my brother's son
It rains downright.
How now? a conduit, girl? What, still in tears?
130 Evermore show'ring? In one little body
Thou counterfeitst a bark, a sea, a wind:
For still thy eyes, which I may call the sea,
Do ebb and flow with tears; the bark thy body is,
Sailing in this salt flood; the winds, thy sighs,
135 Who, raging with thy tears and they with them,
Without a sudden calm will overset
Thy tempest-tossed body. How now, wife?
Have you delivered to her our decree?

Lady Capulet. Ay, sir; but she will none, she gives you thanks.
140 I would the fool were married to her grave!

Capulet. Soft! take me with you, take me with you, wife.
How? Will she none? Doth she not give us thanks?
Is she not proud? Doth she not count her blest,
Unworthy as she is, that we have wrought
145 So worthy a gentleman to be her bridegroom?

Juliet. Not proud you have, but thankful that you have.
Proud can I never be of what I hate,
But thankful even for hate that is meant love.

Capulet. How, how, how, how, choplogic? What is this?
150 "Proud"—and "I thank you"—and "I thank you not"—
And yet "not proud"? Mistress minion you,
Thank me no thankings, nor proud me no prouds,
But fettle your fine joints 'gainst Thursday next
To go with Paris to Saint Peter's Church,
155 Or I will drag thee on a hurdle thither.
Out, you green-sickness carrion! out, you baggage!

127 the sunset ... son: the death of Tybalt.

129–137 conduit: fountain. Capulet compares Juliet to a boat (**bark**), an ocean, and the wind because of her excessive crying.

141 take me with you: let me understand you.

146–148 Not proud ... meant love: I'm not pleased, but I am grateful for your intentions.

149–157 Capulet calls Juliet a person who argues over fine points (**choplogic**) and a spoiled child (**minion**). He tells her to prepare herself (**fettle your fine joints**) for the wedding or he'll haul her there in a cart for criminals (**hurdle**). He calls her a piece of dead flesh (**green-sickness carrion**) and a coward (**tallow-face**).

© Houghton Mifflin Harcourt Publishing Company

You tallow-face!

Lady Capulet. Fie, fie; what, are you mad?

Juliet. Good father, I beseech you on my knees,

[*She kneels down.*]

Hear me with patience but to speak a word.

160 **Capulet.** Hang thee, young baggage! disobedient wretch!
I tell thee what—get thee to church a Thursday
Or never after look me in the face.
Speak not, reply not, do not answer me!
My fingers itch. Wife, we scarce thought us blest

165 That God had lent us but this only child;
But now I see this one is one too much,
And that we have a curse in having her.
Out on her, hilding!

    Nurse.   God in heaven bless her!
You are to blame, my lord, to rate her so.

170 **Capulet.** And why, my Lady Wisdom? Hold your tongue,
Good Prudence. Smatter with your gossips, go!

Nurse. I speak no treason.

Capulet.   O, God-i-god-en!

Nurse. May not one speak?

Capulet.   Peace, you mumbling fool!
Utter your gravity o'er a gossip's bowl,

175 For here we need it not.

    Lady Capulet.   You are too hot.

Capulet. God's bread! it makes me mad. Day, night, late, early,
At home, abroad, alone, in company,
Waking or sleeping, still my care hath been
To have her matched; and having now provided

180 A gentleman of princely parentage,
Of fair demesnes, youthful, and nobly trained,
Stuffed, as they say, with honorable parts,
Proportioned as one's thought would wish a man—
And then to have a wretched puling fool,

185 A whining mammet, in her fortunes tender,
To answer "I'll not wed, I cannot love;
I am too young, I pray you pardon me"!
But, an you will not wed, I'll pardon you.
Graze where you will, you shall not house with me.

190 Look to't, think on't; I do not use to jest.
Thursday is near; lay hand on heart, advise:
An you be mine, I'll give you to my friend;

164 My fingers itch: I feel like hitting you.

168 hilding: a good-for-nothing person.

171 smatter: chatter.

174 Utter ... bowl: Save your words of wisdom for a gathering of gossips.

179 matched: married.

184 puling: crying.
185 mammet: doll.

189–195 Capulet swears that he'll kick Juliet out and cut her off financially if she refuses to marry.

© Houghton Mifflin Harcourt Publishing Company

An you be not, hang, beg, starve, die in the streets,
For, by my soul, I'll ne'er acknowledge thee,
195 Nor what is mine shall never do thee good.
Trust to't. Bethink you. I'll not be forsworn.

[*Exit.*]

Juliet. Is there no pity sitting in the clouds
That sees into the bottom of my grief?
O sweet my mother, cast me not away!
200 Delay this marriage for a month, a week;
Or if you do not, make the bridal bed
In that dim monument where Tybalt lies.

Lady Capulet. Talk not to me, for I'll not speak a word.
Do as thou wilt, for I have done with thee.

[*Exit.*]

205 **Juliet.** O God!—O nurse, how shall this be prevented?
My husband is on earth, my faith in heaven.
How shall that faith return again to earth
Unless that husband send it me from heaven
By leaving earth? Comfort me, counsel me.
210 Alack, alack, that heaven should practice stratagems
Upon so soft a subject as myself!
What sayst thou? Hast thou not a word of joy?
Some comfort, nurse.

Nurse.   Faith, here it is.
Romeo is banish'd; and all the world to nothing
215 That he dares ne'er come back to challenge you;
Or if he do, it needs must be by stealth.
Then, since the case so stands as now it doth,
I think it best you married with the County.
O, he's a lovely gentleman!
220 Romeo's a dishclout to him. An eagle, madam,
Hath not so green, so quick, so fair an eye
As Paris hath. Beshrew my very heart,
I think you are happy in this second match,
For it excels your first; or if it did not,
225 Your first is dead—or 'twere as good he were
As living here and you no use of him.

Juliet. Speakst thou this from thy heart?

Nurse. And from my soul too; else beshrew them both.

Juliet. Amen!

230 **Nurse.** What?

Juliet. Well, thou hast comforted me marvelous much.
Go in; and tell my lady I am gone,
Having displeased my father, to Laurence' cell,

196 I'll not be forsworn: I will not break my promise to Paris.

207–211 Juliet is worried about the sin of being married to two men. She asks how heaven can play such tricks (**practice stratagems**) on her.

222 beshrew: curse.

223–225 This new marriage will be better than the first, which is as good as over.

229 Amen: I agree—that is, curse your heart and soul.

To make confession and to be absolved.

235 **Nurse.** Marry, I will; and this is wisely done.

[*Exit.*]

Juliet. Ancient damnation! O most wicked fiend!
Is it more sin to wish me thus forsworn,
Or to dispraise my lord with that same tongue
Which she hath praised him with above compare
240 So many thousand times? Go, counselor!
Thou and my bosom henceforth shall be twain.
I'll to the friar to know his remedy.
If all else fail, myself have power to die.

[*Exit.*]

236–238 Ancient damnation: old devil; **dispraise:** criticize.

241 Thou . . . twain: I'll no longer tell you my secrets.

CHECK YOUR UNDERSTANDING

Answer these questions before moving on to the **Analyze the Text** section on the following page.

1 When the act begins, Benvolio is —

   A trying to persuade Mercutio to avoid the Capulets

   B arguing with Mercutio about how best to help Romeo

   C explaining why he is eager to get into a brawl

   D joking about how Mercutio always wants to fight

2 What is a sign in Act III that the story of Romeo and Juliet is turning into a tragedy?

   F Juliet begs the Nurse to tell her what happened to Romeo.

   G Romeo breaks his vow to love Tybalt and not to fight with him.

   H Friar Laurence gets frustrated with how Romeo is acting.

   J Lord and Lady Capulet become furious with Juliet.

3 In Scene 5, lines 1–35, Juliet wants the darkness to continue because —

   A she is playfully trying to hide from Romeo

   B she and Romeo are trying to escape together

   C she wants Romeo to stay with her a little longer

   D she knows she may not live to see the morning

ANALYZE THE TEXT

Support your responses with evidence from the text. NOTEBOOK

1. **Interpret** What is the meaning of Mercutio's repeated curse, "A plague o' both your houses!" (Scene 1, lines 85, 93)? What might this curse foreshadow? What other moments in Act III have similar foreshadowing?

2. **Evaluate** What is Romeo's motivation for killing Tybalt? Is his action justified or a mistake? Explain your response.

3. **Cite Evidence** In what ways do Romeo and Juliet need the help of Friar Laurence and the Nurse in order to save their love and to move forward? Support your response with evidence from the text.

4. **Analyze** In Scene 5, Lord Capulet becomes enraged when Juliet says she will not marry Paris. In what way are his words and actions in this scene like those of Romeo and Juliet? What are the likely consequences of his actions?

5. **Notice & Note** In Scene 5, how and why does the Nurse's behavior contrast with or contradict her earlier behavior? How does this contrast or contradiction affect Juliet? Explain, citing details from the text.

CREATE AND PRESENT

Write a Journal Entry Explore the parallel feelings of despair that Romeo and Juliet feel in Act III by writing a journal entry for each character. Base your journal entries on evidence from the text.

- ❏ Write a one-page journal entry from the point of view of Juliet when she learns of the death of Tybalt.

- ❏ Write a one-page journal entry from the point of view of Romeo when he is awaiting exile at the friar's cell.

- ❏ If you don't know the word for something or the way to express an idea, ask for assistance from your teacher or peers.

Present to a Partner Share your journal entries by reading them aloud to a partner.

- ❏ Read clearly, at an appropriate volume, and with proper expression.

- ❏ Listen carefully to your partner's journal entries.

- ❏ Ask questions about anything you do not understand.

SETTING A PURPOSE

Note the details of the plan Juliet and Friar Laurence initiate in this act.
Pay attention to the reactions of other characters as the plan unfolds.
Write down any questions you generate during reading.

ACT IV

Scene 1 *Friar Laurence's cell.*

[*Enter* Friar Laurence *and* Paris.]

Friar Laurence. On Thursday, sir? The time is very short.

Paris. My father Capulet will have it so,
And I am nothing slow to slack his haste.

Friar Laurence. You say you do not know the lady's mind.
5 Uneven is the course; I like it not.

Paris. Immoderately she weeps for Tybalt's death,
And therefore have I little talked of love;
For Venus smiles not in a house of tears.
Now, sir, her father counts it dangerous
10 That she do give her sorrow so much sway,
And in his wisdom hastes our marriage
To stop the inundation of her tears,
Which, too much minded by herself alone,
May be put from her by society.
15 Now do you know the reason of this haste.

Friar Laurence [*aside*]. I would I knew not why it should be
        slowed.—
Look, sir, here comes the lady toward my cell.

[*Enter* Juliet.]

Paris. Happily met, my lady and my wife!

Juliet. That may be, sir, when I may be a wife.

20 **Paris.** That may be must be, love, on Thursday next.

Juliet. What must be shall be.

Friar Laurence.   That's a certain text.

Paris. Come you to make confession to this father?

Juliet. To answer that, I should confess to you.

Paris. Do not deny to him that you love me.

2–3 My . . . haste: Capulet is eager to have the wedding on Thursday and so am I.

4–5 You . . . course: You don't know how Juliet feels about this. It's a very uncertain (**uneven**) plan.

13–14 Which . . . society: which, thought about too much by her in privacy, may be put from her mind if she is forced to be with others.

ANALYZE LITERARY DEVICES

Annotate: Mark two instances of dramatic irony in lines 18–25.

Analyze: What information does the audience have that a character doesn't? How does this information create suspense?

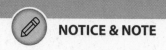
Juliet. I will confess to you that I love him.

   Paris. So will ye, I am sure, that you love me.

   Juliet. If I do so, it will be of more price,
   Being spoke behind your back, than to your face.

   Paris. Poor soul, thy face is much abused with tears.

30 **Juliet.** The tears have got small victory by that,
   For it was bad enough before their spite.

   Paris. Thou wrongst it more than tears with that report.

   Juliet. That is no slander, sir, which is a truth;
   And what I spake, I spake it to my face.

35 **Paris.** Thy face is mine, and thou hast slandered it.

   Juliet. It may be so, for it is not mine own.
   Are you at leisure, holy father, now,
   Or shall I come to you at evening mass?

   Friar Laurence. My leisure serves me, pensive daughter, now.
40 My lord, we must entreat the time alone.

   Paris. God shield I should disturb devotion!
   Juliet, on Thursday early will I rouse ye.
   Till then, adieu, and keep this holy kiss.

   [*Exit.*]

   Juliet. O, shut the door! and when thou hast done so,
45 Come weep with me—past hope, past cure, past help!

   Friar Laurence. Ah, Juliet, I already know thy grief;
   It strains me past the compass of my wits.
   I hear thou must, and nothing may prorogue it,
   On Thursday next be married to this County.

50 **Juliet.** Tell me not, friar, that thou hearest of this,
   Unless thou tell me how I may prevent it.
   If in thy wisdom thou canst give no help,
   Do thou but call my resolution wise
   And with this knife I'll help it presently.
55 God joined my heart and Romeo's, thou our hands;
   And ere this hand, by thee to Romeo's sealed,
   Shall be the label to another deed,
   Or my true heart with treacherous revolt
   Turn to another, this shall slay them both.
60 Therefore, out of thy long-experienced time,
   Give me some present counsel; or, behold,
   'Twixt my extremes and me this bloody knife
   Shall play the umpire, arbitrating that
   Which the commission of thy years and art

30–31 The tears . . . spite: The tears haven't ruined my face; it wasn't all that beautiful before they did their damage.

35 Paris says he owns Juliet's face (since she will soon marry him). Insulting her face, he says, insults him, its owner.

47–48 compass: limit; **prorogue:** postpone.

52–53 If in . . . wise: If you can't find a way to help me, at least agree that my plan is wise.

56–67 And ere this hand . . . of remedy: Before I sign another wedding agreement (**deed**), I will use this knife to kill myself. If you, with your years of experience (**long-experienced time**), can't help me, I'll end my sufferings (**extremes**) and solve the problem myself.

© Houghton Mifflin Harcourt Publishing Company

65 Could to no issue of true honor bring.
Be not so long to speak. I long to die
If what thou speak'st speak not of remedy.

Friar Laurence. Hold, daughter, I do spy a kind of hope,
Which craves as desperate an execution
70 As that is desperate which we would prevent.
If, rather than to marry County Paris,
Thou hast the strength of will to slay thyself,
Then is it likely thou wilt undertake
A thing like death to chide away this shame,
75 That copest with death himself to scape from it;
And, if thou darest, I'll give thee remedy.

Juliet. O, bid me leap, rather than marry Paris,
From off the battlements of yonder tower,
Or walk in thievish ways, or bid me lurk
80 Where serpents are; chain me with roaring bears,
Or shut me nightly in a charnel house,
O'ercovered quite with dead men's rattling bones,
With reeky shanks and yellow chapless skulls;
Or bid me go into a new-made grave
85 And hide me with a dead man in his shroud—
Things that, to hear them told, have made me tremble—
And I will do it without fear or doubt,
To live an unstained wife to my sweet love.

Friar Laurence. Hold, then. Go home, be merry, give consent
90 To marry Paris. Wednesday is tomorrow.
Tomorrow night look that thou lie alone:

71–76 If, rather than . . . remedy: If you are desperate enough to kill yourself, then you'll be daring enough to try the deathlike solution that I propose.

77–88 Juliet lists the things she would do rather than marry Paris. **charnel house:** a storehouse for bones; **reeky shanks:** stinking bones; **chapless:** without jaws.

© Houghton Mifflin Harcourt Publishing Company • Image Credits: ©Paramount/Kobal Collection/REX/Shutterstock

93 vial: small bottle.

Let not the nurse lie with thee in thy chamber.
Take thou this vial, being then in bed,
And this distilled liquor drink thou off;
95 When presently through all thy veins shall run
A cold and drowsy humor; for no pulse
Shall keep his native progress, but surcease;
No warmth, no breath, shall testify thou livest;
The roses in thy lips and cheeks shall fade

96–106 humor: liquid; **no pulse . . . pleasant sleep:** Your pulse will stop (**surcease**), and you will turn cold, pale, and stiff, as if you were dead; this condition will last for 42 hours.

100 To paly ashes, thy eyes' windows fall
Like death when he shuts up the day of life;
Each part, deprived of supple government,
Shall, stiff and stark and cold, appear like death;
And in this borrowed likeness of shrunk death
105 Thou shalt continue two-and-forty hours,
And then awake as from a pleasant sleep.
Now, when the bridegroom in the morning comes
To rouse thee from thy bed, there art thou dead.
Then, as the manner of our country is,
110 In thy best robes uncovered on the bier

111–112 same ancient vault . . . lie: same ancient tomb where all members of the Capulet family are buried.

Thou shalt be borne to that same ancient vault
Where all the kindred of the Capulets lie.
In the meantime, against thou shalt awake,
Shall Romeo by my letters know our drift;

114 drift: plan.

115 And hither shall he come; and he and I
Will watch thy waking, and that very night
Shall Romeo bear thee hence to Mantua.
And this shall free thee from this present shame,
If no inconstant toy nor womanish fear

119–120 inconstant toy: foolish whim; **abate thy valor:** weaken your courage.

120 Abate thy valor in the acting it.

Juliet. Give me, give me! O, tell me not of fear!

Friar Laurence. Hold! Get you gone, be strong and prosperous
In this resolve. I'll send a friar with speed
To Mantua, with my letters to thy lord.

125 **Juliet.** Love give me strength! and strength shall help afford.
Farewell, dear father.

[*Exeunt*]

Scene 2 *Capulet's house.*

[*Enter* Capulet, Lady Capulet, Nurse, *and* Servingmen.]

Capulet. So many guests invite as here are writ.

[*Exit a* Servingman.]

Sirrah, go hire me twenty cunning cooks.

1–8 Capulet is having a cheerful conversation with his servants about the wedding preparations. One servant assures him that he will test (**try**) the cooks he hires by making them taste their own food (**lick their fingers**).

Servingman. You shall have none ill, sir; for I'll try if they can lick their fingers.

5 **Capulet.** How canst thou try them so?

Servingman. Marry, sir, 'tis an ill cook that cannot lick his own fingers. Therefore he that cannot lick his fingers goes not with me.

Capulet. Go, begone.

[*Exit a* Servingman.]

10 We shall be much unfurnished for this time. What, is my daughter gone to Friar Laurence?

10 unfurnished: unprepared.

Nurse. Ay, forsooth.

Capulet. Well, he may chance to do some good on her. A peevish self-willed harlotry it is.

14 A silly, stubborn girl she is.

[*Enter* Juliet.]

15 **Nurse.** See where she comes from shrift with merry look.

Capulet. How now, my headstrong? Where have you been gadding?

Juliet. Where I have learnt me to repent the sin Of disobedient opposition To you and your behests, and am enjoined

19 behests: orders; **enjoined:** commanded.

20 By holy Laurence to fall prostrate here To beg your pardon. Pardon, I beseech you! Henceforward I am ever ruled by you.

Capulet. Send for the County. Go tell him of this. I'll have this knot knit up tomorrow morning.

24 I'll have this wedding scheduled for tomorrow morning.

25 **Juliet.** I met the youthful lord at Laurence' cell And gave him what becomed love I might, Not stepping o'er the bounds of modesty.

Capulet. Why, I am glad on't. This is well. Stand up. This is as't should be. Let me see the County.

30 Ay, marry, go, I say, and fetch him hither. Now, afore God, this reverend holy friar, All our whole city is much bound to him.

Juliet. Nurse, will you go with me into my closet To help me sort such needful ornaments

35 As you think fit to furnish me tomorrow?

36–39 Lady Capulet urges her husband to wait until Thursday as originally planned. She needs time to get food (**provision**) ready for the wedding party.

Lady Capulet. No, not till Thursday. There is time enough.

Capulet. Go, nurse, go with her. We'll to church tomorrow.

[*Exeunt* Juliet *and* Nurse.]

Lady Capulet. We shall be short in our provision. 'Tis now near night.

39–46 Capulet is so set on Wednesday that he promises to make the arrangements himself.

Capulet. Tush, I will stir about,

© Houghton Mifflin Harcourt Publishing Company

© Houghton Mifflin Harcourt Publishing Company

ANALYZE PARALLEL PLOTS

Annotate: Mark evidence of Lord Capulet's feelings regarding Juliet's wedding to Paris.

Compare: How does Shakespeare contrast Juliet's wedding to Romeo with her upcoming wedding to Paris?

3 orisons: prayers.

7–8 we have . . . tomorrow: We have picked out (**culled**) everything appropriate for the wedding tomorrow.

ANALYZE LITERARY DEVICES

Annotate: Mark an instance of foreshadowing in the text.

Analyze: What does this detail imply about how Juliet's plan will ultimately result?

23 This shall forbid it: A dagger will be her alternative means of keeping from marrying Paris.

24–58 Juliet lists her various doubts and fears about what she is about to do.

40 And all things shall be well, I warrant thee, wife.
    Go thou to Juliet, help to deck up her.
    I'll not to bed tonight; let me alone.
    I'll play the housewife for this once. What, ho!
    They are all forth; well, I will walk myself
45 To County Paris, to prepare him up
    Against tomorrow. My heart is wondrous light,
    Since this same wayward girl is so reclaimed.

[*Exeunt.*]

Scene 3 *Juliet's bedroom.*

[*Enter* Juliet *and* Nurse.]

Juliet. Ay, those attires are best; but, gentle nurse,
    I pray thee leave me to myself tonight;
    For I have need of many orisons
    To move the heavens to smile upon my state,
5 Which, well thou knowest, is cross and full of sin.

[*Enter* Lady Capulet.]

Lady Capulet. What, are you busy, ho? Need you my help?

Juliet. No madam; we have culled such necessaries
    As are behooveful for our state tomorrow.
    So please you, let me now be left alone,
10 And let the nurse this night sit up with you;
    For I am sure you have your hands full all
    In this so sudden business.

Lady Capulet.   Good night.
    Get thee to bed and rest, for thou hast need.

[*Exeunt* Lady Capulet *and* Nurse.]

Juliet. Farewell! God knows when we shall meet again.
15 I have a faint cold fear thrills through my veins
    That almost freezes up the heat of life.
    I'll call them back again to comfort me.
    Nurse!—What should she do here?
    My dismal scene I needs must act alone.
20 Come, vial.
    What if this mixture do not work at all?
    Shall I be married then tomorrow morning?
    No, no! This shall forbid it. Lie thou there.

[*lays down a dagger*]

    What if it be a poison which the friar
25 Subtly hath ministered to have me dead,
    Lest in this marriage he should be dishonored
    Because he married me before to Romeo?

I fear it is; and yet methinks it should not,
For he hath still been tried a holy man.
30 How if, when I am laid into the tomb,
I wake before the time that Romeo
Come to redeem me? There's a fearful point!
Shall I not then be stifled in the vault,
To whose foul mouth no healthsome air breathes in,
35 And there die strangled ere my Romeo comes?
Or, if I live, is it not very like
The horrible conceit of death and night,
Together with the terror of the place—
As in a vault, an ancient receptacle
40 Where for this many hundred years the bones
Of all my buried ancestors are packed;
Where bloody Tybalt, yet but green in earth,
Lies fest'ring in his shroud; where, as they say,
At some hours in the night spirits resort—
45 Alack, alack, is it not like that I,
So early waking—what with loathsome smells,
And shrieks like mandrakes torn out of the earth,
That living mortals, hearing them, run mad—
O, if I wake, shall I not be distraught,
50 Environed with all these hideous fears,
And madly play with my forefathers' joints,
And pluck the mangled Tybalt from his shroud,
And, in this rage, with some great kinsman's bone

36–43 Juliet fears the vision (**conceit**) she might have on waking in the family tomb and seeing the rotting body of Tybalt.

45–54 She fears that the smells together with the sounds of ghosts screaming might make her lose her mind and commit bizarre acts. Mandrake root was thought to look like the human form and to scream when pulled from the ground.

© Houghton Mifflin Harcourt Publishing Company

As with a club dash out my desp'rate brains?
55 O, look! methinks I see my cousin's ghost
Seeking out Romeo, that did spit his body
Upon a rapier's point. Stay, Tybalt, stay!
Romeo, I come! this do I drink to thee.

[*She drinks and falls upon her bed within the curtains.*]

Scene 4 *Capulet's house.*

[*Enter* Lady Capulet *and* Nurse.]

Lady Capulet. Hold, take these keys and fetch more spices, nurse.

Nurse. They call for dates and quinces in the pastry.

[*Enter* Capulet.]

Capulet. Come, stir, stir, stir! The second cock hath crowed,
The curfew bell hath rung, 'tis three o'clock.
5 Look to the baked meats, good Angelica;
Spare not for cost.

Nurse.   Go, you cot-quean, go,
Get you to bed! Faith, you'll be sick tomorrow
For this night's watching.

Capulet. No, not a whit. What, I have watched ere now
10 All night for lesser cause, and ne'er been sick.

Lady Capulet. Ay, you have been a mouse-hunt in your time;
But I will watch you from such watching now.

[*Exeunt* Lady Capulet *and* Nurse.]

Capulet. A jealous hood, a jealous hood!

[*Enter three or four* Servants, *with spits and logs and baskets.*]

                                        Now, fellow,

What is there?

15 **First Servant.** Things for the cook, sir; but I know not what.

Capulet. Make haste, make haste. [*Exit* Servant.] Sirrah, fetch
    drier logs.
Call Peter; he will show thee where they are.

Second Servant. I have a head, sir, that will find out logs
And never trouble Peter for the matter.

20 **Capulet.** Mass, and well said, merry whoreson, ha!
Thou shalt be loggerhead. [*Exit* Servant.] Good faith, 'tis day.
The County will be here with music straight,
For so he said he would. [*music within*] I hear him near.
Nurse! Wife! What, ho! What, nurse, I say!

[*Reenter* Nurse.]

---

57 stay: stop.

2 pastry: the room where baking is done.

5 Angelica: In his happy mood, Capulet calls the nurse by her name.

6 cot-quean: a "cottage quean," or housewife. This is a joke about Capulet doing women's work (arranging the party).

11–13 Lord and Lady Capulet joke about his being a woman chaser (**mouse-hunt**) as a young man. He makes fun of her jealousy (**jealous hood**).

20–23 The joking between Capulet and his servants includes the mild oath **Mass**, short for "by the Mass," and **loggerhead**, a word for a stupid person as well as a pun, since the servant is searching for drier logs. **straight:** right away.

25 Go waken Juliet; go and trim her up.
  I'll go and chat with Paris. Hie, make haste,
  Make haste! The bridegroom he is come already:
  Make haste, I say.

[*Exeunt.*]

Scene 5 *Juliet's bedroom.*

[*Enter* Nurse.]

Nurse. Mistress! what, mistress! Juliet! Fast, I warrant her, she.
  Why, lamb! why, lady! Fie, you slugabed!
  Why, love, I say! madam! sweetheart! Why, bride!
  What, not a word? You take your pennyworths now,
5 Sleep for a week; for the next night, I warrant,
  The County Paris hath set up his rest
  That you shall rest but little. God forgive me,
  Marry and amen, how sound is she asleep!
  I needs must wake her. Madam, madam, madam!
10 Aye, let the County take you in your bed,
  He'll fright you up, i' faith. Will it not be?

[*opens the curtains*]

  What, dressed and in your clothes and down again?
  I must needs wake you. Lady! lady! lady!
  Alas, alas! Help, help! my lady's dead!
15 O well-a-day that ever I was born!
  Some aqua vitae, ho! My lord! my lady!

[*Enter* Lady Capulet.]

Lady Capulet. What noise is here?

Nurse.   O lamentable day!

Lady Capulet. What is the matter?

Nurse.   Look, look! O heavy day!

Lady Capulet. O me, O me! My child, my only life!
20 Revive, look up, or I will die with thee!
  Help! help! Call help.

[*Enter* Capulet.]

Capulet. For shame, bring Juliet forth; her lord is come.

Nurse. She's dead, deceased; she's dead! Alack the day!

Lady Capulet. Alack the day, she's dead, she's dead, she's dead!

25 **Capulet.** Ha! let me see her. Out alas! she's cold,
  Her blood is settled, and her joints are stiff;
  Life and these lips have long been separated.
  Death lies on her like an untimely frost

© Houghton Mifflin Harcourt Publishing Company

1–11 The nurse chatters as she bustles around the room. She calls Juliet a **slugabed**, or sleepyhead, who is trying to get her **pennyworths**, or small portions, of rest now, since after the wedding Paris won't let her get much sleep.

17 lamentable: filled with grief.

Upon the sweetest flower of all the field.

30 **Nurse.** O lamentable day!

Lady Capulet.   O woeful time!

Capulet. Death, that hath ta'en her hence to make me wail,
Ties up my tongue and will not let me speak.

[*Enter* Friar Laurence *and* Paris, *with* Musicians.]

Friar Laurence. Come, is the bride ready to go to church?

Capulet. Ready to go, but never to return.
35 O son, the night before thy wedding day
Hath death lain with thy wife. See, there she lies,
Flower as she was, deflowered by him.
Death is my son-in-law, Death is my heir;
My daughter he hath wedded. I will die
40 And leave him all. Life, living, all is Death's.

40 Life . . . Death's: My life, my possessions, and everything else of mine belongs to Death.

Paris. Have I thought long to see this morning's face,
And doth it give me such a sight as this?

Lady Capulet. Accursed, unhappy, wretched, hateful day!
Most miserable hour that e'er time saw
45 In lasting labor of his pilgrimage!
But one, poor one, one poor and loving child,
But one thing to rejoice and solace in,
And cruel Death hath catched it from my sight!

46–48 But one . . . my sight: I had only one child to make me happy, and Death has taken (**catched**) her from me.

Nurse. O woe! O woeful, woeful, woeful day!
50 Most lamentable day, most woeful day
That ever, ever I did yet behold!
O day! O day! O day! O hateful day!
Never was seen so black a day as this.
O woeful day! O woeful day!

55 Beguiled: tricked

55 **Paris.** Beguiled, divorced, wronged, spited, slain!
Most detestable Death, by thee beguiled,
By cruel, cruel thee quite overthrown!
O love! O life! not life, but love in death!

Capulet. Despised, distressed, hated, martyred, killed!
60 Uncomfortable time, why camest thou now
To murder, murder our solemnity?
O child! O child! my soul, and not my child!
Dead art thou, dead! alack, my child is dead,
And with my child my joys are buried!

60–61 why . . . solemnity: Why did Death have to come to murder our celebration?

65 **Friar Laurence.** Peace, ho, for shame! Confusion's cure lives not
In these confusions. Heaven and yourself
Had part in this fair maid! now heaven hath all,
And all the better is it for the maid.

Your part in her you could not keep from death,
70 But heaven keeps his part in eternal life.
The most you sought was her promotion,
For 'twas your heaven she should be advanced;
And weep ye now, seeing she is advanced
Above the clouds, as high as heaven itself?
75 O, in this love, you love your child so ill
That you run mad, seeing that she is well.
She's not well married that lives married long,
But she's best married that dies married young.
Dry up your tears and stick your rosemary
80 On this fair corse, and, as the custom is,
In all her best array bear her to church;
For though fond nature bids us all lament,
Yet nature's tears are reason's merriment.

    Capulet. All things that we ordained festival
85 Turn from their office to black funeral—
Our instruments to melancholy bells,
Our wedding cheer to a sad burial feast;
Our solemn hymns to sullen dirges change;
Our bridal flowers serve for a buried corse;
90 And all things change them to the contrary.

    Friar Laurence. Sir, go you in; and, madam, go with him;
And go, Sir Paris. Every one prepare
To follow this fair corse unto her grave.
The heavens do lower upon you for some ill;
95 Move them no more by crossing their high will.

65–78 The friar says that the cure for disaster (**confusion**) cannot be found in cries of grief. Juliet's family and heaven once shared her; now heaven has all of her. All the family ever wanted was the best for her; now she's in heaven—what could be better than that? It is best to die young, when the soul is still pure, without sin.

79–80 stick . . . corse: Put rosemary, an herb, on her corpse.

82–83 though . . . merriment: Though it's natural to cry, common sense tells us we should rejoice for the dead.

84 ordained festival: intended for the wedding.

88 sullen dirges: sad, mournful tunes.

94–95 The heavens . . . will: The fates (**heavens**) frown on you for some wrong you have done. Don't tempt them by refusing to accept their will (Juliet's death).

[*Exeunt* Capulet, Lady Capulet, Paris, *and* Friar.]

First Musician. Faith, we may put up our pipes, and be gone.

Nurse. Honest good fellows, ah, put up, put up,
For well you know this is a pitiful case.

[*Exit.*]

Second Musician. Aye, by my troth, the case may be amended.

[*Enter* Peter.]

100 **Peter.** Musicians, oh, musicians, "Heart's ease, heart's ease." Oh,
an you will have me live, play "Heart's ease."

First Musician. Why "Heart's ease"?

Peter. Oh, musicians, because my heart itself plays "My heart is
full of woe." Oh, play me some merry dump, to comfort me.

105 **First Musician.** Not a dump we, 'tis no time to play now.

Peter. You will not, then?

First Musician. No.

Peter. I will then give it you soundly.

First Musician. What will you give us?

110 **Peter.** No money, on my faith, but the gleek. I will give you the
minstrel.

First Musician. Then will I give you the serving creature.

Peter. Then will I lay the serving creature's dagger
on your pate. I will carry no crotchets. I'll re you,
I'll fa you, do you note me?

115 **First Musician.** An you re us and fa us, you note us.

Second Musician. Pray you put up your dagger, and put out your wit.

Peter. Then have at you with my wit! I will drybeat
you with an iron wit, and put up my iron dagger.
Answer me like men:
120   "When griping grief the heart doth wound
           And doleful dumps the mind oppress,
             Then music with her silver sound—
Why "silver sound"? Why "music with her silver sound"? What
say you, Simon Catling?

125 **First Musician.** Marry, sir, because silver hath a sweet sound.

Peter. Pretty! What say you, Hugh Rebeck?

Second Musician. I say "silver sound" because musicians
sound for silver.

Peter. Pretty too! What say you, James Soundpost?

130 **Third Musician.** Faith, I know not what to say.

113 pate: top of the head.

Peter. Oh, I cry you mercy, you are the singer. I will say for you. It is "music with her silver sound" because musicians have no gold for sounding.

    "Then music with her silver sound
135   With speedy help doth lend redress."

[*Exit.*]

First Musician. What a pestilent knave is this same!

Second Musician. Hang him, Jack! Come, we'll in here. Tarry for the mourners, and stay dinner.

[*Exeunt.*]

136 pestilent: bothersome; irritating.

CHECK YOUR UNDERSTANDING

Answer these questions before moving on to the **Analyze the Text** section on the following page.

1 What two possibilities does Juliet worry about when she goes to drink from the vial from Friar Laurence?

  A That she will have to marry Paris or that her marriage to Romeo will be revealed

  B That Paris will learn of her plan or that Friar Laurence will tell her father about it

  C That she won't see her mother or her nurse again

  D That the potion will either do nothing or kill her

2 The playwright has Nurse and Lady Capulet repeat "She's dead" throughout lines 23–24 in Scene 5 order to —

  F make sure the audience knows what happened

  G demonstrate the depth of the characters' grief

  H provide context for the following scene

  J symbolize the finality of death

3 Which statement best summarizes the interaction between Peter and the musicians?

  A Peter tries to get the musicians to play but they refuse.

  B Peter tries to get the musicians to leave but they stay.

  C The musicians try to get Peter to pay them but he leaves.

  D The musicians try to get Peter to join them but he refuses.

ANALYZE THE TEXT

Support your responses with evidence from the text. ⊟ NOTEBOOK

1. **Analyze** Review Juliet's dialogue with Paris in Scene 1. If Juliet had never met Romeo, might she have fallen in love with Paris? Explain your response.

2. **Identify** Shakespeare often employs a literary technique known as dramatic irony. **Dramatic irony** exists when the reader or viewer knows something that one or more of the characters does not. For example, when Paris asks Juliet to confess to Friar Laurence that she loves him, she carefully avoids denying it. We know that Juliet loves Romeo, not Paris. Identify two other examples of dramatic irony in Act IV. Explain how these ironic moments contribute to the building tension in the play.

3. **Analyze** In Scene 2, how does Shakespeare increase the pace of the plot even further? What effect is this likely to have on the audience?

4. **Compare** Juliet drinks the sleeping potion, despite her fears. What does this reveal about her character? Has she changed from the beginning of the play, before she met Romeo? Explain your response.

5. **Notice & Note** Shakespeare includes **comic relief,** a humorous exchange between Peter and the musicians, at the end of Act IV just after Juliet's family discovers her body. What is the impact of this choice on the audience? What message is conveyed by contrasting a humorous scene with a tragic one?

CREATE AND DISCUSS

Participate in a Dramatic Reading In a small group, prepare a dramatic reading of a scene from *The Tragedy of Romeo and Juliet,* Act IV.

- ❏ Choose a scene and assign roles to each member of the group. Include the role of a narrator to read the stage directions.

- ❏ Highlight or underline your character's lines. Mark notes beside the lines to indicate how you think each line should be read. Think about when you might change your tone, adjust your voice, or read more quickly or slowly.

- ❏ Practice reading through the scene as a group a few times until readers chime in smoothly with their lines. Then perform the dramatic reading for the rest of the class.

SETTING A PURPOSE

Notice the unexpected events, misunderstandings, and instances of poor timing that bring the play to its tragic end. Write down any questions you generate during reading.

ACT V

Scene 1 *A street in Mantua.*

[*Enter* Romeo.]

Romeo. If I may trust the flattering truth of sleep,
My dreams presage some joyful news at hand.
My bosom's lord sits lightly in his throne,
And all this day an unaccustomed spirit
5 Lifts me above the ground with cheerful thoughts.
I dreamt my lady came and found me dead
(Strange dream that gives a dead man leave to think!)
And breathed such life with kisses in my lips
That I revived and was an emperor.
10 Ah me! how sweet is love itself possessed,
When but love's shadows are so rich in joy!

[*Enter Romeo's servant,* Balthasar, *booted.*]

News from Verona! How now, Balthasar?
Dost thou not bring me letters from the friar?
How doth my lady? Is my father well?
15 How fares my Juliet? That I ask again,
For nothing can be ill if she be well.

Balthasar. Then she is well, and nothing can be ill.
Her body sleeps in Capels' monument,
And her immortal part with angels lives.
20 I saw her laid low in her kindred's vault
And presently took post to tell it you.
O, pardon me for bringing these ill news,
Since you did leave it for my office, sir.

Romeo. Is it e'en so? Then I defy you, stars!
25 Thou knowst my lodging. Get me ink and paper
And hire posthorses. I will hence tonight.

Balthasar. I do beseech you, sir, have patience.
Your looks are pale and wild and do import
Some misadventure.

17–19 Balthasar replies that Juliet is well, since although her body lies in the Capulets' (**Capels'**) burial vault, her soul (**her immortal part**) is with the angels.

21 presently took post: immediately rode (to Mantua).

23 you did . . . office: you gave me the duty of reporting important news to you.

24 I . . . stars: Romeo angrily challenges fate, which has caused him so much grief.

28–29 import some misadventure: suggest that something bad will happen.

Romeo.   Tush, thou art deceived.

30 Leave me and do the thing I bid thee do.

    Hast thou no letters to me from the friar?

Balthasar. No, my good lord.

Romeo.   No matter. Get thee gone

    And hire those horses. I'll be with thee straight.

[*Exit* Balthasar.]

    Well, Juliet, I will lie with thee tonight.

35 Let's see for means. O mischief, thou art swift

    To enter in the thoughts of desperate men!

    I do remember an apothecary,

    And hereabouts he dwells, which late I noted

    In tattered weeds, with overwhelming brows,

40 Culling of simples. Meager were his looks,

    Sharp misery had worn him to the bones;

    And in his needy shop a tortoise hung,

    An alligator stuffed, and other skins

    Of ill-shaped fishes; and about his shelves

45 A beggarly account of empty boxes,

    Green earthen pots, bladders, and musty seeds,

    Remnants of packthread, and old cakes of roses

    Were thinly scattered, to make up a show.

    Noting this penury, to myself I said,

50 "An if a man did need a poison now

    Whose sale is present death in Mantua,

    Here lives a caitiff wretch would sell it him."

    O, this same thought did but forerun my need,

    And this same needy man must sell it me.

55 As I remember, this should be the house.

    Being holiday, the beggar's shop is shut.

    What, ho! apothecary!

[*Enter* Apothecary.]

Apothecary.   Who calls so loud?

Romeo. Come hither, man. I see that thou art poor.

    Hold, there is forty ducats. Let me have

60 A dram of poison, such soon-speeding gear

    As will disperse itself through all the veins

    That the life-weary taker may fall dead,

    And that the trunk may be discharged of breath

    As violently as hasty powder fired

65 Doth hurry from the fatal cannon's womb.

35–40 Let's . . . means: Let me find a way (to join Juliet in death); **apothecary:** pharmacist; **tattered weeds:** ragged clothes; **culling of simples:** selecting herbs.

47 cakes of roses: rose petals pressed together to create a perfume.

49 penury: poverty.

50–52 "An if a man . . . sell it him": Though it is a crime to sell poison in Mantua, the apothecary is such a miserable (**caitiff**) wretch that he would probably do it for the money.

59 ducats: gold coins.

60–65 Romeo wants fast-acting (**soon-speeding**) poison that will work as quickly as gunpowder exploding in a cannon.

Apothecary. Such mortal drugs I have; but Mantua's law
Is death to any he that utters them.

Romeo. Art thou so bare and full of wretchedness
And fearest to die? Famine is in thy cheeks,

70 Need and oppression starveth in thine eyes,
Contempt and beggary hangs upon thy back;
The world is not thy friend, nor the world's law,
The world affords no law to make thee rich;
Then be not poor, but break it and take this.

75 **Apothecary.** My poverty but not my will consents.

Romeo. I pay thy poverty and not thy will.

Apothecary. Put this in any liquid thing you will
And drink it off, and if you had the strength
Of twenty men, it would dispatch you straight.

80 **Romeo.** There is thy gold—worse poison to men's souls,
Doing more murder in this loathsome world,
Than these poor compounds that thou mayst not sell.
I sell thee poison; thou hast sold me none.
Farewell. Buy food and get thyself in flesh.

85 Come, cordial and not poison, go with me
To Juliet's grave; for there must I use thee.

[*Exeunt.*]

Scene 2 *Friar Laurence's cell in Verona.*

[*Enter* Friar John.]

Friar John. Holy Franciscan friar, brother, ho!

[*Enter* Friar Laurence.]

Friar Laurence. This same should be the voice of Friar John.
Welcome from Mantua. What says Romeo?
Or, if his mind be writ, give me his letter.

5 **Friar John.** Going to find a barefoot brother out,
One of our order to associate me,
Here in this city visiting the sick,
And finding him, the searchers of the town,
Suspecting that we both were in a house

10 Where the infectious pestilence did reign,
Sealed up the doors, and would not let us forth,
So that my speed to Mantua there was stayed.

Friar Laurence. Who bare my letter, then, to Romeo?

Friar John. I could not send it—here it is again—

15 Nor get a messenger to bring it thee,

© Houghton Mifflin Harcourt Publishing Company

So fearful were they of infection.

Friar Laurence. Unhappy fortune! By my brotherhood,
The letter was not nice, but full of charge,
Of dear import, and the neglecting it
20 May do much danger. Friar John, go hence,

Get me an iron crow and bring it straight
Unto my cell.

Friar John.　　　　Brother, I'll go and bring it thee.

[*Exit.*]

Friar Laurence. Now must I to the monument alone.
Within this three hours will fair Juliet wake.
25 She will beshrew me much that Romeo
Hath had no notice of these accidents;
But I will write again to Mantua,
And keep her at my cell till Romeo come—
Poor living corse, closed in a dead man's tomb!

[*Exit.*]

Scene 3 *The cemetery that contains the Capulets' tomb.*

[*Enter* Paris *and his* Page *with flowers and a torch.*]

Paris. Give me thy torch, boy. Hence, and stand aloof.
Yet put it out, for I would not be seen.
Under yond yew tree lay thee all along,
Holding thine ear close to the hollow ground.
5 So shall no foot upon the churchyard tread
(Being loose, unfirm, with digging up of graves)
But thou shalt hear it. Whistle then to me,
As signal that thou hearst something approach.
Give me those flowers. Do as I bid thee, go.

10 **Page** [*aside*]. I am almost afraid to stand alone
Here in the churchyard; yet I will adventure.

[*withdraws*]

Paris. Sweet flower, with flowers thy bridal bed I strew

[*He strews the tomb with flowers.*]

(O woe! thy canopy is dust and stones)
Which with sweet water nightly I will dew;
15 Or, wanting that, with tears distilled by moans.
The obsequies that I for thee will keep
Nightly shall be to strew thy grave and weep.

[*The* Page *whistles.*]

© Houghton Mifflin Harcourt Publishing Company

18–20 The letter wasn't trivial (**nice**) but contained a message of great importance (**dear import**). The fact that it wasn't sent (**neglecting it**) may cause great harm.

21 iron crow: crowbar.

25–26 She . . . accidents: She will be furious with me when she learns that Romeo doesn't know what has happened.

ANALYZE LITERARY DEVICES
Annotate: Mark the oxymoron in line 29. Note that the word *corse* means "corpse."

Analyze: What emotional effect does this oxymoron create?

1 aloof: some distance away.

ANALYZE PARALLEL PLOTS
Annotate: Mark the transition between parallel plots that happens on this page.

Analyze: As the play comes to a close, Shakespeare brings together some parallel plots and the characters associated with them. What is the impact of Paris's entrance at this point in the play?

12–17 Paris promises to decorate Juliet's grave with flowers and sprinkle it with either perfume (**sweet water**) or his tears. He will perform these honoring rites (**obsequies**) every night.

The boy gives warning something doth approach.
What cursed foot wanders this way tonight
20 To cross my obsequies and true love's rite?
What, with a torch? Muffle me, night, awhile.

[*withdraws*]

[*Enter* Romeo *and* Balthasar *with a torch, a mattock, and a crow of iron.*]

Romeo. Give me that mattock and the wrenching iron.
Hold, take this letter. Early in the morning
See thou deliver it to my lord and father.
25 Give me the light. Upon thy life I charge thee,
Whate'er thou hearest or seest, stand all aloof
And do not interrupt me in my course.
Why I descend into this bed of death
Is partly to behold my lady's face,
30 But chiefly to take thence from her dead finger
A precious ring—a ring that I must use
In dear employment. Therefore hence, be gone.
But if thou, jealous, dost return to pry
In what I farther shall intend to do,
35 By heaven, I will tear thee joint by joint
And strew this hungry churchyard with thy limbs.
The time and my intents are savage-wild,
More fierce and more inexorable far
Than empty tigers or the roaring sea.

40 **Balthasar.** I will be gone, sir, and not trouble you.

Romeo. So shalt thou show me friendship. Take thou that.
Live, and be prosperous; and farewell, good fellow.

Balthasar [*aside*]. For all this same, I'll hide me hereabout.
His looks I fear, and his intents I doubt.

[*withdraws*]

45 **Romeo.** Thou detestable maw, thou womb of death,
Gorged with the dearest morsel of the earth,
Thus I enforce thy rotten jaws to open,
And in despite I'll cram thee with more food.

[Romeo *opens the tomb.*]

Paris. This is that banish'd haughty Montague
50 That murdered my love's cousin—with which grief
It is supposed the fair creature died—
And here is come to do some villainous shame
To the dead bodies. I will apprehend him.
Stop thy unhallowed toil, vile Montague!
55 Can vengeance be pursued further than death?

Condemned villain, I do apprehend thee.
Obey, and go with me; for thou must die.

Romeo. I must indeed; and therefore came I hither.
Good gentle youth, tempt not a desp'rate man.
60 Fly hence and leave me. Think upon these gone;
Let them affright thee. I beseech thee, youth,
Put not another sin upon my head
By urging me to fury. O, be gone!
By heaven, I love thee better than myself.
65 For I come hither armed against myself.
Stay not, be gone. Live, and hereafter say
A madman's mercy bid thee run away.

Paris. I do defy thy conjuration
And apprehend thee for a felon here.

70 **Romeo.** Wilt thou provoke me? Then have at thee, boy!

[*They fight.*]

Page. O Lord, they fight! I will go call the watch.

[*Exit.*]

Paris. O, I am slain! [*falls*] If thou be merciful,
Open the tomb, lay me with Juliet.

[*dies.*]

Romeo. In faith, I will. Let me peruse this face.
75 Mercutio's kinsman, noble County Paris!
What said my man when my betossed soul
Did not attend him as we rode? I think
He told me Paris should have married Juliet.
Said he not so? or did I dream it so?
80 Or am I mad, hearing him talk of Juliet,
To think it was so? O, give me thy hand,
One writ with me in sour misfortune's book!
I'll bury thee in a triumphant grave.
A grave? O, no, a lantern, slaughtered youth,
85 For here lies Juliet, and her beauty makes
This vault a feasting presence full of light.
Death, lie thou there, by a dead man interred.

[*lays Paris in the tomb.*]

How oft when men are at the point of death
Have they been merry! which their keepers call
90 A lightning before death. O, how may I
Call this a lightning? O my love! my wife!

68 I reject your appeal.

LANGUAGE CONVENTIONS
Annotate: Parallel structure is the repetition of words, phrases, or grammatical structures to add emphasis or to improve the sound and rhythm of text. Mark the syllable that Romeo repeats several times in his parting speech in lines 74 to 120.

Analyze: What is Shakespeare's purpose in using parallel structure here? What is its impact?

82 Romeo notes that, like himself, Paris has been a victim of bad luck.

84–87 Romeo will bury Paris with Juliet, whose beauty fills the tomb with light. Paris' corpse (**Death**) is being buried (**interred**) by a dead man in that Romeo expects to be dead soon.

© Houghton Mifflin Harcourt Publishing Company

94 ensign: sign

98–100 O, what . . . enemy: I can best repay you (Tybalt) by killing your enemy (myself) with the same hand that cut your youth in two (**twain**).

102–105 Romeo can't get over how beautiful Juliet still looks. He asks whether Death is loving (**amorous**) and whether it has taken Juliet as its lover (**paramour**).

111–112 shake . . . flesh: rid myself of the burden of an unhappy fate (**inauspicious stars**).

115 dateless: eternal; never-ending. Romeo means that what he is about to do can never be undone.

117–118 Romeo compares himself to the pilot of a ship (**bark**) who is going to crash on the rocks because he is so weary and sick.

Death, that hath sucked the honey of thy breath,
Hath had no power yet upon thy beauty.
Thou art not conquered. Beauty's ensign yet
95 Is crimson in thy lips and in thy cheeks,
And death's pale flag is not advanced there.
Tybalt, liest thou there in thy bloody sheet?
O, what more favor can I do to thee
Than with that hand that cut thy youth in twain
100 To sunder his that was thine enemy?
Forgive me, cousin! Ah, dear Juliet,
Why art thou yet so fair? Shall I believe
That unsubstantial Death is amorous,
And that the lean abhorred monster keeps
105 Thee here in dark to be his paramour?
For fear of that I still will stay with thee
And never from this palace of dim night
Depart again. Here, here will I remain
With worms that are thy chambermaids. O, here
110 Will I set up my everlasting rest
And shake the yoke of inauspicious stars
From this world-wearied flesh. Eyes, look your last!
Arms, take your last embrace! and, lips, O you
The doors of breath, seal with a righteous kiss
115 A dateless bargain to engrossing death!
Come, bitter conduct; come, unsavory guide!
Thou desperate pilot, now at once run on
The dashing rocks thy seasick weary bark!
Here's to my love! [*drinks*] O true apothecary!
120 Thy drugs are quick. Thus with a kiss I die.

[*falls*]

[*Enter* Friar Laurence, *with lantern, crow, and spade.*]

Friar Laurence. Saint Francis be my speed! how oft tonight
Have my old feet stumbled at graves! Who's there?

Balthasar. Here's one, a friend, and one that knows you well.

Friar Laurence. Bliss be upon you! Tell me, good my friend,
125 What torch is yond that vainly lends his light
To grubs and eyeless skulls? As I discern,
It burneth in the Capels' monument.

Balthasar. It doth so, holy sir; and there's my master,
One that you love.

Friar Laurence.   Who is it?

Balthasar.   Romeo.

© Houghton Mifflin Harcourt Publishing Company

130 **Friar Laurence.** How long hath he been there?

Balthasar.   Full half an hour.

Friar Laurence. Go with me to the vault.

Balthasar.   I dare not, sir.
My master knows not but I am gone hence,
And fearfully did menace me with death
If I did stay to look on his intents.

135 **Friar Laurence.** Stay then; I'll go alone. Fear comes upon me.
O, much I fear some ill unthrifty thing.

Balthasar. As I did sleep under this yew tree here,
I dreamt my master and another fought,
And that my master slew him.

Friar Laurence.   Romeo!

[*stoops and looks on the blood and weapons*]

140 Alack, alack, what blood is this which stains
The stony entrance of this sepulcher?
What mean these masterless and gory swords
To lie discolored by this place of peace?

[*enters the tomb*]

Romeo! O, pale! Who else? What, Paris too?
145 And steeped in blood? Ah, what an unkind hour
Is guilty of this lamentable chance!
The lady stirs.

[Juliet *rises.*]

Juliet. O comfortable friar! where is my lord?
I do remember well where I should be,
150 And there I am. Where is my Romeo?

Friar Laurence. I hear some noise. Lady, come from that nest
Of death, contagion, and unnatural sleep.
A greater power than we can contradict
Hath thwarted our intents. Come, come away.
155 Thy husband in thy bosom there lies dead;
And Paris too. Come, I'll dispose of thee
Among a sisterhood of holy nuns.
Stay not to question, for the watch is coming.
Come, go, good Juliet. I dare no longer stay.

160 **Juliet.** Go, get thee hence, for I will not away.

[*Exit* Friar Laurence.]

132–134 My master . . . intents: My master told me to go away and threatened me with death if I watched what he did.

136 unthrifty: unlucky.

140–143 Alack . . . place of peace? Why are these bloody swords lying here at the tomb (**sepulcher**), a place that should be peaceful? (The swords are also **masterless**, or without their owners.)

148 comfortable: comforting.

153–154 A greater . . . intents: A greater force than we can fight (**contradict**) has ruined our plans (**thwarted our intents**).

156–157 I'll dispose . . . nuns: I'll find a place for you in a convent of nuns.

What's here? A cup, closed in my true love's hand?
Poison, I see, hath been his timeless end.
O churl! drunk all, and left no friendly drop
To help me after? I will kiss thy lips.
165 Haply some poison yet doth hang on them
To make me die with a restorative.

[*kisses him*]

Thy lips are warm!

Chief Watchman [*within*]. Lead, boy. Which way?

Juliet. Yea, noise? Then I'll be brief. O happy dagger!

[*snatches Romeo's dagger*]

170 This is thy sheath; there rust, and let me die.

[*She stabs herself and falls.*]

[*Enter* Watchmen *with the* Page *of Paris.*]

Page. This is the place. There, where the torch doth burn.

Chief Watchman. The ground is bloody. Search about the
churchyard.

Go, some of you; whoe'er you find attach.

[*Exeunt some of the* Watch.]

Pitiful sight! here lies the County slain;
175 And Juliet bleeding, warm, and newly dead,
Who here hath lain this two days buried.
Go, tell the Prince; run to the Capulets;
Raise up the Montagues; some others search.

[*Exeunt others of the* Watch.]

We see the ground whereon these woes do lie,
180 But the true ground of all these piteous woes
We cannot without circumstance descry.

[*Reenter some of the* Watch, *with* Balthasar.]

Second Watchman. Here's Romeo's man. We found him in the
churchyard.

Chief Watchman. Hold him in safety till the Prince come hither.

[*Reenter* Friar Laurence *and another* Watchman.]

Third Watchman. Here is a friar that trembles, sighs, and weeps.
185 We took this mattock and this spade from him
As he was coming from this churchyard side.

Chief Watchman. A great suspicion! Stay the friar too.

[*Enter the* Prince *and* Attendants.]

162 timeless: happening
before its proper time.

163 churl: miser.

165 Haply: perhaps.

173 attach: arrest.

178 Raise up: awaken.

179–181 We see . . . descry:
We see the earth (**ground**)
these bodies lie on. But the real
cause (**true ground**) of these
deaths is yet for us to discover
(**descry**).

182–187 The guards arrest
Balthasar and Friar Laurence as
suspicious characters.

© Houghton Mifflin Harcourt Publishing Company

Prince. What misadventure is so early up,
That calls our person from our morning rest?

[*Enter* Capulet, Lady Capulet, *and others.*]

190 **Capulet.** What should it be, that they so shriek abroad?

Lady Capulet. The people in the street cry "Romeo,"
Some "Juliet," and some "Paris"; and all run,
With open outcry, toward our monument.

Prince. What fear is this which startles in our ears?

195 **Chief Watchman.** Sovereign, here lies the County Paris slain;
And Romeo dead, and Juliet, dead before,
Warm and new killed.

Prince. Search, seek, and know how this foul murder comes.

Chief Watchman. Here is a friar, and slaughtered Romeo's man,
200 With instruments upon them fit to open
These dead men's tombs.

Capulet. O heavens! O wife, look how our daughter bleeds!
This dagger hath mista'en, for, lo, his house
Is empty on the back of Montague,
205 And it missheathed in my daughter's bosom!

203–205 This dagger . . . in my daughter's bosom: This dagger has missed its target. It should rest in the sheath (**house**) that Romeo wears. Instead it is in Juliet's chest.

Lady Capulet. O me! this sight of death is as a bell
That warns my old age to a sepulcher.

[*Enter* Montague *and others.*]

Prince. Come, Montague; for thou art early up
To see thy son and heir now early down.

210 **Montague.** Alas, my liege, my wife is dead tonight!
Grief of my son's exile hath stopped her breath.
What further woe conspires against mine age?

Prince. Look, and thou shalt see.

Montague. O thou untaught! what manners is in this,
215 To press before thy father to a grave?

214–215 what manners . . . grave: What kind of behavior is this, for a son to die before his father?

Prince. Seal up the mouth of outrage for a while,
Till we can clear these ambiguities
And know their spring, their head, their true descent;
And then will I be general of your woes
220 And lead you even to death. Meantime forbear,
And let mischance be slave to patience.
Bring forth the parties of suspicion.

216–221 Seal . . . patience: Stop your emotional outbursts until we can find out the source (**spring**) of these confusing events (**ambiguities**). Wait (**forbear**) and be patient, and let's find out what happened.

Friar Laurence. I am the greatest, able to do least,
Yet most suspected, as the time and place
225 Doth make against me, of this direful murder;
And here I stand, both to impeach and purge

© Houghton Mifflin Harcourt Publishing Company

Myself condemned and myself excused.

Prince. Then say at once what thou dost know in this.

Friar Laurence. I will be brief, for my short date of breath
230   Is not so long as is a tedious tale.
      Romeo, there dead, was husband to that Juliet;
      And she, there dead, that Romeo's faithful wife.
      I married them; and their stol'n marriage day
      Was Tybalt's doomsday, whose untimely death
235   Banish'd the new-made bridegroom from this city;
      For whom, and not for Tybalt, Juliet pined.
      You, to remove that siege of grief from her,
      Betrothed and would have married her perforce
      To County Paris. Then comes she to me
240   And with wild looks bid me devise some mean
      To rid her from this second marriage,
      Or in my cell there would she kill herself.
      Then gave I her (so tutored by my art)
      A sleeping potion; which so took effect
245   As I intended, for it wrought on her
      The form of death. Meantime I writ to Romeo
      That he should hither come as this dire night
      To help to take her from her borrowed grave,
      Being the time the potion's force should cease.
250   But he which bore my letter, Friar John,
      Was stayed by accident, and yesternight
      Returned my letter back. Then all alone
      At the prefixed hour of her waking
      Came I to take her from her kindred's vault;
255   Meaning to keep her closely at my cell
      Till I conveniently could send to Romeo.
      But when I came, some minute ere the time
      Of her awaking, here untimely lay
      The noble Paris and true Romeo dead.
260   She wakes; and I entreated her come forth
      And bear this work of heaven with patience;
      But then a noise did scare me from the tomb,
      And she, too desperate, would not go with me,
      But, as it seems, did violence on herself.
265   All this I know, and to the marriage
      Her nurse is privy; and if aught in this
      Miscarried by my fault, let my old life
      Be sacrificed, some hour before his time,
      Unto the rigor of severest law.

270   **Prince.** We still have known thee for a holy man.
      Where's Romeo's man? What can he say in this?

223–227 Friar Laurence confesses that he is most responsible for these events. He will both accuse (**impeach**) himself and clear (**purge**) himself of guilt.

236 It was Romeo's banishment, not Tybalt's death, that made Juliet so sad.

248 borrowed: temporary.

254 kindred's: family's.

265–269 and to . . . law: Her nurse can bear witness to this secret marriage. If I am responsible for any of this, let the law punish me with death.

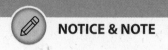
273 in post: at full speed.

279–280 The Prince asks for Paris' servant, who notified the guards (**raised the watch**). Then he asks the servant why Paris was at the cemetery.

283–285 Anon . . . call the watch: Soon (**anon**) someone with a light came and opened the tomb. Paris drew his sword, and I ran to call the guards.

292–295 See what . . . punished: Look at the punishment your hatred has brought on you. Heaven has killed your children (**joys**) with love. For shutting my eyes to your arguments (**discords**), I have lost two relatives. We have all been punished.

297–298 jointure: dowry, the payment a bride's father traditionally made to the groom. Capulet means that no one could demand more of a bride's father than he has already paid.

301 at such rate be set: be valued so highly.

303–304 Capulet promises to do for Romeo what Montague will do for Juliet. Their children have become sacrifices to their hatred (**enmity**).

Balthasar. I brought my master news of Juliet's death;
And then in post he came from Mantua
To this same place, to this same monument.
275 This letter he early bid me give his father,
And threatened me with death, going in the vault,
If I departed not and left him there.

Prince. Give me the letter. I will look on it.
Where is the County's page that raised the watch?
280 Sirrah, what made your master in this place?

Page. He came with flowers to strew his lady's grave;
And bid me stand aloof, and so I did.
Anon comes one with light to ope the tomb;
And by-and-by my master drew on him;
285 And then I ran away to call the watch.

Prince. This letter doth make good the friar's words,
Their course of love, the tidings of her death;
And here he writes that he did buy a poison
Of a poor 'pothecary, and therewithal
290 Came to this vault to die and lie with Juliet.
Where be these enemies? Capulet, Montague,
See what a scourge is laid upon your hate,
That heaven finds means to kill your joys with love!
And I, for winking at your discords too,
295 Have lost a brace of kinsmen. All are punished.

Capulet. O brother Montague, give me thy hand.
This is my daughter's jointure, for no more
Can I demand.

Montague. But I can give thee more;
For I will raise her statue in pure gold,
300 That whiles Verona by that name is known,
There shall no figure at such rate be set
As that of true and faithful Juliet.

Capulet. As rich shall Romeo's by his lady's lie—
Poor sacrifices of our enmity!

305 **Prince.** A glooming peace this morning with it brings.
The sun for sorrow will not show his head.
Go hence, to have more talk of these sad things;
Some shall be pardoned, and some punished;
For never was a story of more woe
310 Than this of Juliet and her Romeo.

[*Exeunt.*]

CHECK YOUR UNDERSTANDING

Answer these questions before moving on to the **Analyze the Text** section on the following page.

1 The apothecary's role in Act V is to —

   A serve as a foil to Friar John

   B foreshadow the fight between Romeo and Paris

   C give Romeo a practical way to carry out a plan

   D fuel the feud between the Montagues and the Capulets

2 Which line contains an oxymoron?

   F *Under yond yew tree lay thee all along*

   G *Sweet flower, with flowers thy bridal bed I strew*

   H *Nightly shall be to strew thy grave and weep.*

   J *Thou detestable maw, thou womb of death*

3 What important idea does Prince Escalus state at the end of the play?

   A It is dangerous to make assumptions.

   B A person can have only one true love.

   C The body is mortal, but the soul is immortal.

   D Hate between families can lead to tragedy.

ANALYZE THE TEXT

Support your responses with evidence from the text. ☷ NOTEBOOK

1. **Interpret** What dream does Romeo describe at the beginning of Act V, Scene 1? What part of his dream foreshadows events to come?

2. **Synthesize** *Romeo and Juliet* contains many **oxymorons**, expressions that bring together contradictory terms. Choose at least five instances in the play; then explain how this device deepens the play's themes.

3. **Connect** Recall Juliet's response when her mother suggests the idea of marrying Paris (Act I, Scene 3, lines 98–100). What does this reveal about Juliet's character before she meets Romeo? How does this contrast with Romeo's behavior in the parallel plot involving Rosaline? By Act V, how has Juliet changed?

4. **Evaluate** In a tragedy, a hero or heroine's character flaw is usually the cause of his or her downfall. Do you believe Romeo or Juliet has a character flaw that leads to his or her death? Support your response with evidence from the play.

5 **Notice & Note** In Scene 2, why is Friar Laurence in a panic when he finds out that his letter was not delivered to Romeo? Why is this Aha Moment a key turning point in the plot?

RESEARCH

RESEARCH TIP
For a brief research task that involves long literary works, look for **secondary sources,** which summarize or interpret original works. For example, if you are researching *Warm Bodies*, a young-adult novel (and later a movie) based on *Romeo and Juliet*, you can search "warm bodies novel summary" to find sources that address the questions of the research task.

Artists in many media have based works on *The Tragedy of Romeo and Juliet*. Research three of these works—songs, poems, plays, visual works of art, or musicals. Use the chart below to note how these adaptations remain true to Shakespeare's story and how they depart from it or put a different spin on it.

Extend Locate an interview with an artist who based a work of art or literature or art on a Shakespeare play. What was it about Shakespeare's work that spoke to the artist? In what way did the artist seek to transform, emphasize, or extend Shakespeare's message?

TITLE OF WORK	GENRE OF WORK	HOW IS IT TRUE TO SHAKESPEARE?	HOW DOES IT DEPART FROM SHAKESPEARE?

CREATE AND DISCUSS

Write a Eulogy With a partner, write a one-page collective eulogy—a tribute to someone who has died—for Romeo and Juliet.

❑ Brainstorm important details about Romeo, Juliet, their lives, and their relationship. Think about what motivates them, how they fall in love, the challenges they face, and how they change each other. Share information from your annotations and notes on the play.

❑ Craft your eulogy, highlighting key details about the characters of the two young people. Support your ideas with evidence from the play.

❑ If you have difficulty finding the right words to describe a character or express an idea, ask your peers or your teacher for help.

Discuss with a Small Group Share your eulogies with another pair. Discuss the challenges of casting tragic figures in a positive light—as is necessary in a eulogy—despite the fact that their own flaws contributed to their downfall.

❑ Make a collective list of the character traits your eulogies highlighted.

❑ What character traits or plot events did you omit or gloss over in your eulogies and why? Consider the audience of a eulogy, and talk about the challenge of capturing someone's life in a way that is flattering to him or her. Listen respectfully to the contributions of all group members.

❑ Reflect on your role in this activity. Make notes about what you did well and on areas for improvement.

> Go to the **Speaking and Listening Studio** for help with having a small-group discussion.

RESPOND TO THE ESSENTIAL QUESTION

 How can love bring both joy and pain?

Gather Information Review your annotations and notes on *The Tragedy of Romeo and Juliet*. Then, add relevant information to your Response Log. As you determine which information to include, think about:

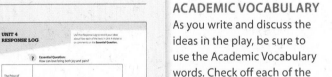

• the joy and pain that come to Shakespeare's characters as they experience love

• the metaphors of love that Shakespeare uses in the play

• the lessons about love implied by Romeo and Juliet's tragic end

At the end of the unit, use your notes to help you write a literary analysis.

ACADEMIC VOCABULARY
As you write and discuss the ideas in the play, be sure to use the Academic Vocabulary words. Check off each of the words that you use.

❑ **attribute**

❑ **commit**

❑ **expose**

❑ **initiate**

❑ **underlie**

VOCABULARY STRATEGY:
Shakespeare's Language

It takes time to get used to Shakespeare's language, but learning to unlock its layers will help you understand his continued popularity and influence. Shakespeare was a master of clever word play, including the use of **puns**. He also used many **foreign words** to add meaning and color to his writing.

A **pun** is a joke built upon multiple meanings of a word or upon two words that sound similar but have different meanings. Near the end of Act IV, Peter challenges the musicians to help him develop a pun based on a verse.

> **Peter.**   "When griping grief the heart doth wound
> And doleful dumps the mind oppress,
> Then music with her silver sound—
>
> Why "silver sound"? Why "music with her silver sound"? What
>   say you, Simon Catling?
>
> **First Musician.** Marry, sir, because silver hath a sweet sound.
>
> **Peter.** Pretty! What say you, Hugh Rebeck?
>
> **Second Musician.** I say "silver sound" because musicians sound
>   for silver.
>
> **Peter.** Pretty too! What say you, James Soundpost?
>
> **Third Musician.** Faith, I know not what to say.
>
> **Peter.** Oh, I cry you mercy, you are the singer. I will say for you.
>   It is "music with her silver sound" because musicians have no
>   gold for sounding.

The English language is filled with words of foreign origin, but Shakespeare takes this a step further and includes words and phrases that many English speakers do not know. Once translated, these lend extra depth of meaning to his work. Here are some examples from *Romeo and Juliet*:

> *ambuscadoes* (Spanish for "ambushes"), Act I, Scene 4
>
> *benedicite* (Latin for "God bless you"), Act II, Scene 3
>
> *passado, punto reverso, hay,* and *alla stoccata* (foreign terms for
> sword-fighting moves), Act II, Scene 4; Act III, Scene 1
>
> *aqua vitae* (Latin for "water of life," signifying brandy), Act III, Scene 2

Practice and Apply With a partner, locate and explain the puns below. Then brainstorm a few words that you could use in original puns. Write a brief dialogue like the one between Peter and the musicians that uses your puns.

1. "You have dancing shoes / With nimble soles; I have a soul of lead / So stakes me to the ground I cannot move." (Act I, Scene 4, lines 14–16)

2. "Ask for me tomorrow, and you/shall find me a grave man." (Act III, Scene 1, lines 91–92)

Now review the word wall that you began in Act I. Which words on your wall are foreign? How do these words enhance your experience of reading Shakespeare?

LANGUAGE CONVENTIONS:
Parallel Structure

Parallel structure is the repetition of words, phrases, or grammatical structures in order to add emphasis or to improve the sound and rhythm of a piece of writing. Shakespeare regularly makes use of parallel structure to create cadence, or a balanced, rhythmic flow of words. Here is an example from Act II, Scene 1, lines 8–11:

> Appear thou in the likeness of a sigh;
> Speak but one rhyme, and I am satisfied!
> Cry but "Ay me!" pronounce but "love" and "dove";
> Speak to my gossip Venus one fair word . . .

Shakespeare repeats the structure of a verb followed by *but*: "Speak but . . . Cry but . . . pronounce but . . ." The parallel grammatical structures give equal weight to each phrase. Any one of these three tiny gestures from Rosaline, Mercutio jokes, would cause lovesick Romeo to rejoice. Read the passage aloud to hear the cadence that the parallel structures lend to the verse.

This example from Act I, Scene 5, lines 10–11 contains a series of four past-tense verbs, each followed by the word *for*.

> You are looked for and called for, asked for
> and sought for, in the great chamber.

In this case, the speaker (a servant) sounds rather ridiculous, as if he is trying to use flowery language to deliver a simple message.

In the next example, from Act IV, Scene 1, lines 102–103, Shakespeare repeats three parallel adjectives:

> Each part, deprived of supple government,
> Shall, stiff and stark and cold, appear like death;

Friar Laurence uses these grim adjectives to describe what Juliet's body will be like once she drinks the potion. The repetition gives his speech a somber rhythm, like a funeral march.

Practice and Apply Write a paragraph about how the themes, events, or characters of *Romeo and Juliet* relate to your life or to the life of someone you know. Include at least two examples of parallel structure in your paragraph. Share your work with a partner and discuss how the parallel structure increases the power and clarity of your language.

SONNET

HAVING IT BOTH WAYS

by **Elizabeth Jennings**
pages 397–399

COMPARE POEMS

As you read, notice the structure and graphic elements of the poems. Then, think about elements the poems share. After you read both poems, you will collaborate with a small group on a final project.

 ESSENTIAL QUESTION:

How can love bring both joy and pain?

SONNET

SUPERHEART

by **Marion Shore**
pages 400–401

QUICK START

Love, in all its forms, is one of the most powerful feelings that humans experience. Whether it is the love between parent and child, a couple, or friends, the emotion of love leaves an indelible mark on everyone who experiences it. Think about examples of love that you have read about or witnessed in movies or in your life. How did those relationships affect the people involved? Share your thoughts and impressions with your group.

ANALYZE POETRY

A **sonnet** is a lyric poem composed of fourteen lines, usually written in **iambic pentameter.** An iamb is a pair of syllables, the first one stressed and the second one unstressed. The pair make up what's called a metrical foot. The *penta* in pentameter tells you there are five iambs, or syllable pairs, per line. Like this:

What liberty we have when out of love.

A sonnet follows a prescribed form and rhyming pattern. You will see different types of rhymes as you read sonnets. Traditional, or "perfect" rhymes are easy to identify. Other rhymes, called off rhymes or slant rhymes, are more subtle. For example:

Like Superman with all his super powers,	A
Cruising at lightning speed around the Earth,	B
Or leaping from Metropolis's towers,	A
Or soaring toward his fortress in the north,	B

In this stanza, *powers* and *towers* are a traditional, or perfect rhyme. But *Earth* and *north* are a rhyme as well. This type of slant rhyme is often called an eye rhyme, because the letters at the ends of the words mirror each other—they rhyme as much because they look alike as because of the way they sound.

The purpose of a sonnet is to set up a contrast between two things that are related but different, like love and vulnerability. That difference is often emphasized with a contextual twist called a *volta*, or turn. The poet can introduce the volta at any point. Often it comes near the rhyming couplet at the end—like the surprise twist at the end of a movie.

GENRE ELEMENTS: LYRIC POETRY

- usually short to convey strong emotions
- written using first-person point of view to express the speaker's thoughts and feelings
- often uses repetition and rhyme to create a melodic quality
- includes many forms, such as sonnets, odes, and elegies

CONNECT IDEAS

When reading texts, good readers look for **connections** between them, as well as connections to texts they already know. Readers may note similar themes, styles, or text structures. This similarity may not be an accident: writers are often inspired by authors who came before them. For example, Shakespeare wrote over 100 sonnets. Modern-day writers, including Elizabeth Jennings and Marion Shore, have drawn inspiration from this traditional poetic form and used it to express the universal experience of love.

ANNOTATION MODEL

NOTICE & NOTE

As you read, notice the poetic elements each writer uses. In this model, you can see one reader's notes about "Having It Both Ways."

What liberty we have when out of <u>love,</u>
Our heart's back in its place, our nerves (unstrung,)
Time cannot tease us, and once more we <u>move</u>
In step with it. Out of love we're (strong,)

Lines 1 and 3 end in the near-rhymes "love" and "move." Lines 2 and 4 also end in near-rhymes that end in an "ng" sound.

I also notice that the syllables of of these lines alternate between unstressed and stressed.

BACKGROUND

Elizabeth Jennings *(1926–2001) is known as a traditional poet who excelled at the use of meter and rhyme. She spent most of her life in Oxford, England, and published her first book of poetry at age 27. Over her lifetime, Jennings published more than twenty-five books of poetry for which she received numerous awards. She said that while her life did influence her writing, her poetry is not autobiographical.*

HAVING IT BOTH WAYS
Sonnet by Elizabeth Jennings

PREPARE TO COMPARE

As you read, note how the poet makes language choices to communicate message and tone. Specifically, think about how she uses diction and syntax to give voice to thoughts and feelings about love.

What liberty we have when out of love,
Our heart's back in its place, our nerves unstrung,
Time cannot tease us, and once more we move
In step with it. Out of love we're strong,

5 Without its yearnings and the way it makes
All virtues vices. Steady liberty
Is our element and no heartbreaks
Can touch or take us. We are nobly free.

Notice & Note

You can use the side margins to notice and note signposts in the text.

CONNECT IDEAS

Annotate: Underline the first stanza.

Respond: What do you think the poet is saying in this part of the poem? How does it connect to experiences with love that you may have read about or observed?

CONTRASTS AND CONTRADICTIONS

Notice and Note: Underline the first line of the third stanza.

Respond: What internal contrast or contradiction about her feelings is the poet revealing?

But how long can we live within this state?
10 Don't we miss the slow encroachment of
Possessive passion? Don't we half-await

Its cruel enchantments which no longer have
Power over us? O we are obdurate,
Begging for freedom, hankering for love.

CHECK YOUR UNDERSTANDING

Answer these questions about "Having It Both Ways" before moving on to the next selection.

1 In the second stanza, the poet is explaining —

   A how it feels when one sets off on a new adventure

   B how it feels when one is unencumbered by fluctuating emotions

   C how it feels when one reaches a goal before setting a new one

   D how it feels when one is constantly desiring what he does not have

2 In the fourth stanza, the poet uses the word <u>obdurate</u> to show —

   F how people repeatedly make choices that are not always wise

   G how people stubbornly pursue relationships that are not always pleasurable

   H how people repeatedly try to obtain possessions that cost too much money

   J how people stubbornly stay in relationships longer than they should

3 An important message in "Having It Both Ways" is —

   A the connection between the freedom of being able to do what you want and living by the rules of a relationship

   B the tension between wanting your partner to understand the intensity of your feelings for them and not wanting to overpower them

   C the virtuousness of liberty versus the vices of romantic love

   D the conflicting desires for emotional freedom and the feelings of being in love

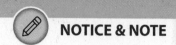
BACKGROUND

Marion Shore *(b. 1952) is an award-winning American poet and translator. Her poems—and her translations of the work of other poets—have appeared in numerous journals and anthologies. Shore's first book of original poetry,* Sand Castle, *was published in 2010. A native of Queens, New York, she lives in Belmont, Massachusetts, with her husband and two sons.*

SUPERHEART
Sonnet by Marion Shore

PREPARE TO COMPARE

As you read, look for how the poet uses contemporary pop culture references to communicate the age-old experience of being in love.

> Like Superman with all his super powers,
> Cruising at lightning speed around the Earth,
> Or leaping from Metropolis's towers,
> Or soaring toward his fortress in the north,
> 5 His mighty prowess never falling victim
> To any weapon save for (strangely enough)
> A fragment of his long-lost planet Krypton,
> Wounded by what he could not help but love,
> So I too had lately come to feel
> 10 Invulnerable, the enemy subdued,
> The bullets bouncing off my heart of steel,
> Safe in its arctic fortress of solitude,
> Or rising up in solitary flight —
> And then you came along: my kryptonite.

Notice & Note

You can use the side margins to notice and note signposts in the text

WORD GAPS

Notice and Note: Underline the word that means "in total control" or "strong" in Line 10.

Respond: How does the use of that word reinforce the imagery of Superman?

ANALYZE POETRY

Annotate: Underline the words that help you determine the rhyming pattern of the final two lines of the poem.

Respond: How does this rhyming pattern reinforce the shift introduced in these lines?

CHECK YOUR UNDERSTANDING

Answer these questions before moving on to the **Analyze the Texts** section on the following page.

1 In Lines 1 through 4, the poet —

    A asks the reader to believe that she really is a superhero

    B starts to build a simile between a superhero and the speaker

    C contrasts herself to a superhero who can do anything

    D describes how a superhero struggles to meet expectations

2 The author uses pop-culture references to —

    F explain how being in love makes people feel like a superhero

    G illustrate the theme of vulnerability in love

    H try to get graphic novel readers to read poetry

    J explain how writing makes her feel like a superhero

3 How does the last line of the poem contrast with what has come before?

    A The description of outlandish behavior at the beginning of the poem contrasts with the everyday activities at the end of the poem.

    B The calming tone at the beginning of the poem contrasts with the feelings of action at the end of the poem.

    C The discussion of a superhero at the beginning of the poem contrasts with the description of a villain at the end of the poem.

    D The image of a being who cannot be wounded contrasts with the image of one who is vulnerable.

RESPOND

ANALYZE THE TEXTS

Support your responses with evidence from the text. ⎙ NOTEBOOK

1. **Analyze** In "Having It Both Ways," lines 9-13 consist of a series of questions. How do these questions represent a shift in thought from the ideas stated in the first eight lines?

2. **Interpret** What message do you think the author of "Superheart" is trying to communicate by combining the sonnet form with a modern-day pop culture **allusion,** or reference, to Superman?

3. **Explain** In "Having It Both Ways," why does the poet extend some thoughts across two lines, rather than completing them on one line?

4. **Analyze** The author of "Having It Both Ways" uses "we" and "our" as she describes contrary desires for romantic love and independence. What is the effect of this choice on the sonnet's tone?

5. **Notice & Note** What is the effect in "Superheart" of the first 13 lines building toward one image, only to be contradicted by the last line?

RESEARCH

Poets first began to write sonnets in Italy in the 1200s. Since then, countless poets have used sonnets to communicate their messages.

Read "Having It Both Ways" and "Superheart" aloud. Then, find at least three other sonnets. Read each of them aloud several times, paying attention to **prosody**—the timing, phrasing, emphasis, and intonation appropriate to each poem. Briefly describe the theme of each. Use the chart below for your notes.

TITLE	POET	THEME
Having It Both Ways	Elizabeth Jennings	
Superheart	Marion Shore	

Extend Think about how the sonnets are similar to and different from each other. With a group, discuss how the form of the sonnet affects the message the poet is trying to communicate.

CREATE AND DISCUSS

Discuss the Poems Have a group discussion about the messages conveyed in the two sonnets.

- ❏ Think about what each poet says about love.

- ❏ Reflect on whether you agree or disagree with each poet's feelings about love. Explain why you feel that way.

- ❏ As a group, discuss what messages society communicates to us about love and relationships.

Create a Visual Response With your group, create a visual response to the messages that society communicates to us about love and relationships.

- ❏ With your group, locate five images that reflect messages society sends about love and relationships.

- ❏ Note what each image says and explain why you chose it.

Go to the **Speaking and Listening Studio** for help having a group discussion.

RESPOND TO THE ESSENTIAL QUESTION

? How can love bring both joy and pain?

Gather Information Review your annotations and notes on "Having It Both Ways" and "Superheart" and highlight those that help answer the Essential Question. Then, add relevant details to your Response Log.

As you determine which evidence to include, think about:

- what each poem says about being in love
- how each poet uses the sonnet form to communicate her message

At the end of the unit, you will use your notes to write a literary analysis.

ACADEMIC VOCABULARY

As you write and discuss what you learned from the poems, be sure to use the Academic Vocabulary words. Check off each of the words that you use.

- ❏ **attribute**
- ❏ **commit**
- ❏ **expose**
- ❏ **initiate**
- ❏ **underlie**

© Houghton Mifflin Harcourt Publishing Company

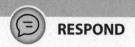

HAVING IT BOTH WAYS
Sonnet by Elizabeth Jennings

SUPERHEART
Sonnet by Marion Shore

Collaborate & Compare

COMPARE POEMS

Both "Having It Both Ways" and "Superheart" are poems about love. Even though the sonnets share a topic, they may express different themes, or messages about life. They may also differ in tone and mood. Finally, the poets may use language—diction, syntax, and figures of speech, for instance—to convey their particular messages.

Complete the chart below to examine the two poems. Be sure to support your ideas with text evidence.

	HAVING IT BOTH WAYS	SUPERHEART
Theme, or Message about Life		
Tone		
Mood		
Use of Language		

ANALYZE THE TEXTS

Discuss these questions in your group.

1. **Compare** Both poems address the highs and lows of love. Compare the **mood,** the feeling or atmosphere created; and the **tone**, or attitude, each writer takes toward the topic of love. In what ways are they similar or different?

2. **Interpret** What is the theme of each poem? Try to state each theme in one sentence. Cite text evidence in your discussion.

3. **Critique** Discuss the language that each poet uses to convey her message. Which poem do you think uses language more effectively? Why? Use text evidence to support your opinion.

4. **Evaluate** Does one poem tell the "truth" about love better than the other? Discuss this question using text evidence as well as what you have observed or read about love.

© Houghton Mifflin Harcourt Publishing Company • Image Credits: (t) ©KarenHBlack/Shutterstock; (b) ©Rawpixel.com/Adobe Stock

COLLABORATE AND PRESENT

Your group can continue exploring the ideas in these texts by collaborating on a sonnet. Follow these steps:

1. **Decide on the Topic** With your group, decide what aspect of love you would like to address. Think about how your group can bring a fresh interpretation to an age-old feeling and experience.

2. **Freewrite** Individually, take some time to freewrite about the topic. You can begin in poetic form, bullet points, or prose.

3. **Develop a Plan** Share your drafts, building on ideas from each group member to develop a final plan.

4. **Plan your sonnet** Review the elements of a sonnet:
   - 14 lines
   - Repetition of unstressed and stressed syllables
   - Often introduces a turn of thought near the end

   Decide what ideas you want to address in which stanzas, or groups of lines.

5. **Compose** Work together to write your sonnet. Your group may want to work individually or in pairs on separate stanzas or work together on the entire poem.

6. **Polish and Present** Make any needed revisions to the sonnet and share it with the class.

 Go to the **Speaking and Listening Studio** for help with giving a presentation.

INDEPENDENT READING

Reader's Choice

Setting a Purpose   Select one or more of these options from your eBook to continue your exploration of the Essential Question.

- Read the descriptions to see which text grabs your interest.
- Think about which genres you enjoy reading.

Notice & Note

In this unit, you practiced asking **Big Questions** and noticing and noting two signposts: **Word Gap** and **Numbers and Stats.** As you read independently, these signposts and others will aid your understanding. Below are the anchor questions to ask when you read literature and nonfiction.

Reading Literature: Stories, Poems, and Plays		
Signpost	**Anchor Question**	**Lesson**
Contrasts and Contradictions	Why did the character act that way?	p. 419
Aha Moment	How might this change things?	p. 171
Tough Questions	What does this make me wonder about?	p. 494
Words of the Wiser	What's the lesson for the character?	p. 171
Again and Again	Why might the author keep bringing this up?	p. 170
Memory Moment	Why is this memory important?	p. 418

Reading Nonfiction: Essays, Articles, and Arguments		
Signpost	**Anchor Question(s)**	**Lesson**
Big Questions	What surprised me? What did the author think I already knew? What challenged, changed, or confirmed what I already knew?	p. 248 p. 2 p. 84
Contrasts and Contradictions	What is the difference, and why does it matter?	p. 3
Extreme or Absolute Language	Why did the author use this language?	p. 85
Numbers and Stats	Why did the author use these numbers or amounts?	p. 249
Quoted Words	Why was this person quoted or cited, and what did this add?	p. 85
Word Gaps	Do I know this word from someplace else? Does it seem like technical talk for this topic? Do clues in the sentence help me understand the word?	p. 3 p. 249

© Houghton Mifflin Harcourt Publishing Company

You can preview these texts in Unit 4 of your eBook.

Then, check off the text or texts that you select to read on your own.

MYTH

Pyramus and Thisbe from *Metamorphoses*
Ovid

Pyramus and Thisbe have grown up as neighbors, but their families despise each other. When Pyramus and Thisbe fall in love, the result is tragedy.

SONNET

Sonnet 71
Pablo Neruda

The poet explores how we can't love in a vacuum. The world creeps into and affects our relationships.

SCIENCE WRITING

Why Love Literally Hurts
Eric Jaffe

Older couples who have been together for a long time frequently die within months or even days of each other. What does love have to do with that?

SHORT STORY

The Bass, the River, and Sheila Mant
W.D. Wetherell

What will a person sacrifice for love? Is the sacrifice always worth it?

Collaborate and Share With a partner, discuss what you learned from at least one of your independent readings.

- Give a brief synopsis or summary of the text.

- Describe any signposts that you noticed in the text and explain what they revealed to you.

- Describe what you most enjoyed or found most challenging about the text. Give specific examples.

- Decide whether you would recommend the text to others. Why or why not?

Go to the **Reading Studio** for more resources on **Notice & Note.**

Write a Literary Analysis

Go to the **Writing Studio** for help writing your literary analysis.

This unit explores the many facets of love—joy, pain, passion, and conflict— to name just a few. For this writing task, you will write a literary analysis on a topic based on this idea. Look back at the texts in the unit and consider the aspects or characteristics of love that are represented in each text. Synthesize your ideas by writing a literary analysis. For an example of a well-written analytical text you can use as a mentor text, review the essay "Love's Vocabulary." You can also use the notes you made in your Response Log after reading the texts in this unit.

Writing Prompt

Read the information in the box below.

This is the topic or context for your literary analysis.

> Love is an emotion that is easy to feel but sometimes difficult to endure.

Think carefully about the following question.

Circle the two most important words, phrases, or ideas in the prompt.

> How can love bring both joy and pain?

Think about the ideas about love you have encountered in this unit and how they are similar to and different from one another.

Write a literary analysis comparing two selections in this unit. Explain how the portrayal of love is similar and different in each text.

Review these points as you write and again when you finish. Make any needed changes.

Be sure to—

❑ provide an introduction that catches the reader's attention, clearly states the topic, and includes a clear controlling idea or thesis statement

❑ develop a comparison using examples from the texts

❑ organize central ideas in a logically structured body

❑ use appropriate register, vocabulary, tone, and voice

❑ use transitions to create connections between sections of your analysis

❑ end by summarizing ideas or drawing an overall conclusion that synthesizes the comparisons you made

① Plan

Preparation is crucial in writing a literary analysis. Review each of the selections you plan to write about. Then start to analyze similarities and differences in the way they portray the topic of love.

- What ideas about love are explored in each text?
- Take notes on how the portrayal of love is similar and different in each. In your notes, list details, examples, and quotations that support your points.

As you prepare, keep in mind your purpose and your audience. Use the chart below to help you in planning your draft.

Literary Analysis: The Nature of Love		
Aspect or Characteristic of Love:		
Text Title	**Ideas about Love**	**Details, Examples, and Quotations**
First Text:		
Second Text:		

Background Reading Review the notes you have taken in your Response Log after reading the texts in this unit. These texts provide background reading that will help you think about what you want to say in your analysis.

Go to **Writing as a Process: Introduction** for help planning your literary analysis.

Notice & Note

From Reading to Writing

As you plan your literary analysis, apply what you've learned about signposts to your own writing. Remember that writers use common features, called signposts, to help convey their message to readers.

Think about how you can incorporate **Contrasts and Contradictions** into your literary analysis.

Go to the **Reading Studio** for more resources on **Notice & Note**.

Use the notes from your Response Log as you plan your analysis.

UNIT 4
RESPONSE LOG

Essential Question:
How can love bring both joy and pain?

The Price of Freedom

Love's Vocabulary

My Shakespeare

The Tragedy of Romeo and Juliet

Having It Both Ways

Superheart

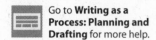

Go to **Writing as a Process: Planning and Drafting** for more help.

Organize Your Ideas After you have examined your chosen texts for ideas and evidence, organize them using the chart below. Write a clear thesis statement about how a particular aspect of love is depicted in each text. Search for an interesting quotation or detail to introduce your thesis statement. Then decide which organizational pattern you will use for the body, or middle section, of your literary analysis. You might present all your ideas about one text first, and then write about the second text. Or, you could discuss the similar ideas both texts, followed by a discussion of their differences. In the last box, write down some ideas for what you want to say in your concluding section.

Literary Analysis
Interesting Quotation or Detail to Introduce Your Thesis Statement
Thesis Statement
Body of the Analysis
Conclusion

You might prefer to draft your analysis online.

② Develop a Draft

Once you have completed your planning activities, you will be ready to begin drafting your literary analysis. Refer to your Graphic Organizers, as well as any notes you took as you studied the texts in the unit. Remember to present your ideas in logically ordered paragraphs, with one central idea for each paragraph. Use transitions to create clear connections between paragraphs and ideas. Using a word processor or online writing application makes it easier to make changes or move sentences around later when you are ready to revise your first draft.

Use the Mentor Text

Genre Characteristics

In a literary analysis, you need to support your statements with examples and evidence. Note how the author of "Love's Vocabulary" uses this example to support her statement that poets have had to "create their own private vocabularies" for love.

> Mrs. Browning sent her husband a poetic abacus of love, which in a roundabout way expressed the sum of her feelings.

The author gives an example of how Elizabeth Barrett Browning found a unique way to describe love in her poetry.

Apply What You've Learned In order to support your thesis statement, choose clear examples from the texts you are analyzing.

Author's Craft

The ideas you're presenting deserve your best efforts to express them clearly. To do that, you will need to use precise and descriptive language. Notice how the author of "Love's Vocabulary" uses language that is both expressive and exact.

> Love is the white light of emotion. It includes many feelings which, out of laziness and confusion, we crowd into one simple word.

The author uses a vivid analogy ("white light") to describe love; and she identifies two specific factors ("laziness and confusion") in our misuse of the word "love."

Apply What You've Learned State your ideas clearly, using precise language.

③ Revise

Go to **Writing as a Process: Revising and Editing** for help revising your literary analysis.

On Your Own A draft is where you get your ideas down on paper. It is the process of revision that turns that draft into a powerful piece of writing that really communicates what you're trying to say. The Revision Guide will help you focus on specific elements to make your writing stronger.

REVISION GUIDE

Ask Yourself	Tips	Revision Techniques
1. Does my introduction use an example or detail to introduce my thesis statement and make people want to read my analysis?	**Mark** the introduction.	**Add** an interesting example or detail from one of the texts you are analyzing.
2. Have I stated my thesis in a clear, coherent way?	**Underline** the thesis statement.	**Reword** the statement to make the central idea clearer.
3. In the body of the text, have I presented my key ideas in a logical, organized way?	**Mark** the sentence that introduces each important idea.	**Reorganize** your ideas to make the structure more logical.
4. Have I used effective details and examples from the literary texts to support my ideas?	**Underline** details and examples that support each idea.	**Add** more support for your ideas if necessary.
5. Are appropriate and varied transitions used to connect and contrast ideas?	**Note** transitions from paragraph to paragraph.	**Add** transition words and phrases to provide continuity.
6. Does the conclusion give the reader something to think about?	**Underline** the concluding insight offered to readers.	**Add** a final, thought-provoking statement about love.

ACADEMIC VOCABULARY

As you conduct your **peer review**, try to use these words.

❑ attribute

❑ commit

❑ expose

❑ initiate

❑ underlie

With a Partner After you have worked through the Revision Guide on your own, exchange papers with a partner. Evaluate each other's drafts in a **peer review**. Give constructive feedback to help your partner better accomplish his or her purpose in writing. Explain how you think your partner's draft should be revised and what your specific suggestions are.

④ Edit

The final step in writing your literary analysis is editing for the proper use of standard English conventions and correcting any misspellings or grammatical errors. This process helps to ensure that readers will not be confused and will be able to understand your ideas and insights.

Language Conventions

Capitalization Capitalizing certain kinds of nouns is important to provide clarity and ease of reading. In a literary analysis, there are important capitalization conventions to pay attention to.

> ❗ Go to Capital Letters in the **Grammar Studio** to learn more about capitalization.

- In **titles of literary works**, capitalize the first and last words and all other important words. Do not capitalize conjunctions, articles, and prepositions shorter than five letters.
- Capitalize the first letters of names and titles used before names.
- Capitalize the first letters of adjectives made from proper nouns.

The chart contains examples of properly capitalized names and titles.

Capitalization Type	Example
Titles	"The Price of Freedom" *The Tragedy of Romeo and Juliet* "Why Love Literally Hurts"
Names and titles	Professor Susan Holmes Doctor Kim Hong Friar Laurence
Proper Adjectives	Shakespearean British Elizabethan

⑤ Publish

Finalize your literary analysis and choose a way to share it with your audience. Consider these options:

- Present your analysis as a speech to the class.
- Post your analysis as a blog on a classroom or school website.

Use the scoring guide to evaluate your literary analysis.

WRITING TASK SCORING GUIDE: LITERARY ANALYSIS		
Organization/Progression	**Development of Ideas**	**Use of Language and Conventions**
4 • The organization is effective and appropriate to the purpose. • All ideas are focused on the topic specified in the prompt. • Transitions clearly show the relationship among ideas.	• The introduction catches the reader's attention and clearly states the central insight. • The body of the analysis compares key ideas from two texts in a clear and logical way. • The ideas are well supported by examples and details from the literary texts. • The conclusion presents a thought-provoking statement about the topic.	• Language and word choice is purposeful and precise. • The style is appropriately formal. • Spelling, capitalization, and punctuation are correct. • Grammar, usage, and mechanics are correct.
3 • The organization is, for the most part, effective and appropriate to the purpose. • Most ideas are focused on the topic specified in the prompt. • A few more transitions are needed to show the relationship among ideas.	• The introduction could be more engaging. The central insight is stated. • The body of the analysis compares key ideas from two texts in a fairly logical way. • The ideas are supported by examples and details. • The conclusion presents a statement about the topic.	• Language is for the most part specific and clear. • The style is formal, for the most part. • Some spelling, capitalization, and punctuation mistakes are present. • Some grammar and usage errors occur.
2 • The organization is evident but is not always appropriate to the purpose. • Only some ideas are focused on the topic specified in the prompt. • More transitions are needed to show the relationship among ideas.	• The introduction is not engaging. The central insight is stated, but not clearly. • The body of the analysis compares key ideas from two texts, but not in a logical way. • The ideas are supported by a few examples and details. • The statement in the conclusion is not clearly related to the topic.	• Language is somewhat vague and unclear. • The style is often informal. • Spelling, capitalization, and punctuation are often incorrect but do not make reading difficult. • Grammar and usage are often incorrect, but the writer's ideas are still clear.
1 • The organization is not appropriate to the purpose. • Ideas are not focused on the topic specified in the prompt. • No transitions are used, making the analysis difficult to follow.	• The introduction is missing or confusing. • The body of the text does not effectively compare ideas from two texts. • The conclusion is missing.	• Language is inappropriate for the text. • The style is too informal. • Many spelling, capitalization, and punctuation errors are present. • Many grammatical and usage errors confuse the writer's ideas.

Reflect on the Unit

The literary analysis that you created pulls together and expresses your thoughts about two texts in this unit. Now is a good time to reflect on what you have learned.

Reflect on the Essential Question

- How can love bring both joy and pain? How has your answer to this question changed since you first considered it when you started this unit?

- What are some examples from the texts you've read that show how love affects our lives?

Reflect on Your Reading

- Which selections were the most interesting or surprising to you?

- From which selection did you learn the most about the nature of love?

Reflect on the Writing Task

- What difficulties did you encounter while working on your literary analysis? How might you avoid them next time?

- What part of the literary analysis was the easiest and what part was the hardest to write? Why?

- What improvements did you make to your analysis as you were revising?

© Houghton Mifflin Harcourt Publishing Company

UNIT 4 SELECTIONS
- **"The Price of Freedom"**
- **"Love's Vocabulary"**
- **"My Shakespeare"**
- *The Tragedy of Romeo and Juliet*
- **"Having It Both Ways"**
- **"Superheart"**

A MATTER OF LIFE OR DEATH

? ESSENTIAL QUESTION:

What does it take to survive in a crisis?

" To endure what is unendurable is true endurance. "

Japanese proverb

© Houghton Mifflin Harcourt Publishing Company • Image Credits: (t) ©Hulton Archive/Getty Images; (b) ©duncan1890/E+/Getty Images

ACADEMIC VOCABULARY

Academic Vocabulary words are words you use when you discuss and write about texts. In this unit you will practice and learn five words.

☑ **dimension** ❑ **external** ❑ **statistic** ❑ **sustain** ❑ **utilize**

Study the Word Network to learn more about the word **dimension**.

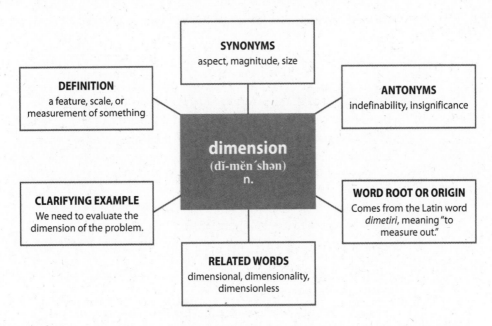

SYNONYMS
aspect, magnitude, size

DEFINITION
a feature, scale, or measurement of something

ANTONYMS
indefinability, insignificance

dimension
(dĭ-mĕn´shən)
n.

CLARIFYING EXAMPLE
We need to evaluate the dimension of the problem.

WORD ROOT OR ORIGIN
Comes from the Latin word *dimetiri*, meaning "to measure out."

RELATED WORDS
dimensional, dimensionality, dimensionless

Write and Discuss Discuss the completed Word Network with a partner, making sure to talk through all of the boxes until you both understand the word, its synonyms, antonyms, and related forms. Then, fill out Word Networks for the remaining four words. Use a dictionary or online resource to help you complete the activity.

 Go online to access the Word Networks.

RESPOND TO THE ESSENTIAL QUESTION

In this unit, you will explore how different people survive a crisis. As you read, you will revisit the **Essential Question** and gather your ideas about it in the **Response Log** that appears on page R5. At the end of the unit, you will have the opportunity to write an **argument** about whether or not survival is selfish. Filling out the Response Log will help you prepare for this writing task.

 You can also go online to access the Response Log.

UNIT 5 RESPONSE LOG

Use this Response Log to record your ideas about how each of the texts in Unit 5 relates to or comments on the **Essential Question.**

? Essential Question:
What does it take to survive in a crisis?

The Leap	
Is Survival Selfish?	
The End and the Beginning	
from Night	
from The Pianist	

Notice & Note

For more information on these and other signposts to Notice & Note, visit the **Reading Studio**.

THE LEAP

You are about to read the short story "The Leap." In it, you will notice and note signposts that provide clues about the story's characters and themes. Here are three key signposts to look for as you read this story and other works of fiction.

When you see phrases like these, pause to see if it's a **Memory Moment** signpost:

"I remember when . . ."

"That reminded me of . . ."

"This is just like when . . ."

"My mother used to tell me . . ."

Memory Moment You're telling a friend a great story about your weekend. You realize you need to tell about something that happened earlier, so your friend will get the point of the story. An author does the same thing in a Memory Moment, interrupting the narrative to tell readers a story from the past.

When an author introduces a blast from the past, it's for a good reason. Paying attention to a **Memory Moment** can:

- provide insight into the current situation
- explain character motivation, either now or in a situation still to come
- offer insight into theme
- explain one aspect of a relationship between character and plot

The paragraph below illustrates a student's annotation within "The Leap" and a response to a Memory Moment signpost.

Anchor Question
When you notice this signpost, ask: Why might this memory be important?

> I would, in fact, tend to think that all memory of double somersaults and heartstopping catches had left her arms and legs were it not for the fact that sometimes, as I sit sewing in the room of the rebuilt house in which I slept as a child, <u>I hear the crackle, catch a whiff of smoke from the stove downstairs and suddenly the room goes dark,</u> the stitches burn beneath my fingers, and I am sewing with a needle of hot silver, a thread of fire.

What memory is introduced?	The narrator remembers a house fire that occurred when she was a child.
Why do you think this memory is important to the story? What might it tell us about characters or plot?	The narrator, an adult, still remembers a childhood fire. That tells her that her mother still remembers her earlier life as a trapeze artist. The fire connects the mother and daughter in some way, but we don't yet know how.

Again and Again When something happens over and over in a text, pay attention to it. There is a reason the author chose to repeat that element, and a message you as the reader should take from it.

- Look for a recurring word, phrase, image, or event.
- If it provides insight into character motivation or theme, it may be an important element in the story.
- Ask yourself: Why might the author keep bringing this up?

Here a student marked an instance of Again and Again:

> I owe her [the narrator's mother] my existence three times. The first was when . . .

Pause to see if it's an **Again and Again** signpost when you see repetition of:

- words
- phrases
- colors
- images

Anchor Question
When you notice this signpost, ask: Why might the author keep bringing this up?

What does the narrator recognize?	three times her mother saved her or did something that led to her "existence"
What do you think this could mean? How might it change things?	These events could explain the mother/daughter relationship and why they're together now. The story may provide details about some or all of the events.

Contrasts And Contradictions What if your good friend met you every day at the same time and place to walk to class together—then one day she does not show up and she is not answering your texts. You would probably wonder what was going on: Is she okay? Is she mad at me?

A shift in a character's behavior—or a disconnect between what you expect to happen and what actually does—can grab your attention in a story the same way it does in real life. When a character thinks or does something unexpected, take the time to figure out what it means. In this example a student marked a Contrast and Contradiction.

When you see phrases like these, pause to see if it's a **Contrasts and Contradictions** signpost:

"This seems different from . . ."

"This is puzzling because . . ."

"This goes against . . ."

"This surprised me because . . ."

> . . . she shows so little of the drama or flair one might expect from a performer that I tend to forget the Flying Avalons. She has kept no sequined costume, no photographs, no fliers or posters from that part of her youth.

Anchor Question
When you notice this signpost, ask: Why would the character act or feel this way?

What contradiction is expressed here?	The narrator's mother was once a highly skilled performer in a glamorous circus act. She doesn't talk about that part of her life and has kept no mementos of that time.
What insight might this provide about the narrator's mother?	Maybe something happened while she was in the circus that she wants to forget.

© Houghton Mifflin Harcourt Publishing Company

THE LEAP

Short Story by **Louise Erdrich**

? **ESSENTIAL QUESTION:**

What does it take to survive in a crisis?

QUICK START

Examine the photographs that accompany the selection. Then read the first paragraph and predict what the story will be about. Note your prediction in the margin of your text so you can check it after you finish the story.

ANALYZE PLOT

The **plot** is the sequence of events in a work of fiction. A typical plot is linear—it evolves in chronological order in fairly predictable stages. "The Leap" has a non-linear plot that begins at the end: the adult daughter has moved home to care for her blind, elderly mother. Events that lead up to this situation are revealed in a series of **flashbacks**—interruptions in the chronological narrative—that describe events at different points in the past.

As the narrator's flashbacks reveal events in "The Leap," use a chart like this one to record events. When you finish the story, number the events in chronological order and write a summary of events in the order they occurred.

EVENTS BEFORE NARRATOR'S BIRTH	EVENTS DURING NARRATOR'S CHILDHOOD	EVENTS DURING NARRATOR'S ADULTHOOD

MAKE INFERENCES

In a short story, the **theme,** or underlying message, usually emerges through inference. An **inference** is a logical conclusion based on what you already know plus what the text tells you. To uncover themes in "The Leap," first examine the story's title. You might note, for example, that the speaker's mother would have made many fairly spectacular leaps in her career as a trapeze artist. But could *leap* also have one or more figurative meanings? Then, look for clues in the story that hint at its meaning. For example, character or plot developments may help reveal a story's themes.

As you read, use a chart like the one below to track your ideas and inferences about the story's themes.

STORY ELEMENTS OR CLUES	MY INFERENCES	POSSIBLE THEME
1		
2		
3		

GENRE ELEMENTS: SHORT STORY

- includes the basic elements of fiction—setting, characters, plot, conflict, and theme
- centers on a particular moment or event in life
- can be read in one sitting

CRITICAL VOCABULARY

encroach	extricate	constrict	comply	tentative

Answer the questions, using a dictionary or thesaurus as needed. Make sure answers reflect understanding of each Critical Vocabulary word's meaning.

1. My backyard hedge is beginning to **encroach** upon my neighbor's yard. Is my neighbor happy about this? Why or why not?

2. My neighbor wants to install a fence to **constrict** the growth of my hedge. What does my neighbor hope that fence will do?

3. The defendant had to **extricate** herself from the crush of news reporters and photographers outside the courthouse. Was this easy to do? Why?

4. Zach is a great bass player, but he doesn't **comply** with the band's rehearsal schedule. What might happen as a result?

5. We have **tentative** plans to visit the Grand Canyon this summer. Are we sure we're going to go? How do you know this?

LANGUAGE CONVENTIONS

Relative Clauses In this lesson you will learn about the **relative clause.** Relative clauses function as an adjective and describe a noun. A relative clause begins with a signal word: a relative pronoun *(that, which, who, whom, whose)* or a relative adverb *(when, where, why).* In this sentence from "The Leap," the relative clause is underlined:

It commemorates the disaster <u>that put our town smack on the front page of the Boston and New York tabloids.</u>

As you read "The Leap," look for the signal words that indicate a relative clause may follow a noun or noun phrase.

ANNOTATION MODEL

NOTICE & NOTE

As you read, note your own questions and observations, and signposts, including **Memory Moment, Again and Again,** and **Contrasts and Contradictions.** Here is one reader's response to the first paragraph of "The Leap."

My mother is the <u>surviving half</u> of a blindfold <u>trapeze act</u>, not a fact I think about much even now that <u>she is sightless</u>, the result of encroaching and stubborn cataracts. She walks slowly through <u>her house here in New Hampshire.</u> . . . <u>She has never upset an object</u> or as much as brushed a magazine onto the floor. She has never lost her balance or <u>bumped into a closet door</u> left carelessly open.

"Surviving" means the mother's partner is dead. Trapeze accident?

"The mother is blind, but has never bumped into anything" Contradiction?

BACKGROUND

Louise Erdrich *(b. 1954) is best known for exploring the Native American experience in her novels, poetry, and children's books. Born in Little Falls, Minnesota, she grew up in North Dakota. Of German American and Ojibwa (Chippewa) descent, her writing reflects a fascination with the influence of family and heritage on individuals and community. She lives in Minneapolis, Minnesota, where she owns a bookstore and continues to write. Her best-known works include the novels* Love Medicine, The Beet Queen, *and* The Round House.

THE LEAP

Short Story by Louise Erdrich

SETTING A PURPOSE

Unraveling the truth about the past and deciding how the past informs the present are often steps of a journey. As you read "The Leap," consider how this story illustrates those steps in the speaker's journey.

1   My mother is the surviving half of a blindfold trapeze act, not a fact I think about much even now that she is sightless, the result of **encroaching** and stubborn cataracts. She walks slowly through her house here in New Hampshire, lightly touching her way along walls and running her hands over knickknacks, books, the drift of a grown child's belongings and castoffs. She has never upset an object or as much as brushed a magazine onto the floor. She has never lost her balance or bumped into a closet door left carelessly open.

2   It has occurred to me that the catlike precision of her movements in old age might be the result of her early training, but she shows so little of the drama or flair one might expect from a performer that I tend to forget the Flying Avalons. She has kept no sequined costume, no photographs, no fliers or posters from that part of her youth. I would, in fact, tend to think that all memory of double somersaults and heartstopping catches had

© Houghton Mifflin Harcourt Publishing Company • Image Credits: (c) ©Swim Ink 2, LLC/Corbis Historical/Getty Images; (tr) ©Ulf Andersen/Getty Images

Notice & Note

You can use the side margins to notice and note signposts in the text.

encroach
(ĕn-krōch´) *v.* to gradually intrude upon or invade.

CONTRASTS AND CONTRADICTIONS

Notice & Note: What mementos from her past life does the narrator's mother keep?

Analyze: Why do you think this might be the case?

© Houghton Mifflin Harcourt Publishing Company • Image Credits: ©Underwood Archives/Archive Photos/Getty Images

ANALYZE PLOT

Annotate: Mark the clue in paragraph 3 that tells you about when this flashback took place.

Cite Evidence: When did this scene take place? How do you know?

left her arms and legs were it not for the fact that sometimes, as I sit sewing in the room of the rebuilt house in which I slept as a child, I hear the crackle, catch a whiff of smoke from the stove downstairs and suddenly the room goes dark, the stitches burn beneath my fingers, and I am sewing with a needle of hot silver, a thread of fire.

3   I owe her my existence three times. The first was when she saved herself. In the town square a replica tent pole, cracked and splintered, now stands cast in concrete. It commemorates the disaster that put our town smack on the front page of the Boston and New York tabloids. It is from those old newspapers, now historical records, that I get my information. Not from my mother, Anna of the Flying Avalons, nor from any of her in-laws, nor certainly from the other half of her particular act, Harold Avalon, her first husband. In one news account it says, "The day was mildly overcast, but nothing in the air or temperature gave any hint of the sudden force with which the deadly gale would strike."

4   I have lived in the West, where you can see the weather coming for miles, and it is true that out here we are at something of a disadvantage. When extremes of temperature collide, a hot and cold front, winds generate instantaneously behind a hill and crash upon you without warning. That, I think, was the likely situation on that day in June. People probably commented on the pleasant air, grateful that no hot sun beat upon the striped tent that stretched over the

entire center green. They bought their tickets and surrendered them in anticipation. They sat. They ate caramelized popcorn and roasted peanuts. There was time, before the storm, for three acts. The White Arabians of Ali-Khazar rose on their hind legs and waltzed. The Mysterious Bernie folded himself into a painted cracker tin, and the Lady of the Mists made herself appear and disappear in surprising places. As the clouds gathered outside, unnoticed, the ringmaster cracked his whip, shouted his introduction, and pointed to the ceiling of the tent, where the Flying Avalons were perched.

5   They loved to drop gracefully from nowhere, like two sparkling birds, and blow kisses as they threw off their plumed helmets and high-collared capes. They laughed and flirted openly as they beat their way up again on the trapeze bars. In the final vignette[1] of their act, they actually would kiss in midair, pausing, almost hovering as they swooped past one another. On the ground, between bows, Harry Avalon would skip quickly to the front rows and point out the smear of my mother's lipstick, just off the edge of his mouth. They made a romantic pair all right, especially in the blindfold sequence.

6   That afternoon, as the anticipation increased, as Mr. and Mrs. Avalon tied sparkling strips of cloth onto each other's face and as they puckered their lips in mock kisses, lips destined "never again to meet," as one long breathless article put it, the wind rose, miles

---

[1] **vignette:** (vĭn-yĕt´) a brief scene.

MAKE INFERENCES

Annotate: In paragraph 6, mark lines that reveal the daughter's feelings about her mother.

Infer: What does she admire about her mother?

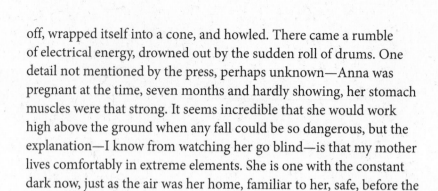
off, wrapped itself into a cone, and howled. There came a rumble of electrical energy, drowned out by the sudden roll of drums. One detail not mentioned by the press, perhaps unknown—Anna was pregnant at the time, seven months and hardly showing, her stomach muscles were that strong. It seems incredible that she would work high above the ground when any fall could be so dangerous, but the explanation—I know from watching her go blind—is that my mother lives comfortably in extreme elements. She is one with the constant dark now, just as the air was her home, familiar to her, safe, before the storm that afternoon.

7   From opposite ends of the tent they waved, blind and smiling, to the crowd below. The ringmaster removed his hat and called for silence, so that the two above could concentrate. They rubbed their hands in chalky powder, then Harry launched himself and swung once, twice, in huge calibrated[2] beats across space. He hung from his knees and on the third swing stretched wide his arms, held his hand out to receive his pregnant wife as she dove from her shining bar.

8   It was while the two were in midair, their hands about to meet, that lightning struck the main pole and sizzled down the guy wires, filling the air with a blue radiance that Harry Avalon must certainly have seen through the cloth of his blindfold as the tent buckled and the edifice toppled him forward, the swing continuing and not returning in its sweep, and Harry going down, down into the crowd with his last thought, perhaps, just a prickle of surprise at his empty hands.

9   My mother once said that I'd be amazed at how many things a person can do within the act of falling. Perhaps, at the time, she was teaching me to dive off a board at the town pool, for I associated the idea with midair somersaults. But I also think she meant that even in that awful doomed second one could think, for she certainly did. When her hands did not meet her husband's, my mother tore her blindfold away. As he swept past her on the wrong side, she could have grasped his ankle, the toe-end of his tights, and gone down clutching him. Instead, she changed direction. Her body twisted toward a heavy wire and she managed to hang on to the braided metal, still hot from the lightning strike. Her palms were burned so terribly that once healed they bore no lines, only the blank scar tissue of a quieter future. She was lowered, gently, to the sawdust ring just underneath the dome of the canvas roof, which did not entirely settle but was held up on one end and jabbed through, torn, and still on fire in places from the giant spark, though rain and men's jackets soon put that out.

10   Three people died, but except for her hands my mother was not seriously harmed until an overeager rescuer broke her arm in **extricating** her and also, in the process, collapsed a portion of the

---

[2] **calibrated:** checked or determined by comparison with a standard.

CONTRASTS AND CONTRADICTIONS

Notice & Note: In paragraph 9, what observation does the daughter reveal that the mother has shared?

Analyze: Why would the mother say this? How does she know?

extricate
(ĕk´strĭ-kāt) *v.* to release or disentangle from.

tent bearing a huge buckle that knocked her unconscious. She was taken to the town hospital, and there she must have hemorrhaged,[3] for they kept her, confined to her bed, a month and a half before her baby was born without life.

11   Harry Avalon had wanted to be buried in the circus cemetery next to the original Avalon, his uncle, so she sent him back with his brothers. The child, however, is buried around the corner, beyond this house and just down the highway. Sometimes I used to walk there just to sit. She was a girl, but I rarely thought of her as a sister or even as a separate person really. I suppose you could call it the egocentrism[4] of a child, of all young children, but I considered her a less finished version of myself.

12   When the snow falls, throwing shadows among the stones, I can easily pick hers out from the road, for it is bigger than the others and in the shape of a lamb at rest, its legs curled beneath. The carved lamb looms larger as the years pass, though it is probably only my eyes, the visions shifting, as what is close to me blurs and distances sharpen. In odd moments, I think it is the edge drawing near, the edge of everything, the unseen horizon we do not really speak of in the eastern woods. And it also seems to me, although this is probably an idle fantasy, that the statue is growing more sharply etched, as if, instead of weathering itself into a porous mass, it is hardening on the hillside with each snowfall, perfecting itself.

13   It was during her confinement in the hospital that my mother met my father. He was called in to look at the set of her arm, which was complicated. He stayed, sitting at her bedside, for he was something of an armchair traveler and had spent his war quietly, at an air force training grounds, where he became a specialist in arms and legs broken during parachute training exercises. Anna Avalon had been to many of the places he longed to visit—Venice, Rome, Mexico, all through France and Spain. She had no family of her own and was taken in by the Avalons, trained to perform from a very young age. They toured Europe before the war, then based themselves in New York. She was illiterate.

14   It was in the hospital that she finally learned to read and write, as a way of overcoming the boredom and depression of those weeks, and it was my father who insisted on teaching her. In return for stories of her adventures, he graded her first exercises. He bought her her first book, and over her bold letters, which the pale guides of the penmanship pads could not contain, they fell in love.

15   I wonder if my father calculated the exchange he offered: one form of flight for another. For after that, and for as long as I can remember, my mother has never been without a book. Until now, that is, and it remains the greatest difficulty of her blindness. Since

© Houghton Mifflin Harcourt Publishing Company

LANGUAGE CONVENTIONS
Annotate: Mark the two relative clauses in paragraph 13.

Analyze: How and why did the speaker's mother meet her second husband?

---
[3] **hemorrhaged** (hĕm´ər-ĭjd): bled heavily.
[4] **egocentrism:** belief in the primary or sole importance of the self.

constrict
(kən-strĭkt´) *v.* to limit or
impede growth.

AGAIN AND AGAIN

Notice & Note: The ideas
in paragraph 17 suggest at
least one theme. Mark the
relevant ideas.

Infer: What is one theme
suggested here? What other
theme might be suggested?

my father's recent death, there is no one to read to her, which is why
I returned, in fact, from my failed life where the land is flat. I came
home to read to my mother, to read out loud, to read long into the
dark if I must, to read all night.

16   Once my father and mother married, they moved onto the old
farm he had inherited but didn't care much for. Though he'd been
thinking of moving to a larger city, he settled down and broadened
his practice in this valley. It still seems odd to me, when they could
have gone anywhere else, that they chose to stay in the town where
the disaster had occurred, and which my father in the first place
had found so **constricting**. It was my mother who insisted upon it,
after her child did not survive. And then, too, she loved the sagging
farmhouse with its scrap of what was left of a vast acreage of woods
and hidden hay fields that stretched to the game park.

17   I owe my existence, the second time then, to the two of them and
the hospital that brought them together. That is the debt we take for
granted since none of us asks for life. It is only once we have it that we
hang on so dearly.

18   I was seven the year the house caught fire, probably from
standing ash. It can rekindle, and my father, forgetful around the
house and perpetually exhausted from night hours on call, often
emptied what he thought were ashes from cold stoves into wooden or
cardboard containers. The fire could have started from a flaming box,
or perhaps a buildup of creosote[5] inside the chimney was the culprit.
It started right around the stove, and the heart of the house was
gutted. The baby-sitter, fallen asleep in my father's den on the first
floor, woke to find the stairway to my upstairs room cut off by flames.
She used the phone, then ran outside to stand beneath my window.

19   When my parents arrived, the town volunteers had drawn water
from the fire pond and were spraying the outside of the house,
preparing to go inside after me, not knowing at the time that there
was only one staircase and that it was lost. On the other side of the
house, the superannuated[6] extension ladder broke in half. Perhaps the
clatter of it falling against the walls woke me, for I'd been asleep up to
that point.

MAKE INFERENCES

Annotate: Mark lines in
paragraph 20 that describe the
daughter's reaction to the fire.

Infer: How is the narrator
like her mother? What
characteristics do they share?

20   As soon as I awakened, in the small room that I now use for
sewing, I smelled the smoke. I followed things by the letter then,
was good at memorizing instructions, and so I did exactly what was
taught in the second-grade home fire drill. I got up, I touched the
back of my door before opening it. Finding it hot, I left it closed and
stuffed my rolled-up rug beneath the crack. I did not hide under my
bed or crawl into my closet. I put on my flannel robe, and then I sat
down to wait.

---

[5] **creosote:** a flammable, oily byproduct of burning carbon-based fuels like coal,
peat, and wood.
[6] **superannuated:** obsolete; ready for retirement.

© Houghton Mifflin Harcourt Publishing Company

© Houghton Mifflin Harcourt Publishing Company • Image Credits: ©Sandra Baker/Photographer's Choice/getty Images

21   Outside, my mother stood below my dark window and saw clearly that there was no rescue. Flames had pierced one side wall, and the glare of the fire lighted the massive limbs and trunk of the vigorous old elm that had probably been planted the year the house was built, a hundred years ago at least. No leaf touched the wall, and just one thin branch scraped the roof. From below, it looked as though even a squirrel would have had trouble jumping from the tree onto the house, for the breadth of that small branch was no bigger than my mother's wrist.

22   Standing there, beside Father, who was preparing to rush back around to the front of the house, my mother asked him to unzip her dress. When he wouldn't be bothered, she made him understand. He couldn't make his hands work, so she finally tore it off and stood there in her pearls and stockings. She directed one of the men to lean the broken half of the extension ladder up against the trunk of the tree. In surprise, he **complied**. She ascended. She vanished. Then she could be seen among the leafless branches of late November as she made her way up and, along her stomach, inched the length of a bough that curved above the branch that brushed the roof.

23   Once there, swaying, she stood and balanced. There were plenty of people in the crowd and many who still remember, or think they do, my mother's leap through the ice-dark air toward that thinnest extension, and how she broke the branch falling so that it cracked in her hands, cracked louder than the flames as she vaulted with

ANALYZE PLOT

Annotate: Mark the mother's assessment of the situation outside the daughter's window.

Draw Conclusions: Based on what you know about the mother's character, what do you think she is going to do?

comply
(kəm-plī´) *v.* to obey an instruction or command.

CONTRASTS AND CONTRADICTIONS

Notice & Note: What is unusual about the mother's demeanor in paragraph 24?

Evaluate: Why does the mother react this way? What does her demeanor tell you about her character?

tentative
(tĕn´tə-tĭv) *adj.* with caution and without confidence.

MEMORY MOMENT

Notice & Note: In paragraph 26, what does the narrator remember about something her mother once told her?

Evaluate: What does the daughter think about during her fall toward the firefighters' net?

it toward the edge of the roof, and how it hurtled down end over end without her, and their eyes went up, again, to see where she had flown.

24   I didn't see her leap through air, only heard the sudden thump and looked out my window. She was hanging by the backs of her heels from the new gutter we had put in that year, and she was smiling. I was not surprised to see her, she was so matter-of-fact. She tapped on the window. I remember how she did it, too. It was the friendliest tap, a bit **tentative**, as if she was afraid she had arrived too early at a friend's house. Then she gestured at the latch, and when I opened the window she told me to raise it wider and prop it up with the stick so it wouldn't crush her fingers. She swung down, caught the ledge, and crawled through the opening. Once she was in my room, I realized she had on only underclothing, a bra of the heavy stitched cotton women used to wear and step-in, lace-trimmed drawers. I remember feeling light-headed, of course, terribly relieved, and then embarrassed for her to be seen by the crowd undressed.

25   I was still embarrassed as we flew out the window, toward earth, me in her lap, her toes pointed as we skimmed toward the painted target of the fire fighter's net.

26   I know that she's right. I knew it even then. As you fall, there is time to think. Curled as I was, against her stomach, I was not startled by the cries of the crowd or the looming faces. The wind roared and beat its hot breath at our back, the flames whistled. I slowly wondered what would happen if we missed the circle or bounced out of it. Then I wrapped my hands around my mother's hands. I felt the brush of her lips and heard the beat of her heart in my ears, loud as thunder, long as the roll of drums.

© Houghton Mifflin Harcourt Publishing Company • Image Credits: ©FPG/Archive Photos/Getty Images

CHECK YOUR UNDERSTANDING

Answer these questions before moving on to the **Analyze the Text** section on the following page.

1 Which of these is true about Harold Avalon?

A He is the narrator's father.

B He is killed in combat.

C He is buried near his uncle, founder of the Flying Avalons.

D He is a doctor who specializes in setting broken bones.

2 Chronologically, which of these events happens first?

F Anna Avalon's first child is stillborn.

G The narrator moves back into her childhood home in New Hampshire.

H The narrator's father dies.

J Ashes ignite a fire in the New Hampshire farmhouse.

3 Which of these statements is true about a character in "The Leap"?

A The father achieves a daring act of bravery.

B The mother achieves a daring act of bravery.

C The narrator loses her eyesight.

D The narrator does not get along with her mother.

ANALYZE THE TEXT

Support your responses with evidence from the text. ☰ NOTEBOOK

1. **Infer** In paragraph 9, Anna decides to reach for the hot braided metal rather than for her husband as he falls. What does this reveal about her character?

2. **Interpret** Identify the leaps in the story. Which leaps are literal? Which are figurative?

3. **Infer** Reread paragraph 26. What does the narrator learn? What inferences can you make about the story's theme or themes?

4. **Compare** Compare the description of the trapeze accident with the description of the house fire. What do these descriptions reveal about the mother's character?

5. **Notice & Note** The narrator speaks of the three ways that she owes her existence to her mother. Identify the three ways and the plot-related literary technique used to reveal them.

RESEARCH

How much do you know about traditional circuses? Research images of vintage circuses as well as any circus-related terms from the text that you are curious about or unfamiliar with. Record what you learn in a graphic organizer. Then reread the story, this time noting instances of circus imagery and how each instance contributes to character, theme, or another aspect of the story.

CIRCUS TERM OR IMAGE	WHAT RESEARCH REVEALS

CREATE AND DISCUSS

Write a Research Summary Write a four- to five-paragraph summary of your research results.

❏ Introduce the topic and share the goals of your research.

❏ Decide on an organizational strategy, then in your two to three body paragraphs, share what your questions were and the details of what you learned.

❏ In your final paragraph, state your conclusion about the use of circus imagery in "The Leap."

Discuss with a Group Have a group discussion about the topics and terms you and your group members chose to research and the information you discovered.

❏ First, share what questions you and your group members researched. If another student researched a question similar to yours, you may choose to collaborate with that student for a portion of the discussion.

❏ As a group, decide on the order in which you and your group members will present your results.

❏ Keep your presentation brief, and listen closely as others share theirs. Write down at least one relevant question or meaningful observation you might contribute to each presentation.

Go to the **Writing Studio** for more on writing a research summary.

Go to the **Speaking and Listening Studio** for help having a group discussion.

RESPOND TO THE ESSENTIAL QUESTION

? ### What does it take to survive in a crisis?

Gather Information Review your annotations and notes on "The Leap." Then, add relevant information to your Response Log. As you determine which information to include, think about:

• What crises the narrator faces and how she handles them

• What crises the mother faces and how she handles them

• What you know about responding to a crisis

At the end of the unit, use your notes to help you write an argument.

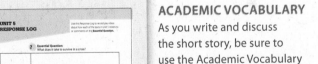

ACADEMIC VOCABULARY

As you write and discuss the short story, be sure to use the Academic Vocabulary words. Check off the words that you use.

❏ **dimension**

❏ **external**

❏ **statistic**

❏ **sustain**

❏ **utilize**

 **RESPOND**

© Houghton Mifflin Harcourt Publishing Company

WORD BANK
encroach
extricate
constrict
comply
tentative

 Go to the **Vocabulary Studio** for more help with prefixes.

CRITICAL VOCABULARY

Practice and Apply Answer these questions, using a dictionary or thesaurus as needed. Make sure your answers reflect your understanding of each Critical Vocabulary word's meaning.

1. Should a rescue crew provide a **tentative** response to an **encroaching** forest fire? Why or why not?

2. Would it feel **constricting** to always **comply** with the wishes of others? Explain.

3. Why would you **extricate** yourself from a planned road trip upon learning of an approaching blizzard?

VOCABULARY STRATEGY:
Prefixes

The Critical Vocabulary words *encroach, extricate, constrict,* and *comply* all contain a **prefix,** an affix added to the beginning of a base word. Knowing the meaning of common prefixes, such as *en-, ex-, con-,* and *com-,* will help you clarify the meaning of unknown words. Here are the meanings of some common prefixes and examples of other words that contain the prefixes:

PREFIXES	MEANINGS	EXAMPLES
en-	to go into or onto	encapsulate, encircle
ex-	out of or away from	exchange, exterminate
con-	together, with, jointly	consensus, congenial

If a base word is unfamiliar, use your knowledge of the word's prefix and how the word is used in context to clarify its meaning. If necessary, consult a dictionary to determine the precise meaning of the word.

Practice and Apply For each prefix in the chart, identify one word that contains it. The word may be in the text, or it may be a word of your own choosing. For each word you choose, follow these steps:

1. Identify the base word, the main word part. For example, the base word of *exchange* is *change*

2. Write a definition for each word that incorporates the prefix meaning and the base word meaning. Use a dictionary to check your definition. Make changes if needed.

3. Finally, write a sample sentence for each word you choose.

LANGUAGE CONVENTIONS:
Relative Clauses

A **clause** is a group of words that contains a subject and a predicate. **Relative clauses** describe nouns and function as adjectives. Here are the characteristics of a relative clause:

- It begins with a signal word: a relative pronoun (*that, which, who, whom, whose*) or a relative adverb (*when, where, or why*).

- It follows a noun or a noun phrase.

- It provides extra information about a noun or a noun phrase, or it answers the questions *What kind? How many? Which one?*

Authors use relative clauses not only to convey specific meanings, but also to add interest and variety to their work. Read this sentence from "The Leap":

> It commemorates the disaster <u>that put our town smack on the front page of the Boston and New York tabloids.</u>

The clause contains all the elements of a relative clause: it begins with a relative pronoun—*that;* it follows a noun—*disaster*; it answers the question *Which one?*—the disaster that put the town in the tabloids.

Erdrich could have expressed the same ideas this way:

> It commemorates the disaster. The disaster put our town smack on the front page of the Boston and New York tabloids.

Notice how the sentence with the relative clause is smoother and easier to read. Here are some other examples of relative clauses from the "The Leap":

RELATIVE CLAUSES		
SIGNAL WORD	EXAMPLE IN SELECTION	WORDS MODIFIED
which	He was called in to look at the set of her arm, <u>which was complicated.</u>	"the set of her arm"
who	…and it was my father <u>who insisted on teaching her.</u>	"father"
where	…they chose to stay in the town <u>where the disaster had occurred…</u>	"town"

Practice and Apply Look back at the summary you created in response to this selection's Write a Research Summary task. Revise your summary to include at least two relative clauses. With a partner, discuss your revised summaries. Then work together to identify three or four more relative clauses in "The Leap" that are not included as examples in this lesson.

© Houghton Mifflin Harcourt Publishing Company

IS SURVIVAL SELFISH?

Argument by **Lane Wallace**

? **ESSENTIAL QUESTION:**

What does it take to survive in a crisis?

QUICK START

Most people have either read or heard about life-threatening situations. What survival stories can you tell? Share them with the class.

ANALYZE ARGUMENTS

In an **argument,** an author expresses a position on an issue and then attempts to support that position. A successful argument persuades readers to agree with the author's claim, or position. To analyze arguments, you must first outline its basic parts.

- The **claim** is the author's position on the topic or issue. It is the central idea around which the argument is structured.

- **Reasons** are explanations that support the claim by answering the question. Why does the author hold that opinion? An author's reasoning must be clear and logical to create a valid argument.

- **Evidence** includes facts, statistics, personal experiences, statements by experts, and other information. The evidence supports the reasons and, ultimately, the author's claim.

- The argument ends with a persuasive **conclusion,** which revisits the claim.

Most arguments begin by stating a claim and presenting reasons and evidence for it. To be persuasive, an argument must include evidence that is valid, relevant, and sufficient. Facts must be true and provable through research. Opinions are beliefs, but do not support reasons and aren't evidence.

ANALYZE RHETORICAL DEVICES

Authors often use **rhetorical devices** when they write arguments. Some devices, such as **rhetorical questions,** are intended to engage the audience and make a point. In other cases, an author may rely on faulty logic or rhetorical devices meant to deceive the audience. Always read arguments critically in order to assess the accuracy and validity of the author's argument. In particular, be on the lookout for instances and effects of logical fallacies or **faulty reasoning**, which are errors in reasoning.

GENRE ELEMENTS: ARGUMENT

- presents a claim or position on an issue
- includes reasons or evidence that support the claim
- may include rhetorical devices or other persuasive strategies

TECHNIQUE	EXAMPLE	EXPLANATION
False Cause and Effect	I ate shrimp last night and feel sick today. The shrimp must have been bad.	A connection between two ideas does not always mean that one causes the other.
Circular Reasoning	Ms. Vasquez is a great teacher because she does a great job teaching.	Circular reasoning restates the argument as a reason to support it.
Overgeneralization	I saw three shooting stars this past winter. Shooting stars appear in winter.	Generalizations based on limited data may not be accurate. Stereotypes are a form of generalization.
Straw Man	My opponent believes all state laws are unnecessary.	Misstating an opposition's position so it is easy to attack or tear down.
Red Herring	Although we are meeting to talk about club rules, let's discuss upcoming projects.	Bringing up a topic that distracts from the real topic.
Begging the Question	Everyone will agree that my position is valid.	Assumption by the writer that a claim or other statement is true.

CRITICAL VOCABULARY

berate	**consume**	**edict**	**laud**	**transfix**

To see how many Critical Vocabulary words you know, discuss answers to the questions below.

1. If fans **laud** an actor for her roles, what would they do?

2. What might **transfix** a person?

3. If a fire were to **consume** something, what would be happening?

4. If you **berate** another person, what would you be doing?

5. When someone delivers an **edict**, what is the intent?

LANGUAGE CONVENTIONS

Commas Authors use commas to achieve two purposes. First, commas show where the reader should pause. If the text were being read aloud, the reader would hesitate at each comma. Authors also use commas to signal a break in thought and make the sentence easier to read.

ANNOTATION MODEL

NOTICE & NOTE

As you read, note the author's claim and her use of rhetorical devices. Here you can see one reader's notes about "Is Survival Selfish?"

The "women and children first" protocol of the *Titanic* may not be as strong a social stricture as it was a century ago. <u>But we still tend to laud those who risk or sacrifice themselves to save others in moments of danger or crisis and look less kindly on those who focus on saving themselves, instead.</u>

But is survival really selfish and uncivilized? Or is it smart? And is going in to rescue others always heroic? [Or is it sometimes just stupid?] . . .

<u>In July 2007, I was having a drink with a friend in Grand Central Station when an underground steam pipe exploded just outside.</u>

the author is preparing to make her claim

the author uses loaded language; she calls survival stupid

author backs up her claim with facts from a personal experience

BACKGROUND

Lane Wallace *is an author, speaker, and adventurer. She writes for* The Atlantic *magazine,* The New York Times, *and many aviation magazines. She survived a horrible car crash at age 20 in New Zealand, and after nearly dying, she quit her job in hospital administration and became an airplane pilot. She decided to combine a passion for writing, exploring, and seeking adventures. She has gone wreck-diving in the South Pacific, has flown a spy plane 70,000 feet above Earth, and has flown relief missions into Africa. She is the author of* Surviving Uncertainty *and* Unforgettable.

IS SURVIVAL SELFISH?

Argument by Lane Wallace

SETTING A PURPOSE

As you read, think about how you would react in a life-threatening situation. Would you save yourself? Or would you save others, and risk your own life?

1   When the ocean liner *Titanic* sank in April of 1912, one of the few men to survive the tragedy was J. Bruce Ismay, the chairman and managing director of the company that owned the ship. After the disaster, however, Ismay was savaged by the media and the general public for climbing into a lifeboat and saving himself when there were other women and children still on board. Ismay said he'd already helped many women and children into lifeboats and had only climbed in one himself when there were no other women or children in the area and the boat was ready to release. But it didn't matter. His reputation was ruined. He was labeled an uncivilized coward and, a year after the disaster, he resigned his position at White Star.

2   The "women and children first" protocol of the *Titanic* may not be as strong a social stricture[1] as it was a century ago. But we

---

[1] **social stricture:** behavioral restriction placed on society.

Notice & Note

Use the side margins to notice and note signposts in the text.

ANALYZE ARGUMENTS

Annotate: In paragraph 1, underline the topic the author introduces with an anecdote.

Analyze: Consider the title of this selection. Why might the author have chosen to begin her argument with this example?

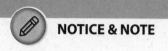

laud
(lôd) *v.* to praise.

ANALYZE ARGUMENTS

Annotate: In paragraph 3, underline a statement the author can build on to create a full claim.

Analyze: How do the rhetorical devices in the questions that precede the statement set up the author's claim?

LANGUAGE CONVENTIONS

Annotate: Mark the commas in the last sentence of paragraph 5.

Analyze: What is the purpose of these commas?

transfix
(trăns-fĭks´) *v.* to captivate or make motionless with awe.

consume
(kən-soom´) *v.* to completely destroy or eradicate.

ANALYZE RHETORICAL DEVICES

Annotate: In paragraph 8, mark the question the author poses.

Evaluate: What rhetorical device is she using? Is it effective?

berate
(bĭ-rāt´) *v.* to criticize or scold.

still tend to **laud** those who risk or sacrifice themselves to save others in moments of danger or crisis and look less kindly on those who focus on saving themselves, instead.

3   But is survival really selfish and uncivilized? Or is it smart? And is going in to rescue others always heroic? Or is it sometimes just stupid? It's a complex question, because there are so many factors involved, and every survival situation is different.

4   Self-preservation is supposedly an instinct. So one would think that in life-and-death situations, we'd all be very focused on whatever was necessary to survive. But that's not always true. In July 2007, I was having a drink with a friend in Grand Central Station[2] when an underground steam pipe exploded just outside. From where we sat, we heard a dull "boom!" and then suddenly, people were running, streaming out of the tunnels and out the doors.

5   My friend and I walked quickly and calmly outside, but to get any further, we had to push our way through a crowd of people who were staring, **transfixed,** at the column of smoke rising from the front of the station. Some people were crying, others were screaming, others were on their cell phones . . . but the crowd, for the most part, was *not* doing the one thing that would increase everyone's chances of survival, if in fact a terrorist bomb with god knows what inside it had just gone off—namely, moving away from the area.

6   We may have an instinct for survival, but it clearly doesn't always kick in the way it should. A guy who provides survival training for pilots told me once that the number one determining factor for survival is simply whether people hold it together in a crisis or fall apart. And, he said, it's impossible to predict ahead of time who's going to hold it together, and who's going to fall apart.

7   So what is the responsibility of those who hold it together? I remember reading the account of one woman who was in an airliner that crashed on landing. People were frozen or screaming, but nobody was moving toward the emergency exits, even as smoke began to fill the cabin. After realizing that the people around her were too paralyzed to react, she took direct action, crawling over several rows of people to get to the exit. She got out of the plane and survived. Very few others in the plane, which was soon **consumed** by smoke and fire, did. And afterward, I remember she said she battled a lot of guilt for saving herself instead of trying to save the others.

8   Could she really have saved the others? Probably not, and certainly not from the back of the plane. If she'd tried, she probably would have perished with them. So why do survivors **berate** themselves for not adding to the loss by attempting the impossible? Perhaps it's because we get very mixed messages about survival ethics.

---

[2] **Grand Central Station:** a large commuter-rail and subway terminal in New York City.

Survivors of the *Titanic* disaster in a lifeboat.

9   On the one hand, we're told to put our own oxygen masks on first, and not to jump in the water with a drowning victim. But then the people who ignore those **edicts** and survive to tell the tale are lauded as heroes. And people who do the "smart" thing are sometimes criticized quite heavily after the fact.

10   In a famous mountain-climbing accident chronicled in the book and documentary *Touching the Void*, climber Simon Yates was attempting to rope his already-injured friend Joe Simpson down a mountain in bad weather when the belay[3] went awry. Simpson ended up hanging off a cliff, unable to climb up, and Yates, unable to lift him up and losing his own grip on the mountain, ended up cutting the rope to Simpson to save himself. Miraculously, Simpson survived the 100 foot fall and eventually made his way down the mountain. But Yates was criticized by some for his survival decision, even though the alternative would have almost certainly led to both of their deaths.

11   In Yates' case, he had time to think hard about the odds, and the possibilities he was facing, and to realize that he couldn't save anyone but himself. But what about people who have to make more instantaneous decisions? If, in fact, survivors are driven by instinct not civilization, how do you explain all those who choose

edict
(ē′dĭkt) *n.* an official rule or proclamation.

CONTRASTS AND CONTRADICTIONS

Notice & Note: Mark the sentence in paragraph 10 that shows something unexpected that happened.

Respond: Does this unexpected event support or refute the author's claim?

---

[3] **belay:** the securing of a rope to a cleat or another object.

© Houghton Mifflin Harcourt Publishing Company • Image Credits: ©sezer66/iStock/Getty Images Plus/Getty Images

**ANALYZE
RHETORICAL DEVICES**

Annotate: In paragraph 12, mark the sentence that appears to contradict the author's argument about how people behave in a crisis.

Analyze: Why is this an example of a false cause and effect as far as confirming the author's claim about bravery vs. selfishness?

otherwise? Who would dive into icy waters or onto subway tracks or disobey orders to make repeat trips onto a minefield to bring wounded to safety? Are they more civilized than the rest of us? More brave? More noble?

12   It sounds nice, but oddly enough, most of the people who perform such impulsive rescues say that they didn't really think before acting. Which means they weren't "choosing" civilization over instinct. If survival is an instinct, it seems to me that there must be something equally instinctive that drives us, sometimes, to run into danger instead of away from it.

13   Perhaps it comes down to the ancient "fight or flight" impulse. Animals confronted with danger will choose to attack it, or run from it, and it's hard to say which one they'll choose, or when. Or maybe humans are such social herd animals, dependent on the herd for survival, that we feel a pull toward others even as we feel a contrary pull toward our own preservation, and the two impulses battle it out within us . . . leading to the mixed messages we send each other on which impulse to follow.

14   Some people hold it together in a crisis and some people fall apart. Some people might run away from danger one day, and toward

it the next. We pick up a thousand cues in an instant of crisis and respond in ways that even surprise ourselves, sometimes.

15   But while we laud those who sacrifice themselves in an attempt to save another, there is a fine line between brave and foolish. There can also be a fine line between smart and selfish. And as a friend who's served in the military for 27 years says, the truth is, sometimes there's no line at all between the two.

CHECK YOUR UNDERSTANDING

Answer these questions before moving on to the **Analyze the Text** section on the following page.

1 How does the author support her claim that people are sometimes blamed for saving themselves?

  A By arguing that some people are heroes and other people are not

  B By asking the reader questions that force them to assign blame

  C By giving examples of what happened during and after a crisis

  D By showing that it takes selfishness to want to save yourself

2 The author included the information in paragraph 7 to —

  F demonstrate that in some circumstances saving your life is the right action

  G argue that this woman cost other people their lives by her actions

  H offer an example of what you should do in an airplane fire

  J criticize the other passengers for not trying to save themselves

3 The author concludes her argument with —

  A recommendations for what you should do in a live-or-die situation

  B another example that explains what being selfish in a crisis means

  C a story about a friend who says you have to be brave and foolish

  D generalizations arguing that the issue is not so simple

ANALYZE THE TEXT

Support your responses with evidence from the text. 📓 NOTEBOOK

1. **Synthesize** Lane Wallace begins her argument with a series of questions to get her readers thinking about what is selfish and what is heroic. In your own words, state the claim that she expresses in paragraph 3. Take into account the information she presents in the rest of her argument, including her conclusions at the end.

2. **Analyze** Wallace writes that "the number one determining factor for survival is simply whether people hold it together in a crisis or fall apart." Is this an example of a claim, a reason, or evidence? Explain with an example from the text.

3. **Critique** Review the list of rhetorical devices in the Get Ready section of this selection. Identify at least two that Wallace uses in her argument. Are they effective in advancing her argument? Explain.

4. **Evaluate** Reread paragraph 12. As evidence for Wallace's claim, is this paragraph valid and relevant? Explain.

5. **Notice & Note** In the final paragraph, Wallace writes that there can be "a fine line between smart and selfish," and that "sometimes there's no line at all between the two." What does she mean by this apparent contradiction? How does her conclusion restate her claim? Note the sentence at the beginning of the selection that states this claim.

RESEARCH

RESEARCH TIP
If you are having trouble finding enough information on a topic, research a related topic and expand your search to include other aspects.

Accounts of different individuals who have lived through life-threatening or even deadly crises often provide very different tales of survival. With a partner, research stories of survivors and take notes in first column of the chart below.

SURVIVOR EXPERIENCE	MY RESPONSE TO SURVIVOR'S ACTION

Extend Explore the recent work being done to treat victims of Post-Traumatic Stress Disorder (PTSD), which has been recognized as the psychiatric reaction to surviving a life-threatening experience.

CREATE AND DISCUSS

Prepare for Discussion Review the examples you researched. With your partner, discuss whether or not you would describe each survivor's actions as selfish. Fill in the second column of the chart on the previous page.

Class Discussion Hold a class discussion on the issues of survival introduced in the selection.

Review the author's claim and her evidence and reason. Then use your charts to further the discussion about how issues of saving oneself versus saving others play out in specific circumstances.

❏ As a group, set rules and guidelines. Decide on your goals, taking votes on key issues. During your discussion, use appropriate content-area vocabulary. Allow members to express their views, responding thoughtfully.

❏ Have group members ask clarifying questions and respond to other's questions. Be sure to build on the ideas of others as you participate in the discussion.

❏ Review your discussion to determine any points of group consensus.

> Go to the **Speaking and Listening Studio** for help with having a group discussion.

RESPOND TO THE ESSENTIAL QUESTION

? What does it take to survive in a crisis?

Gather Information Review your annotations and notes on "Is Survival Selfish?" Then, add relevant information to your Response Log. As you determine which information to include, think about:

- what characteristics enable survivors to survive
- what role luck or fate plays in surviving disaster
- why a person would feel guilt for surviving a life-threatening situation

At the end of the unit, use your notes to help you write an argument.

UNIT 5
RESPONSE LOG

Essential Question:
What does it take to survive in a crisis?

The Leap	
Is Survival Selfish?	
The End and the Beginning	
from Night	
from The Pianist	

ACADEMIC VOCABULARY
As you write and discuss what you learned from the argument, be sure to use the Academic Vocabulary words. Check off each of the words that you use.

❏ **dimension**
❏ **external**
❏ **statistic**
❏ **sustain**
❏ **utilize**

WORD BANK
laud
transfix
consume
berate
edict

CRITICAL VOCABULARY

Practice and Apply Circle the letter of the best answer to each question. Then, explain your response.

1. Which of the following would be something you might **laud**?
   a. a supreme accomplishment   **b.** a failure to complete

2. If something were to **transfix** you, how would you react?
   a. stand in awe   **b.** run in fear

3. Which of the following would be likely to **consume** something?
   a. a cloud of fog   **b.** a forest fire

4. If I **berate** another person, how would that person feel?
   a. humiliated   **b.** delighted

5. If a king issued an **edict**, what would it be like?
   a. an opinion   **b.** a law

VOCABULARY STRATEGY:
Synonyms

Go to the **Vocabulary Studio** for more on synonyms.

Words that share the same or nearly the same meaning are called **synonyms**. Authors sometimes use synonyms to vary word choice and make their writing more interesting. For example, in paragraph 7 of "Is Survival Selfish?" the author uses the word *paralyzed*. The synonym *transfixed* might also have worked, but the author had already used it in paragraph 5.

If you come across an unfamiliar word in a text, try to think of another word that would make sense in the context of the sentence. Then check a dictionary or a thesaurus to see if your word is truly a synonym for the unfamiliar word. Note any subtle differences between the synonyms and try to understand why the author chose that precise word. Ask yourself whether the context sentence has the same or a slightly different meaning with your synonym as with the author's original word.

Practice and Apply Use a print or online thesaurus to complete this activity.

1. Create a two-column chart. In the first column, write the Critical Vocabulary words. In the second column, write at least two synonyms for each word.

2. Write a sentence using each Critical Vocabulary word.

3. For each sentence you write, exchange the Critical Vocabulary word for one of its synonyms. Work together with a partner to choose the best synonym for each sentence. Discuss whether using a synonym changes the meaning of each original sentence.

LANGUAGE CONVENTIONS:
Commas

A writer's use of punctuation not only helps readers to understand the writer's message, but it also signals how the writer wants the text to be read. In your writing, you can use commas to signal a break or a pause to the reader. When you write, read your sentences out loud, noticing where you pause. The parts where you pause probably need to be punctuated by a comma. Commas are also used to distinguish and divide main and subordinate clauses. Look at these examples from "Is Survival Selfish?"

> **Simpson ended up hanging off a cliff, unable to climb up, and Yates, unable to lift him up and losing his own grip on the mountain, ended up cutting the rope to Simpson to save himself.**

> **If she'd tried, she probably would have perished with them.**

Read the two sentences out loud, noticing where you pause. The commas after "cliff" and "up" in the first sentence signal to the reader to pause. The comma after "mountain" signals a break in thought and makes the sentence easier to understand. The comma after "tried" in the second sentence separates a subordinate clause from the main clause.

Additional examples from "Is Survival Selfish" are shown in the following chart.

PURPOSE OF COMMA	EXAMPLE FROM THE SELECTION
to signal a break in thought	**And afterward, I remember she said she battled a lot of guilt for saving herself instead of trying to save the others.**
to signal the reader to pause	**He was labeled an uncivilized coward and, a year after the disaster, he resigned his position at White Star.**
to divide main and subordinate clauses	**If survival is an instinct, it seems to me that there must be something equally instinctive that drives us, sometimes, to run into danger instead of away from it.**

Practice and Apply These sentences include words, phrases, and clauses that need to be punctuated with commas. Rewrite the sentences, inserting the needed punctuation. If you get stuck, try reading the sentence out loud.

1. Yes I absolutely want to survive.

2. Beyond saving your own life people expect you to be a hero and save others.

3. If you survive people think you should have saved others.

4. If she'd tried to help others she probably would have perished with them.

5. Surviving danger what everyone hopes for changes the rest of a person's life.

Go to the **Grammar Studio** for more on commas.

© Houghton Mifflin Harcourt Publishing Company

THE END AND THE BEGINNING

Poem by **WISŁAWA SZYMBORSKA**

? **_ESSENTIAL QUESTION:_**

What does it take to survive in a crisis?

QUICK START

Think about the aspects of daily life that are disrupted by war or mass violence. What kinds of challenges do people face in the aftermath of such events?

ANALYZE POETIC LANGUAGE

"The End and the Beginning" is a **lyric poem,** one in which a single speaker expresses his or her personal ideas and feelings. Lyric poetry can take many forms and can address all types of topics, from everyday experiences to complex ideas. Most poems—except narrative poems, which tell a story—are lyric poems.

Poetry is highly concentrated as far as language used, so poets must be precise and economical about the words they choose and how they use them. As Szymborska said in her Nobel Prize acceptance speech, "every word is weighed." Analyzing an author's language choices—and the literary effect of those choices—can deepen your understanding of a poem. You can analyze Wisława Szymborska's poetic language in "The End and the Beginning" by looking at the elements outlined in the chart below.

GENRE ELEMENTS: LYRIC POETRY

- usually short to convey strong emotions

- written using first-person point of view to express the speaker's thoughts and feelings

- often uses repetition and rhyme to create a melodic quality

- includes many forms, such as sonnets, odes, and elegies

TONE	IMAGERY	DICTION/SYNTAX
Tone refers to the author's attitude toward the subject. Authors shape a work's tone through topics they choose to explore, word choices, and images those words create. Recognizing tone in literature is essential to gaining meaning, just as recognizing a person's tone of voice is essential to understanding what is said and meant. Elements to consider when evaluating tone include: • words with positive or negative connotations • use of informal language, such as idioms or colloquial expressions • repetition of significant words or phrases	Poets often use **imagery,** or descriptive words and phrases that create sensory experiences for the reader. Imagery usually appeals to one or more of the five senses to help readers imagine exactly what is being described. For example, the striking image of "corpse-filled wagons" passing through rubble-lined roads calls to mind photographs that most readers will have seen of war-torn, bombed-out cities. The image helps the reader envision what the speaker observes. Look for other images in the poem that engage your senses and evoke a strong emotional response.	Two closely related elements of an author's style that affect the tone of their work are diction and syntax. **Diction** is the writer's choice of specific words, and **syntax** is the way those words are arranged into phrases and sentences. A writer's choices regarding diction and syntax can reflect a tone that is formal or informal, concrete or abstract, or literal or figurative. Look for the specific words the author chose for the poem and how she chose to arrange them. What tone do those carefully chosen words create?

ANALYZE POETIC STRUCTURE

Poets use rhetorical devices such as repetition and parallelism to convey meaning. **Repetition** is the use of a word or phrase two or more times. **Parallelism** is the use of the same grammatical or metrical structure within and across lines and verses. Parallelism can provide rhythmic symmetry and balance to a piece, and often shows that two or more ideas are similar or connected. Repetition and parallelism are often used together.

Below are the third and fourth stanzas of "The End and the Beginning." Find and underline examples of repetition and parallelism.

> Someone has to get mired
> in scum and ashes,
> sofa springs,
> splintered glass,
> and bloody rags.
>
> Someone has to drag in a girder
> to prop up a wall.
> Someone has to glaze a window,
> rehang a door.

As you read "The End and the Beginning," look for the use of repetition and parallelism. Think about the effect of these and other elements of the author's style; and how that style conveys information about the speaker and message.

ANNOTATION MODEL   NOTICE & NOTE

As you read, note your observations about the poem's tone, the use of sensory imagery, and the author's choice of diction and syntax. Here is how one reader responded to the first stanzas of "The End and the Beginning."

After every war

someone has to clean up.

Things won't

straighten themselves up, after all.

Someone has to push the rubble

to the side of the road,

so the corpse-filled wagons

can pass.

There have been multiple wars. This suggests a cycle. Calling the aftereffects of war "cleaning up" and "straightening" seems ironic.

Rubble = debris from bombed-out buildings? I see powerful language: "corpse-filled."

BACKGROUND

Wisława Szymborska *(1923–2012) was born in Poland. Her first two published volumes of poetry, written in post-World War II Communist-dominated Poland, were written in the style of Socialist Realism. Szymborska later disowned these works. Her disillusionment with communism was reflected in* Calling Out to Yeti, *published in 1957. Her poems, noted for their unique, ironic tone, have been translated into many languages. Szymborska won the Nobel Prize in Literature in 1996.*

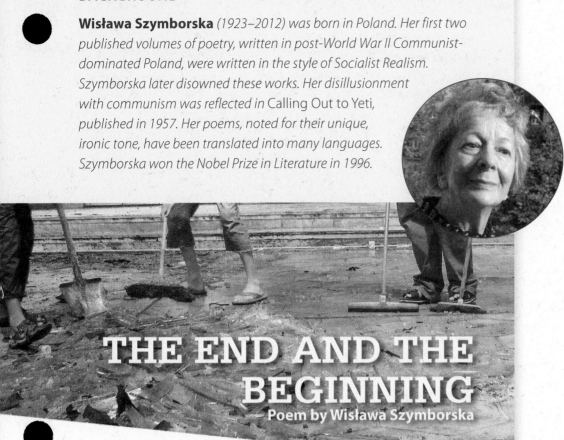

THE END AND THE BEGINNING
Poem by Wisława Szymborska

SETTING A PURPOSE

As you read, think about the aspects of daily life that are disrupted by a war or mass violence. What kind of challenges do people confront in the immediate aftermath of such an event? Note your observations and any questions you have as you read.

After every war
someone has to clean up.
Things won't
straighten themselves up, after all.

5 Someone has to push the rubble
to the side of the road,
so the corpse-filled wagons
can pass.

Someone has to get mired
10 in scum and ashes,
sofa springs,
splintered glass,
and bloody rags.

Notice & Note

You can use the side margins to notice and note signposts in the text.

ANALYZE POETIC LANGUAGE
Annotate: Underline words and phrases in lines 1–13 that appeal to the reader's senses.

Interpret: What general picture do these words or phrases create in your mind?

© Houghton Mifflin Harcourt Publishing Company

ANALYZE POETIC STRUCTURE

Annotate: Mark the use of repetition and parallelism in the first four stanzas of the poem.

Interpret: What is the effect of these devices?

ANALYZE POETIC LANGUAGE

Annotate: Mark the use of figurative language in lines 33–36.

Interpret: Reread lines 26–42. What might people be figuratively throwing on garbage piles along with the rubble of war?

Someone has to drag in a girder
15 to prop up a wall.
Someone has to glaze a window,
rehang a door.

Photogenic it's not,
and takes years.
20 All the cameras have left
for another war.

We'll need the bridges back,
and new railway stations.
Sleeves will go ragged
25 from rolling them up.

Someone, broom in hand,
still recalls the way it was.
Someone else listens
and nods with unsevered[1] head.
30 But already there are those nearby
starting to mill about[2]
who will find it dull.

From out of the bushes
sometimes someone still unearths
35 rusted-out arguments
and carries them to the garbage pile.

---

[1] **unsevered:** not cut off; not separated.
[2] **mill about:** move idly or aimlessly.

Those who knew
what was going on here
must make way for
40 those who know little.
And less than little.
And finally as little as nothing.

In the grass that has overgrown
causes and effects,
45 someone must be stretched out
blade of grass in his mouth
gazing at the clouds.

NOTICE & NOTE

CONTRASTS AND CONTRADICTIONS

Notice & Note: Mark the passages in lines 37-42 that tell what the speaker thinks needs to happen.

Interpret: Why should "those who knew" make way for "those who know little"?

CHECK YOUR UNDERSTANDING

Answer these questions before moving on to the **Analyze the Text** section on the following page.

1 The tone of the poem's speaker is best described as —

   A grateful and relieved—she's happy to be alive

   B resolute and enthusiastic—she's ready to get on with the rebuilding

   C angry and harsh—she's bitter about what has happened

   D ironic—she notices people's tendency to forget about war

2 The word <u>mired</u> in line 9 means —

   F permanently stuck

   G at a disadvantage

   H deeply sunk into

   J dirty or slimy

3 What is an important idea in the poem?

   A The cyclical nature of war and recovery from it

   B The abuse of government power

   C The excitement of war makes a good news story.

   D The importance of antiwar protests

ANALYZE THE TEXT

Support your responses with evidence from the text. ☰ NOTEBOOK

1. **Analyze** Answer these questions to explore how Szymborska creates the tone of the poem. Cite words and phrases from the poem to support your answers.

   • Does the speaker use formal or informal language? What is the effect of this choice?

   • What is the speaker's attitude toward the situation he or she is describing?

   • How does the tone of the poem change beginning with line 30?

2. **Infer** Notice the repetition of the word "someone" throughout the poem. What statement is the speaker making by using an indefinite pronoun rather than referring to a specific person?

3. **Interpret** In line 18, the speaker says that the aftermath of war is not "photogenic." What images in the poem reinforce this idea about war? How does the poet show the extent of the devastation?

4. **Interpret** Reread the last stanza of the poem. What does the grass symbolize, or represent? What does the speaker mean when she describes this "someone" as being "stretched out / blade of grass in his mouth / gazing at the clouds"?

5. **Notice & Note** In lines 37–42, the speaker contrasts "those who knew" with those who know "as little as nothing"? How are these two groups of people different from each other?

RESEARCH

Research at least three images of people in the aftermath of war. If you have a particular area of interest, pursue it. If not, search for images of the aftermath of World War II from a city in Europe or Asia. Later, you'll write photo captions that incorporate literal and figurative language. As you search, use a chart like the one below to track your results.

WHAT I LOOKED FOR	WHAT I FOUND	WHERE I FOUND IT	WHAT I LEARNED ABOUT IT

RESEARCH TIP
The information on the Internet is not regulated for accuracy. Be sure to use only credible sources for your information, including sites you know and trust, those your teachers recommend, and those with .edu, .org, or .gov addresses.

CREATE AND PRESENT

Write Photo Captions In "The End and the Beginning," Wisława Szymborska describes scenes of the aftermath of war using language that works at two levels: literal and figurative.

❏ Gather the photos you found in your research. Think of words that describe those images literally, as well as words that evoke figurative meanings.

❏ Write captions for up to three of your images, describing each image in both literal and figurative language. You may choose to write one literal and one figurative caption per image or combine them in some creative way.

Share with a Group Have a group discussion about the images, your captions, and the literal and figurative interpretations of those images.

❏ As a group, decide on the order in which you and your group members will present your images and captions. Will you share all three of your images or choose just one or two?

❏ Share your research experience and caption-writing thought process in a brief presentation. Point out the ways in which your caption(s) suggest both literal and figurative interpretations of those images.

❏ Listen closely as others share their work. For each presentation, write down at least one question that you would like to follow up with research.

> Go to **Giving a Presentation** in the **Speaking and Listening Studio** to learn more.

RESPOND TO THE ESSENTIAL QUESTION

? What does it take to survive in a crisis?

Gather Information Review your annotations and notes on "The End and the Beginning." Then, add relevant information to your Response Log. As you determine which information to include, think about:

- what it must be like to live in the aftermath of war
- the cleaning up and rebuilding of physical surroundings required of people
- the emotional rebuilding and recovery required of survivors

At the end of the unit, use your notes to help you write an argument.

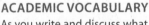

ACADEMIC VOCABULARY

As you write and discuss what you learned from the poem, be sure to use the Academic Vocabulary words. Check off each of the words that you use.

❏ **dimension**

❏ **external**

❏ **statistic**

❏ **sustain**

❏ **utilize**

MEMOIR

from
NIGHT
by **Elie Wiesel**
pages 459–465

Drawings by former
concentration camp
inmates.

COMPARE MEMOIRS

As you read, notice similarities in the settings,
characters, points of view, and author's purpose
in two memoirs set during the same time period
and country. Think about how each author's
use of language contributes to the tone of each
text. After you read both selections, you will
collaborate with a small group on a final project.

? *ESSENTIAL*
QUESTION:

What does it take
to survive in a
crisis?

MEMOIR

from
THE PIANIST
by **Władysław Szpilman**
pages 466–473

©Houghton Mifflin Harcourt Publishing Company • Image Credits: (t) ©dpa picture alliance/Alamy;
(b) ©Roger Viollet/Getty Images

QUICK START

In school and through different texts and works of art, you have learned about World War II and the European front. What do you know about the plight of Jewish communities in Europe shortly before and during the war? Talk with a partner about your understanding of the Holocaust and other atrocities during that time.

ANALYZE MEMOIRS

A **memoir** is an autobiographical account of a person's experiences and observations of an event. As you read the following memoirs, use these questions to help you think about both authors' purposes for writing:

- What is the historical context for the memoir? About what significant events and people is the author sharing memories?
- What perspective do you understand from reading a first-person account?
- What makes the author a reliable authority on writing about these events?
- Who is the audience for the memoir?
- What do you learn about the impact on people of the historical events described?

GENRE ELEMENTS: MEMOIR
- records actual events based on the writer's observations
- reveals the writer's feelings
- provides historical context for the events described

ANALYZE WORD CHOICE

The **tone** of a work is the author's attitude toward the subject. A writer's tone may be described by a single word, such as formal, informal, serious, angry, or lighthearted. The **mood** of a work is the emotional atmosphere the writer creates. Writers shape tone and mood through word choice. Similar words can describe both tone and mood—for example, *fear*, *dread*, *amusement*—but mood relates to how the author's words affect the reader. Which words help create the tone or mood?

TONE OR MOOD	EXAMPLE FROM SELECTIONS
Tone: Fear and dread	**One more hour. Then we would know the verdict: death or reprieve.**
Tone: Despair	**He felt time was running out. He was speaking rapidly, he wanted to tell me so many things. His speech became confused, his voice was choked.**
Mood: Suspense	**There was no time to stop and think: my last hiding place in this building had been discovered, and I must leave it at once.**

As you read the excerpts from *Night* and from *The Pianist*, identify specific words that contribute to each text's tone and mood.

CRITICAL VOCABULARY

reprieve	emaciated	execute	decisive	din
isolation	conscientiously	deprecating	naïve	

To preview the Critical Vocabulary words, use the words to complete the sentences.

1. I could not hear him over the _____ of the music.

2. The _____ of being home alone all day was starting to bother me.

3. After we found the _____ stray cat, we immediately gave it food.

4. _____ checking over the test for mistakes, I felt confident that I had aced it.

5. It is _____ to trust someone who keeps betraying you.

6. All day, I dreaded the teacher's punishment, but I received a(n) _____ .

7. Which steps do I need to follow to _____ the task properly?

8. The boxing match lasted a long time, but one boxer finally landed a(n) _____ blow that ended it.

9. My _____ tone as I criticized his work discouraged him.

LANGUAGE CONVENTIONS

A **dependent clause** has a subject and verb, but can not stand alone as a sentence. Read the following sentences from the texts. How do the dependent clauses add meaning to these sentences from the selection?

> **We had risen at dawn**, **as we did every day**.

> **I was wandering among the walls of totally burnt-out buildings where there could not possibly be any water or remnants of food, or even a hiding place.**

As you read the texts, notice how the authors use dependent clauses to express meaning and add interest.

ANNOTATION MODEL

NOTICE & NOTE

In the model, see one student's notes about the first part of *Night*.

The SS offered us a <u>beautiful</u> present for the new year. We had just returned from work. As soon as we passed the camp's entrance, we <u>sensed something out of the ordinary</u> in the air. The roll call was shorter than usual. The evening soup was distributed at great speed, swallowed as quickly. We were <u>anxious</u>.

Wiesel is using the word "beautiful" ironically; he is describing the SS using a sarcastic tone. The prisoners sense that something is different and they are "anxious" about it.

BACKGROUND

Elie Wiesel *(1928–2016) was a teacher, writer, and Nobel Peace Prize winner. Born in Romania, Wiesel and his family were among millions of European Jews deported to concentration camps during the Holocaust. In 1944, the Nazis sent the family to Auschwitz, where Wiesel's mother and sister perished. Months later, when Wiesel and his father were moved to Buchenwald concentration camp, his father also died. Buchenwald was eventually liberated, and Wiesel went on to write about his experience. His many works include* Dawn *and* The Accident, *both sequels to* Night.

from NIGHT
Memoir by Elie Wiesel

PREPARE TO COMPARE

As you read, make note of Wiesel's point of view and possible purpose for writing this memoir. Notice details that help you understand the setting, characters, and events in this excerpt from Night. *Additionally, pay attention to how Wiesel uses word choice to achieve a certain tone.*

Notice & Note

You can use the side margins to notice and note signposts in the text.

1 The SS[1] offered us a beautiful present for the new year. We had just returned from work. As soon as we passed the camp's entrance, we sensed something out of the ordinary in the air. The roll call was shorter than usual. The evening soup was distributed at great speed, swallowed as quickly. We were anxious.

2 I was no longer in the same block as my father. They had transferred me to another Kommando,[2] the construction one, where twelve hours a day I hauled heavy slabs of stone. The head of my new block was a German Jew, small with piercing eyes. That evening he announced to us that henceforth no one was allowed to leave the block after the evening soup. A terrible word began to circulate soon thereafter: selection.

---

[1] **SS:** abbreviation of *Schutzstaffel,* German for "defense force"; an armed unit of the Nazi Party that controlled concentration camps.

[2] **Kommando** (kə-măn´dō): German for "command," a small-group organization for laborers in the camps.

3   We knew what it meant. An SS would examine us. Whenever he found someone extremely frail—a "Muselman" was what we called those inmates—he would write down his number: good for the crematorium.

4   After the soup, we gathered between the bunks. The veterans told us: "You're lucky to have been brought here so late. Today, this is paradise compared to what the camp was two years ago. Back then, Buna[3] was a veritable hell. No water, no blankets, less soup and bread. At night, we slept almost naked and the temperature was thirty below. We were collecting corpses by the hundreds every day. Work was very hard. Today, this is a little paradise. The Kapos[4] back then had orders to kill a certain number of prisoners every day. And every week, selection. A merciless selection . . . Yes, you are lucky."

5   "Enough! Be quiet!" I begged them. "Tell your stories tomorrow, or some other day."

6   They burst out laughing. They were not veterans for nothing.

7   "Are you scared? We too were scared. And, at that time, for good reason."

8   The old men stayed in their corner, silent, motionless, hunted-down creatures. Some were praying.

9   One more hour. Then we would know the verdict: death or **reprieve**.

10   And my father? I first thought of him now. How would he pass selection? He had aged so much. . . .

11   Our *Blockälteste*[5] had not been outside a concentration camp since 1933. He had already been through all the slaughterhouses, all the factories of death. Around nine o'clock, he came to stand in our midst:

12   "*Achtung!*"[6]

WORDS OF THE WISER

Notice & Note: Underline what the author learns from the veteran inmates.

Respond: How does Wiesel use the words of the inmates to provide context for the reader? How does his reaction to the advice contribute to the tone of the text?

reprieve
(rĭ-prēv´) *n.* the cancellation or postponement of punishment.

---

[3] **Buna** (boo´nə): a section of the concentration camp at Auschwitz.
[4] **Kapos** (kä´pōs): prisoners who performed certain duties for the guards.
[5] **Blockälteste** (blŏk ĕl´təs-tə): a rank of Kapos; a prisoner designated by the Nazis to be the leader or representative of a block, or group of barracks.
[6] **Achtung!** (äk´toong): German command for "Attention!"

13   There was instant silence.

14   "Listen carefully to what I am about to tell you." For the first time, his voice quivered. "In a few moments, selection will take place. You will have to undress completely. Then you will go, one by one, before the SS doctors. I hope you will all pass. But you must try to increase your chances. Before you go into the next room, try to move your limbs, give yourself some color. Don't walk slowly, run! Run as if you had the devil at your heels! Don't look at the SS. Run, straight in front of you!"

15   He paused and then added:

16   "And most important, don't be afraid!"

17   That was a piece of advice we would have loved to be able to follow.

18   I undressed, leaving my clothes on my cot. Tonight, there was no danger that they would be stolen.

19   Tibi and Yossi, who had changed Kommandos at the same time I did, came to urge me:

20   "Let's stay together. It will make us stronger."

21   Yossi was mumbling something. He probably was praying. I had never suspected that Yossi was religious. In fact, I had always believed the opposite. Tibi was silent and very pale. All the block inmates stood naked between the rows of bunks. This must be how one stands for the Last Judgment.

22   "They are coming!"

23   Three SS officers surrounded the notorious Dr. Mengele,[7] the very same who had received us in Birkenau. The *Blockälteste* attempted a smile. He asked us:

24   "Ready?"

---

[7] **Dr. Mengele** (mĕn-gə′lə): Josef Mengele (1911–1979), Nazi physician at Auschwitz known for conducting cruel experiments on prisoners.

25   Yes, we were ready. So were the SS doctors. Dr. Mengele was holding a list: our numbers. He nodded to the *Blockälteste*: we can begin! As if this were a game.

26   The first to go were the "notables" of the block, the *Stubenälteste*,[8] the Kapos, the foremen, all of whom were in perfect physical condition, of course! Then came the ordinary prisoners' turns. Dr. Mengele looked them over from head to toe. From time to time, he noted a number. I had but one thought: not to have my number taken down and not to show my left arm.

27   In front of me, there were only Tibi and Yossi. They passed. I had time to notice that Mengele had not written down their numbers. Someone pushed me. It was my turn. I ran without looking back. My head was spinning: you are too skinny . . . you are too weak . . . you are too skinny, you are good for the ovens . . . The race seemed endless; I felt as though I had been running for years . . . You are too skinny, you are too weak . . . At last I arrived. Exhausted. When I had caught my breath, I asked Yossi and Tibi:

28   "Did they write me down?"

29   "No," said Yossi. Smiling, he added, "Anyway, they couldn't have. You were running too fast . . ."

30   I began to laugh. I was happy. I felt like kissing him. At that moment, the others did not matter! They had not written me down.

31   Those whose numbers had been noted were standing apart, abandoned by the whole world. Some were silently weeping.

32   THE SS OFFICERS left. The *Blockälteste* appeared, his face reflecting our collective weariness.

33   "It all went well. Don't worry. Nothing will happen to anyone. Not to anyone . . ."

34   He was still trying to smile. A poor **emaciated** Jew questioned him anxiously, his voice trembling:

35   "But . . . sir. They *did* write me down!"

36   At that, the *Blockälteste* vented his anger: What! Someone refused to take his word?

37   "What is it now? Perhaps you think I'm lying? I'm telling you, once and for all: nothing will happen to you! Nothing! You just like to wallow in your despair, you fools!"

38   The bell rang, signaling that the selection had ended in the entire camp.

39   With all my strength I began to race toward Block 36; midway, I met my father. He came toward me:

40   "So? Did you pass?"

41   "Yes. And you?"

42   "Also."

43   We were able to breathe again. My father had a present for me: a half ration of bread, bartered for something he had found at the depot, a piece of rubber that could be used to repair a shoe.

ANALYZE MEMOIRS

Annotate: Mark details that help you better understand Wiesel's character at the time of the events.

Evaluate: How has the passage of time given Wiesel insight into what he experienced at the end of the "selection"?

emaciated
(ĭ-mā′shē-āt id) *adj.* made extremely thin and weak.

---

8 **Stubenälteste** (shtyōō′bə-nĭl-tŭs -tə): a rank of Kapos; prisoners designated by the Nazis to be the leaders of their barracks, or rooms.

44   The bell. It was already time to part, to go to bed. The bell regulated everything. It gave me orders and I **executed** them blindly. I hated that bell. Whenever I happened to dream of a better world, I imagined a universe without a bell.

45   A FEW DAYS passed. We were no longer thinking about the selection. We went to work as usual and loaded the heavy stones onto the freight cars. The rations had grown smaller; that was the only change.

46   We had risen at dawn, as we did every day. We had received our black coffee, our ration of bread. We were about to head to the work yard as always. The *Blockälteste* came running:

47   "Let's have a moment of quiet. I have here a list of numbers. I shall read them to you. All those called will not go to work this morning; they will stay in camp."

48   Softly, he read some ten numbers. We understood. These were the numbers from the selection. Dr. Mengele had not forgotten.

49   The *Blockälteste* turned to go to his room. The ten prisoners surrounded him, clinging to his clothes:

50   "Save us! You promised . . . We want to go to the depot, we are strong enough to work. We are good workers. We can . . . we want . . ."

51   He tried to calm them, to reassure them about their fate, to explain to them that staying in the camp did not mean much, had no tragic significance: "After all, I stay here every day . . ."

52   The argument was more than flimsy. He realized it and, without another word, locked himself in his room.

53   The bell had just rung.

54   "Form ranks!"

55   Now, it no longer mattered that the work was hard. All that mattered was to be far from the block, far from the crucible[9] of death, from the center of hell.

56   I saw my father running in my direction. Suddenly, I was afraid.

57   "What is happening?"

58   He was out of breath, hardly able to open his mouth.

---

[9] **crucible:** a vessel used for melting materials at high temperatures.

execute
(ĕk´sĭ-kyōot) *v.* to carry out, or accomplish.

LANGUAGE CONVENTIONS
Annotate: Underline the dependent clause in paragraph 44.

Analyze: How does this complex sentence contribute to the tone of the paragraph?

59   "Me too, me too . . . They told me too to stay in the camp."

60   They had recorded his number without his noticing.

61   "What are we going to do?" I said anxiously.

62   But it was he who tried to reassure me:

63   "It's not certain yet. There's still a chance. Today, they will do another selection . . . a **decisive** one . . ."

64   I said nothing.

65   He felt time was running out. He was speaking rapidly, he wanted to tell me so many things. His speech became confused, his voice was choked. He knew that I had to leave in a few moments. He was going to remain alone, so alone . . .

66   "Here, take this knife," he said. "I won't need it anymore. You may find it useful. Also take this spoon. Don't sell it. Quickly! Go ahead, take what I'm giving you!"

67   My inheritance . . .

68   "Don't talk like that, Father." I was on the verge of breaking into sobs. "I don't want you to say such things. Keep the spoon and knife. You will need them as much as I. We'll see each other tonight, after work."

69   He looked at me with his tired eyes, veiled by despair. He insisted:

70   "I am asking you . . . Take it, do as I ask you, my son. Time is running out. Do as your father asks you . . ."

71   Our Kapo shouted the order to march.

The Kommando headed toward the camp gate. Left, right!

72 I was biting my lips. My father had remained near the block, leaning against the wall. Then he began to run, to try to catch up with us. Perhaps he had forgotten to tell me something . . . But we were marching too fast . . . Left, right!

73   We were at the gate. We were being counted. Around us, the **din** of military music. Then we were outside.

---

decisive
(dĭ-sī′sĭv) *adj.* final or concluding.

ANALYZE WORD CHOICE

Annotate: Mark words in this section that contribute to the tone of the text.

Analyze: How does the word *inheritance* communicate the author's tone?

din
(dĭn) *n.*
loud noise.

74   ALL DAY, I PLODDED AROUND like a sleepwalker. Tibi and Yossi would call out to me, from time to time, trying to reassure me. As did the Kapo who had given me easier tasks that day. I felt sick at heart. How kindly they treated me. Like an orphan. I thought: Even now, my father is helping me.

75   I myself didn't know whether I wanted the day to go by quickly or not. I was afraid of finding myself alone that evening. How good it would be to die right here!

76   At last, we began the return journey. How I longed for an order to run! The military march. The gate. The camp. I ran toward Block 36.

77   Were there still miracles on this earth? He was alive. He had passed the second selection. He had still proved his usefulness . . . I gave him back his knife and spoon.

CHECK YOUR UNDERSTANDING

Choose the best answer to each question.

1 The guards separate the inmates by —

  A age

  B occupation

  C physical condition

  D observance of authority

2 After the first selection, why doesn't the author mind his work assignment?

  F It is easier than what he had been doing.

  G It gives him a chance to be with his father.

  H It keeps his mind occupied.

  J It means he has been spared.

3 What does Wiesel's father give him?

  A Coins

  B Letters

  C His watch and comb

  D A spoon and knife

BACKGROUND

Władysław Szpilman *(1911–2000) was a Polish musician and composer who lived through the atrocities of the Holocaust. Before the war, Szpilman had been a professional pianist who performed on Polish radio and in front of large crowds. Since he was of Jewish descent, he was confined to a ghetto in Warsaw after Germany invaded Poland in 1939. Szpilman's family was taken away to the death camps; afterward, the Nazis assigned him to work groups in Warsaw. After a rebel uprising, Szpilman managed to hide in a series of abandoned buildings, constantly searching for food and water while evading Nazi patrols. After the war, Szpilman lived a long life, during which he published his memoir, The Pianist, which was turned into an award-winning film in 2002.*

from THE PIANIST

Memoir by Władysław Szpilman

PREPARE TO COMPARE

As you read, make note of how Szpilman establishes setting and character. Notice how his descriptions compare to those of Wiesel. Also pay attention to how Szpilman's word choices reveal his attitudes about the events he experiences.

Notice & Note

You can use the side margins to notice and note signposts in the text.

ANALYZE MEMOIRS

Annotate: Mark details Szpilman uses to establish setting.

Analyze: How does Szpilman's description of the setting contribute to the mood of the text?

1   I was alone: alone not just in a single building or even a single part of a city, but alone in a whole city that only two months ago had a population of a million and a half and was one of the richer cities of Europe. It now consisted of the chimneys of burnt-out buildings pointing to the sky, and whatever walls the bombing had spared: a city of rubble and ashes under which the centuries-old culture of my people and the bodies of hundreds of thousands of murdered victims lay buried, rotting in the warmth of these late autumn days and filling the air with a dreadful stench. . .

2   The first day of November was approaching, and it was beginning to get cold, particularly at night. To keep myself from going mad in my **isolation**, I decided to lead as disciplined a life as possible. I still had my watch, the pre-war Omega I treasured as the apple of my eye, along with my fountain pen. They were my sole personal possessions. I **conscientiously** kept the watch wound and drew up a timetable by it. I lay motionless all day long to conserve what little strength I had left, putting out my hand only once, around midday, to fortify myself with a rusk[1] and a mug of water sparingly portioned out. From early in the morning until I took this meal, as I lay there with my eyes closed, I went over in my mind all the compositions I had ever played, bar by bar. Later, this mental refresher course turned out to have been useful: when I went back to work I still knew my repertory and had almost all of it in my head, as if I had been practising all through the war. Then, from my midday meal until dusk, I systematically ran through the contents of all the books I had read, mentally repeating my English vocabulary. I gave myself English lessons, asking myself questions and trying to answer them correctly and at length.

3   When darkness came I fell asleep. I would wake around one in the morning and go in search of food by the light of matches—I had found a supply of them in the building, in a flat that had not been entirely burnt out. I looked in cellars and the charred[2] ruins of the flats, finding a little oatmeal here, a few pieces of bread there, some dank[3] flour, water in tubs, buckets and jugs. I don't know how many times I passed the charred body on the stairs during these expeditions. He was the sole companion whose presence I need not fear. Once I found an unexpected treasure in a cellar: half a litre of spirits.[4] I decided to save it until the end of the war came. . .

4   What tormented me most was not knowing what was happening in the battle areas, both on the front and among the rebels. The Warsaw rebellion itself had been put down. I could cherish no illusions about that. But perhaps there was still resistance outside the city, in Praga on the other side of the Vistula. I could still hear artillery fire over there now and then, and shells would explode in the ruins, often quite near me, echoing harshly in the silence amidst the burnt-out buildings. What about resistance in the rest of Poland? Where were the Soviet troops? What progress was the Allied offensive making in the west? My life or death depended on the answer to these questions, and even if the Germans did not discover my hiding place it was soon going be my death—of cold if not starvation. . .

---

[1] **rusk:** sweet biscuit or bread.
[2] **charred:** burned.
[3] **dank:** damp in an unpleasant way.
[4] **spirits:** alcoholic beverages.

isolation
(ī-sə-lā´shən) *n.* the condition of being alone or apart from others.

conscientiously
(kŏn-shē-ĕn´shəs-ly) *adj.* doing something thoroughly.

ANALYZE WORD CHOICE

Annotate: Mark the author's description of the body on the stairs.

Interpret: How does the word *companion* contribute to the tone of the text?

5   Today the SS were driving a group of men in civilian clothing to work on the hospital. It was nearly ten in the morning, and I was lying flat on the steep roof when I suddenly heard a volley of firing quite close to me, from a rifle or machine pistol: it was a sound between whistling and twittering, as if a flock of sparrows were flying overhead, and shots fell around me. I looked round: two Germans were standing on the hospital roof opposite, firing at me. I slid back down into the attic and ran to the trapdoor, ducking. Shouts of, 'Stop, stop!' pursued me as bullets flew overhead. However, I landed in the stairway safely.

6   There was no time to stop and think: my last hiding place in this building had been discovered, and I must leave it at once. I raced down the stairs and out into Sędziowska Street, ran along the road and plunged into the ruins of the bungalows that had once been the Staszic estate.[5]

---

[5] **the ruins of the bungalows that had once been the Staszic estate:** referring to the housing complex owned by the family of Stanislaw Staszic, a prominent Polish scholar from the 19th century. Staszic was in favor of forcible assimilation of Jews into Polish society.

7   Yet again my situation was hopeless, as it had been so often before. I was wandering among the walls of totally burnt-out buildings where there could not possibly be any water or remnants of food, or even a hiding place. After a while, however, I saw a tall building in the distance, facing Aleja Niepodległości and backing on to Sędziowska Street, the only multi-storey building in the area. I set off. On closer inspection I saw that the centre of the building had been burnt out, but the wings were almost intact. There was furniture in the flats, the tubs were still full of water from the time of the rebellion, and the looters had left some provisions in the larders.[6]

8   Following my usual custom, I moved into the attic. The roof was quite intact, with just a few holes left in it by splinters of shrapnel. It was much warmer here than in my previous hiding place, although flight from it would be impossible. I could not even escape into death by jumping off the roof. There was a small stained-glass window on the last mezzanine floor of the building, and I could observe the neighbourhood through it. Comfortable as my new surroundings

---

[6] **larders:** places where food is stored.

LANGUAGE CONVENTIONS
Annotate: Underline the dependent clauses in the first two sentences of paragraph 7.

Analyze: How do these clauses contribute to Szpilman's message?

ANALYZE WORD CHOICE
Annotate: Mark words in paragraphs 7 and 8 that reveal Szpilman's thoughts and feelings.

Analyze: What do these words tell you about Szpilman's thoughts and feelings at this moment?

© Houghton Mifflin Harcourt Publishing Company · Image Credits: © Rahul Barcja/Shutterstock

were, I did not feel at ease here—perhaps just because I was now used to the other building. All the same, I had no choice: I must stay here. . .

9   After two days, I went in search of food. This time I planned to lay in a good supply so that I did not have to leave my hiding place too often. I would have to search by day, since I did not know this building well enough to find my way around it by night. I found a kitchen, and then a larder containing several cans of food and some bags and boxes. Their contents would have to be carefully checked. I untied strings and lifted lids. I was so absorbed in my search that I never heard anything until a voice right behind me said, 'What on earth are you doing here?'

10   A tall, elegant German officer was leaning against the kitchen dresser, his arms crossed over his chest.

11   'What are you doing here?' he repeated. 'Don't you know the staff of the Warsaw fortress commando unit is moving into this building any time now?'

12   I slumped on the chair by the larder door. With the certainty of a sleepwalker, I suddenly felt that my strength would fail me if I tried to escape this new trap. I sat there groaning and gazing dully at the officer. It was some time before I stammered, with difficulty, 'Do what you like to me. I'm not moving from here.'

13   'I've no intention of doing anything to you!' The officer shrugged his shoulders. 'What do you do for a living?'

14   'I'm a pianist.'

15   He looked at me more closely, and with obvious suspicion. Then his glance fell on the door leading from the kitchen to the other rooms. An idea seemed to have struck him.

16   'Come with me, will you?'

17   We went into the next room, which had obviously been the dining room, and then into the room beyond it, where a piano stood by the wall. The officer pointed to the instrument.

18   'Play something!'

19   Hadn't it occurred to him that the sound of the piano would instantly attract all the SS men in the vicinity? I looked enquiringly at him and did not move. He obviously sensed my fears, since he added reassuringly, 'It's all right, you can play. If anyone comes, you hide in the larder and I'll say it was me trying the instrument out.'

20   When I placed my fingers on the keyboard they shook. So this time, for a change, I had to buy my life by playing the piano! I hadn't practised for two and a half years, my fingers were stiff and covered with a thick layer of dirt, and I had not cut my nails since the fire in the building where I was hiding. Moreover, the piano was in a room without any window panes, so its action was swollen by the damp and resisted the pressure of the keys.

21   I played Chopin's Nocturne in C sharp minor. The glassy, tinkling sound of the untuned strings rang through the empty flat and the stairway, floated through the ruins of the villa on the other side of the street and returned as a muted, melancholy echo. When I had

CONTRASTS AND CONTRADICTIONS

Notice & Note: Mark the contrast Szpilman sets up in paragraph 21.

Evaluate: How does this contrast contribute to the memoir's tone?

© Houghton Mifflin Harcourt Publishing Company

finished, the silence seemed even gloomier and more eerie than before. A cat mewed in a street somewhere. I heard a shot down below outside the building—a harsh, loud German noise.

22   The officer looked at me in silence. After a while he sighed, and muttered, 'All the same, you shouldn't stay here. I'll take you out of the city, to a village. You'll be safer there.'

23   I shook my head. 'I can't leave this place,' I said firmly.

24   Only now did he seem to understand my real reason for hiding among the ruins. He started nervously.

25   'You're Jewish?' he asked.

26   'Yes.'

27   He had been standing with his arms crossed over his chest; he now unfolded them and sat down in the armchair by the piano, as if this discovery called for lengthy reflection.

28   'Yes, well,' he murmured, 'in that case I see you really can't leave.'

29   He appeared to be deep in thought again for some time, and then turned to me with another question. 'Where are you hiding?'

30   'In the attic.'

31   'Show me what it's like up there.'

32   We went upstairs. He inspected the attic with a careful and expert eye. In so doing he discovered something I had not yet noticed: a kind of extra floor above it, a loft made of boards under the roof valley and directly above the entrance to the attic itself. At first glance

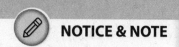
you hardly noticed it because the light was so dim there. The officer said he thought I should hide in this loft, and he helped me look for a ladder in the flats below. Once I was up in the loft I must pull the ladder up after me.

33   When we had discussed this plan and put it into action, he asked if I had anything to eat.

34   'No,' I said. After all, he had taken me unawares while I was searching for supplies.

35   'Well, never mind,' he added hastily, as if ashamed in retrospect of his surprise attack. 'I'll bring you some food.'

36   Only now did I venture a question of my own. I simply could not restrain myself any longer. 'Are you German?'

37   He flushed, and almost shouted his answer in agitation, as if my question had been an insult. 'Yes, I am! And ashamed of it, after everything that's been happening.'

38   Abruptly, he shook hands with me and left.

39   Three days passed before he reappeared. It was evening, and pitch dark, when I heard a whisper under my loft. 'Hello, are you there?'

40   'Yes, I'm here,' I replied.

41   Soon afterwards something heavy landed beside me. Through the paper, I felt several loaves and something soft, which later turned out to be jam wrapped in greaseproof paper. I quickly put the package to one side and called, 'Wait a moment!'

42   The voice in the dark sounded impatient. 'What is it? Hurry up. The guards saw me come in here, and I mustn't stay long.'

43   'Where are the Soviet troops?'

44   'They're already in Warsaw, in Praga on the other side of the Vistula. Just hang on a few more weeks—the war will be over by spring at the latest.'

45   The voice fell silent. I did not know if the officer was still there, or if he had gone. But suddenly he spoke again, 'You must hang on, do you hear?' His voice sounded harsh, almost as if he were giving an order, convincing me of his unyielding belief that the war would end well for us. Only then I did hear the quiet sound of the attic door closing . . .

46   On 12 December, the officer came for the last time. He brought me a larger supply of bread than before and a warm eiderdown. He told me he was leaving Warsaw with his detachment, and I must on no account lose heart, since the Soviet offensive was expected any day now.

47   'In Warsaw?'

48   'Yes.'

49   'But how will I survive the street fighting?' I asked anxiously.

50   'If you and I survived this inferno for over five years.' he replied, 'it's obviously God's will for us to live. Well, we have to believe that, anyway.'

51   'We had already said goodbye, and he was about to go, when an idea came to me at the last moment. I had long been racking

© Houghton Mifflin Harcourt Publishing Company

ANALYZE MEMOIRS

Annotate: Underline details that help you understand the character of the officer.

Describe: Describe how Szpilman views the officer. How does he communicate this feeling to the reader?

my brains for some way of showing him my gratitude, and he had absolutely refused to take my only treasure, my watch.

52   'Listen!' I took his hand and began speaking urgently. 'I never told you my name—you didn't ask me, but I want you to remember it. Who knows what may happen? You have a long way to go home. If I survive, I'll certainly be working for Polish Radio again. I was there before the war. If anything happens to you, if I can help you then in any way, remember my name. Szpilman, Polish Radio.'

53   He smiled his usual smile, half **deprecating**, half shy and embarrassed, but I felt I had given him pleasure with what, in the present situation, was my **naïve** wish to help him.

deprecating
(dĕp´rĭ-kāt-ing) *adj.* belittling or downplaying something.

naïve
(nī-ēv´) *adj.* lacking in experience and everyday knowledge.

CHECK YOUR UNDERSTANDING

Answer these questions before moving on to the **Analyze the Text** section on the following page.

1 Why does the narrator have to move to new hiding places?

  A Other refugees needs to hide there.

  B The Germans have found him.

  C The corpse is bothering him.

  D He has run out of food.

2 When the officer finds the narrator he asks him to —

  F play the piano

  G turn himself in

  H hand over his watch

  J inform him of anyone else hiding

3 How does the narrator keep his mind occupied while hiding?

  A Helping others

  B Spying on the Germans

  C Writing poems and stories

  D Going over compositions in his head

© Houghton Mifflin Harcourt Publishing Company

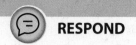

ANALYZE THE TEXT

Support your responses with evidence from the text. ☰ NOTEBOOK

1. **Infer** In paragraph 8 of *Night*, Wiesel writes "The old men stayed in their corner, silent, motionless, hunted-down creatures. Some were praying." Which words in this quotation have strong connotations? How do these words convey the tone and mood of Wiesel's narrative?

2. **Analyze** Look back at the scene in which Wiesel must run before the SS doctors during selection. Why does Wiesel repeat his thoughts, "you are too skinny, you are too weak"? How do these words—and Wiesel's frenzied repetition of them—help the reader relate to Wiesel's experience?

3. **Analyze** What makes Wiesel a reliable authority on life in the prison camp? From what other prisoners does he incorporate statements and perspectives and why do you think he includes them in his memoir?

4. **Evaluate** In *The Pianist*, Szpilman writes about a great deal of time he spent in isolation, without interacting with anyone else. How does he draw the reader into the experience without the benefit of dialogue or much action?

5. **Notice & Note** Reread *The Pianist*, paragraphs 10–18. What is the tone of Szpilman's description of the German officer and of the dialogue between the two men? Why do you think Szpilman included the dialogue with the officer in his memoir?

RESEARCH

Both memoirs are set within the historical events of World War II and the Holocaust. Find a detail or event in one of the texts that you would like to know more about. What questions do you have about it? Search for answers to your questions and record your findings in a chart like the one below.

QUESTIONS:	
Findings:	Source:

Connect Share your findings with a partner and show the sources you used. Critique each other's sources, keeping the following questions in mind:

- Do the authors of the source have credibility and the expertise to address this topic? What is their point of view, or perspective, on the topic?
- Do other sources back up the accuracy of their information? Does the source appear to offer a balanced view, or is it biased?

CREATE AND DISCUSS

Write an Introduction Reread the Background paragraph that appears before each selection. With a group, expand one of them into a longer introduction, using information from your research.

Go to the **Writing Studio** for more on using research in your writing.

- ❏ Choose the Background for either *Night* or *The Pianist*.

- ❏ Share information group members gathered during their research time. Discuss how this information adds context to the author's experiences.

- ❏ Work individually to incorporate the pieces of information into an expanded introduction that could appear before the memoir.

Discuss with a Small Group Now that you've used each other's research to write individual introductions to the text, share what you've written.

Go to the **Speaking and Listening Studio** for help with sharing ideas as a group.

- ❏ Take turns reading aloud your texts.

- ❏ As a group, reflect on how you incorporated the research in different ways. How do the different introductions provide the reader with helpful context?

RESPOND TO THE ESSENTIAL QUESTION

? What does it take to survive in a crisis?

Gather Information Review your annotations and notes on *Night* and *The Pianist* and highlight those that help answer the Essential Question. Then, add relevant details to your Response Log.

ACADEMIC VOCABULARY

As you write and discuss what you learned from the memoirs, be sure to use the Academic Vocabulary words. Check off each of the words that you use.

- ❏ **dimension**
- ❏ **external**
- ❏ **statistic**
- ❏ **sustain**
- ❏ **utilize**

RESPOND

WORD BANK

emaciated	isolation
decisive	conscientiously
execute	deprecating
din	naïve
reprieve	

CRITICAL VOCABULARY

Practice and Apply Use your knowledge of the Critical Vocabulary words to respond to each question.

1. Wiesel describes one of the prisoners as **emaciated**. What does the prisoner look like?

2. When Wiesel's father passes the second **decisive** selection, Wiesel is relieved. Explain why.

3. While a prisoner, Wiesel **executes** his work tasks. Do the guards likely have a complaint about his work? Explain.

4. The narrator can hear the **din** of military music in the background. What does the music sound like?

5. The prisoners at the concentration camp hope for a **reprieve** from death. What do they hope will happen?

6. Szpilman spends a lot of time in **isolation**. What ends that isolation?

7. Why do you think Szpilman treats the watch **conscientiously**?

8. The officer smiles in a **deprecating** way. What does that reveal about his view of himself?

9. What makes Szpilman's offer to help the officer **naïve**?

VOCABULARY STRATEGY:
Multiple-Meaning Words

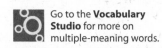

Go to the **Vocabulary Studio** for more on multiple-meaning words.

The Critical Vocabulary word *execute* means "to accomplish or carry out fully." *Execute* has another definition, "to put to death." Like *execute*, many words have **multiple meanings**. Use the strategies below to determine or clarify the meaning of multiple-meaning words.

- Use context, or the way the word is used in a sentence or paragraph, to determine meaning. Look at the words and sentences around the unknown word to clarify its meaning. For example, look at the following sentence: *Mountain climbing was her passion, and she wanted to scale every peak.* The context tells you that *scale* refers to climbing.

- Consult general and specialized reference materials, particularly glossaries and dictionaries, to determine or clarify the precise meaning of a word. Dictionary entries provide all the definitions of a word, as well as its part of speech, so select the definition that makes sense.

Practice and Apply Work in a group to locate these words from *Night*: *present* (paragraph 1) and *block* (paragraph 2), and these words from *The Pianist*: *mad* (paragraph 2) and *flat* (paragraph 3). Use context clues or reference materials to determine the precise meaning for each word.

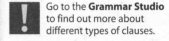

LANGUAGE CONVENTIONS
Clauses

A **clause** is a group of words with a subject and a verb. There are two types of clauses: an **independent clause** can stand alone as a sentence; a **dependent clause** cannot. Instead, dependent clauses act as modifiers, adding meaning to independent clauses. Dependent clauses often begin with these words: *as if, as, since, than, that, though, until, whenever, where, while, who,* and *why.* These words are subordinating conjunctions that clarify the connection between the clauses.

Go to the **Grammar Studio** to find out more about different types of clauses.

Read the following sentence from *Night*:

> **They had transferred me to another Kommando, the construction one, <u>where twelve hours a day I hauled heavy slabs of stone.</u>**

This sentence contains one independent clause and one dependent clause. Notice how the independent clause *They had transferred me to another Kommando, the construction one* forms a complete thought and can stand alone as a sentence. The dependent clause, which is underlined, provides additional information about the independent clause, but it cannot stand alone.

The two types of clauses function together to convey the author's meaning. Without the clause, the author's ideas might be presented this way:

> **They had transferred me to another Kommando, the construction one. The Kommando was where twelve hours a day I hauled heavy slabs of stone.**

These simple sentences are choppy, repetitive, and less interesting to read. Here are more examples of effective independent and dependent clauses from *The Pianist*. The dependent clauses are underlined.

> **He obviously sensed my fears, <u>since he added reassuringly,</u> "It's all right, you can play."**

> **<u>When I had finished,</u> the silence seemed even gloomier and more eerie than before.**

Practice and Apply Write three to four sentences, each with at least one independent and one dependent clause, about your reaction to the two memoirs. Try to use different subordinating conjunctions in your sentences.

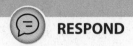

from **NIGHT**
Memoir by
Elie Wiesel

from **THE PIANIST**
Memoir by
Władysław Szpilman

Collaborate & Compare

COMPARE MEMOIRS

When you compare two or more texts on the same topic, you **synthesize** the information: you make connections and extend key ideas. It's easier to do this when the texts you're comparing are the same genre, or type of writing.

In a small group, complete the chart with details from both memoirs. Some of these details are easy to find in the text. For others, you will need to make inferences or draw conclusions using the details that do appear in the text. Discuss elements the memoirs share. Support your ideas with specific evidence from the texts. After hearing other views, you may want to adjust the responses in your chart.

LITERARY ELEMENT	*NIGHT*	*THE PIANIST*
Setting		
Point of View		
How the Narrator Reacts to His Circumstance		
Characterization		
Author's Purpose		
Word Choice		
Tone		

ANALYZE THE TEXTS

Discuss these questions in your group.

1. **Analyze** Both authors describe characters other than themselves. How do these different characters' perspectives add to the texts' meanings?

2. **Contrast** What differences do you notice between the authors' styles and tones?

3. **Compare** What themes do the two texts share?

4. **Synthesize** What have you learned from these memoirs about the events of World War II and the Holocaust?

COLLABORATE AND PRESENT

With your group, present your findings as you compared the memoirs. Use the information in your charts to plan a presentation to the rest of the class about how the memoirs have some common elements but differ in other ways.

1. **Plan Your Presentation** As a group, choose the most important ideas that you discussed, and write a summary of each. Use the following questions to prepare your presentation:
   - ❏ In what order will we present these ideas?
   - ❏ What will each group member say?
   - ❏ How will we conclude our presentation?
   - ❏ How can we use precise vocabulary and language, with evidence from the texts, to help the audience understand our points?

2. **Present and Discuss** Deliver your presentation to the rest of the class and listen to the other presentations. Then, with your group, discuss whether you think that the memoir is an appropriate genre for both writers to use to explore the events of the Holocaust. Explain your thinking.

3. **Reflect** On your own, write your thoughts on how you helped your group prepare and present the material.

INDEPENDENT READING

Reader's Choice

Setting a Purpose Select one or more of these options from your eBook to continue your exploration of the Essential Question.

• Read the descriptions to see which text grabs your interest.

• Think about which genres you enjoy reading.

Notice & Note

In this unit, you practiced noticing and noting these signposts and strategies: **Memory Moment, Again and Again,** and **Contrasts and Contradictions**. As you read independently, these signposts and others will aid your understanding. Below are the anchor questions to ask when you read literature and nonfiction.

Reading Literature: Stories, Poems, and Plays		
Signpost	**Anchor Question**	**Lesson**
Contrasts and Contradictions	Why did the character act that way?	p. 419
Aha Moment	How might this change things?	p. 171
Tough Questions	What does this make me wonder about?	p. 494
Words of the Wiser	What's the lesson for the character?	p. 171
Again and Again	Why might the author keep bringing this up?	p. 170
Memory Moment	Why is this memory important?	p. 418

Reading Nonfiction: Essays, Articles, and Arguments		
Signpost	**Anchor Question(s)**	**Lesson**
Big Questions	What surprised me? What did the author think I already knew? What challenged, changed, or confirmed what I already knew?	p. 248 p. 2 p. 84
Contrasts and Contradictions	What is the difference, and why does it matter?	p. 3
Extreme or Absolute Language	Why did the author use this language?	p. 85
Numbers and Stats	Why did the author use these numbers or amounts?	p. 249
Quoted Words	Why was this person quoted or cited, and what did this add?	p. 85
Word Gaps	Do I know this word from someplace else? Does it seem like technical talk for this topic? Do clues in the sentence help me understand the word?	p. 3

You can preview these texts in Unit 5 of your eBook.

Then, check off the text or texts that you select to read on your own.

ARTICLE

Adventurers Change. Danger Does Not.
Alan Cowell

Which is more important—to reach the summit of Mount Everest or to save the life of a fellow climber in trouble?

MEMOIR

from An Ordinary Man
Paul Rusesabagina

A Rwandan hotel owner of mixed Hutu and Tutsi descent saves more than a thousand refugees and survives the 1994 genocide.

POEM

Who Understands Me But Me
Jimmy Santiago Baca

When a young man is sentenced to prison, he loses a lot but gains even more.

SPEECH

Truth at All Costs
Marie Colvin

Is it worth the risk to report from a war zone? Do war correspondents make a difference?

INFORMATIONAL TEXT

from Deep Survival
Laurence Gonzales

Is a positive mental attitude really the key to survival? The author explores how disaster survivors manage to beat the odds.

Collaborate and Share   Work with a partner to discuss what you learned from at least one of your independent readings.

- Give a brief synopsis or summary of the text.

- Describe any signposts that you noticed in the text and explain what they revealed to you.

- Describe what you most enjoyed or found most challenging about the text. Give specific examples.

- Decide whether you would recommend the text to others. Why or why not?

Go to the **Reading Studio** for more resources on **Notice & Note.**

Write an Argument

Go to the **Writing Studio** for help writing your argument.

This unit explores the idea of survival and what it takes to endure an extreme situation. Look back at the texts you read, and think about the events that place the people and characters in danger and what their reactions are. Then decide for yourself whether the desire for survival can be selfish. Write an argument that explains your position, using evidence from at least two texts in this unit. For an example of a well-written argumentative text you can use as a mentor text, review Lane Wallace's "Is Survival Selfish?"

As you write your argument, you will want to look at the notes you made in your Response Log.

Writing Prompt

Read the information in the box below.

This is the topic or context for your argument.

> **Survival may be instinctive, but it is not simple.**

Think carefully about the following question.

This is the essential question for the unit.

> **What does it take to survive in a crisis?**

Mark the question you must answer in your essay.

Write an argument stating your position on the question "Does survival require selfishness?"

An effective argument:

- ☐ makes a clear, specific claim
- ☐ develops the claim with valid reasons and relevant evidence
- ☐ anticipate and address counterclaims, or opposing arguments, by providing counterarguments
- ☐ includes a logically structured body, including transitions
- ☐ concludes with an effective summary of the claim
- ☐ demonstrates an appropriate, clear use of language, maintaining a formal style (register), voice, and tone through the use of standard academic English

Review these points as you write and again when you finish. Make any needed changes.

1 Plan

Writing an argument involves a lot of thought and planning. Think about the selections you've read in this unit and the questions they raise about what it takes to survive. Is a focus on saving oneself selfish, or is it a healthy, even smart, human instinct? Does it depend on the circumstances? Use the word web below to help you explore your thoughts and feelings about survival. Include ideas from the unit texts.

You also need to think about what you hope to achieve in your argument and for whom you are writing—your purpose and your audience.

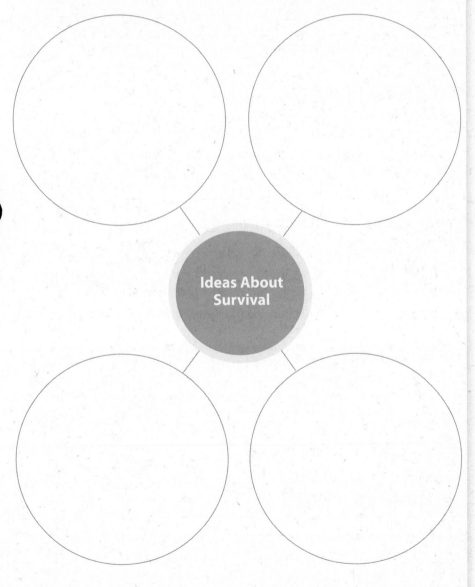

 Go to **Writing Arguments: Planning and Drafting** for help planning your argument.

Notice & Note

From Reading to Writing

As you plan your argument, apply what you've learned about signposts to your own writing. Remember that writers use common features, called signposts, to help convey their message to readers.

Think about how you can incorporate **Quoted Words** into your argument.

 Go to the **Reading Studio** for more resources on **Notice & Note**.

Use the notes from your Response Log as you plan your argument.

Background Reading To find evidence for your argument, go back to the notes you have taken in your Response Log for this unit. If needed, do additional research.

© Houghton Mifflin Harcourt Publishing Company

WRITING TASK

Go to **Writing Arguments: Reasons and Evidence** for more help.

Organize Your Ideas Organize the ideas for your argument in the chart below. Write a clear claim, or thesis statement. Acknowledge a counterclaim, or opposing view, that you will address by providing a counterargument. Then, clearly organize your reasons and relevant details, examples, and evidence, progressing logically from one reason to the next. Refer to at least three of the selections in the unit. When you write your conclusion, summarize your position in a persuasive way.

Argument: Does Survival Require Selfishness?		
Claim, or thesis statement		
Why the audience might not agree (counterclaim)		
Why the audience should agree with you		
Reason 1	**Reason 2**	**Reason 3**
Evidence	**Evidence**	**Evidence**
Conclusion		

2 Develop a Draft

You might prefer to draft your argument online.

Write a well-organized draft of your argument, keeping your purpose and audience in mind as you write. Introduce your argument in a memorable way. Use formal language and a respectful tone. Refer to your graphic organizers and the outline you have created, as well as any notes you took as you studied the texts in the unit. These will provide a kind of map for you to follow as you write. Using a word processor or online writing application makes it easier to make changes or move sentences around later when you are ready to revise your first draft.

Use the Mentor Text

Genre Characteristics

Introduce your argument in a memorable way that will grab your reader's attention. You want your readers to be involved in what you have to say from the very beginning. Note how the opening lines of "Is Survival Selfish?" capture the reader's attention.

> When the ocean liner *Titanic* sank in April of 1912, one of the few men to survive the tragedy was J. Bruce Ismay, the chairman and managing director of the company that owned the ship.

The writer uses a surprising and intriguing fact to immediately draw in the reader.

Apply What You've Learned Draw your reader into your argument quickly with an interesting fact or example.

Author's Craft

It's important to help your reader move smoothly through your argument. One way to do that is to use transitions—words that connect reasons and evidence to the claim and express the relationship between words, sentences, and paragraphs.

> In Yates' case, he had time to think hard about the odds, and the possibilities he was facing, and to realize that he couldn't save anyone but himself. But what about people who have to make more instantaneous decisions?

See how this example makes smooth transitions from one idea to the next.

Apply What You've Learned Use transitions effectively in your argument.

© Houghton Mifflin Harcourt Publishing Company

Go to **Writing Arguments: Revising and Editing** for more help.

③ Revise

On Your Own Getting your ideas down on paper is the purpose of a draft. Revising that draft is where your ideas are polished and improved. The Revision Guide will help you focus on specific elements to make your writing stronger.

REVISION GUIDE

Ask Yourself	Tips	Revision Techniques
1. Does my introduction include a clearly stated claim?	**Underline** the introduction. **Highlight** the claim.	**Reword** the claim to make the idea clearer.
2. Do at least two valid reasons support the claim? Is each reason supported by relevant and sufficient evidence?	**Highlight** each reason. **Underline** each piece of evidence.	**Add** reasons or revise existing ones to make them more valid. **Insert** relevant evidence to ensure that your support is sufficient.
3. Have I addressed one or more counterclaims?	**Mark** both the counterclaims and your responses to them.	**Add** a counterclaim and counterargument that addresses the counterclaim.
4. Do I maintain a formal style throughout the argument?	**Highlight** slang and informal language.	**Reword** text to replace informal language with formal language.
5. Are appropriate and varied transitions used to connect reasons and evidence to the claim?	**Mark** each transition.	**Add** transition words and phrases to provide continuity.
6. Does the conclusion effectively summarize my argument?	**Underline** the summary of your argument.	**Add** or **reword** sentences to strengthen your summary.

ACADEMIC VOCABULARY
As you conduct your **peer review**, try to use these words.

❏ dimension
❏ external
❏ statistic
❏ sustain
❏ utilize

With a Partner After you have addressed all the points in the Revision Guide, exchange papers with a partner. Evaluate each other's drafts in a **peer review**. Look for places that need transitions and be ready to make suggestions of connecting words that might help. Pay attention to the style of the writing and notice any language that is too informal. As you make your suggestions for changes, be sure to bring up things your partner did well.

When you are receiving feedback, listen respectfully and consider your partner's points thoughtfully.

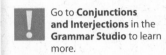

 Edit

Once you have addressed the organization, development, and flow of ideas in your essay, you have one last step to take. Edit for the proper use of standard English conventions and make sure to correct any misspellings or grammatical errors.

Language Conventions

Look for places in your argument where you can use **transition words**, also known as **connecting words**, to link ideas, events, or reasons.

- **Contrast** Connecting words and phrases can show that two ideas are being contrasted. Some examples include *but, on the one hand, conversely, however, but then, nonetheless, in spite of, in contrast to.*

- **Sequence** Connecting words and phrases can also show time relationships between ideas. Some examples include *then, when, first, second, next, last, finally.* Dates are also sequence connectors.

Other types of connecting words indicate cause and effect, reasons, examples, and comparison. The chart contains examples of connecting words from "Is Survival Selfish?" and *Deep Survival* (in the online Independent Reading).

> Go to **Conjunctions and Interjections** in the **Grammar Studio** to learn more.

Connecting words showing sequence	In July 2007, I was having a drink with a friend in Grand Central Station when an underground steam pipe exploded just outside. From where we sat, we heard a dull "boom!" and then suddenly, people were running, streaming out of the tunnels and out the doors.
Connecting words showing contrast	Survivors aren't fearless. They *use* fear: they turn it into anger and focus. Conversely, searchers are always amazed to find people who have died while in possession of everything they needed to survive.

⑤ **Publish**

Finalize your argument and choose a way to share it with your audience. Consider these options:

- Deliver your argument to your class.

- Present your argument as a letter to the editor. Submit it to your school or community newspaper or an online magazine.

Use the scoring guide to evaluate your argument.

WRITING TASK SCORING GUIDE: ARGUMENT

	Organization/Progression	Development of Ideas	Use of Language and Conventions
4	• The organization is effective and appropriate to the purpose. • All ideas center on a specific claim. • Transitions clearly show the relationships among ideas.	• The introduction catches the reader's attention and clearly states the claim. • Reasons are compelling and supported by evidence including quotations and facts. • A counterclaim is effectively presented and addressed. • The conclusion synthesizes the ideas, effectively summarizes the argument, and provides a thought-provoking insight.	• Language and word choice is purposeful and precise. • The style is appropriately formal. • Spelling, capitalization, and punctuation are correct. • Grammar and usage are correct.
3	• The organization is, for the most part, effective and appropriate to the purpose. • Most ideas are focused on the claim. • A few more transitions are needed to show the relationship among ideas.	• The introduction could be more engaging. The claim is stated. • Appropriate reasons for the claim are supported by relevant evidence. • A counterclaim is presented and addressed. • The conclusion summarizes the argument effectively.	• Language is for the most part specific and clear. • The style is generally formal. • Minor spelling, capitalization, and punctuation mistakes do not interfere with the message. • Some grammar and usage errors occur but do not cause confusion.
2	• The organization is evident but is not always appropriate to the purpose. • Only some ideas are focused on the claim presented in the thesis. • Relationships among ideas are sometimes unclear.	• The introduction is not engaging. A vague claim is stated. • One or more reasons may be provided but lack sufficient evidence. • A counterclaim may be hinted at or not adequately addressed. • The conclusion merely restates the claim.	• Language is somewhat vague and unclear. • The style is often informal. • Spelling, capitalization, and punctuation are often incorrect. • Several errors in grammar and usage appear.
1	• The organization is not apparent. • Ideas are often tangential to a claim. • No transitions are used, making the argument difficult to understand.	• The introduction is missing or fails to make a claim. • Reasons are irrelevant or unsupported by evidence. • A counterclaim is either absent or not addressed. • The conclusion is missing.	• The style of language is inappropriate for the text. • Many spelling, capitalization, and punctuation errors make reading difficult. • Grammatical and usage errors cause significant confusion.

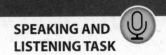
Present and Respond to an Argument

You will now prepare to deliver your argument as an oral presentation.

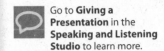
Go to **Giving a Presentation** in the **Speaking and Listening Studio** to learn more.

1 Adapt Your Argument for Presentation

Review your argument, thinking about how you can condense and clarify it for presentation. Use the chart below as you adapt your argument.

Argument Presentation Planning Chart		
Title and Introduction	How will you revise your title and introductory paragraph to capture the listener's attention and make a powerful statement of your claim?	
Audience	What information will your audience already know? What will they think about your claim? What counterclaims could they make?	
Effective Language and Organization	Which parts of your argument should be simplified? Where can you add connecting words such as "first, second, third" to clarify your main points?	
Visuals	What images could you use to illustrate your points or make your argument more convincing?	

2 Practice with a Partner or Group

After you have adapted your argument for presentation, practice with a partner or group to improve both the argument and your delivery. Remember to use appropriate content and academic vocabulary, and ask for help if you do not know the words to express your ideas.

Practice Effective Verbal Techniques

❏ **Enunciation** Practice saying difficult words aloud. If there are words that you stumble over, consider replacing them.

❏ **Voice Modulation and Pitch** Raise and lower your voice to emphasize points and make your arguments persuasive.

© Houghton Mifflin Harcourt Publishing Company

SPEAKING AND LISTENING TASK

As you work to improve your own delivery and that of your classmates, follow these discussion rules:

❏ point out strengths as well as weaknesses

❏ only contribute information that is relevant to the discussion

❏ avoid generalizations like, "It was good," or "It could be better."

❏ include suggestions for improvement in a considerate and tactful manner

❏ **Speaking Rate** Speak slowly enough that listeners understand you. Speak fast enough so that listeners don't fall asleep.

❏ **Volume** Have your partner or a group member go to the back of the room to see whether you can be heard.

Practice Effective Nonverbal Techniques

❏ **Eye Contact** Try to make eye contact with everyone in your audience at least once.

❏ **Facial Expression** Practice using facial expressions that mirror the emotions to which you are appealing with your argument.

❏ **Gestures** Gesture naturally with your hands, your shoulders, and your head, in ways that add meaning and interest to your delivery.

Provide and Consider Advice for Improvement

As a listener, pay close attention and listen respectfully. Take notes about ways that presenters can improve their deliveries and verbal and nonverbal techniques. Paraphrase and summarize each presenter's key ideas and main points, and ask questions to clarify ideas.

As a presenter, listen closely to questions and consider ways to revise your delivery to make sure your points are clear and logically sequenced. Remember to ask for suggestions about how you might make your delivery clearer and more interesting.

❸ Deliver Your Argument

Use the advice you received during practice to make final changes to your argument. Then, using effective verbal and nonverbal techniques, present it to your classmates.

Listen for rhetorical appeals presenters use to support a claim. These strategies appeal to the reader's logic, ethics, or emotions. When writers use emotional appeals, they should offer evidence. Notice persuasive techniques presenters may use to manipulate your emotions:

- **Bandwagon** (everyone is doing it)
- **Personal attack** (discrediting an idea by attacking the person who expressed it)
- **Transfer** (connecting feelings about one thing to something else)
- **Loaded language** (choosing words that elicit strong feelings)
- **Understatement** (deliberately saying less than you mean)
- **Overstatement** (purposefully exaggerating or hyping)
- **Ad Hominem** (an argument directed against a person rather than an issue)
- **Testimonial** (relying on endorsements by well-known people)

© Houghton Mifflin Harcourt Publishing Company

Reflect on the Unit

In this writing task, you wrote about survival in the light of ideas and insights from the readings in this unit. Now is a good time to reflect on what you have learned.

Reflect on the Essential Question

- What does it take to survive in a crisis? How has your answer to this question changed since you first considered it when you started this unit?

- What are some examples from the texts you've read that show what it takes to survive in a crisis?

Reflect on Your Reading

- Which selections were the most interesting or surprising to you?

- From which selection did you learn the most about survival and survivors?

Reflect on the Writing Task

- What difficulties did you encounter while working on your argument? How might you avoid them next time?

- What part of the argument was the easiest and what part was the hardest to write? Why?

- What improvements did you make to your argument as you were revising?

UNIT 5 SELECTIONS
- "The Leap"
- "Is Survival Selfish?"
- "The End and the Beginning"
- from *Night*
- from *The Pianist*

HEROES AND QUESTS

© Houghton Mifflin Harcourt Publishing Company • Image Credits: (t) ©Carlos Amarillo/Shutterstock; (inset) ©Baranov E/Shutterstock; (b) ©MR1805/iStock/Getty Images Plus/Getty Images

? ESSENTIAL QUESTION:

What drives us to take on a challenge?

> " If a journey doesn't have something to teach you about yourself, then what kind of journey is it? "
>
> **Kira Salak**

ACADEMIC VOCABULARY

Academic Vocabulary words are words you use when you discuss and write about texts. In this unit you will practice and learn five words.

☑ **motivate** ☐ **objective** ☐ **pursuit** ☐ **subsequent** ☐ **undertake**

Study the Word Network to learn more about the word **motivate**.

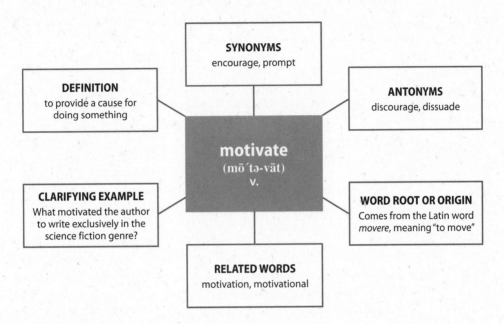

SYNONYMS
encourage, prompt

DEFINITION
to provide a cause for doing something

ANTONYMS
discourage, dissuade

motivate
(mō´tə-vāt)
v.

CLARIFYING EXAMPLE
What motivated the author to write exclusively in the science fiction genre?

WORD ROOT OR ORIGIN
Comes from the Latin word *movere*, meaning "to move"

RELATED WORDS
motivation, motivational

Write and Discuss Discuss the completed Word Network with a partner, making sure to talk through all of the boxes until you both understand the word, its synonyms, antonyms, and related forms. Then, fill out a Word Network for each of the four remaining words. Use a dictionary or online resource to help you complete the activity.

Go online to access the Word Networks.

RESPOND TO THE ESSENTIAL QUESTION

In this unit, you will explore what motivates people to take on a challenge. As you read, you will revisit the **Essential Question** and gather your ideas about it in the **Response Log** that appears on page R6. At the end of the unit, you will have the opportunity to write an **explanatory essay** exploring the human need for challenges. Filling out the Response Log will help you prepare for this writing task.

You can also go online to access the Response Log.

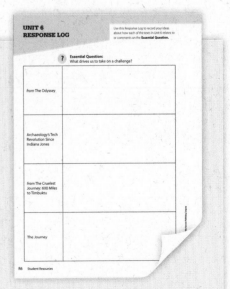

Notice & Note

from THE ODYSSEY

For more information on these and other signposts to Notice & Note, visit the **Reading Studio**.

You are about to read a selection from the epic poem *The Odyssey*. In it, you will notice and note signposts that will give you clues about the poem's characters and themes. Here are three signposts to look for as you read this epic poem and other works of fiction.

When you read an epic poem, pause to see if the hero is facing a **Tough Question:**

"What could I could possibly do . . ."

"I am not sure what the right decision is . . ."

"How will I ever understand why . . ."

"Never have I been so confused about . . ."

Tough Questions Have you ever faced a difficult choice and asked a friend or yourself, "What should I do?" Questions such as these have no simple answers but make us consider our options.

When a character of a poem or story asks a tough question when facing a difficult choice, it reveals an internal conflict that the character is struggling to resolve. Authors may have characters ask an explicit question, or the question may be implied in a statement that suggests confusion or doubt.

One of the characteristics of an epic hero is the ability to respond to tough questions by taking swift action to overcome dangerous situations. Odysseus must prove his cleverness in facing tough choices many times throughout the course of *The Odyssey*. The lines below illustrate a student's annotation and a response to a **Tough Questions** signpost.

> 'Old shipmates, friends,
> the rest of you stand by; I'll make the crossing
> in my own ship, with my own company,
> and find out what the mainland natives are—
> for they may be wild savages, and lawless, or
> hospitable and god fearing men.'

Anchor Question
When you notice this signpost, ask: What does this make me wonder about?

What tough questions does Odysseus face here?	Are the natives dangerous or hospitable? Who should go find out?
What does Odysseus' decision make you wonder about?	Is it wise for Odysseus to go with only a few people?

Again and Again Song lyrics tend to include repetitive words and phrases which help us remember them. Songwriters use repeated words to enhance rhythm and rhyme and emphasize ideas and themes. Poets and authors create patterns by using situations, objects, and words or phrases **Again and Again** to make a point. Paying attention to instances of repetition can:

- provide insight into character, theme, or conflict
- reveal symbols or events being foreshadowed
- emphasize important ideas
- display literary artistry, such as rhyme, rhythm, or imagery

In this example, a student underlined an instance of Again and Again.

> When <u>Dawn spread out her finger tips of rose</u>
> the rams began to stir, moving for pasture . . .

When you see a word, phrase, or image appearing **Again and Again** as you read, pause to note:

"The author is repeating this phrase because . . ."

"This repeated phrase seems odd at this moment because . . ."

"Again the author is bringing up the image of . . ."

Anchor Question
When you notice this signpost, ask: Why might the author keep bringing this up?

What is occurring again and again?	the reference to Dawn spreading out her "finger tips of rose"
Why do you think the author keeps using this phrase?	to add rhythm and incorporate imagery that describes the dawn

Contrasts and Contradictions Imagine watching a movie with a character who has been a bully, but is suddenly acting kind. You wonder why the character actions contradict previous behavior. Use **Contrasts and Contradictions** to draw conclusions and make predictions about characters. Authors often use Contrasts and Contradictions to:

- create complex characters
- show character development and growth
- build mystery and tension
- develop conflict
- provide insight into themes

Here a student marked a Contrast and Contradiction.

> He seized and drained the bowl, and it went down
> so fiery and smooth he called for more:
> 'Give me another, <u>thank you kindly. Tell me, how are you called?</u>
> <u>I'll make a gift will please you.</u>

When you see **Contrasts and Contradictions** as you read, pause to note:

"Until now, the character has acted . . ."

"I expected the character to . . ."

"This character is very different than . . ."

Anchor Question
When you notice this signpost, ask: Why did the character act that way?

What is the contrast or contradiction?	Suddenly the Cyclops is being polite and friendly
Why is the character acting this way? What does this tell you about the character?	He wants more wine. I can infer that the Cyclops has a weakness, and Odysseus can manipulate him.

THE EPIC

Extraordinary heroes in pursuit of hideous monsters. Brutal battles fought and perilous quests undertaken. Spectacular triumphs and crushing defeats. The epic, still very much alive in today's novels and movies, began thousands of years ago in the oral tradition of ancient Greece. There, listeners gathered around poet-storytellers to hear the daring exploits of the hero Odysseus. Across storm-tossed seas, through wild forests, amid countless dangers and subsequent narrow escapes, the hero, motivated by a singular focus on his objective, prevails against all odds. It's no wonder that Homer's Odyssey *remains one of the most beloved epics in Western literature. It captivates us and carries us off into a time and place quite different from—yet somehow similar to—our own.*

CHARACTERISTICS OF THE EPIC

An **epic** is a long narrative poem. It recounts the adventures of an epic hero, a larger-than-life figure who undertakes great journeys and performs deeds requiring remarkable bravery and cunning. As you begin your own journey through Homer's epic, you can expect to encounter the following elements.

ELEMENTS OF THE EPIC	
Epic Hero • Possesses superhuman strength, craftiness, and confidence • Helped or harmed by gods or fate • Embodies qualities valued by the culture • Overcomes perilous situations	**Archetypes** Characters and situations recognizable across times and cultures • brave hero • evil temptress • sea monster • loyal servant • suitors' contest • buried treasure
Epic Plot Depicts a long, strange journey filled with such complications as • strange creatures • divine intervention • treacherous weather • large-scale events	**Epic Themes** Reflect universal concerns, such as • courage • the fate of a nation • loyalty • beauty • life and death • a homecoming
Epic Setting • Includes fantastic or exotic lands • Involves more than one nation or culture	

THE LANGUAGE OF HOMER

The people of ancient Greece who first experienced *The Odyssey* heard it sung in a live performance. The poet, or another performer, used epic similes, epithets, and allusions to help keep the audience enthralled.

- A **simile** is a comparison between two unlike things, using the word *like* or *as*. Homer often employs the **epic simile**, a comparison developed at great length over several lines. For example, the epic simile in the passage on the right compares an angry Odysseus to a roasting sausage.

> His rage
> held hard in leash, submitted to his mind,
> while <u>he himself rocked, rolling from side to side,</u>
> <u>as a cook turns a sausage, big with blood</u>
> <u>and fat, at a scorching blaze, without a pause,</u>
> <u>to broil it quick</u>: so he rolled left and right, . . .

- An **epithet** renames a person or thing with a descriptive phrase. To maintain the meter of the poem or complete a line of verse, the poet would often use an epithet containing the necessary number of syllables. For example, Homer often refers to Odysseus by such epithets as "son of Laertes" and "raider of cities."

- An **allusion** is a reference to a literary or historical person, place, event, or composition. For example, when Telemachus, Odysseus' son, beholds the palace of Menelaus, he exclaims, "This is the way the court of Zeus must be." Every listener in Greece immediately understood the allusion to Zeus, the ruler of the gods.

EXAMINING THE HOMERIC EPICS

Considered the greatest masterpieces of the epic form, *The Iliad* and *The Odyssey* present high drama and intense emotions. In both books, important plot elements include the interference of gods in human affairs, the epic heroism of the central characters, and the saga of the Trojan War and its aftermath.

THE TROJAN WAR The legendary conflict between Greece (or Achaea) and Troy began around 1200 BC. Paris, a Trojan prince, kidnapped Helen, the wife of Menelaus, king of Sparta. Menelaus recruited the armies of allied kingdoms to attack Troy and recover his wife. For ten years the Greek forces held Troy under siege, but they could not penetrate the walls of the city.

Finally, Odysseus, king of Ithaca, came up with a plan to break the stalemate. He ordered his men to build a giant wooden horse. One morning the people of Troy awoke to find that horse outside the city gates—and no Greeks in sight. Assuming the Greeks had retreated and had left the horse as a peace offering, they brought the horse inside the gates. They soon discovered, too late, that the horse was filled with Greek soldiers and that their city was doomed.

HEROISM *The Odyssey* recounts Odysseus' adventures as he struggles to make his way home from post-war Troy, along with the conflicts that arise in Ithaca just before and after his return. He prevails against gruesome monsters, enchanting women, and greedy rivals intent on preventing him from reaching his objective. Odysseus employs cleverness and guile to get out of difficult situations.

© Houghton Mifflin Harcourt Publishing Company • Image Credits: ©Leemage/Universal Images Group/Getty Images

from

THE ODYSSEY

Epic Poem by **Homer**
translated by Robert Fitzgerald

? ***ESSENTIAL QUESTION:***

What drives us to take on a challenge?

QUICK START

Think about someone you think is a hero. What qualities or characteristics do you admire in this person? Brainstorm a list of up to 20 heroic traits. Share your list with a partner, and note any overlapping traits. Ask your classmates or teacher to explain any terms you are not familiar with.

EPIC HEROES

Odysseus is an **epic hero**—a larger-than-life character who embodies the ideals of a nation or race. Epic heroes take part in long, dangerous adventures and accomplish great deeds. They are considered **archetypes** because they can be found in many works from different cultures throughout the ages. Often their character traits provide clues to the epic's **themes**. In addition, the form, style, and point of view of epics provides insight into the historical time in which they were written.

Although epic heroes may have superhuman abilities, they still have human flaws. These flaws make them more complex and also more believable. For example, Odysseus demonstrates extraordinary strength and courage, but his overconfidence results in a tendency to dismiss warnings. His imperfections help make him more likable than a perfect character would be, and the audience can relate to his mistakes.

As you read, take notes in the chart below to help you analyze how the complex character of Odysseus develops over the course of the epic.

© Houghton Mifflin Harcourt Publishing Company

GENRE ELEMENTS: EPIC POEM

- a long, narrative poem on a serious subject in an elevated or formal style
- tells adventures of a hero whose traits reflect the ideals of a nation or race
- addresses universal themes
- occurs across cultures and time periods

QUESTION ABOUT ODYSSEUS	NOTES FROM THE EPIC
What do you learn about Odysseus' character through how he faces various conflicts?	
What traits, or qualities, does Odysseus show through his interactions with other characters?	
What do Odysseus' character traits tell you about what the ancient Greeks found admirable? What themes do you predict Homer might develop?	

EPIC POETRY

An **epic** is a long narrative poem, usually an adventure story. An epic plot spans many years and involves a long journey. Often, the fate of an entire nation is at stake. An epic **setting** spans great distances and foreign lands. Epic **themes** reflect timeless concerns, such as courage, honor, life, and death. To appreciate *The Odyssey* as poetry, follow these steps:

- Read the epic aloud. Listen for sound devices, such as alliteration, meter, and rhyme, and notice how they reflect and enhance meaning.

- Pay attention to structure by following punctuation closely. Remember that the end of a line does not indicate the end of a thought.

- Consider how imagery and figurative language, including epic similes, develop characters and reveal plot events. Note allusions and epithets.

As you read, make notes in the chart about poetic elements you notice.

POETIC DEVICE	EXAMPLE
Sound devices	
Imagery and figurative language	
Allusions and epithets	
Other poetic elements	

LANGUAGE CONVENTIONS

Absolute Phrases In this lesson, you will learn about the usefulness of **absolute phrases** in adding information and imagery to writing. An absolute phrase consists of a noun and a participle, a verb form ending in *-ed* or *-ing* that acts as an adjective. An absolute phrase describes the main clause. As you read, note Homer's use of absolute phrases. Here is an example.
I drove them, <u>all three wailing</u>, to the ships . . .

ANNOTATION MODEL

NOTICE & NOTE

As you read, notice and note signposts, including **Tough Questions, Again and Again,** and **Contrasts and Contradictions.** Here is how one reader responded to the beginning of *The Odyssey*.

He saw the townlands
and learned the minds of many distant men,
and <u>weathered many bitter nights and days</u>
in his deep heart at sea, while he <u>fought only</u>
<u>to save his life, to bring his shipmates home.</u>

epic poem setting--a wanderer who sees many lands

"fought"-Odysseus will perform heroic deeds

BACKGROUND

Homer *may have lived sometime between 900 and 800 BC—if he ever lived at all. Although the ancient Greeks credited him with composing* The Iliad *and* The Odyssey, *people have long argued about whether or not he really existed. Many theorists speculate on who Homer may have been and where he may have lived. Details in the stories suggest that he was born and lived in the eastern Aegean Sea, either on the island of Chios or in Smyrna, and that he was blind.*

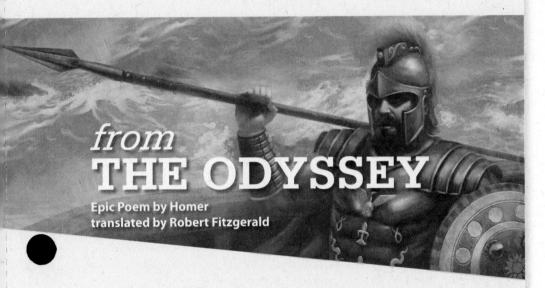

from
THE ODYSSEY

Epic Poem by Homer
translated by Robert Fitzgerald

Whatever position modern scholars take on the debate, most believe that one or two exceptionally talented individuals created the Homeric epics. The Iliad *and* The Odyssey *each contain 24 books of verse, but they probably predate the development of writing in Greece. The verses, which were originally sung, gradually became part of an important oral tradition. Generations of professional reciters memorized and performed the poems at festivals throughout Greece. By 300 BC, several versions of the books existed, and scholars undertook the job of standardizing the texts.*

Homer's poems profoundly influenced Greek culture and, as a result, contributed to the subsequent development of Western literature, ideas, and values. The Roman poet Virgil wrote a related poem, the Aeneid, *in Latin, and Odysseus appears in Dante's* Inferno. *Poets throughout English literature, from Geoffrey Chaucer in the Middle Ages to William Shakespeare in the Renaissance to John Keats in the Romantic era, have found inspiration in Homer. James Joyce's 1922 novel* Ulysses *(the Latin form of Odysseus' name) transforms one ordinary Dublin day into an Odyssean journey. Dozens of movies have retold the saga of the Trojan War and the long journey home, both directly and symbolically. For thousands of years people have taken the tales of a wandering Greek bard and made them their own.*

Notice & Note

You can use the side margins to notice and note signposts in the text.

SETTING A PURPOSE

As you read, monitor your comprehension by rereading and referring to the explanatory notes in the margins. Ask for help from a peer or teacher when you come across other unfamiliar words or phrases.

IMPORTANT CHARACTERS IN THE ODYSSEY
(in order of mention)

Book 1

Helios (hē′lē-ŏs), the sun god, who raises his cattle on the island of Thrinacia (thrĭ-nā′shə)

Zeus (zōōs), the ruler of the Greek gods and goddesses; father of Athena and Apollo

Telemachus (tə-lĕm′ə-kəs), Odysseus' son

Penelope (pə-nĕl′ə-pē), Odysseus' wife

Book 9

Alcinous (ăl-sĭn′ō-əs), the king of the Phaeacians (fē-ā′shənz)

Cyclopes (sī-klō′pēz), a race of one-eyed giants; an individual member of the race is a Cyclops (sī′klŏps)

Apollo (ə-pŏl′ō), the god of music, poetry, prophecy, and medicine

Poseidon (pō-sīd′n), the god of the seas, earthquakes, and horses; father of the Cyclops who battles Odysseus

Athena (ə-thē′nə), the goddess of war, wisdom, and cleverness; goddess of crafts

Book 12

Circe (sûr′sē), a goddess and enchantress who lives on the island of Aeaea (ē-ē′ə)

Sirens (sī′rənz), creatures, part woman and part bird, whose songs lure sailors to their death

BOOK 1

A GODDESS INTERVENES

Sing in me, Muse, and through me tell the story
of that man skilled in all ways of contending,
the wanderer, harried for years on end,
after he plundered the stronghold
5 on the proud height of Troy.

                                        He saw the townlands

and learned the minds of many distant men,
and weathered many bitter nights and days
in his deep heart at sea, while he fought only
to save his life, to bring his shipmates home.
10 But not by will nor valor could he save them,
for their own recklessness destroyed them all—
children and fools, they killed and feasted on
the cattle of Lord Helios, the Sun,
and he who moves all day through heaven
15 took from their eyes the dawn of their return.

Of these adventures, Muse, daughter of Zeus,
tell us in our time, lift the great song again. . . .

The story of Odysseus begins with the goddess Athena appealing to
Zeus to help Odysseus, who has been wandering for ten years on the
seas, to find his way home to his family on Ithaca. While Odysseus has
been gone, his son, Telemachus, has grown to manhood and Odysseus'
wife, Penelope, has been besieged by suitors wishing to marry her and
gain Odysseus' wealth. The suitors have taken up residence in her home
and are constantly feasting on the family's cattle, sheep, and goats. They
dishonor Odysseus and his family. Taking Athena's advice, Telemachus
travels to Pylos for word of his father. Meanwhile, on Ithaca, the evil
suitors plot to kill Telemachus when he returns.

1 Muse: a daughter of Zeus, credited with divine inspiration.

3 harried: tormented; harassed.

11–13 their own recklessness . . . the Sun: a reference to an event occurring later in the poem—an event that causes the death of Odysseus' entire crew.

BOOK 9

NEW COASTS AND POSEIDON'S SON
The Cyclops

*Odysseus has spent ten years wandering the Mediterranean Sea. By
Book 9, he has reached the island of Scheria, where King Alcinous has
welcomed him with a banquet. Odysseus agrees to tell King Alcinous
stories about his adventures, including the following story about a race
of creatures called the Cyclopes.*

1 Cyclopes (sī-klō′pēz): refers
to the creatures in plural;
Cyclops is singular.

In the next land we found were Cyclopes,
giants, louts, without a law to bless them.
In ignorance leaving the fruitage of the earth in mystery
to the immortal gods, they neither plow
5 nor sow by hand, nor till the ground, though grain—
wild wheat and barley—grows untended, and
wine-grapes, in clusters, ripen in heaven's rain.
Cyclopes have no muster and no meeting,
no consultation or old tribal ways,
10 but each one dwells in his own mountain cave
dealing out rough justice to wife and child,
indifferent to what the others do. . . ."

*Across the bay from the land of the Cyclopes is a lush, deserted
island. Odysseus and his crew land on the island in a dense fog
and spend days feasting on wine and wild goats and observing the
mainland, where the Cyclopes live. On the third day, Odysseus
and his company of men set out to learn if the Cyclopes are friends
or foes.*

"When the young Dawn with finger tips of rose
came in the east, I called my men together
15 and made a speech to them:

        'Old shipmates, friends,

the rest of you stand by; I'll make the crossing
in my own ship, with my own company,
and find out what the mainland natives are—
for they may be wild savages, and lawless,
20 or hospitable and god fearing men.'
At this I went aboard, and gave the word
to cast off by the stern. My oarsmen followed,
filing in to their benches by the rowlocks,
and all in line dipped oars in the gray sea.

22 stern: the rear end of a ship.

© Houghton Mifflin Harcourt Publishing Company

25 As we rowed on, and nearer to the mainland,
at one end of the bay, we saw a cavern
yawning above the water, screened with laurel,
and many rams and goats about the place
inside a sheepfold—made from slabs of stone
30 earthfast between tall trunks of pine and rugged
towering oak trees.

A prodigious man

slept in this cave alone, and took his flocks
to graze afield—remote from all companions,
knowing none but savage ways, a brute
35 so huge, he seemed no man at all of those
who eat good wheaten bread; but he seemed rather
a shaggy mountain reared in solitude.
We beached there, and I told the crew
to stand by and keep watch over the ship;
40 as for myself I took my twelve best fighters
and went ahead. I had a goatskin full
of that sweet liquor that Euanthes' son,
Maron, had given me. He kept Apollo's
holy grove at Ismarus; for kindness
45 we showed him there, and showed his wife and child,
he gave me seven shining golden talents
perfectly formed, a solid silver winebowl,
and then this liquor—twelve two-handled jars
of brandy, pure and fiery. Not a slave
50 in Maron's household knew this drink; only
he, his wife and the storeroom mistress knew;
and they would put one cupful—ruby-colored,
honey-smooth—in twenty more of water,
but still the sweet scent hovered like a fume
55 over the winebowl. No man turned away
when cups of this came round.

A wineskin full

I brought along, and victuals in a bag,
for in my bones I knew some towering brute
would be upon us soon—all outward power,
60 a wild man, ignorant of civility.

We climbed, then, briskly to the cave. But Cyclops
had gone afield, to pasture his fat sheep,
so we looked round at everything inside:
a drying rack that sagged with cheeses, pens
65 crowded with lambs and kids, each in its class:
firstlings apart from middlings, and the 'dewdrops,'

27 screened with laurel: partially hidden by laurel trees.

42–43 Euanthes (yoo-ăn´thēz); **Maron** (mâr´ŏn).

46 talents: bars of gold or silver of a specified weight, used as money in ancient Greece.

57 victuals (vĭt´lz): food.

66–67 The Cyclops has separated his lambs into three age groups.

© Houghton Mifflin Harcourt Publishing Company

68 whey: the watery part of milk, which separates from the curds, or solid part, during the making of cheese.

74 good salt water: the open sea.

EPIC HEROES
Annotate: Mark foreshadowing in lines 75–77 suggesting that Odysseus has a weakness that may bring trouble to him and his men.

Evaluate: What flaws might be revealed in these lines?

78 burnt an offering: burned a portion of the food as an offering to secure the gods' goodwill. (Such offerings were frequently performed by Greek sailors during difficult journeys.)

or newborn lambkins, penned apart from both.
And vessels full of whey were brimming there—
bowls of earthenware and pails for milking.
70 My men came pressing round me, pleading:
                                                'Why not
take these cheeses, get them stowed, come back,
throw open all the pens, and make a run for it?
We'll drive the kids and lambs aboard. We say
put out again on good salt water!'

75 how sound that was! Yet I refused. I wished
to see the caveman, what he had to offer—
no pretty sight, it turned out, for my friends.
We lit a fire, burnt an offering,
and took some cheese to eat; then sat in silence
80 around the embers, waiting. When he came
he had a load of dry boughs on his shoulder
to stoke his fire at suppertime. He dumped it
with a great crash into that hollow cave,
and we all scattered fast to the far wall.
85 Then over the broad cavern floor he ushered
the ewes he meant to milk. He left his rams
and he-goats in the yard outside, and swung
high overhead a slab of solid rock
to close the cave. Two dozen four-wheeled wagons,
90 with heaving wagon teams, could not have stirred

the tonnage of that rock from where he wedged it
over the doorsill. Next he took his seat
and milked his bleating ewes. A practiced job
he made of it, giving each ewe her suckling;
95 thickened his milk, then, into curds and whey,
sieved out the curds to drip in withy baskets,
and poured the whey to stand in bowls
cooling until he drank it for his supper.
When all these chores were done, he poked the fire,
100 heaping on brushwood. In the glare he saw us.

'Strangers,' he said, 'who are you? And where from?
What brings you here by sea ways—a fair traffic?
Or are you wandering rogues, who cast your lives
like dice, and ravage other folk by sea?'

105 We felt a pressure on our hearts, in dread
of that deep rumble and that mighty man.
But all the same I spoke up in reply:

'We are from Troy, Achaeans, blown off course
by shifting gales on the Great South Sea;
110 homeward bound, but taking routes and ways
uncommon; so the will of Zeus would have it.
We served under Agamemnon, son of Atreus—
the whole world knows what city
he laid waste, what armies he destroyed.
115 It was our luck to come here; here we stand,
beholden for your help, or any gifts
you give—as custom is to honor strangers.
We would entreat you, great Sir, have a care
for the gods' courtesy; Zeus will avenge
120 the unoffending guest.'

                                        He answered this

from his brute chest, unmoved:

                                        'You are a ninny,

or else you come from the other end of nowhere,
telling me, mind the gods! We Cyclopes
care not a whistle for your thundering Zeus
125 or all the gods in bliss; we have more force by far.
I would not let you go for fear of Zeus—
you or your friends—unless I had a whim to.
Tell me, where was it, now, you left your ship—
around the point, or down the shore, I wonder?'

96 withy baskets: baskets made from twigs.

102 fair traffic: honest trading.

117–120 It was a sacred Greek custom to honor strangers with food and gifts. Odysseus is reminding the Cyclops that Zeus will punish anyone who mistreats a guest.

130 He thought he'd find out, but I saw through this,
and answered with a ready lie:

'My ship?

Poseidon Lord, who sets the earth a-tremble,
broke it up on the rocks at your land's end.
A wind from seaward served him, drove us there.
135 We are survivors, these good men and I.'

Neither reply nor pity came from him,
but in one stride he clutched at my companions
and caught two in his hands like squirming puppies
to beat their brains out, spattering the floor.
140 Then he dismembered them and made his meal,
gaping and crunching like a mountain lion—
everything: innards, flesh, and marrow bones.
We cried aloud, lifting our hands to Zeus,
powerless, looking on at this, appalled;
145 but Cyclops went on filling up his belly
with manflesh and great gulps of whey,
then lay down like a mast among his sheep.
My heart beat high now at the chance of action,
and drawing the sharp sword from my hip I went
150 along his flank to stab him where the midriff
holds the liver. I had touched the spot
when sudden fear stayed me: if I killed him
we perished there as well, for we could never
move his ponderous doorway slab aside.
155 So we were left to groan and wait for morning.

When the young Dawn with fingertips of rose
lit up the world, the Cyclops built a fire
and milked his handsome ewes, all in due order,
putting the sucklings to the mothers. Then,
160 his chores being all dispatched, he caught
another brace of men to make his breakfast,
and whisked away his great door slab
to let his sheep go through—but he, behind,
reset the stone as one would cap a quiver.
165 There was a din of whistling as the Cyclops
rounded his flock to higher ground, then stillness.
And now I pondered how to hurt him worst,
if but Athena granted what I prayed for.
Here are the means I thought would serve my turn:

170 a club, or staff, lay there along the fold—
an olive tree, felled green and left to season
for Cyclops' hand. And it was like a mast

© Houghton Mifflin Harcourt Publishing Company

TOUGH QUESTIONS

Notice and Note: Mark the question Odysseus faces in lines 151–168.

Evaluate: What does it say about his approach to problems that Odysseus "pondered"?

---

154 ponderous: heavy in a clumsy way; bulky.

161 brace: pair.

163–164 The Cyclops reseals the cave with the massive rock as easily as an ordinary human places the cap on a container of arrows.

171 left to season: left to dry out and harden.

a lugger of twenty oars, broad in the beam—
a deep-sea-going craft—might carry:
175 so long, so big around, it seemed. Now I
chopped out a six foot section of this pole
and set it down before my men, who scraped it;
and when they had it smooth, I hewed again
to make a stake with pointed end. I held this
180 in the fire's heart and turned it, toughening it,
then hid it, well back in the cavern, under
one of the dung piles in profusion there.
Now came the time to toss for it: who ventured
along with me? whose hand could bear to thrust
185 and grind that spike in Cyclops' eye, when mild
sleep had mastered him? As luck would have it,
the men I would have chosen won the toss—
four strong men, and I made five as captain.

At evening came the shepherd with his flock,
190 his woolly flock. The rams as well, this time,
entered the cave: by some sheep-herding whim—
or a god's bidding—none were left outside.
He hefted his great boulder into place
and sat him down to milk the bleating ewes
195 in proper order, put the lambs to suck,
and swiftly ran through all his evening chores.
Then he caught two more men and feasted on them.
My moment was at hand, and I went forward
holding an ivy bowl of my dark drink,
200 looking up, saying:

                              'Cyclops, try some wine.
Here's liquor to wash down your scraps of men.
Taste it, and see the kind of drink we carried
under our planks. I meant it for an offering
if you would help us home. But you are mad,
205 unbearable, a bloody monster! After this,
will any other traveller come to see you?

He seized and drained the bowl, and it went down
so fiery and smooth he called for more:

'Give me another, thank you kindly. Tell me,
210 how are you called? I'll make a gift will please you.
Even Cyclopes know the wine-grapes grow
out of grassland and loam in heaven's rain,
but here's a bit of nectar and ambrosia!'

© Houghton Mifflin Harcourt Publishing Company

173 lugger: a small, wide sailing ship.

182 profusion: abundance.

EPIC POETRY

Annotate: In lines 198–208, mark a passage indicating one of Odysseus' character traits.

Analyze: How does Odysseus' behavior in this passage reflect Greek ideas and values and suggest a theme?

213 nectar (nĕk´tər) **and ambrosia** (ăm-brō´zhə): the drink and food of the gods.

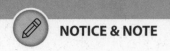
215 **fuddle and flush:** the state of confusion and redness of the face caused by drinking alcohol.

LANGUAGE CONVENTIONS

Annotate: Mark the absolute phrase in lines 221–226.

Analyze: How does the absolute phrase add to the meaning of the sentence?

231 **the pike:** the pointed stake.

244 **smithy:** blacksmith's shop.

245 **adze** (ădz): an axlike tool with a curved blade.

Three bowls I brought him, and he poured them down.
215 I saw the fuddle and flush come over him,
then I sang out in cordial tones:

                              'Cyclops
you ask my honorable name? Remember
the gift you promised me, and I shall tell you.
My name is Nohbdy: mother, father, and friends,
220 everyone calls me Nohbdy.'

                              And he said:
'Nohbdy's my meat, then, after I eat his friends.
Others come first. There's a noble gift, now.'

Even as he spoke, he reeled and tumbled backward,
his great head lolling to one side: and sleep
225 took him like any creature. Drunk, hiccupping,
he dribbled streams of liquor and bits of men.

Now, by the gods, I drove my big hand spike
deep in the embers, charring it again,
and cheered my men along with battle talk
230 to keep their courage up: no quitting now.
The pike of olive, green though it had been,
reddened and glowed as if about to catch.
I drew it from the coals and my four fellows
gave me a hand, lugging it near the Cyclops
235 as more than natural force nerved them; straight
forward they sprinted, lifted it, and rammed it
deep in his crater eye, and I leaned on it
turning it as a shipwright turns a drill
in planking, having men below to swing
240 the two-handled strap that spins it in the groove.
So with our brand we bored that great eye socket
while blood ran out around the red hot bar.
Eyelid and lash were seared; the pierced ball
hissed broiling, and the roots popped.

                              In a smithy
245 one sees a white-hot axehead or an adze
plunged and wrung in a cold tub, screeching steam—
the way they make soft iron hale and hard—:
just so that eyeball hissed around the spike.
The Cyclops bellowed and the rock roared round him,
250 and we fell back in fear. Clawing his face
he tugged the bloody spike out of his eye,
threw it away, and his wild hands went groping;
then he set up a howl for Cyclopes
who lived in caves on windy peaks nearby.

255 Some heard him; and they came by divers ways
to clump around outside and call:

                                   'What ails you,
Polyphemus? Why do you cry so sore
in the starry night? You will not let us sleep.
Sure no man's driving off your flock? No man
260 has tricked you, ruined you?'

                              Out of the cave
the mammoth Polyphemus roared in answer:

'Nohbdy, Nohbdy's tricked me, Nohbdy's ruined me!'

To this rough shout they made a sage reply:

'Ah well, if nobody has played you foul
265 there in your lonely bed, we are no use in pain

---

255 **divers:** various.

257 **Polyphemus** (pŏl-ə-fē´məs): the name of the Cyclops.

263 **sage:** wise.

264–267 Odysseus' lie about his name has paid off.

© Houghton Mifflin Harcourt Publishing Company

272 breach: opening.

Notice & Note: Mark the question Odysseus asks himself while he is trapped in the Cyclops's cave.

Analyze: How does Odysseus' strategy reflect traits he has shown previously?

298 pectoral fleece: the wool covering a sheep's chest.

given by great Zeus. Let it be your father,
Poseidon Lord, to whom you pray.'

                    So saying
they trailed away. And I was filled with laughter
to see how like a charm the name deceived them.
270 Now Cyclops, wheezing as the pain came on him,
fumbled to wrench away the great doorstone
and squatted in the breach with arms thrown wide
for any silly beast or man who bolted—
hoping somehow I might be such a fool.
275 But I kept thinking how to win the game:
death sat there huge; how could we slip away?
I drew on all my wits, and ran through tactics,
reasoning as a man will for dear life,
until a trick came—and it pleased me well.
280 The Cyclops' rams were handsome, fat, with heavy
fleeces, a dark violet.

                      Three abreast
I tied them silently together, twining
cords of willow from the ogre's bed;
then slung a man under each middle one
285 to ride there safely, shielded left and right.
So three sheep could convey each man. I took
the woolliest ram, the choicest of the flock,
and hung myself under his kinky belly,
pulled up tight, with fingers twisted deep
290 in sheepskin ringlets for an iron grip.
So, breathing hard, we waited until morning.
When Dawn spread out her finger tips of rose
the rams began to stir, moving for pasture,
and peals of bleating echoed round the pens
295 where dams with udders full called for a milking.
Blinded, and sick with pain from his head wound,
the master stroked each ram, then let it pass,
but my men riding on the pectoral fleece
the giant's blind hands blundering never found.
300 Last of them all my ram, the leader, came,
weighted by wool and me with my meditations.
The Cyclops patted him, and then he said:

'Sweet cousin ram, why lag behind the rest
in the night cave? You never linger so,
305 but graze before them all, and go afar
to crop sweet grass, and take your stately way
leading along the streams, until at evening

you run to be the first one in the fold.
Why, now, so far behind? Can you be grieving
310 over your Master's eye? That carrion rogue
and his accurst companions burnt it out
when he had conquered all my wits with wine.
Nohbdy will not get out alive, I swear.
Oh, had you brain and voice to tell
315 where he may be now, dodging all my fury!
Bashed by this hand and bashed on this rock wall
his brains would strew the floor, and I should have
rest from the outrage Nohbdy worked upon me.'

He sent us into the open, then. Close by,
320 I dropped and rolled clear of the ram's belly,
going this way and that to untie the men.
With many glances back, we rounded up
his fat, stiff-legged sheep to take aboard,
and drove them down to where the good ship lay.
325 We saw, as we came near, our fellows' faces
shining; then we saw them turn to grief
tallying those who had not fled from death.
I hushed them, jerking head and eyebrows up,
and in a low voice told them: 'Load this herd;
330 move fast, and put the ship's head toward the breakers.'
They all pitched in at loading, then embarked
and struck their oars into the sea. Far out,
as far off shore as shouted words would carry,
I sent a few back to the adversary:

335 'O Cyclops! Would you feast on my companions?
Puny, am I, in a Caveman's hands?
How do you like the beating that we gave you,
you damned cannibal? Eater of guests
under your roof! Zeus and the gods have paid you!'

340 The blind thing in his doubled fury broke
a hilltop in his hands and heaved it after us.
Ahead of our black prow it struck and sank
whelmed in a spuming geyser, a giant wave
that washed the ship stern foremost back to shore.
345 I got the longest boathook out and stood
fending us off, with furious nods to all
to put their backs into a racing stroke—
row, row, or perish. So the long oars bent
kicking the foam sternward, making head
350 until we drew away, and twice as far.
Now when I cupped my hands I heard the crew
in low voices protesting:

AGAIN AND AGAIN

Notice & Note: Mark the name the Cyclops repeats.

Analyze: What effect does the repeated pun have?

---

330 put . . . the breakers: turn the ship around so that it is heading toward the open sea.

334 adversary: opponent; enemy.

335–339 Odysseus assumes that the gods are on his side.

340–348 The hilltop thrown by Polyphemus lands in front of the ship, causing a huge wave that carries the ship back to the shore. Odysseus uses a long pole to push the boat away from the land.

351 cupped my hands: put his hands on either side of his mouth in order to magnify his voice.

        'Godsake, Captain!
Why bait the beast again? Let him alone!'
'That tidal wave he made on the first throw
355 all but beached us.'

        'All but stove us in!'
'Give him our bearing with your trumpeting,
he'll get the range and lob a boulder.'

        'Aye
He'll smash our timbers and our heads together!'

I would not heed them in my glorying spirit,
360 but let my anger flare and yelled:

        'Cyclops,
if ever mortal man inquire
how you were put to shame and blinded, tell him
Odysseus, raider of cities, took your eye:
Laertes' son, whose home's on Ithaca!'

365 At this he gave a mighty sob and rumbled:

'Now comes the weird upon me, spoken of old.
A wizard, grand and wondrous, lived here—Telemus,
a son of Eurymus; great length of days
he had in wizardry among the Cyclopes,
370 and these things he foretold for time to come:
my great eye lost, and at Odysseus' hands.
Always I had in mind some giant, armed
in giant force, would come against me here.
But this, but you—small, pitiful and twiggy—
375 you put me down with wine, you blinded me.
Come back, Odysseus, and I'll treat you well,
praying the god of earthquake to befriend you—
his son I am, for he by his avowal
fathered me, and, if he will, he may
380 heal me of this black wound—he and no other
of all the happy gods or mortal men.'

Few words I shouted in reply to him:
'If I could take your life I would and take
your time away, and hurl you down to hell!
385 The god of earthquake could not heal you there!'

At this he stretched his hands out in his darkness
toward the sky of stars, and prayed Poseidon:
'O hear me, lord, blue girdler of the islands,

366 Now comes . . . of old:
Now I recall the destiny
predicted long ago.

**367–375 A wizard . . . you
blinded me:** Polyphemus tells
of a prophecy made long ago
by Telemus, a prophet who
predicted that Polyphemus
would lose his eye at the hands
of Odysseus.

377 the god of earthquake:
Poseidon.
378 avowal: honest admission.

if I am thine indeed, and thou art father:
390 grant that Odysseus, raider of cities, never
see his home: Laertes' son, I mean,
who kept his hall on Ithaca. Should destiny
intend that he shall see his roof again
among his family in his father land,
395 far be that day, and dark the years between.
Let him lose all companions, and return
under strange sail to bitter days at home.'

In these words he prayed, and the god heard him.
Now he laid hands upon a bigger stone
400 and wheeled around, titanic for the cast,
to let it fly in the black-prowed vessel's track.

But it fell short, just aft the steering oar,
and whelming seas rose giant above the stone
to bear us onward toward the island.

                                                    There
405 as we ran in we saw the squadron waiting,
the trim ships drawn up side by side, and all
our troubled friends who waited, looking seaward.
We beached her, grinding keel in the soft sand,
and waded in, ourselves, on the sandy beach.
410 Then we unloaded all the Cyclops' flock
to make division, share and share alike,
only my fighters voted that my ram,
the prize of all, should go to me. I slew him
by the sea side and burnt his long thighbones
415 to Zeus beyond the stormcloud, Cronus' son,
who rules the world. But Zeus disdained my offering;
destruction for my ships he had in store
and death for those who sailed them, my companions.

Now all day long until the sun went down
420 we made our feast on mutton and sweet wine,
till after sunset in the gathering dark
we went to sleep above the wash of ripples.

When the young Dawn with finger tips of rose
touched the world, I roused the men, gave orders
425 to man the ships, cast off the mooring lines;
and filing in to sit beside the rowlocks
oarsmen in line dipped oars in the gray sea.
So we moved out, sad in the vast offing,
having our precious lives, but not our friends."

© Houghton Mifflin Harcourt Publishing Company

Notice & Note: How does the Cyclops's behavior in lines 386–397 contrast with his previous behavior? Mark key details.

Infer: Based on what you know of epic poetry, what do you think will happen as a result of Cyclops's prayer?

400 titanic for the cast: drawing on all his enormous strength in preparing to throw.

402 aft: behind.

404 the island: the deserted island where most of Odysseus' men had stayed behind.

415 Cronus' son: Zeus' father, Cronus, was a Titan, one of an earlier race of gods.

428 offing: the part of the deep sea visible from the shore.

BOOK 12

SEA PERILS AND DEFEAT

The Sirens

Odysseus and his men continue their journey home toward Ithaca.
They spend a year with the goddess Circe on the island of Aeaea. Circe
sends Odysseus and his crew to the Land of the Dead (the underworld),
after which they return to Circe's island. While the men sleep, Circe
takes Odysseus aside to hear about the underworld and to offer advice.

                    "Then said the Lady Circe:

'So: all those trials are over.

                      Listen with care

    to this, now, and a god will arm your mind.
    Square in your ship's path are Sirens, crying
5 beauty to bewitch men coasting by;
    woe to the innocent who hears that sound!
    He will not see his lady nor his children
    in joy, crowding about him, home from sea;
    the Sirens will sing his mind away
10 on their sweet meadow lolling. There are bones
    of dead men rotting in a pile beside them
    and flayed skins shrivel around the spot.

                       Steer wide;

    keep well to seaward; plug your oarsmen's ears
    with beeswax kneaded soft; none of the rest
15 should hear that song.

                But if you wish to listen,

    let the men tie you in the lugger, hand
    and foot, back to the mast, lashed to the mast,
    so you may hear those harpies' thrilling voices;
    shout as you will, begging to be untied,

2–3 In Circe, Odysseus has found a valuable ally. In this section, she describes in detail the dangers that he and his men will meet on their way home.

CONTRASTS AND CONTRADICTIONS

Notice and Note: According to lines 4–12, how does the Sirens' song sharply contrast with the effect the song has on men who listen to it?

Analyze: Why do you think the author introduces such a contrast at this point in the poem?

18 those harpies' thrilling voices: the delightful voices of those horrible female creatures.

20 your crew must only twist more line around you
and keep their stroke up, till the singers fade.

*At dawn, Odysseus and his men continue their journey. Odysseus
decides to tell the men of Circe's warnings about the Sirens, whom they
will soon encounter. He is fairly sure that they can survive this peril if he
keeps their spirits up. Suddenly, the wind stops.*

"The crew were on their feet
briskly, to furl the sail, and stow it; then,
each in place, they poised the smooth oar blades
and sent the white foam scudding by. I carved

30–31 plumb amidships:
exactly in the center of the ship.

39 Perimedes (pĕr-ĭ-mē´dēz).

25 a massive cake of beeswax into bits
and rolled them in my hands until they softened—
no long task, for a burning heat came down
from Helios, lord of high noon. Going forward
I carried wax along the line, and laid it
30 thick on their ears. They tied me up, then, plumb
amidships, back to the mast, lashed to the mast,
and took themselves again to rowing. Soon,
as we came smartly within hailing distance,
the two Sirens, noting our fast ship
35 off their point, made ready, and they sang. . . .

The lovely voices in ardor appealing over the water
made me crave to listen, and I tried to say
'Untie me!' to the crew, jerking my brows;
but they bent steady to the oars. Then Perimedes
40 got to his feet, he and Eurylochus,
and passed more line about, to hold me still.
So all rowed on, until the Sirens
dropped under the sea rim, and their singing
dwindled away.
                                    My faithful company
45 rested on their oars now, peeling off
the wax that I had laid thick on their ears;
then set me free.

© Houghton Mifflin Harcourt Publishing Company

CHECK YOUR UNDERSTANDING

Answer these questions before moving on to the **Analyze the Text** section on the following page.

1 Which of the following sentences shows how Odysseus first uses his cleverness to outwit the Cyclops?

    A *Steer wide; keep well to seaward; plug your oarsmen's ears with beeswax kneaded soft.*

    B *If I could take your life I would and take your time away, and hurl you down to hell!*

    C *Why not take these cheeses, get them stowed, come back, throw open all the pens, and make a run for it?*

    D *Poseidon Lord, who sets the earth a-tremble, broke it up on the rocks at your land's end.*

2 Odysseus and his surviving men ultimately escape from the Cyclops by —

    F hiding underneath the Cyclops's sheep

    G removing the door to the Cyclops's cave

    H promising the Cyclops that they will return

    J giving the Cyclops the rest of their wine

3 Odysseus is tied to the mast because he —

    A ran out of beeswax and cannot cover his own ears

    B did not want to leave Circe's island

    C is offering himself as a sacrifice to Helios, lord of high noon

    D wants to hear the song of the Sirens without dying

ANALYZE THE TEXT

Support your responses with evidence from the text. 📓 NOTEBOOK

1. **Interpret** In the opening lines of Book 1, the poet calls upon Muse, a daughter of Zeus often credited with inspiration. Why would he open the epic in this way? What does this allusion tell you about him as a poet?

2. **Analyze** How does Odysseus regard the Cyclops, based on the description in lines 1–12 of Book 9? What does this description reveal about Odysseus' values as well as the values of the ancient Greeks?

3. **Analyze** Why does Odysseus continue to taunt the Cyclops as he pulls away from the shore? What traits does he demonstrate through this behavior, and what are the consequences?

4. **Evaluate** One theme in *The Odyssey* is that a hero must rely on clever deceit, or guile, to survive. Explain how this theme is conveyed. What other themes can you identify?

5. **Notice & Note** The author uses many epithets for Odysseus, such as "carrion rogue" and "raider of cities." What effect does the repetition of these epithets have on your understanding of the character of Odysseus?

RESEARCH

RESEARCH TIP
When researching audio recordings, keep in mind that some readings may be of higher quality than others. A classic such as *The Odyssey* has been recorded by several organizations and actors with varying success. Look for audio recordings with positive reviews or those that have received awards.

Like other classic epic poems, *The Odyssey* was spoken before it was written. This great adventure was passed down orally from generation to generation. Find two audio recordings of *The Odyssey* and listen to the parts you have read in this unit. Pay attention to elements of **prosody**—timing, phrasing, emphasis, and intonation—the readers use. Use the chart below to make notes about how the audio version makes the action and/or the characters more vivid; and how it helps you better understand the text.

	HOW IT INCREASES MY ENJOYMENT OF THE TEXT	HOW IT HELPS ME UNDERSTAND THE TEXT
Audio Recording 1		
Audio Recording 2		

Extend With a small group, create your own audio recording of the selections from *The Odyssey* in this unit. When planning your own recording, integrate the qualities you appreciated most about the two recordings you researched. Play your recording for the class.

CREATE AND PRESENT

Write a Narrative The point of view in *The Odyssey* rarely wavers from that of Odysseus. Nevertheless, other characters' words and actions hint at what they are thinking. Write a one-page narrative of an event from *The Odyssey* from the point of view of a character or object other than Odysseus. For example, you could narrate Odysseus's escape from the Cyclops from the point of view of the Cyclops, one of the rams, or one of the Sirens as Odysseus and his crew sailed by.

❏ Review the main events covered in the selections from *The Odyssey*. Choose an event and a point of view.

❏ Write your narrative. Speak in the voice of the character you chose.

❏ Use dialogue and description to engage and orient the reader, set up the situation, and create a smooth progression of events.

❏ Use precise words and phrases, telling details, and sensory language to convey a vivid picture of the events.

Deliver a Presentation With a group, create and deliver a 3- to 5-minute multimodal presentation of your narrative. A multimodal presentation includes two or more media, such as audio elements, written elements, visual aids, lighting effects, and presentation software.

❏ Research ways to integrate your the media you choose. Look for images online or create your own graphics to illustrate your presentation.

❏ Rehearse your presentation, including all multimedia elements. Share your presentation with the class. If time allows, offer to answer questions from the audience about your work.

 Go to the **Writing Studio** for more on writing a narrative.

 Go to the **Speaking and Listening Studio** for help with using media in a presentation.

RESPOND TO THE ESSENTIAL QUESTION

 What drives us to take on a challenge?

Gather Information Review your annotations and notes on the selection from *The Odyssey*. Then, add relevant information to your Response Log. As you determine which information to include, think about:

• Odysseus' motivations as he takes on challenges

• flaws that hold Odysseus back on his quest to return home

• how cultures might influence what people take on as challenges

At the end of the unit, use your notes to help you write an explanatory essay.

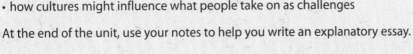

ACADEMIC VOCABULARY

As you write and discuss what you learned from the narrative presentations, be sure to use the Academic Vocabulary words. Check off each of the words that you use.

❏ **motivate**

❏ **objective**

❏ **pursuit**

❏ **subsequent**

❏ **undertake**

Go to the **Vocabulary Studio** for more on words from Latin.

VOCABULARY STRATEGY:
Words from Latin

Recognizing **word roots** can help you determine the meanings of unfamiliar words. For example, the word *desolation*, meaning "a feeling of loneliness," contains the Latin root *sol*, which means "alone." This root is found in numerous other English words. Study the Latin roots and their meanings in the chart, along with example words that contain each root.

LATIN ROOT	MEANING	EXAMPLES
sol-	alone	soliloquy, solo
trem-	tremble	tremor, tremulous
plac-	calm	implacable, placate
vers	turn	adversity, versatile

Practice and Apply For each Latin root in the chart, follow these steps:

1. Look online or in print resources for one additional example of a word that uses the Latin root.

2. Use your knowledge of the root's meaning to write a definition for each example word.

3. Consult a dictionary to confirm each example word's meaning.

4. Use each example word in a sentence.

LANGUAGE CONVENTIONS:
Absolute Phrases

An **absolute phrase** consists of a noun and a participle, a verb form ending in *-ed* or *-ing* that acts as an adjective. Absolute phrases must be set off with commas and may also contain objects of the participle and any modifiers. Rather than modifying a specific word in a sentence, absolute phrases describe the main clause of a sentence. Absolute phrases are a helpful way to add information to a sentence.

Look at this example of an absolute phrase from *The Odyssey*.

> There
> as we ran in we saw the squadron waiting,
> <u>the trim ships drawn up side by side,</u> and all
> our troubled friends who waited, looking seaward.

In this sentence, the absolute phrase *the trim ships drawn up side by side* is a description. The phrase adds information and helps explain how the waiting squadron looked. The noun *ships* is modified by the adjective *trim*, the participle *drawn*, and the additional modifiers *up side by side*. The absolute phrase modifies the first part of the sentence: *There as we ran in we saw the squadron waiting.*

Practice and Apply Look back at the narrative you wrote for Create and Present. Revise your narrative to include one or two absolute phrases. Share your revised narrative with a partner and discuss how your revisions add variety and interest.

Go to the **Grammar Studio** for more on participial phrases.

ARCHAEOLOGY'S TECH REVOLUTION SINCE INDIANA JONES

Informational Text by **Jeremy Hsu**

? ESSENTIAL QUESTION:

What drives us to take on a challenge?

QUICK START

Look at the title, headings, and images in this article. What do you predict it will be about? Discuss your prediction with the class.

MAKE PREDICTIONS

We make predictions every day—about our lives, about current events, and about texts we are reading. When we **predict** while reading, we make a reasonable guess about what is likely to happen next in a text. We usually base our predictions on several factors:

- prior knowledge—what we already know about a situation or subject
- information gleaned from scanning a text to read titles, headings, and photos or illustrations
- details from the text

As we gather more information, our predictions may change.

ANALYZE TECHNICAL TEXTS

Authors of informational or technical texts often present one central idea or make one central claim. They can't however, just make their claim or present their idea. They must provide relevant examples and evidence to support those claims.

As you read, note the central ideas the author presents and the evidence and relevant examples he provides to support those ideas. Also, think about the organizational design the author uses to present the thesis and supporting information. Use a chart like the one below to help you analyze the structure and characteristics of technical texts as they appear in Jeremy Hsu's article.

GENRE ELEMENTS: INFORMATIONAL TEXT

- provides factual information
- includes evidence to support ideas
- may contain text features to organize and clarify ideas
- includes domain-specific vocabulary

Introduction: What is this article mostly about? What is the central thesis?	
Central Ideas	**Supporting Evidence and Relevant Examples**
1.	
2.	
3.	
4.	
Conclusion: How does the author pull it all together?	

CRITICAL VOCABULARY

| innovation | GPS | artifact | infrared | forensic analysis |

To see how many Critical Vocabulary words you already know, use them to complete the sentences.

1. The _____ camera produced high-contrast photographs.

2. Most new cars come equipped with _____ as standard equipment.

3. That ancient carving tool was an interesting _____.

4. The medical examiner performed extensive _____ on the remains.

5. Satellite imaging is an _____ that has had a major effect in many areas of life and work.

LANGUAGE CONVENTIONS

Appositives In this lesson, you will learn about the effective use of appositives. An **appositive** is a noun or pronoun that writers use to identify, rename, or provide extra information about a noun. An appositive phrase includes an appositive and modifiers of it.

The movie, **a documentary about inventors,** has won several awards.

Rachel, **the chef,** prepared a delicious dinner for her guests.

Most appositives are set off with commas. As you read "Archaeology's Tech Revolution Since Indiana Jones," note the author's use of appositives.

ANNOTATION MODEL

NOTICE & NOTE

As you read, develop your understanding of this technical text by noting examples and details of central ideas. In the model, you can see one reader's notes about the text's main ideas.

Let's face it, Indiana Jones was a pretty [lousy archaeologist. He destroyed his sites, used a bullwhip instead of a trowel and was more likely to kill his peers than co-author a paper with them.] Regardless, "Raiders of the Lost Ark," which celebrates its 30th anniversary on June 12, did make studying the past cool for an entire generation of scientists. Those modern archaeologists whom "Raiders" inspired luckily learned from the mistakes of Dr. Jones, and [use advanced technology such as satellite imaging, airborne laser mapping, robots and full-body medical scanners] instead of a scientifically useless whip.

> things a good archaeologist shouldn't do

> things a good archaeologist should do

BACKGROUND

Jeremy Hsu *has been working as a science and technology journalist since 2008, and has written on subjects as diverse as supercomputing and wearable electronics. He contributes to a variety of publications, including* Scientific American, Discover, *and* Popular Science. *In this article, Hsu uses Indiana Jones, the iconic archaeologist of a series of popular movies, to introduce how the field of archaeology has changed with advancements in technology.*

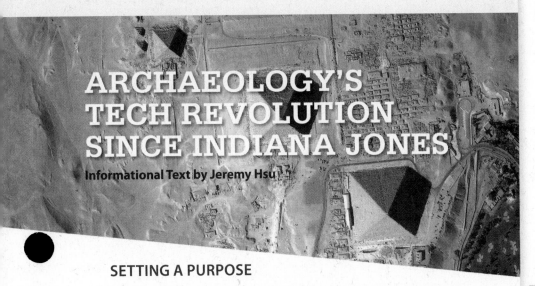

ARCHAEOLOGY'S TECH REVOLUTION SINCE INDIANA JONES

Informational Text by Jeremy Hsu

SETTING A PURPOSE

As you read, pay attention to examples the author gives to build the central idea. Many of those examples include technical terms. When you come across an unfamiliar term, ask your teacher or a peer for help or consult reference material.

1   Let's face it, Indiana Jones was a pretty lousy archaeologist. He destroyed his sites, used a bullwhip instead of a trowel[1] and was more likely to kill his peers than co-author a paper with them. Regardless, "Raiders of the Lost Ark," which celebrates its 30th anniversary on June 12, did make studying the past cool for an entire generation of scientists. Those modern archaeologists whom "Raiders" inspired luckily learned from the mistakes of Dr. Jones, and use advanced technology such as satellite imaging,[2] airborne laser mapping, robots and full-body medical scanners instead of a scientifically useless whip.

2   Such **innovations** have allowed archaeologists to spot buried pyramids from space, create 3-D maps of ancient Mayan ruins from the air, explore the sunken wrecks of Roman ships and find

---

[1] **trowel** (trou´əl): a small implement with a pointed, scoop-shaped blade used for digging.

[2] **satellite imaging**: the scanning of the earth by satellite or high-flying aircraft to obtain information about it.

Notice & Note

You can use the side margins to notice and note signposts in the text.

MAKE PREDICTIONS

Annotate: Mark words or phrases in the title and paragraph 1 that help you predict what this article is about.

Predict: What do you expect to learn from reading this article?

innovation
(ĭn-ə-vā´shən) *n.* something newly introduced.

A LIDAR (Light Detection and Ranging) image created with data from NOAA's National Geodetic Survey.

GPS
n. Global Positioning System, a utility that provides positioning, navigation, and timing services.

artifact
(är´tə-făkt) *n.* an object produced or shaped by human workmanship.

infrared
(ĭn´ frə-rĕd) *adj.* pertaining to electromagnetic radiation having wavelengths greater than those of visible light and shorter than those of microwaves.

LANGUAGE CONVENTIONS

Annotate: Mark a sentence in paragraph 5 where the author has used an appositive.

Analyze: Which part of the sentence is the appositive? What noun does it describe?

evidence of heart disease in 3,000-year-old mummies. Most of the new toolkit comes from fields such as biology, chemistry, physics or engineering, as well as commercial gadgets that include **GPS**, laptops and smartphones.

3   "If we dig part of a site, we destroy it," said David Hurst Thomas, a curator in anthropology at the American Museum of Natural History in New York. "Technology lets us find out a lot more about it before we go in, like surgeons who use CT and MRI scans.[3]"

4   Archaeologists have harnessed such tools to find ancient sites of interest more easily than ever before. They can dig with greater confidence and less collateral damage[4], apply the latest lab techniques to ancient human **artifacts** or remains, and better pinpoint when people or objects existed in time.

Satellites mark the spot

5   One of the current revolutions in archaeology relies upon satellites floating in orbit above the Earth. Sarah Parcak, an Egyptologist at the University of Alabama in Birmingham, and an international team recently used **infrared** satellite imaging to peer as far down as 33 feet (10 meters) below the Egyptian desert. They found 17 undiscovered pyramids and more than 1,000 tombs.

6   The images also revealed buried city streets and houses at the ancient Egyptian city of Tanis, a well-known archaeological site that was featured in "Raiders of the Lost Ark" three decades ago.

7   Even ordinary satellite images used by Google Earth have helped. Many of the old Egyptian sites have buried mud brick architecture

---

[3] **CT and MRI scans:** special X-ray tests that produce cross-sectional images.
[4] **collateral damage** (kə-lăt´ər-əl dăm´-ĭj): unintended injury or damage.

Satellite imagery of the Giza pyramid complex on the outskirts of Cairo, Egypt.

that crumbles over time and mixes with the sand or silt above them. When it rains, soils with mud brick hold moisture longer and appear discolored in satellite photos.

8   "In the old days, I'd jump into the Land Rover and go look at a possible site," said Tony Pollard, director of the Centre for Battlefield Archaeology at the University of Glasgow in Scotland. "Now, before that, I go to Google Earth."

Digging with less damage

9   Tools such as ground-penetrating radar can also help archaeologists avoid destroying precious data when they excavate ancient sites, Thomas said.

10   "Many Native American tribes are very interested in remote sensing that is noninvasive and nondestructive, because many don't like the idea of disturbing the dead or buried remains," Thomas explained.

11   Magnetometers[5] can distinguish between buried metals, rocks and other materials based on differences in the Earth's magnetic field. Soil resistivity surveys detect objects based on changes in electrical current speed.

Dusting off old bones

12   Once objects or bones have surfaced, archaeologists can return them to the lab for **forensic analysis** that would impress any CSI[6] agent. Computed tomography (CT) scanners commonly used in

---

[5] **magnetometer** (măg-nĭ-tom´ĭ-tər): an instrument for comparing the intensity and direction of magnetic fields.

[6] **CSI:** crime scene investigator.

© Houghton Mifflin Harcourt Publishing Company • Image Credits: ©DigitalGlobe/ScapeWare3d/Getty Images

ANALYZE TECHNICAL TEXTS

Annotate: Mark words and phrases that explain magnetometers.

Analyze: How could the use of a magnetometer help preserve Native American sites?

forensic analysis
(fə-rěn´sĭk ə-năl´ĭ-sĭs) *n.* the scientific collection and analysis of physical evidence in criminal cases.

A rover robot to be sent into an air shaft of the Pyramid of Khufu in Giza, Egypt.

ANALYZE TECHNICAL TEXTS

Annotate: Mark text that describes the kinds of information archaeologists can obtain from bones.

Analyze: What does this text reveal about the use of technology in archaeology?

medicine have revealed blocked arteries in an ancient Egyptian princess who ended up mummified 3,500 years ago.

13   Looking at the ratios of different forms of elements, called isotopes, in the bones of ancient people may reveal what they ate. The dietary details can include whether they favored foods such as corn or potatoes, or if they were strictly hunters.

14   A similar chemical signature[7] based on the isotope ratio of different geographical locations can reveal where humans originally grew up. Archaeologists used it to identify the origins of dozens of soldiers found in a 375-year-old mass grave in Germany.

15   "Once they excavated them, they did analysis on bones and identified in most cases where individual soldiers came from," Pollard said. "Some came from Finland, some came from Scotland."

Back to the future

16   Archaeologists have many other new tools in the toolkit. The laser mapping technique used on the Mayan ruins, called LIDAR (Light Detection And Ranging), has become a norm for archaeology in just a few years. Robots have begun exploring pyramids and caves as well as underwater shipwrecks.

---

[7] **chemical signature:** a unique pattern, produced by an analytical instrument, indicating the presence of a particular molecule.

17   "When I was a bad boy and went into archaeology instead of med school, my mother thought I'd spent all my time in the past," Thomas said. "It couldn't be further from the truth; we do all we can to keep up technologically."

18   Technology won't eliminate the need to dig anytime soon, archaeologists say. But if that day comes, "archaeology will get a lot more boring," Pollard said. He wasn't alone with that sentiment.

19   "It's all very well to use satellite imaging, but until you get out into the field, you're stuck in your lab," Parcak said. "It's a constant in archaeology; you've got to dig and explore."

CHECK YOUR UNDERSTANDING

Answer these questions before moving on to the **Analyze the Text** section on the next page.

1 Which of the following is true?

A Archaeologists have little regard for preserving sites.

B Archaeologists are technologically savvy scientists.

C Archaeology is a science developed by Native Americans.

D The tech revolution has made archaeology boring.

2 Which of the sentences from the selection most strongly supports the idea that some people miss the way archaeology used to be practiced?

F *In the old days, I'd jump into the Land Rover and go look at a possible site*

G *It's all very well to use satellite imaging, but until you get out into the field, you're stuck in your lab*

H *When I was a bad boy and went into archaeology instead of med school, my mother thought I'd spend all my time in the past*

J *Now, before that, I go to Google Earth.*

3 Which of these is not an important idea in the article?

A Archaeologists do not like to damage precious sites.

B Archaeologists do much of their work in a lab.

C Indiana Jones used a bullwhip instead of a trowel.

D Archaeologists use tools from a variety of fields.

ANALYZE THE TEXT

Support your responses with evidence from the text. 🗐 NOTEBOOK

1. **Confirm Predictions** Recall the predictions you made before reading the article. Which ones can you confirm? Which do you need to correct?

2. **Draw Conclusions** What is the author's main idea about the technology revolution in archaeology?

3. **Summarize** What would you say is the most significant result of the technology revolution in archaeology?

4. **Cite Evidence** Describe one of the images in the article. How does it help support the author's claims?

5. **Notice & Note** The article contains several numbers and statistics. Find one instance, and explain how it supports the author's main idea.

RESEARCH

Jeremy Hsu mentions a variety of technologies that are available to archaeologists today. To understand the changes those technologies have brought to archaeology, you need to know how archaeologists worked in the past. Research some of the tools and technologies available to archaeologists 100 years ago, around the early 1900s. Record what you learn in the chart.

TASK	TOOL OR TECHNOLOGY USED 100 YEARS AGO
Locating a site	
Field work	
Lab work	

Connect Share your findings with classmates. You will incorporate some of your findings into the slideshow presentation you will create.

CREATE AND DISCOVER

Present a Slideshow Work with a partner or a small group to research one of the technologies Jeremy Hsu mentions in his article. Then create a slideshow to accompany instructions for the technology or process.

- ❏ Work with your classmates to create a list of these technologies.
- ❏ In small groups or pairs choose one of the technologies to research.
- ❏ Consult at least three sources.
- ❏ Use the information to create a slideshow you will share with the class. In your show, give oral instructions on how the tool or technology is used.
- ❏ Remember to use appropriate technical vocabulary in your presentation.

Write a Summary Write a summary of what you learn from your classmates.

- ❏ Take notes as each pair or group of classmates gives its presentation.
- ❏ Review your notes and write a summary of what you learned.
- ❏ Share what you learned during a class discussion.

Go to **Using Media in a Presentation** in the **Speaking and Listening Studio** for more help.

Go to **Using Textual Evidence: Paraphrasing and Summarizing** in the **Writing Studio** for more on writing a summary.

RESPOND TO THE ESSENTIAL QUESTION

 What drives us to take on a challenge?

Gather Information Review your annotations and notes on "Archaeology's Tech Revolution Since Indiana Jones." Then add relevant information to your Response Log. As you determine which information to include, think about:

- the challenges that archaeologists face
- changes in archaeology
- what quests motivate archaeologists

At the end of the unit, use your notes to help you write an explanatory essay.

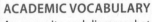

ACADEMIC VOCABULARY

As you write and discuss what you learned from the text, be sure to use the Academic Vocabulary words. Check off each of the words that you use.

- ❏ **motivate**
- ❏ **objective**
- ❏ **pursuit**
- ❏ **subsequent**
- ❏ **undertake**

CRITICAL VOCABULARY

Practice and Apply Answer each question to demonstrate your understanding of the Critical Vocabulary words. Then, explain your responses.

1. The automobile was once an **innovation**. Is it still?

2. Why is **GPS** a popular utility?

3. Imagine your class is gathering **artifacts** for a time capsule. What will you contribute?

4. How is **infrared** satellite imaging able to see underground?

5. **Forensic analysis** is used in criminal cases. Why do archaeologists use it?

VOCABULARY STRATEGY:
Use References

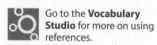

Go to the **Vocabulary Studio** for more on using references.

The author of the article you have just read incorporates popular, historical, and scientific references into the text. Though you may be able to understand the author's main idea without knowing what these references are, knowing them will enhance your comprehension and make the article more interesting to you.

Practice and Apply Use print or digital resource materials, including glossaries, dictionaries, and encyclopedias, to define or explain each reference from the article.

1. *Raiders of the Lost Ark*

2. curator

3. Google Earth

4. isotopes

5. Mayan ruins

6. LIDAR (Light Detection and Ranging)

LANGUAGE CONVENTIONS:
Use Appositives Effectively

An **appositive** is a noun or pronoun that identifies or renames another noun or pronoun. An **appositive phrase** includes an appositive and modifiers of it.

An appositive can be either essential or nonessential. An essential appositive provides information that is needed to identify what is referred to by the preceding noun or pronoun.

> **The author Jeremy Hsu has written several articles about technology.**

A nonessential appositive adds extra information about a noun or pronoun whose meaning is already clear.

> **Indiana Jones, played by Harrison Ford, was a popular movie character.**

In "Archaeology's Tech Revolution Since Indiana Jones," the author uses appositives in the following ways.

- To name or identify

> **Looking at the ratios of different forms of elements, called isotopes, in the bones of ancient people may reveal what they ate.**

> **"If we dig part of a site, we destroy it," said David Hurst Thomas, a curator in anthropology at the American Museum of Natural History in New York.**

- To describe or explain

> **The images also revealed buried city streets and houses at the ancient Egyptian city of Tanis, a well-known archaeological site that was featured in "Raiders of the Lost Ark" three decades ago.**

Practice and Apply Write your own sentences with appositives, using the examples from "Archaeology's Tech Revolution Since Indiana Jones" as models. Your sentences can be about your own experiences with technology. When you have finished, share your sentences with a partner and compare your use of appositives.

> Go to the **Grammar Studio** for more on appositives.

TRAVEL WRITING

from

THE CRUELEST JOURNEY: 600 MILES TO TIMBUKTU

by **Kira Salak**

pages 539–547

COMPARE THEME AND MAIN IDEA

As you read, notice how the ideas in both texts relate to the topic of a personal journey or quest. Then, look for ways that the ideas in the two texts relate to each other. After you read both selections, you will collaborate with a small group on a final project.

? **ESSENTIAL QUESTION:**

What drives us to take on a challenge?

POEM

THE JOURNEY

by **Mary Oliver**

pages 555–557

from **The Cruelest Journey: 600 Miles to Timbuktu**

QUICK START

Traveling provides us with enduring memories, but it can also lead to some uncomfortable experiences and feelings. With a group, discuss your most memorable travel experiences.

ANALYZE TRAVEL WRITING

Travel writing is a type of nonfiction that records an author's experiences exploring new places. Travel writers don't just present a series of facts; they present a narrative that describes a setting, reflects a purpose, and communicates messages about life. In this excerpt, Kira Salak uses narrative techniques to reveal her reflections about her journey. She doesn't just tell you what she sees, she shows you how she feels. By including vivid details and **imagery** to describe people, places, and events, Salak builds tension and gets readers involved in her adventure. In addition to imagery, Salak's narrative reflects other literary elements:

- **Mood:** The mood of a work is the emotional response it creates in readers. What details does Salak include to create the mood of her narrative?
- **Central Idea:** The central idea of a work refers to a larger message about life. How is the setting of the narrative important to Salak's central idea?
- **Purpose:** When reading, think about why Salak wrote the narrative. Look for how she uses text structure and language to achieve her purpose.

EVALUATE GRAPHIC FEATURES

Graphic features help a reader better understand what a text is trying to communicate. They may include diagrams, charts, tables, time lines, illustrations, photographs, and maps. In particular, maps that accompany travel writing help the reader better understand where the narrative occurs geographically.

As you read the excerpt from *The Cruelest Journey: 600 Miles to Timbuktu*, note how the graphic features help the author achieve her purpose.

GENRE ELEMENTS: TRAVEL WRITING

- type of narrative nonfiction
- usually illustrated with photographs, maps, or other visuals that help the reader visualize the places being described
- provides author's impressions about places visited
- includes vivid details and imagery to describe people, places, and events

CRITICAL VOCABULARY

To preview the Critical Vocabulary words, match the words to their definitions

1. circuitously	a. consistency and strength of purpose
2. disingenuous	b. not flowing or progressing
3. integrity	c. in an indirect and lengthy manner
4. embark	d. lacking in honesty
5. stagnant	e. to begin a journey or project

LANGUAGE CONVENTIONS

Authors often use **sentence variety** to keep their writing from becoming monotonous. In addition, sometimes they introduce varied sentences to mirror the ideas they describe.

- Long, winding sentences slow down a reader. They may also reflect a long journey or a detailed plot.
- Short, choppy sentences can be read more quickly. They can be used to add tension to a plot or reflect on quickly moving events.
- Breaks in sentences, such as the use of dashes, cause readers to pause and reflect on what they have just read.

As you read the excerpt from *The Cruelest Journey: 600 Miles to Timbuktu*, watch for how the author uses varying sentence length—and punctuation breaks within sentences—to effectively express her ideas.

ANNOTATION MODEL

NOTICE & NOTE

Here is an example of how one student annotated the beginning of "The Cruelest Journey: 600 Miles to Timbuktu."

In the beginning, <u>my journeys feel at best ludicrous, at worst insane.</u> This one is no exception. The idea is to <u>paddle nearly 600 miles on the Niger River in a kayak, alone, from the Malian town of Old Ségou to Timbuktu.</u> And now, at the very hour when I have decided to leave, a thunderstorm bursts open the skies, sending down apocalyptic rain, washing away the very ground beneath my feet.

When the author says her "journeys feel at best ludicrous, at worst insane" I think she is creating a mood of chaos. This is reinforced by the thunderstorm at the beginning of the journey.

The purpose of the text is to describe the author's kayaking trip from Old Ségou to Timbuktu.

© Houghton Mifflin Harcourt Publishing Company

BACKGROUND

Kira Salak *(b. 1971) wrote her book,* The Cruelest Journey: 600 Miles to Timbuktu, *to document her 600-mile solo kayak trip on the Niger River. The first person to ever achieve this feat, she traveled through a remote and dangerous region in Africa. Salak is an adventurer, an explorer, and a journalist. She has covered the civil war in the Democratic Republic of Congo, traveled across Papua New Guinea, and biked across Alaska. In 2005, she received a National Geographic Emerging Explorer Award, which recognizes people who are helping build knowledge about the world through exploration. This selection is an excerpt from her book.*

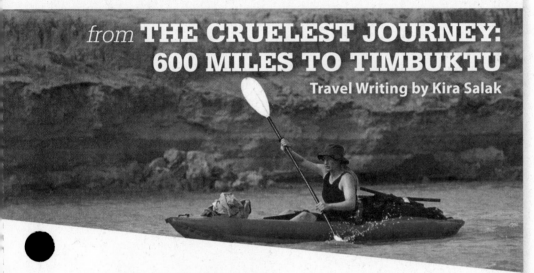

from **THE CRUELEST JOURNEY: 600 MILES TO TIMBUKTU**

Travel Writing by Kira Salak

PREPARE TO COMPARE

What does Salak think and feel about her journey? Make note of her thoughts, comments, and any telling details you notice. Write down any questions you generate during reading.

1 In the beginning, my journeys feel at best ludicrous, at worst insane. This one is no exception. The idea is to paddle nearly 600 miles on the Niger River in a kayak, alone, from the Malian town of Old Ségou to Timbuktu. And now, at the very hour when I have decided to leave, a thunderstorm bursts open the skies, sending down apocalyptic rain, washing away the very ground beneath my feet. It is the rainy season in Mali, for which there can be no comparison in the world. Lightning pierces trees, slices across houses. Thunder racks the skies and pounds the earth like mortar fire, and every living thing huddles in tenuous shelter, expecting the world to end. Which it doesn't. At least not this time. So that we all give a collective sigh to the salvation of the passing storm as it rumbles its way east, and I survey the river I'm to leave on this morning. Rain or no rain, today is the day for the journey to begin.

Notice & Note

You can use the side margins to notice and note signposts in the text.

ANALYZE TRAVEL WRITING
Annotate: Mark the author's description of the rainstorm.

Respond: How does she use details to create a mood?

LANGUAGE CONVENTIONS

Annotate: Mark the author's description of walking through Old Ségou.

Respond: How does the sentence structure mirror the topic?

And no one, not even the oldest in the village, can say for certain whether I'll get to the end.

2   "Let's do it," I say, leaving the shelter of an adobe hut. My guide from town, Modibo, points to the north, to further storms. He says he will pray for me. It's the best he can do. To his knowledge, no man has ever completed such a trip, though a few have tried. And certainly no woman has done such a thing. This morning he took me aside and told me he thinks I'm crazy, which I understood as concern and thanked him. He told me that the people of Old Ségou think I'm crazy too, and that only uncanny[1] good luck will keep me safe.

3   Still, when a person tells me I can't do something, I'll want to do it all the more. It may be a failing of mine. I carry my inflatable kayak through the narrow passageways of Old Ségou, past the small adobe huts melting in the rains, past the huddling goats and smoke of cooking fires, people peering out at me from the dark entranceways. It is a labyrinth[2] of ancient homes, built and rebuilt after each storm, plastered with the very earth people walk upon. Old Ségou must look much the same as it did in Scottish explorer Mungo Park's time

---

[1] **uncanny:** mysterious or impossible to explain.
[2] **labyrinth:** a complex collection of paths, such as a maze.

when, exactly 206 years ago to the day, he left on the first of his two river journeys down the Niger to Timbuktu, the first such attempt by a Westerner. It is no coincidence that I've planned to leave on the same day and from the same spot. Park is my benefactor of sorts, my guarantee. If he could travel down the Niger, then so can I. And it is all the guarantee I have for this trip—that an obsessed 19th-century adventurer did what I would like to do. Of course Park also died on this river, but I've so far managed to overlook that.

4   I gaze at the Niger through the adobe passageways, staring at waters that began in the mountainous rain forests of Guinea and traveled all this way to central Mali—waters that will journey northeast with me to Timbuktu before cutting a great circular swath through the Sahara and retreating south, through Niger, on to Nigeria, passing **circuitously** through mangrove swamps and jungle, resting at last in the Atlantic in the Bight of Benin.[3] But the Niger is more than a river; it is a kind of faith. Bent and plied by Saharan sands, it perseveres more than 2,600 miles from beginning to end through one of the hottest, most desolate regions of the world. And when the rains come each year, it finds new strength of purpose, surging through the sunbaked lands, giving people the boons of crops and livestock and fish, taking nothing, asking nothing. It humbles all who see it.

5   If I were to try to explain why I'm here, why I chose Mali and the Niger for this journey—now that is a different matter. I can already feel the resistance in my gut, the familiar clutch of fear. I used to avoid stripping myself down in search of motivation, scared of what I might uncover, scared of anything that might suggest a taint of the pathological.[4] And would it be enough to say that I admire Park's own trip on the river and want to try a similar challenge? That answer carries a whiff of the **disingenuous**; it sounds too easy to me. Human motivation, itself, is a complicated thing. If only it was simple enough to say, "Here is the Niger, and I want to paddle it." But I'm not that kind of traveler, and this isn't that kind of trip. If a journey doesn't have something to teach you about yourself, then what kind of journey is it? There is one thing I'm already certain of: Though we may think we choose our journeys, they choose us.

6   Hobbled donkeys cower under a new onslaught of rain, ears back, necks craned. Little children dare each other to touch me, and I make it easy for them, stopping and holding out my arm. They stroke my white skin as if it were velvet, using only the pads of their fingers, then stare at their hands to check for wet paint.

7   Thunder again. More rain falls. I stop on the shore, near a centuries-old kapok tree under which I imagine Park once took shade. I open my bag, spread out my little red kayak, and start to pump it up. I'm doing this trip under the sponsorship of *National*

circuitously
(sər-kyoōˊĭ-təs-lē) *adv.*
in an indirect and lengthy manner.

ANALYZE TRAVEL WRITING
Annotate: In Paragraph 5, underline the author's strongest belief about travel.

Respond: Why do you think she chose to make this trip?

disingenuous
(dĭs-ĭn-jĕnˊyoō-əs) *adj.*
insincere, deceitful.

---

[3] **Bight of Benin:** a gulf on Africa's west coast between Ghana and Nigeria.
[4] **taint of the pathological:** trace of mental illness.

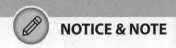
integrity
(ĭn-tĕg´rĭ-tē) *n.*
consistency and strength of
purpose.

Geographic Adventure, which hopes to run a magazine story about
it. This means that they need photos, lots of photos, and so a French
photographer named Rémi Bénali feverishly snaps pictures of me. I
don't know what I hate more—river storms or photo shoots. I value
the privacy and **integrity** of my trips, and I don't want my journey
turning into a circus. The magazine presented the best compromise it
could: Rémi, renting a motor-driven pirogue,[5] was given instructions
to find me on the river every few days to do his thing.

8   My kayak is nearly inflated. A couple of women nearby, with
colorful cloth wraps called *pagnes* tied tightly about their breasts,
gaze at me cryptically, as if to ask: *Who are you and what do you think
you're doing?* The Niger churns and slaps the shore, in a surly mood.
I don't pretend to know what I'm doing. Just one thing at a time now,
kayak inflated, kayak loaded with my gear. Paddles fitted together and
ready. Modibo is standing on the shore, watching me.

9   "I'll pray for you," he reminds me.

10   I balance my gear, adjust the straps, get in. And, finally,
irrevocably, I paddle away. . . .

11   The storm erupts into a new overture. Torrential rains. Waves
higher than my kayak, trying to capsize me. But my boat is self-
bailing[6] and I stay afloat. The wind drives the current in reverse,
tearing and ripping at the shores, sending spray into my face. I paddle
madly, crashing and driving forward. I travel inch by inch, or so it
seems, arm muscles smarting and rebelling against this journey. I
crawl past New Ségou, fighting the Niger for more distance. Large
river steamers rest in jumbled rows before cement docks, the town
itself looking dark and deserted in the downpour. No one is out in
their boats. The people know something I don't: that the river dictates
all travel.

12   A popping feeling now and a screech of pain. My right arm
lurches from a ripped muscle. But this is no time and place for such
an injury, and I won't tolerate it, stuck as I am in a storm. I try to
get used to the pulses of pain as I fight the river. There is only one
direction to go: forward. Stopping has become anathema.[7]

embark
(ĕm-bärk´) *v.*
to set out on a course or a
journey (often aboard a boat).

13 I wonder what we look for when we **embark** on these kinds of trips.
There is the pat answer that you tell the people you don't know: that
you're interested in seeing a place, learning about its people. But then
the trip begins and the hardship comes, and hardship is more honest:
it tells us that we don't have enough patience yet, nor humility, nor
gratitude. And we thought that we did. Hardship brings us closer
to truth, and thus is more difficult to bear, but from it alone comes
compassion. And so I've told the world that it can do what it wants
with me during this trip if only, by the end, I have learned something
more. A bargain, then. The journey, my teacher.

---

[5] **pirogue** (pĭ-rōg´): a canoe made from a hollowed tree trunk.
[6] **self-bailing:** the boat has holes, or scuppers, that allow water to drain from the
cockpit.
[7] **anathema:** something hated or despised.

14   And where is the river of just this morning, with its whitecaps that would have liked to drown me, with its current flowing backward against the wind? Gone to this: a river of smoothest glass, a placidity unbroken by wave or eddy, with islands of lush greenery awaiting me like distant Xanadus.[8] The Niger is like a mercurial god, meting out punishment and benediction on a whim. And perhaps the god of the river sleeps now, returning matters to the mortals who ply its waters? The Bozo and Somono[9] fishermen in their pointy canoes. The long passenger pirogues, overloaded with people and merchandise, rumbling past, leaving diesel fumes in their wake. And now, inexplicably, the white woman in a little red boat, paddling through waters that flawlessly mirror the cumulus clouds above. We all belong here, in our way. It is as if I've entered a very lucid dream, continually

---

[8] **Xanadus** (zăn´ə-dōōz): Xanadu, the summer palace of Kublai Khan; connotes an elaborate, ideal paradise.

[9] **Bozo and Somono**: ethnic groups native to Mali and the Niger River delta.

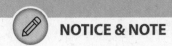

LANGUAGE CONVENTIONS

Annotate: Notice the punctuation within the last two sentences of Paragraph 14. Mark each one.

Respond: How does each one affect how you read these sentences?

surprised to find myself here on this river—I've become a hapless actor in a mysterious play, not yet knowing what my part is, left to gape at the wonder of what I have set in motion. Somehow: I'm in a kayak, on the Niger River, paddling very slowly but very surely to Timbuktu.

15   *As Salak continues on her journey—including a side trip on a tributary of the Niger—she encounters raging storms, dangerous hippos, and unrelenting heat. Because she is traveling in a small kayak and unable to carry many supplies, she comes ashore each night, seeking shelter and food from the locals, who live along the banks of the river. The locals are very curious about a woman undertaking such a dangerous journey alone. Some of them greet her warmly and generously; others with hostility. Finally, weak from dysentery, she approaches her final destination—Timbuktu.*

from Chapter Thirteen

16   "This river will never end," I say out loud, over and over again, like a mantra. My map shows an obvious change to the northeast, but that turn hasn't come for hours, may never come at all. To be so close to Timbuktu, and yet so immeasurably far away. All I know is that I must keep paddling. I *have* to be close. Determined still to get to Timbuktu's port of Korioumé by nightfall, I shed the protection of my long-sleeved shirt, pull the kayak's thigh straps in tight, and prepare for the hardest bout of paddling yet.

17   I paddle like a person possessed. I paddle the hours away, the sun falling aside to the west but still keeping its heat on me. I keep up a cadence in my head, keep my breaths regular and deep, in synch with my arm movements. The shore passes by slowly, but it passes. As the sun gets ominously low, burning a flaming orange, the river turns almost due north and I can see a distant, square-shaped building

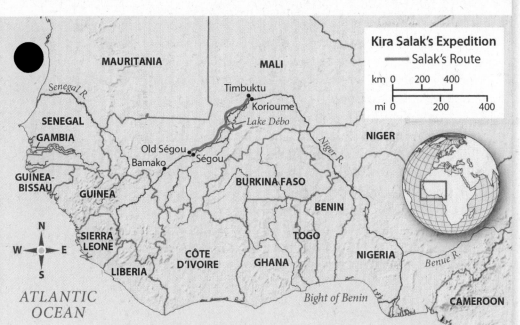

Kira Salak's Expedition
—— Salak's Route

EVALUATE GRAPHIC
FEATURES

Annotate: Trace the route of the
Niger River on the map.

Respond: How does the map
help you better understand the
author's journey?

made of cement: the harbinger of what can only be Korioumé. Hardly
a tower of gold, hardly an El Dorado, but I'll take it. I paddle straight
toward it, ignoring the pains in my body, my raging headache.
Timbuktu, Timbuktu! Bozo fishermen ply the river out here, and they
stare at me as I pass. They don't ask for money or cadeaux[10]—can they
see the determination in my face, sense my fatigue? All they say is,
"Ça va, madame?"[11] with obvious concern. One man actually stands
and raises his hands in a cheer, urging me on. I take his kindness with
me into the final stretch, rounding the river's sharp curve to the port
of Korioumé. . . .

WORD GAPS

Notice & Note: Mark the
footnote for "cadeaux."

Respond: Why do you think
the author chooses to use the
French word for "gifts" instead
of the English one?

18   Just as the last rays of the sun color the Niger, I pull up beside
a great white river steamer, named, appropriately, the *Tombouctou.*
Rémi's boat is directly behind me, the flash from his camera lighting
up the throng of people gathering on shore. There is no more
paddling to be done. I've made it. I can stop now. I stare up at the
familiar crowd waiting in the darkness. West African pop music
blares from a party on the *Tombouctou.*

19   Slowly, I undo my thigh straps and get out of my kayak, hauling
it from the river and dropping it onshore for the last time. A huge
crowd has gathered around me, children squeezing in to stroke my
kayak. People ask where I have come from and I tell them, "Old
Ségou." They can't seem to believe it.

20   "Ségou?" one man asks. He points down the Niger. His hand
waves and curves as he follows the course of the river in his mind.

21   "Oui," I say.

22   "Ehh!" he exclaims.

23   "Ségou, Ségou, Ségou?" a woman asks.

_____
[10]**cadeaux** (kə-dō′): French word meaning "gifts."
[11]**Ça va, madame?** (sä vä, mä-däm′): French for "How are you, madam?"

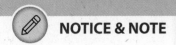
24   I nod. She runs off to tell other people, and I can see passersby rushing over to take a look at me. What does a person look like who has come all the way from Ségou? They stare down at me in my sweat-stained tank top, my clay-smeared skirt, my sandals both held together with plastic ties.

25   I unload my things to the clamor of their questions, but even speaking seems to pain me now. Such a long time getting here. And was the journey worth it? Or is it blasphemy to ask that now? I can barely walk, have a high fever. I haven't eaten anything for more than a day. How do you know if the journey is worth it? I would give a great deal right now for silence. For stillness.

26   My exhaustion and sickness begin to alter this arrival, numbing the sense of finish and self-congratulation and replacing it with only the most important of questions. I've found that illness does this to me, quiets the busy thoughts of the mind, gives me a rare clarity

that I don't usually have. I see the weeks on the river, the changing tribal groups, the lush shores down by Old Ségou metamorphosing[12] slowly into the treeless, sandy spread near Timbuktu. I'm wishing I could explain it to people—the subtle yet certain way the world has altered over these past few weeks. The inevitability of it. The grace of it. Grace, because in my life back home every day had appeared the same as the one before. Nothing seemed to change; nothing took on new variety. It had felt like a **stagnant** life.

27   I know now, with the utter conviction of my heart, that I want to avoid that stagnant life. I want the world to always be offering me the new, the grace of the unfamiliar. Which means—and I pause with the thought—a path that will only lead through my fears. Where there are certainty and guarantees, I will never be able to meet that unknown world.

---

[12] **metamorphosing:** completely changing into another form.

stagnant
(stăg´nənt) *adj.*
unchanging; without activity or development.

CHECK YOUR UNDERSTANDING

Answer these questions before moving on to the **Analyze the Text** section on the following page.

1 What mood is conveyed as the excerpt from Chapter 13 begins?

A Enjoyment and excitement

B Serenity and uncertainty

C Calm and quiet

D Tedium and exhaustion

2 How does the author mainly support her ideas?

F With descriptions of her experiences

G With facts about geography

H With impressions of other writers

J With information about the region

3 What is the purpose of the map in the text?

A It shows the reader the geography of the continent.

B It helps the reader visualize what the author saw.

C It shows the reader where the author traveled.

D It helps the reader plan a trip similar to the author.

ANALYZE THE TEXT

Support your responses with evidence from the text. NOTEBOOK

1. **Interpret** Reread paragraphs 5 and 6. What reasons does Salak give for making this trip? Why does she really undertake this journey? What does she expect to learn from the experience?

2. **Analyze** What does the dialogue in paragraphs 19–23 add to the narrative? How does it contribute to the central idea of the selection?

3. **Cite Evidence** The text includes both facts and opinions. Identify two facts and two opinions from the text.

4. **Critique** The selection includes a map showing Salak's journey. What other visual aids would you have found helpful in visualizing her journey?

5. **Notice & Note** In paragraph 2, why does the author point out the number of people who have completed the journey?

RESEARCH

Find out about the places in your community by learning how to travel around it.

- Think about two places in your community that students might like to visit.
- How could students travel to each place? Could they walk, use public transportation, or bike? Is a car necessary? Research online as needed.
- Think about how easy or confusing it would be to give directions to each location. Write positives and negatives about giving directions to each place.

LOCATIONS	TRANSPORTATION OPTIONS	POSITIVES AND NEGATIVES

Extend As a group, discuss the locations and transportation options in the chart. Choose a place for which you will provide directions using a mode of transportation the group agrees on.

CREATE AND GIVE INSTRUCTIONS

Create Directions With your group, create a set of directions that you will deliver orally to another group.

- ❏ Decide what the group will create to accompany your oral instructions. Consider a written version of the directions, a map or maps, clues, and pictures.
- ❏ Then, create clear, detailed directions for another team to travel from school to the location using your chosen mode of transportation.

Give Directions Present your directions to another group.

- ❏ Be sure to give the group all the information they need to follow the directions.
- ❏ Speak slowly and clearly, using appropriate vocabulary.
- ❏ Answer any clarifying questions the group may have.

Receive Directions Use another group's directions to find a place of interest in your community.

- ❏ Listen carefully and examine the directions thoroughly.
- ❏ Ask questions to clarify anything you do not understand.

Discuss the Directions As a class, discuss the processes of creating and following directions.

- ❏ What was the hardest part about giving and/or following directions?
- ❏ What surprised you the most about giving and/or following directions?

RESPOND TO THE ESSENTIAL QUESTION

? What drives us to take on a challenge?

Gather Information Review your annotations and notes on the excerpt from *The Cruelest Journey: 600 Miles to Timbuktu* and highlight those that help answer the Essential Question. Then, add relevant details to your Response Log.

ACADEMIC VOCABULARY

As you write and discuss what you learned from travel writing, be sure to use the Academic Vocabulary words. Check off each of the words that you use.

- ❏ **motivate**
- ❏ **objective**
- ❏ **pursuit**
- ❏ **subsequent**
- ❏ **undertake**

CRITICAL VOCABULARY

WORD BANK
circuitously
disingenuous
integrity
embark
stagnant

Practice and Apply Answer each question in a way that demonstrates your comprehension of the Critical Vocabulary word.

1. What might be the benefits of traveling *circuitously* to an unfamiliar destination?

2. Have you ever given a *disingenuous* answer? Explain.

3. When have you acted with *integrity*? Explain.

4. What would you do to get ready to *embark* on a trip around the world?

5. What would you do if you felt your life was *stagnant*?

VOCABULARY STRATEGY:
Foreign Words

Did you notice how Kira Salak worked foreign words into the text? Take a look at how one student marked an example.

A couple of women nearby, with colorful cloth wraps called *pagnes* tied tightly around their breasts, gaze at me cryptically, as if to ask: *Who are you and what do you think you're doing?*	Pagnes is not an English word. By reading the context around the word, I can figure out that pagnes are a type of colorful cloth that women wrap around themselves to create a dress.

In addition to using context clues, footnotes also sometimes provide definitions of foreign words. If neither of those is included in the text, you can often use an online translation tool to figure out the meaning of a non-English word.

Practice and Apply Use context clues, footnotes, and a dictionary if needed, to determine the meaning of the following French words.

1. cadeaux (paragraph 17)

2. Ça va? (paragraph 17)

3. Bon appétit!

LANGUAGE CONVENTIONS:
Sentence Variety

Authors vary **sentence length and style** to keep a piece from becoming monotonous. Authors also use sentence length to achieve a specific effect. For example, long sentences tend to slow readers down, while short sentences are read more quickly. A series of short, choppy sentences can also add tension.

Read this sentence from the selection:

> I gaze at the Niger through the adobe passageways, staring at waters that began in the mountainous rain forests of Guinea and traveled all this way to central Mali—waters that will journey northeast with me to Timbuktu before cutting a great circular swath through the Sahara and retreating south, through Niger, on to Nigeria, passing circuitously through mangrove swamps and jungle, resting at last in the Atlantic in the Bight of Benin.

Salak could have written the passage this way:

> I gaze at the Niger through the adobe passageways. I stare at waters that began in the mountainous rain forests of Guinea and traveled all this way to central Mali. These waters will journey northeast with me to Timbuktu. Then they will cut a great circular swath through the Sahara and retreat south, through Niger, on to Nigeria. Along the way, they will pass circuitously through mangrove swamps and jungle. They will rest at last in the Atlantic in the Bight of Benin.

By using a long, winding sentence, the author mirrors the flow of the river she is describing.

Later, Salak changes her sentence style as shown in this example:

> Just one thing at a time now, kayak inflated, kayak loaded with my gear. Paddles fitted together and ready.

Here, Salak uses shorter phrases and sentences to mirror the sequence of quick actions she is performing.

Authors also use breaks in sentences for effect. Consider this sentence:

> Which means—and I pause with the thought—a path that will only lead through my fears.

The use of dashes to offset Salak's side comment causes readers to pause with her and think carefully about the insight she is sharing.

Practice and Apply Write a short narrative about a trip you have taken or something meaningful you have experienced. In the narrative, use a variety of sentence lengths to mirror what you describe.

© Houghton Mifflin Harcourt Publishing Company

POEM

THE JOURNEY

by **Mary Oliver**

pages 555–557

COMPARE THEME AND MAIN IDEA

Now that you've read the excerpt from *The Cruelest Journey: 600 Miles to Timbuktu*, read "The Journey" and consider how this poem explores some of the same ideas. As you read, think about how "The Journey" relates to the idea of a journey or quest as well to your own experiences. After you are finished, you will collaborate with a small group on a final project that involves an analysis of both texts.

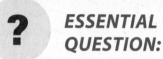 **ESSENTIAL QUESTION:**

What drives us to take on a challenge?

TRAVEL WRITING

from

THE CRUELEST JOURNEY: 600 MILES TO TIMBUKTU

by **Kira Salak**

pages 539–547

The Journey

QUICK START

Journeys can involve physical travel or they can be more metaphorical. During the course of their lives, many people pursue emotional journeys that lead to great change in their lives. Think about a period of time when you have changed. In a small group, describe your journey.

ANALYZE LANGUAGE

Figurative language is language that communicates meanings beyond the literal meanings of words. In figurative language, words are often used to represent ideas and concepts they would not otherwise be associated with. Poets use figurative language to make revealing comparisons and to help readers see subjects in a new light.

In "The Journey," Mary Oliver uses two types of figurative language: personification and metaphor.

PERSONIFICATION	METAPHOR
Authors use **personification** to give human qualities to an object, animal, or idea. For example, Oliver describes the wind as having stiff fingers, like a human.	Authors use **metaphors** to compare two things that are basically unlike but have something in common. Unlike similes, metaphors do not use the words *like* or *as*. In "The Journey," Oliver compares the subject's emotional state to a trembling house. An **extended metaphor** is a longer metaphor that continues the comparison at length, even throughout an entire poem or literary work.

GENRE ELEMENTS: POEM
- uses figurative language
- uses structure to communicate ideas
- expresses a theme, or a message about life
- uses imagery, rhythm, and word choice to elicit emotion from readers

MAKE CONNECTIONS

As a good reader, you make connections between the text and issues outside of the text. Doing so broadens your understanding of the text and helps you see how the text applies to the human experience.

- **Personal experiences:** Think about whether the text reminds of anything you have personally experienced in your life. Consider how your experiences influence your understanding or impressions of the text.
- **Other texts:** Notice if the text reminds you of something else you have read. Perhaps it is similar in genre, or maybe the theme reminds you of another text you have read.
- **Society at large:** Consider whether the text comments on or relates to issues in society at large. Remember that while the text may not seem to resonate with one particular group, people in another group may strongly identify with the text.

When reading "The Journey," think about any personal connections that you can make with the ideas in the poem.

ANNOTATION MODEL

NOTICE & NOTE

As you read, make notes about how ideas in the poem relate to your personal experiences. In the model, you can see one reader's notes about a portion of "The Journey."

> One day you finally knew
>
> what you had to do, and began,
>
> though the voices around you
>
> kept shouting
>
> their bad advice—

This reminds me of the time I decided to try a new sport. I felt it was important to challenge myself to try something new, even though many people thought that I should just keep playing the same sports I always had.

BACKGROUND

Mary Oliver (b.1935) is known for observing the natural world in a way that is both romantic and unflinchingly honest. Oliver's poems often draw attention to small details—a bird calling, a still pond, a grasshopper. Her vivid imagery of the natural world opens a window for her to explore larger issues, such as love, loss, wonder, and grief. Oliver has published numerous other collections, and has won the Pulitzer Prize for Poetry and a National Book Award. She has also written many essays, as well as two books about the craft of writing poetry. Oliver has taught at colleges and universities including Bennington College in Vermont.

THE JOURNEY
Poem by Mary Oliver

PREPARE TO COMPARE

Pay attention to details that describe barriers to the journey in the poem. Write down any questions you generate during reading.

© Houghton Mifflin Harcourt Publishing Company • Image Credits: (t) ©Frederick M. Brown/Getty Images Entertainment/ Getty Images; (c) ©4tomania/Shutterstock

One day you finally knew
what you had to do, and began,
though the voices around you
kept shouting
5 their bad advice—
though the whole house
began to tremble
and you felt the old tug
at your ankles.
10 "Mend my life!"
each voice cried.
But you didn't stop.

ANALYZE LANGUAGE

Annotate: Mark the metaphor in lines 19–22.

Infer: What is the speaker comparing in this metaphor?

AHA MOMENT

Annotate: Mark the moment when the speaker begins to come to a new realization.

Infer: What is the speaker beginning to recognize?

You knew what you had to do,
though the wind pried
15 with its stiff fingers
at the very foundations—
though their melancholy
was terrible.
It was already late
20 enough, and a wild night,
and the road full of fallen
branches and stones.
But little by little,
as you left their voices behind,
25 the stars began to burn
through the sheets of clouds,
and there was a new voice,
which was slowly
recognized as your own,
30 that kept you company
as you strode deeper and deeper
into the world,
determined to do
the only thing you could do—
30 determined to save
the only life you could save.

CHECK YOUR UNDERSTANDING

Answer these questions before moving on to the **Analyze the Text** section on the following page.

1 In lines 6–9, what is the speaker revealing?

A The speaker knows from experience that it is time to make a change.

B The speaker is afraid of an approaching tornado and is trying to escape.

C The speaker feels concerned and has decided to resist the upcoming changes.

D The speaker is worried about how the house will survive the coming storm.

2 Which of the following is an example of personification?

F *One day you finally knew / what you had to do*

G *the wind pried / with its stiff fingers / at the very foundations*

H *But little by little, / as you left their voices behind*

J *as you strode deeper and deeper / into the world*

3 An important message in "The Journey" is —

A people should take advice from those around them

B storms are frightening to experience

C it is always rewarding to make changes

D it can be difficult to do what is best for oneself

ANALYZE THE TEXT

Support your responses with evidence from the text. 🗒 NOTEBOOK

1. **Analyze** How does Oliver personify the wind? What is the figurative meaning of this strong wind outside the home of a person who is undertaking a journey?

2. **Interpret** Notice that the poem is written in one long stanza, not broken into smaller stanzas. How does Oliver use this structure to develop an extended metaphor?

3. **Synthesize** Trace the nature images that occur throughout the poem. How does Oliver use each image to develop the extended metaphor in the poem?

4. **Infer** What is the **theme**, or underlying message, of the poem? How do the title and structure of the poem help convey the theme?

5. **Notice & Note** In the last line the speaker expresses determination to "save / the only life you could save." How does this expand on the speaker's Aha Moment that a change had to be made?

RESEARCH

In the chart below, write a paraphrase for "The Journey." Remember that when you **paraphrase** a text, you put the text in your own words. The paraphrase should capture the essential points of the text without using the exact words from it. A paraphrase, even of a poem, should be written in prose.

Next, think about how the poem reminds you of experiences in your life. Select images to create a visual personal response to the poem. The images may be photographs you take, photos from magazines, drawings, or images in the public domain.

MY PARAPHRASE

CREATE AND DISCUSS

Create a Visual Response Use images to create a visual personal response to "The Journey."

❏ Arrange the images in a logical order in a visual display, whether the order mirrors the poem or the chronological order of the event about which they remind you.

❏ Using your paraphrase, develop a theme statement for "The Journey." Remember the **theme** of a text is the larger message it states about humanity. Add your theme statement to your visual display.

Discuss Visuals and Theme In small groups, share your theme statements and personal visual responses.

❏ Discuss each group member's theme statement. Notice how people may interpret the theme in different ways.

❏ Allow each member to share and discuss his or her visuals and how they connect to the poem.

❏ Reflect on similarities and differences in how group members reacted to the poem.

 Go to the **Speaking and Listening Studio** for help with having a group discussion.

RESPOND TO THE ESSENTIAL QUESTION

? What drives us to take on a challenge?

Gather Information Review your annotations and notes on "The Journey" and highlight those that help answer the Essential Question. Then, add relevant details to your Response Log.

ACADEMIC VOCABULARY

As you write and discuss what you learned about "The Journey," be sure to use the Academic Vocabulary words. Check off each of the words that you use.

❏ **motivate**

❏ **objective**

❏ **pursuit**

❏ **subsequent**

❏ **undertake**

Collaborate & Compare

COMPARE THEME AND MAIN IDEA

from
**THE CRUELEST JOURNEY:
600 MILES TO TIMBUKTU**
Travel Writing by
Kira Salak

THE JOURNEY
Poem by
Mary Oliver

Think about the journey portrayed in "The Journey" and the journey Kira Salak undertakes in the excerpt from *The Cruelest Journey: 600 Miles to Timbuktu*. What similarities and differences are there between the journeys? How have you connected with each journey?

Review both selections and consider how you might answer the questions. To develop your response, complete the graphic organizer below.

	THE CRUELEST JOURNEY	THE JOURNEY
Purpose		
Message		
Text Structure		
Language		
Personal Connection		

ANALYZE THE TEXTS

Discuss these questions in your group.

1. **Connect** What similarities do you see between the journey described by Salak and the journey discussed in the poem?

2. **Compare and Contrast** How would you describe each writer's purpose? How are Salak's and Oliver's purposes similar and different?

3. **Infer** How does each author use language to effectively convey her point?

4. **Synthesize** What have you learned from these sources together about how to take on a challenge?

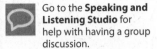

COLLABORATE AND PRESENT

Now your group can continue exploring the ideas in these texts by collaborating on a response to the text. Follow these steps:

1. **Discuss** In your group, discuss which journey you more closely identify with. Think about how these and similar journeys can apply to the broader human experience.

2. **Use Text Evidence** Support your response with evidence from the texts. Refer to your notes in the graphic organizer on the previous page.

3. **Listen** Consider your group members' points of view. Think about how personal experiences have shaped each person's point of view. Adjust your own response as you reflect on your classmates' comments.

4. **Ask Questions** Ask questions for clarification or to gain information.

5. **Write** In the chart below, take notes on the discussion. Then compose a brief summary of your group's discussion. Include what you have learned and what insights you have gained.

Go to the **Speaking and Listening Studio** for help with having a group discussion.

NOTES FROM THE DISCUSSION

SUMMARY

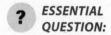

ESSENTIAL QUESTION:

What drives us to take on a challenge?

Reader's Choice

Setting a Purpose Select one or more of these options from your eBook to continue your exploration of the Essential Question.

- Read the descriptions to see which text grabs your interest.
- Think about which genres you enjoy reading.

Notice & Note

In this unit, you practiced noticing and noting these signposts: **Tough Questions, Again and Again,** and **Contrasts and Contradictions.** As you read independently, these signposts and others will aid your understanding. Below are the anchor questions to ask when you read literature and nonfiction.

Reading Literature: Stories, Poems, and Plays		
Signpost	**Anchor Question**	**Lesson**
Contrasts and Contradictions	Why did the character act that way?	p. 419
Aha Moment	How might this change things?	p. 171
Tough Questions	What does this make me wonder about?	p. 494
Words of the Wiser	What's the lesson for the character?	p. 171
Again and Again	Why might the author keep bringing this up?	p. 170
Memory Moment	Why is this memory important?	p. 418

Reading Nonfiction: Essays, Articles, and Arguments		
Signpost	**Anchor Question(s)**	**Lesson**
Big Questions	What surprised me? What did the author think I already knew? What challenged, changed, or confirmed what I already knew?	p. 248 p. 2 p. 84
Contrasts and Contradictions	What is the difference, and why does it matter?	p. 3
Extreme or Absolute Language	Why did the author use this language?	p. 85
Numbers and Stats	Why did the author use these numbers or amounts?	p. 249
Quoted Words	Why was this person quoted or cited, and what did this add?	p. 85
Word Gaps	Do I know this word from someplace else? Does it seem like technical talk for this topic? Do clues in the sentence help me understand the word?	p. 3

You can preview these texts in Unit 6 of your eBook.

Then, check off the text or texts that you select to read on your own.

EPIC POEM

from **The Odyssey**
Homer

Odysseus faces daunting challenges as he tries to return home to Ithaca after the Trojan War.

POEM

Siren Song
Margaret Atwood

What is it really like to be a Siren stuck on an island? Not as glamorous as it might seem.

DRAMA

from **The Odyssey: A Dramatic Retelling of Homer's Epic**
Simon Armitage

What's the best path between two evils? Odysseus orders his ship to sail straight between an abyss and a monster!

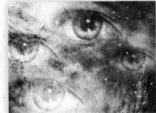

SHORT STORY

Ilse, Who Saw Clearly
E. Lily Yu

A traveling magician steals the eyes from everyone in Ilse's village, so Ilse goes on a quest to get them back.

ARGUMENT

The Real Reasons We Explore Space
Michael Griffen

What is it about space that challenges us to go there?

Collaborate and Share   Get with a partner to discuss what you learned from at least one of your independent readings.

- Give a brief synopsis or summary of the text.

- Describe any signposts that you noticed in the text and explain what they revealed to you.

- Describe what you most enjoyed or found most challenging about the text. Give specific examples.

- Decide whether you would recommend the text to others. Why or why not?

Go to the **Reading Studio** for more resources on **Notice & Note.**

Write an Explanatory Essay

This unit focuses on the very human need to pit ourselves against forces that may be stronger than we are. These challenges might be more than we can meet; or they might provide us with the most satisfying moments of our lives. For this writing task, you will write an explanatory essay focusing on one of the challenges you have read about in the unit. In your essay, you will give a clear explanation of how that particular activity might meet the human need for challenge. For an example of a well-written explanatory essay you can use as a mentor text, review the article "Archaeology's Tech Revolution Since Indiana Jones."

As you write your essay, you will want to look at the notes you made in your Response Log after reading the texts in this unit.

Writing Prompt

Read the information in the box below.

This is the topic or context for your essay.

> **The human need for challenge takes many forms, from traveling through forbidding places to exploring the mind.**

This is the Essential Question for the unit. How would you answer this question, based on the texts in this unit?

Think carefully about the following question.

> **What drives us to take on a challenge?**

Mark the words that describe exactly what you are supposed to write.

Write an explanatory essay about how an activity described in one of the unit selections meets the human need for challenge.

Be sure to—

Review these points as you write and again when you finish. Make any needed changes.

- ❑ include a clear thesis about the activity and the need for challenge
- ❑ engage readers with an interesting observation, quotation, or detail
- ❑ organize central ideas in a logically structured body that clearly develops the thesis
- ❑ use domain-specific vocabulary and logical transitions to clarify and connect ideas
- ❑ include evidence from the texts to illustrate central ideas
- ❑ have a concluding section that follows logically from the body of the essay and sums up the central ideas of the explanation

① **Plan**

Begin the planning process by choosing your topic. Go over your notes from this unit to see what appeals to your personal interests or engages you emotionally and intellectually. It may help to discuss the selections in this unit with a partner to generate ideas. Then choose a topic, keeping in mind your purpose for writing and your audience. Write a thesis statement and consider how you can explore and support it. A hierarchy diagram like the one below can help you organize your ideas and develop evidence for the body of your essay.

Go to **Writing Informative Texts: Developing a Topic** for help planning your essay.

From Reading to Writing

As you plan your explanatory essay, apply what you've learned about signposts to your own writing. Remember that writers use common features, called signposts, to help convey their message to readers.

Think about how you can incorporate **Numbers and Stats** into your argument.

 Go to the **Reading Studio** for more resources on **Notice & Note**.

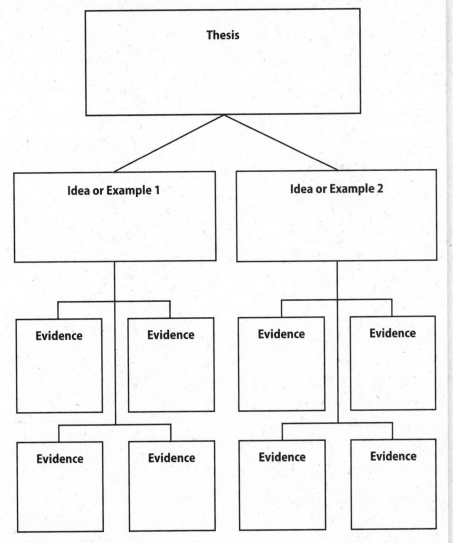

Use the notes from your Response Log as you plan your essay.

Background Reading Review the notes you have taken in your Response Log after reading the texts in this unit. These texts provide background reading that will help you think about what you want to say in your essay.

Go to **Writing Informative Texts: Organizing Ideas** for more help.

Organize Your Ideas Now it's time to take the ideas and information from your planning activities and organize them in a way that will help you draft your essay. First, decide what organizational pattern best serves your purpose—chronology, main idea and supporting details, cause and effect, or another organizing structure. You may use the chart below to organize your ideas, or create an outline of your own. Present your information in logically ordered paragraphs. Each paragraph should have a central idea related to your thesis with relevant evidence, details, quotations, and examples to support it. Write a conclusion that summarizes your thesis and presents a final synthesis of your central ideas.

EXPLANATORY ESSAY
Introduction
Body
Point 1:
Point 2:
Point 3:
Conclusion

2 Develop a Draft

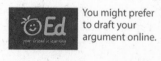

You might prefer to draft your argument online.

Once you have completed your planning activities, you will be ready to begin drafting your explanatory essay. Be sure to use precise language, including domain-specific terms, to make your explanation clear for readers. Use transitions to connect the main sections of your essay and to clarify the relationships among your ideas. Refer to your Graphic Organizer and the outline you have created, as well as any notes you took as you studied the texts in this unit.

Use the Mentor Text

Author's Craft

You can use narrative text effectively when you write an explanatory essay. A longer piece of narrative can present important information. Just a tiny piece of a story can engage the reader, as it does in the mentor text "Archaeology's Tech Revolution Since Indiana Jones."

> … Indiana Jones was a pretty lousy archaeologist. He destroyed his sites, used a bullwhip instead of a trowel and was more likely to kill his peers than co-author a paper with them.

I never thought about Indiana Jones that way!

Apply What You've Learned Use a narrative structure, when it's appropriate, to make your ideas clear and draw in your reader.

Genre Characteristics

An explanatory narrative is built on a thesis and ideas, but evidence is always necessary for support. Here is how the author of "Archaeology's Tech Revolution Since Indiana Jones" supports one idea with evidence.

> Those modern archaeologists whom "Raiders" inspired luckily learned from the mistakes of Dr. Jones, and use advanced technology such as satellite imaging, airborne laser mapping, robots and full-body medical scanners …

These examples show the kinds of technology that archaeologists use now. They support the idea that there has been a "tech revolution" in archaeology..

Apply What You've Learned Support your thesis and central ideas with evidence.

3 Revise

Go to **Writing as a Process: Revising and Editing** for help revising your essay.

On Your Own A draft is where you get your ideas down on paper. It is the process of revision that allows you to go back and find ways to improve your explanatory essay. The Revision Guide will help you focus on specific elements to make your writing stronger.

REVISION GUIDE

Ask Yourself	Tips	Revision Techniques
1. Does the introduction engage readers and state a clear thesis?	**Underline** the thesis statement and **mark** an engaging idea in the introduction.	**Add** an attention-getting detail to the introduction and **add** a thesis statement.
2. Are ideas organized logically and linked with transitions?	**Note** the idea explored in each paragraph. **Mark** transitional words and phrases.	**Reorder** evidence to center each paragraph on one idea. **Add** appropriate transitions to connect ideas and clarify the organization.
3. Does text evidence support the ideas in each paragraph?	**Underline** each supporting fact, definition, example, or quotation.	**Add** facts, details, examples, or quotations to support ideas.
4. Does the conclusion effectively summarize ideas?	**Underline** the restated thesis or summary of ideas in the conclusion.	**Add** a restatement of the thesis or summary of the essay's ideas.
5. Is the style appropriately formal, including domain-specific vocabulary?	**Note** slang or informal word choices. **Underline** domain-specific terms.	**Replace** informal language. **Add** scientific or academic language as appropriate.

ACADEMIC VOCABULARY

As you conduct your **peer review**, try to use these words.

❑ motivate
❑ objective
❑ pursuit
❑ subsequent
❑ undertake

With a Partner After you have worked through the Revision Guide on your own, exchange papers with a partner. Evaluate each other's drafts in a **peer review**. Pay particular attention to the organization of the ideas and the style. Think about ways your partner could better accomplish his or her purpose in writing.

In your discussion, describe your specific revisions suggestions and explain how they would improve the essay. As you give feedback, include praise for what he or she has done well.

④ Edit

Edit for the proper use of standard English conventions and make sure to correct any misspellings or grammatical errors. One of the most common causes of spelling errors is confusing one word for another. These types of errors will not show up in a computer spell check.

Go to **Commonly Misspelled Words** in the **Grammar Studio** to learn more.

Spelling Commonly Confused Words

There are many words in the English language that are pronounced the same way but are spelled differently and have different meanings. These types of words are called **homophones.** You are familiar with some of them, such as *your* and *you're*. There are also many words that are close in pronunciation, but different in spelling and meaning. When you're editing, make sure you have used the right word. This chart includes a few that you might use in an explanatory essay.

WORDS	DEFINITIONS	EXAMPLES
accept / except	*Accept* is a verb meaning "to receive or believe," while *except* is a preposition meaning "excluding."	**Except** for some of the more extraordinary events, I can **accept** that *The Odyssey* recounts a real journey.
affect/ effect	As a verb, *affect* means "to influence," while *effect* as a verb means "to cause." If you want a noun, you will almost always want *effect*.	Did Circe's wine **affect** Odysseus' mind? It did **effect** a change in Odysseus' men. In fact, it had an **effect** on everyone else who drank it.
loose / lose	*Loose* is an adjective that means "free, not restrained," while *lose* is a verb meaning "to misplace or fail to find."	Who turned the horses **loose**? I hope we won't **lose** any of them.
than / then	Use *than* in making comparisons. On all other occasions, use *then*.	I enjoyed this story more **than** that one. **Then** I read a third one and liked it best of all.

⑤ Publish

Finalize your essay and choose a way to share it with your audience. Consider these options:

- Post your essay as a blog.
- Participate in a Collaborative Discussion with your peers.

Use the scoring guide to evaluate your essay.

WRITING TASK SCORING GUIDE: EXPLANATORY ESSAY

	Organization/Progression	Development of Ideas	Use of Language and Conventions
4	• The organization is effective and appropriate to the purpose. • All ideas are focused on the topic specified in the prompt. • Varied transitions clearly show the relationship among ideas.	• The introduction catches the reader's attention and clearly states the thesis. • The topic is well developed with clear main ideas supported by specific and well-chosen facts, details, examples, etc. • The conclusion effectively summarizes the information.	• Language and word choice is purposeful and precise. • Care has been taken to avoid errors with commonly confused words. • Spelling, capitalization, and punctuation are correct. • Grammar, usage, and mechanics are correct.
3	• The organization is, for the most part, effective and appropriate to the purpose. • Most ideas are focused on the topic specified in the prompt. • Transitions generally clarify the relationships between ideas.	• The introduction could be more engaging. The thesis statement identifies the topic but may be cursory. • Most ideas are adequately developed and supported with facts, details, examples, and quotations. • The conclusion summarizes the information presented.	• Language is for the most part specific and clear. • Generally, care has been taken to avoid errors with commonly confused words. • There are some spelling, capitalization, and punctuation mistakes. • Some grammar and usage errors occur.
2	• The organization is evident but is not always appropriate to the purpose. • Only some ideas are focused on the topic specified in the prompt. • More transitions are needed to show the relationship among ideas.	• The introduction is not engaging. The topic is not clear and the thesis statement does not express a clear point. • The development of ideas is minimal. The writer uses facts, details, examples, etc. that are inappropriate or ineffectively presented. • The conclusion is only partially effective.	• Language is somewhat vague and unclear. • There are problems with commonly confused words. • Spelling, capitalization, and punctuation, as well as grammar and usage, are often incorrect but do not make reading difficult.
1	• The organization is not appropriate to the purpose. • Ideas are not focused on the topic specified in the prompt. • No transitions are used, making the essay difficult to understand.	• The introduction is missing or confusing and the thesis statement is missing. • The development of ideas is weak. Supporting facts, details, examples, or quotations are unreliable, vague, or missing. • The conclusion is missing.	• Language is inappropriate for the text. • There are many problems with commonly confused words. • Many spelling, capitalization, and punctuation errors are present. • Grammatical and usage errors confuse the writer's ideas.

Participate in a Collaborative Discussion

This unit focuses on ways people seek out and often thrive during life's challenges. Look back at the Reading Model text, "Archaeology's Tech Revolution Since Indiana Jones," and at the other texts in the unit. How do different people meet the need for challenges in life? Synthesize your ideas by holding a collaborative discussion on how the different selections explore the answers to this crucial question. As you discuss, share findings from your essay.

Go to **Participating in Collaborative Discussions** in the **Speaking and Listening Studio** to learn more.

1 Use Your Essay as the Basis for Your Participation

Review your essay, and use the chart below to guide you as you make notes to use in the collaborative discussion.

NOTES FOR COLLABORATIVE DISCUSSION	
Key Point	**Evidence**
Key Point	**Evidence**
Key Point	**Evidence**

© Houghton Mifflin Harcourt Publishing Company

As you work to improve your presentations, be sure to follow discussion rules:

❑ **listen closely to each other**

❑ **don't interrupt**

❑ **stay on topic**

❑ **ask helpful, relevant questions**

❑ **provide clear, thoughtful answers**

② Get Organized and Practice

Join a group of four classmates. Try to include students who have chosen different selections to write about in their explanatory essays. Each student will be the expert on the text.

Present your ideas to your group, using content and academic vocabulary that is appropriate to your topic. Encourage classmates to ask questions about your ideas and examples, preparing you to "think on your feet" during the large-group discussion.

As a group, choose one or two questions you would like to pose to the class for further discussion.

Participate in the Collaborative Discussion

Present your group's discussion questions to the class. Help make the questions clear to other students and participate actively in the discussion that follows. Refer to your notes when needed.

An effective participant in a collaborative discussion

❑ makes a clear, logical, and well-defended generalization about the challenges people seek and meet

❑ uses relevant quotations and specific examples to illustrate ideas

❑ listens actively and responds thoughtfully and politely to the ideas of other speakers

❑ builds on the ideas of other speakers' contributions

❑ summarizes the discussion by synthesizing ideas

After the discussion, think about what you learned. Were there interesting new insights into the theme of the unit? Did you learn about ideas you had not thought of on your own by participating in the discussion? Write a paragraph about what you learned. Include any follow-up questions you would like to pursue further.

Reflect on the Unit

When you were writing your explanatory essay, you pulled together and expressed many of your thoughts about the reading you have done in this unit. Now is a good time to reflect on what you have learned.

Reflect on the Essential Question

- What drives us to take on a challenge? How has your answer to this question changed since you first considered it when you started this unit?

- What are some examples from the texts you've read that show the human need to seek and meet challenges?

Reflect on Your Reading

- Which selections were the most interesting or surprising to you?

- From which selection did you learn the most about why challenges are important to us?

Reflect on the Writing Task

- What difficulties did you encounter while working on your explanatory essay? How might you avoid them next time?

- What part of the essay was the easiest and what part was the hardest to write? Why?

- What improvements did you make to your essay as you were revising?

UNIT 6 SELECTIONS
- The Epic
- from *The Odyssey*
- "Archaeology's Tech Revolution Since Indiana Jones"
- from *The Cruelest Journey: 600 Miles to Timbuktu*
- "The Journey"

RESOURCES

HMH *INTO LITERATURE* STUDIOS

For more instruction and practice, visit the HMH *Into Literature* Studios.

 Reading Studio

 Writing Studio

 Speaking & Listening Studio

 Grammar Studio

 Vocabulary Studio

UNIT 1
RESPONSE LOG

? **Essential Question:**
How can we come together despite our differences?

A Quilt of a Country	
Unusual Normality	
Once Upon a Time	
The Vietnam Wall	
The Gettysburg Address	
from Saving Lincoln	

UNIT 2
RESPONSE LOG

Use this Response Log to record your ideas about how each of the texts in Unit 2 relates to or comments on the **Essential Question.**

? Essential Question:
How do people find freedom in the midst of oppression?

I Have a Dream	
Interview with John Lewis	
from Hidden Figures	
The Censors	
Booker T. and W.E.B.	
from Reading Lolita in Tehran	
from Persepolis 2: The Story of a Return	

© Houghton Mifflin Harcourt Publishing Company

UNIT 3
RESPONSE LOG

? **Essential Question:**
How do we form and maintain our connections with others?

The Grasshopper and the Bell Cricket	
Monkey See, Monkey Do, Monkey Connect	
With Friends Like These . . .	
AmeriCorps NCCC: Be the Greater Good	
Loser	
At Dusk	

Use this Response Log to record your ideas about how each of the texts in Unit 4 relates to or comments on the **Essential Question.**

? **Essential Question:**
How can love bring both joy and pain?

The Price of Freedom	
Love's Vocabulary	
My Shakespeare	
The Tragedy of Romeo and Juliet	
Having It Both Ways	
Superheart	

Use this Response Log to record your ideas about how each of the texts in Unit 5 relates to or comments on the **Essential Question.**

? Essential Question:
What does it take to survive in a crisis?

The Leap	
Is Survival Selfish?	
The End and the Beginning	
from Night	
from The Pianist	

UNIT 6
RESPONSE LOG

? **Essential Question:**
What drives us to take on a challenge?

from The Odyssey	
Archaeology's Tech Revolution Since Indiana Jones	
from The Cruelest Journey: 600 Miles to Timbuktu	
The Journey	

© Houghton Mifflin Harcourt Publishing Company

Using a Glossary

A glossary is an alphabetical list of vocabulary words. Use a glossary just as you would a dictionary—to determine the meanings, parts of speech, pronunciation, and syllabification of words. (Some technical, foreign, and more obscure words in this book are defined for you in the footnotes that accompany many of the selections.)

Many words in the English language have more than one meaning. This glossary gives the meanings that apply to the words as they are used in the selections in this book.

The following abbreviations are used to identify parts of speech of words:

adj. adjective *adv.* adverb *n.* noun *v.* verb

Each word's pronunciation is given in parentheses. A guide to the pronunciation symbols appears in the Pronunciation Key below. The stress marks in the Pronunciation Key are used to indicate the force given to each syllable in a word. They can also help you determine where words are divided into syllables.

For more information about the words in this glossary or for information about words not listed here, consult a dictionary.

Pronunciation Key

Symbol	Examples	Symbol	Examples	Symbol	Examples
ă	pat	m	mum	ûr	urge, term, firm, word, heard
ā	pay	n	no, sudden* (sud´n)	v	valve
ä	father	ng	thing	w	with
âr	care	ŏ	pot	y	yes
b	bib	ō	toe	z	zebra, xylem
ch	church	ô	caught, paw	zh	vision, pleasure, garage
d	deed, milled	oi	noise	ə	about, item, edible, gallop, circus
ĕ	pet	ŏŏ	took	ər	butter
ē	bee	ōō	boot		
f	fife, phase, rough	ŏŏr	lure		
g	gag	ôr	core	**Sounds in Foreign Words**	
h	hat	ou	out	KH	*German* ich, ach; *Scottish* loch
hw	which	p	pop	N	*French,* bon (bôn)
ĭ	pit	r	roar	œ	*French* feu, œuf; *German* schön
ī	pie, by	s	sauce		
îr	pier	sh	ship, dish	ü	*French* tu; *German* über
j	judge	t	tight, stopped		
k	kick, cat, pique	th	thin		
l	lid, needle* (nēd´l)	*th*	this		
		ŭ	cut		

*In English the consonants *l* and *n* often constitute complete syllables by themselves.

Stress Marks

The relative emphasis with which the syllables of a word or phrase are spoken, called stress, is indicated in three different ways. The strongest, or primary, stress is marked with a bold mark (´). An intermediate, or secondary, level of stress is marked with a similar but lighter mark (´). The weakest stress is unmarked. Words of one syllable show no stress mark.

GLOSSARY OF ACADEMIC VOCABULARY

attribute (ătʹrə-byōōt) *n.* a characteristic, quality, or trait.

capacity (kə-păsʹĭ-tē) *n.* the ability to contain, hold, produce, or understand.

commit (kə-mĭtʹ) *v.* to carry out, engage in, or perform.

confer (kən-fûrʹ) *v.* to grant or give to.

decline (dĭ-klīnʹ) *v.* to fall apart or deteriorate slowly.

dimension (dĭ-mĕnʹshən) *n.* a feature, scale, or measurement of something.

emerge (ĭ-mûrjʹ) *v.* to come forth, out of, or away from.

enable (ĕ-nāʹbəl) *v.* to give the means or opportunity.

enforce (ĕn-fôrsʹ) *v.* to compel observance of or obedience to.

entity (ĕnʹtĭ-tē) *n.* a thing that exists as a unit.

expose (ĭk-spōzʹ) *v.* to make visible or reveal.

external (ĭk-stûrʹnəl) *adj.* related to, part of, or from the outside.

generate (jĕnʹə-rāt) *v.* to produce or cause something to happen or exist.

impose (ĭm-pōzʹ) *v.* to bring about by force.

initiate (ĭ-nĭshʹē-āt) *v.* to start or cause to begin.

integrate (ĭnʹtĭ-grāt) *v.* to pull together into a whole; unify.

internal (ĭn-tûrʹnəl) *adj.* inner; located within something or someone.

motivate (mōʹtə-vāt) *v.* to provide a cause for doing something.

objective (əb-jĕkʹtĭv) *n.* an intention, purpose, or goal.

presume (prĭ-zōōmʹ) *v.* to take for granted as being true; to assume something is true.

pursuit (pər-sōotʹ) *n.* the action of chasing or following something.

resolve (rĭ-zŏlvʹ) *v.* to decide or become determined.

reveal (rĭ-vēlʹ) *v.* to show or make known.

statistic (stə-tĭsʹtĭk) *n.* a piece of numerical data.

subsequent (sŭbʹsĭ-kwĕnt) *adj.* coming after or following.

sustain (sə-stānʹ) *v.* to support or cause to continue.

trace (trās) *v.* to discover or determine the origins or developmental stages of something.

underlie (ŭn-dər-līʹ) *v.* to be the cause or support of.

undertake (ŭn-dər-tākʹ) *v.* to assume responsibility for or take on a job or course of action.

utilize (yōotʹl-īz) *v.* to make use of.

GLOSSARY OF CRITICAL VOCABULARY

adulate (ăj´ə-lāt) *v.* to praise or admire excessively.

allocate (ăl´ə-kāt) *v.* to assign or designate for.

analytical (ăn-ə-lĭt´ĭ-kəl) *adj.* able to analyze, or understand something by breaking it down into parts.

annihilate (ə-nī´ə-lāt) *v.* to destroy completely.

artifact (är´tə-făkt) *n.* an object produced or shaped by human workmanship.

assess (ə-sĕss´) *v.* to determine the qualities or abilities of something.

audacious (ô-dā´shəs) *adj.* bold, rebellious.

berate (bĭ-rāt´) *v.* to criticize or scold.

circuitously (sər-kyōō´ĭ-təs-lē) *adv.* in an indirect and lengthy manner.

cognition (kŏg-nĭsh´ən) *n.* the process or pattern of gaining knowledge.

comply (kəm-plī´) *v.* to obey an instruction or command.

conceive (kən-sēv´) *v.* to form or develop in the mind: devise.

conscientiously (kŏn-shē-ĕn´shəs-ly) *adj.* doing something thoroughly.

constrict (kən-strĭkt´) *v.* to limit or impede growth.

consume (kən-sōōm´) *v.* to completely destroy or eradicate.

contagion (kən-tā´jən) *n.* the spreading from one to another.

convert (kən-vûrt´) *v.* to change one's system of beliefs.

counterparts (koun´tər-pärts) *n.* people or things that have the same characteristics and function as another.

decisive (dĭ-sīs´ĭv) *adj.* final or concluding.

decoy (dē´koi) *n.* a means to trick or attract.

default (dĭ-fôlt´) *v.* to fail to keep a promise to repay a loan.

degenerate (dĭ-jĕn´ər-āt) *v.* to decline morally.

demented (dĭ-mĕn´tĭd) *adj.* suffering from dementia, crazy, foolish.

deprecating (dĕp´rĭ-kāt-ing) *adj.* belittling or downplaying something.

derive (dĭ-rīv´) *v.* to obtain or extract from.

desolate (dĕs´ə-lĭt) *adj.* unhappy; lonely.

detract (dĭ-trăkt´) *v.* to take away from.

din (dĭn) *n.* loud noise.

discernable (dĭ-sûr´nə-bəl) *adj.* recognizable or noticeable.

discordant (dĭ-skôr´dnt) *adj.* conflicting or not harmonious.

GLOSSARY OF CRITICAL VOCABULARY

disingenuous (dĭs-ĭn-jĕn´yoͦo-əs) *adj.* insincere, deceitful.

distend (dĭ-stĕnd´) *v.* to bulge or expand.

diversity (dĭ-vûr´sĭ-tē) *n.* having varied social and/or ethnic backgrounds.

edict (ē´dĭkt) *n.* an official rule or proclamation.

emaciated (ĭ-mā´shē-āt-id) *adj.* made extremely thin and weak.

emanate (ĕm´ə-nāt) *v.* to emit or radiate from.

embark (ĕm-bärk´) *v.* to set out on a course or a journey (often aboard a boat).

empathy (ĕm´pə-thē) *n.* the ability to understand and identify with another's feelings.

encroach (ĕn-krōch´) *v.* to gradually intrude upon or invade.

execute (ĕk´sĭ-kyoͦot) *v.* to carry out, or accomplish.

extricate (ĕk´strĭ-kāt) *v.* to release or disentangle from.

forensic analysis (fə-rĕn´sĭk ə-năl´ĭ-sĭs) *n.* the scientific collection and analysis of physical evidence in criminal cases.

GPS *n.* Global Positioning System, a utility that provides positioning, navigation, and timing services.

gradation (grā-dā´shən) *n.* a slight, successive change in color, degree or tone.

horde (hôrd) *n.* a large group or crowd; a swarm.

implication (ĭm-plĭ-kā´shən) *n.* consequence or effect.

increment (ĭn´krə-mənt) *n.* an addition or increase by a standard measure of growth.

inextricably (ĭn-ĕk´strĭ-kə-blē) *adv.* in a way impossible to untangle.

infiltration (ĭn-fĭl-trā´shən) *n.* the act or process of passing in secret through enemy lines.

infrared (ĭn´frə-rĕd) *adj.* pertaining to electromagnetic radiation having wavelengths greater than those of visible light and shorter than those of microwaves.

innovation (ĭn-ə-vā´shən) *n.* something newly introduced.

insistent (ĭn-sĭs´tənt) *adj.* demanding that something happen or refusing to accept that it will not happen.

intangible (ĭn-tăn´jə-bəl) *n.* something that is difficult to grasp or explain.

integrity (ĭn-tĕg´rĭ-tē) *n.* consistency and strength of purpose.

intention (ĭn-tĕn´shən) *n.* purpose or plan.

interwoven (ĭn-tər-wō´vən) *adj.* blended or laced together.

intrusion (ĭn-troͦo´shən) *n.* act of trespass or invasion.

irrelevant (ĭr-rĕl´ə-vənt) *adj.* insignificant, unimportant.

irreproachable (ĭr-ĭ-prō′chə-bəl) *adj.* without fault or blame; perfect.

isolation (ī-sə-lā′shən) *n.* the condition of being alone or apart from others.

knack (năk) *n.* a special talent for doing something.

laud (lôd) *v.* to praise.

loiter (loi′tər) *v.* to stand or wait idly.

lozenge (lŏz′ĭnj) *n.* a diamond-shaped object.

maneuver (mə-nōō′vər) *v.* to make a series of controlled movements.

naïve (nī-ēv′) *adj.* lacking in worldly experience, everyday knowledge, or understanding.

perish (pĕr′ĭsh) *v.* to die or come to an end.

pluralistic (plŏŏr′ə-lĭs′tĭc) *adj.* consisting of many ethnic and cultural groups.

redemptive (rĭ-dĕmp′tĭv) *adj.* causing freedom or salvation.

rehabilitation (rē-hə-bĭl-ĭ-tā′shən) *n.* the act of being restored to good health or condition.

reprieve (rĭ-prēv′) *n.* the cancellation or postponement of punishment.

resolve (rĭ-zŏlv′) *v.* to decide or become determined.

sabotage (săb′ə-täzh) *n.* deliberate destruction of property; an act of damage to stop something.

scam (skăm) *n.* a plan to cheat others, often out of money.

seductive (sĭ-dŭk′tĭv) *adj.* tempting, alluring.

segregate (sĕg rĭ-gāt) *v.* to cause people to be separated based on gender, race, or other factors.

serrated (sĕr′ā-tĭd) *adj.* having a jagged, saw-toothed edge.

sheepish (shē′pĭsh) *adj.* showing embarrassment.

simulate (sĭm′yə-lāt) *v.* to create in a controlled setting conditions similar to those a person or machine might face in the real world.

skeptic (skĕp′tĭk) *n.* someone who doubts something.

stagnant (stăg′nənt) *adj.* unchanging; without activity or development.

stereotype (stĕr′ē-ə-tīp) *n.* one that is thought of as conforming to a set type or image.

subversive (səb-vûr′sīv) *adj.* intending to undermine or overthrow those in power.

supple (sŭp′əl) *adj.* flexible or easily adaptable.

synchronization (sing-krə-nĭ-zā′shən) *n.* coordinated, simultaneous action.

tentative (tĕn′tə-tĭv) *adj.* with caution and without confidence.

transfix (trans-fĭks′) *v.* to captivate or make motionless with awe.

validate (văl′ĭ-dāt) *v.* to establish the value, truth, or legitimacy of.

INDEX OF SKILLS

© Houghton Mifflin Harcourt Publishing Company

© Houghton Mifflin Harcourt Publishing Company

mentor text use, 241
organize ideas, 240
peer review, 242
plan, 239–240
publish, 243
reflect on, 245
revise, 242
scoring guide, 244
writing prompt, 238
signal words, 422, 435
similes, 48, 285, 497
epic, 497
situational irony, 117, 122
slant rhymes, 395
small group discussion, 181, 223, 233, 261,
391, 475
soliloquy, 285
sonnet, 395, 405
sound devices, 47, 129, 500
sound effects, 165, 166, 276
sound elements, 100, 276
sources
cite, 142, 158, 160
credible, 102, 134, 142, 454
evaluate, 102, 134, 142, 212, 454
identify bias, 29, 159, 212, 474
omissions in, 159
reference, 28, 114, 208, 432, 476, 534
Speaking and Listening Task
argument presentation, 489
collaborative discussion, 571
podcast, 165
speaking, discussion rules for, 69, 166,
445, 490, 572
speaking strategies, 489–490. *See also*
nonverbal cues and techniques; verbal
cues and techniques
special effects
computer-generated imagery, 66
in multimodal texts, 210, 212, 276
practical effect, 66
spelling
commonly confused words, 569
plural nouns, 243
storyboards, 155
straw man, 437
structure
parallel, 56, 58, 63, 286, 326, 342, 381, 393
sentence, 17, 45, 253, 263, 266, 538, 540
text, 105, 108, 109
subordinate clauses, 6
subplot, 33, 36, 215
suffixes, 126
summarize. See also paraphrase
Analyze the Text, 12, 96, 212, 532
information, 29, 533
texts, 199, 201, 205
support for claims, 5, 185
suspense, 117, 282, 285, 457

symbols, 152, 234, 495
synonyms, 274, 446
syntax, 17, 130, 397, 404, 449
analyze, 227, 230
synthesize, 70, 71, 234, 235, 408, 478
Analyze the Text, 28, 134, 154, 212, 280,
390, 444, 478, 558, 560

T

technical texts, analyze, 525, 529, 530
tense of verbs, 138, 139, 145
testimonial, 490
text evidence. *See* evidence
text meaning
analyze, 251, 253
draw conclusions, 251, 254
explicit, 251
implicit, 251
infer, 251, 253
text structures
analyze, 105, 108, 109
cause and effect, 105
main idea and details, 105
narrative, 105
thesis/important ideas, 105
theme, 173, 176, 222, 235, 312, 421
across texts, 214, 226, 234
analyze, 33, 37, 38, 120, 173, 178
characterization and, 215, 234, 235
infer, 173, 176
plot and, 173, 234, 235, 421
setting and, 33, 37, 38, 40, 117, 120, 173,
178
thesis statement, 159, 265, 410, 484, 565
tone, 17, 19, 21, 22, 26, 74, 119, 130, 135
165, 166, 227, 233, 263, 273, 276, 374,
404. 408, 449, 457, 478, 482, 484
analyze, 17, 19, 21, 22, 26, 117
Tough Questions (Notice & Note),
494, 508, 512
transfer (emotional appeal), 490
transitions, 165, 242, 485, 487

U

understatement, 55, 130, 490

V

verbal cues and techniques
enunciation, 166, 489
microphone skills, 166
pitch, 166, 489
register, 29, 166, 273
speaking rate, 166, 490
volume, 61, 103, 135, 213, 490
verbal irony, 117, 123
verb phrases, 174, 183
verb tense, 138, 145
video, 276
producing, 281

vocabulary
Glossary of Academic Vocabulary, R8
Glossary of Critical Vocabulary,
R9–R11
specialized/technical, 3, 114, 208, 249,
527, 533
Vocabulary Strategy
antonyms, 98
context clues, 182, 224
denotative and connotative meanings,
30, 144
foreign words, 262, 550
multiple-meaning words, 62, 476
patterns of word changes, 14
prefixes, 434
reference sources, 114, 208, 534
resources, print and digital, 114, 208,
534
Shakespeare's language, 392
suffixes that form nouns, 126
synonyms, 274, 446
words from Greek, 196
words from Latin, 522
voice, 17, 19, 21, 22, 26, 74, 103, 135, 165,
166, 227, 233, 243, 273, 276, 374, 408,
482, 489, 490, 521
active, 18, 31, 79, 216, 225
analyze, 22, 26
passive, 18, 20, 31, 79, 216, 217, 225
volume of speech, 490

W

word choice, 457, 464, 467, 469
Word Gaps, 3, 11, 188, 249, 257, 270,
400, 545
Word Network, 1, 83, 169, 247, 417, 493
words
affixes, 434
antonyms, 98, 182
commonly confused, 569
connotations, 30, 144
denotations, 30, 144
etymology, 44
from Greek, 196
from Latin, 44, 522
multiple-meaning, 62, 476
parallel, 56, 63
patterns of change, 14
prefixes, 196, 434
roots, 196, 522
suffixes, 126
synonyms, 272, 446
Words of the Wiser (Notice & Note), 171,
179, 324, 345, 460
writing activities
argument, 153, 482–488
blog post, 113
eulogy, 391
explanatory essay, 564–570

© Houghton Mifflin Harcourt Publishing Company

INDEX OF TITLES AND AUTHORS

ACKNOWLEDGMENTS

ACKNOWLEDGMENTS

Excerpt from *Persepolis 2: The Story of a Return* by Marjane Satrapi, translated by Anjali Singh. Text copyright © by Marjane Satrapi. Translation copyright © 2004 by Anjali Singh. Any third party use of this material, outside of this publication, is prohibited. Interested parties must apply directly to Penguin Random House LLC for permission. Reprinted by permission of Pantheon Books, an imprint of the Knopf Doubleday Publishing Group, a division of Penguin Random House LLC, The Random House Group, Limited, and Marjane Satrapi. All rights reserved.

Excerpt from *The Pianist* by Władysław Szpilman. Text Copyright © 1999 by Władysław Szpilman. Used by permission of St. Martin's Press.

"The Price of Freedom" by Noreen Riols, from *The Moth Presents All These Wonders: True Stories About Facing The Unknown,* edited by Catherine Burns. Text copyright © 2017 by Noreen Riols. Any third party use of this material, outside of this publication, is prohibited. Interested parties must apply directly to Penguin Random House LLC for permission. Reprinted by permission of Crown Archetype, an imprint of the Crown Publishing Group, a division of Penguin Random House LLC, Serpant's Tail Press, and The Moth. All rights reserved.

"A Quilt Of A Country" from *The Daily Beast* by Anna Quindlen. Text copyright © 2001 by Anna Quindlen. Reprinted by permission of ICM Partners.

Quote by Kofi Annan from "What Can I Do to Make Things Better?" by Kofi Annan from *Parade Magazine*. Text copyright © by Kofi Annan. Reprinted by permission of Kofi Annan.

Excerpt from *Reading Lolita in Tehran: A Memoir in Books* by Azar Nafisi. Text copyright © 2002 by Azar Nafisi. Any third party use of this material, outside of this publication, is prohibited. Interested parties must apply directly to Penguin Random House LLC for permission. Reprinted by permission of Random House, an imprint and division of Penguin Random House LLC and Penguin Books UK. All rights reserved.

"Superheart" by Marion Shore. Text copyright © by Marion Shore. Reprinted by permission of Marion Shore.

"Unusual Normality" by Ishmael Beah from *All These Wonders* edited by Catherine Burns. Text copyright © 2017 by Ishmael Beah. Reprinted by permission of SLL/Sterling Lord Literistic, Inc.

"The Vietnam Wall" from *The Lime Orchard Woman* by Alberto Ríos. Text copyright © 1988 by Alberto Ríos. Reprinted by permission of the author.

Excerpt from "With Friends Like These . . ." by Dorothy Rowe from the series "How to Understand People," from *The Observer*, March 8, 2009. Text copyright © 2009 by Guardian News and Media Ltd. Reprinted by permission of Guardian News and Media Limited.